Intercultural
Communication:
A Reader

Intercultural Communication: A Reader

Fourth Edition

LARRY A. SAMOVAR
San Diego University

RICHARD E. PORTER
California State University,
Long Beach

Wadsworth Publishing Company
Belmont, California
A Division of Wadsworth, Inc.

Communications Editor: Kristine Clerkin
Production Editor: Vicki Friedberg
Text and Cover Designer: MaryEllen Podgorski
Copy Editor: Jeff Van Bueren
Print Buyer: Karen Hunt
Photo Researcher: Lindsay Kefauver
Cover Photos: Left: United Nations/M. Grant, Saw Iwin;
   Right: Jeroboam/Bob Clay

Printed in the United States of America

1 2 3 4 5 6 7 8 9 10—89 88 87 86 85

ISBN 0-534-04293-7

Library of Congress Cataloging in Publication Data
   Main entry under title:

Intercultural communication.

   Includes bibliographies and indexes.
   1. Intercultural communication—Addresses,
essays, lectures.   I. Samovar, Larry A.
II. Porter, Richard E.
HM258.I523   1985   302.2   84-19567
ISBN 0-534-04293-7

Preface   ix

Contents

v

Chapter 3 Nondominant Domestic Cultures   116

Chapter 4 Cultural Contexts   158

PART THREE
INTERCULTURAL INTERACTION:
TAKING PART IN INTERCULTURAL COMMUNICATION   200

Chapter 5   Verbal Interaction   202

Chapter 6   Nonverbal Interaction   254

Preface

The occasion of the fourth edition of our reader on intercultural communication is both pleasant and exciting because it indicates an ongoing acceptance of our ideas and views about intercultural communication among a wide variety of scholars and teachers in a field that has great personal meaning to us. We are also pleased that the intercultural communication field is continuing to grow and that we have helped shape and define that field. This fourth edition represents our continuing attempt to refine our thoughts and feelings about the field and to share them with you.

As in the past, we intend this anthology to be for the general reader. Consequently, we have selected materials that are broadly based and comprehensive, which are suitable for both undergraduate and graduate students. Although the level of difficulty varies from article to article, we believe that, with only one or two exceptions, we have not gone beyond the difficulty level found in most texts for advanced undergraduate students. Twenty-two essays are new to this edition, eleven of which were written especially for this volume.

Intercultural Communication: A Reader is designed to meet three specific needs. The first comes from our belief that successful intercultural communication is a matter of the highest importance if humankind and society are to survive. This book, then, is designed to serve as a *basic anthology* for courses providing theoretical and practical knowledge about intercultural communication processes. Our intention is to make this book useful not only to students of communication theory, but also to readers seeking practical and immediately usable knowledge. Second, the book may be used as a *supplementary text* in existing service and basic communication skills courses and in interpersonal communication courses. Third, the book provides *resource material* for advanced courses in public speaking, communication theory, small group communication, organizational and business communication, and mass communication, as well as for courses in anthropology, sociology, social psychology, social welfare, business, and political science or international relations. It also may serve as a resource manual for people who find themselves in programs or situations involving intercultural communication.

The book is organized into four closely related parts. In Part One, "Intercultural Communication: An Introduction," the first chapter contains essays that examine the philosophical basis for intercultural communication and discuss what intercultural communication is, what it tries to accomplish, and the nature of intercultural communication. Parts Two, Three, and Four trace the intercultural communication experience by means of a topical sequence. Part Two, "Socio-Cultural Backgrounds: What We Bring to Intercultural Communication," examines the influences of socio-cultural factors on intercultural interaction. In this section, Chapter 2 deals with the understanding of international cultures while Chapter 3 explores nondominant domestic cultures, subcultures, and deviant subgroups. Chapter 4 continues with an exploration of the cultural contexts within which intercultural communication occurs. We believe that through an examination of the cultural differences in what we bring to our intercultural communication acts, we are better able to understand and to appreciate what goes on during the communication event itself. In Part Three, "Intercultural Interaction: Taking Part in Intercultural Communication," our analysis focuses on the problems of intercultural interaction. Chapter 5 in this section examines cultural differences in verbal interaction; Chapter 6 focuses on differences in nonverbal interaction. Part Four, "Intercultural Communication: Becoming More Effective," is concerned with improving intercultural communication. In Chapter 7 the readings offer the knowledge and experiences of successful intercultural communicators and practical suggestions for improving intercultural communication. Chapter 8, the final chapter, examines the ethical dimensions of intercultural communication, the future of intercultural communication, and possible directions for change and improvement.

This book continues to be the outcome of a joint venture. The ideas reflected in it and the decisions necessary for its development and preparation grew out of an association and a dialogue that have persisted since 1967. Both of us share a mutual concern that if the human race is to endure in the decades ahead—decades that will, in both time and space, bring all humans closer together in a global community—we must all be able to communicate with people from cultures far removed from our own.

We wish to express our appreciation to the many authors, professional associations, and publishers whose cooperation has helped make this book possible. In addition, various individuals have played a significant role in the development and completion of this project. Especially, we should like to acknowledge the thoughtful reviews of the manuscript by Mary Jane Collier, California State University, Los Angeles; Jolene Koester, California State University, Sacramento; and Felipe Korzeny, Michigan State University.

Larry A. Samovar
Richard E. Porter

Intercultural Communication:
A Reader

Part One

Intercultural Communication: An Introduction

Precision of communication is important, more important than ever, in our era of hair-trigger balances, when a false or misunderstood word may create as much disaster as a sudden thoughtless act.

—*James Thurber*

Intercultural communication, as we might rightly suspect, is not new. As long as people from different cultures have been encountering one another there has been intercultural communication. What is new, however, is the systematic study of exactly what happens when cross-cultural contacts and interaction take place—when message producer and message receiver are from different cultures.

Perhaps the knowledge that technology has produced the means of our own self-destruction has prompted this concern. Historically, intercultural communication, more often than not, has employed a rhetoric of force rather than reason. Maybe we are now seeking something other than traditional force. Or perhaps the reason for this new study is more pragmatic, brought about by our mobility, increased contact among cultures, and a widening world marketplace. Traditionally, intercultural communication took place only within an extremely small minority. Ministers of government and certain merchants were the travelers and visitors to foreign lands. Until rather recently, we Americans had little contact with other cultures even within our own country. The ghetto or barrio dwellers remained in the ghetto or barrio. If they did emerge, it was to serve the upper class, not to interact as equals. And those who made up the vast white middle America remained at home, rarely leaving their own county. But this has changed markedly; we are now a mobile society among ever-increasing mobile societies.

This increased contact with other cultures, subcultures, and deviant subgroups makes it imperative for us to make a concerted effort to get along with and understand people whose beliefs

1

and backgrounds may be vastly different from our own. The ability, through increased awareness and understanding, to coexist peacefully with people who do not necessarily share our life styles or values not only could benefit us in our own neighborhoods but also could be the decisive factor in forestalling nuclear annihilation.

There remains a great need to specify the nature of intercultural communication and to recognize the various viewpoints that see it somewhat differently. From what we have already said, you should suspect that there are a variety of ways in which the topic of intercultural communication can be explored. There are perspectives that look at intercultural communication from a mass media point of view. Scholars who follow this approach are concerned with issues such as international broadcasting, worldwide freedom of the press, the Western domination of information, and the use of modern electronic technologies for the instantaneous worldwide transmission of information. Other groups investigate international communication. Here the emphasis is on communication between nations and between governments. It is the communication of diplomacy and propaganda. Although both of these approaches are of great value, they are not the domain of this book. Our concern is with the more personal aspects of communication—what happens when people from different cultures interact face-to-face. Hence, we identify our approach as one that examines the *interpersonal dimensions* of intercultural communication. For this reason, the articles and essays we have selected for this collection have been selected because we believe they focus on those variables of both culture and communication that come into play *during* the communication encounter—during the time that participants from different cultures are trying to share ideas, information, and feelings.

Inquiry into the nature of intercultural communication has raised many questions, but it has produced only a few theories and far fewer answers. Most of the inquiry has been associated with fields other than communication: primarily anthropology, international relations, social psychology, and socio- and psycholinguistics. Although the direction of research has been diverse, the knowledge has not been coordinated. There is still a great need to specify the nature of intercultural communication and to recognize various viewpoints that see the phenomenon somewhat differently. Much that has emerged has been more a reaction to current socio-racial-ethnic concerns than an attempt to define and to explain intercultural communication. But, it is quite clear that knowledge of intercultural communication can aid in solving communication problems before they arise. School counselors who understand some of the reasons why the poor perceive schools as they do might be better able to treat young truants. Those who know that native Americans and Mexicans use eye contact in ways that differ from other Americans may be able to avert misunderstandings. In essence, what we are saying is that many problems can be avoided by understanding the components of intercultural communication.

1

Approaches

We begin this exploration of intercultural communication with a series of diverse articles that (1) introduce the philosophy that underlies our concept of intercultural communication, (2) provide a general orientation and overview of intercultural communication, (3) theorize about the analysis of intercultural transactions, (4) provide insight into cultural differences, and (5) demonstrate the relationships between culture and perception. Our purpose at this point is to give you a sufficient introduction to the many wide and diverse dimensions of intercultural communication so that you will be able to approach the remainder of this volume with an appropriate frame of reference to make your further inquiry interesting, informative, and useful.

Dean C. Barnlund in "Communication in a Global Village" traces communication and transportation developments that have led to the apparent shrinking of the contemporary world and the emergence of the global community. He points out the ramifications of the global village in terms of the forms and kinds of interactions that necessarily accompany such a new community of people. Barnlund considers problems of meaning associated with cultural differences, interpersonal encounters, intercultural encounters, and the role of the "collective unconscious" in intercultural interactions.

In the next article, "Approaching Intercultural Communication," we introduce some of the *specific* topics and issues associated with the study of intercultural communication and present in rather broad terms what it involves. We start by defining and explaining the role of human communication. We then turn our attention to the specific areas of culture and communication and show how they interrelate to form the field of intercultural communication. By examining the major variables that affect intercultural communication, we better understand how it operates. By knowing at the outset of the book what the study of intercultural communication entails, you should have a greater appreciation for the selections that follow.

Next, Dorthy L. Pennington presents us with a somewhat different approach to staking out the territory of intercultural communication. In a manner similar to the previous approach by Porter and Samovar, Pennington begins with the assumption that to understand intercultural communication attention must be paid to the concept of culture and its major components. She identifies nine categories of components: (1) existential world-view; (2) language and symbol systems; (3) schemas (cultural patterns of interpreting, organizing, and classifying data); (4) beliefs, attitudes, and values; (5) temporality (concept of, attitude toward, and use of time); (6) space, proxemics (spatial behavior); (7) religion, myths, and expressive forms; (8) social relationships and communication networks; and (9) interpolation patterns. Following a descriptive discussion of these components, Pennington offers a model of culture and an explanation of what transpires when two or more cultures come together.

The importance of culture in human interaction is underscored by Edward T. Hall in his selection "Context and Meaning." The grand connection between culture and human communicative behavior is revealed when Hall demonstrates how culture provides a highly selective screen between people and their outside worlds. This cultural filter effectively designates what people attend to as well as what they choose to ignore. This link between culture and behavior is further illustrated through Hall's discussion of high- and low-context communication, in which he shows how people from different cultural backgrounds learn to concentrate on unique aspects of their environments.

Anne Pedersen and Paul Pedersen continue the general theme of this chapter as they offer yet another approach to the study and understanding of intercultural communication. Although their approach is more practical than theoretical, it nevertheless presents information concerning the operating ingredients when people from different cultures interact. The Pedersen approach is based on what they call a "Cultural Grid." In a single framework, the grid combines a personal (individual) perspective of specific behaviors, expectations, and values with a cultural (group) perspective of social system variables. By *combining* the individual and the group perspective, the Cultural Grid can be used to describe a distinctive cultural orientation in each communication situation and to suggest how specific behaviors, expectations, and values are related to social system variables.

Like past experiences, perception also plays a role in human interaction. This influence and impact serves as the nucleus for Marshall R. Singer's article "Culture: A Perceptual Approach." He begins his analysis with two important premises. First, individual patterns of behavior are based on individual perceptions of the external world. Second, because these patterns are learned, they are culturally based. These two ideas lead Singer through a model of culture and perception that helps explain why communication between members of contrasting cultures is often so difficult. The problem, as this essay suggests, is that our view of reality is shaped by our cultural experiences.

Communication in a Global Village

DEAN C. BARNLUND

Nearing Autumn's close.
My neighbor—
How does he live, I wonder?

—*Bashō*

These lines, written by one of the most cherished of *haiku* poets, express a timeless and universal curiosity in one's fellow man. When they were written, nearly three hundred years ago, the word "neighbor" referred to people very much like one's self—similar in dress, in diet, in custom, in language—who happened to live next door. Today relatively few people are surrounded by neighbors who are cultural replicas of themselves. Tomorrow we can expect to spend most of our lives in the company of neighbors who will speak in a different tongue, seek different values, move at a different pace, and interact according to a different script. Within no longer than a decade or two the probability of spending part of one's life in a foreign culture will exceed the probability a hundred years ago of ever leaving the town in which one was born. As our world is transformed our neighbors increasingly will be people whose life styles contrast sharply with our own.

The technological feasibility of such a global village is no longer in doubt. Only the precise date of its attainment is uncertain. The means already exist:

From Dean C. Barnlund, *Public and Private Self in Japan and the United States* (Tokyo: Simul Press, Inc., 1975), pp. 3–24. Reprinted by permission of the publisher. Professor Barnlund teaches at San Francisco State University. Footnotes deleted.

in telecommunication systems linking the world by satellite, in aircraft capable of moving people faster than the speed of sound, in computers which can disgorge facts more rapidly than men can formulate their questions. The methods for bringing people closer physically and electronically are clearly at hand. What is in doubt is whether the erosion of cultural boundaries through technology will bring the realization of a dream or a nightmare. Will a global village be a mere collection or a true community of men? Will its residents be neighbors capable of respecting and utilizing their differences, or clusters of strangers living in ghettos and united only in their antipathies for others?

Can we generate the new cultural attitudes required by our technological virtuosity? History is not very reassuring here. It has taken centuries to learn how to live harmoniously in the family, the tribe, the city state, and the nation. Each new stretching of human sensitivity and loyalty has taken generations to become firmly assimilated in the human psyche. And now we are forced into a quantum leap from the mutual suspicion and hostility that have marked the past relations between peoples into a world in which mutual respect and comprehension are requisite.

Even events of recent decades provide little basis for optimism. Increasing physical proximity has brought no millenium in human relations. If anything, it has appeared to intensify the divisions among people rather than to create a broader intimacy. Every new reduction in physical distance has made us more painfully aware of the psychic distance that divides people and has increased alarm over real or imagined differences. If today people occasionally choke on what seem to be indigestible differences between rich and poor, male and female, specialist and nonspecialist within cultures, what will happen tomorrow when people must assimilate and cope with still greater contrasts in life styles? Wider access to more people will be a doubtful victory if human beings find they have nothing to say to one another or cannot stand to listen to each other.

Time and space have long cushioned intercultural encounters, confining them to touristic exchanges. But this insulation is rapidly wearing thin. In the world of tomorrow we can expect to live— not merely vacation—in societies which seek different values and abide by different codes. There we will be surrounded by foreigners for long periods of time, working with others in the closest possible relationships. If people currently show little tolerance or talent for encounters with alien cultures, how can they learn to deal with constant and inescapable coexistence?

The temptation is to retreat to some pious hope or talismanic formula to carry us into the new age. "Meanwhile," as Edwin Reischauer reminds us, "we fail to do what we ourselves must do if 'one world' is ever to be achieved, and that is to develop the education, the skills and the attitudes that men must have if they are to build and maintain such a world. The time is short, and the needs are great. The task faces all men. But it is on the shoulders of people living in the strong countries of the world, such as Japan and the United States, that this burden falls with special weight and urgency."

Anyone who has truly struggled to comprehend another person—even those closest and most like himself—will appreciate the immensity of the challenge of intercultural communication. A greater exchange of people between nations, needed as that may be, carries with it no guarantee of increased cultural empathy; experience in other lands often does little but aggravate existing prejudices. Studying guidebooks or memorizing polite phrases similarly fails to explain differences in cultural perspectives. Programs of cultural enrichment, while they contribute to curiosity about other ways of life, do not cultivate the skills to function effectively in the cultures studied. Even concentrated exposure to a foreign language, valuable as it is, provides access to only one of the many codes that regulate daily affairs; human understanding is by no means guaranteed because conversants share the same dictionary. (Within the United States, where people inhabit a common territory and possess a common language, mutuality of meaning among Mexican-Americans, White-Americans, Black-Americans, Indian-Americans—to say nothing of old and young, poor and rich, pro-establishment and anti-establishment cultures—is a sporadic and unreliable occurrence.) Useful as all these measures are for enlarging appreciation of diverse cultures, they fall short of what is needed for a global village to survive.

What seems most critical is to find ways of gaining entrance into the assumptive world of another culture, to identify the norms that govern face-to-face relations, and to equip people to function within a social system that is foreign but no longer incomprehensible. Without this kind of insight people are condemned to remain outsiders no matter how long they live in another country. Its institutions and its customs will be interpreted inevitably from the premises and through the medium of their own culture. Whether they notice something or overlook it, respect or ridicule it, express or conceal their reaction will be dictated by the logic of their own rather than the alien culture.

There are, of course, shelves and shelves of books on the cultures of the world. They cover the history, religion, political thought, music, sculpture, and industry of many nations. And they make fascinating and provocative reading. But only in the vaguest way do they suggest what it is that really distinguishes the behavior of a Samoan, a Congolese, a Japanese, or an American. Rarely do the descriptions of a political structure or religious faith explain precisely when and why certain topics are avoided or why specific gestures carry such radically different meanings according to the context in which they appear.

When former President Nixon and former Premier Sato met to discuss a growing problem concerning trade in textiles between Japan and the United States, Premier Sato announced that since they were on such good terms with each other the deliberations would be "three parts talk and seven parts 'haragei'." Translated literally, "haragei" means to communicate through the belly, that is to feel out intuitively rather than verbally state the precise position of each person.

Subscribing to this strategy—one that governs many interpersonal exchanges in his culture—Premier Sato conveyed without verbal elaboration his comprehension of the plight of American textile firms threatened by accelerating exports of Japanese fabrics to the United States. President Nixon—similarly abiding by norms that govern interaction within his culture—took this comprehension of the American position to mean that new export quotas would be forthcoming shortly.

During the next few weeks both were shocked at the consequences of their meeting: Nixon was infuriated to learn that the new policies he expected were not forthcoming, and Sato was upset to find that he had unwittingly triggered a new wave of hostility toward his country. If prominent officials, surrounded by foreign advisers, can commit such grievous communicative blunders, the plight of the ordinary citizen may be suggested. Such intercultural collisions, forced upon the public consciousness by the grave consequences they carry and the extensive publicity they receive, only hint at the wider and more frequent confusions and hostilities that disrupt the negotiations of lesser officials, business executives, professionals and even visitors in foreign countries.

Every culture expresses its purposes and conducts its affairs through the medium of communication. Cultures exist primarily to create and preserve common systems of symbols by which their members can assign and exchange meanings. Unhappily, the distinctive rules that govern these symbol systems are far from obvious. About some of these codes, such as language, we have extensive knowledge. About others, such as gestures and facial codes, we have only rudimentary knowledge. On many others—rules governing topical appropriateness, customs regulating physical contact, time and space codes, strategies for the management of conflict—we have almost no systematic knowledge. To crash another culture with only the vaguest notion of its underlying dynamics reflects not only a provincial naïveté but a dangerous form of cultural arrogance.

It is differences in meaning, far more than mere differences in vocabulary, that isolate cultures, and that cause them to regard each other as strange or even barbaric. It is not too surprising that many cultures refer to themselves as "The People," relegating all other human beings to a subhuman form of life. To the person who drinks blood, the eating of meat is repulsive. Someone who conveys respect by standing is upset by someone who conveys it by sitting down; both may regard kneeling as absurd. Burying the dead may prompt tears in one society, smiles in another, and dancing in a third. If spitting on the street makes sense to some, it will appear bizarre that others carry their spit in their pocket; neither may quite appreciate someone who spits to express gratitude. The bullfight that constitutes an almost religious ritual for some seems a cruel and inhumane way of destroying a defenseless animal to others. Although staring is acceptable social behavior in some cultures, in others it is a thoughtless invasion of privacy. Privacy, itself, is without universal meaning.

Note that none of these acts involves an insurmountable linguistic challenge. The words that describe these acts—eating, spitting, showing respect, fighting, burying, and staring—are quite translatable into most languages. The issue is more conceptual than linguistic; each society places events in its own cultural frame and it is these frames that bestow the unique meaning and differentiated response they produce.

As we move or are driven toward a global village and increasingly frequent cultural contact, we need more than simply greater factual knowledge of each other. We need, more specifically, to identify what might be called the "rulebooks of meaning" that distinguish one culture from another. For to grasp the way in which other cultures perceive the world, and the assumptions and values that are the foundation of these perceptions, is to gain access to the experience of other human beings. Access to the world view and the communicative style of other cultures may not only enlarge our own way of experiencing the world but enable us to maintain constructive relationships with societies that operate according to a different logic than our own.

SOURCES OF MEANING

To survive, psychologically as well as physically, human beings must inhabit a world that is relatively free of ambiguity and reasonably predictable. Some sort of structure must be placed upon the endless profusion of incoming signals. The infant, born into a world of flashing, hissing, moving images, soon learns to adapt by resolving this chaos into toys and tables, dogs and parents. Even adults who have had their vision or hearing restored through surgery describe the world as a frightening and sometimes unbearable experience; only after days of effort are they able to transform blurs and noises into meaningful and therefore manageable experiences.

It is commonplace to talk as if the world "has" meaning, to ask what "is" the meaning of a phrase, a gesture, a painting, a contract. Yet when thought about, it is clear that events are devoid of meaning until someone assigns it to them. There is no appropriate response to a bow or a handshake, a shout or a whisper, until it is interpreted. A drop of water and the color red have no meaning, they simply exist. The aim of human perception is to make the world intelligible so that it can be managed successfully; the attribution of meaning is a prerequisite to and preparation for action.

People are never passive receivers, merely absorbing events of obvious significance, but are active in assigning meaning to sensation. What any event acquires in the way of meaning appears to reflect a transaction between what is there to be seen or heard, and what the interpreter brings to it in the way of past experience and prevailing motive. Thus the attribution of meanings is always a creative process by which the raw data of sensation are transformed to fit the aims of the observer.

The diversity of reactions that can be triggered by a single experience—meeting a stranger, negotiating a contract, attending a textile conference—is immense. Each observer is forced to see it through his own eyes, interpret it in the light of his own values, fit it to the requirements of his own circumstances. As a consequence, every object and message is seen by every observer from a somewhat different perspective. Each person will note some features and neglect others. Each will accept some relations among the facts and deny others. Each will arrive at some conclusion, tentative or certain, as the sounds and forms resolve into a "temple" or "barn," a "compliment" or "insult."

Provide a group of people with a set of photographs, even quite simple and ordinary photographs, and note how diverse are the meanings they provoke. Afterward they will recall and forget different pictures, they will also assign quite distinctive meanings to those they do remember. Some will recall the mood of a picture, others the actions; some the appearance and others the attitudes of persons portrayed. Often the observers cannot agree upon even the most "objective" details—the number of people, the precise location and identity of simple objects. A difference in frame of mind—fatigue, hunger, excitement, anger—will change dramatically what they report they have "seen."

It should not be surprising that people raised in different families, exposed to different events, praised and punished for different reasons, should come to view the world so differently. As George Kelly has noted, people see the world through templates which force them to construe events in unique ways. These patterns or grids which we fit over the realities of the world are cut from our own experience and values, and they predispose us to certain interpretations. Industrialist and farmer do not see the "same" land; husband and wife do not plan for the "same" child; doctor and patient do not discuss the "same" disease; borrower and creditor do not negotiate the "same" mortgage; daughter and daughter-in-law do not react to the "same" mother.

The world each person creates for himself is a distinctive world, not the same world others occupy. Each fashions from every incident whatever meanings fit his own private biases. These biases, taken together, constitute what has been called the "assumptive world of the individual." The world each person gets inside his head is the only world he knows. And it is this symbolic world, not the real world, that he talks about, argues about, laughs about, fights about.

Interpersonal Encounters

Every communication, interpersonal or intercultural, is a transaction between these private worlds. As people talk they search for symbols that will enable them to share their experience and converge upon a common meaning. This process, often long and sometimes painful, makes it possible finally to reconcile apparent or real differences between them. Various words are used to describe this moment. When it involves an integration of facts or ideas, it is usually called an "agreement"; when it involves sharing a mood or feeling, it is referred to as "empathy" or "rapport." But "understanding" is a broad enough term to cover both possibilities; in either case it identifies the achievement of a common meaning.

If understanding is a measure of communicative success, a simple formula—which might be called the *Interpersonal Equation*—may clarify the major factors that contribute to its achievement:

Interpersonal Understanding = ƒ (Similarity of Perceptual Orientations, Similarity of Belief Systems, Similarity of Communicative Styles)

That is, "Interpersonal Understanding" is a function of or dependent upon the degree of "Similarity of Perceptual Orientations," "Similarity of Systems of Belief," and "Similarity in Communicative Styles." Each of these terms requires some elaboration.

"Similarity in Perceptual Orientations" refers to a person's prevailing approach to reality and the degree of flexibility he manifests in organizing it. Some people can scan the world broadly, searching for diversity of experience, preferring the novel and unpredictable. They may be drawn to new foods, new music, new ways of thinking. Others seem to scan the world more narrowly, searching to confirm past experience, preferring the known and predictable. They secure satisfaction from old friends, traditional art forms, familiar life styles. The former have a high tolerance for novelty; the latter a low tolerance for novelty.

It is a balance between these tendencies, of course, that characterizes most people. Within the same person attraction to the unfamiliar and the familiar coexist. Which prevails at any given moment is at least partly a matter of circumstance: when secure, people may widen their perceptual field, accommodate new ideas or actions; when they feel insecure they may narrow their perceptual field to protect existing assumptions from the threat of new beliefs or life styles. The balance may be struck in still other ways: some people like to live in a stable physical setting with everything in its proper place, but welcome new emotional or intellectual challenges; others enjoy living in a chaotic and disordered environment but would rather avoid exposing themselves to novel or challenging ideas.

People differ also in the degree to which their perceptions are flexible or rigid. Some react with curiosity and delight to unpredictable and uncategorizable events. Others are disturbed or uncomfortable in the presence of the confusing and complex. There are people who show a high degree of tolerance for ambiguity; others manifest a low tolerance for ambiguity. When confronted with the complications and confusions that surround many daily events, the former tend to avoid immediate closure and delay judgment while the latter seek immediate closure and evaluation. Those with little tolerance for ambiguity tend to respond categorically, that is, by reference to the class names for things (businessmen, radicals, hippies, foreigners) rather than to their unique and differentiating features.

It would be reasonable to expect that individuals who approach reality similarly might understand each other easily, and laboratory research confirms this conclusion: people with similar perceptual styles attract one another, understand each other better, work more efficiently together and with greater satisfaction than those whose perceptual orientations differ.

"Similarity in Systems of Belief" refers not to the way people view the world, but to the conclusions they draw from their experience. Everyone develops a variety of opinions toward divorce, poverty, religion, television, sex, and social customs. When belief and disbelief systems coincide, people are likely to understand and appreciate each other better. Research done by Donn Byrne and replicated by the author demonstrates how powerfully human beings are drawn to those who hold the same beliefs and how sharply they are repelled by those who do not.

Subjects in these experiments were given questionnaires requesting their opinions on twenty-six topics. After completing the forms, each was asked to rank the thirteen most important and least important topics. Later each person was given four forms, ostensibly filled out by people in another group but actually filled out to show varying degrees of agreement with their own answers, and invited to choose among them with regard to their attractiveness as associates. The results were clear: people most preferred to talk with those whose attitudes duplicated their own exactly, next chose those who agreed with them on all important issues, next chose those with similar views on unimportant issues, and finally and reluctantly chose those who disagreed with them completely. It appears that most people most of the time find satisfying relationships easiest to achieve with someone who shares their own hierarchy of beliefs. This, of course, converts many human encounters into rituals of ratification, each person looking to the other only to obtain endorsement and applause for his own beliefs. It is, however, what is often meant by "interpersonal understanding."

Does the same principle hold true for "Similarity of Communicative Styles"? To a large extent, yes. But not completely. By "communicative style" is meant the topics people prefer to discuss, their favorite forms of interaction—ritual, repartee, argument, self-disclosure—and the depth of involvement they demand of each other. It includes the extent to which communicants rely upon the same channels—vocal, verbal, physical—for conveying information, and the extent to which they are tuned to the same level of meaning, that is, to the factual or emotional content of messages. The use of a common vocabulary and even preference for similar metaphors may help people to understand each other.

But some complementarity in conversational style may also help. Talkative people may prefer quiet partners, the more aggressive may enjoy the less aggressive, those who seek affection may be drawn to the more affection-giving, simply because both can find the greatest mutual satisfaction when interpersonal styles mesh. Even this sort of complementarity, however, may reflect a case of similarity in definitions of each other's conversational role.

This hypothesis, too, has drawn the interest of communicologists. One investigator found that people paired to work on common tasks were much more effective if their communicative styles were similar than if they were dissimilar. Another social scientist found that teachers tended to give higher grades on tests to students whose verbal styles matched their own than to students who gave equally valid answers but did not phrase them as their instructors might. To establish common meanings seems to require that conversants share a common vocabulary and compatible ways of expressing ideas and feelings.

It must be emphasized that perceptual orientations, systems of belief, and communicative styles do not exist or operate independently. They overlap and affect each other. They combine in complex ways to determine behavior. What a person says is influenced by what he believes and what he believes, in turn, by what he sees. His perceptions and beliefs are themselves partly a product of his manner of communicating with others. The terms that compose the Interpersonal Equation constitute not three isolated but three interdependent variables. They provide three perspectives to use in the analysis of communicative acts.

The Interpersonal Equation suggests there is an underlying narcissistic bias in human societies that draws similar people together. Each seeks to find in the other a reflection of himself, someone who views the world as he does, who interprets it as he does, and who expresses himself in a similar way. It is not surprising, then, that artists should be drawn to artists, radicals to radicals, Jews to Jews—or Japanese to Japanese and Americans to Americans.

The opposite seems equally true: people tend to avoid those who challenge their assumptions, who dismiss their beliefs, and who communicate in strange and unintelligible ways. When one reviews history, whether he examines crises within or between cultures, he finds people have consistently shielded themselves, segregated themselves, even fortified themselves, against wide differences in modes of perception or expression (in many cases, indeed, have persecuted and conquered the infidel and afterwards substituted their own cultural ways for the offending ones). Intercultural defensiveness appears to be only a counterpart of interpersonal defensiveness in the face of uncomprehended or incomprehensible differences.

INTERCULTURAL ENCOUNTERS

Every culture attempts to create a "universe of discourse" for its members, a way in which people can interpret their experience and convey it to one another. Without a common system of codifying sensations, life would be absurd and all efforts to share meanings doomed to failure. This universe of discourse—one of the most precious of all cultural legacies—is transmitted to each generation in part consciously and in part unconsciously. Parents and teachers give explicit instruction in it by praising or criticizing certain ways of dressing, of thinking, of gesturing, of responding to the acts of others. But the most significant aspects of any cultural code may be conveyed implicitly, not by rule or lesson but through modelling behavior. The child is surrounded by others who, through the mere consistency of their actions as males and females, mothers and fathers, salesclerks and policemen, display what is appropriate behavior. Thus the grammar of any culture is sent and received largely unconsciously, making one's own cultural assumptions and biases difficult to recognize. They seem so obviously right that they require no explanation.

In *The Open and Closed Mind*, Milton Rokeach poses the problem of cultural understanding in its simplest form, but one that can readily demonstrate the complications of communication between cultures. It is called the "Denny Doodlebug Problem." Readers are given all the rules that govern his culture: Denny is an animal that always faces North, and can move only by jumping; he can jump large distances or small distances, but can change direction only after jumping four times in any direction; he can jump North, South, East or West, but not diagonally. Upon concluding a jump his master places some food three feet directly West of him. Surveying the situation, Denny concludes he must jump four times to reach the food. No more or less. And he is right. All the reader has to do is explain the circumstances that make his conclusion correct.

The large majority of people who attempt this problem fail to solve it, despite the fact that they are given all the rules that control behavior in this culture. If there is difficulty in getting inside the simplistic world of Denny Doodlebug—where the cultural code has already been broken and handed to us—imagine the complexity of comprehending behavior in societies where codes have not yet been deciphered. And where even those who obey these codes are only vaguely aware and can rarely describe the underlying sources of their own actions.

If two people, both of whom spring from a single culture, must often shout to be heard across the void that separates their private worlds, one can begin to appreciate the distance to be overcome when people of different cultural identities attempt to talk. Even with the most patient dedication to seeking a common terminology, it is surprising that people of alien cultures are able to hear each other at all. And the peoples of Japan and the United States would appear to constitute a particularly dramatic test of the ability to cross an intercultural divide. Consider the disparity between them.

Here is Japan, a tiny island nation with a minimum of resources, buffeted by periodic disasters, overcrowded with people, isolated by physical fact and cultural choice, nurtured in Shinto and Buddhist religions, permeated by a deep respect for nature, nonmaterialist in philosophy, intuitive in thought, hierarchical in social structure. Eschewing the explicit, the monumental, the bold and boisterous, it expresses its sensuality in the form of impeccable gardens, simple rural temples, asymmetrical flower arrangements, a theatre unparalleled for containment of feeling, an art and literature remarkable for their delicacy, and crafts noted for their honest and earthy character. Its people, among the most homogeneous of men, are modest and apologetic in manner, communicate in an ambiguous and evocative language, are engrossed in interpersonal rituals and prefer inner serenity to influencing others. They occupy unpretentious buildings of wood and paper and live in cities laid out as casually as farm villages. Suddenly from these rice paddies emerges an industrial giant, surpassing rival nations with decades of industrial experience, greater resources, and a larger reserve of technicians. Its labor, working longer, harder and more frantically than any in the world, builds the earth's largest city, constructs some of its ugliest buildings, promotes the most garish and insistent advertising anywhere, and pollutes its air and water beyond the imagination.

And here is the United States, an immense country, sparsely settled, richly endowed, tied through waves of immigrants to the heritage of Europe, yet forced to subdue nature and find fresh solutions to the problems of survival. Steeped in the Judeo-Christian tradition, schooled in European abstract and analytic thought, it is materialist and experimental in outlook, philosophically pragmatic, politically equalitarian, economically competitive, its raw individualism sometimes tempered by a humanitarian concern for others. Its cities are studies in geometry along whose avenues rise shafts of steel and glass subdivided into separate cubicles for separate activities and separate people. Its popular arts are characterized by the hugeness of Cinemascope, the spontaneity of jazz, the earthy loudness of rock; in its fine arts the experimental, striking, and monumental often stifle the more

subtle revelation. The people, a smorgasbord of races, religions, dialects, and nationalities, are turned expressively outward, impatient with rituals and rules, casual and flippant, gifted in logic and argument, approachable and direct yet given to flamboyant and exaggerated assertion. They are curious about one another, open and helpful, yet display a missionary zeal for changing one another. Suddenly this nation whose power and confidence have placed it in a dominant position in the world intellectually and politically, whose style of life has permeated the planet, finds itself uncertain of its direction, doubts its own premises and values, questions its motives and materialism, and engages in an orgy of self criticism.

It is when people nurtured in such different psychological worlds meet that differences in cultural perspectives and communicative codes may sabotage efforts to understand one another. Repeated collisions between a foreigner and the members of a contrasting culture often produce what is called "culture shock." It is a feeling of helplessness, even of terror or anger, that accompanies working in an alien society. One feels trapped in an absurd and indecipherable nightmare.

It is as if some hostile leprechaun had gotten into the works and as a cosmic caper rewired the connections that hold society together. Not only do the actions of others no longer make sense, but it is impossible even to express one's own intentions clearly. "Yes" comes out meaning "No." A wave of the hand means "come," or it may mean "go." Formality may be regarded as childish, or as a devious form of flattery. Statements of fact may be heard as statements of conceit. Arriving early, or arriving late, embarrasses or impresses. "Suggestions" may be treated as "ultimatums," or precisely the opposite. Failure to stand at the proper moment, or failure to sit, may be insulting. The compliment intended to express gratitude instead conveys a sense of distance. A smile signifies disappointment rather than pleasure.

If the crises that follow such intercultural encounters are sufficiently dramatic or the communicants unusually sensitive, they may recognize the source of their trouble. If there is patience and constructive intention the confusion can sometimes be clarified. But more often the foreigner, without knowing it, leaves behind him a trail of frustration, mistrust, and even hatred *of which he is totally unaware*. Neither he nor his associates recognize that their difficulty springs from sources deep within the rhetoric of their own societies. Each sees himself as acting in ways that are thoroughly sensible, honest and considerate. And—given the rules governing his own universe of discourse—each is. Unfortunately, there are few cultural universals, and the degree of overlap in communicative codes is always less than perfect. Experience can be transmitted with fidelity only when the unique properties of each code are recognized and respected, or where the motivation and means exist to bring them into some sort of alignment.

THE COLLECTIVE UNCONSCIOUS

Among the greatest insights of this modern age are two that bear a curious affinity to each other. The first, evolving from the efforts of psychologists, particularly Sigmund Freud, revealed the existence of an "individual unconscious." The acts of human beings were found to spring from motives of which they were often vaguely or completely unaware. Their unique perceptions of events arose not from the facts outside their skins but from unrecognized assumptions inside them. When, through intensive analysis, they obtained some insight into these assumptions, they became free to develop other ways of seeing and acting which contributed to their greater flexibility in coping with reality.

The second of these generative ideas, flowing from the work of anthropologists, particularly Margaret Mead and Ruth Benedict, postulated a parallel idea in the existence of a "cultural unconscious." Students of primitive cultures began to see that there was nothing divine or absolute about cultural norms. Every society had its own way of viewing the universe, and each developed from its premises a coherent set of rules of behavior. Each tended to be blindly committed to its own style of life and regarded all others as evil. The fortunate person who was able to master the art of living in foreign cultures often learned that his own mode of life was only one among many. With this insight he became free to choose from among cultural values those that seemed to best fit his peculiar circumstances.

Cultural norms so completely surround people, so permeate thought and action, that few ever recognize the assumptions on which their lives and their sanity rest. As one observer put it, if birds were suddenly endowed with scientific curiosity they might examine many things, but the sky itself would be overlooked as a suitable subject; if fish were to become curious about the world, it would never occur to them to begin by investigating water. For birds and fish would take the sky and sea for granted, unaware of their profound influence because they comprise the medium for every act. Human beings, in a similar way, occupy a symbolic universe governed by codes that are unconsciously acquired and automatically employed. So much so that they rarely notice that the ways they interpret and talk about events are distinctively different from the ways people conduct their affairs in other cultures.

As long as people remain blind to the sources of their meanings, they are imprisoned within them. These cultural frames of reference are no less confining simply because they cannot be seen or touched. Whether it is an individual neurosis that keeps an individual out of contact with his neighbors, or a collective neurosis that separates neighbors of different cultures, both are forms of blindness that limit what can be experienced and what can be learned from others.

It would seem that everywhere people would desire to break out of the boundaries of their own experiential worlds. Their ability to react sensitively to a wider spectrum of events and peoples requires an overcoming of such cultural parochialism. But, in fact, few attain this broader vision. Some, of course, have little opportunity for wider cultural experience, though this condition should change as the movement of people accelerates. Others do not try to widen their experience because they prefer the old and familiar, seek from their affairs only further confirmation of the correctness of their own values. Still others recoil from such experiences because they feel it dangerous to probe too deeply into the personal or cultural unconscious. Exposure may reveal how tenuous and arbitrary many cultural norms are; such exposure might force people to acquire new bases for interpreting events. And even for the many who do seek actively to enlarge the variety of human beings with whom they are capable of communicating there are still difficulties.

Cultural myopia persists not merely because of inertia and habit, but chiefly because it is so difficult to overcome. One acquires a personality and a culture in childhood, long before he is capable of comprehending either of them. To survive, each person masters the perceptual orientations, cognitive biases, and communicative habits of his own culture. But once mastered, objective assessment of these same processes is awkward since the same mechanisms that are being evaluated must be used in making the evaluations. Once a child learns Japanese or English or Navaho, the categories and grammar of each language predispose him to perceive and think in certain ways, and discourage him from doing so in other ways. When he attempts to discover why he sees or thinks as he does, he uses the same techniques he is trying to identify. Once one becomes an Indian, an Ibo, or a Frenchman—or even a priest or scientist—it is difficult to extricate oneself from that mooring long enough to find out what one truly is or wants.

Fortunately, there may be a way around this paradox. Or promise of a way around it. It is to expose the culturally distinctive ways various peoples construe events and seek to identify the conventions that connect what is seen with what is thought with what is said. Once this cultural grammar is assimilated and the rules that govern the exchange of meanings are known, they can be shared and learned by those who choose to work and live in alien cultures.

When people within a culture face an insurmountable problem they turn to friends, neighbors, associates, for help. To them they explain their predicament, often in distinctive personal ways. Through talking it out, however, there often emerge new ways of looking at the problem, fresh incentive to attack it, and alternative solutions to it. This sort of interpersonal exploration is often successful within a culture for people share at least the same communicative style even if they do not agree completely in their perceptions or beliefs.

When people communicate between cultures, where communicative rules as well as the substance of experience differs, the problems multiply. But so, too, do the number of interpretations and alternatives. If it is true that the more people differ the harder it is for them to understand each other, it is equally true that the more they differ the more they have to teach and learn from each other. To do so, of course, there must be mutual respect and sufficient curiosity to overcome the frustrations that occur as they flounder from one misunderstanding to another. Yet the task of coming to grips with differences in communicative styles—between or within cultures—is prerequisite to all other types of mutuality.

Approaching Intercultural Communication

RICHARD E. PORTER
LARRY A. SAMOVAR

In the decades of the 1960s and 1970s, numerous events had profound effects on the world and humankind. Rapid and wide-ranging improvements in forms of transportation and communication caused the world to shrink in a figurative sense; we entered the era of the global village. Our mobility improved until distances no longer mattered. Jet airplanes can put us anywhere within hours. This newfound mobility is not exclusively ours; people around the world are on the move. International tradesmen, foreign students, diplomats, and especially tourists are moving in and out of an assortment of cultures—cultures that often appear unfamiliar, alien, and at times mysterious. Additional cultural contact also has emerged through the influx of refugees into the United States. People from Vietnam, Cambodia, Laos, Cuba, and Haiti, to name just a few countries, have entered the United States and are trying to adjust to life in their new homes. As these people try to assimilate into this culture, we will have many opportunities for intercultural contacts in our daily lives.

This original essay appeared in print for the first time in the third edition. All rights reserved. Permission to reprint must be obtained from the publisher and the authors. Professor Porter teaches in the Speech Communication Department at California State University, Long Beach. Professor Samovar teaches in the Speech Communication Department, San Diego State University.

While this global phenomenon was taking place, there was also a kind of cultural revolution within our own boundaries. Domestic events made us focus our attention upon new and often demanding cultures, subcultures, and deviant subgroups. Blacks, Chicanos, women, homosexuals, the poor, the Weatherman underground, the Symbionese Liberation Army, the drug culture, youth, and countless other groups became highly visible and vocal, and they disturbed many of us. Frequently, their communicative behaviors seemed strange, even bizarre, and failed to meet our normal expectations.

This attention to minority subcommunities made us realize that intercultural contact not only is inevitable but often is unsuccessful. We discovered, in short, that intercultural communication is difficult. Even when the natural barrier of language is overcome, we can still fail to understand and to be understood. These failures, both in the international arena and on the domestic scene, give rise to the marriage of culture and communication and to the recognition of intercultural communication as a field of study. Inherent in this fusion is the idea that intercultural communication entails the investigation of culture and the difficulties of communicating across cultural boundaries.

Intercultural communication occurs whenever a message producer is a member of one culture and a message receiver is a member of another. Our discussion, therefore, will deal with intercultural communication and point out the relationships among communication, culture, and intercultural communication.

COMMUNICATION

To understand intercultural interaction we must first understand human communication. Understanding human communication means knowing something about what happens during an encounter, why it happens, what can happen, the effects of what happens, and finally what we can do to influence and maximize the results of that event.

Understanding and Defining Communication

We begin with a basic assumption that communication has something to do with human behavior and the satisfaction of a need to interact with other human beings. Almost everyone needs social contact with other people, and this need is met through the exchange of messages that serve as bridges to unite otherwise isolated individuals. Messages come into being through human behavior. When we talk, we obviously are behaving, but when we wave, smile, frown, walk, shake our heads, or gesture, we also are behaving. Frequently these actions are messages; they are used to communicate something to someone else.

Before these behaviors can be called messages, they must meet two requirements. First, they must be observed by someone, and second, they must elicit meaning. In other words, any behavior to which meaning is given is a message.

If we examine this last statement for a moment we can see several implications. First, the word *any* tells us that both verbal and nonverbal behaviors may function as messages. Verbal messages consist of spoken or written words (speaking and writing are word-producing behaviors) while nonverbal messages consist of the entire remaining repertory of behaviors.

Second, behavior may be either conscious or unconscious. We occasionally do something without being aware of it. This is especially true of nonverbal behavior. Habits such as fingernail biting, toe tapping, leg jiggling, head shaking, staring, and smiling, for instance, occur many times without conscious awareness. Even such things as slouching in a chair, chewing gum, or adjusting glasses are frequently unconscious behaviors. And since a message consists of behaviors to which meaning may be attributed, we must acknowledge the possibility of producing messages unknowingly.

A third implication of behavior-message is that we frequently behave unintentionally. For instance, if we are embarrassed we may blush or speak with vocal disfluencies. We do not intend to blush or to stammer, but we do so anyway. Again, these unintentional behaviors become messages if someone sees them and gives meaning to them.

With this concept of conscious-unconscious, intentional-unintentional behavior relationships, we are ready to formulate a definition of communication. Here, *communication* is defined as that which happens whenever meaning is attributed to behavior or to the residue of behavior. When someone observes our behavior or its residue and gives meaning to it, communication has taken place regardless of whether our behavior was conscious or unconscious, intentional or unintentional. If we think about this for a moment, we must realize that it is impossible for us not to behave. The very act of being is a form of behavior. And if behavior has communication potential, then it is also impossible for us not to communicate; in other words, *we cannot not communicate*.

The notion of behavior residue mentioned in our definition refers to those things that remain as a record of our actions. For instance, this article is a behavior residue resulting from certain behaviors; as the authors we had to think, write, and type. Another example of behavior residue might be the odor of cigar smoke lingering in an elevator after the cigar smoker has departed. Smoking the cigar was the behavior; the odor is the residue. The meaning you give to that smell is a reflection of your past experiences and attitudes toward cigars, smoking, smoking in public elevators, and, perhaps, people who smoke cigars.

Our approach to communication has focused on the attribution of meaning to behavior. Attribution means that we take meaning that we already have and give it to behavior we observe in our environment. We might imagine that somewhere in each of our brains is a meaning reservoir in which we have stored all of the meanings we possess. These various meanings have developed throughout our lifetimes as a result of our culture acting upon us as well as the result of our individual experiences within that culture. Meaning is relative to each of us because each of us is a unique human being with a unique background and experiences.

When we encounter a behavior in our environment we each dip into our individual, unique meaning reservoirs and select the meaning we believe is most likely to be most appropriate for the behavior encountered and the social context in which it occurred. Usually this works quite well, but at other times it fails and we misinterpret a message—we attribute the wrong meaning to the behavior we have observed.

Our definition of communication has been general, thus far, in order to accommodate the many circumstances under which communication may occur. We now are going to propose a modified definition that assumes a conscious intention to communicate yet realizes that unconscious and unintentional behavior may complicate communication situations. Our definition also will specify the ingredients of communication and some of the dynamics present in communication.

The Ingredients of Communication

Before we examine the ingredients of communication, we must have a definition that specifies the ingredients and their relationships. As our purpose in studying intercultural communication is to develop communication skills to apply with conscious intent, our working definition of communication specifies intentional communication. *Communication* is now defined as a dynamic transactional behavior-affecting process in which sources and receivers intentionally code their behavior to produce messages that they transmit through a channel in order to induce or elicit particular attitudes or behaviors. Communication is complete only when the intended message recipient perceives the coded behavior, attributes meaning to it, and is affected by it. In these transactions must be included all conscious or unconscious, intentional or unintentional, verbal, nonverbal, and contextual stimuli that act as cues to both the source and the receiver about the quality and credibility of the message.

This definition allows us to identify eight specific ingredients of communication within the context of intentional communication. First is the *source*. A source is a person who has a need to communicate. This need may range from a social desire for recognition as an individual to the desire to share information with others or to influence the attitudes and behaviors of one or more others. The source's wish to communicate is a desire to share an internal state of being with another human being. Communication, then, really is concerned with the sharing of internal states of being with varying degrees of intention to influence the information, attitudes, and behaviors of others.

Internal states of being cannot be shared directly, however. We must rely on symbolic representations of our internal states. This brings us to the second ingredient, *encoding*. Encoding is an internal activity in which verbal and nonverbal behaviors are selected and arranged according to the rules of grammar and syntax applicable to the language being used to create a message.

The result of encoding behavior is a *message*. A message is a set of verbal and/or nonverbal symbols that represent a source's particular state of being at a particular moment in time and space. Although encoding is an internal act that produces a message, a message is external to the source; the message is what must pass between a source and a receiver if the source is to influence the receiver.

Messages must have a means by which they move from source to receiver. The fourth communication ingredient is the *channel* that provides the connection between source and receiver. A channel is the physical means by which the message moves between source and receiver.

The fifth ingredient is the *receiver*. Receivers are the people who intercept messages and as a consequence become linked to the message source. Receivers may be those intended by the source or they may be others who, by whatever circumstance, come in contact with the message once it has entered the channel.

Receivers have problems with messages not unlike the problems sources have with internal states of being. Messages usually impinge on receivers in the form of light waves and sound waves although they may be in forms that stimulate any of the senses. Whatever the form of sensory stimulation, receivers must convert these energies into meaningful experiences.

Converting external energies into a meaningful experience is the sixth ingredient, called *decoding*. It is akin to the source's act of encoding, as it also is an internal activity. Decoding is the internal processing of a message and the attribution of meaning to the source's behaviors that represent the source's internal state of being.

The seventh ingredient we need to consider is *receiver response*. This is most easily thought of as what a receiver decides to do about the message. Response may vary along a minimum-maximum dimension. Minimum response is the receiver's decision to ignore or to do nothing about the message. Maximum response, in contrast, is an immediate overt physical act of possibly violent proportion. If communication has been somewhat successful, the response of the receiver, to some degree, will resemble that desired by the source who created the response-eliciting message.

The final ingredient we consider is *feedback*. This is information available to a source that permits qualitative judgments about communication effectiveness in order to adjust and adapt to an ongoing situation. Although feedback and response are not the same thing, they are clearly related. Response is what the receiver decides to do about the message while feedback is information about communication effectiveness. They are related because receiver response is a normal source of feedback.

The eight ingredients just discussed are only a partial list of the factors that function during a communication event. In addition to these elements, when we conceive of communication as a process there are several other characteristics that help us understand how communication actually works.

First, communication is *dynamic*. It is an ongoing, ever-changing activity. As participants in communication we constantly are affected by other people's messages and, as a consequence, we undergo continual change. Each of us in our daily lives meets and interacts with people and these people exert some influence over us. Each time we are influenced we are changed in some way, which means that as we go through life we do so as continually changing individuals—dynamic persons.

A second characteristic of communication is that it is *interactive*. Communication must take place between a source and a receiver. This implies two or more people who bring to a communication event their own unique backgrounds and experiences that serve as a backdrop for communicative interaction. Interaction also implies a reciprocal situation in which each party attempts to influence the other. That is, each party simultaneously creates messages designed to elicit specific responses from the other.

Third, communication is *irreversible*. Once we have said something and someone has received and decoded the message, we cannot retrieve it. This circumstance is sometimes called "putting your foot in your mouth." The point is that because of the process nature of communication, once a receiver has been affected by a message, that result cannot be called back. The source may send other messages in attempts to modify the effect, but it cannot be eliminated. This frequently is a problem when we unconsciously or unintentionally send a message to someone. We may affect them adversely and not even know it. Then during future interaction we may wonder why that someone is reacting to us in an unusual way.

Fourth, communication takes place in both a *physical* and a *social* context. When we interact with someone it is not in isolation but within specific physical surroundings and under a set of specific social dynamics. Physical surroundings include specific physical objects such as furniture, window coverings, floor coverings, lighting, noise levels, acoustics, vegetation, presence or absence of physical clutter, as well as competing messages. Many aspects of the physical environment can and do affect communication—the comfort or discomfort of a chair, the color of the walls, or total atmosphere of a room are but a few. Also affecting communication is the symbolic meaning of the physical surroundings—a kind of nonverbal communication. To illustrate, recall briefly the Paris Peace Talks in which much time was spent in deciding on a table shape acceptable to all parties. While this may seem trivial, it was very important to the negotiators because a table with equal sides symbolically represented an equality of all parties at the table. The South Vietnamese did not want to give this recognition to the Viet Cong any more than North Vietnam wished to give this recognition to the United States.

Social context defines the social relationships that exist between source and receiver. In our American culture we tend to be somewhat cavalier toward social hierarchies and pay much less attention to them than do people in other cultures. Nevertheless, such differences as teacher-student, employer-employee, parent-child, Admiral-Seaman, senator-citizen, friend-enemy, physician-patient, and judge-attorney affect the communication process. And, quite frequently, the physical surroundings help define the social context. The employer may sit behind a desk while the employee stands before the desk to receive an admonition. Or, in the courtroom, the judge sits elevated facing the courtroom, jurors, and attorneys, indicating the social superiority of the judge relative to the other officers of the court. The attorneys sit side by side indicating a social equality between accuser and accused until such time as the jury of peers renders a verdict.

No matter what the social context, it will have some effect on communication. The form of language used, the respect or lack of respect shown one another, the time of day, personal moods, who speaks to whom and in what order, and the degree of nervousness or confidence people express are but a few of the ways in which the social context can affect communication.

At this point, we should see clearly that human communication does not take place in a social vacuum. Rather, communication is an intricate matrix of interacting social acts that occur in a complex social environment. This social environment reflects the way people live, how they come to interact with and get along in their world. This social environment is culture, and if we truly are to understand communication, we also must understand culture.

CULTURE

When we begin to consider culture, we are concerned with the way people live because culture is the form or pattern for living. People learn to think, feel, believe, and strive for what their culture considers proper. Language habits, friendships, eating habits, communication practices, social acts, economic and political activities, and technology all follow the patterns of culture. If people speak Tagalog, shun members of another race, eat snakes, avoid wine, live in communal housing, bury their dead, talk on the telephone, or rocket to the moon, it is because they have been born into or at least reared in a culture that contains these elements. What people do, how they act, and how they live and communicate are both responses to and functions of their culture.

Culture is an intriguing concept. Formally defined, *culture* is the deposit of knowledge, experiences, beliefs, values, attitudes, meanings, hierarchies, religion, timing, roles, spatial relations, concepts of the universe, and material objects and possessions acquired by a large group of people in the course of generations through individual and group striving. Culture manifests itself in patterns of language and in forms of activity and behavior that act as models for both the common adaptive acts and the styles of communication that enable people to live in a society within a given geographic environment at a given state of technical development at a particular moment in time. Culture also specifies and is defined by the nature of material things that play an essential role in common life. Such things as houses, instruments and machines used in industry and agriculture, forms of transportation, and instruments of war provide a material foundation for social life. Culture is persistent, enduring, and omnipresent; it includes all of the behavioral reinforcements received during the course of a lifetime. Culture also dictates the form and structure of our physical realm, and it encompasses and specifies the social environment permeating our lives. The effect of culture on our lives is largely unrealized. Perhaps a way to understand cultural influences is by way of analogy with electronic computers: As we program computers to do what they do, our culture to a great extent programs us to do what we do and to be what we are. Our culture affects us in a deterministic manner from conception to death—and even after death in terms of funeral rites.

Culture and communication are inseparable because culture not only dictates who talks with whom, about what, and how the communication proceeds, it also helps to determine how people encode messages, the meanings they have for messages, and the conditions and circumstances under which various messages may or may not be sent, noticed, or interpreted. In fact, our entire repertory of communicative behaviors is dependent largely on the culture in which we have been raised. Culture, consequently, is the foundation of communication. And, when cultures vary, communication practices also vary.

Subcultures and Subgroups

A *subculture* is a racial, ethnic, regional, economic, or social community exhibiting characteristic patterns of behavior sufficient to distinguish it from others within an embracing culture or society. Subcultures in the United States include, for example, Oriental Americans, Polish Americans, Jews, the urban poor, Hare Krishnas, and the Mafia.

Another important societal element that does not meet criteria necessary to be called a subculture, but nevertheless poses similar communication problems, is the *deviant subgroup*. Included among the deviant subgroups are gays, pimps and prostitutes, the drug community, youth gangs, religious cults, and revolutionary organizations. These subgroups are products of the dominant culture, but their group existence has not persisted long enough nor developed a sufficiently wide enough pattern of deviant behaviors to qualify as a culture or subculture. The main distinguishing feature of subgroups is that their values, attitudes, and behavior or elements of their behavior are at odds

with the majority community. Subgroups exist within a community that is displeased with them, generally disagrees with them, and has difficulty understanding and communicating with them. But, from the point of view of commuication, these subgroups can be considered as if they are subcultures.

Each subculture or subgroup is a social entity that, although a part of the dominant main culture, is unique and provides its members with a set of experiences, backgrounds, social values, and expectations that may not be found elsewhere in the dominant culture. Hence, communication between people who appear similar may not be easy because in reality they are members of very different subcultures or subgroups and their experiential backgrounds are so different they may be unable to relate meaningfully.

INTERCULTURAL COMMUNICATION

In all respects, everything so far said about communication applies to intercultural communication. The functions and relationships between the components of communication obviously apply. But what especially characterizes intercultural communication is that sources and receivers come from different cultures. This alone is sufficient to identify a unique form of communicative interaction that must take into account the role and function of culture in the communication process. In this section, intercultural communication will first be defined and discussed through the perspective of a model and then its various forms will be shown.

Intercultural Communication Model

Intercultural communication occurs whenever a message producer is a member of one culture and a message receiver is a member of another. In this circumstance, we immediately are faced with the problems inherent in a situation where a message encoded in one culture must be decoded in an-

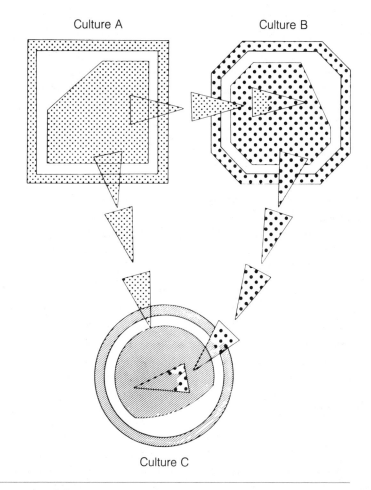

Figure 1 Model of Intercultural Communication

other. As we have already seen, culture shapes the individual communicator. It largely is responsible for the entire repertory of communicative behaviors and meanings each person possesses. Consequently, those repertories possessed by two people from different cultures will be very different, which can lead to all sorts of difficulties. But, through the study and understanding of intercultural communication, we can reduce or nearly eliminate these difficulties.

The influence of culture on the individual and the problems of encoding and decoding messages across cultures are illustrated in Figure 1. Three cultures are represented in this model by three distinct geometric shapes. Cultures A and B are relatively similar to one another and they are represented by a square and an irregular octagon that is nearly square. Culture C is quite different from cultures A and B. This greater difference is represented both by the circular shape of culture C and its physical distance from cultures A and B.

Within each culture is another shape somewhat similar to the shape of the culture. This represents an individual who has been shaped by the culture. The shape of the individual is slightly different from that of the influencing culture. This suggests two things. First, there are other affecting influences besides culture that help shape the individual. And, second, although culture is a dominant shaping force on an individual, people vary to some extent from each other within any culture.

Message encoding and decoding across cultures is illustrated by a series of arrows connecting them. These arrows indicate the transmission of messages between cultures. When a message leaves the culture in which it was encoded, it contains the meaning intended by the encoder. This is represented by the arrows leaving a culture containing the same pattern as that within the individual encoder. When a message reaches the culture where it is to be decoded, it undergoes a transformation in which the influence of the decoding culture becomes a part of the message meaning. The meaning content of the original message becomes modified during the decoding phase of intercultural communication because the culturally different repertory of communicative behaviors and meanings possessed by the decoder does not contain the same cultural meanings possessed by the encoder.

The degree to which culture influences intercultural communication situations is a function of the dissimilarity between the cultures. This is indicated in the model by the degree of pattern change shown in the message arrows. The change between cultures A and B is much less than the change between cultures A and C and between cultures B and C. This is due to the greater similarity of cultures A and B. The repertory of communicative behaviors and meanings is similar and the decoding effort therefore produces results more nearly like those intended in the original message encoding. But since culture C is represented as being vastly different from cultures A and B, the decoding also is vastly different and more nearly represents the pattern of culture C.

The model suggests that there can be wide variation in cultural differences during intercultural communication. This is due in part to circumstances. Intercultural communication takes place in a wide variety of situations that range from interactions between people in whom cultural differences are extreme to interactions between people who are members of the same dominant culture and whose differences are reflected by membership in different subcultures or subgroups. If we think of differences varying along a minimum-maximum dimension (see Figure 2), the amount of difference between two cultural groups can be seen to depend on the comparative social uniqueness of the two groups. Although this scale is crude, it permits us to examine an intercultural communication act and gain insight into the effect of cultural differences. In order to understand this scale, we will look at some of the examples of cultural differences positioned along the scale.

The first example represents a maximum difference—differences between Asian and Western cultures. This is typified in a conversation between two farmers, one from a communal farm on the outskirts of Beijing and the other from a large mechanized wheat and corn farm near Des Moines. In this example, we find the greatest number of cultural factors subject to variation. Physical appearance, religion, philosophy, social attitudes, language, heritage, basic concepts of self and the universe, and degree of technological development are among the cultural factors that differ sharply. We also must recognize that these two farmers share the commonality of farming and a rural life style. In some aspects of cultural patterns they may be more closely related to each other than they are to members of their own cultures who live in a large urban metropolis. In other words, across some cultural dimensions, the Iowa farmer may share more in common with the Chinese farmer than with a New York City stockbroker.

An example closer to the center of the scale is the difference between American culture and German culture. Less variation is found—physical characteristics are similar, and the English language is derived in part from German and its ancestor languages. The roots of German and American philosophies lie in ancient Greece, and most Americans and Germans share the Christian religion.

Examples near the minimal end of the scale are characterized in two ways. First are variations found between members of separate but similar cultures—for instance, between U.S. Americans

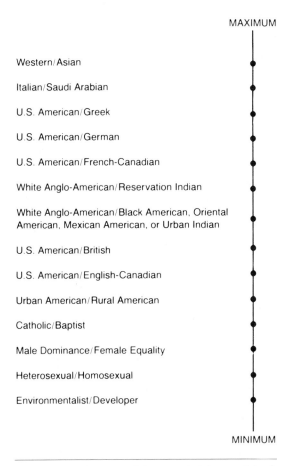

MAXIMUM

Western/Asian

Italian/Saudi Arabian

U.S. American/Greek

U.S. American/German

U.S. American/French-Canadian

White Anglo-American/Reservation Indian

White Anglo-American/Black American, Oriental
American, Mexican American, or Urban Indian

U.S. American/British

U.S. American/English-Canadian

Urban American/Rural American

Catholic/Baptist

Male Dominance/Female Equality

Heterosexual/Homosexual

Environmentalist/Developer

MINIMUM

Figure 2 Arrangement of Compared Cultures, Subcultures, and Subgroups along a Scale of Minimum to Maximum Socio-cultural Differences

and English-Canadians. The difference is less than that found between American and German cultures, between American and Greek cultures, or even between American and British cultures but greater than that generally found within a single culture. Second, minimal differences may be seen between subcultures or deviant subgroups of the same dominant culture. Socio-cultural differences can be found between members of the Catholic church and members of the Baptist church, between members of the Sierra Club and advocates of offshore oil drilling, between middle-class Americans and the urban poor, between mainstream

Americans and the homosexual community, or between male dominance advocates and female equality advocates.

In any of these examples—comparisons between separate but similar cultures or between subcultures or subgroups—members of each cultural group share much more in common than compared groups in the examples at the maximum end of the scale. They probably speak the same language, share the same general religion, attend the same schools, and inhabit the same geographical area. Yet, these groups are still somewhat culturally different; they do not share the same experiences nor do they share the same perceptions. They see the world differently. Their life styles may be different, and their beliefs, values, and attitudes are not all the same. Because of their cultural similarity, they differ primarily in limited aspects of their social perceptions.

Social perception is the process by which we attach meanings to the social objects and events we encounter in our environments and is an extremely important aspect of communication. Culture conditions and structures our perceptual processes in such a way that we develop culturally determined perceptual sets. These perceptual sets not only influence which stimuli reach our awareness, but more important, they have a great influence on the judgmental aspect of perception—the attachment of meaning to these stimuli. It is our contention that *intercultural communication* can best be understood as *cultural variance in the perception of social objects and events*. The barriers to communication caused by this perceptual variance can best be lowered by a knowledge and understanding of cultural factors that are subject to variance, coupled with an honest and sincere desire to communicate successfully across cultural boundaries.

A sincere desire for effective communication is critical because a successful exchange may be hampered not only by cultural variations but also by unfriendly or hostile attitudes. Problems of racial and ethnic prejudice can inhibit communication between cultures and races. If these problems are present, no amount of cultural knowledge or communication skill will make the encounter a pleasant one. Our major concern then is with those situations where there are cultural differences in the encoding and decoding of verbal and nonverbal messages during intercultural interaction and the problems inherent in the varying situations.

CULTURE AND COMMUNICATION

The link between culture and communication is crucial to understanding intercultural communication because it is through the influence of culture that people learn to communicate. A Korean, an Egyptian, or an American learns to communicate like other Koreans, Egyptians, or Americans. Their behavior can convey meaning because it is learned and shared; it is cultural. People view their world through categories, concepts, and labels that are products of their culture.

Cultural similarity in perception makes the sharing of meaning possible. The ways in which we communicate, the circumstances of our communication, the language and language style we use, and our nonverbal behaviors are all primarily a response to and a function of our culture. Communication is cultural. And, as cultures differ from one another, the communication practices and behaviors of the individuals reared in those cultures also will vary.

Culture is an all-encompassing form or pattern for living. It is complex, abstract, and pervasive. Numerous aspects of culture help to determine communicative behavior. These socio-cultural elements are diverse and cover a wide range of human social activity. For the sake of simplicity and to put some limitation on our discussion, we will examine a few of the socio-cultural elements associated with *perception*, *verbal processes*, and *nonverbal processes*.

These socio-cultural elements are the constituent parts of intercultural communication. When we combine them, as we do when we communicate, they are like the components of a stereo system—each one relates to and needs the other. In our discussion, the elements will be separated in order to identify and discuss them. In actuality, however, they do not exist in isolation nor do they function alone. They all form a complex matrix of interacting elements that operate together to constitute the complex phenomenon called intercultural communication.

Perception

In its simplest sense, perception is the internal process by which we select, evaluate, and organize stimuli from the external environment. In other words, perception is the way in which we convert the physical energies of our environment into meaningful experience. A number of corollary issues arise out of this definition that help explain the relationship between perception and culture. It is generally believed that people behave as they do because of the ways in which they perceive the world, and that these behaviors are learned as part of their cultural experience. Whether in judging beauty or describing snow, we respond to stimuli as we do primarily because our culture has taught us to do so. We tend to notice, reflect on, and respond to those elements in our environment that are important to us. In the United States we might respond principally to a thing's size and cost while to the Japanese, color might be the important criterion. Culture tends to determine which are the important criteria of perception.

Intercultural communication can best be understood as cultural variance in the perception of social objects and events. A central tenet of this position is that minor problems in communication often are exaggerated by these perceptual differences. To understand others' worlds and actions, we must try to understand their perceptual frames of reference. We must learn to understand how they perceive the world. In the ideal intercultural encounter we would hope for many overlapping experiences and a commonality of perceptions. The nature of culture, however, tends to introduce us to dissimilar experiences, and hence, to varied perceptions of the external world.

Three major socio-cultural elements have a direct and major influence on the meanings we develop for our percepts. These elements are our *belief, value, attitude systems*, our *world view*, and our *social organization*. When these three elements influence our perceptions and the meanings we develop for them, they are affecting our individual, subjective aspects of meanings. We all may see the same social entity and agree upon what it is in objective terms, but what the object or event means to us individually may differ considerably. Both a Saudi Arabian and an American would agree in the objective sense that a particular person is a woman. But they most likely would disagree completely on what a woman is in a social sense. Each of the three major socio-cultural elements will be considered individually to show how they affect perception.

Belief, Value, Attitude Systems. *Beliefs*, in a general sense, can be viewed as individually held subjective probabilities that some object or event possesses certain characteristics. A belief involves a link between the belief object and the characteristics that distinguish it. The degree to which we believe that an event or an object possesses certain characteristics reflects the level of our subjective probability and, consequently, the depth or intensity of our belief. That is, the more certain we are in a belief, the greater is the intensity of that belief.

Culture plays an important role in belief formation. Whether we accept the *New York Times*, the Bible, the entrails of a goat, tea leaves, the visions induced by peyote, or the changes specified in the Taoist *I Ching* as sources of knowledge and beliefs depends on our cultural backgrounds and experiences. In matters of intercultural communication there are no rights or wrongs as far as beliefs are concerned. If someone believes that voices in the wind can guide one's behavior along the proper path, we cannot throw up our hands and declare the belief wrong; we must be able to recognize and to deal with that belief if we wish to obtain satisfactory and successful communication.

Values are the evaluative aspect of our belief, value, attitude systems. Evaluative dimensions include qualities such as usefulness, goodness, aesthetics, need satisfaction ability, and pleasure production. Although each of us has a unique set of values, there also are values that tend to permeate a culture. These are called *cultural values*.

Cultural values usually are derived from the larger philosophical issues that are part of a culture's milieu. These values generally are normative in that they inform a member of a culture what is good and bad, right and wrong, true and false, positive and negative, and so on. Cultural values define what is worth dying for, what is worth protecting, what frightens people and their social systems, what are considered proper subjects for study and ridicule, and what types of events lead individuals to group solidarity. Cultural values also specify which behaviors are important and which should be avoided within a culture. Cultural values are a set of organized rules for making choices and reducing conflicts within a given society.

Values express themselves within a culture by prescribing behaviors that members of the culture are expected to perform. These are called *normative values*. Thus, Catholics are supposed to attend Mass, motorists are supposed to stop at stop signs, and workers in our culture are supposed to arrive at work at the designated time. Most people follow normative behaviors; a few do not. Failure to do so may be met with either informal or codified sanctions. Thus the Catholic who avoids Mass may receive a visit from the priest, the driver who runs a stop sign may receive a traffic ticket, and the employee who is tardy may be fired. Normative behavior also extends itself into everyday manners and becomes a guide to individual and group behavior that minimizes or prevents harm to individual sensitivities within cultural groups.

Beliefs and values contribute to the development and content of our *attitudes*. We may define an attitude formally as a learned tendency to respond in a consistent manner with respect to a given object of orientation. Attitudes are learned within a cultural context. Whatever cultural environment surrounds us helps shape and form our attitudes, our readiness to respond, and ultimately our behavior.

The cultural bias of belief, value, attitude systems can be seen in the example of bullfighting. Many North Americans believe that cruelty to animals is wrong and that the systematic wearing down and killing of a bull is an example of that cruelty. Consequently, many North Americans view bullfighting within a negative attitude frame and will actively avoid attending bullfights or even viewing them on television. Some even campaign to have bullfights banned. To most Latin Americans, however, bullfighting is a contest of courage between man and beast. It is evaluated positively, and the triumph of the matador is not seen as cruelty to animals but as the exercise of courage, skill, and physical agility. In this cultural context, to witness a bullfight is to witness one of life's finer moments when man again demonstrates his dominance over the beast. This mastery of the bull even has metaphorical overtones of good triumphing over evil.

World View. This cultural element, though abstract in concept and description, is one of the most important elements found in the perceptual aspects of intercultural communication. World view deals with a culture's orientation toward such things as God, humanity, nature, the universe, and the other philosophical issues that are concerned with the concept of being. In short, our world view helps us locate our place and rank in the universe. Because world view is so complex, it is often difficult to isolate during an intercultural interaction. In this examination, we seek to understand its substance and its elusiveness.

World view issues are timeless and represent the most fundamental basis of a culture. A Catholic surely has a different world view than does a Moslem, Hindu, Jew, Taoist, or atheist. The way in which native American Indians view the individual's place in nature differs sharply from the middle-class Euro-American's view. Native Americans have a world view that places them at one with nature. They perceive a balanced relationship between man and the environment, a partnership of equality and respect. In other words, middle-class Euro-Americans have a human-centered picture of the world. Because of their profound belief that humans are supreme and are apart from nature, they treat the universe as theirs—a place to

carry out their desires and wishes through the power of science and technology.

World view influences a culture at a very deep and profound level. Its effects often are quite subtle and not revealed in such obvious and often superficial ways as dress, gestures, and vocabulary. Think of a culture's world view as being analogous to a pebble tossed into a pond. Just as the pebble causes ripples that spread and reverberate over the entire surface of the pond, world view spreads itself over a culture and permeates every facet of it. World view influences beliefs, values, attitudes, uses of time, and many other aspects of culture. In many subtle and often not obvious ways, it is a powerful influence in intercultural communication because as a member of a culture, each communicator's world view is so deeply imbedded in the psyche that it is taken completely for granted, and the communicators each assume automatically that everyone else views the world as they do.

Social Organization. The manner in which a culture organizes itself and its institutions also affects how members of the culture perceive the world and how they communicate. It might be helpful to look briefly at two of the dominant social units found in a culture.

The *family*, although it is the smallest social organization in a culture, is one of the most influential. Families set the stage for a child's development during the formative periods of life. The family presents the child with a wide range of cultural influences that affect almost everything from a child's first attitudes to the selection of toys. The family also guides the child's acquisition of language. Skills from vocabulary building to dialects are the purview of the family. Even the amount of emphasis placed on language is governed by the family. The family also offers and withholds approval, support, rewards, and punishments, which have a marked effect on the values children develop and the goals they pursue. If, for example, children by observation and communication learn that silence is paramount in their culture, as it is in Japan, they will reflect that aspect of culture in their behavior and bring it to intercultural settings.

The *school* is another social organization that is important. By definition and history, schools are endowed with a major portion of the responsibility for passing on and maintaining a culture. They are a community's basic link with its past as well as its taskmaster for the future. Schools maintain a culture by relating to new members what has happened, what was important, and what one as a member of the culture must know. Schools may teach geography or wood carving, mathematics or nature lore; they may stress revolution based on peace or predicated on violence. Or they may relate a particular culturally accepted version of history. But whatever is taught in a school is determined by the culture in which that school exists. Recognition of this fact has motivated some black communities in the United States to open storefront alternative schools that stress black power and "black is beautiful." These concerns are strictly a part of the black cultural experience and are not found as integrated components of the dominant U.S. culture's school functions.

Having shown the importance of perceptual systems to our understanding of culture and intercultural communication, we next turn our attention to verbal processes.

Verbal Processes

Verbal processes include not only how we talk to each other but also the internal activities of thinking and meaning development for the words we use. These processes (*verbal language* and *patterns of thought*) are vitally related to perception and the attachment and expression of meaning.

Verbal Language. Any discussion of language in intercultural settings must include an investigation of language issues in general before dealing with specific problems of foreign language, language translation, and the argot and vernacular of subcultures and subgroups. Here, in our introduction to the various dimensions of culture, we will look at verbal language as it relates to our understanding of culture.

In the most basic sense, language is an organized, generally agreed upon, learned symbol system used to represent human experiences within a geographic or cultural community. Each culture places its own individual imprint on word symbols. Objects, events, experiences, and feelings have a particular label or name solely because a community of people have arbitrarily decided to so name them. Thus, because language is an inexact system of symbolically representing reality, the meanings for words are subject to a wide variety of interpretations.

Language is the primary vehicle by which a culture transmits its beliefs, values, and norms. Language gives people a means of interacting with other members of their culture and a means of thinking. Thus, language serves both as a mechanism for communication and as a guide to social reality. Language influences perceptions and transmits and helps pattern thoughts.

Patterns of Thought. The mental processes, forms of reasoning, and approaches to problem solution prevalent in a community are another major component of culture. Unless they have had experiences with people from other cultures who follow different patterns of thought, most people assume everyone thinks in much the same way. But we should be aware that there are cultural differences in aspects of thinking. These differences can be clarified and related to intercultural communication by making a general comparison between Western and Eastern patterns of thought. In most Western thought there is an assumption of a direct relationship between mental concepts and the concrete world of reality. This orientation places great stock in logical considerations and rationality. There is a belief that truth is out there somewhere, that it can be discovered by following the correct logical sequences. One need only turn over the right rock and it will be there. The Eastern view, best illustrated by Taoist thought, holds that problems are solved quite differently. To begin with, people are not granted instant rationality. Truth is not found by active searching and the application of Aristotelian modes of reasoning. On the contrary, one must wait, and if truth is to be known it will make itself apparent. The major difference in these two views is in the area of activity. To the Western mind, human activity is paramount and ultimately will lead to the discovery of truth. In the Taoist tradition, truth is the active agent, and if it is to be known it will be through the activity of truth making itself apparent.

A culture's thought patterns affect the way individuals in that culture communicate, which in turn will affect the way each person responds to individuals from another culture. We cannot expect everyone to employ the same patterns of thinking, but understanding that many patterns exist and learning to accommodate them will facilitate our intercultural communication.

Nonverbal Processes

Verbal processes are the primary means for the exchange of thoughts and ideas, but closely related nonverbal processes often can overshadow them. Although there is not complete agreement as to what constitutes the province and domain of nonverbal processes, most authorities agree that the following topics must be included: gestures, facial expressions, eye contact and gaze, posture and movement, touching, dress, objects and artifacts, silence, space, time, and paralanguage. As we turn to the nonverbal processes relevant to intercultural communication, we will consider three aspects: *nonverbal behavior* that functions as a silent form of language, *concepts of time*, and the *use and organization of space*.

Nonverbal Behavior. It would be foolish for us to try to examine all of the elements that constitute nonverbal behavior because of the tremendous range of activity that constitutes this form of human activity. An example or two should enable us to visualize how nonverbal issues fit into the overall scheme of intercultural understanding. Touch as a

form of communication can demonstrate how nonverbal communication is a product of culture. In Germany, women as well as men shake hands at the outset of every social encounter; in the United States, women seldom shake hands. In Thailand, people do not touch in public, and to touch someone on the head is a major social transgression. You can imagine the problems that could arise if one did not understand some of the variances.

Another illustrative example is eye contact. In the United States we are encouraged to maintain good eye contact when we communicate. In Japan eye contact often is not important. And in some American Indian tribes young children are taught that eye contact with an elder is a sign of disrespect. A white school teacher working on an Indian reservation was not aware of this and thought her students were not interested in school because they never looked at her.

As a component of culture, nonverbal expression has much in common with language. Both are coding systems that are learned and passed on as part of cultural experience. Just as we learn that the word *stop* can mean to halt or to cease, we also have learned that an arm held up in the air with the palm facing another person frequently means the same thing. Because most nonverbal communication is culturally based, what it symbolizes often is a case of what a culture has transmitted to its members. The nonverbal symbol for suicide, for example, varies among cultures. In the United States it is a finger pointed at the temple, in Japan it is a hand thrust into the stomach, and in New Guinea, it is symbolized by a hand on the neck. Both nonverbal symbols and the responses they generate are part of cultural experience—what is passed from generation to generation. Every symbol takes on significance because of one's past experience with it. Culture influences and directs those experiences, and is, therefore, a major contributor to how we send, receive, and respond to these nonverbal symbols.

Concept of Time. A culture's concept of time is its philosophy toward the past, present, and future, and the importance or lack of importance it places on time. Most Western cultures think of time in lineal-spatial terms. We are timebound and well aware of the past, present, and future. In contrast, the Hopi Indians pay very little attention to time. They believe that each thing—whether a person, plant, or animal—has its own time system.

Even within the dominant American culture we find groups that have learned to perceive time in ways that appear strange to many outsiders. Mexican-Americans frequently speak of Chicano time when their timing varies from the predominant Anglo concept. And blacks often use what is referred to as BPT (black people's time) or hang-loose time—maintaining that priority belongs to what is happening at that instant.

Time, like other components of culture, serves to underscore a basic theme of this book—vast differences exist between diverse cultures, and those differences affect communication.

Use of Space. The way in which people use space as a part of interpersonal communication is called *proxemics*. It involves not only the distance between people engaged in conversation but also their physical orientation. We all most likely have some familiarity with the fact that Arabs and Latins tend to interact physically closer together than do North Americans. What is important is to realize that people of different cultures do have different ways in which they relate to one another spatially and that when talking to someone from another culture we must expect what in our culture would be violations of our personal space and be prepared to continue our interaction without reacting adversely. We may experience feelings that are difficult to handle; we may believe that the other person is overbearing, boorish, or even making unacceptable sexual advances when indeed the other person' movements are only manifestations of his or her cultural learning about how to use space.

Physical orientation is also culturally influenced, and it helps to define social relationships. North Americans prefer to sit where they are face to face or at right angles to one another. We seldom seek side-by-side arrangements. Chinese, however, often prefer and feel more comfortable in a side-by-side arrangement and may feel uncomfortable when placed in a face-to-face situation.

We also tend to define social hierarchies through our nonverbal use of space. Sitting behind a desk while speaking with someone who is standing is usually a sign of a superior-subordinate relationship with the socially superior person seated. This same behavior, however, can also be used to convey disapproval, disrespect, or insult if one violates cultural norms. Misunderstandings easily occur in intercultural settings when two people, each acting according to the dictates of their cultures, violate each other's expectations. If we were to remain seated when expected to rise, we could easily violate a cultural norm and insult our host or guest unknowingly.

How we organize space also is a function of our culture. Our homes, for instance, nonverbally preserve our cultural beliefs and values. South American house designs are extremely private with only a door opening directly onto the street and everything else behind walls. North Americans are used to large unwalled front yards with windows looking into the house allowing passersby to see what goes on inside. In South America, a North American is liable to feel excluded and wonder about what goes on behind all those closed doors.

SUMMARY

In many respects the relationship between culture and communication is reciprocal. They affect and influence each other. What we talk about, how we talk about it, what we see, attend to, or ignore, how we think, and what we think about are influenced by our culture. In turn, what we talk about, how we talk about it, and what we see help shape, define, and perpetuate our culture. One cannot exist without the other. One cannot change without causing change in the other.

We have suggested that the chief problem associated with intercultural communication is error in social perception brought about by cultural variations that affect the perceptual process. The attribution of meaning to messages is in many respects influenced by the culture of the message decoder.

When the message being interpreted was encoded in another culture, the cultural influences and experiences that produced that message may be entirely different from the cultural influences and experiences that are being drawn upon to decode the message. Consequently, grave errors in meaning may arise that are neither intended nor really the fault of the communicators. These errors are the result of people with entirely different backgrounds being unable to understand one another accurately.

The approach we have taken also is based on a fundamental assumption: The parties to intercultural communication must have an honest and sincere desire to communicate and seek mutual understanding. This assumption requires favorable attitudes on the part of intercultural communicators and an elimination of superior-inferior relationships based on membership in particular cultures, races, or ethnic groups. Unless this basic assumption has been satisfied, our theory of cultural variance in social perception will not produce improvement in intercultural communication.

We have discussed several socio-cultural variables that are major sources of communication difficulty. Although they were discussed in isolation, we cannot allow ourselves to conclude that they are unrelated. They all are related in a matrix of cultural complexities. For successful intercultural communication, we must be aware of these cultural factors affecting communication in both our own culture and in the culture of the other party. We need to understand not only cultural differences but also cultural similarities. While understanding differences will help us determine sources of potential problems, understanding similarities may help us become closer to one another.

Intercultural Communication

DORTHY L. PENNINGTON

Is intercultural communication something that one does consciously or something that occurs automatically when members of two or more cultures interact?

Any good definition of intercultural communication requires both description and prescription. The descriptive level aids in showing what occurs naturally in intercultural communication. From the point of view of description, it is more appropriate, for several reasons, to treat intercultural communication as something that occurs, rather than as something that one does consciously. First, treating intercultural communication prescriptively, that is, as something that one should do, leads to the assumption that once a prescribed set of steps is followed, communication takes place. This formula-like approach may be misleading, if not disappointing, when the desired results are not achieved as expected. Second, treating intercultural communication as something that should occur in a certain way focuses undue attention on the procedure itself, rather than on the end result.

By the same token, however, prescriptive definitions are needed to serve as correctives for habitual blunders made both in the past and in the present, and as a basis for improving these interactions. That is, because intercultural communication has occurred in certain ways previously is not justification enough for continuing such behaviors and for regarding them as sacred, simply because tradition has sanctioned them. These behaviors must be subjected to evaluation and the ineffective ones should be replaced with carefully prescribed alternatives.

Some approaches to intercultural communication begin with attention to what is meant by the term *culture* and then proceed to examining what happens when two or more cultures come together. What occurs at the point of intersect can be called communication. It is safe to presume that neither group remains unaffected; something of each is consumed in the dynamic. Real intercultural communication is not so much the idea of cultural entities coming together and merely alternating in their influence upon one another; it is, rather, the transactions that occur at the point of intersect. Each culture is in some way different as a result of the interaction.

Although this operational definition of intercultural communication simplifies the issue, it results not from a lack of awareness of more "scientific" definitions of culture, but rather from a familiarity with the abundant definitions of culture identified by such scholars as Kroeber and Kluckhohn.[1] In general terms, culture may be defined as learned and shared behaviors and perceptions transmitted from generation to generation through a shared symbol system.

There are equally many definitions of the term *communication*. The one requirement that must be met for communication, however, is that some type of meaning must be derived and shared.

To understand intercultural communication in greater detail, attention must be devoted to the concept of culture and to its major components. Two approaches that are available for achieving such an understanding are a global, undifferentiated one in which culture is mentioned as an abstracted whole, and a differentiated approach in which significant, though not exhaustive, configurations are pointed out and then comprehensively linked into a whole. Because of the nature of the task at hand—providing specific ways to conceptualize intercultural communication so that applied operationalizations can be made—the latter of the two approaches will be used here. The assumption is that the beginning of intercultural communication is cultural understanding—of culture in general, of one's own culture in particular, and of another's culture. Before understanding another culture, one must fully understand one's own, and therefore, a historical background leading to the present state of a culture is necessary. The approach that will be used here may be called a "cultural-historical" one. What might in some instances seem like extreme polarizations are made for purposes of comparison only, and the components listed are not exclusive, but may overlap one another.

SIGNIFICANT CULTURAL COMPONENTS

Existential World-View, Cosmology, Ontology

This component has to be given high, if not first, priority in the study of a culture. Because this component permeates all others, its significance cannot be underestimated. If one understands a culture's world-view and cosmology, reasonable accuracy can be attained in predicting behaviors and motivations in other dimensions. Too often intercultural study is confined to a description and awareness of the differences between or among cultures. Although necessary, this treatment alone is inadequate. Beyond recognizing differences, which is analogous to noticing the tip of the iceberg while the bottom goes unseen, there is the need to understand the reasons for and the nature of the differences. Probing cosmological issues allows one to penetrate deeper, to really begin to understand the nature of culture.

Included in the study of world-view and cosmology are questions such as, What are the dominant beliefs and attitudes of a group, concerning the place of humans in nature and in society? What is the general pattern of ideas concerning the relations of humans to one another and to the world as they perceive and experience it? For each culture, for example, one can construct an existential, ontological hierarchy, such as: (1) Supreme Being,

(2) supernatural beings, (3) humans, (4) lower forms of life, (5) inanimate objects, and (6) nature.[2]

Humans' perceptions of their relation to the other forms of existence is very important, as is the hierarchical order in which they are ranked. For example, what do humans consider to be their relation to God or to the being identified as supreme for that culture? Is the Supreme Being considered to be the ultimate controller of life and events or do humans perceive themselves as exercising great control over their destiny? And likewise, do humans seek to gain dominion over nature, to blend harmoniously with it in a complementary sense, or do they subdue themselves to it? Is their relation with other humans one of competition in which the needs of the individual are placed above those of the group, or is it a communal, cooperative one in which individual needs are subordinated to those of the welfare of the group? In short, does the world-view show the world as a place to be conquered, manipulated, or dominated in order to be negotiated, or does it show the world as being negotiable, but by petition, placation, or working with nature in a complementary sense? A capitalistic world-view, for example, supports the social darwinistic notion of survival of the fittest (based upon what it perceives as innate qualities), and this leads to the formation of hierarchies among people.

Other relevant questions include: How are the beliefs of a culture expressed formally and implicitly in the customs and ethical prescriptions in both ritualistic and secular contexts? What is the relation between (1) the major attitudes toward social relations, (2) the proper use of resources, and (3) the established beliefs about the nature of human society and its place in a wider universe of cosmic forces? How do the beliefs relate to the construction of ethical standards and to the prescribed courses of action? Is the relation reciprocal? (If a group believes that an omniscient, omnipresent Supreme Being intervenes in the affairs of humans to avenge injustice, members of that group are likely to emphasize compassion and regard for their fellows.)

How have the beliefs and attitudes of a people been conditioned by their natural, material, and cultural background? What are the myths of the origin of a people and how do such myths express and sustain beliefs and attitudes? What is the relation between myths, rituals, and rites, and the local resources (a culture's dependence or independence)? For example, is the rain dance thought to bring forth the rain, and the rain, the harvest? In times of drought, why do some believe in cloud seeding, some in irrigation, and others in the rain dance that placates the natural forces to prompt rain? Why are certain life-symbols thought to bring forth fertility among some peoples, whereas others rely more on drugs or chemicals to enhance fertility?

How and to what extent does a group rationalize its fate by postulating mysterious forces and beings in nature and mysterious powers among their fellows? What are the beliefs in the supernatural and in the ability of humans to control it? In what contexts is the supernatural evoked? Is this done through rituals, prayers, or other ceremonies? How is this related to the rest of the cultural pattern and to social activity? How does a group base its living patterns on the perceived causal factors linking events, on the logical implications of ideas, and on an understanding of mechanical and organic processes?[3] (One simplified example in our society, of a change in the understanding of processes, seems to be a conscious move back to organic production where food is grown in natural ways, without mechanization or artificial stimulants. More complicated and less superficial examples can be chosen to capture the patterns of reasoning, causality, and activity within a culture.)

Questions of world-view and cosmology such as those listed above are central to the understanding of a culture, and it is important to determine in-depth world-view identities and relational habits.

Language, Symbol System

The development of language in a culture is an issue that has interested semanticists for quite some time. Included in the issue is the question of the relationship between symbols and referents, between words and the things for which they stand.

Explanations of the origin of language lead to a circle, "for the end and goal of language formation, the act of denotation by specific properties, must be regarded as also the principle of its beginning."[4] Whatever its origin, however, language is the medium through which a culture expresses its world-view; it is the process of mediation between thought and natural surroundings. Like culture in general, language is learned and it serves to convey thoughts; in addition it transmits values, beliefs, perceptions, norms, and so on. Through sharing in the language, one becomes a part of a cultural community and has existence in relation to it. While to an outsider the language may seem strange, to the insider it has assumed symbolic significance and often mythic power, such as in a culture where it is believed that the success of a hunt depends upon uttering the right words. And just as language is the medium through which the world-view of a culture is expressed, because of the circular relationship between the two, world-view influences the nature of language.

Nonverbal and extra-verbal communication patterns are also learned. Kinesics, gestures, eye contact and behavior, as well as pictoral and geometric shapes and designs, tend to have significance unique to a particular culture. The same holds true for tactile communication and for vocal inflections and stress. Built into both the verbal and nonverbal language of a culture are perceptions, stored judgments, expectations, and of equal importance, the process of reasoning, the structural means by which decisions are arrived at.

Schemas

Each culture has previous learnings and perceptions that influence its intake of new information and phenomena. These may be called its schemas[5] or its schematic pattern of interpreting, organizing, and classifying data. Each culture places priorities and values in different places. Even hierarchical ranking of the same items may differ from group to group. Going beyond the basic need for food, clothing, and shelter, for example, which is shared

by all cultures, a culture will rank such things as competition, cooperation, material acquisitions, male dominance, individual rights vis-à-vis societal rights, colors, tastefulness, timeliness, and so on, in its own preferential way. Though schemas can be modified by learning, they are culturally based and are influenced by world-view, in terms of the ways in which information and data are reconciled and fitted together.

Beliefs, Attitudes, and Values

Beliefs are judgments, expectancies, or implicit sets, and belief systems have three major dimensions: a belief-disbelief dimension, a central-peripheral dimension, and a time-perspective dimension.[6] Beliefs may be isolated judgments about isolated events, phenomena, or data, whereas attitudes represent tendencies or predispositions to relate events, phenomena, or data to one another and to regard them in a rather predictable way. A series of beliefs, therefore, may comprise an attitude. Values are related to beliefs in that they too are based upon judgments. Consequently, certain things are held in esteem and regarded with merit and worth. A culture's values are symbolized in its behavioral expectations and norms.

Beliefs, attitudes, and values are formed not only through the direct experiences of an individual, but also through vicarious and shared cultural experiences and perceptions. It is through language and myths, among other primary means of learning, that they are shared and transmitted. And like language and schemas, beliefs, attitudes, and values are influenced by a culture's cosmology and world-view. For instance, if members of a culture believe that a Supreme Being controls their existence and that their power vis-á-vis such a Being is limited, their reverence will probably be reflected not only in their honor and submission to the deity, but also by the attitude of "what will be, will be" in their relations with their fellows and in their mundane encounters. Thus the culture will adopt as a value the honoring of the deity and the anticipation of the role of fate, suggesting a belief in an external locus of control.

We can see, then, how beliefs become attitudes and how both serve to mold cultural values. Beliefs are the seeds that are nurtured into attitudes that grow into values.

Temporality

Temporality refers to the concept of, attitude toward, and use of time. Each culture has a concept of past, present, and future, and treats time in a unique way:

Fundamental to the understanding of any group is knowledge of how that group structures time and space. To those outside the group, a different time or space orientation often appears bizarre simply because the outsider doesn't understand the different set of cultural rules regulating and directing the behavior of the insider.[7]

Time-binding is a cultural phenomenon that is "tied up into life in so many ways that it is difficult to ignore it."[8] And since time-binding is a cultural phenomenon, we can gain insight by specifying those features of a culture that are believed to influence its time-binding, and by showing, as claimed in the basic thesis posited here, that time-binding, like the other components, is shaped by world-view and cosmology.

One explanation holds that a culture's religious and philosophical doctrines provide the basis for its temporality. More specifically, the parts of religious doctrines considered relevant are those pertaining to existence and to being, to the soul, to the ego, to the place of humans in the ontological order, to their relationship to higher beings, and so on. For example, Western religious doctrines teach that the soul extends its existence infinitely into the future. This belief comes not only from the influence of Christianity on the West, but also from the teachings of Judaic and other peoples who preceded Christianity.[9] Like the soul, in Western religious philosophy, the ego is also organized in terms of a "unilinear progression"[10] toward the future.

Hence, a culture's concept of time (past, present, and future) is determined by its philosophy of ego-extension, as shown, for instance, in Western tradition where there is a futuristic attitude and a preoccupation with what is to come and with planning for it. Humans' perceptions of their place in the ontology and their perceived ability to master their existence will influence the extent to which they attempt to control and plan for the future or to which they dwell on the past or present.

An additional explanation, different from that of religious doctrines providing the basis for a culture's temporality, attributes time-usage to the nature of the activities in which a group is engaged and to its geographical location. Commercialization and technology are given as some of the reasons for the way time is regarded in America, for example. Years ago in an agrarian, unhurried life style, promptness was not a premium and agrarian people, such as farmers, often approximated the correct time by looking at the position of the sun. With increased commercialization of activities, however, standardization of time became necessary.

Also important in the study of time is the degree to which a group feels a sense of progress, when comparing one generation to the next. Those groups that feel that their existence from generation to generation is not marked by significant changes (that is, measured along a linear dimension) but that instead see their existence in terms of a circular, déjà vu pattern will tend to regard time in a cavalier manner, especially if they believe in an external locus of control. The contrary will usually be true for groups that feel a definite sense of progress through generations.[11]

Space, Proxemics

Just as each culture has its own orientation toward time, it also has a set of rules governing spatial behaviors. What, for instance, is considered to be the appropriate distance between persons interacting within a given culture?

Edward Hall has noted four distances for Americans interacting, each of which has a different use: (1) intimate distance (six to eighteen inches), (2) personal distance (eighteen inches to four feet),

(3) social distance (four to seven feet), and (4) public distance (twelve to twenty-five feet or more).[12] To persons of other cultures whose members stand closer when interacting, American distances are greater and seem less personal.

Not only are the spaces between interacting persons unique to different cultures, but also the ordering of the surrounding space in terms of material objects and openness. The sense of boundaries and territoriality may be less tangible and the property lines and measured borders may be less distinctly defined in some cultures. What is seen as empty space in one culture may not be considered so in another. For example, unoccupied areas in Africa, which to an outsider are open space, are to the African "the forest," a sacred place. One American student who visited Nigeria expressed having a different sense of spatiality when riding in automobiles there, because speed limits were not always defined and one drove where there was open space, rather than according to center lines. Or consider Native American cultures, whose traditional perception of boundaries differs from other cultures' perception.

In addition to the concept of physical space is that of psychological space. Psychological security is provided by such things as feelings of mental safety and comfort with one's surroundings, by having one's beliefs, attitudes, values, and identity remain intact and unthreatened. Each culture's learned and shared features "become its basis of identity. These may be such things as a common background, experiences, language, world-view, schemas, social organization, et cetera. A race thus becomes defensive when others intrude upon its psychological space."[13]

Religion, Myths, and Expressive Forms

Each culture has phenomena and events that are not explainable in rational terms; they must be accounted for in other ways, such as through religion and one of its expressive forms, myths:

While religion grows from the blind worship of Life and magic "aversion" of Death to a definite totem-cult or other sacramentalism, another sort of "life-symbol" develops in its own way, starting also in quite unintentional processes, and culminating in permanent significant forms. This medium is myth.[14]

A genuine myth is said to contain a measure of truth and is perceived to be a satisfying and true answer to questions that a group deems important.[15] Mythic truths, however, are of a different kind, revealed only in a festive atmosphere.[16]

Myth is related to language in that myth "is an inherent necessity of language, if we recognize in language the outward form and manifestation of thought; it is in fact the dark shadow which language throws upon thought and which can never disappear till language becomes commensurate with thought, which it never will."[17]

Religion and myth in a culture are significant forms and are a part of the cultural cosmology. Myths are functionally basic and account for such fundamental questions as the origin of the universe and how its various configurations are related to each other, including a culture's beliefs about its own origin. Myths create a sense of social consciousness.

Closely allied to religion and myths are the various expressive and presentational forms such as music, art, poetry, dance, and so on.

Social Relationships and Communication Networks

The family, which is often referred to as the smallest unit in society, is also one of the agencies of socialization within a culture. By the same token, the culture determines the nature of the family structure and of the communication networks. In some cultures the family structure is nuclear, and in others, it is more extended. The former is built around the relationship between parents and children, whereas the latter incorporates other relatives such as aunts, uncles, grandparents, cousins, and so on. Extended families are believed to foster a greater sense of community, of involvement with others, and of shared responsibility for the welfare of others.

Community relations may be communal and cooperative or competitive and individualistic, depending in large part upon whether the culture is an oral or a literate one. Oral cultures, compared to those that emphasize literacy, are believed to foster a greater sense of communalism and cooperation. Since in oral cultures much communication takes place by spoken words, members feel a greater sense of participation in the information and with one another and, according to McLuhan, this sense of interdependency is created because no one is able to know appreciably more or less than anyone else—meaning that there is little individualism and specialization.[18] The ear, which is sensitive, hyperaesthetic, and all-inclusive, is the primary medium in oral cultures. Literate cultures, on the other hand, use the eye, which is said to be cool and neutral. And as McLuhan further states, when humans become phonetically literate, they may have an intellectual grasp of the world, but most of the deeply emotional corporate family feeling is excised from their relationship with their social milieu, since the alphabet, a part of literate cultures, translates otherwise rich divergencies into visual form; and the visual sense is the only one that allows us to detach.[19]

Although oral and literate media are not mutually exclusive, but may be viewed as different degrees on the same continuum, they greatly affect the type of communication relationships within a culture. Those cultures oriented toward oral media will undoubtedly begin to value relationships and the need for interdependency and cooperation in a manner different from literate cultures that emphasize individualism and competition; what were once quantitative points on the continuum eventually become qualitative ones, and the design of social relationships becomes principally one of inclusion versus one of exclusion. Because a culture is "massaged" by the type of media with which it communicates, the role of media in shaping the nature, views, and relationships in a culture must be acknowledged and examined.

Examining communication networks and dynamics within a culture also provides insights into other types of social structure. For example, is the flow of communication downward through a vertical hierarchy, from the older members to the younger or from the more powerful to the less powerful, or can the flow be described as horizontal? If communication is initiated by and is more easily accessible to certain groups or individuals, what does this reflect about status differences?

A culture's social relationships and communication networks, like its other significant components, are related to its cosmology, and they fall at the anthropomorphic level of the ontology where humans' relationship to other persons is the concern.

Interpolation Patterns

As a concept, interpolation is used by social psychologists, but it is also relevant for the study of culture. Interpolation, as used here, refers to the handling of new or unanticipated matter that appears between a group and its ultimate goal. It is what transpires or how the group makes the necessary interventions between itself and its final goal or destination. For example, let us suppose that a group of boys is going on a fishing trip and they suddenly discover that in order to proceed in the desired direction, they must cross a wire fence otherwise used to contain cattle. How they choose to do so is a matter of interpolation. They may stoop between two rows of wire as someone raises the top string of wire, or they may choose to find a gate and open it in order to pass through. The interpolation may be a matter for conversation on the first trip, but the more often the fishing trips are taken, the less the crossing of the fence is a separate act; it becomes integrated into the fishing trip. It then becomes a reflex-like action which no longer enters the conversation. To use another example, going on a canoeing expedition may be a different type of experience for one cultural group than for another. Negotiating the rough currents may serve for one group as an appropriate time to communicate verbally with one another and with nature, whereas another group may emphasize complete silence.

Interpolation, therefore, is a crucial factor to consider in the study of a culture, for although cultures often work toward the same ends, the means by which interventions are made to handle unanticipated matter, and the complementary behaviors surrounding the completion of the task, may bear little similarity.

MODEL OF CULTURE

The significant, though not exhaustive, configurations of a culture discussed above can be holistically linked in the following model (Figure 1), which pictorially summarizes the relationship of the parts to the whole. The model portrays a culture's world-view, its cosmology, and its ontological perceptions as being the central base in which the other components are grounded. The essence of cosmology and world-view is, therefore, primary to the understanding of any cultural conceptualizations and to the more observable behavioral manifestations. While behaviorally the parts may interact as an abstracted whole, this model helps in diagramming or focusing on any component as a unit of analysis.

INTERCULTURAL COMMUNICATION

In intercultural communication, we are concerned with what transpires when two or more cultures come together. What occurs at the point of intersection? What behaviors are engendered by the encounter itself? Assuming that there are differences among groups, how are they handled? The phenomenon of difference is a critical one—humans have a hard time when others are different from them.

Sociologically, history informs us that we should expect several results when groups with differences come together: (1) the formation of some

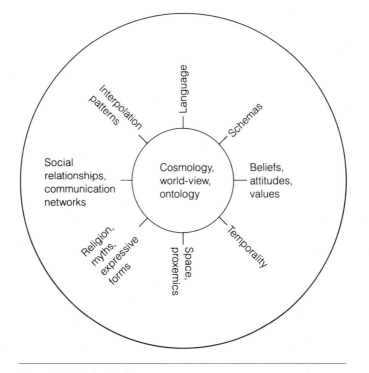

Figure 1 Model of Culture

type of hierarchy, (2) power relationships, (3) prejudice, and (4) persuasion or other means of enforcing the hierarchy.

Hierarchies will inevitably develop in any social order for various reasons: (1) fate, (2) destiny, (3) historical necessity, or (4) social equilibrium.[20] Consequently, categories of superiors, equals, and inferiors will emerge. The superiors gain and retain their power by persuading inferiors that they have the right to rule—they create a perception of legitimate power. Those at the top of the hierarchy ostensibly "know" that they represent the virtue of the order, but their "knowledge" cannot be accounted for by any rational means, for it is beyond the kind of reason used to explore space, time, and motion.[21]

Through the hierarchy, power relationships develop and some portion of the population becomes a distinctive entity. The means of differentiation may be social or physical, and the "inferior" group will be assigned roles by members of the "superior" group. For example, in America, religion and color were rationales used to enslave and subordinate Africans and to try to instill within them a sense of inferiority because of their different religion and color. Realizing that they are seen as being different, either the "inferiors" will try to emulate the behaviors of the large group to prove that they are not different, or they will form a distinctive social structure that to them assumes symbolic significance.

By controlling the advanced technology, the superior weapons, the means of production, and the images that the mass media project, the "superiors" can retain their power and can use these means along with prejudice to reinforce the distance between themselves and other groups. While the "superior" group may often accomplish its ends by its power of persuasion, coercion may be necessary in some cases to reinforce the status differences, as was the case between early Americans and the Africans brought here for servitude.

Therefore, in studying the relations between two or more cultural groups, one can and should historically trace the formation of the hierarchy or the source of difficulty; often the origin was purely arbitrary. If there are problems between groups, one can then discover that many of the existing and problematic attitudes of one group toward another had arbitrary origins and that there should be nothing sacred or unchangeable about them.

Such a historical approach to intercultural communication has proven valid for this writer and has been reconfirmed in several ways. For example, at a meeting of American historians, the question was posed as to the worth of using the historical methodology of reconstructing the formation of relationships and events among groups—to achieve understanding and generate information about intercultural relations—in hopes that the understanding and information would serve as corrective mechanisms for attitude change. The response of the historians present was quite encouraging. They concurred that historically reconstructing relations between groups as they developed chronologically can, in fact, serve as a basis of attitude change, by allowing one to trace the origin of present difficulties and to seriously examine the often arbitrary formation of existing attitudes. A second corrective function derived from historical reconstruction, as vividly pointed out by one historian, is that it allows a sense of identification between people. He related a classroom experience that after having read the life story of the famous black leader Frederick Douglass, one of the white students in the class expressed an identification with Douglass as a human being and as a man, the type of identification that the hierarchical structure of superior-inferior would normally preclude. The historical approach seems to be valid for understanding the relations between any given cultures, for attitude examination, and for needed change. This approach assumes that there has been some previous relationship between the groups in question, that the question of power has come to bear on the relationship, and that some type of hierarchical relationship is apparent.

To summarize, one can conceptualize intercultural communication on four levels: (1) the cosmological, which means providing a thorough understanding of culture and its universal features, and viewing its bases in cosmological beliefs, as shown in the discussion and model of culture presented here; (2) the historical, which involves determining objective facts and data about previous communication between or among the cultures in question (can historical reconstruction of the relations between the groups be used to trace the source of any present difficulties, and if so, what advantages are provided by doing so?); (3) the theoretical, or determining what systems of analysis can be applied to communication between the groups, and what theories, models, postulates, hypotheses, and so on can aid in analyzing the process; and (4) the practical, which involves determining what types of exercises, simulations, controlled and real-life experiences to use to buttress the learning experiences of participants in intercultural communication.

As a final note, it should be pointed out that teachers, facilitators, and participants should be prepared to handle the risks and apprehensions that may be felt when undergoing new growth and learning experiences in intercultural communication.

NOTES

1. A. L. Kroeber and Clyde Kluckhohn, *Culture, A Critical Review of Concepts and Definitions* (New York: Random House, Vintage Books, n.d.).

2. Adapted from John S. Mbiti, *African Religions and Philosophy* (New York: Doubleday & Company, 1969), p. 20.

3. *African Worlds*, edited by Darryl Forde (London: Oxford University Press, 1954), vii–xii.

4. Ernest Cassirer, *Language and Myth* (New York: Dover Publications, 1953), p. 30.

5. John Parry. *The Psychology of Human Communication* (New York: American Elsevier Publishing Company, 1967), p. 97.

6. Milton Rokeach, *The Open and Closed Mind* (New York: Basic Books, 1960), pp. 32–53.

7. Thomas Kochman, *Rappin' and Stylin' Out* (Urbana: University of Chicago Press, 1972), p. 19.

8. Edward Hall, *The Silent Language* (New York: Fawcett, 1969), p. 52.

9. Marian W. Smith, "Different Cultural Concepts of Past, Present, and Future," *Psychiatry* XV, no. 4, November 1952, p. 396.

10. Ibid., p. 397.

11. Dorthy L. Pennington, "Temporality Among Black Americans: Implications for Intercultural Communication," unpublished doctoral dissertation, University of Kansas, 1974.

12. Edward Hall, *The Hidden Dimension* (New York: Doubleday, 1969), pp. 113–129.

13. Jon A. Blubaugh and Dorthy L. Pennington, *Crossing Difference: Interracial Communication* (Columbus, Ohio: Charles E. Merrill, 1976), p. 76.

14. Suzanne K. Langer, *Philosophy in a New Key* (New York: New American Library, 1951), p. 148.

15. Adolph E. Jensen, *Myth and Cult Among Primitive Peoples* (Chicago: University of Chicago Press, 1963), p. 41.

16. Ibid.

17. Cassirer, *Language and Myth*, p. 5.

18. "Playboy Interview: Marshall McLuhan," reprint from the March 1969 issue of *Playboy Magazine*. Copyright © 1969 by HMH Publishing Company, 12pp. unnumbered.

19. Ibid.

20. Hugh Duncan, *Communication and Social Order* (New York: Bedminister Press, 1962), pp. 253–256.

21. Ibid.

Context and Meaning

EDWARD T. HALL

One of the functions of culture is to provide a highly selective screen between man and the outside world. In its many forms, culture therefore designates what we pay attention to and what we ignore.[1] This screening function provides structure for the world and protects the nervous system from "information overload."[2] Information overload is a technical term applied to information processing systems. It describes a situation in which the system breaks down when it cannot properly handle the huge volume of information to which it is subjected. Any mother who is trying to cope with the demands of small children, run a house, enjoy her husband, and carry on even a modest social life knows that there are times when everything happens at once and the world seems to be closing in on her. She is experiencing the same information overload that afflicts business managers, administrators, physicians, attorneys, and air controllers. Institutions such as stock exchanges, libraries, and telephone systems also go through times when the demands on the system (inputs) exceed capacity. People can handle the crunch through delegating and establishing priorities; while institutional solutions are less obvious, the high-context rule seems to apply. That is, the only way to increase information-handling capacity without increasing the mass and complexity of the system is to program the memory of the system so that less information is required to activate the system, i.e., make it more

From Edward T. Hall, *Beyond Culture* (Garden City, N.Y.: Doubleday & Company, 1976), pp. 85–103. Copyright © 1976 by Edward T. Hall. Reprinted by permission of Doubleday & Company, Inc. and The Lescher Agency. Professor Hall teaches at Northwestern University.

like the couple that has been married for thirty-five years. The solution to the problem of coping with increased complexity and greater demands on the system seems to lie in the preprogramming of the individual or organization. This is done by means of the "contexting" process. . . .

The importance of the role of context is widely recognized in the communication fields, yet the process is rarely described adequately, or if it is, the insights gained are not acted upon. Before dealing with context as a way of handling information overload, let me describe how I envisage the contexting process, which is an emergent function; i.e., we are just discovering what it is and how it works. Closely related to the high–low-context continuum is the degree to which one is aware of the selective screen that one places between himself and the outside world.[3] As one moves from the low to the high side of the scale, awareness of the selective process increases. Therefore, what one pays attention to, context, and information overload are all functionally related.

In the fifties, the United States government spent millions of dollars developing systems for machine translation of Russian and other languages. After years of effort on the part of some of the most talented linguists in the country, it was finally concluded that the only reliable, and ultimately the fastest, translator is a human being deeply conversant not only with the language but with the subject as well. The computers could spew out yards of print-out but they meant very little. The words and some of the grammar were all there, but the sense was distorted. That the project failed was not due to lack of application, time, money, or talent, but for other reasons, which are central to the theme of this [article].

The problem lies not in the linguistic code but in the context, which carries varying proportions of the meaning. Without context, the code is incomplete since it encompasses only part of the message. This should become clear if one remembers that the spoken language is an abstraction of an event that happened, might have happened, or is being planned. As any writer knows, an event is usually infinitely more complex and rich than the language used to describe it. Moreover, the writing system is an abstraction of the spoken system and is in effect a reminder system of what somebody said or could have said. In the process of abstracting, as contrasted with measuring, people take in some things and unconsciously ignore others. This is what intelligence is: paying attention to the right things. The linear quality of a language inevitably results in accentuating some things at the expense of others. Two languages provide interesting contrasts. In English, when a man says, "It rained last night," there is no way of knowing how he arrived at that conclusion, or if he is even telling the truth, whereas a Hopi cannot talk about rain at all without signifying the nature of his relatedness to the event—firsthand experience, inference, or hearsay. This is a point made by the linguist Whorf[4] thirty years ago. However, selective attention and emphasis are not restricted to language but are characteristic of the rest of culture as well.

The rules governing what one perceives and [what one] is blind to in the course of living are not simple; at least five sets of disparate categories of events must be taken into account. These are: the subject or activity, the situation, one's status in a social system, past experience, and culture. The patterns governing juggling these five dimensions are learned early in life and are mostly taken for granted. The "subject" or topic one is engaged in has a great deal to do with what one does and does not attend. People working in the "hard" sciences, chemistry and physics, which deal with the physical world, are able to attend and integrate a considerably higher proportion of significant events observed than scientists working with living systems. The physical scientist has fewer variables to deal with; his abstractions are closer to the real events; and context is of less importance. This characterization is, of course, oversimplified. But it is important to remember that the laws governing the physical world, while relatively simple compared to those governing human behavior, may seem complex to the layman, while the complexity of language appears simple to the physicist, who, like everyone else, has been talking all his life. In these terms it is all too easy for the person who is in full command

of a particular behavioral system, such as language, to confuse what he can *do* with a given system, with the unstated rules governing the way the system operates. The conceptual model I am using takes into account not only what one takes in and screens out but what one does not know about a given system even though one has mastered that system. The two are *not* the same. Michael Polanyi[5] stated this principle quite elegantly when he said, "The structure of a machine cannot be defined in terms of the laws which it harnesses."

What man chooses to take in, either consciously or unconsciously, is what gives structure and meaning to his world. Furthermore, what he perceives is "what he intends to do about it." Setting aside the other four dimensions (situation, status, past experience, and culture), theoretically it would be possible to arrange all of man's activities along a continuum ranging from those in which a very high proportion of the events influencing the outcome were consciously considered to those in which a much smaller number were considered. In the United States, interpersonal relations are frequently at the low end of the scale. Everyone has had the experience of thinking that he was making a good impression only to learn later that he was not. At times like these, we are paying attention to the wrong things or screening out behavior we should be observing. A common fault of teachers and professors is that they pay more attention to their subject matter than they do to the students, who frequently pay too much attention to the professor and not enough to the subject.

The "situation" also determines what one consciously takes in and leaves out. In an American court of law, the attorneys, the judge, and the jury are compelled by custom and legal practice to pay attention only to what is legally part of the record. Context, by design, carries very little weight. Contrast this with a situation in which an employee is trying to decipher the boss's behavior—whether he is pleased or not, and if he is going to grant a raise. Every little clue is a story in itself, as is the employee's knowledge of behavior in the past.

One's status in a social system also affects what must be attended. People at the top pay attention to different things from those at the middle or the bottom of the system. In order to survive, all organizations, whatever their size, have to develop techniques not only for replacing their leader but for switching the new leader's perceptions from the internal concerns he focused on when he was at the lower and middle levels to a type of global view that enables the head man or woman to chart the course for the institution.

The far-reaching consequences of what is attended can be illustrated by a characteristic fault in Western thinking that dates back to the philosophers of ancient Greece. Our way of thinking is quite arbitrary and causes us to look at ideas rather than events—a most serious shortcoming. Also, linearity can get in the way of mutual understanding and divert people needlessly along irrelevant tangents. The processes I am describing are particularly common in the social sciences; although the younger scientists in these fields are gradually beginning to accept the fact that when someone is talking about events on one level this does not mean that he has failed to take into account the many other events on different levels. It is just that one can talk about only a single aspect of something at any moment (illustrating the linear characteristic of language).

The results of this syndrome (of having to take multiple levels into account when using a single-level system) are reflected in a remark made by one of our most brilliant and least appreciated thinkers in modern psychiatry, H. S. Sullivan,[6] when he observed that as he composed his articles, lectures, and books the person he was writing to (whom he projected in his mind's eye) was a cross between an imbecile and a bitterly paranoid critic. What a waste. And so confusing to the reader who wants to find out what the man is really trying to say.

In less complex and fast-moving times, the problem of mutual understanding was not as difficult, because most transactions were conducted with people well known to the speaker or writer, people with similar backgrounds. It is important for conversationalists in any situation—regardless of the area of discourse (love, business, science)—

to get to know each other well enough so that they realize what each person is and is not taking into account. This is crucial. Yet few are willing to make the very real effort—life simply moves too fast—which may explain some of the alienation one sees in the world today.

Programming of the sort I am alluding to takes place in all normal human transactions as well as those of many higher mammals. It constitutes the unmeasurable part of communication. This brings us to the point where it is possible to discuss context in relation to meaning, because what one pays attention to or does not attend is largely a matter of context. Remember, contexting is also an important way of handling the very great complexity of human transactions so that the system does not bog down in information overload.

Like a number of my colleagues, I have observed that meaning and context are inextricably bound up with each other. While a linguistic code can be analyzed on some levels independent of context (which is what the machine translation project tried to accomplish), *in real life the code, the context, and the meaning can only be seen as different aspects of a single event*. What is unfeasible is to measure one side of the equation and not the others.[7]

Earlier, I said that high-context messages are placed at one end and low-context messages at the other end of a continuum. A high-context (HC) communication or message is one in which most of the information is either in the physical context or internalized in the person, while very little is in the coded, explicit, transmitted part of the message. A low-context (LC) communication is just the opposite; i.e., the mass of the information is vested in the explicit code. Twins who have grown up together can and do communicate more economically (HC) than two lawyers in a courtroom during a trial (LC), a mathematician programming a computer, two politicians drafting legislation, two administrators writing a regulation, or a child trying to explain to his mother why he got into a fight.

Although no culture exists exclusively at one end of the scale, some are high while others are low. American culture, while not on the bottom, is toward the lower end of the scale. We are still considerably above the German-Swiss, the Germans, and the Scandinavians in the amount of contexting needed in everyday life. While complex, multi-institutional cultures (those that are technologically advanced) might be thought of as inevitably LC, this is not always true. China, the possessor of a great and complex culture, is on the high-context end of the scale.

One notices this particularly in the written language of China, which is thirty-five hundred years old and has changed very little in the past three thousand years. This common written language is a unifying force tying together half a billion Chinese, Koreans, Japanese, and even some of the Vietnamese who speak Chinese. The need for context is experienced when looking up words in a Chinese dictionary. To use a Chinese dictionary, the reader must know the significance of 214 radicals (there are no counterparts for radicals in the Indo-European languages). For example, to find the word for star one must know that it appears under the sun radical. To be literate in Chinese, one has to be conversant with Chinese history. In addition, the spoken pronunciation system must be known, because there are four tones and a change of tone means a change of meaning; whereas in English, French, German, Spanish, Italian, etc., the reader need not know how to pronounce the language in order to read it. Another interesting sidelight on the Chinese orthography is that it is also an art form.[8] To my knowledge, no low-context communication system has ever been an art form. Good art is always high-context; bad art, low-context. This is one reason why good art persists and art that releases its message all at once does not.

The level of context determines everything about the nature of the communication and is the foundation on which all subsequent behavior rests (including symbolic behavior). Recent studies in sociolinguistics have demonstrated how context-dependent the language code really is. There is an excellent example of this in the work of the linguist Bernstein,[9] who has identified what he terms "restricted" (HC) and "elaborated" (LC) codes in which vocabulary, syntax, and sounds are all altered: In the restricted code of intimacy in the home, words and sentences collapse and are shortened. This even applies to the phonemic structure of the language. The individual sounds begin to merge, as does the vocabulary, whereas in the highly articulated, highly specific, elaborated code of the classroom, law, or diplomacy, more accurate distinctions are made on all levels. Furthermore, the code that one uses signals and is consistent with the situation. A shifting of code signals a shift in everything else that is to follow. "Talking down" to someone is low-contexting him—telling him more than he needs to know. This can be done quite subtly simply by shifting from the restricted end of the code toward the elaborated forms of discourse.

From the practical viewpoint of communications strategy, one must decide how much time to invest in contexting another person. A certain amount of this is always necessary, so that the information that makes up the explicit portions of the message is neither inadequate nor excessive. One reason most bureaucrats are so difficult to deal with is that they write for each other and are insensitive to the contexting needs of the public. The written regulations are usually highly technical on the one hand, while providing little information on the other. That is, they are a mixture of different codes or else there is incongruity between the code and the people to whom it is addressed. Modern management methods, for which management consultants are largely responsible, are less successful than they should be, because in an attempt to make everything explicit (low-contexting again) they frequently fail in their recommendations to take into account what people already know. This is a common fault of the consultant, because few consultants take the time (and few clients will pay for the time) to become completely contexted in the many complexities of the business.

There is a relationship between the worldwide activism of the sixties and where a given culture is situated on the context scale, because some are more vulnerable than others. HC actions are by definition rooted in the past, slow to change, and highly stable. Commenting on the need for the stabilizing effect of the past, anthropologist Loren Eiseley[10] takes an anti-activist position and points out how vulnerable our own culture is:

Their world (the world of the activist), therefore, becomes increasingly the violent, unpredictable world of the first men simply because, in lacking faith in the past, one is inevitably forsaking all that enables man to be a planning animal. For man's story,[11] in brief, is essentially that of a creature who has abandoned instinct *and replaced it with cultural tradition and the hard-won increments of contemplative thought. The lessons of the past have been found to be a reasonably secure construction for proceeding against an unknown future.*[12]

Actually, activism is possible at any point in the HC–LC continuum, but it seems to have less direction or focus and becomes less predictable and more threatening to institutions in LC systems. Most HC systems, however, can absorb activism without being shaken to their foundations.

In LC systems, demonstrations are viewed as the last, most desperate act in a series of escalating events. Riots and demonstrations in the United States, particularly those involving blacks,[13] are a message, a plea, a scream of anguish and anger for the larger society to *do something*. In China (an HC culture), the Red Guard riots apparently had an entirely different significance. They were promulgated from the top of the social order, not the bottom. They were also a communication from top to bottom: first, to produce a show of strength by Mao Tse-tung; second, to give pause to the opposition and shake things up at the middle levels—a way of mobilizing society, not destroying it. Chinese friends with whom I have spoken about these riots took them much less seriously than I did. I was, of course, looking at them from the point of view of one reared in a low-context culture, where such riots can have disastrous effects on the society at large.

Wherever one looks, the influence of the subtle hand of contexting can be detected. We have just spoken of the effects of riots on high- and low-context political systems, but what about day-to-day matters of perception? On the physiological level of color perception, one sees the power of the brain's need to perceive and adjust everything in terms of context. As any interior designer knows, a powerful painting, print, or wall hanging can change the perceived color of the furnishings around it. The color psychologist Faber Birren[14] demonstrated experimentally that the perceived shade of a color depends upon the color context in which it occurs. He did this by systematically varying the color of the background surrounding different color samples.

Some of the most impressive demonstrations of the brain's ability to supply the missing information—the function of contexting—are the experiments of Edwin Land, inventor of the Land camera. Working in color photography using a single red filter, he developed a process that is simple, but the explanation for it is not. Until Land's experiments, it was believed that color prints could be made only by superimposing transparent images of three separate photographs made with the primary colors—red, blue, and yellow. Land made his color photographs with two images: a black-and-white image to give light and shadow, and a single, *red* filter for color. When these two images were projected, superimposed on a screen, even though red was the only color, they were perceived in full color with all the shades and gradations of a three-color photograph![15] Even more remarkable is the fact that the objects used were deliberately chosen to provide no cues as to their color. To be sure that his viewers didn't unconsciously project color, Land photographed spools of plastic and wood and geometric objects whose color would be unknown to the viewer. How the eye and the visual centers of the brain function to achieve this remarkable feat of internal contexting is still only partially understood. But the actual stimulus does only part of the job.

Contexting probably involves at least two entirely different but interrelated processes—one inside the organism and the other outside. The first takes place in the brain and is a function of either past experience (programmed, internalized contexting) or the structure of the nervous system (innate contexting), or both. External contexting comprises the situation and/or setting in which an event occurs (situational and/or environmental contexting).[16]

One example of the growing interest in the relationship of external context to behavior is the widespread interest and concern about our public-housing disasters. Pruitt-Igoe Homes in St. Louis is only one example. This $26-million fiasco imposed on poor blacks is now almost completely abandoned. All but a few buildings have been dynamited, because nobody wants to live there.

Objections and defects in high-rise public housing for poor families are legion: Mothers can't supervise their children; there are usually no community service agencies nearby and no stores or markets; and quite often there is no access to any public transportation system. There are no recreation centers for teenagers and few places for young children to play. In any budget crunch, the first thing to be cut is maintenance and then the disintegration process starts; elevators and hallways turn into death traps. The case against high-rise housing for low-income families is complex and underscores the growing recognition that environments are not behaviorally neutral.

Although situational and environmental context has only recently been systematically studied, environmental effects have been known to be a factor in behavior for years. Such men as the industrialist Pullman[17] made statements that sounded very advanced at the time. He believed that if workers were supplied with clean, airy, well-built homes in pleasant surroundings, this would exert a positive influence on their health and general sense of well-being and would make them more productive as well. Pullman was not wrong in his analysis. He simply did not live up to his stated ideals. The main street of his company town, where supervisors lived, was everything he talked about. But his workers were still poorly housed. Being isolated in a company town in close proximity to the plush home of managers made their inadequate living conditions more obvious by way of contrast, and the workers finally embarked on a violent strike. There were many other human, economic, and political needs, which Pullman had not taken into account, that led to worker dissatisfaction. Pullman's professed idealism backfired. Few were aware of the conditions under which his laborers actually lived and worked, so that the damage done to the budding but fragile environmentalist position was incalculable and gave ammunition to the "hard-nosed," "practical" types whose minds were focused on the bottom-line figures of profit and loss.

Quite often, the influence of either programmed contexting (experience) or innate contexting (which is built in) is brushed aside. Consider the individual's spatial needs and his feelings about certain spaces. For example, I have known women who needed a room to be alone in, whose husbands did not share this particular need, and they brushed aside their wives' feelings, dismissing them as childish. Women who have this experience should not let my talking about it raise their blood pressure. For it is very hard for someone who does not share an unstated, informal need with another person to experience that need as tangible and valid. Among people of northern European heritage, the only generally accepted proxemic needs are those associated with status. However, status is linked to the ego. Therefore, while people accept that the person at the top gets a large office, whenever the subject of spatial needs surfaces it is likely to be treated as a form of narcissism. The status and organizational aspects are recognized while internal needs are not.

Yet, people have spatial needs independent of status. Some people can't work unless they are in the midst of a lot of hubbub. Others can't work unless they are behind closed doors, cut off from auditory and visual distractions. Some are extraordinarily sensitive to their environments, as though they had tentacles from the body reaching out and touching everything. Others are impervious to environmental impact. It is these differences, when and if they are understood at all, that cause trouble for architects. Their primary concern is with aesthetics, and what I am talking about lies underneath aesthetics, at a much more basic level.

As often happens, today's problems are being solved in terms of yesterday's understanding. With few exceptions, most thinking on the man-environment relationship fails to make the man-environment (M-E) transaction specific, to say nothing of taking it into account. The sophisticated architect pays lip service to the M-E relationship and then goes right on with what he was going to do anyway, demonstrating once more that people's needs, cultural as well as individual—needing a room of one's own—are not seen as real. Only the building is real! (This is extension transference again.)

Of course, the process is much more complex than most people think. Until quite recently, this whole relationship had been unexplored.[18] Perhaps those who eschewed it did so because they unconsciously and intuitively recognized its complexity. Besides, it is much easier to deal with such simple facts as a balance sheet or the exterior design of a building. Anyone who begins to investigate context and contexting soon discovers that much of what is examined, even though it occurs before his eyes, is altered in its significance by many hidden factors. Support for research into these matters is picayune. What has to be studied is not only very subtle but is thought to be too fine-grained, or even trivial, to warrant serious consideration.

One hospital administrator once threw me out of his office because I wanted to study the effects of space on patients in his hospital. Not only was he not interested in the literature, which was then considerable, but he thought I was a nut to even suggest such a study. To complicate things further, proxemics research requires an inordinate amount of time. For every distance that people use, there are at least five major categories of variables that influence what is perceived as either correct or improper. Take the matter of "intrusion distance" (the distance one has to maintain from two people who are already talking in order to get attention

but not intrude). How great this distance is and how long one must wait before moving in depends on: what is going on (activity), your status, your relationship in a social system (husband and wife or boss and subordinate), the emotional state of the parties, the urgency of the needs of the individual who must intrude, etc.

Despite this new information, research in the social and biological sciences has turned away from context. In fact, attempts are often made to consciously exclude context. Fortunately, there are a few exceptions, men and women who have been willing to swim against the main currents of psychological thought.

One of these is Roger Barker, who summarized twenty-five years of observations in a small Kansas town in his book *Ecological Psychology*.[19] Starting a generation ago, Barker and his students moved into the town and recorded the behavior of the citizens in a wide variety of situations and settings such as classrooms, drugstores, Sunday-school classes, basketball games, baseball games, club meetings, business offices, bars, and hangouts. Barker discovered that much of people's behavior is situation-dependent (under control of the setting), to a much greater degree than had been supposed. In fact, as a psychologist, he challenged many of the central and important tenets of his own field. In his words:

The view is not uncommon among psychologists that the environment of behavior is a relatively unstructured, passive, probabilistic arena of objects and events upon which man behaves in accordance with the programming he carries about within himself. . . . When we look at the environment of behavior as a phenomenon worthy of investigation for itself, and not as an instrument for unraveling the behavior-relevant programming within persons, the situation is quite different. From this viewpoint the environment is seen to consist of highly structured, improbable arrangements of objects and events which coerce behavior in accordance with their own dynamic patterning. . . . We found

... that we could predict some aspects of children's behavior more adequately from knowledge of the behavior characteristics of the drugstores, arithmetic classes, and basketball games they inhabited than from knowledge of the behavior tendencies of particular children.... (emphasis added) (p. 4)

Later Barker states,

The theory and data support the view that the environment in terms of behavior settings is much more than a source of random inputs to its inhabitants, or of inputs arranged in fixed array and flow patterns. They indicate, rather, that the environment provides inputs with controls that regulate the inputs in accordance with the systemic requirements of the environment, on the one hand, and in accordance with the behavior attributes of its human components, on the other. This means that the same environmental unit provides different inputs to different persons, and different inputs to the same person if his behavior changes; and it means, further, that the whole program of the environment's inputs changes if its own ecological properties change; if it becomes more or less populous, for example. (p. 205)[20]

Barker demonstrates that in studying man *it is impossible to separate the individual from the environment in which he functions.* Much of the work of the transactional psychologists Ames, Ittelson, and Kilpatrick,[21] as well as my earlier work,[22] leads to the same conclusion.

In summary, regardless of where one looks, one discovers that a universal feature of information systems is that meaning (what the receiver is expected to do) is made up of: the communication, the background and preprogrammed responses of the recipient, and the situation. (We call these last two the internal and external context.)

Therefore, what the receiver actually perceives is important in understanding the nature of context. Remember that what an organism perceives is influenced in four ways—by status, activity, setting,

and experience. But in man one must add another crucial dimension: *culture.*

Any transaction can be characterized as high-, low-, or middle-context [Figure 1]. HC transactions feature preprogrammed information that is in the receiver and in the setting, with only minimal information in the transmitted message. LC transactions are the reverse. Most of the information must be in the transmitted message in order to make up for what is missing in the context (both internal and external).

In general, HC communication, in contrast to LC, is economical, fast, efficient, and satisfying; however, time must be devoted to programming. If this programming does not take place, the communication is incomplete.

HC communications are frequently used as art forms. They act as a unifying, cohesive force, are long-lived, and are slow to change. LC communications do not unify; however, they can be changed easily and rapidly. This is why evolution by extension is so incredibly fast; extensions in their initial stages of development are low-context. To qualify this statement somewhat, some extension systems are higher on the context scale than others. A system of defense rocketry can be out of date before it is in place and is therefore very low-context. Church architecture, however, was for hundreds of years firmly rooted in the past and was the material

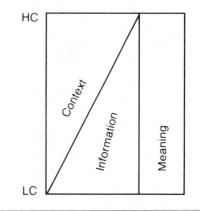

Figure 1

focus for preserving religious beliefs and ideas. Even today, most churches are still quite traditional in design. One wonders if it is possible to develop strategies for balancing two apparently contradictory needs: the need to adapt and change (by moving in the low-context direction) and the need for stability (high-context). History is replete with examples of nations and institutions that failed to adapt by holding on to high-context modes too long. The instability of low-context systems, however, on the present-day scale is quite new to mankind. And furthermore, there is no reservoir of experience to show us how to deal with change at this rate.

Extensions that now make up most of man's world are for the most part low-context. The question is, how long can man stand the tension between himself and his extensions? This is what *Future Shock*[23] and *Understanding Media*[24] are all about. Take a single example, the automobile, which completely altered the American scene in all its dimensions—exploded communities, shredded the fabric of relationships, switched the rural-urban balance, changed our sex mores and churchgoing habits, altered our cities, crime, education, warfare, health, funerals. (One undertaker recently experimented with drive-in viewing of the corpse!) In summary:

The screens that one imposes between oneself and reality constitute one of the ways in which reality is structured.

Awareness of that structure is necessary if one is to control behavior with any semblance of rationality. Such awareness is associated with the low-context end of the scale.

Yet there is a price that must be paid for awareness—instability, obsolescence, and change at a rate that may become impossible to handle and result in information overload.

Therefore, as things become more complex, as they inevitably must with fast-evolving, low-context systems, it eventually becomes necessary to turn life and institutions around and move toward the greater stability of the

high-context part of the scale as a way of dealing with information overload.

NOTES

1. *The Hidden Dimension* discusses this quality of culture in more detail.

2. Meier (1963)

3. Man also imposes a selective screen between the conscious part of his mind and the unconscious part. Sullivan (1947) and Freud (1933)

4. Whorf (1956)

5. Polanyi (1968)

6. Sullivan (1947)

7. The linguist Noam Chomsky (1968) and his followers have tried to deal with the contexting feature of language by eliminating context and going to so-called "deep structure." The results are interesting but end up evading the main issues of communication and to an even greater extent stress ideas at the expense of what is actually going on.

8. For further information on Chinese, see Wang (1973).

9. Bernstein (1964)

10. Eiseley (1969)

11. I do not agree with Eiseley's generalizing about all of mankind, because activism, like everything else, has to be taken in context. As we will see, LC cultures appear to be more vulnerable to violent perturbations than HC cultures.

12. Saul Bellow's (1974) article on the role of literature in a setting of changing times is also relevant to this discussion. Bellow makes the point that for some time now there has been a conscious effort on the part of avant-garde Western intellectuals to obliterate the past. "Karl Marx felt in history the tradition of all dead generations weighing like a nightmare on the brain of the living. Nietzsche speaks movingly of 'it was,' and Joyce's Stephen

Dedalus also defines history as a 'nightmare from which we are trying to awaken.'" Bellow points out, however, that there is a paradox that must be met, for to do away with history is to destroy one's own part in the historical process. It is reasonably certain, however, that what these men were trying to do was to redefine context in order to reduce its influence on men's actions. Simply to do away with the past would lead to an incredibly unstable society, as we shall see.

13. Black culture is much higher on the context scale than white culture, and one would assume from our model that riots do not have the same meaning for blacks as they do to the white society in which the blacks are imbedded.

14. Birren (1961)

15. For further details on this fascinating set of experiments, see Land (1959).

16. These distinctions are completely arbitrary and are for the convenience of the writer and the reader. They do not necessarily occur in nature. The inside-outside dichotomy has been struck down many times, not only by the perceptual transactionalists (Kilpatrick, 1961) following in Dewey's footsteps but in my own writings as well. Within the brain, experience (culture) acts on the structure of the brain to produce mind. It makes little difference *how* the brain is modified; what is important is that modification does take place and is apparently continuous.

17. Buder (1967)

18. See Hall (1966a) for a comprehensive treatment of man's relationship to the spaces he builds as well as a bibliography on the subject.

19. Barker (1968) and Barker and Schoggen (1973)

20. The interested reader will find it worthwhile to consult Barker's works directly.

21. Kilpatrick (1961)

22. Hall (1966a)

23. Toffler (1970)

24. McLuhan (1964)

BIBLIOGRAPHY

Barker, Roger G. *Ecological Psychology*. Stanford, Calif.: Stanford University Press, 1968.

———, and Schoggen, Phil. *Qualities of Community Life*. San Francisco: Jossey-Bass, 1973.

Bellow, Saul. "Machines and Story Books," *Harper's Magazine*, Vol. 249, pp. 48–54, August 1974.

Bernstein, Basil. "Elaborated and Restricted Codes: Their Social Origins and Some Consequences." In John J. Gumperz and Dell Hymes (eds.). The Ethnography of Communication, *American Anthropologist*, Vol. 66, No. 6, Part II, pp. 55–69, 1964.

Birren, Faber. *Color, Form and Space*. New York: Reinhold, 1961.

Buder, Stanley. "The Model Town of Pullman: Town Planning and Social Control in the Gilded Age," *Journal of the American Institute of Planners*, Vol. 33, No. 1, pp. 2–10, January 1967.

Chomsky, Noam. *Language and Mind*. New York: Harcourt, Brace & World, Inc., 1968.

Eiseley, L. "Activism and the Rejection of History," *Science*, Vol. 165, p. 129, July 11, 1969.

Freud, Sigmund. *New Introductory Lectures on Psychoanalysis*. New York: W. W. Norton & Company, Inc. 1933.

Hall, Edward T. "Art, Space and the Human Experience." In Gyorgy Kepes (ed.). *Arts of the Environment*. New York: George Braziller, Inc., 1972.

———. *The Hidden Dimension*. Garden City, N.Y.: Doubleday, 1966(a).

———. "Human Needs and Inhuman Cities." In *The Fitness of Man's Environment, Smithsonian Annual II*. Washington, D.C.: Smithsonian Institution Press, 1968. Reprinted in *Ekistics*, Vol. 27, No. 160, March 1969.

Kilpatrick, F. P. *Explorations in Transactional Psychology* (contains articles by Adelbert Ames, Hadley Cantril, William Ittelson, and F. P.

Kilpatrick). New York: New York University Press, 1961.

McLuhan, Marshall. *Understanding Media*. New York: McGraw-Hill, 1964.

Meier, Richard. "Information Input Overload: Features of Growth in Communications-Oriented Institutions," *Libri* (Copenhagen), Vol. 13, No. 1, pp. 1–44, 1963.

Polanyi, M. "Life's Irreducible Structure," *Science*, Vol. 160, pp. 1308–12, June 21, 1968.

Sullivan, Harry Stack. *Conceptions of Modern Psychiatry*. New York: William Alanson White Psychiatric Foundation, 1947.

Toffler, Alvin. *Future Shock*. New York: Bantam Books, 1970.

Wang, William. "The Chinese Language," *Scientific American*, Vol. 228, No. 2, February 1973.

Whorf, Benjamin Lee. *Language, Thought, and Reality*. New York: The Technology Press of M.I.T. and John Wiley, 1956.

The Cultural Grid: A Personal Cultural Orientation

ANNE B. PEDERSEN
PAUL B. PEDERSEN

Cultural identities are more complex than the boundaries of national or ethnic difference would lead us to believe. Managers of multinational corporations are being persuaded by economic interests to recognize three important and related features about culture. (1) There is evidence, replicated in many countries, that effective communication between employees is strongly related to productivity (Coch & French 1948, the Scanlon Plan, and Quality Circles). (2) There is increased attention to the importance of specific skills for interacting with persons from different nationalities. (3) Sophisticated executives realize that a culture is no longer described solely by ethnic or nationality characteristics such as language, race, color of skin, or geographic origin. In fact "culture" is an integration of ideological and social system variables acting together in a kaleidoscope of changing patterns.

For example, the Tai Pan in James Clavell's novel *Noble House* belongs to a multinational Hong Kong dynasty with conglomerate corporate interests. His "culture" is reflected by his status and prestige among the Chinese in one context and among the Scot Highland chiefs in another; among the Mt. Victoria upper class in one encounter and among the wharfside smugglers in another. The Tai

Pan is a married Scot of forty years, fluent in multiple Chinese dialects, the fifth generation of his clan to rule in Hong Kong. To understand his culture in any specific situation requires integrating many factors other than Scot ethnicity and Chinese fluency.

The implication of this example is that the boundaries on one's "personal cultural orientation" are complex and ever-changing. In fact, it is this very dynamic complexity of cultural data that has frustrated the accurate prediction of role behaviors, expectations, and values across situations.

The Cultural Grid combines an individual perspective of social system variables in the same interacting framework. By combining the individual and group perspective the Cultural Grid can be used to describe a distinctive personal cultural orientation in each situation, and to suggest how specific behaviors, expectations, and values are related to social system variables.

1. DIFFERENCES FROM OTHER APPROACHES

The Cultural Grid differs from other models of personality in several ways. First, the Cultural Grid is uniquely interactional. Whereas other approaches describe behavior as a function of the whole person, or as a function of the situation, the Cultural Grid combines the perspective of the person within the situation in an operational context.

Second, the Cultural Grid combines the cultural universal with the culture specific perspective in a "personal cultural orientation." Approaches that focus on the "emic" or culture specific variables, such as behaviors of an ethnic group, have a tendency to stereotype. Approaches that focus on the "etic" or culturally universal variables, such as values clarification and human relations training, have a tendency to be insensitive toward unique perspectives. The personal cultural orientation combines the general and specific perspectives in one framework.

Third, the Cultural Grid combines the changing of the person with the changing of the system. The proactive "alloplastic" perspective focuses on changing the system by anticipating the effects of

intercultural contact on the individual. The group temporarily bends its rules; for example, it becomes more lenient in toleration of another's perceived eccentricities. The reactive "autoplastic" perspective of changing the individual to fit the system emphasizes remedial strategies for the individual in reconciling differences.

Fourth, the Cultural Grid adds an explanation to the description of intercultural relationships. Descriptive approaches focus on values, expectations, behaviors, or social systems variables without suggesting hypotheses for how and why cognitive and environmental variables are interrelated.

2. THEORETICAL FOUNDATIONS

Cognitive Perspective

Social scientists have demonstrated that we are to a large extent not only what we do, but what we think, feel, intuit, expect, and value about our behavior. Much of our activity and thought concerning this activity is mediated by our perception of intentional interaction with persons and objects in our environment.

For example, a young employee who jumps from a sitting to a standing position at the entrance of a mature chief executive is engaging in an activity that gains the approval of the older person in Western European culture. Standing, then, becomes associated in thought with the socially desirable approval outcome. Thus, the younger individual comes to expect the tactic of standing to win approval. Further, a value is assigned to the execution and social outcome of this act. Standing in this situation becomes the socially correct thing to do and gives one a sense of personal goodness. It symbolizes respect for wisdom, age, and experience. The employee and the executive share similar expectations and values.

In the above instance, standing assumed a connotation of "goodness." However, in some Pacific Island cultures, activities such as standing until told to sit, or direct eye contact, are socially inappropriate forms of behavior among unequals. Each culture defines its own rules for each situation.

Behavior, expectation, and value, then, become patterned in thought. They are cognitive perspectives that match social system variables requiring both cultural and contextual interpretation.

Social System Perspective

Sociologists use the terms *status* and *role* as concepts connecting culturally defined expectations to the pattern of behavior within a particular social system. Every person occupies multiple status levels. Each of the status levels has an associated role behavior on which our expectations are based. An example of many distinct statuses held by one person is a combination such as International Marketing executive, husband, father, Red Cross volunteer, church warden, Republican party member, and military reservist. The activities associated with being or acting as a father are quite different from those expected when in the marketing officer capacity. The executive may be a firm believer in participative management principles. The tactics he applies when acting as chairman of a marketing group meeting will probably differ from those he uses as a father. In the father role, he may use the tactics of immediate reward when the children cooperate in tidying a room for a visitor, while as an executive, he may wait a longer time before praising his colleagues in collaborative effort for a task well done. Both tactics reflect appropriate decision-making principles.

Pattern Salience

Behavior in similar situations may differ according to the priority or saliency of one or more of the constellation of social system variables such as socioeconomic status, age, education, and so forth (see Figure 1). In the first example, the entrance of a mature chief executive engages in the other person the standing behavior associated with the status of employee.

In a similar situation, the employee may be greeted by another typist from the typing pool.

Standing up most likely would not occur, all other factors being equal. The salient pattern arises from friend or colleague status interacting with informal role behavior and the expectation of reciprocal treatment, indicating, perhaps, a value of trust.

Our behaviors, expectations, and values are the internalized patterns of those groups with which we have affiliated and by which we are described—for example, age. Much demographic detail is readily observable. Like it or not, most middle-aged persons are starting to look middle aged. British males can be distinguished from their American counterparts by accent, and few have difficulty identifying the appropriate racial categories. However, some social system–role behavior interactions are less fixed and more difficult to detect. For example, a Continental education is a plausible cause for the numeral seven to be crossed 7; the word "zed" may be used as the equivalent of zero.

Clusters, then, of individual behaviors, expectations, and values are embedded in the complex mosaic of an everchanging social system saliency. To this extent our self-orientation, or image, is derived from our many group identifications. As a bicultural person may pattern the behaviors of two groups, the multicultural person is versatile in matching the patterns of many groups.

3. ACCULTURATION PROCESS

The expected direction of the bi- or multi-culturation process depends upon the type of cultural encounter. For example, a British executive in Iran will expect and be expected to acculturate from his home to his host culture. Cocktail parties or other forms of alcohol consumption may not be met with social approval. However, British and Iranian executives working closely with one another in Paris may be expected to adapt mutually to one another's culture. Each most likely will come to know and to accommodate the behaviors, expectations, and values of the other's culture.

In the above example of the cultural differentiation process the more usual "nationality" categories were used. A more complex typology includ-

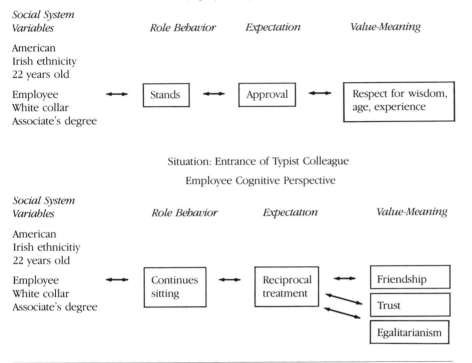

Situation: Entrance of Western European Chief Executive

Employee Cognitive Perspective

Social System Variables	*Role Behavior*	*Expectation*	*Value-Meaning*
American Irish ethnicity 22 years old			
Employee White collar Associate's degree	Stands	Approval	Respect for wisdom, age, experience

Situation: Entrance of Typist Colleague

Employee Cognitive Perspective

Social System Variables	*Role Behavior*	*Expectation*	*Value-Meaning*
American Irish ethnicitiy 22 years old			
Employee White collar Associate's degree	Continues sitting	Reciprocal treatment	Friendship / Trust / Egalitarianism

Figure 1

ing physical, nationality, economic, and behavioral categories is presented by Kinloch (1979). Physiological types might include men, women, young people, old people, the handicapped, and others. Nationality types might include the variety of Anglo and non-Anglo Europeans such as Italians and Greeks. Economic types might include the poor and lower middle and upper class of society. Behavioral types might include criminals, psychotics, geniuses, addicts, and so forth. These special groups combine to function in behavioral patterns that place them in readily recognizable social groups.

The boundaries of some of these social categories—for example, economic—are relatively fluid and unfixed. As a result of excess production capacity, managers and administrators in many fields of endeavor are making difficult but necessary decisions that ultimately result in staff joining the growing group of the executive unemployed. Acquiring the requisite behavioral patterns of this culture is often difficult, painful, and less a matter of personal choice. Upon reabsorption into the executive status, the experience is not likely to be forgotten.

4. BEHAVIOR, EXPECTATION, VALUE, AND INTERACTION

How does cultural orientation affect interaction? Erickson (1975) and Abromowitz and Dokecki (1977) suggest that similarity in social class, cultural communication style, intelligence, temperament, and social identity are more significant than race or gender in influencing the outcome of interactions. Personnel recruitment officers regularly report that initial impressions and "looking for someone similar to me" tend to influence the outcome of selection interviews. As a result of perceived "dissimilarity," interactions may produce the undesirable outcomes of personal or cross-cultural conflict.

Cross-Cultural Conflict

The particular pattern of behaviors that we activate most frequently defines our personal cultural orientation. Through this orientation we perceive any situation. *Cross-cultural conflict* occurs when two persons or groups with different cultural orientations know what the other expects of them but disagree in their selection of a behavior appropriate to their encounter. For example, you may know that your host culture expects you to be polite but are not sure which behaviors demonstrate politeness. Two salesmen, a Japanese and an American, meet in Hong Kong. Both expect politeness. The Japanese bows; the American holds out his hand. The result is a *cross-cultural conflict situation*. The behaviors differ; the expectations are the same.

Personal Conflict

By contrast, a more individually based *personal conflict* is more likely to be the result of disagreement in expectations. For example, both salesmen known which behaviors are necessary to demonstrate politeness, but one chooses not to display them for reasons of his own. Owing to higher occupational status, or not willing to look weak, the American may delay extending his hand. Their behavior patterns are normally the same; the expectations are quite different.

Importance of Analysis to Outcome

Cross-cultural conflict may occur without either person being wrong, given their differing perspectives. However, if we assume that there are no "cultural" differences we usually assume that one person is right and the other wrong in their different understanding of the same situation. To the

extent that a situation is viewed as a *personal conflict*, there is likely to be much less tolerance of subtleties between persons because both believe that they share the same expectations about the situation. This "intolerance" has been noted to characterize British/American interaction over the years.

Bi-Orientation Model

Accuracy in defining the appropriate behaviors and agreement in expectations of both parties, then, are useful concepts in defining communication interactions. A Bi-orientation Model, derived from the ideas of Newcomb (1953) and Chaffee, McLeod, and Guerrero (1969), suggests a type of intervention or resolution (see Figure 2). Bi-orientation is the degree to which both persons in the interaction *agree* on their expectations for the exchange, and the extent to which each *accurately* views the role behaviors, expectations, and values of the other. The following examples describe typical communicator–communicatee transactions. The actors may represent a project manager and a host country national, a human resource counselor and a client, a provider and a consumer, a salesperson and a potential customer, or a superior-subordinate relationship.

TYPE I High Agreement, High Accuracy. Both parties in a two-person interaction have accurate and complete information, communication behaviors interweave, and both agree that the success of the exchange meets their expectations. The next step is understood and is generally followed. This is the "ideal" case. The caveat is that this surface agreement may cover a great deal of resistance to change. The host country national may continue tardy behavior. The client may not return. The customer may decide against the product. Subordinates may not increase their production.

TYPE II High Agreement, Low Accuracy. Here, the foreign project manager does not understand the host country national's problem and

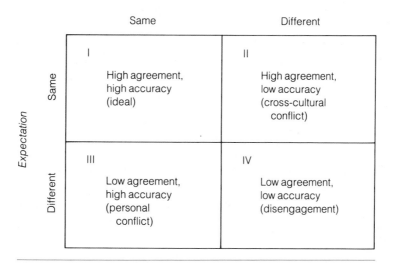

Figure 2 Similar and Dissimilar Behaviors and Expectations

the national misinterprets the manager's behavior. For example, the national, the client, the customer, or the subordinate may interpret nervousness in conversation as agitation, an eagerness to be rid of him or her. The expectations are the same— perhaps both expect facilitation of helping—but they are inaccurate in viewing the role behaviors of the other. The behaviors differ; the expectations are the same. This is a typical *cross-cultural conflict* situation. Intervention by a third party—a supervisor, one from the consumer's support system, or one of the subordinate's colleagues—may increase the likelihood that both parties will see that they are in agreement with regard to their expectations for the situation.

TYPE III Low Agreement, Low Accuracy. This situation is likely to result in confusion and hostility. Both the provider and the consumer will continually apply different assumptions to the encounter which will sooner or later explode or disengage. For example, at the international governmental level, a multinational corporation in a lesser-developed country may assume that greater production and efficiency in assembling auto-

mobiles will lead to greater retail sales. By contrast, the host country may apply a differential tax to shield the home market from overseas domination. Different behaviors; different expectations. At another level of interaction, the superior may assume that the employee needs more access to the decision-making process. The subordinate may want less responsibility and may resent the ensuing transfer of the work to the personal domain.

TYPE IV Low Agreement, High Accuracy. This type of interaction may be quite healthy indeed, as it permits the intrusion of different points of view in the discussion without necessarily creating explosive friction. For example, both provider and consumer may know that the effort of international sales activity tires the provider considerably, but they may not agree on their expectations for that situation. This is descriptive of a *personal conflict* situation. The salesperson may feel that the standard showroom display is sufficient. The potential customer may feel slighted unless invited to an all star dinner/dance/showgirl revue. Another customer may expect to be invited to the home of the salesperson.

5. PERSONAL CULTURAL ORIENTATION

It is apparent that accurate perception of another person's cultural orientation is an important skill. The Cultural Grid aids in the organization of social system information to enable the executive to more quickly grasp another's personal cultural orientation. It helps in forming hypotheses about the types of conflict that are likely to occur, or that are already occurring in a particular interaction. This, in turn, aids the formulation of an appropriate response.

For example, when a young South Pacific Island employee throws himself immediately into a chair in the office of a personnel officer while she remains standing, no disrespect may have been intended. From his cultural orientation, he may have been demonstrating behavior that was not extraordinary, but *expected* and *valued* as a socially correct demonstration of respect. Although both the personnel officer and the employee expect displays of politeness, they are inaccurate in understanding the other's interpretation of the appropriate behavior to match this expectation.

The Cultural Grid captures the flexible and dynamic patterns of person-environment interaction (see Figure 3). The Grid represents a few of the multiplicity of variables that complicate one's cultural orientation. The list is not exhaustive. For example, religion is an obvious category as an important social system variable (SSV), and beliefs might be useful as a fourth category in personal cultural orientation.

Social System Variables (SSV)		Role Behavior	Expectation	Value-Meaning
	Demographic race gender age other			
	Ethnographic ethnicity nationality language			
	Status level economic social educational			
	Affiliation formal non-formal informal			

Figure 3 The Cultural Grid: Matching Social System Variables with Behavior Expectation and Value

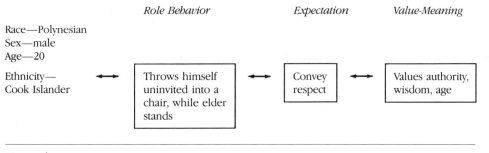

	Role Behavior	*Expectation*	*Value-Meaning*
Race—Polynesian Sex—male Age—20 Ethnicity— Cook Islander	Throws himself uninvited into a chair, while elder stands	Convey respect	Values authority, wisdom, age

Figure 4

6. CATEGORIES FROM FIRSTHAND EXPERIENCE

When used in the cross-cultural management education situation, trainees and, indeed, the trainer, should be encouraged to generate categories of their own. These may be obtained from firsthand experience with distinct groupings or knowledge presented by resource persons drawn from different populations. As an interview schedule, the Cultural Grid prepares the personnel manager or the human resource counselor to detect the categories that are important to the interviewee. These may confirm or support data already gathered from other cells.

We can use the earlier employment interview as a sample of particular knowledge patterned by the Grid framework (see Figure 4).

An interview between a Caucasian male personnel manager of fifty years and a twenty-year-old Caucasian male, a Harvard graduate who exhibits the same sitting behavior at the entrance of a senior member of the firm should flag the interviewer's attention (see Figure 5).

If the manager ascertains that the young man is: (1) serious in his intention to join the company, (2) does not wish to convey disrespect, and (3) attends to the authority dimension but (4) is inaccurate in his understanding of how his actions are interpreted by the manager, then we have a *cross-cultural conflict* situation.

On the other hand, should it be discovered that the young man knows the appropriate "courtesy" response yet chooses to throw himself into a chair, perhaps ignoring the manager's entrance for reasons of his own, the personnel officer is facing a *personal conflict* situation. The ensuing decision will surely consider how desperately the firm needs this young man's talents. Is there some other facet of this person's orientation unaccounted for?

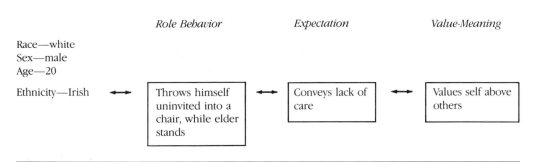

	Role Behavior	*Expectation*	*Value-Meaning*
Race—white Sex—male Age—20 Ethnicity—Irish	Throws himself uninvited into a chair, while elder stands	Conveys lack of care	Values self above others

Figure 5

If so, this may change the manager's conclusions as to the expectations and value-meaning that this man's action was intended to portray. Admittedly, inference is difficult in the best of situations. Knowing the categories of the Cultural Grid will help the manager to search for a more accurate interpretation of the applicant's personal cultural orientation.

As an educational technique, the Grid is useful for several purposes. (1) Managers are able to portray their own cultural orientation for personal insight. (2) Comparisons can be made among trainees to heighten awareness and knowledge of all human interactions. (3) Seemingly arbitrary changes of behavior become more predictable in different situations based on expectations or values. Additionally, the joint impact of demographic–social system variables and role behavior, expectations, and values is more easily appreciated. (4) It helps in the description of cross-cultural situations for case study generation, analysis, and decision making. (5) Using the Grid as an interview schedule provides a framework for incorporating complexity in the management of cross-cultural or other forms of interpersonal interaction.

There are numerous possibilities for application of the Cultural Grid both in describing the cultural orientation of any particular person and in describing the areas of similarity or dissimilarity between persons. The Grid may be used as a training needs assessment tool. It may help the trainer identify those behaviors, expectations, or values that are organizationally inappropriate and might require change in relation to wider social system variables. For example, promotion from waiter to maître d' might require a more distant, dignified behavior than the more personal, friendly style used previously.

In addition, the Grid helps in the anticipation of certain changes in behavior, expectations, and values as a result of organizational development. It becomes possible to anticipate more accurately the changed, complex, multicultural orientation of the previously worry-free mechanic turned garage supervisor. Hence, in the evaluation of training needs or results, the Grid encourages a balanced assessment of the interacting variables. Finally, the Cul-

tural Grid provides a structure for training managers and administrators in interpersonal interaction skills.

7. PERSONAL CULTURAL ORIENTATION AND SITUATION ANALYSIS

The Personal Cultural Orientation framework is useful for situation definition and understanding.

G. M. Foster (1962, p. 61) relates the social-psychological barriers to public health clinic use by the local peoples in Tzintzuntzan, Mexico. A young child becomes ill. The parents, poor farm laborers, know that clinic physicians sometimes cure children when folk medicine fails. However, they fear that the cost of town medicine may be high. There are five other small children in the family. They require food, clothing, shelter. Their well-being may be put in jeopardy if the parents turn toward a potentially costly treatment. This, then, is the dilemma—the social cost of trying to save one child versus the total well-being of the entire family (see Figure 6).

Such a diagram should stimulate discussion of the types of patterns likely to be evoked with a change in priorities of the interactive variables. For example, should parent status assume dominance, the subsequent role behavior might be a struggle to obtain medical care at all costs, as they value each child equally. A change in the situation, such as a gift of good farm land to the parents, might alter their total point of view. Essentially, the modeling and rotation of categories of personal perspective facilitates inference and understanding of another's cultural orientation.

8. CULTURAL GRID AND INCIDENT EXPLANATION

The Cultural Grid assists in the description and explanation of cross-cultural conflict incidents.

An American male project director working with the Agency for International Development (AID) and the Ministry of Health of a Latin American country was asked at short notice to make a formal

Situation: Sick Child versus Public Health Clinic

Mexican Parents' Cognitive Perspective

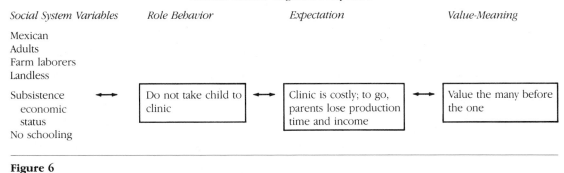

Social System Variables	Role Behavior	Expectation	Value-Meaning

Mexican
Adults
Farm laborers
Landless

Subsistence economic status ⟷ Do not take child to clinic ⟷ Clinic is costly; to go, parents lose production time and income ⟷ Value the many before the one
No schooling

Figure 6

presentation to government officials. Being conscientious and desiring to make the best possible showing, the American hired two local young ladies, design specialists, to prepare the charts and graphs. These were expertly created and the bill presented. The American felt that the payment requested was outlandishly high for a Latin country. In fact, he felt that the young ladies were trying to "do him out of his money"; they "saw an American coming." Determined to charm them into a reduction in the bill, he arranged to meet the two at a neighborhood cafe. The women, in turn, appeared very matter of fact about the bill and stood firm, (see Figure 7).

The Cultural Grid of two contrasting orientations describes a situation in which underlying expectations and values are somewhat similar, but the behaviors differ. This is a cross-cultural conflict situation. Neither party was "right" or "wrong" given their cultural understandings.

Using the Grid, the AID project director was able to stand back and analyze the situation from the design specialists' perspective. He concluded that in his status as a representative of the American government he would pay up. In other words, this status factor triggered a pattern of cognitive variables in support of this behavior. He expected thus to maintain a good public relations image with these people.

The American noted that if he had been acting as a private citizen and businessman, a different

mosaic would have been enacted. He would have told the women to "take it or leave it." This change in pattern saliency could have downgraded the situation from one of cross-cultural conflict to personal conflict and hostile disengagement.

9. CULTURAL GRID AND CASE STUDY ANALYSIS

The Cultural Grid is useful for intervention and resolution practice in case study exercises. For example, the following incident occurred at the Overseas Training Institute (OTI) of a major multinational business specializing in agricultural machinery.

A white male human-resource–development trainer in his mid-thirties is confronted by a black male engineering graduate of about the same age, who is now participating in training prior to advancement to the International Sales Division as Assistant Manager. The trainee hesitates when the HRD trainer asks about the reason for his visit. The trainee then talks about his failure on objective measures that test his knowledge of technical specification, about his difficulty in reacquiring study skills, about his fear of coping with racial prejudice against himself and his family in his designated post in Australia, and about his indecision concerning choice of career path and overseas duty. The HRD specialist, trained in nondirective counseling traditions, alternates positions from

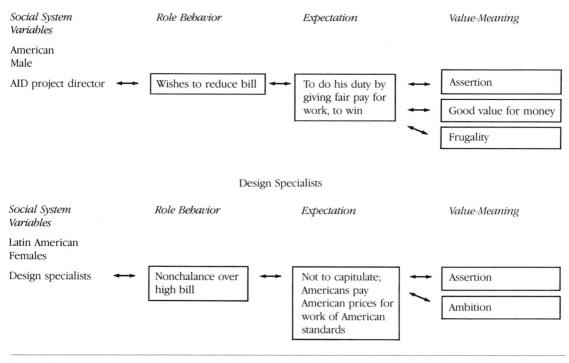

AID Project Director

Social System Variables	*Role Behavior*	*Expectation*	*Value-Meaning*
American Male			
AID project director ↔	Wishes to reduce bill ↔	To do his duty by giving fair pay for work, to win ↔	Assertion
		↔	Good value for money
		↘	Frugality

Design Specialists

Social System Variables	*Role Behavior*	*Expectation*	*Value-Meaning*
Latin American Females			
Design specialists ↔	Nonchalance over high bill ↔	Not to capitulate; Americans pay American prices for work of American standards ↔	Assertion
		↘	Ambition

Figure 7

leaning back to hands on knees to leaning forward, as the trainee, ever more loudly, demands advice and information. Focusing on feelings, the specialist adroitly reflects and paraphrases the trainee's thoughts and emotions. As the hour progresses, tension increases. Finally, the trainer decides to reflect the apparent tension he feels. At this point, the trainee angrily retorts, "Forget it, man! I don't have time to play your silly games," and abruptly leaves the office.

The Cultural Grid is useful as an analytical tool in graphing the complexity and movement of this interpersonal interaction. A comparison of the social system variable aspect of the Grid for the HRD specialist and for the trainee would look something like Table 1.

Much similarity is evident. However, there is sufficient information, for managers knowledgeable about authority/responsibility relationships in organizations to search for factors impinging on the immediate situation—perhaps the feeling of debasement for the trainee, accustomed to controlling the situation, who is now suffering the stress of seeking help. Initially the interview takes the form of a Type II cross-cultural conflict situation.

Both the trainee and the HRD specialist would agree on the expectations for their interaction; however, they are inaccurate in the mutual perception of the behaviors demonstrating a "helping" situation. The specialist continues to reflect; the trainee demands an answer. This is a typical cross-cultural conflict interaction. The expectations are the same, but the behaviors differ. The conflict is most likely not one of ethnicity.

At this point the HRD specialist needs the flexible tactical ability acquired by cross-cultural training to control the situation. However, if this opportunity is lost, the interaction will degenerate. The two men move to the Type III interaction. Both the manager and the trainee continue to apply differ-

Table 1 Personal Cultural Orientation

	Social System Variables	
	Trainee	*HRD Trainer*
Sex	Male	Male
Age	Mid-30s	Mid-30s
Ethnicity	Black	White
Nationality	American	American
Language	English	English
Education	M.Sc.	M.A.
Status	International sales trainee	Human resource trainer
Affiliation	Mid-career executive	Training and development staff

ent assumptions to the situation, leading to the predictable hostile disengagement. Both continue to hold inaccurate perceptions of what the other person considers helping behaviors. Additionally, they would now disagree on a description of the set of expectations for the interaction.

The description of this incident by means of the Cultural Grid is a first-step learning exercise for cross-cultural managers. The reality of the analytical situation is far more complex. However, the Grid does capture the changing nature of interpersonal interaction. The skilled HRD specialist can move the conflict from the cross-cultural to the interpersonal interaction domain, subsequent to moving toward a Type I solution.

10. CONCLUSION

In conclusion, contact with persons of differing cultural orientations provides managers with a certain dilemma. Most recognize that differences do exist and must be accounted for in interaction. However, attempts to describe and explain cultural differences raise accusations of stereotyping and racism. As a result, indirect measures have been developed that use indicators of nationality/ethnic background to predict some performance criteria.

The fear that causality is implied in cultural identification is understandable.

The Cultural Grid theory is explicitly derived from a multi-disciplinary body of theory and research. It does not move from classification to behavior but derives classification from behavior. The Cultural Grid consequently allows us to account for the very real and important differences in cultural orientation within the context of the social system structure. Nationality and ethnicity are seen in balance with other significant characteristics that help describe and understand behavior. No matter what the manager's work responsibility in the multinational corporation, the direct and comprehensive accounting for complex personal cultural orientations must be recognized as important.

REFERENCES

Ambrowitz, C., and Dokecki, P. "The politics of clinical judgment: Early empirical returns." *Psychological Bulletin* 84, 1977, pp. 469–476.

Blake, R., and Mouton, J. "How to choose a leadership style." *Training and Development Journal*, February 1982, pp. 38–46.

Chaffie, S.; McLeod, J.; and Guerrero, J. "Origins and implications of the co-orientational approach in communication research." Paper presented to the Association for Educational Journalism, Berkeley, California, 1969. Expanded in Farace, R.; Monge, P.; and Russell, M. *Communicating and Organizing*. Reading, Mass.: Addison-Wesley, 1977.

Coch, L, and French, J. R. P., Jr. "Overcoming resistance in change." *Human Relations* 1, 1948, pp. 512–532.

Erickson, F. "Gatekeeping and the melting pot." *Harvard Educational Review* 45, 1975, pp. 44–71.

Foster, G. M. *Traditional Cultures: And the Impact of Technological Change*. New York: Harper and Brothers, 1962.

Hines, A. "Cross-cultural communication concepts for executive decision making. Module for cultural effects on executive decision making." Honolulu, Hawaii, 1981.

Hines, A., and Pedersen, P. "The cultural grid: Management guidelines for a personal cultural orientation." *The Culture Learning Institute* Report. Honolulu, Hawaii: East West Center, Spring 1982.

Hines, A., and Pedersen, P. "The cultural grid: Matching social systems variables and cognitive perspectives." *Asian Pacific Training and Development Journal*, 1981, vol. 1.

Kinloch, C. *The sociology of minority group relations*. Englewood Cliffs, N.J.: Prentice-Hall, 1979.

Lambert, M. J. "The implications of psychotherapy outcome research on cross-cultural psychotherapy." In A. Marsella and P. Pedersen, eds., *Cross-cultural counseling and psychotherapy*. New York: Pergamon Press, 1981.

Marsella, A., and Pedersen, A. *Cross-cultural counseling and psychotherapy*. New York: Pergamon Press, 1982.

Newcomb, T. M. "An approach to the study of communicative acts." *Psychological Review* 60, 1953, pp. 393–404.

Pedersen, P.; Draguns, J.; Lonner, W.; and Trimble, J. *Counseling across cultures: Revised and expanded edition*. Honolulu: University Press of Hawaii, 1981.

Culture: A Perceptual Approach

MARSHALL R. SINGER

THE PERCEPTUAL MODEL[1]

It is a basic premise of this paper that man behaves as he does because of the ways in which he perceives the external world. By perception we mean here the process by which an individual selects, evaluates, and organizes stimuli from the external environment.[2] While individuals and the groups which they constitute can only act or react on the basis of their perceptions, the important point is that the "same" stimuli are often perceived differently by different individuals and groups. Whether or not an objective "reality" exists apart from man's perception of that reality need not concern us here. In terms of human behavior, however, there exists, for man, only subjective reality— i.e., the universe as individual men perceive it. The question then becomes: How does man form his perception of the external world and how do those perceptions affect his behavior?

We would argue (rather simplistically here, because it is not the main purpose of the paper) that man is inescapably a social animal. Particularly in his earliest years, but throughout his entire life as well, man must exist in relationship with other human beings. Each of the humans with whom he comes into contact brings to that relationship his own perceptual view of the universe. More impor-

From *Readings in Intercultural Communication*, Vol 1, edited by David S. Hoopes, pp. 6–20. Reprinted by permission of the author. Professor Singer teaches in the Graduate School of Public and International Affairs, University of Pittsburgh.

tant, perhaps, each of the groups in which he has been raised will have conditioned him to view the world from their perspective. Will he regurgitate or salivate at the thought of eating the flesh of a cow or of a kitten? It will depend on how thoroughly he has internalized the attitudes and values which he has been taught by his groups. Not only the languages he speaks and the way in which he thinks, but even *what* he sees, hears, tastes, touches, and smells are conditioned by the cultures[3] in which he has been raised.

Benjamin Lee Whorf, the noted linguist, has written: "We are thus introduced to a new principle of relativity, which holds that all observers are not led by the same physical evidence to the same picture of the universe, unless their linguistic backgrounds are similar, or can in some way be calibrated."[4] We would go a step further and substitute the word "perceptual" for the word "linguistic." We would argue that every culture has its own language[5] or code, to be sure, but that a language is the manifestation—verbal or otherwise—of the perceptions which the group holds. Language, once established, further constrains the individual to perceive in certain ways, but we would insist that language is merely one of the ways in which groups maintain and reinforce similarity of perception.

Specifically our model is based on the following set of premises, some of which are quite generally accepted; some of which are, at this stage, only hypotheses; and others of which are merely definitional. As the model is refined and further developed, some of these will undoubtedly be dropped, others will probably be rephrased, and still others may be added. While we believe that the approach is more important than the specific components, we present them here in order to make our model as explicit as is possible.[6]

1. Individual patterns of behavior are based on individual perceptions[7] of the external world, which are largely learned.

2. Because of biological and experiential differences, no two individuals perceive the external world exactly identically.

3. The greater the biological and experiential differences between individuals, the greater is the disparity in perceptions likely to be. Conversely, the more similar the biological and experiential background, the more similarly are individuals likely to perceive.

4. A perceptual group may be defined as a number of individuals who perceive some aspects of the external world more or less similarly.[8]

5. A number of people who perceive some aspects of the external world more or less similarly, and recognize (communicate) that they share that similarity or perception, may be termed an identity group.

6. The higher the degree of similarity of perception that exists among a number of individuals, other things being equal: (a) the easier is communication among them likely to be; (b) the more communication among them is likely to occur; and (c) the more likely it is that this similarity of perception will be recognized—that an identity group will form.[9]

7. Ease of communications will allow for constant increase in degree of similarity of perception (through feedback mechanisms) which in turn allows for still further ease of communication. Thus, there tends to be a constant reinforcement of group identity.[10]

8. The greater the number and the degree of intensity of perceptual groups which individuals share—the more overlapping of important perceptual groups which exists among a number of individuals—the more likely they are to have a high degree of group identity.[11]

9. A pattern of perceptions and behavior which is accepted and expected by an identity group is called a culture. Since by definition each identity group has its own pattern of behaviorial norms, each group may be said to have its own culture.[12]

10. Since communication tends to be easiest among individuals who identify most closely with each other, and most difficult among individuals who perceive more or less dissimilarly, this tends

to reinforce and exacerbate awareness of group differences. Any "we" (identity group) comes into much sharper focus when juxtaposed against "they" (a different identity group).

11. An individual must inevitably be a member of a myriad of different perceptual and identity groups simultaneously, by definition. However, he shares a higher degree of similarity of perception, and a higher degree of group identity, with some groups that with others. Consciously or otherwise, he rank orders his various group identities.[13]

12. Because environmental and biological factors are ever changing, perceptions, attitudes and values are ever changing. Consequently, the rank ordering of group identities is ever changing and new perceptual groups are constantly being formed, while existing groups are constantly in a state of flux.[14]

We know from the study of genetics that no two individuals are physiologically completely identical. Certainly if the skin on the tips of the fingers is different for each individual then each person's sense of touch must be presumed to be individual and unique. Yet far more important for the way men view the universe are the still unanswered questions of physical variations in other sensory receptors. What about the configuration of cones and rods in the retina of the eye, or taste buds on the tongue, or fibers in the ear, or any of the other physical receptors of external stimuli? If no two individuals have identical receptors of stimuli, then it must follow, on the basis of physiological evidence alone, that no two individuals perceive the external world completely identically. Yet biological differences probably account for only the smallest fraction of the perceptual distinctions made by man.

Far more important is determining an individual's perceptions of the external world are the experiential factors involved in the incorporation, organization and processing of sensory data. Genetically, we inherit from our parents those physical characteristics that distinguish us as their offspring. Admittedly there is a good deal of individual variation biologically and environmentally, but there is also a good deal of similarity. Given two white parents the overwhelming probability is that the offspring will be white. Given two English speaking parents the overwhelming probability is that the offspring will speak English. The difference is that biologic identity is—within a given range of probability—fixed, while environmental identity is not. The son of two white parents will always remain white no matter what happens to him after birth, but the son of two English speaking parents may never speak English if immediately after birth he is raised by a totally non-English speaking group. Thus while biologic inheritance is relatively immutable, environmental inheritance is ever changing. The fascinating aspect of environmental conditioning, however, is that while there is theoretically an almost infinite number of possibilities, in fact, the number of environmental factors to which most individuals are exposed is amazingly limited. Thus for example, while there may be a whole world to explore, if not an entire universe, the incredibly overwhelming majority of individuals who inhabit this planet never stray more than a few miles from their place of birth. Indeed each of us is a member of a finite, and comparatively small, number of different identity groups.

If, for biologic and environmental reasons, it is not possible for any two individuals to perceive the universe 100 percent similarly, neither is it possible—for the same reasons—for them to share absolutely no similarity of perception. Hence we are postulating here a continuum of similarity of perception among individuals. At one end we can approach—but never reach—zero; at the other we can approach—but never reach—100 percent. Actually, degree of similarity of perception can probably best be measured not as a point of a continuum, but rather as a range of points. Thus, for example,[15] two Catholics—one from a third generation wealthy Boston family, and the other from an illiterate and impoverished small village in the Congo—may share, as Catholics, no more than perhaps a 10 to 15 percent similarity of perception. Yet we would argue that to the degree that they share an identity (recognize a similarity of perception) as Catholics they are a part of the broad identity group called "Catholics." Teachers, considered as a group, may share an average range of 20–25 percent similarity of perception. If we narrow the group to include only college teachers, the range of similarity of perception may increase to from 40 to 50 percent. If we further specify that the group consists of only Catholic, male, heterosexual college teachers of quantum physics, with Ph.D.'s from M.I.T. between the ages of 35 and 40, the range of similarity of perception might well increase to perhaps 75 to 80 percent. Notice that while we have decreased the number of people who can be included in our group, we have increased the number of group identities which the members of the groups share. By doing so we have greatly increased the likelihood of their sharing still greater similarities of perception in the future. It is no wonder that the smaller the group the greater the group cohesion is likely to be.

By communication we mean here that one individual or a group of individuals more or less understands another's message. Since no two individuals perceive 100 percent similarly, it follows that no individual will perceive another's message 100 percent as the sender intended it to be understood. When we couple this with what Claude Shannon[16] has said about the ever present distortion in the communication process we recognize the potentially high degree of noncommunication inherent in the process. Fortunately, it is not imperative to the functioning of groups that communications be perceived 100 percent accurately. Fortunately too, there are corrective devices inherent in almost any communication system. One such device is the "feedback mechanism" which may allow for continuous testing of accuracy of perception.[17] Another is redundancy. Most verbal languages are themselves more than one-half redundant. Thus, if part of the message is lost, either due to differing perceptions or to distortions within the system, enough of the message usually gets through th convey the general meaning intended. At least in face to face communication and to some extent in television and movies, there is repetition of the same message over a number of channels.

Thus, both audio and visual channels may simultaneously convey and reinforce the same message. Regardless of the type of media available in any society, however, face to face communications will remain the most effective form of communication.

But verbal communication comprises only a portion—and it may perhaps be the smallest portion—of the communication that goes on in any society. Far more important are the silent, nonverbal communications which we only half consciously or unconsciously transmit and receive. Perhaps a million persons intersect at the corner of Broadway and 42nd Street in New York City each day, and yet, the nonverbal communication process is so accurate that without a word being spoken they filter past each other in orderly fashion, only rarely touching. A glance, a shrug, time and spatial communication,[18] indeed an endless number of nonverbal cues which are often too subtle even to be conscious, may communicate far more than words. There is mounting evidence that within any given group nonverbal communications may account for the overwhelming majority of the communication which occurs. It is precisely because we communicate and perceive so well within our own groups that we feel so comfortable there. We can communicate effectively with a minimum of effort and frustration because the patterns of behavior of the members of our own groups are so predictable to us that a minimum of effort is required for effective functioning.

It is precisely such shared, often unarticulated, and sometime unarticulatable patterns of perception, communication, and behavior which are referred to as "a culture." But group identities do not necessarily recognize the integrity of national boundaries. In the hypothetical case of the college teachers of quantum physics cited above, no mention was made of nationality. To be sure, if we were to stipulate that they all be Americans, the percentage of their shared similarity of perception would probably rise still higher. But the fact is that there is a considerably higher degree of similarity of perception among college teachers of quantum physics—regardless of nationality—than there could possibly be between them and, let us say, uneducated sharecroppers or perhaps barbers in the same society. It is for this reason that we consider only each group as having its own culture, rather than attempting to consider only each society as having its own culture, and then being forced to consider deviations from the societal norms as "sub-cultural." This is not to say that societal cultures do not exist. On the contrary; to the degree that an entire society shares and communicates certain similarities of perception and behavior it may itself be considered as an identity group—and thus to have a common culture of its own.

But we would argue, there is greater analytical and operational utility in considering each society as the aggregate of the identity (cultural) groups which exist within it. From there we may proceed to compare and analyze whole societies to determine which identity groups are present in each and—

1. how the presence or absence of certain groups in a given society affects that entire society

2. what other clusters of groups may always, often, rarely or never be found in societies containing certain groups

3. the differences and similarities between the same groups in different societies[19]—why they are different, how they relate to the whole society, and how the whole society is related to them

4. the differences and similarities between different groups in the same society

While we believe that the implications of this formulation of the problem to the study of the process of social change are indeed significant, they fall outside the scope of this paper.[20]

IMPLICATIONS FOR CROSS-CULTURAL OPERATIONS

Implicit in the perceptual model outlined above is the proposition that an individual is in fact functioning somewhat "cross-culturally" whenever he communicates with another individual. The fewer group identities he shares (and the less intensely he held the identities which exist) with the individuals with whom he must communicate the more "cross-culturally" he is operating. We are dealing here with a continuum and not with dichotomies. The important point to note, however, is that some *intranational* communications can be far more cross-cultural than other *international* communications.

Workers in various anti-poverty programs have sometimes been chagrined and shocked to find their well-intentioned plans utterly rejected by the very people whom they were intended to help. What they have often overlooked—and what any experienced social worker knows—is the fact that the white, urban, middle-class, well-educated professional probably has a totally different set of perceptions (and hence values, attitudes, and modes of behavior) than his Negro, rural, lower-class, uneducated client.[21] Merely because the professional sees merit in a particular proposal in no way ensures that the client will view the proposal in the same way. Indeed, it would be nearly miraculous if he did. It is precisely because of this that the demand has grown for greater participation of clients in the planning of proposals intended for their benefit. To some degree this may alleviate the problem. But until the cause of the problem is recognized clearly, it is doubted that significant progress will be made. Until one of the groups concerned (and it can only be the professional group) recognizes that their perceptions differ markedly from those of the other—and recognize that different is not the same as bad—and makes a concerted attempt to understand the other's perceptions, the incidence of friction and frustration is likely to continue. What is more, now that the Negro in the United States has begun to organize to defend the validity of his identity, the white population has begun to sense an urgency for understanding these perceptions.

International cross-cultural operations are often more complicated and more difficult than domestic cross-cultural operations—not necessarily because the individuals involved share fewer perceptions, but rather because it is often extremely difficult to adjust levels of expectation of communication in unfamiliar environments. Within our own society there are a multitude of familiar silent and/or subtle cues which tell us at which levels of sophistication we may communicate. When the physicist talks to his barber in the United States, he knows that he is expected to discuss baseball, the weather, and women. He also knows that it would be futile for him to attempt to discuss quantum physics. Thus he adjusts his communication expectations accordingly and leaves the barber shop a little wiser about the league standing of the home team, a little apprehensive about the impending winter, and a little titillated by the cover of *Playboy*. But he certainly has no feeling of frustration at not having been able to discuss physics. He knows his own society well enough to know with whom he may discuss baseball and with whom he may discuss physics. In a foreign environment, on the other hand, it is difficult—particularly for the newcomer—to assess at which level he may communicate. The same physicist operating outside of his own country may be pleasantly surprised to find that his foreign counterpart not only speaks his language, but *appears* to have the same problems, aspirations, and values as he himself has. He, therefore, expects to be readily understood, even when discussing the most complicated intellectual problems. If he later finds that he was not completely understood, he may feel hurt, cheated, and frustrated. Because of the outward *appearance* of similarity based on common perceptions which the two share as quantum physicists, he may not have taken into account the fact that there are a myriad of other group identities—and consequently many other patterns of perception and behavior—which they do *not* have in common.

But there is another reason for the increased difficulty of international cross-cultural operations. While two individuals in the same society may be a cultural world away from each other educationally, physically they may reside in the same city, in the same mass culture. If the physicist eats in the barber's home, he will know approximately what to expect and how to behave. When he leaves the barber's house he will drive down familiar streets with familiar faces, places, and smells to the security and com-fort of his own home. In the home of another physicist in, say, Bombay, on the other hand, he will not only have to remember the specifics of not eating with his left hand (and any other specific cross-cultural data that he may have acquired) but he must be prepared for the totally unexpected. It is simply not possible to teach someone from one culture the perhaps hundreds of millions of discrete "bits" of information he would have to know to truly understand another culture. Yet it is precisely because he does not know what it is about another culture that he does not know that his anxiety level must perforce be high. Further, as soon as the hypothetical American physicist leaves the home of his counterpart in Bombay, he must wander through strange streets, with strange faces, places, and smells. All the silent little cues which would come to him subliminally in the United States would be missing. In Bombay it would be necessary for him to expend an enormous amount of energy merely making explicit all of those myriad little cues which in his own culture can remain implicit and subconscious. But, obviously, the lack of reception of silent cues is not all that complicates international cross-cultural operations. The matter of adjusting to unfamiliar food, climate, and other physical differences can be a very real problem. Further there is the additional real burden of functioning in a society in which one may be totally or partially unfamiliar with the spoken or written language.

There is one additional factor which tends to make international cross-cultural operations more emotionally taxing than most domestic cross-cultural operations. While we have argued that, analytically, all communications are to some degree cross-cultural, within our own society contact with significantly different groups can be kept to a minimum. At home we tend to spend most of our leisure time, at least, surrounded by individuals who perceive more or less as we do. Even if our work is of the nature which forces us to deal with people significantly different from ourselves during the day, in the evening we can retreat to the comfort and ease of our own groups. Internationally this is not always possible.[22] Aside from possible contact with fellow countrymen (the connotation of the terms *landsmann* is significant here) when working or living in a foreign environment one can expect no relief from the strain of uncertainty— either until his task is accomplished and he returns home or until he has lived in that environment long enough to increase his own range of similarity of perception with those around him to the point where, if not everything, at least most things need no longer be made conscious and explicit.

In short, while some communications within the same society can be more cross-cultural than other international communications, international cross-cultural operations tend to be significantly more difficult because we tend to share a higher degree of similarity of perception with more groups in our own society than we do in a foreign environment.

NOTES

1. The perceptual model presented here, as well as several experimental applications of that model are currently being developed in considerable detail by the author and are scheduled to appear in a forthcoming work tentatively entitled *Group Perception and Social Action*. Pages 1–6 of this paper are taken from an article "Perception and Social Change in Ceylon," soon to appear in a special issue of the *International Journal of Comparative Sociology*.

2. Thus, our use of the term "perception" includes "memory" (in the cybernetic sense) and "cognition" in the interpretative sense.

3. In our list of propositions presented below, we define each group as having its own culture.

4. From *Collected Papers on Metalinguistics*, quoted by Franklin Fearing in "An Examination of the Conceptions of Benjamin Whorf in the Light of Theories on Perception and Cognition," in *Language in Culture* edited by Harry Hoijer, University of Chicago Press, Chicago, 1954, p. 48.

5. Here we are using language in the broadest sense. This may include the jargon or symbols used by social scientists or mathematicians, for example, to express the concepts peculiar to their group.

6. These premises draw rather heavily on the extensive literature produced by the cultural anthropologists, sociologists, psychologists, communications theorists, and linguists. In particular the model is strongly influenced by the notion of perceptual constancies. See F. P. Kilpatrick (ed), *Explorations in Transactional Psychology*, New York University Press, NY, 1961.

7. As used here perception includes attitudes and values.

8. While the terms "more" and "less" are vaguely quantitative, they are clearly inadequate for a precise science of social action. Unfortunately, they are often the best that the social scientist can produce, given the current state of our knowledge. A good deal of serious research being done by psychologists today, however, indicates that they are finding ways of measuring perceptions more and more precisely. For some suggestive approaches to this problem, see B. Berelson and G. A. Steiner, *Human Behavior: An Inventory of Scientific Findings*, Harcourt Brace and World, Inc., New York, 1964.

9. The converse of this is also true.

10. Where there is little or no communication among individuals there tends to be a decrease in similarity of perception which in turn tends to make further communications more difficult. See premise 10.

11. In most societies the family enjoys the highest degree of group identity. Among the reasons that this is so is the fact that the family tends to combine a great many different perceptual groups simultaneously. Thus, with rare exception, all adult members of the family speak the same language, are from the same place of residence, are of the same religious persuasion, have approximately the same educational level, are of the same socioeconomic class, are very likely to be employed in the same occupational grouping, and so on at incredible length. In other words, the family enjoys one of the highest possible degrees of group identity precisely because the members of that group are also concurrently members of so many

other perceptual groups. Indeed, family identity as the superordinant identification for the individual tends to break down precisely in those more mobile societies (particularly in urban, industrial areas) where the family combines fewer similarities of perception.

12. For a further discussion of this approach, see below.

13. It often happens that individuals and/or groups exist, having internalized elements of several differing or even conflicting value systems simultaneously. Individuals and groups are able to survive and function under these conditions primarily because: (a) they are able to identify in differing degrees—and at differing levels of consciousness—with each of the value systems with which they identify; and (b) because most group identities which are simultaneously held only rarely come into direct *conscious* conflict. When two equally held value systems do come into conflict, a high degree of personal and/or group anxiety (conscious or otherwise) may result. The individual and/or group often seeks some third identity which can accommodate, neutralize, rationalize, and/or synthesize these conflicting value systems. For some individuals and/or groups it could produce an inability to act. For still others, it might mean rather erratic behavior, alternately overstressing one value system at the expense of the other. In any one of these cases, however, it would probably be diagnosed as ambivalence.

14. Small, isolated, and relatively undifferentiated societies may often seem to be almost totally unchanging and unchangeable just because there a high degree of shared perceptions among most of the members of those societies. It is precisely because there is such a high degree of identity and such a high degree of reinforcement of similarity of perception that it is so difficult to introduce change into those societies.

15. Any figures used in our examples are completely hypothetical, and are included merely to illustrate a concept. They are not based on any known research.

16. See Claude E. Shannon and Warren Weaver, *The Mathematical Theory of Communication*, University of Illinois Press, Urbana, 1949.

17. For a dramatic demonstration of the necessity of feedback for even partial similarity of perception between sender and receiver, see Harold Levitt, *Managerial Psychology*, University of Chicago Press, second edition, 1964, chapter 9.

18. See Edward T. Hall, *The Silent Language*, Doubleday & Co., New York, 1959.

19. For example, the family, students, businessmen, industrial workers, bureaucrats, the military, the clergy, etc., in different societies.

20. To some degree this aspect of the problem has been discussed in the author's "Group Perception and Social Change in Ceylon," cited above.

21. The extreme contrast is used here merely for illustrative purposes. Although perhaps in differing degrees the same holds true for clients from other groups as well.

22. It does help to explain, however, the prevalence of the American, German, British, and other foreign ghettoes and clubs one finds abroad.

CONCEPTS AND QUESTIONS
FOR CHAPTER 1

1. How does the concept of a global village affect your view of international relations and your ability to relate to world events?

2. What does Barnlund's discussion of meaning imply when it is applied to intercultural interactions?

3. What does Barnlund mean by the "collective unconscious" and how does it relate to intercultural communication?

4. In what ways are intercultural communication and communication alike? In what way are they different?

5. What is meant by social perception and how does it relate to intercultural communication?

6. How are economic and class factors related to intercultural communication?

7. What is the relationship between culture and perception?

8. How does Hall's discussion of high- and low-context communication relate to Singer's analysis of the twelve premises of intercultural perception?

9. What is the cultural grid and how can you use it personally to improve your ability to be an intercultural communicator?

10. How would someone from an extremely different cultural background respond to your city on a first visit? To your home?

11. What does Singer mean by "subjective reality"? How does that relate to intercultural communication?

12. Do you agree with the twelve premises found in Singer's analysis? Which ones, if any, do you find tenuous?

SUGGESTED READINGS

Asante, M. K., E. Newmark, and C. A. Blake, eds. *Handbook of Intercultural Communication.* Beverly Hills, Calif.: Sage Publications, 1979. This collection of 25 original essays is a state-of-the-art review of theoretical and methodological findings in the field of intercultural communication. The book is divided into six parts: theoretical considerations, conceptual frameworks, issues in intercultural communication, general problems with data, research in specific cultures, and practical applications. Each of these parts contains well-written selections that introduce the reader to some of the main issues and topics of intercultural communication.

Brislin, R. W. *Cross-Cultural Encounters: Face-to-Face Interaction.* New York: Pergamon Press, 1981. The major purpose of this book is to examine the commonalities in the experiences of diverse people; experiences that can, according to Brislin, improve intergroup interaction. Among other topics, the book covers the influence of history on behavior, individual attitudes, traits, and skills, thought and attribution processes, and membership and reference groups.

Casse, P. *Training for the Cross-Cultural Mind.* Washington, D.C.: Society for Intercultural Education, Training, and Research, 1979. This book is based on the premise that everything we say and do is cultural. By emphasizing commonality among human beings, Casse is unsurprisingly optimistic in his outlook toward the intercultural experience and believes it can be a rewarding one if properly managed or handled.

Condon, J. C., and F. Yousef. *An Introduction to Intercultural Communication.* New York: Bobbs-Merrill, 1975. This book serves as an introduction to the field of intercultural communication. The authors write in a casual manner that makes the book very readable. Besides having a pleasant style, the book examines essential ingredients of intercultural communication such as values, language, nonverbal behaviors, and social organization.

Dodd, C. H. *Dynamics of Intercultural Communication.* Dubuque, Iowa: William C. Brown Publishers, 1982. This book is a "basic text" in intercultural communication. The author's main theme is that the impact of culture becomes especially obvious when people from different cultures interact. Dodd looks at various components of culture, such as belief systems, credibility, language, and nonverbal communication.

Fischer, H. D., and J. Merrill. *International Communication.* New York: Hastings House, 1970. This book surveys the broad and varied aspect of international communication. Containing 49 diverse essays, the book covers the field of international communication with an emphasis on mass media.

Ganst, F. C., and E. Morbeck, eds. *Ideas of Culture*. New York: Holt, Rinehart & Winston, 1976. This collection of 38 essays examines culture from a variety of perspectives. It explores the nature of culture, culture as symbols, social order as culture, the patterns of culture, and many other dimensions that help explain the role of culture in our daily lives.

Glenn, E. S., and C. G. Glenn. *Man and Mankind: Conflict and Communication Between Cultures*. Norwood, N.J.: Abey, 1981. In this volume the authors introduce a new theoretical model for communication analysis embodying a cognitive approach to cultural contact. The model not only defines an overall methodology of the acquisition and storage of information, it also determines the cognitive "styles" of various cultures and subcultures, links them to their attendant communication processes, and predicts areas of conflict.

Gudykunst, W. B., and S. J. Halsall. "The application of a theory of contraculture to intercultural communication: Searching for isomorphic processes" in D. Nimmo, ed., *Communication Yearbook* 4. New Brunswick, N.J.: Transaction, 1980, 427–436. This paper addresses itself to one of the major problems plaguing the field of intercultural communication—the lack of overarching theoretical perspectives. The authors agree that there is a need for such frameworks, but suggest that new perspectives do not always have to be developed from scratch. Specifically, the authors use a "theory" of contraculture generated from the prison literature to integrate the diverse findings of sojourner adjustment research.

Harms, L. S. *Intercultural Communication*. New York: Harper & Row, 1973. This introductory text focuses on intercommunity communication, international and world communication, the relationship between communication and culture, and the future of intercultural communication.

Keesing, R. M., and F. M. Keesing. *New Perspectives in Cultural Anthropology*. New York: Holt, Rinehart & Winston, 1971. The authors introduce the concepts of culture with emphasis on the social aspects. Relationships between socio-cultural elements and communication are well defined.

Kluckhohn, C. *Culture and Behavior*. New York: Free Press, 1965. Kluckhohn was one of the most respected anthropologists in the world. This classic volume is a collection of his most famous articles. The first part of the book offers an excellent analysis of culture, while the second half examines various aspects of Navajo culture.

Merritt, R. I., ed. *Communication in International Politics*. Champaign, Ill.: University of Illinois Press, 1972. Merritt has edited an excellent collection of readings in the area of international political communication. This volume is comprehensive and attempts not only to define the area of international communication but also to examine some of its main concerns.

Munroe, R. H., R. L. Munroe, and B. B. Whiting, eds. *Handbook of Cross-Cultural Human Development*. New York: Garland, 1980. This volume consists of 26 chapters intended to focus on the influences culture can have on human development. The editors note that cross-cultural research may help "unpackage" the mechanisms underlying the operation of globally defined environmental variables. and may distinguish what seems to be universally true of development from what is malleable in varying environments.

Oliver, R. T. *Culture and Communication*. Springfield, Ill.: Charles C. Thomas, 1962. An excellent approach to an understanding of rhetorical systems in different cultures is given in this volume. Oliver analyzes how differences in Oriental and Western cultures call for different "logics" and strategies of persuasion.

Prosser, M. H., ed. *Intercommunication Among Nations and People*. New York: Harper & Row, 1973. This collection seeks to define international and intercultural communication as a field of study. Prosser's selections cover a wide range of intercultural topics including attitude formation, leadership, conflict resolution, rights and censorship, and many others.

Prosser, M. H. *The Cultural Dialogue: An Introduction to Intercultural Communication*. Boston: Houghton Mifflin, 1978. This well-written text serves as an excellent introduction to the field of intercultural communication. Prosser examines the basic components of communication and intercultural communication.

Renwick, G. W. "Intercultural communication—state of the art study" in N. C. Jain, ed., *International and Intercultural Communication Annual*, vol. 5. Falls Church, Va.: Speech Communication Association, 1979, 92–100. This essay describes the purpose, methods, and products of a three-year comprehensive study designed to describe and assess the current status of the field of intercultural communication. The study has involved three surveys gathering data on 700 individuals, 500 organizations, and 3,000 courses and training programs in the field.

Rich, A. *Interracial Communication*. New York: Harper & Row, 1974. This book is well written and well researched. It describes various interracial interaction situations and explores possible reasons for the problems that occur when people from different races attempt to communicate.

Sarbaugh, L. E. "A systematic framework for analyzing intercultural communication" in N. C. Jain, ed., *International and Intercultural Communication Annual*, vol. 5. Falls Church, Va.: Speech Communication Association, 1979, 11–22. This article presents a systematic conceptualization for understanding and analyzing intercultural and intracultural communication. The author proposes establishing levels of interculturalness rather than thinking of intercultural and intracultural as discrete categories of communication.

Sarbaugh, L. E. *Intercultural Communication*. Rochelle Park, N.J.: Hayden Books, 1979. This text seeks to serve as an introduction to the study of intercultural communication. The author attempts to answer two important questions: First, what is the difference, if any, between what we label intercultural and what we label intracultural? And second, how differently do we communicate in each of these situations?

Segall, M. H. *Cross-Cultural Psychology: Human Behavior in Global Perspective*. Monterey, Calif.: Brooks/Cole, 1979. This excellent text covers such vital areas as perception, cognition, and personality. These and other topics are all treated in the cultural setting. The major thesis is that human behavior is primarily of cultural origin.

Smith, A. G., ed. *Communication and Culture*. New York: Holt, Rinehart & Winston, 1966. This classic text is a comprehensive volume which contains the efforts of many distinguished scholars in the field of communication. Especially useful is the paradigm for arranging the readings because it helps clarify the relationships between various components of the communication process.

Smith, E. C., and L. F. Luce, eds. *Toward Internationalism: Readings in Cross-Cultural Communication*. Rowley, Mass.: Newbury House, 1979. This collection of 14 articles introduces the student of intercultural communication to some of the major ideas found in the field. Specifically it focuses on value orientations, role expectations, perceptions, nonverbal patterns, and language behavior as they affect the international cross-cultural encounter.

Triandis, H. C. "Cultural influences on social behavior," *Revista Interamericana de Psicologia* 15 (1981), 1–28. Variations in ecology and culture are discussed in this essay. A number of dimensions are presented in summarizing cultural differences. Among the topics treated are: (1) how cultural groups differ in the relative emphases they place on attributes of others, (2) ingroup and outgroup definitions, (3) the way groups process information about others, and (4) their values.

Triandis, H. C., and J. W. Berry, eds. *Handbook of Cross-Cultural Psychology*. Boston: Allyn & Bacon, 1980. This text contains over 40 articles dealing with topics such as ethnographic field techniques, systematic observation techniques, and holocultural research methods. All of these subjects help explain various research tools that might be useful to anyone wishing to conduct research in cross-cultural psychology and/or intercultural communication.

ADDITIONAL READINGS

Abe, H., and R. L. Wiseman. "A cross-cultural confirmation of the dimensions of intercultural effectiveness." *International Journal of Intercultural Relations* 7 (1983), 53–68.

Althen, G., ed. *Learning Across Cultures: Intercultural Communication and International Education Exchange*. Washington, D.C.: National Association for Foreign Student Affairs, 1981.

Barnouw, V. *Culture and Personality*. Homewood, Ill.: Dorsey Press, 1979.

Bochner, S., ed. *Cultures in Contact: Studies in Cross-Cultural Interaction*. Oxford: Pergamon, 1982.

Brislin, R. W. "Cross-cultural research in psychology." *Annual Review of Psychology* 34 (1983), 363–400.

Brislin, R. W., ed. *Culture Learning: Concepts and Research*. Honolulu: University of Hawaii Press, 1977.

Burgoon, M., J. Dillard, N. Doran, and M. Miller. "Cultural and situational influences of the process of persuasive strategy selection." *International Journal of Intercultural Relations* 6 (1982), 85–100.

Casmir, F. L. "Phenomenology and Hermeneutics: Evolving approaches to the study of intercultural and international communication." *International Journal of Intercultural Relations* 7 (1983), 309–324.

Casmir, F. L., ed. *Intercultural and International Communication*. Washington, D.C.: University Press of America, 1978.

Doob, L. W. "The inconclusive struggles of cross-cultural psychology." *Journal of Cross-Cultural Psychology* 11 (March 1980), 59–73.

Dubbs, P. J., and D. D. Whatney. *Cultural Contexts: Making Anthropology Personal*. Boston: Allyn & Bacon, 1980.

Fersh, S., ed. *Learning About Peoples and Cultures*. Evanston, Ill.: McDongal, Littell, 1976.

Gardner, G. H. "Cross-cultural communication." *Journal of Social Psychology* 58 (1962), 241–256.

Geertz, D. *The Interpretation of Culture*. New York: Basic Books, 1973.

Goodman, M. E. *The Individual and Culture*. Homewood, Ill.: Dorsey Press, 1967.

Gudykunst, W. B., and T. Nishida. "Constructing a theory of intercultural communication: The promise and paradox." *Speech Education: Journal of the Communication Association of the Pacific* 7 (1978), 13–25.

Hall, E. T. *Beyond Culture*. Garden City, N.Y.: Doubleday/Anchor Books, 1976.

Hall, E. T. *The Hidden Dimension*. New York: Doubleday, 1966.

Hammet, M. P., and R. W. Brislin, eds. *Research in Culture Learning*. Honolulu, Hawaii: The University of Hawaii Press, 1980.

Hayes, A. S. "A tentative schematization for research in the teaching of cross-cultural communication." *American Journal of Linguistics* 28 (1962), 155–167.

Hori, T. "Culture and personality: Standpoints of cultural anthropology." *Japanese Psychological Review* 23 (1980), 382–391.

Hui, C. H. "Locus of control: A review of cross-cultural research." *International Journal of Intercultural Relations* 6 (1982), 301–323.

Hymes, D. "The anthropology of communication" in F. E. X. Dance, ed. *Human Communication Theory*. New York: Holt, Rinehart & Winston, 1967.

LaBarre, W. *Culture in Context*. Durham, N.C.: Duke University Press, 1980.

Marsella, A., R. G. Tharp, and T. Ciboronski. *Perspectives on Cross-Cultural Psychology*. New York: Academic Press, 1979.

Neff, C. B., ed. *New Directions for Experimental Learning: Cross-Cultural Learning*, no. II. San Francisco: Jossey-Bass, 1981.

Nishida, H., and T. Nishida. "Values and intercultural communication." *Communication: The Journal of the Communication Association of the Pacific* 10, (1981), 50–58.

Osgood, C.E., H.H. May, and M. Murray. *Cross-Cultural Universals of Affective Meaning*. Urbana, Ill.: University of Illinois Press, 1975.

Price-Williams, D. "Toward the idea of a cultural psychology." *Journal of Cross-Cultural Psychology* 11 (1980), 75–88.

Rogers, E. M., and D. L. Kincaid. *Communication Networks: Toward a New Paradigm for Research*. New York: Free Press, 1980.

Rohrlic, R. E. "Toward a unified conception of intercultural communication: An integrated systems approach." *International Journal of Intercultural Relations* 7 (1983), 191–210.

Rotberg, R. I., ed. *The Mixing of Peoples: Problems of Identity and Ethnicity*. Stamford, Conn.: Greylock, Inc., 1978.

Saral, T.B. "Intercultural communication theory and research: An overview of challenges and opportunities" in D. Nimmo, ed., *Communication Yearbook* 3. New Brunswick, N.J.: Transaction, 1979, 395–405.

Sarbaugh, L. E. "A systematic framework for analyzing intercultural communication" in N.C. Jain, ed., *International and Intercultural Communication Annual*, vol. 5. Falls Church, Va.: Speech Communication, 1979, 11–22.

Smith, A.G. "Taxonomies for planning intercultural communication" in N.C. Jain, ed., *International and Intercultural Communication Annual*, vol. 5. Falls Church, Va.: Speech Communication Association, 1979, 1–10.

Smith, E.C., and L.B. Luce, eds. *Toward Internationalism: Readings in Cross-Cultural Communication*. Rowley, Mass.: Newbury House, 1979.

Szalzy, L.B. "Intercultural Communication—A process model." *International Journal of Intercultural Relations* 5 (1981), 133–146.

Triandis, H. *Analysis of Subjective Culture*. New York: John Wiley, 1972.

Triandis, H.C., and W. W. Lambert, eds. *Handbook of Cross-Cultural Psychology*, vol. I. Boston: Allyn & Bacon, 1980.

Trimillos, R.D. "One formalized transmission of culture." *East-West Culture Learning Institute* 9 (1983).

Webb, H. "Cross-cultural awareness: A framework for interaction." *Personnel and Guidance Journal* 61 (1983), 498–500.

Williams, R. *Culture*. London: Fortana Books, 1981.

Part Two

Socio-Cultural Backgrounds: What We Bring to Intercultural Communication

The most immutable barrier in nature is between one man's thoughts and another's.

—*William James*

One of the most important aspects of human communication is the fact that the experiential backgrounds participants bring to a communication experience will affect their behavior during the encounter. Psychologists A. H. Hastorf and H. Cantril underscore this issue when they note that each person acts according to the personal uniqueness he or she brings to the occasion. Think about those countless situations when you and some friends shared an experience and found that there were major differences in your reactions. What you deemed dull your companions found exciting; what you considered pointless they found meaningful. The messages being received were the same for all participants; yet, because each of you has a unique personality and background, you experienced a variety of feelings, sensations, and responses. Each of you brought different backgrounds to the event and as a result attributed individual meanings to the shared experience. In short, the event meant what it did to you because of your own unique past history.

We contend that in order to understand any communication encounter you must appreciate the idea that there is much more to communication than the mere analysis of messages. Messages and the responses you make to them are products of your unique past experiences. And it is this uniqueness of experience that greatly contributes to the "immutable barriers in nature" between each individual's thoughts.

Individual past experience takes on added significance when we introduce the many dimensions of culture. Individuals are influenced not only by personal experiences but by their culture as well. As we suggested in Part One, culture refers to those cumulative deposits of knowledge, values, and behaviors acquired by a large group of people and passed on from one generation to the next. In this sense, culture, in both conscious and unconscious ways, not only teaches you how to think and what to think about, it also dictates such values as what is attractive and what is ugly. In addition, culture teaches you such things as how close to stand next to strangers and even the various ways you can display your anger. When you are interacting with others and become disturbed by their actions you can, for instance, cry, become physically violent, shout, or remain silent. Each of these behaviors, depending on your culture, is a manifestation of what you have learned; it is culturally influenced. These cultural influences affect your ways of perceiving and acting; they contain the societal experiences and values that are passed from generation to generation. Because these behaviors are so much a part of your thinking, you might forget they vary from culture to culture. This is why a person from Japan, for example, might remain silent if disturbed by someone's actions while an Israeli or an Italian would more likely verbalize such displeasure.

Whatever the culture, you can better understand your behavior and the reactions of others if you realize that what you are hearing and seeing is a reflection of that culture. As you might predict, this understanding is greatly facilitated when your cultural experiences are similar to those of the people you are interacting with. Conversely, when different and diverse backgrounds are brought to a communication encounter, it is often difficult to share internal states and feelings. In this section we focus on those difficulties by examining some of the experiences and perceptual backgrounds found in a variety of foreign cultures as well as those found in several American subcommunities.

2

International Cultures

Communication between members of international cultures poses one of the most perplexing intercultural communication problems. How we are to understand others when they come from different sections of our "global village" is a most difficult question. We need only to look around the world at any particular moment in time to find disagreement, strife, and fighting. The locations may change, but the problems persist. Nations become prominent in the news, and what happens within them and between them directly affects the entire world. Although few of us are directly involved with these countries, we may be in contact with students from them who are studying in the United States. They may be our class mates or our students.

To help us better understand people from other cultures and the diverse personalities they can produce, and to give us a perspective from which we may be able to learn how to interact with those with whom we do come in contact, this chapter offers articles that will introduce us to six different international cultures. We begin with Fathi S. Yousef who gives us an insight into Arabic culture in his article "North Americans in the Middle East: Aspects of the Roles of Friendliness, Religion, and Women in Cross-Cultural Relations." Yousef examines the purpose and meaning of behaviors of North Americans and Middle Easterners in the light of Edward T. Hall's high- and low-context cultures. Illustrations involving friendliness, religion, and women are presented, analyzed, and explained. Middle Eastern programmed and internalized cultural patterns of behavior are contrasted with the North American spelled-out and legislated patterns of interaction.

In the next article, "'. . . So Near the United States,'" John Condon focuses on communication between Mexicans and Americans. Condon analyzes the cultural relations between Americans and Mexicans, concentrating on differences in how they perceive things in the context of working relationships.

Nemi C. Jain shifts our attention to the Indian subcontinent as he provides a glimpse of Hindu culture in his article "Some Basic Cultural Patterns of India." Here he examines what it means to be Hindu and discusses how the Hindu tradition contributes to the culture of India and provides a basis for the perceptual frames of reference common to India.

Our understanding of communicative behavior in another culture may be enhanced through the study of that culture's particular thought patterns. A simple fact, yet one that is often overlooked, is that the "steps of reasoning" are not the same in each culture. A prime example of this point is given through an examination of Japanese culture. In his article about patterns of thought in Japan, Professor Satoshi Ishii underscores this idea when he writes, "Logic, which is the basis of rhetoric, is evolved out of a culture; it is not universal." He demonstrates this point by comparing the typical thought patterns found in the United States with those of Japan.

Being aware of how a culture transmits ideas and information to its members is essential to understanding how that culture communicates. Most of the ingredients of culture, both tangible and intangible, are passed on by language and observation. We are born with the tools to speak and listen, hence that dimension of learning is universal. Reading and writing is yet another way in which culture is transmitted. Literacy, however, entails more than learning how to read and write; it influences thinking patterns, perceptions, cultural values, communication styles, and social organization as well. But literacy is not universal; we find that there are cultural groups that do not have a written language. It is therefore useful to know something of these types of cultures. This is especially true because many of the Southeast Asian refugees who have migrated to the United States are from oral cultures—cultures without a written history. To help us gain this insight, Robert Shuter examines the Hmong of Laos, a culture that is predominantly preliterate.

China is the world's most populous country (over one billion people), yet it is one the rest of the world has know very little about. However, now that the "sleeping giant" is awake, more and more attention is being paid to China and to its people. Tourists, businesspersons, and government officials have increasing personal contact with China. Because of this contact they are becoming increasingly concerned with intercultural issues. They are discovering, however, that China is different from other international cultures with which they have interacted; it poses some serious and unique problems. Traditional methods for examining intercultural communication do not always seem to apply in the case of China. In our final essay Stephen W. King explains some of this problem. His thesis is that in the People's Republic of China actual communication exchanges between Chinese and non-Chinese may or may not reflect the traditionally considered aspects of culture, but such exchanges *will* be affected by and reflect the political structures and policies of the government. To support his view, King examines interaction between Chinese and non-Chinese by looking at how the government's position can influence who talks to whom, when and where, about what, and in what way.

North Americans in the Middle East: Aspects of the Roles of Friendliness, Religion, and Women in Cross-Cultural Relations

FATHI S. YOUSEF

INTRODUCTION AND MATRIX

Early in the day, as he walked toward his office off the large room, Bill McCarthy's voice boomed at the Indian, Pakistani, and Middle Eastern support staff. "Good morning Mr. Pasha, Mr. Chishty, Mrs. Khan. Did you have a good weekend?" Bill slowed down by the desk of Ali Abdulla, the Bahraini national, and asked in general, "Are you still keeping Ramadan?" There were mumbled sounds of response and Bill walked on, turning and saying, "Saud, how's the wife today?" Saud blushed and nodded, and Bill entered his office saying, "Good, good!"

Bill McCarthy worked for a North American company in a Middle Eastern, oil rich, Gulf state. He came from a solid Midwestern background. Management thought highly of Bill and considered him friendly, outgoing, and considerate. However, the employees from the Middle East and other traditional societies thought Bill was loud, phony, and insensitive. Bill's greeting voice was high pitched, and as he walked he addressed several people simultaneously without stopping to talk to them.

This original essay appeared in print for the first time in the third edition. All rights reserved. Permission to reprint must be obtained from the publisher and the author. Professor Yousef teaches in the Speech Communication Department at California State University, Long Beach.

The message from a Middle Easterner's perspective was insincere and the greeting was impersonal and unmeant. Bill also embarrassed the staff by asking about keeping Ramadan. During the holy month of Ramadan, Moslems fast from sunrise to sunset. Those who don't fast, generally don't confess to it and abstain from eating or drinking in public. Keeping Ramadan is one of the tenets of Islam and the behavior is rather strictly adhered to particularly by Moslems in the Eastern hemisphere. Bill McCarthy's behavior seemed insensitive and rather insulting because, from a Middle Eastern perspective, it implied that Ali Abdulla or the others may not be fasting or obeying one of the major dictates of their religion. And, in the Middle East, an individual's appeal, reliability, and soundness of character are considered directly related to how religious the individual is. (A case in point is the frequent admiring allusions by President Sadat of Egypt to the moral personality of born again, former U.S. President Jimmy Carter.) Bill McCarthy was also rather offensive when he asked Saud in public about his wife who was sick.

Bill did not intend to offend. He simply engaged in typical North American phatic communion. He wanted to tell the group he was there, he recognized them, and was as friendly and caring as the last time they saw him. However, from the group's cultural perspective, if he was sincere, Bill should approach every individual with a handshake followed probably by a pat on the shoulder and a personal greeting in a voice meant only for the individual to hear and respond to. Whether it is a quick greeting or a query about the health of a family member, especially a female family member, privacy and the interpersonal dimension are the essence of the message (Yousef, 1968, 1974, 1976). The reaction to Bill McCarthy's pleasant North American behavior reflects two different cultural orientations: a North American pattern of loose expectations and casual relations and a Middle Eastern pattern of involved expectations and intense relations (Hall, 1977; Yousef, 1978).

In this article, the role and meaning of behaviors involving North Americans and Middle Easterns are examined in reference to three areas: friendliness, religion, and women. The matrix in Table 1 reflects different cultural orientations and major assumptions underlying observable behaviors involved in cross-cultural relations. Of course, in communication contexts, several variables are frequently involved simultaneously in a complex manner. For the sake of identification and interpretation, however, the following major points are presented as discrete entities.

FRIENDLINESS

It is hard for a North American to conceive of cultures that do not place a high premium on friendliness. Politicians and salesmen, corporate managers and artists, teachers and policemen, along with members of most occupations learn early in life the value of friendliness. The concept itself is considered part and parcel of popularity, which is a prime ingredient of success in democracies. From their early years in the United States, children are taught to believe in friendliness. At homes, in schools, in social groups, in clubs and business environments, and in queues in supermarkets and department stores, proper behavior is friendly behavior. Smiles, greetings, noncommittal small talk, and current jokes about the weather, the World Series, and the news are manifestations of friendliness. The emphasis is on informality, and the tone of voice is loud enough for one and all who are around to participate. Further nonverbal clues such as facial expression, eye contact, and body orientation emphasize the message that all present are included and invited in the interaction. To the North American, the message is direct and the intent is clear: "I'm friendly. I'm just like you. I share similar interests and problems." The behavior reflects an almost overriding preoccupation with a desire to be popular, liked, and accepted. Informality, a prime ingredient of friendliness American-style, is the norm in these casual and fast relationships.

In traditional Middle Eastern societies, the same behaviors lauded in the United States are frequently regarded as flippant and undignified. For example, the friendly North American who walks into

Table 1

Area Examined	Friendliness	Religion	Women
North American orientation	1. A highly regarded desirable quality. 2. Friendliness is extended to one and all; emphasis is on informality most of the time. 3. Manifestation of friendliness reflects almost a preoccupation with a desire to be popular and liked by all.	1. Religious values and beliefs are strictly personal, rarely referred to in daily interactions. 2. Society usually views integrity, ethics, and proper behavior as individual character traits not necessarily linked to one's atheistic or religious beliefs. 3. People regard and expect each other to have control over their actions.	1. Women's status is professedly equal to that of men. 2. A woman's behavior is her own responsibility. 3. A woman's dress and appearance is usually what she wants, likes, and is most comfortable in.
Middle Eastern traditional society orientation	1. Frequently regarded as flippant behavior lacking in dignity. 2. Friendliness is shown to select people; emphasis is on formality most of the time. 3. Manifestation of friendliness reflects consciousness of vertical social and business hierarchies in one's relationships.	1. Religious norms and beliefs are often publicly affirmed and quoted in daily interactions. 2. Society frequently links integrity, ethics, and proper behavior to the degree of one's atheistic or religious beliefs. 3. People regard what happens in life as an expression of God's will.	1. Women's position is assumed to be behind their men. 2. A woman's behavior is viewed as the responsibility of her male family and clan members. 3. A woman's dress and appearance is regarded as a reflection of her character. A woman in immodest or revealing clothes brings shame to herself and her family since her attire would be considered too conspicuous and inviting to the men around.

the company's cafeteria greeting the waiters and those on the serving line with high-pitched "Hello, hello, how're you?" etc., does not create a very positive impression. At best, the individual is regarded as a "crazy American." By and large, one would be looked down upon, sometimes joked with patronizingly, and frequently made fun of by the nationals. The behavior that is usually regarded and rewarded positively in the United States is considered improper and viewed negatively in the Middle East where at a very early age children are taught that in public one looks serious and acts somberly. Among Middle Easterners, public manifestations of friendliness American-style invite opprobrium and disrespect.

The manner of expressing friendliness in the Middle East is a function of one's position in the vertical hierarchies of business and social relationships. However, whether it is friendliness between peers or in superior-subordinate relationships, manifestations of the behavior are generally governed by whether the context is public or private.

Friendly behavior in public is usually formal. Individuals refer to each other by excessive use of honorific or earned titles and official positions. Casual conversations are sprinkled with abundant compliments and testimonials by the interactants about each other's expertise, status, power, influence, or such similar accomplishments. Peers laud each other's work and stances, superiors have kind words for those below them, and subordinates refer to the moral and/or material support of the higher-ups present. In similar contexts, North Americans would be kidding each other about some gaffes or social blunders before attending to the day's business.

In private in the Middle East, behavior is less formal and more relaxed. Although honorifics and titles are not infrequently used thus reflecting society's constant involvement and awareness of the vertical hierarchies in relationships, behavior patterns are rather informal. Peers joke and kid each other about weaknesses as do superiors with each other. Subordinates present, however, refer to funny situations that superiors shared with them and relished.

In public and in private interactions in the Middle East, North American, friendly, put-down humor is usually taken as a form of censure if not insult. Preoccupation with the question of "face" is one of the main reasons why innocuous, American-style humor could be misunderstood by Middle Easterns and taken as deliberate criticism intended to disgrace the receiver.

In general in the United States, society's high compliment is for the individual who is popular and well liked, while in Middle Eastern societies the compliment is for the individual who is respected and dignified. The implication and interpretation is that such an individual is usually mindful of status boundaries in formal and informal interpersonal relations. Through such "proper" behavior the individual earns respect, admiration, and affection—not popularity whose connotations are not always positive for Middle Easterners. In general, friendliness is personal and specific. And its expression and contextual expectations are functions of the status of the interactants.

RELIGION

"Omar, aren't you going to quit smoking?"

"I've been thinking about it. But, you know, John, whatever is written will be."

John Smith looked at his Middle Eastern friend and foreign student at U.C.L.A. and said, "You know what the research says." Omar's response was, "John, if I'm destined to die of cancer, I will, no matter what!"

John dismissed the subject and thought that his Middle Eastern friend who had a degree in aerodynamics was simply being flippant. Although Omar's retort sounded facetious, however, the behavior reflects a cultural orientation and a belief in predestination. Yet, in a way, though paradoxical, to the Middle Easterner the belief does not negate individual choice and freedom. Unlike the North American child growing in a culture whose technological accomplishments constantly emphasize and reinforce one's belief in science and human control of human actions, the Middle Easterner is usually raised in an environment that emphasizes the notion that whatever happens in life is an expression of God's will. Thus, in the Middle Eastern culture, human choices and attempts, successes and failures are regarded as manifestations of God's plan and will.

In contrast, in the United States separation between the roles and domains of church and state is such an ingrained concept that it is not easy for a North American to comprehend cultures where the differentiation is diffused. In the United States religious values and beliefs are viewed as strictly personal matters. They are rarely referred to in daily interactions. As a matter of fact, "good" social manners prohibit discussion of religion or politics. U.S. society regards integrity, ethics, and proper behavior as individual character traits not necessarily linked to one's religious orientation or beliefs. To the Middle Easterner, however, the degree of an individual's religiosity is an indicator of character forthrightness and ethicality. In evaluating people and their actions, religious and secular behaviors are viewed as a diffused entity that is a reflection of the same thing.

Unlike the United States, in the Middle East different social groupings form different sovereign states and countries. In most countries, however, the people are, by and large, ethically homogeneous. In many of these countries civil laws are extensions and operational interpretations of religious and theological rulings. Daily social and business verbal interactions are frequently sprinkled with religious invocations, examples, sayings, and quotations. For instance, expressions of appreciation and admiration start with "Glory be to the Lord"; expressions of disappointment or sorrow usually end with "God's will be done"; and reference to the future is accompanied by the words "God willing."

In the Middle Eastern area, most countries are predominantly Islamic, and Islam is not only a religion but a religious, political, and cultural way of life. The three areas overlap, interact, and imperceptibly affect and reflect on each other. As a religion, Islam is a system of beliefs and practices enshrined in the Koran. The system has been clarified and supplemented by tradition and modified through the ages in response to changes in time and place. Islam is a monotheistic religion. It is a historical offshoot of Judaism and Christianity and is most closely related to them. Currently, it is estimated that the total Moslem population of the world is about 600 million, that is to say, in general, one person out of every six in the world is a Moslem. The largest Moslem community, totaling about 150 million in one geographic location, is on the Indian subcontinent. The Islamic community in the Middle East, including Turkey and Iran, is almost as large (Christopher, 1972). As a political entity, Islam provides an aggregate of institutions and rulings based on Koranic law. Today, several states with populations from different backgrounds style and call themselves Islamic. They range from Hamites in Egypt and Semites in Saudi Arabia to Aryans in Iran and Dravidians in Pakistan. As a culture, Islam is a compound of various ancient Semitic, Indo-Persian, and classical Greek elements that are synthesized and expressed primarily through the medium of the Arabic language. It is a culture that was mainly formulated by conquered peoples from different races and ethnic groups. The people were linguistically Arabicized and religiously Islamized (Hitti, 1970).

In Arabic, a Moslem is literally one who surrenders himself to the will of God, and Islam is the religion of surrender to God's will. The reference is to the surrender that was implicit in the Biblical submission of Abraham and his son to the Lord's command for sacrifice in that Old Testament supreme test. The noun form from Moslem is Islam, a religion whose name is an allusion to Abraham's willingness to sacrifice for the Lord, and the state is *as-salama*, which means peace in Arabic. In other words, an individual's state of peace on earth is a state of submission to God's will, and whatever happens to one in life is an expression of the Lord's will. It is in essence a form of belief in predestination as opposed to the North American view of man as master of nature in a sort of junior partnership with God. Examples from Western thought and culture are reflected in sayings such as "God is my co-pilot," "Somebody up there likes me," etc. (Condon and Yousef, 1975). In the Middle East, however, the culture views a man's behavior as a reflection of his religious beliefs, and whatever happens to him as a manifestation of what is preordained.

WOMEN

An anthropologist friend once commented facetiously to this writer, "In the Middle East and the Third World, the woman walks six feet behind the man, in Europe she walks next to him, and in America she pulls him on a leash." Humor aside, the joke refers to different cultural views of the role and position of women. On a continuum, in considering the North American and Middle Eastern values regarding women, on the one side, in the United States women's behavioral norms and expectations are almost all legislated and written up while on the other side of the continuum, in the Middle East, the same entities are primarily pre-programmed by society in the minds of the members of the culture.

For example, in the United States, concepts of

apple pie and home making, motherhood and family happiness may evoke vague images and associations of women's romantic role in the culture. Legislation, however, and equal opportunity guidelines spell out equality of the sexes, and the culture's social, educational, and business institutions profess, teach, and abide by the laws. The underlying cultural assumption is that of independence and individual responsibility for one's actions and behaviors whether social, sexual, religious, or economic.

In the Middle East, the role and societal position of women is rather paradoxical and undefined. A woman's behavior is primarily the responsibility of the males in her family. However, according to the teachings of Islam, Middle Eastern women have always enjoyed great measures of economic independence. They are entitled to buy and sell, inherit and dispose of their property at will. And, with present emphasis on education and political rights, in many Middle Eastern countries women vote and hold degrees and positions in almost all fields and institutions. Women work as physicians and university professors, engineers and chemists and teachers, etc. The cultural unwritten rules of social behavior, however, shape a picture of a societal position for women different from its counterpart in the United States. For example, despite a woman's educational attainments and economic independence and political status, Middle Eastern cultures expect the woman's social and sexual behavior to be the responsibility of the males in her family. The unmarried woman in Dhahran, Saudi Arabia, who may unhesitatingly chair a business meeting of several male subordinates in her division at 8:00 A.M. is unlikely to accept or be seen having dinner in public with a male friend at 8:00 P.M. without a chaperone. The behavior would reflect on the woman's reputation and affect the "honor" of the males in her nuclear and extended family. By the same token, a Middle Eastern male does not expect a "respectable" woman to accept an invitation to go out with him alone. The notions of honor and shame are unwritten and already pre-programmed in the minds of Middle Easterners. Women's social and sexual behavior is a prime in-

gredient in the structure of relationships in Middle Eastern societies. A woman who engages in culturally unsanctioned behaviors brings shame and dishonor to herself, family, and clan. The woman's "improper" behavior decreases the group's status and societal effectiveness, and could even reflect negatively on the perception of competence of the professionals in the group. For example, the expertise of a male physician or architect or lawyer may be viewed as questionable if a woman or the women in his family are considered "loose" since a woman's "improper" behavior stigmatizes her whole clan. And, in the highly interdependent societies of the Middle East, women's behavior is the central link in the culture's social fabric.

The impact and reflection of a woman's "improper" behavior is such that until restitution takes place, all women in the nuclear and extended family are regarded as "easy," "loose," and "shameless"—terms that reflect terrible and most stinging insults in the culture. The male relatives of an "improperly" behaved woman—the father, the brothers, the husband, the sons, the uncles, the cousins—are dishonored and considered lacking in manliness until the cause or source of shame is rectified or eradicated. The task is the responsibility of the immediate male family members. However, should they seem to hesitate or ignore their "honorable" duty, the next male members in line step in and assume the responsibility. Frequently, punishment is severe and difficult to understand from a North American perspective. The behavior, however, is not unusual or alien to traditional cultures that place a high premium on the behavior of women as a determinant of social relationships (Peristiany, 1965; Yousef, 1978).

The importance of women's behavior in the Middle East is also reflected in the emphasis placed on women's appearance in public. In the culture, what a woman wears is a nonverbal message sent to the environment around her. Revealing clothes connote sexual looseness and availability. Although among the upper and middle classes in the Middle East there is a widespread and heightened awareness of fashions from Rome, Paris, London, and New York, "respectable" women are supposed to have discriminating tastes in public. Halters, tight outfits, and short shorts are considered indirect invitations for male advances. And, since the culture does not have recognized male-female courtship places such as the singles bars in the United States, a woman in revealing or suggestive attire in public is considered not uninterested or unwilling. Whether in a street or a supermarket, a college campus or a gas station, the message in the Middle East is the same—a woman's "improper" dress connotes availability. The view is the same whether one considers the behavior in ultraconservative Riyadh, Saudi Arabia, where Saudi women are usually veiled in public, or in modern Cairo, Egypt, where a veiled woman is a curiosity in a city swarming with all kinds of contemporary dress fashions.

North American families moving to the Middle East as part of educational development, industrial joint ventures, or business investment programs frequently receive what look like restrictive dictates about women's behavior and attire. The message is often regarded as interfering or infringing on personal freedom. The intent in reality is to protect the naive visitor from the ramifications of unintended behaviors. For example, in the midst of her daily chores the North American housewife who finds she has to dash to the supermarket in her halter and shorts shouldn't expect to engage in the same behavior in the Middle East without facing some raised eyebrows. Nor could an innocent bachelor who sees an attractive woman alone in a store or at a bus stop expect to meet or befriend her through engaging her in some form of casual conversation. In the Middle East, "respectable" women do *not* meet men without being formally introduced. Thus while in the United States women share equal rights with men on all levels, in the Middle East women participate on equal footing with men on the business and professional levels and defer to the culture's sexual norms in social life.

On the surface, it might look as though women in the Middle East do not have as much say in society as they do in the United States. In reality,

women wield a lot of power from behind the scenes. Extended family relations are frequently expanded and cemented by marriages arranged by women in the clan. They also play a role in establishing business contracts and help with finding jobs and work contracts for different family members. Societal coalitions and alliances between different clans are many times the results of women's communication and influence with their fathers, brothers, husbands, sons, cousins, and in-laws in different families, tribes, clans, and powerful parties. Women are not taken lightly in Middle Eastern societies though their power in the sociocultural equation is often exercised on the personal level and through the men. The major demand, however, on women's behavior in the Middle East lies in society's expectation of female chastity for, by and large, while the role of women may not at times seem very visible, in the culture, women's social and sexual behavior is most of the time the central fabric of the intensely involved interpersonal relations and expectations.

PATTERNS IN CROSS-CULTURAL COMMUNICATION

The behaviors presented and discussed in this article deal with three patterns of social interaction in the low-context culture of the United States as compared to the high-context culture of the Middle East. First, while the expression of friendliness in the United States is a reflection of the explicit social rules and laws of equality and principles of relating to one and all on a horizontal level, the role and manner of expressing friendliness in the Middle East is preprogrammed in the minds of the people and is an implicit function of one's position in the vertical hierarchy of social and business relationships. The second pattern deals with the role and place of religion in the United States and in the Middle East. Clearly spelled-out rules separate church and state matters in the United States. In the Middle East, the view is frequently diffused into a single entity, and an individual's degree of religiosity is often regarded as an indicator of the individual's moral character. In the third pattern, the laws and rules clarifying equality of the sexes in the United States contrast with the Middle Eastern unwritten norms of women's behavior.

In cross-cultural relations, misinterpretation, frustration, and misunderstanding occur when rational, reasonable behavior in one culture connotes a different meaning in another culture. Frequently, people examine sets of behavior and analyze the isolated components without trying to study the underlying, intangible, cultural pattern that ties and explains the sets together (Hall, 1959). In his book *Beyond Culture* (1977), Hall introduces and contrasts types of low- and high-context cultures. He considers: "American culture, while not on the bottom, is toward the low end of the scale." (Hall, 1977:91). Hall explains that in low-context cultures, frequently, written-up, explicit codes spell out the behavioral norms. In high-context cultures [such] as in the Middle East, the information is either internalized in the individual or is in the physical context itself. In the Middle East the internalization process is a function of the psychological and physical proximity in which people grow up. The environment there provides and rewards intense interpersonal relationships and emphasizes mutual dependence on one's immediate and extended family, tribe, or clan.

Basically, differences in the interpretation of the behavioral expectations and patterns presented in this article reflect different cultural frames of reference. In the low-context culture of the United States relations are rather loose, not too binding, and emphasize independence and equality. In the high-context culture of the Middle East people are intensely involved with each other, constantly aware of their vertical social and business hierarchies and their interdependence in binding relationships. And, whether in the manner and expression of friendliness, or in assessing the role and impact of religion, or in considering the position and behavior of women in the Middle East, cultural norms reflect an abundance of unwritten rules and expectations unlike the wealth of published laws and behavioral guides that spell out and clarify expectations in the United States.

REFERENCES

Condon, J. C., and F. S. Yousef. *An Introduction to Intercultural Communication*. Indianapolis: Bobbs-Merrill, 1975.

Cristopher, J. B. *The Islamic Tradition*. New York: Harper & Row, 1972.

Hall, E. T. *Beyond Culture*. Garden City, N.Y.: Anchor, 1977.

——— *The Silent Language*. Greenwich, Conn.: Fawcett, 1959.

Hitti, P. K. *Islam—A Way of Life*. Minneapolis: University of Minnesota Press, 1970.

Peristiany, J. G., ed. *Honour and Shame: The Values of the Mediterranean*. London: Weiderfield and Nicolson, 1965.

Yousef, F. S. "Communication Patterns: Some Aspects of Nonverbal Behavior in Intercultural Communication." In *Interethnic Communication*, ed. E. Lamar Ross. Athens, Georgia: The University of Georgia Press, 1978.

——— "Cross-Cultural Communication: Aspects of Contrastive Social Values between North Americans and Middle Easterners." *Human Organization*, 33 (1974), 383–387.

——— "Cross-Cultural Testing: An Aspect of the Resistance Reaction." *Language Learning*, 18 (1968), 227–234.

——— "Nonverbal Behavior: Some Intricate and Diverse Dimensions in Intercultural Communication." In *Intercultural Communication: A Reader*, ed. Larry A Samovar and Richard E. Porter. Belmont, Calif.: Wadsworth, 1976.

Yousef, F. S., and N. E. Briggs. "The Multinational Business Organization: A Schema for the Training of Overseas Personnel in Communication." In *International and Intercultural Communication Annual*, Vol. II. Falls Church, Va.: Speech Communication Association, 1975.

"...So Near the United States": Notes on Communication between Mexicans and North Americans

JOHN CONDON

"Poor Mexico," said Porfirio Diaz, "so far from God, so near the United States." In the years since Mexico's last pre-Revolutionary president said these words the nations on both sides of the border have been greatly altered. Some might speculate on the resulting changes in Mexico's proximity to the Lord, but none would deny that geographically and commercially Mexico has never been so near the United States. The cultural distance, however, is something else, for in many respects the cultural gaps between these societies are as great as ever. Thus when President Kennedy said during his highly successful visit to Mexico in 1962 that "geography has made us neighbors, tradition has made us friends," many Mexicans thought it more accurate to say that "geography has made us close but tradition has made us more distant than ever."

Not that there has been any shortage of contact between people of these two cultures. The fifteen hundred mile border that spans the continent is crossed in both directions by more people than any other international border on the globe. These include millions of tourists annually who venture south into Mexico to make up more than 80 percent of that nation's primary source of revenue, tourism. It also includes the countless numbers of workers, both legally admitted and undocumented, business people, students and tourists, too, who cross from Mexico into the United States. Quite apart from this daily traffic, the cultural presence of each society is to be found across the border. The capital city of Mexico is that nation's, and soon the world's, largest metropolis; but the second largest number of Mexicans reside in Los Angeles. And it is worth recalling that scarcely a century and a half ago half of the land that had been Mexico became a part of the U.S., a fact remembered more in Mexico than north of the border. Intercultural contact is hardly a phenomenon of the jet age.

Information about and from each society has never been greater than one finds today. Studies show that the average Mexico City daily newspaper contains a greater percentage of news about the U.S. than the average *New York Times* reports about all the rest of the world combined. North American foods, fashions, products and loan words are enough in evidence in the cities of Mexico to make the casual visitor overlook some significant differences in values and beliefs. Indeed, many veteran observers of relations between Mexicans and North Americans believe that the increase in superficial similarities actually contributes to culture-based misunderstandings.

Insights into contrasting cultural assumptions and styles of communication cannot be gained without an appreciation of the history and geography of the two societies. One quickly learns that where there are intersections, such as the major river that marks a good part of the border or the major war that literally gave shape to each nation, the interpretations and even the names are different in each society. The name "America" itself is one that many Mexicans feel should not be limited to the United States of America alone, particularly since culturally the "anglo" culture is a minority among the nations of the Americas. "North America" and "North American" may be more appreciated.

From *The Bridge,* Spring 1980. Reprinted by permission of the publisher. John Condon has taught at Northwestern University and the International Christian University in Tokyo. He is currently a communication consultant in San Diego, California.

North Americans trace their history from the time of the first English settlers. The people already living on the continent possessed no great cities or monuments to rival anything in Europe, and they held little interest for the European colonists so long as they could be displaced and their land cultivated. The North American Indian has remained excluded from the shaping of the dominant culture of the new nation just as he had been excluded from the land. With political independence and the continuous arrival of immigrants, largely from Northern Europe, the nation took shape in a steady westward pattern. The outlook was to the future, to new land and new opportunities. The spirit was of optimism.

When the Spanish soldiers arrived in Mexico in the 16th century they found cities and temples of civilizations that had flourished for thousands of years. In what some have called a holy crusade, the Spanish attempted to destroy the old societies and reconstruct a new order on top. In religion, in language, in marriage, there was a fusion of Indian and European which was totally different from the pattern in the United States. While Cortés is no hero in Mexico—there are no statues of him anywhere in the country—the fusion of European and native American cultures is a source of great pride, not only in Mexico but extending throughout the Latin American republics. This is the spirit of *la raza* which serves in part to give a sense of identification with other Latin Americans and a sense of separateness from those of the anglo world.

There are other contrasts to be noted as well. The land that became the United States was for the most part hospitable and, for much of the country's history, seemingly endless. Less than a fifth of the land in Mexico, in contrast, is arable.

The images which the people on each side of the border hold of the other differ. Mexico's image of the United States was to a great extent shaped in Europe, formed at a time when European writers had little good to say about the anglo-American world. Even today when Mexicans speak of the ideals of freedom and democracy, their inspiration is more likely to be French than North American. The rivalry between England and Spain, compounded by the religious hostility between Protestants and Catholics, influenced in a comparable way the North American's image of Mexico.

Finally, by way of introduction, we should note that regional differences are pronounced and of importance in understanding the people of Mexico. Social and economic differences vary considerably, and even in language, with perhaps 150 different languages still spoken in the country, there are truly "many Mexicos." Thus it is not surprising that for years there has been a serious interest among Mexicans to find "the Mexican." Some say this search for identity began even before the Conquest, for the 16th century Spaniard was himself unsure of his identity: he arrived in Mexico less than 25 years after driving out the last of the Moors from his own homeland.

An early Adlerian analysis of "the Mexican" by Samuel Ramos found the essence of the Mexican national character in the *pelado*, "the plucked one," at the bottom of the pecking order. While the Ramos thesis has been reconsidered over the years, some of the same themes of doubt and frustration and of a tragic outlook on life continue in contemporary Mexican interpretations.

The history of relations between the United States and Mexico has not been one of understanding and cooperation, though many persons on both sides of the border are working toward those ends. Even under the best of conditions and with the best of intentions, Mexicans and North Americans working together sometimes feel confused, irritated, distrustful. The causes lie not within either culture but rather can be best understood interculturally. Here are four perspectives.

INDIVIDUALISM

In the North American value system are three central and interrelated assumptions about human beings. These are (1) that people, apart from social and educational influences, are basically the same; (2) that each person should be judged on his or her own individual merits; and (3) that these "merits," including a person's worth and character, are revealed through the person's actions. Values of equality and independence, constitutional rights, laws and social programs arise from these assumptions. Because a person's actions are regarded as so important, it is the comparison of accomplishments—Mr. X compared to Mr. X's father, or X five years ago compared to X today, or X compared to Y and Z—that provides a chief means of judging or even knowing a person.

In Mexico it is the uniqueness of the individual which is valued, a quality which is assumed to reside within each person and which is not necessarily evident through actions or achievements. That inner quality which represents the dignity of each person must be protected at all costs. Any action or remark that may be interpreted as a slight to the person's dignity is to be regarded as a grave provocation. Also, as every person is part of a larger family grouping, one cannot be regarded as a completely isolated individual.

This contrast, which is sometimes expressed as the distinction between "individualism" in the case of the North American, and "individuality" in the case of the Mexican, frequently leads to misunderstandings in intercultural encounters ranging from small talk to philosophical arguments.

Where a Mexican will talk about a person's inner qualities in terms of the person's soul or spirit (*alma* or *espiritu*), North Americans are likely to feel uncomfortable using such words to talk about people. They may regard such talk as vague or sentimental, the words seeming to describe something invisible and hence unknowable, or at the very least "too personal." The unwillingness to talk in this way only confirms the view held by many Mexicans that North Americans are insensitive. "Americans are corpses," said one Mexican.

Even questions about the family of a person one does not know well may discomfit many North Americans, since asking about a person's parents or brothers or sisters may also seem too personal. "I just don't know the person well enough to ask about his family," a North American might say, while the Mexican may see things just the opposite: "If I don't ask about the person's family, how will I really know him?"

The family forms a much less important part of an individual's frame of reference in the U.S. than is usually the case in Mexico. Neighbors, friends or associates, even some abstract "average American," may be the basis for the comparison needed in evaluating oneself or others. "Keeping up with the Joneses" may be important in New York or Chicago, but keeping up with one's brother-in-law is more important in Mexico City. In the same way, the Mexican depends upon relatives or close friends to help "arrange things" if there is a problem, or to provide a loan. While this is by no means rare in the United States, the dominant values in the culture favor institutions which are seen as both efficient and fair.

So it is that tensions may arise between Mexicans and North Americans over what seems to be a conflict between trusting particular individuals or trusting abstract principles. In a business enterprise, the North American manager is likely to view the organization and its processes as primary, with the role of specific people being more or less supportive of that system. People can be replaced if need be; nobody is indispensable. When one places emphasis on a person's spirit or views an organization as if it were a family, however, then it seems just as clear that nobody can be exactly replaced by any other person.

Both North Americans and Mexicans may speak of the need to "respect" another person, but here too the meanings of the word respect (or *respeto*) differ somewhat across the cultures. In a study of associations with this word conducted in the U.S. and Mexico, it was found that North Americans regarded "respect" as bound up with the values of equality, fair play and the democratic spirit. There were no emotional overtones. One respects others as one might respect the law. For Mexicans, however, "respect" was found to be an emotionally charged word involving pressures of power, possible threat and often a love-hate relationship. The meaning of respect arises from powerful human relationships such as between father and son or *patrón* and *péon*, not a system of principles to which individuals voluntarily commit themselves.

STRAIGHT TALK

Last year the leaders of both the United States and France visited Mexico. A prominent writer for the distinguished Mexican daily, *Excelsior*, commented on their visits and on the words they spoke. Interpreting the impressions they made on Mexicans, the writer alluded to cultural differences. President Carter was seen as following the anglo-saxon values of his culture as he spoke bluntly of realities. President Giscard d'Estaing, as a product of a cultural tradition which was more familiar to that of Mexico, spoke in a style far more grand, and if his words were in some way further from realities they were at least more beautiful. When all was said and done and the two leaders returned to their capitals, the writer concluded, the world had been little changed as a result of their visits but the French leader's words had at least made his Mexican listeners feel better for awhile.

The ceremonial speaking of heads of state actually shows fewer differences between Mexican and North American styles than do routine conversations. It is not simply that two styles, plain and fancy, contrast; rather, persons from each culture will form judgments about the personality and character of the other as a result. The Mexican is far more likely to flatter, tease or otherwise attempt to charm another than is the North American whose culture has taught him to distrust or poke fun at anyone who "really lays it on."

Often the problem is heightened when there is a difference in the sex, status or age of the two persons in conversation. Mexicans may want to maximize those differences while North Americans often make a great effort to minimize them. North Americans may at present be most sensitive to the way in which a businessman talks to a businesswoman, lest he be accused of "sexism," but the same values apply to "making too much" of one's age or status. Thus the very style which is called for in one culture may be regarded as quite uncalled for in the other culture. North Americans are often suspicious of one who seems effusive in praise; they are also likely to make light of one who seems

too enamored of titles. Mexicans, on the other hand, value one who has the wit and charm to impress another. Nor are titles or other indications of one's status, age or ability to be slighted. The owner of an auto repair shop may defer to a mechanic who is older and more experienced as *maestro*; doctors, lawyers and other professional people will take their titles seriously. To make light of them is to challenge one's dignity.

THE TRUTH

During the world congress held in Mexico for the International Women's Year, some first time visitors experienced the kind of problem that many North Americans have long complained about in Mexico. The visitors would be told one thing only to discover that what they were told seemed to bear no resemblance to the facts. A delegate who would ask where a meeting was being held might be given clear directions, but upon reaching the destination she would find no such meeting. "It was not that the Mexicans were unfriendly or unhelpful—just wrong!" North American managers working with Mexicans have sometimes voiced similar complaints: an employee says something is finished when in fact it has not even been begun.

Rogelio Díaz-Guerrero, head of the psychology department at the National University of Mexico and a foremost interpreter of Mexican behavior patterns, offers this explanation. There are two kinds of "realities" which must be distinguished, objective and interpersonal. Some cultures tend to treat everything in terms of the objective sort of reality; this is characteristic of the United States. Other cultures tend to treat things in terms of interpersonal relations, and this is true of Mexico. This distinction, we may note, bears some resemblance to the distinction made by the *Excelsior* columnist.

Viewed from the Mexican perspective, a visitor asks somebody for information which that person doesn't know. But wanting to make the visitor happy and to enjoy a few pleasant moments together, the Mexican who was asked does his best to say something so that for a short while the visitor is made happy. It is not that Mexicans have a monopoly on telling another person what that person wants to hear: perhaps in all cultures the truth is sometimes altered slightly to soften the impact of a harsh word or to show deference to one's superior. It is the range of situations in which this occurs in Mexico and the relatively sharper contrast of "truth-telling" standards in U.S.-Mexican encounters that is so notable.

In value, if not always in fact, North Americans have given special importance to telling the truth. The clearest object lessons in the lives of the nation's two legendary heroes, Washington and Lincoln, concern honesty, while the presidents who have been most held in disrepute, Harding and Nixon, are held up to scorn because of their dishonesty.

Francisco Gonzales Pineda has written at length about lying. Starting from premises similar to those offered by Samuel Ramos mentioned earlier, including the idealization of manliness of the *pelado*, Gonzalez Pineda says that a Mexican must be able to lie if he is to be able to live without complete demoralization. He says that general recognition of this has made the lie in Mexico almost an institution. He describes variations of lies in different regions of Mexico, including the capital in which he says the use of the lie is socially acceptable in all its forms. He contrasts the Mexican style of lie to that which is used by North Americans. In the United States the lie is little used aggressively or defensively or to express fantasy. The more common form of defense is the expression of the incomplete truth or an evasion of truth. There are stereotyped expressions which are purposefully ambiguous and impersonal, so lacking in emotional content that they do not conflict with the emotional state of the liar.

Whether or not one supports the interpretation of Gonzalez Pineda, an examination of difficulties between North Americans and Mexicans is to be found in the broad area of matching words, deeds and intentions. The North American in a daily routine has a much narrower range of what he considers permissible than is found in similar situations in Mexico.

TIME

If a culture is known by the words exported, as one theory has it, then Mexico may be best known as the land of *mañana*. Differences in the treatment of time may not be the most serious source of misunderstanding between people of the two cultures but it is surely the most often mentioned. Several issues are actually grouped under the general label of "time."

In Edward Hall's influential writings on time across culture, he has distinguished between "monochronic" (M-time) and "polychronic" (P-time) treatments of time; these correspond to the North American and Mexican modes respectively. M-time values take care of "one thing at a time." Time is lineal, segmented. (American football is a very "M-time" game.) It may not be that time is money but M-time treats it that way, with measured precision. M-time people like neat scheduling of appointments and are easily distracted and often very distressed by interruptions.

In contrast, P-time is characterized by many things happening at once, and with a much "looser" notion of what is "on time" or "late." Interruptions are routine, delays to be expected. Thus it is not so much that putting things off until *mañana* is valued, as some Mexican stereotypes would have it, but that human activities are not expected to proceed like clock-work. It should be noted in this regard that the North American treatment of time appears to be the more unusual on a world scale. This writer discovered that even in Japan, a culture not known for its imprecision or indolence, U.S. business people were seen by Japanese colleagues as much too time-bound, driven by schedules and deadlines which in turn thwarted an easy development of human relationships.

North Americans express special irritation when Mexicans seem to give them less than their undivided attention. When a young woman bank teller, awaiting her superior's approval for a check to be cashed, files her nails and talks on the phone to her boyfriend, or when one's taxi driver stops en route to pick up a friend who seems to be going in the

10. Smith, pp. 27–28.

11. Smith, p. 85.

12. Smith, p. 76.

13. Smith, p. 77.

14. Smith, p. 79.

15. S. Radhakrishnan, *Indian Religions* (New Delhi: Vision Books Private Ltd., 1979), pp. 52–53.

16. Radhakrishnan, pp. 70–71.

17. Radhakrishnan, p. 61.

18. Radhakrishnan, p. 62.

19. Smith, p. 62.

20. Smith, pp. 62–63.

21. Radhakrishnan, pp. 63–64.

22. S. N. Chopra, *India: An Area Study* (New Delhi: Vikas Publishing House Private Ltd., 1977), pp. 26–27.

23. Chopra, pp. 27–28.

24. Fersh, pp. 17–21.

25. Murthy and Kamath, p. 5.

26. Murthy and Kamath, p. 8.

Thought Patterns as Modes of Rhetoric: The United States and Japan

SATOSHI ISHII

The second half of the twentieth century can be said to be the age of international communication and global mobility. The rapid progress in communication technology has made it possible for us to exchange and share a tremendous amount of information with people from a variety of different cultural backgrounds. The wide-ranging improvements in transportation have made our world much "smaller" than it once was; people from around the world are freely moving in and out of their homelands. Apparently, this international and intercultural phenomenon will continue to take place in the era of the "global village."

From a historical point of view, communication with people from different cultures is not new. Since ancient times people in North Africa, Europe, Asia, and the Middle East have developed intercultural exchanges in forms of trade and war. In the present century, the United States plays one of the most important roles in the international arena. Today, no nation can depend solely on itself in isolation from others. In this sense, the history of intercultural communication is very long.

The systematic study of this field, however, is rather new. Scholars are still in the stage of defining "culture," "communication," and "inter-

From *Communication* XI (December 1982), 81–86. Reprinted by permission of the publisher. Satoshi Ishii is a professor at Otsuma Women's University, Tokyo, Japan.

cultural." We are still attempting to frame a reliable taxonomy and establish the field as a discipline.[1] Furthermore, recent intercultural communication difficulties raise new questions, and many of these questions need further study if they are to be answered. The interrelationship between "culture" and "thought patterns" is prominent among the intercultural problems facing us.

The Sapir-Whorf hypothesis concerning the vocabulary and sentence structures of a language and *weltanschauung* has long provoked scholars' interest and thought, but what is needed today is a more "macro" study of cultural impacts on thought patterns or discourse patterns in communication situations. The major purpose of the present paper, therefore, is twofold: (1) to review recent movements, from universal reasoning and thought patterns to cultural modes of thought, and (2) to suggest for later studies contrastive patterns of thought as cultural modes of rhetoric in American and Japanese societies. By suggesting the contrastive United States–Japan thought patterns, this writer hopes to delineate some of the major factors influencing the current bilateral communication problems.

RECENT MOVEMENT

John Morrison pronounces that Japanese culture has no rhetorical traditions because of the hierarchical family structure, the tightly knit dominant-submissive society, and the linguistic characteristics of Japanese.[2] These days, however, an increasing number of speech communication scholars are interested in forms of relativistic reasoning and thinking as one of the major components in intercultural communication. People in general have come to realize that there are differences in aspects of thought and that these differences cause various misunderstandings in intercultural communication. A general comparison of Western and Eastern thought patterns serves as a good introductory example. "To the Western mind, human activity is paramount and ultimately will lead to the discovery of truth. In the Taoist tradition, truth is the active agent, and if it is to be known it will be through the activity of truth making itself apparent."[3]

Speech communication scholars who at one time supported only traditional Greco-Roman rhetoric are today more willing to use rhetoric in the plural. Robert Oliver, one of the forerunners in these movements, states:

If the Speech profession is to make a helpful contribution to internationalism—if we are to be able to help our diplomats to do a better job in our multiple and ever-increasing dealings with peoples around the world—it is my belief that we shall have to stop using rhetoric in the singular and commence using it in the plural. I think the facts of life indicate that there is not just one rhetoric—instead, there are many different modes of thinking, and many different ways in which influence must be exerted if it is to be effective.[4]

From the same perspective, Huber W. Ellingsworth proposes the concept of what may be called rhetorical relativity based on cultural influences and thought patterns. He observes:

Anthropologists, perhaps the most exciting and imaginative scholars working in the field of rhetorical theory, have defined national (or cultural) rhetorics as the communication styles of a particular culture, including appropriate themes, modes of expression, standards, purposes, sources, and receivers of communication. Each culture has its own styles, and standards which make its system unique.[5]

In the Western philosophy of rhetoric, Aristotelian logic is represented by the syllogism and the enthymeme which have been widely and unquestionably accepted. Logic, however, is a cultural product, and not universal. "Logic, which is the basis of rhetoric, is evolved out of a culture; it is not universal. *Rhetoric*, then, is not universal either, but varies from culture to culture and even from time to time within a given culture."[6]

Furthermore, Ryomin Akizuki, attempting to explain Daisetz Suzuki's discovery of a new Zen logic, has the following to say: "Being is Being because Being is not Being; i.e., A is A because A is not A."[7] Suzuki's logic is in absolute contrast with Aristotelian dichotomous antimony.

These observations have two important points in common: first, patterns of thinking as rhetorical reasoning are a cultural product and not universal; and second, speech communication scholars of traditional Greco-Roman rhetoric have come to realize and study these differences in intercultural communication situations.

THOUGHT PATTERNS: UNITED STATES VERSUS JAPAN

Despite its increasing significance and interest, the systematic study of cultures and thought pattern has not progressed as it should have. Karl Pribram, one of the pioneers in this field, isolates four distinctive thought patterns or ways of reasoning for persuasive, influential purposes.[8] The four patterns are:

1. Universalistic reasoning, in which "reason is credited with the power to know the truth with the aid of given general concepts" (French, Mediterranean, and other Romance language countries, including Latin America).

2. Nominalistic reasoning, which is distrustful of abstract concepts, emphasizing induction and empiricism (Anglo-American societies).

3. Intuitional reasoning, which stresses the harmony between the whole and its parts, utilizing ideas from authority (Germanic and Slavic Europe).

4. Dialectical reasoning, whose system is located in naturally antagonistic forces (Marxism).

Although Pribram's major focus is on Western cultures, the third reasoning by means of intuition is also common and prevalent in Japanese society.

Robert Kaplan, after a series of analyses of paragraphs written by American and foreign students, concluded that the English speaker's thought pattern is linear, while the Oriental pattern is like a "gyre." He introduces graphic models to explain the thought patterns:[9]

Figure 1 The English "Linear" Pattern

The typical English paragraph consists of (1) a topic statement, (2) subdivisions of the topic statement, (3) examples to support each idea, and (4) examples of the relationships between ideas.

Figure 2 The Oriental "Gyre" Pattern

Oriental writing is marked by what may be called an approach by indirection. In this kind of writing, the development of a paragraph may be said to be "turning and turning in a widening gyre."

We often hear Americans complain that they get confused and frustrated with the Japanese speaker's ambiguity and nontraditional logic. On the other hand, Japanese typically find the average American to be loud and aggressive. This writer argues that these complaints from both sides are largely due to the differences in thought patterns, as well as differences in the modes of rhetoric and the values that function underneath them.

Shigehiko Toyama contends that Anglo-Americans think in "line" while Japanese think in "dots."[10] Along this same line, this writer suggests that the concepts of the American "bridge" and the Japanese "stepping stone" reflect the patterns of thought characteristic of each culture.

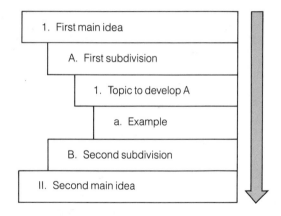

Figure 3 The American "Bridge" Pattern

Using the American bridge model, the speaker or writer organizes his or her ideas and tries to send them explicitly and directly, as if building a bridge from point I to point II. The listener or reader is to cross the bridge by receiving the messages as they are explicitly sent.

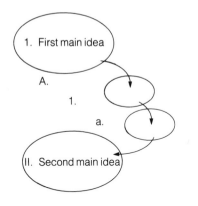

Figure 4 The Japanese "Stepping Stone" Pattern

Using the Japanese "Stepping Stone" approach, the speaker or writer organizes his or her ideas and sends them implicitly and indirectly, as if arranging stepping stones from point I to point II. Sometimes the arrangement itself is not clear and the listener or reader must infer or surmise the intended meaning. Haiku poems serve as good examples.

The distinction between these two rhetorical patterns may be supported by Edward Hall's discussion of "high contexts" and "low contexts."[11] A high context communication is one in which most of the information is either in the physical context or internalized in the communicating persons. In such contexts very little is coded and explicitly transmitted. The Japanese "stepping stone" pattern is an example of a high communication context. A low context communication is the opposite; most of the information is in the explicit message. The American "bridge" pattern is apparently toward the low context end of the high-low continuum. The "bridge" and "stepping stone" concepts are further evidenced by a survey recently conducted by Dr. Donald W. Klopf of the University of Hawaii and this writer. The survey results indicate that the average American adult in Hawaii spends 6 hours and 43 minutes each day in conversation, while the average Japanese adult spends only 3 hours and 31 minutes each day talking to others informally.[12]

COMPARING THE TWO PATTERNS

The description and discussion of the two cultural thought patterns have clarified an important part of the communication difficulties between the two cultures. There are, however, still questions about why and how these differences exist. [Table 1 shows] a list of contrastive cultural backgrounds of the American and the Japanese rhetorical patterns.

The Nippon Steel Corporation generalizes the items in Table 1 as follows:

In contrast to Western people who are more likely to express their opinions in a self-asserting way, Japanese tend to speak and act only after due consideration has been given to the other person's feelings and points of view. Furthermore, there is a habit of not giving a clear-cut yes or no answer, a habit on a long tradition of avoiding unnecessary friction.[13]

It is an interesting and important fact that the Nippon Steel Corporation provides this information to employees who work interculturally in Japan as well as overseas.

Table 1 Contrastive Backgrounds of the Two Patterns

United States	Japan
1. High value for speech.	1. Low value for speech.
2. Strong necessity of speech.	2. Weak necessity of speech.
3. Negative attitude toward silence.	3. Positive attitude toward silence.
4. General preference for overstatements and exaggerations.	4. General preference for understatements and non-exaggerations.
5. Positive attitude toward clear and direct expressions.	5. Negative attitude toward clear and direct expressions.
6. General tendency to analytical reasoning.	6. General tendency to intuitional reasoning.
7. High value for mutual confrontation to keep things moving.	7. High value for mutual dependency to keep interpersonal harmony.
8. Symmetrical human relations.	8. Complementary human relations.

CONCLUSION

Intercultural communication difficulties are not simply a matter of different languages, but of different thought patterns, different values, and different communication styles. The study and teaching of intercultural communication is of vital importance for all speech communication scholars in today's "global village." Patterns of thought as different modes of rhetoric vary from culture to culture, and now need quantitative as well as qualitative research evidence to test them. Hawaii—where various ethnic and cultural groups live and a great number of foreign tourists stay—is an ideal place to promote intercultural communication research and instruction for both academic and practical purposes. The basic problem is not how to integrate different cultures into a larger system but how to preserve their diversity. The real value of intercultural communication is not to attack the other culture's traditions, but to promote mutual understanding and learning.

NOTES

1. Robert Nwankwo, "Interpersonal Communication: A Critical Review," *Quarterly Journal of Speech* 65 (1979), pp. 324–333.

2. Jonn Morrison, "The Absence of a Rhetorical Tradition in Japanese Culture," *Western Speech* 36 (1972), pp. 89–102.

3. Richard Porter and Larry Samovar, "Approaching Intercultural Communication," in *Intercultural Communication: A Reader*, ed. Larry Samovar and Richard Porter, 3rd ed. (Belmont, Calif.: Wadsworth Publishing Co., 1982), p. 40.

4. Robert Oliver, *Culture and Communication* (Springfield, Ill.: Charles Thomas, 1962), pp. 79–80.

5. Huber W. Ellingsworth, "National Rhetorics and Inter-Cultural Communication," *Today's Speech* 17 (1969), p. 35.

6. Robert Kaplan, "Cultural Thought Patterns in Inter-Cultural Communication," *Language Learning* 16 (1970), p. 3.

7. Ryomin Akizuki, *Suzuki Zengaku to Nishida Tetsugaku* (Suzuku Zen and Nishida Philosophy) (Tokyo: Shunju-sha, 1971).

8. Karl Pribram, *Conflicting Patterns of Thought* (Washington, D.C.: Public Affairs Press, 1949).

9. Kaplan, p. 10.

10. Shigehiko Toyama, *Nihongo no Ronri* (The

Logic of the Japanese Language) (Tokyo: Chuokor-on-sha, 1973), pp. 12–15.

11. Edward T. Hall, *Beyond Culture* (Garden City, N.Y.: Doubleday, 1976), pp. 85–103.

12. Satoshi Ishii and Donald Klopf, "A Comparison of Communication Activities of Japanese and American Adults," *ELEC Bulletin* (Spring 1976), pp. 22–26.

13. Nippon Steel Corporation, Personnel Development Office, *Nippon: The Land and Its People* (Tokyo: Gakusei-sha, 1982), p. 297.

The Hmong of Laos: Orality, Communication, and Acculturation

ROBERT SHUTER

Although human beings have inhabited this planet for between thirty thousand and fifty thousand years, the first written scripts date back to 3500 B.C. and only during the last fifteen hundred years has writing been used extensively. In fact, of three thousand reported languages currently in use, only 78 possess a written literature and hundreds may have no written component to their language.[1] Evidently orality is the foundation of all languages, with written codes emerging late in the development of most languages.

It has been argued that acquiring literacy entails more than learning how to read and write, for literacy appears to influence thinking patterns, perception, cultural values, communication style, and the social organization of societies.[2] For example, it has been reported that people from oral cultures—societies that do not have a written language—are inextricably bound to social context and are incapable of conceiving of spoken words as separate from objects or deeds.[3] Hence, unlike literates, oral people are reportedly unable to identify abstract geometric shapes or to classify objects. Instead, the shape is identified as an object familiar to them, and classification is supplanted by function (i.e., saw cuts logs). Similarly, oral and literate communication may also reflect differences in so-

This original essay appears here in print for the first time. All rights remain with the author. Permission to reprint must be obtained from the author. Robert Shuter teaches at Marquette University and is Director of the Center for Intercultural Communication.

cial contexting, with oral people, for example, communicating in narratives bereft of detail that describe critical incidents, while literates use more sequential speech that is often abstract and non-situational.[4]

Despite the prevalence of cultures in the developing world that are either exclusively oral or possess a high degree of orality, few field studies have been conducted on oral societies.[5] In addition, no reported research has limited its scope to the interpersonal patterns of oral people or examined how these patterns influence acculturation into a literate society, the focus of this study. Instead, reported studies on orality have been limited to ethnographic and historical analysis of oral literature and investigation of oral traditions in ancient Greece.[6]

This paper examines the influence of orality on communication and acculturation by focusing on the Hmong of Laos, a predominantly preliterate culture that has over 68,000 people living in the U.S. Since many of the most recent Southeast Asian refugees who have migrated to the U.S. are from oral cultures, an understanding of orality in Hmong society should provide insight into the acculturation of oral people who have settled in literate societies.[7]

The immigration of the Hmong to the U.S. occurred in the late 1970s after they were attacked by Communist Laotians and Vietnamese regimes for assisting the U.S. during the Vietnam war. Apparently, the Hmong were trained first by the CIA and then by the American military to serve as flight personnel on bombing missions to Laos and Vietnam. They also engaged in ground surveillance and guided U.S. pilots by radio to enemy targets deep in the jungles of Laos and Vietnam. After the U.S. pulled out of Vietnam, Hmong villages in Laos were frequently attacked by Laotians and Vietnamese. As a result, the Hmong fled to Thailand where they lived in refugee camps.[8]

The Hmong lived isolated in the mountains of northern Laos in a traditional society characterized by slash-and-burn cultivation, a kinship-based social and political organization, and an animistic belief system consisting of spirit curing, shamanism, and ancestor worship.[9] In addition, the Hmong are essentially an oral people who had no written language until the 1950s when a missionary developed rudimentary written Hmong, which is still unfamiliar to most Hmong.

Field research for this study began in January, 1983 with the selection of 22 interviewees from the Hmong community in Milwaukee, Wisconsin where about two thousand Hmong refugees reside. Ranging in age from 31 to 68, fifteen oral and seven literate Hmong were interviewed using in-depth interview techniques.[10] Subjects were interviewed twice for approximately three hours per session; interviews were taped and then transcribed; and selected interviews were videotaped. The principal investigator conducted all interviews over eight months and was assisted by two Hmong translators.

Interviews probed various dimensions of Hmong culture, but primarily examined five research questions, the focus of the study.

1. What is the structure and content of interpersonal messages communicated in an oral society?

2. How do communicators in an oral society transmit information? Do types of communication transmission affect the selection of cultural values regarding individualism and group centeredness?

3. How do communicators in an oral society retain information?

4. Do communicators from oral societies retain distinct oral communication patterns after they become literate?

5. How do the communication patterns of an oral society affect the acculturation of oral people into a literate society?

RESULTS

Oral Hmong are narrative communicators; that is, the structure and content of their interpersonal messages is generally in the form of a story. Structurally, a typical interpersonal disclosure consists of a plot, normally a critical incident, and a cast of characters, either living or dead. Description of the event or deed is highlighted, and details about time, date, and even place are often omitted. While the content of these stories varies, the plot generally focuses on events or deeds that occurred during the communicator's day or consists of stories about past ancestors and/or memorable events.

For the older oral Hmong, the past is communicated through stories about agriculture, war, and migration—dominant historical themes—and the activities and role responsibilities of significant ancestors. Consider the following description of grandfather provided by Wang, a 68-year-old oral Hmong who has lived in the U.S. for seven years.

"My grandfather was born in Laos. He was a leader of the village when the French came to Laos. He was looked up to by the French soliders. He was a soldier with the French in Laos."

Wang remembered his grandfather through the roles he enacted, principally soldier and village leader, and the activity he engaged in, fighting. Wang could not provide specific information about his grandfather's age, appearance, personality, or the battles in which he fought: he only seemed to know that grandfather was a leader. Similar descriptions of parents who died in Laos are provided by Hmong interviewees: "My parents taught me to be a good person. They also taught me how to do a slash and burn." Like Wang's description of his grandfather, parental memories highlighted farming or fighting activity, and never included character descriptions or other person-centered information.

Hmong communication about the present is also activity oriented and, in Laos, reportedly focused on agriculture, war, migration, climate, and cultural events like funerals, weddings, and animistic rituals. Like communication about the past, interpersonal messages transmitted in Laos generally highlighted what someone *did* and sometimes included a comment about the reactions of others.

"We talked about slash and burn and what we must do tomorrow. We talked about fighting in the war. We talked about leaving the village again. We talked about who will teach our children."

Bereft of detail, these messages focused on the main event, while time, dates, character titles, and sometimes places were normally absent from the communication.

The narrative communication style of the Hmong reflects a central world view of oral people: they tend to "totalize."[11] That is, words cannot be disconnected from deeds and events, and people cannot be separated from social context. The word and the event are one, inextricably united. As a result, the Hmong's interpersonal messages tend to be narrative, situational, activity oriented, and lacking detail, characteristics similar to the oral rhetoric of ancient Greece.[12] In contrast, the communication style of literates tends to be categorical rather than narrative, conceptual not situational. This style may reflect the contextual distance literacy bestows on the speaker, a distance that emerges from being able to think of words as being separate from objects, deeds, and events. Once disconnected from social context, the communicator can think and speak conceptually, and messages need not dwell solely on events and deeds.

Tied to social context, the Hmong culture relies strictly on people and groups to transmit information and consequently places inordinate value on these sources of information. The society is arranged sociologically and politically into groups, with clan and family the preeminent groups. In Laos the Hmong farmed in small groups, socialized in small groups and, as children, were often taught about agriculture, Hmong customs, and animistic beliefs in small groups. Without books, oral people like the Hmong learned only from others and became dependent on people and groups in the community, their only sources of information. For example, consider how the Hmong in Laos learned important cultural customs and sacred beliefs.

"Normally, when the person who knows most of the things in the community, most of the cultural things, when they realize that the man is old, people will go to his house at night and ask him to teach them. As many people that can will go to the house and learn, but they know that a lot of people can go and learn but a few can

*remember. So maybe 10 or 20 will go to an
elderly's house and learn at night, but probably
two or three remember. And there is subject
matter that they should learn at night because it
is sacred, like spiritual beliefs."*

Apparently, small groups were also used extensively to assist individuals to remember information, an enormous problem in oral societies. As a result, the Hmong learned all essential information about cultural events and slash-and-burn agriculture in small groups, often from an elder in the community who was known to have a good memory.

"There are so many things the old man teaches and in different ways. . . . When he realizes that he is old enough and has concerns about the next generation, he will ask the village chief and they should send some of the young men to go to his house and to work with him on the farm and learn the different types of cultural events he knows. When they are 11 to 14 they go and learn. When you and I learn together, you may remember one thing and I remember one thing; we share and discuss. In case I forget something, I ask you—you may remember what I forgot. I may remember what you forgot."

In oral societies like the Hmong, learning must take place in groups since individuals do not have written material to study. Hence, individual study does not exist in an oral society, which promotes group-centered values. In contrast, literacy provides individuals with the opportunity to learn alone, since reading and writing are solitary experiences. As a result, literates are less dependent on groups for information and seem to develop a keener sense of independence than oral people. In fact, becoming literate requires individuals to separate themselves from others and instead to communicate with a new appendage—a pen or pencil. Separation from the group appears to be one of the costs of literacy and may restrict an oral person's acculturation into a literate society, an issue examined later in this paper.

As indicated earlier, memory plays a unique role in oral society: it is the only repository of the past. In Hmong culture, for example, each clan may depend on only one or two persons who remember cultural customs and beliefs. These individuals have no title and do not belong to a particular family, social class, or caste: they are persons who are known to have an extraordinary memory, a highly valued trait.

*"This is a simple society—they know each other.
When they (Hmong community) learn who
remembers better, that one will be famous for it,
and they (Hmong community) know."*

As a result, persons with excellent memories are respected and are the most credible members of the Hmong community. What appears to make these individuals unique is their retention of detail about significant customs and events, an unusual capacity in a society that communicates in narratives. For example, Hmong culture, like many oral societies, has many animistic beliefs that were practiced daily in Laos and that ranged from animal sacrifices when a new home was built to healing rituals like Kakong, an ancient verbal poem used to cure certain sicknesses and physical injuries. These shared beliefs still serve as the ideological cement that binds clan members together and distinguishes one Hmong clan from another. Not surprisingly, individuals who can remember these detailed rituals are vital members of the clan.

Because the Hmong rely strictly on memory, they usually retain deeds, events, and customs that are repeated and, hence, part of their daily activities. Moreover, the rituals that each male in Laos was supposed to retain were limited to selected activities: birth rituals, how to get married, how to arrange a wedding, funeral procedures, burying the dead, and agricultural practices. Hmong frequently communicated in Laos about these subjects, the basics of a "simple" society, and their messages tend to be repetitive, a characteristic of their present communication as well.

*"Here in the United States there's a lot of
difficulty in remembering, but back in Laos, in
the simple society, we are able to remember. . . . In
Hmong society, to me it's because it was so simple
and we use day after day most of the same thing,
that helps the people to remember the different*

steps that we should do. For example, in the procedure of holding a ceremony or whatever, because we use day after day and it was so simple, not so complex that we could remember, but that it was so simple that we could learn easily and we can remember what we learned. And once we got it in the mind, it cannot be forgotten total."

The preceding speaker is Hmong and, though he speaks English and is literate, his message is redundant, for he repeats his thesis, that simplicity aids memory, four times in four consecutive sentences. Similar repetition patterns occur in the messages of oral and literate Hmong interviewees and they are empirical evidence of the narrative, repetitive communication style of oral communicators, a style that seems to be a product of a culture that relies on memory.

That oral and literate Hmong interviewees have similar communication styles suggests that oral stylistic patterns may not disappear after a person becomes literate. This is called residual orality, and it appears to influence more than just communication style for literate Hmong. For example, literate Hmong appear to have difficulty following written directions that explain how to perform an activity, operate a mechanical object, or assemble something. Reared in an oral culture, Hmong traditionally learned through "doing," that is, elders taught Hmong how to perform an activity by involving them in the process: learning was always experiential. For many literate Hmong, the printed word is an inadequate mode of communication, a poor substitute for the oral, experiential learning of the traditional society.

"If Hmong students used to learn by doing and if they went to school and learned just the theory, they have problems when they practice. For example, myself—when I go to school and I learn something by reading, I could understand when I read, but if I was supposed to do it by hand, I didn't know how. So I had to get help from someone in order to be able to do it."

It is difficult to determine which oral patterns of the Hmong survive literacy; nevertheless, residual

orality poses additional obstacles for acculturating oral people into a literate society.

Each oral pattern of the Hmong described in this paper significantly influences their acculturation into the U.S.; consider their communication style, for example. Narrative and situational in nature, the Hmong communication style collides with the communication demands of a literate society that they be categorical, detailed, and, at times, abstract and conceptual. The collision takes place daily in schools and factories, government offices and social service agencies, where the Hmong are required to know birthdates, titles, time of day, definitions; in short, details and categories that are normally omitted from their communication. Lacking temporal and categorical perspective on their past and present, the Hmong cannot provide sufficiently detailed information about age, date of birth, type and dates of employment, children's birthdates—information necessary to survive in a literate society.

In schools they encounter definitions and detailed explanations of words, words that are disconnected from objects and about concepts they cannot see and touch: this is an abstract, categorical world detached from situation and nature. As a result, many older Hmong become frustrated and drop out of school, particularly the men who appear to have less experience with detail and tolerate it less than Hmong women. Females in Hmong society are responsible for cooking, a sequential, categorical activity, and for sewing, a detailed procedure consisting of putting symbolic designs on cloth. These domestic activities may account for Hmong gender differences in becoming literate, and, hence, acculturated.

Literacy threatens the very fabric of Hmong oral society, its group-centeredness, and it is another major obstacle to acculturation. For older Hmong, the very concept of independent study is alien to them, since learning always occurred in the present with cohesive groups of community people. Learning in groups of strangers, homework, independent study—hallmarks of literacy—run counter to the group-centered value of the Hmong and, as a result, many adult Hmong have resisted literacy. For young Hmong, literacy often distances them from their families.

For example, when school-age Hmong begin public school, parents, elders, and the clan—traditionally the only sources of information—now must share their teaching role with groups of strangers: unfamiliar teachers and American peers. As Hmong students become more literate and engage in independent study, they rely less on traditional groups and more on themselves and alien others. This often divides the Hmong family: parents are disturbed by the loss of centrality and power, and often become dependent on literate children, which produces additional family tension. Sensing the consequences of schooling and literacy, Hmong elders want their children to become literate but they do not want it to affect their relationship with them, a difficult request that may impede literacy and acculturation.

Finally, residual orality poses unique acculturation problems for literate Hmong. As indicated earlier, literate Hmong, particularly adults, have difficulty following written instructions unless they are accompanied by oral explanation and demonstrations. This residual pattern, for example, may be an obstacle to certain types of job training, particularly training that is primarily theoretical. As a result, it may limit literate Hmong to occupations that are activity-oriented and taught experientially. Having fewer occupational choices, literate Hmong have less access to American jobs and to goods and services, which may impede their acculturation. Similarly, the narrative, repetitive communication style of many literate Hmong may further narrow job options, since it delays the acquisition of a mainstream American communication style, a prerequisite for employability. Stylistically different from many of their American peers, Hmong literates may have more difficulty acculturating than Southeast Asians from literate societies.

CONCLUSION

Evidently, the oral tradition of the Hmong is reflected in the structure, content, transmission, and retention of interpersonal communication. And be-

cause these oral patterns seem to collide with the values of a literate society and the expected communication of literates, they seem to slow the acculturation of the Hmong into a literate society. This is significant, since a sizable percentage of recent Southeast Asian refugees, possibly as high as 80%, are either exclusively oral or predominantly oral, having grown up in rural oral villages in countries that have a written language, but few schools outside large cities. It is likely that oral patterns and acculturation problems described for the Hmong may be shared by many of the recent Southeast Asian refugees and by others who have migrated from South and Central America, the Middle East, Asia, and Africa, where there seem to be high levels of orality and residual orality.[13]

Conceptually, orality has unique implications for furthering our understanding of communication across cultures. For example, oral cultures may possess significantly different values and communication patterns from literate societies. By being able to classify cultures along an orality continuum, consisting of exclusively oral, high-residual orality, and low-residual orality, a researcher should be able to predict potential intercultural misunderstandings and conflicts. To determine how to classify a culture, communication characteristics of a society can be compared with the list of oral interaction patterns in Table 1, generated from the preceding study.

The table indicates that communicators in each of the three categories may differ in five communication areas: structure of message, content of message, transmission of message, retention of message, and communication world view. In terms of the structure and content of the message, exclusively oral and high-residual oral speakers tend to be narrative communicators emphasizing situational topics, with little temporal and chronological data provided. In contrast, low-residual communicators tend to structure messages categorically and generally provide chronological and temporal information. Societies that are placed in each category also differ in the way information is normally transmitted: exclusively oral and high-residual oral cultures rely primarily on face-to-face interaction,

Table 1

	Exclusively Oral	High-Residual Orality	Low-Residual Orality
Structure of message	Narrative; critical incident; high repetition	Narrative; critical incident; high repetition	Categorical/sequential; detailed; low repetition
Content of message	Situational topics	Primarily situational topics	Abstract and situational topics
	Low in temporal and chronological data	Low in temporal and chronological data	High in temporal and chronological data
Transmission of message	Interpersonal interaction; small group interaction; value group relations	Interpersonal interaction; small group interaction; additional media secondary; value group relations	Multiple media: priority on mass media; value individualism
Retention of message	Memory	Primarily memory	Multiple media
Communication world view	Words, objects, and events inseparable	Words, objects, and events closely connected	Words, objects, and events separate

while low-residual oral societies use multiple media to transmit messages, including print and electronic channels. Reliance on face-to-face transmission in exclusively oral and high-residual oral societies produces group-centered values; in contrast, low-residual oral societies tend to be more individualistic. Without print, exclusively oral cultures depend on memory to retain information. High-residual oral cultures also rely heavily on memory and may also employ other media as a repository of information, though they are of less importance. In contrast, low-residual oral cultures use multiple media to retain information and tend to stress print and electronic media. Finally, communicators from exclusively oral and high-residual oral cultures have varying degrees of difficulty separating spoken words from objects and events and, hence, are tied to social context. Speakers from low-residual oral societies can disconnect words from objects and events.

This paradigm can be used in a variety of ways. For example, in intercultural transactions, researchers may be able to identify areas of potential communication conflict and misunderstandings, once the communicators' cultures have been clas-

sified. Similarly, acculturation problems due to differences in degrees of orality can be isolated with greater ease. Potentially useful, this paradigm should be tested in future studies to determine with greater certainty both the communication patterns of the three types of oral societies and systematic methods for classifying world cultures.

NOTES

1. Munro E. Edmonson, *Lore: An Introduction to the Science of Fiction* (New York: Holt, Rinehart and Winston, 1971).

2. See, for example, John Foley, "The Traditional Oral Audience," *Balkan Studies* 18, 145–153; Jack Goody, *Literacy in Traditional Societies* (Cambridge, England: Cambridge University Press, 1968); Walter Ong, *Orality and Literacy* (London: Methuen, 1982); Sylvia Scriber and Michael Cole, "Literacy Without Schooling: Testing for Intellectual Effects," *Harvard Educational Review* 48, 1978, 448–461.

3. Aleksandr Romanovich Luria, *Cognitive Development: Its Cultural and Social Foundations*,

ed. Michael Cole (Cambridge, Mass.: Harvard University Press, 1976).

4. Ibid.

5. See, for example, Roger Abrahams, "The Training of the Man of Words in Talking Sweet," *Language in Society* 1, 15–29; John Miles Foley, "The Traditional Oral Audience," *Balkan Studies* 18, 1977, 145–153; Aleksandr Romanovich Luria, *Cognitive Development: Its Cultural and Social Foundations*, ed. Michael Cole (Cambridge, Mass.: Harvard University Press, 1976).

6. See, for example, Ruth Finnegan, *Oral Literature in Africa* (Oxford: Clarendon Press, 1970); Eric Havelock, "The Ancient Art of Oral Poetry," *Philosophy and Rhetoric* 19, 187–202, 1979.

7. It is difficult to ascertain the exact percentage of Southeast Asian refugees who are either exclusively oral or predominantly oral. But since most of the recent refugees migrated from rural communities where there were no schools, it has been estimated that most of them are predominantly oral, particularly women, who generally did not receive education even when it was available.

8. Robert William Geddes, *Migrants of the Mountains: The Cultural Ecology of the Blue Miau (Hmong) of Thailand* (Oxford: Clarendon Press, 1976).

9. Timothy Dunnigan, "Segmentary Kinship in an Urban Society: The Hmong of St. Paul, Minneapolis," *Anthropological Quarterly*, 1981, 126–133.

10. Lewis Dexter, *Elite and Specialized Interviewing* (Evanston, Ill.: Northwestern University Press, 1971).

11. Walter Ong, *Orality and Literacy* (London: Methuen, 1982), p. 56.

12. Ibid, pp. 16–30.

13. Walter Ong first used the term residual orality and argues that contemporary cultures have different degrees of residual orality. See Walter Ong, *Orality and Literacy* (London: Methuen, 1982), pp. 28–29.

The Role of Political Structure and Policy in Intercultural Communication in the People's Republic of China: A Personal Note

STEPHEN W. KING

Most contemporary discussions of intercultural communication include advice for understanding cultures and recommendations for improving actual intercultural communication exchanges. This essay will suggest that many such treatments are theoretically short-sighted and practically limited for understanding or improving intercultural communication in the People's Republic of China. The observations supporting this argument are admittedly personal and unabashedly anecdotal, arising from my tenure as a visiting professor of English at Wuhan University in the central Yangtze River valley, and from the opportunity for substantial travel throughout the country.[1] Specifically, I will argue that many treatments of intercultural communication assume a relationship between culture and communication that is inappropriate for the People's Republic of China, because they do not accurately reflect the important role of political structure and policy in communication exchanges within the People's Republic of China.

Most scholars of intercultural communication sensibly suggest that to effectively engage in inter-

This essay was written especially for this volume. All rights reserved. Permission to reprint must be obtained from the publisher and the author. Dr. King teaches at San Diego State University.

cultural communication each participant must attempt to understand the culture of the other person. According to Samovar, Porter, and Jain (1981), to understand another culture one must examine that culture's "world view, activity orientation, time orientation, human nature, perception of self, and social organization" (p. 90). Dodd's (1982) list of factors that require examination is longer, but similar: "cultural roots, cultural personality, material culture, economic organization, roles and culture, kinship relationships, political organization, social control, art, language, stability, and cultural belief system" (p. 28). Brislin (1981) similarly asserted that a "culture can be explained as an identifiable group with shared beliefs and experiencing feelings of worth and value attendant to those experiences, and a shared interest in a common historical background" (p. 23). Once rudimentary knowledge about another's culture is gained, these same scholars have a variety of suggestions for effective intercultural exchanges.

Samovar, Porter, and Jain (1981) advised that successful intercultural communication will be facilitated if you know yourself, use a shared code, take time, consider the physical and human setting, improve your communication skills, encourage feedback, develop empathy, and seek the commonalities among diverse cultures (pp. 202–210). Dodd's (1982) advice ranged from "Be natural but flexible" (p. 147) to "a message should be tailored to fit cultural values and past experiences" (p. 279). Ruben (1981) correctly exhorted sojourners to "Know how respect, empathy, non-judgmentalness, turn-taking, orientation to knowledge, and group and organizational roles are *regarded* and *expressed* in a given culture" (p. 337).

These categories for description of a culture and recommendations for effective intercultural communication have putative utility because the "relationship between culture and communication is reciprocal" (Samovar, Porter, and Jain, 1981, p. 55). That is, as culture determines "what we talk about, how we talk about it, what we see, attend to, ignore, how we think and what we think about," it is obvious that culture affects communication (Samovar, Porter, and Jain, 1981, p. 55). Further-

more, individuals within a culture affect and are affected by the cultural backgrounds of the participants.

This analysis assumes that culture is the collective expression of individual histories, perceptions, values, and beliefs of its members and, further, that an individual's psychology, behavior, and communication will reflect his or her culture. Though this model may be generally accurate for understanding most intercultural communication exchanges around the world, it is notably deficient for understanding or practicing intercultural communication in the People's Republic of China. In the People's Republic of China actual communication exchanges between the Chinese and non-Chinese may or may not reflect the traditionally considered aspects of culture per se, but such exchanges will be affected by and reflect the political structure and policies of the government of the People's Republic of China.[2] Let me briefly illustrate how such fundamental communication issues as Who talks to Whom? When and Where? About What? and In What Way? are affected by the political structure and policies of the People's Republic of China.

WHO TALKS TO WHOM?

Contact between the Chinese and non-Chinese is often strictly controlled or, when not directly controlled, most Chinese behave as if their interactions are being monitored. While teaching at Wuhan University I was housed, along with all the other foreign faculty and consultants, in the Foreign Faculty Residence, which is located in an isolated corner of the campus. My students and other visitors were required to sign in when they wanted to meet with me at the Foreign Faculty Residence, which severely inhibited communication. To avoid the necessity of signing in and the possibility of being questioned about the exchange, some of my students asked to meet elsewhere. On the streets the Chinese people are not at all inhibited about initiating communication, but the publicness of the setting precludes all but the most superficial of exchanges, for example, practicing English. Foreign initiation of communication with the Chinese, other than those with whom the foreigner's work normally brings them in contact, requires prior approval. For example, foreigners do not merely walk into a day-care center or a scientific institute without requesting and receiving prior approval, a process that often takes anywhere from several days to several weeks and ensures the presence of someone from the foreign affairs office. Finally, this constraint on who talks to whom is not limited to exchanges between the Chinese and non-Chinese. Virtually all Chinese are organized into work units, brigades, and communes, and both travel and communication between units are controlled by a bureaucratically complex, vertically integrated system. As a consequence, an individual in one work unit may live close to a person in another work unit of a different brigade or commune and they may never interact. Chinese political structure and policy override physical proximity as a predictor of communication.

WHEN AND WHERE?

Communication between the Chinese and non-Chinese is relatively unconstrained when it occurs at a time and place of approved task interaction. However, foreign-initiated communication at unusual times and places must be approved, or at least most Chinese believe it must be officially blessed. For example, I asked one of my students to accompany me on a car tour of the Wuhan area and, though evidently enthusiastic, he would not accept my invitation until he surreptitiously phoned the foreign affairs office and received official approval. Similarly, the systematic opening and closing of certain areas to foreign visitation illustrates the impact of the government on the issue of where and when intercultural communication takes place within the People's Republic of China.

ABOUT WHAT?

Conversations with the Chinese may involve topics of some political sensitivity and, in such circumstances, the Chinese reflect national policy, even when those policies conflict with either personal feelings or cultural values. For example, when asked about Han Chauvinism (a term describing the prejudice of the dominant Chinese racial group for any racial minority), Chinese faculty and students say that because it was outlawed it does not exist, despite overwhelming evidence to the contrary. Similarly, the Chinese will echo national policy on the desirability of one-child families, despite variations in individual attitudes on the topic and the traditional cultural preference for large families. Indeed, the national policy of the central government is to not present anything Chinese in a bad light in interaction with foreigners. Brislin (1981) correctly observed that the positive views about China reported by American journalists in the mid-1970s were largely the result of tours that were "carefully staged, hosts hand-picked, and aspects of the Chinese culture painstakingly selected to communicate a favorable image" (pp. 163–164). Individual Chinese are more likely to reflect national policy positions about issues than they are to express their own attitudes or attitudes derived from cultural heritage.

HOW?

Even language reflects national policy. "Foreign experts" are accorded considerable prestige in the People's Republic of China. One could conclude that this respect is a reflection of the value the Chinese have traditionally attached to learning and scholarship; however, upon closer examination one discovers that only those talents that contribute to the national objective of economic modernization are respected. Academic achievement is not in and of itself valued, as the cultural value would suggest; only achievements that advance national policy objectives are respected. What is "good" and what is "bad" changes with policy statements emanating from Peking. For example, current pragmatic economic policies are introducing a number of free market–like economic features that have changed the language. *Credit, worker incentives,* and *free markets* were only a few years ago condemnable concepts and linguistically inadmissible.

Now they are openly discussed and encouraged, at least in some of the economic experimental zones.

To summarize, while it may be useful to study Chinese time orientation, history, language, beliefs, kinship relationships, Confucianism, and the writings of Mao Zedong, actual intercultural communication exchanges will be most significantly affected by political realities. The likelihood of one's needing to communicate with one or more of the billion Chinese increases daily as their drive toward modernization brings them into greater contact with the rest of the world. Such contact, and the intercultural communication that results, will be more effective if non-Chinese people study current government structure and policy rather than the socio-cultural elements traditionally recommended by scholars of intercultural communication.

NOTES

1. I am indebted to Wuhan University and the Ministry of Education for the opportunity to teach and travel in the People's Republic of China. My observations about intercultural communication in the People's Republic of China are confirmed by numerous other anecdotal reports of returning Americans. The opportunity for foreigners to conduct systematic social science research in the People's Republic of China is currently very limited, though approval for some of my own research appears imminent.

2. Though this essay examines only the disparity between cultural values and government policy in the People's Republic of China, similar disparity exists in all countries. For example, opinion surveys consistently report Americans favor some form of gun control legislation, yet political reality has precluded its official adoption. The unique aspect of this phenomena in the People's Republic of China is the extent to which official policy is reflected in interpersonal intercultural exchanges.

REFERENCES

Brislin, R. W. *Cross-Cultural Encounters.* New York: Pergamon Press, 1981.

Dodd, C. H. *Dynamics of Intercultural Communication.* Dubuque, IA: William C. Brown Company Publishers, 1982.

Ruben, B. D. "Human communication and cross-cultural effectiveness," in Samovar, L. A., and Porter, R. E. (eds.) *Intercultural Communication: A Reader.* Belmont, CA: Wadsworth Publishing Co., 1982, pp. 331–339.

Samovar, L. A.; Porter, R. E.; and Jain, N. C. *Understanding Intercultural Communication.* Belmont, CA: Wadsworth Publishing Co., 1981.

CONCEPTS AND QUESTIONS FOR CHAPTER 2

1. How might Arabic and North American cultural differences in friendliness behaviors affect intercultural communication?

2. In what ways do the cultural roles for women differ in Arabic and North American cultures? How would these differences affect communication between Arabs and North Americans?

3. What are the basic differences in the role of religion in Arabic and North American cultures? How can these differences affect intercultural interactions?

4. In what areas of interaction are there major problems between Mexicans and North Americans? How might these differences be resolved?

5. How do North American and Mexican views of individualism differ? How might these differences affect intercultural communication?

6. What unique perspectives of world view are inherent in the Hindu culture of India?

7. How might the Hindu perspective on the universe and of humankind's role in the universe affect intercultural communication between Indians and North Americans?

8. How do differences in thought patterns affect intercultural communication?

9. What differences in rhetorical organization, as

exemplified in U.S. and Japanese culture, emerge because of differing thought patterns?

10. How might the oral tradition of the Hmong affect their patterns of communication as immigrants in the United States?

11. What conclusions can be reached about cultural influence on intercultural communication in the People's Republic of China?

12. What are some of the characteristics of the People's Republic of China that affect intercultural communication?

13. What would be different about communicating with someone who lives in the People's Republic of China? How does this differ from the patterns of intercultural communication discussed earlier in this chapter?

SUGGESTED READINGS

Almaney, A. J., and A. J. Alwan. *Communicating with the Arabs: A Handbook for the Business Executive.* Prospect Heights, Ill.: Waveland Press, 1982. The aim of this book is to "enable the businessman to develop a better understanding of the Arabs." Specifically, the authors focus on the fundamental forces that play a major role in influencing Arab thought and actions. Although the book is intended primarily for the businessperson, it can be used profitably by others interested in intercultural communication.

Bauer, W. *China and the Search for Happiness: Recurring Themes in Four Thousand Years of Chinese Cultural History.* New York: Seabury Press, 1976. This impressive volume traces the sources of Chinese culture over the last 4,000 years. The impact of history, religion, and government is treated in great detail.

Clark, A. "African healing and Western psychotherapy." *International Journal of Intercultural Relations* 6 (1982), 5–15. This study looks at the institutions of traditional healing as practiced in Black Africa and at psychotherapy as practiced in Western culture. These two ap-

proaches are compared in terms of their relative positions within the broader health care systems of the respective cultures, and in terms of their therapeutic techniques.

Delgado, M. "Hispanic cultural values: Implications for groups." *Small Group Behavior* 12 (1981), 69–80. This article presents a brief overview of the literature on Hispanic groups, describes a conceptual framework for examining value orientations within the Hispanic culture, and presents a series of recommendations for group leaders interested in developing Hispanic groups.

Diaz-Guerrero, R. *The Psychology of the Mexican: Culture and Personality.* Austin: University of Texas Press, 1967. In an effort to understand and describe the behavior of the Mexican, Diaz-Guerrero looks at the relationship between culture and personality. He examines concepts such as family structure, interpersonal relationships, motivation, values, respect, and status.

Eickelman, F. *The Middle East: An Anthropological Approach.* Englewood Cliffs, N.J.: Prentice-Hall, 1981. Eickelman discusses how the local understandings of Islam affect the Islamic civilization. The local understandings pertain to all aspects of cultural identity, including kin, class distinctions, and interlocking linguistic differences. The emphasis is on the changing interpretations of Middle Eastern societies and culture by Westerners and by Middle Easterners themselves.

Gudykunst, W. B. "Uncertainty reduction and predictability of behavior in low- and high-context cultures: An exploratory study." *Communication Quarterly* 31 (1983), 49–55. This paper presents an exploratory comparison of two aspects of initial interactions in low- and high-context cultures. The types of questions used to reduce uncertainty, and the degree of attributional confidence (based upon background information) is also discussed. The results are discussed in terms of their implications for uncertainty reduction theory and Hall's conceptualization of high- and low-context cultures.

Hingley, R. *The Russian Mind*. Woodbury, N.Y.: The Bodley Head, 1977. This book attempts to look at the Russian personality, character, and mentality. Hingley focuses on the Russian as a person, not on Russia as a country. He is concerned with how Russians show emotion, their attitudes, values, and behavior. In addition, there are chapters that examine communication systems and group consciousness.

Lenero-Otero, L., ed. *Beyond the Nuclear Family Model: Cross Cultural Perspective*. Beverly Hills, Calif.: Sage Publications, 1977. This book is concerned with the concept of the nuclear family in a variety of countries. A special feature of this collection is the series of articles comparing various families across selected cultures.

Lewin, K. "Some social-psychological differences between the United States and Germany," in *Resolving Social Conflicts*. New York: Harper and Brothers, 1948. This classic essay, although written in 1936, is still a valid statement about some of the differing communication patterns between North Americans and Germans. Lewin looks at such communication variables as groups, use of personal space, social distance, and group size; he examines how these and other communication concepts give insight into the people of both North America and Germany.

Nomura, N., and D. Barnlund. "Patterns of interpersonal criticism in Japan and the United States." *International Journal of Intercultural Relations* 7 (1983), 1–18. Preliminary interviews were conducted to look at patterns of interpersonal criticism in Japan and the United States. An Interpersonal Criticism Questionnaire examined sources of dissatisfaction, the status of communication partners, and modes of giving criticism. The results showed a significant difference between the cultures, but no significant difference between the sexes. Both cultures favored expressing dissatisfaction directly. The Japanese expressed criticism passively and Americans more actively. The Japanese adapted messages to the person involved, while Americans adapted messages to the reasons behind the provocations.

Reischauer, E. O. *The Japanese*. Cambridge, Mass.: Harvard University Press, 1972. This book contains a picture of the background culture and values of Japan. Reischauer concentrates on the social organization, values, political system, and international relationships of the Japanese.

Roberts, G. O. *Afro-Arab Fraternity: The Roots of Terramedia*. Beverly Hills, Calif.: Sage Publications, 1980. Roberts discusses the Middle East and Africa as a single unit, focusing on its geography, history, religion, social structures, and ethnic orientations in order to understand the common postcolonial problem faced by the countries in this region of the world.

Ross, S. R., ed. *Views Across the Border: The U.S. and Mexico*. Albuquerque: University of New Mexico Press, 1978. Ross has collected 17 essays that explore the U.S.-Mexican border area in terms of psychology, politics, culture, migration, social class, and personality development.

Stein, H. F. "Adversary symbiosis and complementary group dissociation: An analysis of the U.S./U.S.S.R. conflict." *International Journal of Intercultural Relations* 6 (1982), 55–83. This article examines the psychological basis of the reciprocal stereotyping that governs U.S./Soviet perceptions of each other. It explores the influence of American and Russo-Soviet national psychology and cultural history on present perceptions, expectations, and attitudes.

Wolfson, K., and W. Barnett Pearce. "A cross-cultural comparison of the implications of self-disclosure on conversational logics." *Communication Quarterly* 31 (1983), 249–255. The differences in cultural acts are difficult to describe without using the perspective of one's own culture. "Transcultural concepts" are designed to avoid the ethnocentric attitude. The transcultural concept of "logical force" is discussed between North American and Chinese subjects.

ADDITIONAL READINGS

Bond, M., K. Leung, and W. Kwok Choi. "How does cultural collectivism operate? The impact of task and maintenance contributions of reward distribution." *Journal of Cross-Cultural Psychology* 13 (1982), 186–200.

Cormack, M. L. "American students in India." *International Studies Quarterly* 17 (1973), 337–357.

Dore, R. P. *City Life in Japan*. Berkeley: University of California Press, 1958.

Gardiner, H. W., U. P. Singh, and D. E. D'Orazio. "The liberated woman in three cultures: Marital-role preferences in Thailand, India, and the United States." *Human Organization* 33 (1974), 413–414.

Goldberg, H. "Introduction: Culture and ethnicity in the study of Israeli society." *Ethnic Groups* 1 (1977), 163–186.

Gretler, A., and P. Mandl. *Values, Trends, and Alternatives in Swiss Society*. New York: Praeger Books, 1973.

Hawkins, J. *Mass Communication in China*. New York: Longman, 1982.

Heiliger, W. *Soviet and Chinese Personalities*. Maryland: University Press of America, 1980.

Heisey, D. R. "A Swedish approach to international communication." *Topics in Culture Learning*, vol. 2. Honolulu: East-West Center, 1974, 41–49.

Helm, C. "The German concept of order: The social and physical setting." *Journal of Popular Culture* 13 (1979), 67–80.

Kamikawa, L. M. "Elderly: A Pacific/Asian perspective." *Aging* (July/August, 1981), 2–9.

Kaufman, M. "Reporting from Africa." *The Bridge: A Review of Cultural Affairs and International Training* (Spring 1981), 10–11, 39–40.

Kingston, M. H. *China Man*. New York: Knopf, 1980.

Kitzinger, S. *Women as Mothers: How They See Themselves in Different Cultures*. New York: Random House, 1979.

Klopf, D. W., and R. E. Cambron. "Communication apprehension in foreign settings: The results of exploratory research." *The Journal of the Communication Association of the Pacific* 12 (1983), 37–51.

Korzenny, F., and K. Neuendorf. "The perceived reality of television and aggressive predispositions among children in Mexico." *International Journal of Intercultural Relations* 7 (1983), 33–51.

Lee, E. "Saudis as we, Americans as they." *The Bridge* (Fall, 1980), pp. 3–5, 32–34.

Leung, K., and M. H. Bond. "How Chinese and Americans reward task related contributions: A preliminary study." *Psychologia: An International Journal of Psychology in the Orient* 24 (1982), 32–39.

Liebman, S. *Exploring the Latin American Mind*. Chicago: Nelson-Hall, 1976.

Lindgren, H. C., and A. Tebcheranim. "Arab and American auto- and heterostereotypes: A cross-cultural study of empathy." *Journal of Cross-Cultural Psychology* 2 (1971), 173–180.

Marsella, A. J., D. Kinzie, and P. Gordon. "Ethnic variations in the expression of depression." *Journal of Cross-Cultural Psychology* 4 (1973), 435–458.

Merchant, J. J. "Korean interpersonal patterns: Implications for Korean/American intercultural communication." *Communication* 9 (1980), 60–76.

Mernissi, F. *Beyond the Veil: Male-Female Dynamics in a Modern Muslim Society*. New York: John Wiley, 1975.

Patai, R. *The Arab Mind*. New York: Scribner's Sons, 1973.

Penner, L. A., and T. Any. "A comparison of American and Vietnamese value systems." *Journal of Social Psychology* 101 (1977), 187–204.

Redd, U. V. "How Indians see the world: Communication and perceptions of national groups." *Media Asia* 9 (1982), 32–39.

Rohrlich, B. L. "Contrasting rules: Eastern and Western European women." *International Journal of Intercultural Relations* 3 (1979), 487–496.

Rorer, B. A., and R. C. Ziller. "Iconic communication of values among American and Polish students." *Journal of Cross-Cultural Psychology* 13 (1982), 352–361.

Schneider, M. J., and W. Jordan. "Perceptions of the communicative performance of Americans and Chinese in intercultural dyads." *International Journal of Intercultural Relations* 5 (1981), 175–191.

Smith, H. *The Russians*. New York: Ballantine Books, 1976.

Sobel, M. "Growing old in Great Britain." *Aging* (1981), 8–16.

Yum, J. O. "Communication diversity and information among Korean immigrants in Hawaii." *Human Communication Research* 8 (1982), 154–169.

Nondominant Domestic Cultures

In Chapter 2 we focused on international cultures, that is, cultures which exist beyond the immediate borders of the United States. There are also numerous nondominant cultures, subcultures, and deviant subgroups of various religious, economic, ethnic, age, and racial compositions within U.S. society itself, however, that often bring alien and diverse experiences to a communication encounter. Because these social communities are much more visible than foreign cultures, Americans often take their presence for granted. Yet, if you do not understand the unique experiences of these groups, you can encounter serious communication problems. The articles in this chapter, therefore, will examine some of the cultural experiences inherent in a few of the nondominant communities in the United States. Admittedly there are many more of these social communities than the ones included in our analysis. Our selection, however, was based on three considerations. First, limited space and the necessity for efficiency prohibited a long list of subcultures and subgroups. Second, we decided to include those social communities that are often in conflict with the larger society. And third, we wanted to emphasize the subcultures and subgroups that you are likely to interact with. To this end, we selected some of the major subcommunities of the United States.

Edith A. Folb in "Who's Got the Room at the Top?" begins the chapter with an introduction to the concept of *intra*cultural communication. This is communication between members of the same dominant culture who hold slightly differing values. Folb sees the crucial characteristics of this form of communication as the interrelationships of power, dominance, and nondominance as they are manifest in the particular cultures. She carefully examines these variables as they apply to blacks, native Americans, Chicanos, women, the aged, the physically challenged, and other groups that have been "caste marked and more often negatively identified when it comes to issues of power, dominance, and social control."

The first specific subculture we look at is the economically deprived. Most Americans have been guilty of assuming that because the poor live in America they share a similar culture with the general population. Yet during the last decade sociologists have pointed out the fact that the poor might well be a subculture living both within and apart from the rest of society. This idea serves as the central theme of Jack Daniel's essay, "The Poor: Aliens in an Affluent Society: Cross-Cultural Communication." Daniel looks at the values and experiences that are unique to the poor. He shows that the attitudes of the poor toward education, authority, and the like are often quite different from those of the average American. In addition, he suggests that many of these attitudes are a result of the messages the poor are exposed to— messages that are often at variance with the rest of society. These and other examples demonstrate the large chasm between the poor and the main culture in the United States. Many of these differences are so great that effective communication is often impossible. Daniel maintains that one must understand these "divergent fields of experience" to overcome the barriers that often stifle intercultural communication.

The U.S. population is becoming older. For the first time in history, more than half of the population is over 35 years of age. As this trend continues, new social problems will emerge that must be solved in order to prevent an aged versus youth division in society. Carl W. Carmichael addresses this topic in his essay, "Cultural Patterns of the Elderly," as he examines the problem of "what to do with the aged." Carmichael asserts that aging presents both a cultural and a communication problem because the aging process is related to the beliefs, attitudes, and stereotypes about aging found within the culture and to the interaction patterns prevalent in the culture. Since the increasing population age is a new cultural experience for the United States, the culture must adapt and develop processes to accommodate the increasing proportion of elderly members. Carmichael offers several suggestions on how this might be accomplished.

Recently much attention has been paid to a social community previously taken for granted.

Because women are so much a part of one's perceptual field, and hence part of one's daily life, it was never conceived that the experience of being female was a viable area of investigation. The resurgence of feminism in the last decade, however, has prompted a reexamination of what it means to be a member of that particular social community.

As students of interpersonal communication we recognize that social relationships and communication between the sexes are influenced by the assumptions each makes about the other. Furthermore, these assumptions function in the formation of interpersonal perceptions and in the shaping of messages. Men's assumptions and definitions about women are the focus of our next essay. Marilyn J. Boxer maintains that the assumptions made and held by men are false—false because "women have been named—and defined—by men, and in relation to men." She traces, through a series of historical examples, how this androcentric view of women becomes translated into a social reality that influences communication as well as material culture. The impact of these perceptions as well as their source should be understood by anyone who seeks to improve what Boxer calls "intergender communication."

The gay and lesbian community has recently become a highly visible and controversial component of our society. Their emergence has resulted in a new set of communication situations in which social and interpersonal dialogues are taking place between members of the homo- and heterosexual components of American society. In order to help understand this part of our society better, we have selected as the final article in this chapter Sasha Gregory Lewis's "Lesbians: A Subculture in Hiding." While in recent years more and more lesbians have publicly proclaimed their desire for equal treatment, they are nevertheless still a subculture with experiences and attitudes that keep many of them set apart from the dominant culture. Lewis explores these experiences as she helps us understand the role of the extended family, the importance of the code of silence, attitudes toward sexual indiscretion, and the network system employed by lesbians. By knowing more about the background of this subculture, and hence what they bring to the communication encounter, we might better understand their behavior *during* that encounter.

Who's Got the Room at the Top? Issues of Dominance and Nondominance in Intracultural Communication

EDITH A. FOLB

"If a phenomenon is important, it is perceived, and, being perceived, it is labeled." So notes Nathan Kantrowitz, sociologist and student of language behavior. Nowhere is Kantrowitz's observation more apparent than in that realm of communication studies concerned with the correlates and connections between culture and communication—what the editors of this text have termed "intercultural communication." Our contemporary technology has brought us into both literal and voyeuristic contact with diverse cultures and customs, from the Stone Age Tasaday to the computer age Japanese. Our domestic liberation movements, moreover, have forced upon our consciousness the existence and needs of a multiplicity of groups within our own nation. So, the phenomenon of culture-linked communication is pervasively before us. And, as scholars concerned with culture and communication, we have tried to identify and characterize what we see. This attempt to "label the goods," as it were, has generated a profusion of semantic labels and categories—international communication, cross-cultural communication, intercultural communica-

tion, intracultural communication, trans-racial communication, interracial communication, interethnic communication. What we perceive to be important, we label.

Some may chide us for our penchant for classifications—an example of Aristotelian excessiveness, they may say. However, I see it as a genuine attempt to understand what we do individually and collectively, what we focus on within the field of communication studies. I believe this effort to characterize what we do serves a useful function: It continually prods us to examine and expand our vision of what culture-linked communication is, and, at the same time, it helps us bring into sharper focus the dimensions and differences within this area of study. As Samovar and Porter (1982) remind us, "There is still a great need to specify the nature of intercultural communication and to recognize various viewpoints that see the phenomenon somewhat differently" (p. 2). It is my intention in this essay to attempt what the editors of this text suggest, to look at the correlates and connections between culture and communication from a different point of view, one that examines the properties and issues of dominance and nondominance in communicative exchange. The essay is speculative and sometimes polemical. And the focus of my interest and discussion is the realm of intracultural communication.

THE CONCEPT OF INTRACULTURAL COMMUNICATION

The label "intracultural communication" is not unknown within the field of communication studies, although it is one that has not been widely used. Sitaram and Cogdell (1976) have identified intracultural communication as "the type of communication that takes place between members of the same dominant culture, but with slightly differing values" (p. 28). They go on to explain that there are groups ("subcultures") within the dominant culture who hold a minimal number of values that differ from the mainstream, as well as from other subgroups. These differences are not sufficient to

This original essay appeared in print for the first time in the third edition. All rights reserved. Permission to reprint must be obtained from the publisher and the author. Professor Folb teaches at San Francisco State University.

identify them as separate cultures, but diverse enough to set them apart from each other and the culture at large. "Communication between members of such subcultures is *intracultural communication*" (Sitaram and Cogdell, 1976, p. 28).

In another vein, Sarbaugh (1979) sees intracultural communication as an indicator of the degree of cultural experience shared (or not shared) by two people—the more culturally homogeneous the participants, the greater the level of "intraculturalness" surrounding the communicative act. For Sitaram and Cogdell, then, intracultural communication is a phenomenon that operates within a given culture among its members; for Sarbaugh, it is a measure of homogeneity that well may transcend country or culture.

Like Sitaram and Cogdell, I see intracultural communication as a phenomenon that functions within a single, designated culture. However, like Sarbaugh, I am concerned with the particular variables within that context that importantly influence the degree and kind of cultural homogeneity or heterogeneity that can and does exist among members of the culture. Furthermore, the variables of particular interest to me are those that illuminate and underscore the interrelationship of power, dominance, and nondominance in a particular culture.[1] Finally, I believe that the concept of hierarchy, as it functions within a culture, has a deep impact on matters of power, dominance, and nondominance and, therefore, on both the form and content of intracultural communication.

As a backdrop for the discussion of dominance and nondominance in an intracultural context, I would like to formulate a frame of reference within which to view the discussion.

A FRAME OF REFERENCE FOR INTRACULTURAL COMMUNICATION

Society and Culture

Thomas Hobbes, the seventeenth century political philosopher, left us an intriguing legacy in his work, *Leviathan*. He posited a hypothetical starting point for humankind's march to political and social organization. He called it "the state of nature." In this presocietal state, the biggest club ruled. Kill or be killed was the prevailing modus operandi. Somewhere along the evolutionary road, our ancestors began to recognize a need to change their ways—if any of them were to survive for very long. The principle of enlightened self-interest became the name of the game. Our forebears, however grudgingly, began to curb their inclination to kill, maim, steal, or otherwise aggress upon others and joined together for mutual survival and benefit. The move was one of expediency, not altruism. "Do unto others as you would have them do unto you," whatever its religious import, is a reiteration of the principle of enlightened self-interest.

So, this aggregate of beings came together in order to survive, and, in coming together, gave up certain base instincts, drives, and predilections. "Society" was formed. Those who may scoff at this postulated state of nature need only remember back to the United States' final pullout from Vietnam. The media showed us, in all too brutal detail, the rapidity with which a society disintegrates and we return to the force of the club.

But let us continue with the telling of humankind's tale. It was not sufficient merely to form society; it must be maintained. Controls must be established to ensure its stability. Thus, the social contract was enacted. It was, indeed, the social contract that ensured mutual support, protection, welfare, and survival for the society's members.

However, social maintenance and control did not ensure the perpetuation of the society as an intact entity, carrying along its cumulative and collective experiences, knowledge, beliefs, attitudes, the emergent relationship of self to other, to the group, to the universe, to matters of time and space. That is, it did not ensure the perpetuation of society's accoutrements—its culture. Institutions and structures were needed to house, as it were, the trappings of culture. So, culture was not only embodied in the precepts passed on from one generation to another, but also in the artifacts created by society to safeguard its culture. Looked at in a different light, culture is both a blueprint for continued societal survival as well as the pervasive cement that holds the social mosaic together. Culture daily tells us and shows us how to be in the universe, and it informs future generations how to be.[2]

From the moment we begin life in this world, we are instructed in the cultural ways that govern and hold together our society, ways that ensure its perpetuation. Indeed, the social contract that binds us to our society and our culture from the moment of birth is neither of our own choice nor of our own design. For example, we are labeled by others almost immediately—John, Sandra, Pearl, David. Our genders are determined at once and we are, accordingly, swaddled in appropriate colors and treated in appropriate ways.[3]

As we grow from infancy to childhood, the socialization process is stepped up and we rapidly internalize the rules of appropriate and inappropriate societal behavior. Religion, education, recreation, health care, and many other cultural institutions reinforce our learning, shape and regulate our behavior and thought so they are orderly and comprehensible to other members of our society. Through the socialization process the human animal is transformed into the social animal. Thus, society is maintained through instruction and indoctrination in the ways of the culture.

But the question that pricks and puzzles the mind is: Whose culture is passed on? Whose social order is maintained? Whose beliefs and values are deemed appropriate? Whose norms, mores, and folkways are invoked?

Hierarchy, Power, and Dominance

In most societies, as we know them, there is a hierarchy of status and power. By its very nature, hierarchy implies an ordering process, a sense of the evaluative marketing of those being ordered. Our own vernacular vocabulary abounds with references to hierarchy and concomitant status and power: "top dog," "top banana," "king pin," "king of the mountain."

High status and attendant power may be accorded to those among us who are seen or believed to be great warriors or hunters, those invested with magical, divine, or special powers, those who are deemed wise, or those who are in possession of important, valued, and/or vital societal resources and goods. Of course, power and high status are not necessarily—or even usually—accorded to these specially designated members of the society in some automatic fashion. Power, control, and subsequent high status are often forcibly wrested from others and forcibly maintained. Not everyone abides by the social contract, and strong-arm rule often prevails, as conquered, colonized, and enslaved people know too well.

Whatever the basis for determining the hierarchy, the fact of its existence in a society assures the evolution and continued presence of a power elite—those at the top of the social hierarchy who accrue and possess what the society deems valuable or vital. And, in turn, the presence of a power elite ensures an asymmetrical relationship among the members of the society. In fact, power is often defined as the ability to get others to do what you want and the resources to force them to do your bidding if they resist—the asymmetrical relationship in its extreme form.

But the perpetuation of the power elite through force is not the most effective or efficient way of ensuring one's position at the top of the hierarchy. It is considerably more effective to institute, encourage, and/or perpetuate those aspects of culture—knowledge, experiences, beliefs, values, patterns of social organization, artifacts—that subtly and manifestly reinforce and ensure the continuation of the power elite and its asymmetrical relationship within the society. Though we may dismiss Nazism as a malignant ideology, we should attend to the fact that Hitler well understood the maintenance of the power elite through the manipulation and control of culture—culture as propaganda.

Though I would not imply that all power elites maintain themselves in such an overtly manipulative way, I would at least suggest that the powerful in many societies—our own included—go to great lengths to maintain their positions of power and what those positions bring them. And to that end, they support, reinforce, and, indeed, create those particular cultural precepts and artifacts that are likely to guarantee their continued power. To the extent that the culture reflects implicitly or expressly the needs and desires of the power elite to sustain itself, it becomes a vehicle for propaganda. Thus, cultural precepts and artifacts that govern such matters as social organization and behavior, values, beliefs, and the like can often be seen as rules and institutions that sustain the few at the expense of the many.

So, we come back to the question of whose rules, whose culture? I would suggest that when we in communication studies refer to the "dominant culture" we are, in fact, not talking about numbers. That is why the label "minorities" is misleading when we refer to cultural groups within the larger society. Blacks in South Africa and women in the United States are not numerical minorities—but they are not members of the power elite either. In fact, when we talk about the concept of dominant culture, we are really talking about power—those who *dominate* culture, those who historically or traditionally have had the most persistent and far-reaching impact on culture, on what we think and say, on what we believe and do in our society. We are talking about the culture of the minority and, by extension, the structures and institutions (social, political, economic, legal, religious, and so on) that maintain the power of this minority. Finally, we are talking about rules of appropriate and inappropriate behavior, thought, speech, and action for the many that preserve power for the few. Dominant culture, therefore, significantly reflects the precepts and artifacts of those who dominate culture and is not necessarily, or even usually, a reference to numbers, but to power.

So, coming full circle, I would suggest that our socialization process, our social introduction to this aggregate of people who form society, is an introduction to a rule-governed milieu of asymmetrical societal organization and relationship, and the communicative behaviors and practices found there are likewise asymmetrical in nature. As the witticism goes, "All men (perhaps even women) are created equal—some are just more equal than others."

Given this frame of reference, I would now like to explore some definitions and concepts that, I believe, emerge from this perspective. It is my hope that the discussion will provide the reader with another way to look at intracultural communication.

A NOMENCLATURE FOR INTRACULTURAL COMMUNICATION

The Concept of Nondominance

As already indicated, I view intracultural communication as a phenomenon that operates within a given cultural context. However, my particular focus, as suggested, is not a focus on numbers but an attention to dominance, nondominance, and power in the cultural setting. That is, how do nondominant groups intersect and interact with the dominant culture membership (with those who enact the precepts and support the institutions and systems of the power elite)? For purposes of discussion and analysis, I will take most of my examples from the geopolitical configuration called the United States.

By "nondominant groups" I mean those constellations of people who have not historically or traditionally had continued access to or influence upon or within the dominant culture's (that is, those who dominate culture) social, political, legal, economic, and/or religious structures and institutions. Nondominant groups include people of color, women, gays, the physically challenged,[4] and the aged, to name some of the most prominent. I use the expression "nondominant" to characterize these people because, as suggested, I am referring to power and dominance, not numbers and dominance. Within the United States, those most likely to hold and control positions of real—not token—power and those who have the greatest potential ease of access to power and high status are still generally white, male, able-bodied, heterosexual, and youthful in appearance if not in age.[5]

Nondominant people are also those who, in varying degrees and various ways, have been "invisible" within the society of which they are a part and at the same time bear a visible caste mark. Furthermore, it is this mark of caste identity that is often consciously or habitually assigned low or negative status by members of the dominant culture.

The dimensions of invisibility and marked visibility are keen indicators of the status hierarchy in a given society. In his book, *The Invisible Man*, Ralph Ellison instructs us in the lesson that nondominant people—in this instance, black people—are figuratively "invisible." They are seen by the dominant culture as no one, nobody and therefore go unacknowledged and importantly unperceived.[6] Furthermore, nondominant peoples are often relegated to object status rather than human status. They are viewed as persons of "no consequence," literally and metaphorically. Expressions such as, "If you've seen one, you've seen them all"; "They all look alike to me"; "If you put a bag over their heads, it doesn't matter who you screw" attest to this level of invisibility and dehumanization of nondominant peoples, such as people of color or women. Indeed, one need only look at the dominant culture's slang repertory for a single nondominant group, women, to see the extent of this object status: "tail," "piece of ass," "side of beef," "hole," "gash," "slit," and so on.

At the same time that nondominant peoples are socially invisible, they are often visibly caste marked. Though we tend to think of caste in terms, say, of East Indian culture, we can clearly apply the concept to our own culture. One of the important dimensions of a caste system is that it is hereditary—you are born into a given caste and are usually marked for life as a member. In fact, we are all born into a caste, we are all caste marked. Indeed, some of us are doubly or multiply caste marked. In the United States, the most visible marks of caste relate to gender, race, age, and the degree to which one is able-bodied.

As East Indians do, we too assign low to high status and privilege to our people. The fact that this assignment of status and privilege may be active or passive, conscious or unconscious, malicious or unthinking does not detract from the reality of the act. And one of the major determinants of status, position, and caste marking relates back to who has historically or traditionally had access to or influence upon or within the power elite and its concomitant structures and institutions. So, historically blacks, native Americans, Chicanos, women, the old, the physically challenged have at best been neutrally caste marked and more often negatively identified when it comes to issues of power, dominance, and social control.[7]

Low status has been assigned to those people whom society views as somehow "stigmatized." Indeed, we have labels to identify such stigmatization: "deviant," "handicapped," "abnormal," "substandard," "different"—that is, different from those who dominate. As already suggested, it is the white, male, heterosexual, able-bodied, youthful person who both sets the standards for caste marking and is the human yardstick by which people within the United States are importantly measured and accordingly treated. As Porter and Samovar (1976) remind us, "We [in the United States] have generally viewed racial minorities as less than equal; they have been viewed as second class members of society—not quite as good as the white majority—and treated as such. . . . Blacks, Mexican-Americans, Indians, and Orientals are still subject to prejudice and discrimination and treated in many respects as colonized subjects" (p. 11). I would add to this list of colonized, low status subjects women, the physically challenged, and the aged. Again, our language is a telling repository for illuminating status as it relates to subordination in the social hierarchy: "Stay in your place," "Don't get out of line," "Know your place," "A woman's place is chained to the bed and the stove," "Know your station in life," are just a few sample phrases.

It is inevitable that nondominant peoples will experience, indeed be subjected to and suffer from, varying degrees of fear, denial, and self-hatred of their caste marking. Frantz Fanon's (1963) characterization of the "colonized native"—the oppressed native who has so internalized the power elite's perception of the norm that he or she not only serves and speaks for the colonial elite but is often more critical and oppressive of her or his caste than is the colonial—reveals this depth of self-hatred and denial.

In a parallel vein, the concept of "passing" which relates to a person of color attempting to "pass for" white, is a statement of self-denial. Implicit in the act of passing is the acceptance, if not the belief, that "white is right" in this society, and the closer one can come to the likeness of the privileged caste, the more desirable and comfortable one's station in life will be. So, people of color have passed for white—just as Jews have passed for Gentile or gay males and females have passed for straight, always with the fear of being discovered "for what they are." Physical impairment, too, has been a mark of shame in this country for those so challenged. Even so powerful a figure as F. D. R. refused to be photographed in any way that would picture him to be a "cripple."

If the act of passing is a denial of one's caste, the process of "coming out of the closet" is a conscious acceptance of one's caste. It is an important political and personal statement of power, a vivid metaphor that literally marks a rite of passage. Perhaps, the most striking acknowledgement of one's caste marking in our society relates to sexual preference. For a gay male or lesbian to admit their respective sexual preferences is for them to consciously take on an identity that our society has deemed abnormal and deviant—when measured against the society's standard of what is appropriate. They become, quite literally, marked people. In an important way, most of our domestic liberation movements are devoted to having their membership come out of the closet. That is, these movements seek not only to have their people heard and empowered by the power elite, but to have them reclaim and assert their identity and honor their caste. Liberation movement slogans tell the story of positive identification with one's caste: "Black is beautiful," "brown power," "Sisterhood is powerful," "gay pride," "I am an Indian and proud of it."

The nature and disposition of the social hierarchy in a given society, such as the United States, is reflected not only in the caste structure, but also in the class structure and the role prescriptions and expectations surrounding caste and class. Although the power structure in the United States is a complex and multileveled phenomenon, its predominant, generating force is economic. That is, the power elite is an elite that controls the material resources and goods in this country as well as the means and manner of production and distribution. Though one of our national fictions is that the United States is a classless society, we have, in fact, a well-established class structure based largely on economic power and control. When we talk of lower, middle, and upper classes in this country, we are not usually talking about birth or origins, but about power and control over material resources, and the attendant wealth, privilege, and high status.

There is even a kind of status distinction made within the upper-class society in this country that again relates to wealth and power, but in a temporal rather than a quantitative way—how long one has had wealth, power, and high-class status. So, distinctions are made between the old rich (the Harrimans, the Gores, the Pews) and the new rich (the Hunt family, Norton Simon, and their like).

Class, then, is intimately bound up with matters of caste. Not all, or even most, members of our society have the opportunity—let alone the caste credentials—to get a "piece of the action." It is no accident of nature that many of the nondominant peoples in this country are also poor peoples. Nor is it surprising that nondominant groups have been historically the unpaid, low paid, and/or enslaved work force for the economic power elite.

Finally, role prescriptions are linked to both matters of status and expectations in terms of one's perceived status, class, and caste. A role can be defined simply as a set of behaviors. The set of behaviors we ascribe to a given role is culture-bound and indicative of what has been designated as appropriate within the culture vis-à-vis that role. They are prescriptive, not descriptive, behaviors. We hold certain behavioral expectations for certain roles. It is a mark of just how culture-bound and prescriptive these roles are when someone is perceived to behave inappropriately—for example, the mother who gives up custody of her children in order to pursue her career; she has "stepped out of line."

Furthermore, we see certain roles as appropriate or inappropriate to a given caste. Though another of our national myths—the Horatio Alger myth—tells us that there is room at the top for the industrious, bright go-getter, the truth of the matter is that there is room at the top if you are appropriately caste marked (that is, are white, male, able-bodied, and so on). The resistance, even outright hostility, nondominant peoples have encountered when they aspire to or claim certain occupational roles, for example, is a mark of the power elite's reluctance to relinquish those positions that have been traditionally associated with privileged status and high caste and class ranking. Though, in recent years, there has been much talk about a woman Vice-President of the United States, it has remained just talk. For that matter, there has not been a black Vice-President or a Hispanic or a Jew. The thought of the Presidency being held by most nondominant peoples is still "unspeakable."

The cultural prescription to keep nondominant peoples "in their place" is reinforced by and reinforces what I refer to as the "subterranean self"—the culture-bound collection of prejudices, stereotypes, values, and beliefs that each of us embraces and employs to justify our world view and the place of people in that world. It is, after all, our subterranean selves that provide fuel to fire the normative in our lives—what roles people ought and ought not to perform, what and why certain individuals are ill- or well-equipped to carry out certain roles, and our righteously stated rationalizations for keeping people in their places as we see them. Again, it should be remembered that those who dominate the culture reinforce and tacitly or openly encourage the perpetuation of those cultural prejudices, stereotypes, values, and beliefs that maintain the status quo, that is, the asymmetrical nature of the social hierarchy. Those who doubt the fervent desire of the power elite to maintain things as they are need only ponder the intense and prolonged resistance to the Equal Rights Amendment. If women are already "equal," why not make their equality a matter of record?

The foregoing discussion has been an attempt to illuminate the meaning of nondominance and the position of the nondominant person within our society. By relating status in the social hierarchy to matters of caste, class, and role, it has been my intention to highlight what it means to be a nondominant person within a culture that is dominated by the cultural precepts and artifacts of a power elite. It has also been my intention to suggest that the concept of "dominant culture" is something of a fiction, as we in communication studies traditionally use it. Given my perspective, it is more accurate to talk about those who dominate a culture rather than a dominant culture per se. Finally, I have attempted to point out that cultural dominance is not necessarily, or even usually, a matter of the numbers of people in a given society, but of those who have real power in a society.

Geopolitics

The viewpoint being developed in this essay highlights still another facet of dominance and nondominance as it relates to society and the culture it generates and sustains—namely, the geopolitical facet. The United States is not merely a territory with certain designated boundaries—a geographical entity—it is a geopolitical configuration. It is a country whose history reflects the clear-cut interrelationship of geography, politics, economics, and the domination and control of people. For example, the westward movement and the subsequent takeover of the Indian nations and chunks of Mexico were justified by our doctrine of Manifest Destiny, not unlike the way Hitler's expansionism was justified by the Nazi doctrine of "geopolitik." It is no accident that the doctrine of Manifest Destiny coincides with the rapid growth and development of U.S. industrialization. The U.S. power elite wanted more land in which to expand and grow economically, so it created a rationalization to secure it.

Perhaps nowhere is a dominant culture's (those who dominate culture) ethnocentrism more apparent than in the missionary-like work carried on by its members—whether it be to "civilize" the natives (that is, to impose the conquerors' cultural baggage on them), to "educate them in the ways of the white man," or to "Americanize" them. Indeed, the very term *America* is a geopolitical label as we use it. It presumes that those who inhabit the United States are the center of the Western hemisphere, indeed its only residents.[8] Identifying ourselves as "Americans" and our geopolitical entity as "America," in light of the peoples who live to the north and south of our borders speaks to both our economic dominance in this hemisphere and our ethnocentrism.

Identifying the United States in geopolitical terms is to identify it as a conqueror and controller of other peoples, and suggests both the probability of nondominant groups of people within that territory as well as a polarized, even hostile relationship between these groups and those who dominate culture. What Rich and Ogawa (1982) have pointed out in their model of interracial communication is applicable to most nondominant peoples: "As long as a power relationship exists between cultures where one has subdued and dominated the other . . . hostility, tension and strain are introduced into the communicative situation" (p. 46). Not only were the Indian nations[9] and parts of Mexico conquered and brought under the colonial rule of the United States, but in its industrial expansionism, the United States physically enslaved black Africans to work on the farms and plantations of the South. It also economically enslaved large numbers of East European immigrants, Chinese, Irish, Hispanics (and more recently, Southeast Asians) in its factories, on its railroads, in its mines and fields through low wages and long work hours. It coopted the cottage industries of the home and brought women and children into the factories under abysmal conditions and the lowest of wages.

Indeed, many of the nondominant peoples in this country today are the very same ones whom the powerful have historically colonized, enslaved, disenfranchised, dispossessed, discounted, and relegated to poverty and low caste and class status. So, the asymmetrical relationship between the conquerer and the conquered continues uninterrupted. Although the form of oppression may

change through time, the fact of oppression—and coexistent nondominance—remains.

It has been my desire throughout this essay to speculate about the complex ways in which society, culture, position, and place in the societal hierarchy affect and are affected by the matters of dominance, power, and social control. To this end, I have chosen to identify and characterize configurations of people within a society not only along a cultural axis but along a socio-economic and a geopolitical axis as well. I have tried to reexamine some of the concepts and definitions employed in discussions of culture-linked communication in a different light. And I have chosen the issues and conditions surrounding dominance and nondominance as points of departure and return. As I said at the beginning of this essay, the content is speculative, exploratory, and, hopefully, provocative. Above all, it is intended to encourage dialogue and exchange about the conditions and constraints surrounding intracultural communication.

NOTES

1. See Folb (1980) for another perspective on the intersection of power, dominance, and nondominance as they operate within a discrete microcultural group, the world of the black ghetto teenager.

2. For a fascinating account of how and what kind of culture is transmitted from person to person, see Margaret Mead's *Culture and Commitment* (1970).

3. Mary Ritchie Key's book, *Male/Female Language* (1975), provides an informative discussion of the ways in which females and males are catalogued, characterized, and compartmentalized by our language. She illuminates its effects on how we perceive ourselves, as well as discussing how others perceive us through the prism of language.

4. The semantic marker "physically challenged" is used in lieu of other, more traditional labels such as "handicapped," "physically disabled," or "physically impaired," because it is a designation preferred by many so challenged. It is seen as a positive, rather than a negative, mark of identification.

5. In a country as youth conscious as our own, advanced age is seen as a liability, not as a mark of honor and wisdom as it is in other cultures. Whatever other reservations people had about Ronald Reagan's political aspirations in 1980, the one most discussed was his age. His political handlers went to great lengths—as did Reagan himself—to "prove" he was young in spirit and energy if not in years. It was important that he align himself as closely as possible with the positive mark of youth we champion and admire in this country.

6. It is no mere coincidence that a common thread binds together the domestic liberation movements in this country. It is the demand to be seen, heard, and empowered.

7. See Nancy Henley's *Body Politics* (1977) for a provocative look at the interplay of the variables power, dominance, and sex as they affect nonverbal communication.

8. The current bumper sticker, "Get the United States Out of North America," is a pointed reference to our hemispheric self-centeredness.

9. Neither the label "Indian" nor the label "native American" adequately identifies those people who inhabited the North American continent before the European conquest of this territory. Both reflect the point of view of the labeler, not those so labeled. That is why many who fought for the label "native American" now discount it as not significantly different than "Indian."

BIBLIOGRAPHY

Fanon, Frantz. *Wretched of the Earth*. New York: Grove Press, Inc., 1963.

Folb, Edith A. *Runnin' Down Some Lines: The Language and Culture of Black Teenagers*. Cambridge: Harvard University Press, 1980.

Porter, Richard E. and Larry A. Samovar. "Communicating Interculturally." In *Intercultural Communication: A Reader*, 2nd ed., ed. Larry A. Samovar and Richard E. Porter. Belmont, Calif.: Wadsworth, 1976.

Rich, Andrea L., and Dennis M. Ogawa. "Intercultural and Interracial Communication: An Analytical Approach." In *Intercultural Communication: A Reader*, 3rd ed., ed. Larry A. Samovar and Richard E. Porter. Belmont, Calif.: Wadsworth, 1982.

Samovar, Larry A. and Richard E. Porter, eds. *Intercultural Communication: A Reader*, 3rd ed. Belmont, Calif.: Wadsworth, 1982.

Sarbaugh, L. E. *Intercultural Communication*. Rochelle Park, N.J.: Hayden Book Co., 1979.

Sitaram, K. S., and Roy T. Cogdell. *Foundations of Intercultural Communication*. Columbus, Ohio: Charles E. Merrill, 1976.

The Poor: Aliens in an Affluent Society: Cross-Cultural Communication

JACK DANIEL

INTRODUCTION

Give me your tired, your poor,
Your huddled masses yearning to breathe free,
The wretched refuse of your teeming shore,
Send these, the homeless, tempest-tossed, to me:
I lift my lamp beside the golden door.

—Emma Lazarus 1849–1887

In commemoration of the one hundredth year of American independence, the Statue of Liberty was placed in New York harbor bearing the above inscription. America received its share of the poor but in 1965 Michael Harrington saw fit to write that the poor are internal aliens in an affluent society. This paper is concerned with revealing some possible communication breakdowns resulting from the poor being aliens in an affluent society.

THE GENERAL PROBLEM OF CROSS-CULTURAL COMMUNICATION

Within a given culture, even within the so-called primitive cultures, communication is a highly complex process. From culture to culture, the symbols differ, the channels differ, and messages are encoded and decoded in different fashions. When messages are sent across cultural boundaries, they may be encoded in one context and decoded in another. Wilbur Schramm has described the problem in the following diagram.[1]

Field of Experience   Field of Experience
                    Signal
Source Encoder   Decoder Destination

Schramm states that the source and the receiver are not "in tune" when they have different "fields of experience":

Think of those circles as the accumulated experiences of the two individuals trying to communicate. The source can encode, and the destination can decode, only in terms of the experience each has had. If we have never learned Russian, we can neither code nor decode in that language. If an African tribesman has never seen or heard of an airplane, he can only decode the sight of a plane in terms of whatever experience he has had. The plane may seem to him to be a bird, and the aviator a god borne on wings. If the circles have a large area in common, then communication is easy. If the circles do not meet, if there has been no common experience, then communication is impossible. If the circles have only a small area in common, that is, if the experiences of the source and destination have been strikingly unlike, then it is going to be very difficult to get an intended meaning across from one to the other.[2]

Edward T. Hall and William Foot Whyte provide us with an example of cross-cultural communication in their description of North American–Latin American communication difficulties:

In North America, the "proper" distance to stand when talking to another adult male you do not know well is about two feet, at least in formal business conversation. (Naturally at a cocktail party, the distance shrinks, but anything under eight to ten inches is likely to provoke an apology or an attempt to back up.)

From *Today's Speech*, Vol. 18 (Winter 1970), pp. 15–21. Reprinted by permission of the publisher and the author. Professor Daniel is affiliated with the Black Studies Program at the University of Pittsburgh.

To a Latin American, with his cultural traditions and habits, a distance of two feet seems to him approximately what five feet would to us. To him, we seem distant and cold. To us, he gives an impression of pushiness.

. . . We once observed a conversation between a Latin and a North American which began at one end of a forty-foot hall. At intervals we noticed them again, finally at the other end of the hall. This rather amusing displacement had been accomplished by an almost continual series of small backward steps on the part of the [North] American, trying unconsciously to reach a comfortable talking distance, and an equal closing of the gap by the Latin American as he attempted to reach his accustomed conversation space.[3]

COMMUNICATION BETWEEN PROFESSIONAL AND POOR PEOPLE AS A PROBLEM IN CROSS-CULTURAL COMMUNICATION

Concern for the problem of communication between professionals and the poor as a problem in cross-cultural communication manifests itself in the many community action programs which make use of "indigenous nonprofessionals."

In describing the indigenous nonprofessionals and discussing their usefulness, Reissman said:

The indigenous non-professional is poor, is from the neighborhood, is often a member of a minority group. His family is poor, he is a peer of the client and shares a common background, language, ethnic origin, style and group of interests which it would be impossible and perhaps even undesirable for most professionals to maintain.[4]

Edgar S. and Jean C. Cahn, writing in *The Yale Law Journal*, proposed the establishment of a neighborhood law firm in poor communities and expressed concern about the potential communication problems that might exist between the lawyer and the poor people in the community.[5]

Besides access to grievance, such an institution must be able to establish rapport and communication. Here, the middle class status of professional persons often constitutes an impediment to the development of confidence and identification. This problem has been dealt with by various kinds of outreaching social work carried on by the community organizer, detached worker, and gang or street worker.[6]

It is held here that middle-class oriented professionals and poor people in the United States have such divergent fields of experience that communication between them is in fact a case of cross-cultural communication.

Oscar Lewis' study of poverty has focused primarily on families in Mexico, and recently Puerto Rican families in New York City. His methods consisted of anthropological-psychological field work with much of his time spent living with poor families.[7] According to Lewis:

The culture of poverty is not just a matter of deprivation or disorganization, a term signifying the absence of something. It is a culture in the traditional sense in that it provides human beings with a design for living, with a ready-made set of solutions for human problems, and so serves a significant adaptive function. This style of life transcends national boundaries and regional and rural-urban differences within nations. Wherever it occurs, its practitioners exhibit remarkable similarity in the structure of their families, in interpersonal relations and in their orientation in time.[8]

In further describing the culture of poverty, Lewis offers the following information:

The people do not belong to labor unions or political parties and make little use of banks, hospitals, department stores or museums. . . .

People in a culture of poverty produce little wealth and receive little in return. Chronic unemployment, low wages, lack of property, lack of savings, absence of food reserves in the home, and the chronic shortages of cash imprison the family and the individual in a vicious circle. . . .

Along with disengagement from the larger society, there is hostility to the basic institutions of what are regarded as the dominant classes. There is hatred of the police, mistrust of government and of those in high positions and a cynicism that extends to the church. . . . Yet on the whole it is a comparatively superficial culture. There is in it much pathos, suffering and emptiness. It does not provide much support or satisfaction; its pervading mistrust magnifies individual helplessness and isolation. Indeed, the poverty of the culture is one of the crucial traits of the culture of poverty.[9]

In addition to Oscar Lewis, other writers such as Ben H. Bagdikian[10] and Michael Harrington[11] are inclined to speak of the culture of poverty. Bagdikian writes of the poor among the American Indian and Negro, and the poor city dwellers, while Harrington's focus is primarily on the poor in New York. From his many interviews with poor individuals, Bagdikian presents the following example of an estrangement between the two cultures:

Middle-class assumptions of common sense and social responsibility often make no sense to the poor. What is prudent for the well-fed may be irresponsible for the poor. For most Americans there is something contemptible in the outlook of the impoverished: don't put off until tomorrow any gratification that can be achieved today. For the poor these rules are tried and true. For the poor the future is demonstrably treacherous.[12]

From his analytic description of the poor in New York, Michael Harrington concludes that poverty forms a culture. After vividly describing the poor intellectuals, the poor in the Bowery, and the poor in areas such as Albany and New York, Harrington states:

Perhaps the most important analytic point to have emerged in this description of the other America is the fact that poverty in America forms a culture, a way of life and feeling, that it makes a whole. . . . Then, poverty is a culture in the sense that the mechanism of impoverishment is fundamentally the same in every part of the system. The vicious circle is a basic pattern. It takes different forms for the unskilled workers, for the aged, for the Negroes, for the agricultural workers, but in each case the principle is the same. There are people in the affluent society who are poor because they are poor; and who stay poor because they are poor.[13]

Advocates of the concept of the culture of poverty often will refer to divergent attitudes between the poor people and other parts of the dominant society. An example of this is a study by Ralph Segalman. The summary of the study done by Ralph Segalman appears in Table 1. Segalman's data come from interviewing students at Texas Western College.

Consider Walter B. Miller's discussion of the differences in focal concerns.

The dominant concern over "trouble" involves a distinction of critical importance for the lower class community—that between "law-abiding" and "non-law-abiding" behavior. There is a high degree of sensitivity as to where each person stands in relation to these two classes of activity. Whereas in the middle-class community a major dimension for evaluating a person's status is "achievement" and its external symbols, in the lower class, personal status is very frequently gauged along the law-abiding–non-law-abiding dimension. A mother will evaluate the suitability of her daughter's boyfriend less on the basis of his achievement potential than on the basis of his innate "trouble" potential.

It is being maintained here that the middle-class oriented professional and the poor person are sufficiently different that they can be thought of as representing diverging cultural backgrounds. Consider some of the communication problems of a middle-class oriented professional speaking to a group of sixth grade Negro youngsters who are attending an "inner city" school in Detroit, Michigan, on the topic of good eating habits. If the professional speaks of the vitamins that one can get from cauliflower, eggplant, and broccoli, then there will probably be problems in communication stemming from the fact that "in their culture" the

Table 1 The Cultural Chasm[14]

The concept of	In middle-class terms stands for	But in the lower class is
Authority (courts, police, school principal)	Security—to be taken for granted, wooed	Something hated, to be avoided
Education	The road to better things for one's children and oneself	An obstacle course to be surmounted until the children can go to work
Joining a church	A step necessary for social acceptance	An emotional release
Ideal goal	Money, property, to be accepted by the successful	"Coolness": to "make" out without attracting attention of the authorities
Society	The pattern one conforms to in the interests of security and being "popular"	"The Man," an enemy to be resisted and suspected
Delinquency	An evil originating outside the middle-class home	One of life's inevitable events, to be ignored unless the police get into the act
The future	A rosy horizon	Nonexistent, so live each moment fully
The street	A path for the auto	A meeting place, an escape from a crowded home
Liquor	Sociability, cocktail parties	A means to welcome oblivion
Violence	The last resort of authorities for protecting the law abiding	A tool for living and getting on
Sex	An adventure and binding force for the family—creating problems of birth control	One of life's few free pleasures
Money	A resource to be cautiously spent and saved for the future	Something used now before it disappears

Negro youngsters eat mustard greens, collard greens, and occasionally turnips, kale, and spinach.

Some of the differences between middle-class oriented professionals and the poor, and the resultant communication difficulties might be illustrated by a few statements from a poor but highly verbal individual:

They keep on telling us, those welfare ladies, to take better care of our money, and save it away, and buy what's the best in the stores, and do like them for dresses, and keep the children in school and keep our husbands from leaving us. There isn't nothing they don't have a sermon on. They'll tell you it's bad to spend your money on a smoke or a drink; and it's bad to have your kids sleep alongside you in the bed and you're not supposed to want television because you should be serious with your dollar, and it's wrong for kids, too; and it's bad for you to let them stay out after dark, and they should study their lessons hard and they'll get away ahead and up there.

Well, I'll tell you, they sure don't know what it's about, and they can't know if they come knocking on my door every week until the Lord takes all of us. They have their nice leather shoes, and their smart coats, and they speak the right order of words all right, so I know how many schools they been to. But us? Do they have any idea of what us is about? And let them start at zero the way we do, and see how many big numbers they can become themselves. I mean, if you have got nothing when you're born, and you know you can't get a thing no matter how you tries—well, then you dies with nothing. And no one can deny that arithmetic.

They just don't understand what it's like. You are born in a building where it's cold, and the rats keep you company all day and you are lucky if they don't eat you at night, because they're as hungry as you.

Then the food, it's not always around when you want it, and you don't have money to buy what you do want. Then you go to those schools, and the teachers, they looks down on you, and makes you think you have done something wrong for being born. They shout and make faces, and they treat you like dirt and then tell you to be a doctor or a lawyer; if you just go to the library and stay in school and be neat, that's all it takes. Once in a while lately they want to take you on a trip crosstown, and show you a museum or something. They tell you that you haven't got any pictures at home. So there, take a look and now you own them, and man, you're rich.[15]

If as Oscar Lewis states slum children have usually adopted the attitudes and values of their culture by the time that they are six or seven years old, then one might expect to see cross-cultural communication problems between teacher and students in slum schools. If marked cultural differences exist, then the teachers' methods should be altered from those which are used in middle-class schools. The popular usage of the term "culturally deprived child" partially attests to the fact that such differences in culture do exist between the children who live in poverty and those who are brought up in middle-class homes.

Frank Riessman has defined "culturally deprived" as "those aspects of middle-class culture—such as education, books, formal language—from which these groups have not benefited.[16] By "these

groups," Riessman refers to lower socioeconomic groups of people. In discussing the value of an understanding by the teacher of the culture of the underprivileged, Riessman states:

A sound cultural understanding should enable the teacher to establish a much better relationship with the deprived child who is typically antagonistic toward the school and, on the surface at least, unmotivated to learn. Through an emphatic understanding of his culture, the teacher will begin to see why the deprived child is hostile, what he expects of her, why he wants her to prove herself. The teacher will come to learn why he needs a structured classroom, how she can utilize his in-group loyalty, informality, equalitarianism, humor, and the like. She will come to understand why he does not need love but respect.[17]

Through an understanding of the deprived child's culture, the teacher would not automatically begin to lecture to the child about "delinquency" and his moral character after he has several "unexcused" absences. The child might not have been in school because he has to share one bed with four other brothers and sisters and thereby is not able to sleep in the hot, stuffy, odorous apartment at night. He might not have been in school because his peer group exerts a powerful influence over him, and ascribes status to those who play "hooky." He might have been absent because he found himself in an institution that emphasizes feminine characteristics whereas his culture emphasizes masculinity. As Riessman explains, "Conformity, dependence, neatness, nonaggression—major values in a female school—are not consistent with the masculine stress on vigor and independence."[18] Through an understanding of the deprived child's culture, the teacher could foresee the failure of approaches that emphasized permissiveness and unstructured activity, since the deprived child's culture emphasizes values such as authority, structure, rules, and discipline.

Often teachers of deprived children at the high school level express confusion when they offer to help a student with some problem that exists outside the classroom. I knew a white middle-class teacher who sought employment in one of Pittsburgh's worst slum communities. The teacher desired such a placement because she wanted to "help the children beyond the normal responsibilities of the teacher." However, once she had secured such a position, most of her offers to help were rejected by the students. Had this teacher obtained more information about the attitudes and values of poor people, she would have realized that some poor people have so many needs that haven't been fulfilled for such a long period of time that walking up to them and saying "I've come to help you" is like trying to walk up to a wild lion and petting him. As soon as the offer is made to help, the poor person might become suspicious and begin to look for the "catch."

It is admitted here that the "culture of poverty" is not firmly established as a scientifically useful concept. However, regardless of the term that is used, i.e., *class* or *cultural* differences, *culture* versus *subculture*, etc., significant differences do exist between the "fields of experience" of poor and middle-class people in the United States and elsewhere. That *differences* exist is the major concern of this paper. It is further maintained that these differences, unless taken into consideration, can lead to communication breakdowns between poor and middle-class professionals in America.

As part of communication strategy, the would-be communicator might engage in an audience analysis to determine what channels are being used by his intended audience. If poor people and middle-class people have divergent fields of experience, then one might expect to find differences in channel usage. Researchers in mass communications have found differences in channel usage as a function of social class in America. In the first volume of the "Yankee City Series," Lloyd Warner and Paul S. Lunt described newspaper and magazine subscriptions, motion picture attendance, and book reading according to social class.[19]

Warner and Lunt reported that: (1) There was a high correlation between social class and magazine preference. For example, the *National Geographic* was read mostly by the two upper classes whereas the lower-lower class did not read it at all. (2) There was a definite class bias with regard to the selection of newspapers. Once again, lower classes did not subscribe to the newspapers selected by the upper classes and vice-versa. Warner and Lunt gave similar reports of book reading and movie attendance. In the Hill District of Pittsburgh a brief audience analysis would indicate that if radio is used as the channel for communicating with blacks then one should use radio stations WAMO and WZUM, not just WRYT and KQV. The Hill District is made up of at least 90% Negroes and is considered to be the worst poverty area in Pittsburgh. WAMO and WZUM feature Negro disc jockeys and pop and jazz music whereas WRYT is more of the "silent hour" type and KQV features white disc jockeys playing the "Rolling Stones" and "The Beatles."

In *Social Class in America*, Lloyd W. Warner gives the following account of the soap opera:

The soap opera is a product of contemporary radio. The average upper-middle class radio listener has little interest in soap opera; in fact, most of this group are actively hostile to these curious little dramas that fill the daytime air works. Yet millions and millions of American women listen daily to their favorite soap operas, and advertisers of certain commodities have found them invaluable in selling their products.

Research has shown that the soap opera appeals particularly to the level of the common man. (The common man level is headed by the lower-middle class). The problems raised in these folk dramas, their characters, their plot and values have a strong positive appeal to women of this class level whereas they have little appeal to women above the common man level.[20]

Just as Warner suggests that the soap opera is of little interest to the average upper-middle class radio listener, here it is hypothesized that poor, Negro, six year old Jacks and Jerris have little or no interest in reading about white, six year old Dicks and Janes, their Puffs and Spots and the rest of their middle-class culture. This may contribute to Jack and Jerri becoming "slow readers" who lack motivation.

Margherita MacDonald, Carson McGuire and Robert J. Havighurst investigated the hypothesis that "children of different social classes will belong to different clubs, form different after school play habits, and vary in the movies they attend, the books they read, and the amount of time they spend with their families."[21] They reported that whereas upper-middle and lower-middle class children attend Boy and Girl Scouts, the upper-lower and lower-lower attended neighborhood clubs which were operated by social agencies for serving children who need recreational facilities. Likewise, it was found that the upper class children were more restricted in movie attendance, and that different kinds and numbers of books were read according to the social class of the children.

Lazarsfeld and Kendall[22] focused on variables such as newspaper and magazine reading, movie going, and radio listening of the average American. Again, class distinctions were found. Wilbur Schramm and David M. Whyte[23] found that comic reading declined with higher economic status.[24]

The above studies deal with mass communications in terms of listening and reading habits according to socio-economic status. It is the opinion of this investigator that the communication problems that exist between poor and professional people consist of more than differences in listening and reading habits but also differences in nonverbal forms of communication. In describing the nonverbal aspects of communication, Edward T. Hall says:

Those of us who keep our eyes open can read volumes into what we see going on around us. The citizens of a typical American farming community, for example, do not have to be told why old Mr. Jones is going to town. They know that every other Thursday he makes a trip to the druggist to get his wife a bottle of tonic and that after that he goes around to the feed store, visits with Charley, drops in to call on the sheriff, and then goes home in time for the noonday meal. Jones, in turn, can also tell whenever anything is bothering one of his friends, and the chances are that he will be able to figure out precisely what it

is. He feels comfortable in his way of life because most of the time he "knows what the score is." He doesn't have to say very much to get his point across: a nod of the head or a grunt as he leaves the store is sufficient. People take him as he is. On the other hand, strangers disturb him, not because their mannerisms are different, but because he knows so little about them. When Jones meets a stranger, communication, which is normally as natural as breathing, suddenly becomes difficult and overly complex.[25]

Because of their cultural differences, the professional and the poor person might experience tremendous difficulties in communicating. When a professional makes a poor person wait for six hours in order to obtain a food order for hungry children, when a professional fiddles with papers on his desk while the poor person is talking to him, when the professional works in the poor neighborhood but lives in the suburbs, and when the professional comes to the poor person's home wearing a facial expression of fear and disgust, nonverbal messages are received by the poor person. Moreover, the translation of these messages, by the poor person, may lead to a break in the communication relationship between the poor and the professional person. When a poor person calls in for an emergency appointment but is one half hour late for the appointment, when a poor person claims that his relief check is insufficient yet he takes part of his check and plays the numbers, and when a poor Negro teenager walks into the employment office with his hair processed or natural, again nonverbal messages are received. Once again, depending upon how the professional translates these messages, there may be breaks in the communication relationship.

SUMMARY AND CONCLUSION

The more the overlap in life experiences, the easier it is for two individuals to communicate on an interpersonal basis. Conversely, as the respective source's and receiver's fields of experience have less in common, it becomes more and more difficult for the two individuals to have effective interpersonal communication. In the United States, the middle-class oriented professional and the poor person represent divergent fields of experience, and hence communication between them is very difficult. In one set of experiences one has three balanced meals per day and in the other one is lucky to get one daily plate of beans and a piece of bread. One has individual beds while the other has to share a single bed with a brother and a sister. One person goes in for regular dental and medical check-ups whereas the other views a doctor's bill as missed meals, two more months before you obtain a cheap, new pair of shoes, and one more month behind on the gas bill. The communication difficulties between professional and poor people are increased even more when two different ethnic groups are involved, i.e., Black-White, White-Puerto Rican, Chinese or Black. An essential step to overcoming these barriers will obviously involve people seeking understandings of the divergent cultures in America. On the college campuses this understanding can be enhanced by Black and other ethnic studies.

NOTES

1. Wilbur Schramm, *The Process and Effects of Mass Communication* (Urbana, Illinois, 1955), p. 6.

2. *Ibid.*

3. Edward T. Hall and William Foote Whyte, "Intercultural Communication: A Guide to Men of Action," *Human Organization*, XVIV (1960), pp. 9–10.

4. Frank Reissman, "The Indigenous Nonprofessional—A Strategy of Change for Community Mental Health Programs," Report No. 3, National Institute of Labor, Education, and Mental Health Programs (November, 1964), p. 8.

5. Edgar S. Cahn and Jean C. Cahn, "The War on Poverty: A Civilian Perspective," *Yale Law Journal* LXXIII (July, 1964), pp. 1134–1335.

6. *Ibid.*

7. Oscar Lewis, *Five Families* (New York, 1959).

8. Oscar Lewis, "Culture of Poverty," *Scientific American* (October, 1966), p. 19.

9. *Ibid.*

10. Ben H. Bagdikian, *In the Midst of Plenty: A New Report on the Poor in America* (Baltimore, 1966), p. 49.

11. Michael Harrington, *The Other America* (Baltimore, 1966), p. 156.

12. Bagdikian, p. 49.

13. Harrington, p. 22.

14. Ralph Segalman, "The Cultural Chasm," *Harper's Magazine* (October, 1965).

15. Robert Coles, "The Poor Don't Want to be Middle-Class," *Selective Reading Series*, No. 7, California State Department of Welfare (1965), p. 16.

16. Frank Riessman, *The Culturally Deprived Child* (New York, 1962), pp. 7–8.

17. *Ibid.*

18. *Ibid.*

19. Lloyd W. Warner and Paul S. Lunt, *The Social Life of a Modern Community* (Connecticut, 1941).

20. Lloyd W. Warner, *Social Class in America* (New York, 1960), p. 31.

21. Margherita MacDonald, Carson McGuire, and Robert J. Havighurst, "Leisure Activities and the Socioeconomic Status of Children," *American Journal of Sociology*, LIV (1949), pp. 505–519.

22. Paul F. Lazarsfeld and Patricia Kendall, *Radio Listening in America* (New York, 1948).

23. Wilbur Schramm and David M. Whyte, "Age, Education and Economic Status as Factors in Newspaper Reading," reported in *The Process and Effects of Mass Communication* (Urbana, Illinois, 1955), pp. 71–74.

24. *Ibid.*

25. Edward T. Hall, *The Silent Language* (Connecticut, 1959), pp. 33–34.

Cultural Patterns of the Elderly

CARL W. CARMICHAEL

In the United States, concern for the elderly citizens has grown considerably in the last decade. The overwhelming evidence ranges from the recent emergence of academic departments of gerontology to the hundreds of congressional bills passed and government programs created to aid the elderly. Yet, all this attention hasn't put a dent in the problems of growing old in a youth-oriented culture.

What to do with the aged has been a problem in virtually every society. While treatment of the elderly varies widely from culture to culture, viewing this subpopulation as a "problem" has not varied. Interestingly, one of the related issues on which we do find considerable cultural variance is the degree to which older people are integrated into the mainstream of normal cultural existence—the work force, the family, social life. Or, to look at the other side of that coin, the degree to which older people are *excluded* from the mainstream of their society. It has been argued that the Oriental cultures, though rapidly changing in recent years, have a long history and tradition of utilizing the resources of the older citizens and integrating them more fully into the culture than do Western cultures.[1]

Unquestionably, the United States has not been successful in integrating the elderly into the mainstream of American culture. Three of the major reasons for this are quite relevant to the theme of this book. First, one could argue that integration of the aged is not a cultural goal. Some societal-level policies are intended to have quite the opposite effect, segregation of the aged from the rest of society—for example, mandatory retirement as a means to remove older people from the work force without regard to the individual's desire or ability to continue working. Second, it is not always recognized that this is a cultural-level problem. Our entire culture has placed the aged into a separate, subcultural category—with our attitudes, with our beliefs, and with our stereotypes. Third, many aspects of this cultural problem are communication related and therefore not so obvious to the gerontologist or the legislator who is not tuned to a communication orientation.

I. INTEGRATION NOT A CULTURAL GOAL

As individuals, we may feel great compassion for the plight of our elders and advocate strongly that people should remain in active roles and a viable part of our culture for as long as they live; but as a society we have collectively acted to make it difficult for this to happen. In fact, many of our cultural policies unmistakably are intended to militate against integration of the aged into the mainstream of society.

The most blatant example of this is mandatory retirement. In our culture one's occupation often becomes one's identity. "What do you do?" is the almost rote conversation opener in America because we elevate others in terms of the occupational roles they play in society.

One's job is also a major social outlet. For many people, most of their primary social affiliations are occupationally related, whether they are the breadwinner or the breadwinner's spouse. Obviously, the typical person in our culture depends on the work place to meet the normal needs of affiliation and social attachment. The loss of one's job can be a devastating disruption in the fulfillment of these needs. Such is the case when workers reach retirement age and discover they are no longer part of the social system at the office or the mill.

This original essay appeared in print for the first time in the third edition. All rights reserved. Permission to reprint must be obtained from the publisher and the author. Professor Carmichael is with the Center for Gerontology and the Speech Department at the University of Oregon.

This is not the place to debate the complicated issues relating to retirement. Anyway, the problem is not retirement *per se*, but the fact that retirement is mandatory. The point here is that mandatory retirement is a government-imposed, cultural mechanism the intent of which is to remove people after a certain age from the job market. In our culture, when someone is removed from the job market, he or she is well on the way to being removed from the mainstream of society. Rather than attempt to integrate our elders into the culture, in the United States the goal seems to be to eliminate them from the active roles that contribute to society.

II. AGING AS A CULTURAL PROBLEM

There are times when any one of us feels very much alone; we are born, struggle for survival, and go to our graves alone. Yet, while that kind of feeling may be justified, the reality is that we cannot live in a social vacuum in this complex, interpersonally interdependent culture. Our lives are inextricably interwoven with many other individuals and institutions. We cannot escape the rules, the laws, the social conditioning, the media—the basic socialization process of our culture.

The aging process may appear at first to be a uniquely individual experience, but that is simply not the case. It can be argued that the aging process is very much related to the attitudes toward aging, the beliefs about aging, and the stereotypes of aging found within the culture.

Attitudes

Numerous studies have been conducted in recent years to discover what the attitudes of our culture are toward older people and the aging process. Nearly 300 such studies were reviewed in an exhaustive literature survey conducted by this author.[2] The subjects in these studies ranged in age from preschool to the very elderly in their nineties. While the findings are far too diverse to express in detail here, one general conclusion prevails: From the teenage years and on, the attitudes of people in our culture toward growing old are fairly negative. They don't begin that way, as many of the studies with younger children reveal, but something in our culture changes attitudes negatively around the age of puberty. Communicologists must now seek to learn how these attitudes are communicated, what factors reinforce them, and how they can be changed.

The phenomenon at issue here should be of great concern to us. Although the concept of attitude has been difficult to define, it usually refers to some kind of a cognitive evaluation. An attitude is how we feel about something, how much we like or don't like something. Unquestionably, how we feel about older people and the aging process—the prevailing attitudes toward aging in our culture—relates to how we treat our elderly in this culture, as well as to how we are affected by the aging process ourselves as individuals.

Beliefs

There exists in our culture a broad set of beliefs, or misbeliefs, about aging. Cultural commmunication, from generation to generation, has perpetuated myths of aging that have become so widely accepted they are all but impossible to change, even in the face of recent scientific evidence to the contrary. Consider a few salient examples and check your own beliefs in each case:

When people get old, they can expect increased memory dysfunction.

You can't teach an old dog new tricks.

Intelligence declines in old age.

One of the worst problems in old age is being lonely.

People become more religious as they grow older.

Older people have no interest in sex.

The list could go on; however, these are typical examples of beliefs that are not only widely accepted in our culture but have been disputed in recent gerontological research. Some have even received popular coverage in the media, such as the CBS Special, "Sex After Sixty." Yet, such beliefs are so firmly grounded in the American culture that change does not come easily and many older people are quite directly affected by them. In fact, one could argue quite legitimately that one of the worst problems our culture imposes on its aging members is this belief mythology. Psychologically induced states of "oldness" may occur as a result of the self-fulfilling prophecy phenomenon and a belief system in America that abounds with myths or at least half-truths that are more applicable in the very elderly years than they are at a relatively younger 60 or 62 when the word *old* becomes appropriate in our culture. Quite possibly, many older people have aged prematurely by adopting the age-related characteristics they have come to believe must exist after a certain age.

Stereotyping

In some ways, the stereotyping process is a necessary evil. On the positive side, it enables communication efficiency in the sense that communication about a person or a group of people can be simplified by identifying them in terms of their most basic, widely believed characteristics. One might argue that whether or not those beliefs are accurate is irrelevant, as long as they come from the belief system of the communication receivers. Yet, this process, by nature, invites inaccuracy. So, on the negative side, people who are stereotyped are identified only in terms of those "common denominator" characteristics that are believed but are not necessarily true and that relate to a whole category of people but not necessarily to the individual.

Stereotyping requires cooperation on a cultural level. When an actor portrays an old man, he turns to the most convenient symbols of "oldmanness" his culture provides: white hair, stooped posture, a cane, a hearing aid, a harsh, raspy voice. Note that the culture provided those symbols and therefore the actor was able to communicate the image of this character efficiently to an audience from that culture.

The problem for older people in this regard is obvious. Negative stereotypes, or at least inaccurate ones, are perpetuated by this process. The image that younger people have of their elders, the image that older people have of themselves, is affected by the stereotypes we see through the media and elsewhere. The burning question, of course, is who is at fault? Is the actor guilty of perpetuating a negative image? Or, does he merely reflect cultural beliefs—that just happen to be inaccurate and negative? When Carol Burnett plays her famous crotchety old woman role, should she be faulted for portraying characteristics that are unduly negative and that are not true of most older women? Or, should she be commended for cleverly choosing characteristics that are at least true of some older women and that are hilariously funny to most of her viewers?

While those questions may be unanswerable, at least we must consider the problem the stereotyping process produces for older people. The stereotypes of aging come out of a cultural belief system that is highly inaccurate. Since we relate to others to a great extent on the basis of their image, our relationships with our elders are thereby greatly affected by false and often negative beliefs. That these images can sometimes be portrayed as funny by a comedian is no great solace for one who tries to age gracefully in a culture that sees the aging person as ugly, wrinkled, stooped, deranged, decrepit, slow, sexless, and crotchety.

III. AGING AS A COMMUNICATION PROBLEM

The field of gerontology has focused on a particular population subgroup and has had a "social problem" orientation. The study of aging and problems of the aged necessarily has been an interdisciplinary venture. Unfortunately, until recently, communication has not been included as one of its traditional subdisciplines.

However, the kind of knowledge and the kind of perspective found in communication obviously would be useful in dealing with this or any other social problem. Certainly, one could argue that *any* social problem or cultural phenomenon could not be fully understood without studying the communication systems that relate to it. But, more specifically, many of the problems of the aged are quite directly *communication problems* and should be studied as such.[3]

The relevance and the value of communication to aging begins at the very heart of how the field of communication has defined itself. Two of the major conceptual aspects of communication are: (1) information processing, and (2) human interaction—interpersonally or through media. Not only do many of the traditionally studied problems of aging relate to one or the other of these, but analysis from this "communication perspective" leads to new areas of study that have great potential in gerontological theory development.

Information Processing

Communication—whatever the setting, the level, or the type—inherently involves the processing of information. The individual human organism encodes, decodes, packages, distorts, relays *information*, as does the group, the business organization, the social system, and the culture. Some of the oldest and most researched theories of aging relate to information processing.

Recent research on changes in memory functioning as a result of aging has led to a reevaluation of widely held beliefs previously confirmed by early research.[4] Similarly, intelligence deterioration was always assumed to be a normal function of aging but is now a controversial area thanks to recent findings and improved research techniques.[5] Questions relating to linguistic functioning or "language facility" are now being asked by gerontologists.[6] The processing of nonverbal cues was the focus of a paper delivered by this author at the 1980 national meeting of the Gerontological Society.[7]

One of the most serious communication problems that old people experience is the reduction of information to process because of age-related sensory losses. Under normal conditions of aging, older people can expect noticeable decreases in sensory abilities—hearing, vision, touch sensitivity, and distinguishing tastes and smells. Furthermore, some abnormal conditions of severe health impairment, that are age-related at least in terms of frequency, result in serious communication problems. Strokes often damage the speech centers in the brain. Arteriosclerosis can reduce the oxygen supply to the brain and can affect any of the information processing functions. Surely the communication process is significantly affected when any of these normal or pathological changes in information processing occur. How the process is affected and how improvements can be made in each case are socially relevant research questions for the communicologist.

Human Interaction

While communication, in its broadest sense, can include the study of computer systems or even animal behavior, the bulk of the research and writing in this field has focused on human interaction. Most current definitions of communication contain the concept of interaction (transaction, linking, and so on), and most communicologists are primarily, if not exclusively, concerned with interaction on the human level. In our coursework and in our research, we have studied every type of setting—from the classroom to the business conference room—and every size of group—the dyad, the triad, the small group, the assembly, the social system. Yet, almost none of this tremendous accumulation of knowledge relates specifically to older people.

There is no reason to believe that the basic, human need to communicate—to interact with other human beings for socializing, decision making, or whatever—should change with age. Older people, by virtue of their membership in the human race, are subject to the same communication anxieties, the same communication needs, the same communication breakdowns, the same communication dependencies, the same communication problems in relationships, and in the same kinds of settings—from the family (perhaps now a redefined unit for them) to the classroom—that younger people experience. Older people use the media (some studies indicate they use the media more than younger people do), perhaps even as a substitute for dwindling interpersonal communication.

Our culture has chosen to ignore many of the normal communication needs of our older citizens. After retirement, social contacts decrease. For some, this is a slow process that begins at retirement and continues through the young-old years (60 to 72), but for others the change occurs abruptly at retirement because most of their friendships were job related. Through the middle-old years (72 to 80), most older people experience the death of their closest friends and, perhaps, their spouses. Then, ultimately, in the old-old years (80 and older) most older people experience considerable aloneness or, worse yet, institutionalization—a cultural mechanism to care for the infirmed elderly that has been described by some as inhumane.

Some of the needs of older people get widespread attention, especially the medical and economic problems. But our culture has not shown concern for the communication needs of the elderly. The only communication mechanisms that our culture provides for the older person are the media. But, then, how much of the content of the media is geared to the older audience?

It may very well be that older people in our culture are communication starved. Many experience a state of communication deprivation that could be affecting other aspects of their lives, including such social psychological phenomena as life satisfaction, self-esteem, or even the will to live. If so, as a culture we have not responded to this problem.

Cross-cultural comparisons, many of which are reported in the gerontology literature, show that the United States may have one of the worst track records for integrating the aging population into the mainstream of our culture.[8] This problem is very much a *communication* problem.

The problem could be solved in part by changing the retirement system and enabling part-time employment for older people. Perhaps some assistance could come in the form of increased educational opportunities for the aged, or more organizations for them to join, or even more attention in the media. But, the problem isn't just one of the employment, or education, or clubs. On a cultural level, we must change our attitudes, beliefs, stereotypes, values, and so on that affect the aged on an individual level. Such change begins on the individual level but permeates the communication systems of the culture.

NOTES

1. Erdman Palmore, *The Honorable Elders* (Durham, N.C.: Duke University Press, 1975). Note, however, that this author, from his own research and travel in Japan, does not agree with the overly optimistic views expressed by Palmore. See C. W. Carmichael, "Aging in Japan and America: A Communication Perspective," *Journal of the Communication Association of the Pacific*, Fall 1978.

2. Carl W. Carmichael, "Attitudes Toward Aging Throughout the Life Span," *Journal of the Communication Association of the Pacific*, VIII, August 1979, pp. 129–151.

3. For a more elaborate discussion of this idea, see Carl W. Carmichael, "Communication and Gerontology: Interfacing Disciplines," *Western Speech Communication*, XL, Spring 1976, pp. 121–129.

4. For example, see Jack Adamowicz, "Visual Short-Term Memory and Aging," *Journal of Gerontology*, 31 (1976), 39–46.

5. For example, see Paul Baltes and K. W. Shaie, "Aging and IQ: The Myth of the Twilight Years," *Psychology Today*, March 1974, pp. 35–40.

6. For example, see Frain Pearson, *Language Facility and Aging*, Ph.D. Dissertation, University of Oregon, 1976.

7. Carl W. Carmichael and Jean McGee, "Nonverbal Communication and the Aged," paper presented at

Gerontological Society Conference, San Diego, Calif., 1980.

8. Donald Cowgill and Lowell Holmes (eds.), *Aging and Modernization* (New York: Appleton-Century-Crofts, 1972).

Are Women Human Beings? Androcentricity as a Barrier to Intercultural Communication

MARILYN J. BOXER

The New Woman is Human first, last, and always. Incidentally she is female; as man is male.

—*Charlotte Perkins Gilman, 1910*[1]

Traditional Woman, on the other hand, is "over-sexed." For the contemporary reader this term may evoke an image of a James Bondian female, defying natural elements and espionage rings to bed the lusty hero. When Charlotte Perkins Gilman coined it almost a century ago, she referred to that least "sexy" social creature, the passionless *true woman* of Victorian ideology for whom sexual intercourse represented a fulfillment of duty to man, God, and country, and perhaps, a desire for children.[2] Social analyst Gilman, concerned to place relations between the sexes in a historical, and especially, an evolutionary perspective, believed that the human species had perverted nature by constructing a social order that exaggerated the sex-linked characteristics of women to the exclusion of their basic human traits. As a result, woman was "over-sexed," that is, compelled to live within a constricted, feminine world of domesticity in which her dress, manners, education, work, and social relations all were defined by her sexual function. Unlike man, Gilman said, for whom the whole world was home, the home was woman's world. All else, all other employments, had been labelled by men "man's work." Whenever a woman sought to move beyond her "sex functions," beyond domesticity, she was accused of behaving like a man, of being "de-natured" or "un-sexed." "When a doe wishes to run far and fast," Gilman wrote, "she is not 'unfeminine,' she is not 'making a buck of herself.' She likes to run, not because she is a doe, but because she is a deer, just as much of a deer as he is." But humanness, which Gilman defined as the abilities to devise, utilize, and adapt tools and to invent and develop social relations—the capacities that she assumed distinguished the human species from others—had been defined as male, and woman was considered "but a side-issue (most literally if we accept the Hebrew legend!)"[3] Gilman's conception of woman as "over-sexed" thus implies connotations similar to those that contemporary women find in the term "sex object." Both reflect male-centered, or androcentric, assumptions about women and relations between the sexes. These assumptions, unnamed and rarely examined, influence social relations between the sexes. By labelling the social world androcentric, Gilman hoped to reveal and ultimately to remove attitudes, customs, and institutions that, by denying women their full humanity, hindered the progress of the human species.

In the act of naming, as Edith Folb points out elsewhere in this volume, we assert the importance of a phenomenon.[4] Listing a series of labels for various forms of communication, she includes international, intercultural, intracultural, interracial, interethnic, and others. She offers, however, no category for communication between the sexes. If "intergender communication" remains unnamed, it is perhaps because of the same androcentricity, in the academic as well as the social world, that, until the last fifteen years, led to the virtual exclusion of women-oriented, or gynaecocentric, studies from the humanities and social sciences. And absent for whatever reason, the continuing neglect of essays in women's studies[5] contributes to the perpetuation of male-centered, male-dominated cultures and to bodies of knowledge that are incomplete if not also invalid, while, if present, such new perspectives throw light on old questions. Concepts of society and culture, of hierarchy, power, and dominance, which Folb here establishes as basic to understanding intracultural communication, also determine relations between the sexes. If they help to explain "Whose culture is passed on? Whose social order is maintained?" they also reveal—if we dare to ask the questions—how ideology and institutional power have been invented and structured to serve male interests. Women have been named—and defined—by men and in relation to men. The social, i.e., male, construction of "femininity" has even led to consideration by partisans of both possible answers, of the question, *Are* women human beings?[6]

Feminists have long recognized "femininity" as an androcentric invention.[7] Feminist scholars have demonstrated how relations between the sexes are socially structured to maintain a male-serving balance of power that—rather than "nature"—distorts perceptions of reality, troubles communications between the sexes, and keeps women down. Such analysis also answers the question, Why don't women rebel?

If the origins of language and literature, of history, and of philosophy, remain largely shrouded in obscurity, their power to shape our concepts of ourselves and our social world is quite evident.[8] Applied toward answering the questions at hand, we might begin with a process essential to all humanistic studies, that of naming. The first human being, according to Hebrew myth, was Adam, or "adham," a generic word for humankind applied to the legendary and originally androgynous first creature of God. Following the second, and more familiar version of creation in Genesis, only after God fashioned a second being from Adam's rib did sex appear in human history. Called "wo-man" because she was taken from man, henceforth the generic word "man" would also mean "male" but not female.[9]

It has long been asserted that use of a generic term for all human beings, the old conventional "he/man" approach, includes by intention individuals of both sexes. According to its advocates, it represents a case of "man embracing woman"[10]—while its challengers point out, more literally, that "woman" includes "man."[11] The impossibility of replacing "man" with "woman" in a generic sense, however, has been explained by reference to recent scholarship in linguistics and semiotics. This analysis employs the concept of "markedness" to describe an asymmetrical relationship of complementary opposite terms within a larger class, in which one but not the other of the terms can be used to designate the entire class, and thus subsume its complementary—but unequal—opposite.[12] So "man embraces woman" but woman does not include man.[13]

Although forty years ago the historian Mary Ritter Beard puzzled over the willingness of men of precision—lawyers, literary critics, scientists, and scholars—to tolerate the linguistic ambiguity inherent in the use of "man" to denote both human beings and biological males,[14] it was only with the advent of the women's liberation movement of the 1970s that a broad-based, sustained, and relatively successful attack on sexist language was launched. Whatever the alleged intention of such usage, numerous studies demonstrate that it creates confusion, harms children, and erects a linguistic barrier to intergender communication.

But the recognition that women are considered less generically human than men does not depend on intent and interpretation. It is stated explicitly in the words of the men whose works form the basis of western philosophy and civilization. It is integral to the definitions of womanhood promulgated by the philosophers of antiquity as well as to the social scientists of modernity. The men who have described—and prescribed—women's roles, the philosophers, priests, physicians, psychologists, psychoanalysts, professors, and politicians, have all agreed: "Man is the measure of all things"; women are measured by man's standard. Let men speak for themselves.

First Aristotle, the greatest of Greek philosophers mused:

The female, in fact, is female on account of an inability of a sort, viz, it lacks the power to concoct semen ... We should look upon the female state as being as it were a deformity, though one which occurs in the ordinary course of nature.[15]

Over a millennium later, Aquinas, the greatest of medieval Catholic theologians, wrote:

As regards the individual nature, woman is defective and misbegotten, for the active force in the male seed tends to the production of a perfect likeness in the masculine sex; while the production of woman comes from a defect in the active force or from some material indisposition, or even from some external influence. ... On the other hand, as regards human nature in general, woman is not misbegotten but is included in nature's intention as directed to the work of generation.[16]

If by the twentieth century philosophers and theologians had given way to psychologists and journalists as the sources of popular wisdom, the old ideas remained the basis of much modern thought about the roles of women. The most influential of practitioners of the new "science" of mind, Freud, could escape his androcentricity no more than Aristotle. He defined women in terms of what they lack, women's self-consciousness as a result of a "missing" organ and the:

momentous discovery which little girls are destined to make. They notice the penis of a brother or playmate, strikingly visible and of large proportions, at once recognize it as the superior counterpart of their own small and inconspicuous organ, and from that time forward fall victim to envy for the penis.

Boys, after their analogous discovery of anatomical differences, develop, Freud asserts, "horror of the mutilated creature or triumphant contempt for her." Freud's penis-centered androcentricism so defined his perspective that he saw the female human being as a deficient male, whose personality development followed from "the fact of being castrated," and the resulting "wound to her narcissism . . . [which] she develops, like a scar." The "inferiority of the clitoris" he accepted *a priori*.[17]

The mind of Aristotle thus reached across the centuries to echo in modern social science and reach general audiences through journalism and other mass media. Grant Allen, a well-known American journalist of the early twentieth century, declared that women constituted "not the human race . . . not even half the human race but a sub-species set apart for purposes of reproduction merely.[18] As Gilman observed, men saw in women only their male-defined femininity. The four-hundred-year "Querelle des femmes" concerning women's "nature" and education, the nineteenth century "woman question" about "woman's place,"[19] and their twentieth century imitations make no sense except in a culture that dichotomizes, polarizes, and ascribes social roles and social space on the basis of sex. As Xenophon in the early fourth century B.C. ingeniously claimed that God had endowed women with more natural timidity and less tolerance for harsh weather than men, so that they might be content to stay at home watching men's possessions, so Erik Erikson in the twentieth century A.D. invented an analogy between the "inner space" occupied by women's primary reproductive organs and "feminine" affinity for inward-directed play and social relations.[20]

Translated into social reality, these androcentric prescriptions of woman's place, role, and destiny affect every aspect of human behavior and material culture. Through dichotomization of human characteristics into opposing poles, whose desirability varies by gender, women are deemed more "feminine" and attractive if "not at all aggressive, very emotional, and very dependent," while men are judged more "masculine" and attractive if "very aggressive, not at all emotional, and not at all dependent." Mental health practitioners, moreover, use these stereotypic traits to formulate definitions of mental health which then serve prescriptively to limit the expression of human qualities by both

sexes.[21] But given the differential value placed upon them by (our androcentric) society, women clearly lose more in the process.

Incorporated into social institutions, polarized and androcentric thinking influences not only language, literature, thought, and communication but also architecture, dress, religion, law, school, professions, and even sports and games. In ancient Greece, the houses of citizens included a section called the "gynacaeum," or women's quarters; men's "place" was everywhere else. From the Chador and veil to the "itsy-bitsy, teeny-weeny, yellow polka-dot bikini" of the 1960s song and the torn, off-the-shoulder sweatshirt popularized by a 1983 movie, *Flashdance*, women's garments, not men's, are designed to hinder or to entice men's glances; never was "the center of [man's] dress-consciousness . . . the codpiece.[22] Adam's sin in the garden of Eden was never used to proscribe pulpit or forum for men, while Eve's (though elicited by the devil himself rather than, as Adam's, by mere woman)[23] became the rationalization for centuries of denial of women's religious, political, and educational aspirations. The limitations on women's access to higher learning and better employments all reflect androcentric assumptions about women's "role," justified if not by religion, then by androcentric definitions of "nature." But who defines nature?

The "laws of (woman's) nature" have been prescribed by androcentric philosophers. Women should not, said Rousseau, complain about men's laws; it is nature that decrees women's subordination to men. "Women do wrong to complain of the inequality of man-made laws; this inequality is not of man's making; or at any rate it is not the result of mere prejudice but of reason."[24] One of the stars of the eighteenth-century Enlightenment, Rousseau lit a beacon followed by generations of men who discovered "natural laws" which lent new credibility to old misogyny. Scientists of the social as well as of the natural world, almost exclusively male, they also invented and promulgated a myth of "scientific objectivity" that has served to mask the unacknowledged values and motives which shape the very questions raised, as well as the interpretations of findings.[25] Centering definitions of womanhood on sexual functions, biologists and medical scientists in the nineteenth century replaced the "curse of Eve" with the monthly "curse" as a rationale for women's subordination, and the weakness of Eve's will (in resisting the serpent) with the smallness of the female brain.[26] Recognizing neither the moral choice nor the imbalance of political power reflected in his statement, one typical speaker told his medical college audience in 1847 that:

It would no doubt be a great boon to the human race ... if women could do the marvelous things men have done, like vote, own property, and get a proper education. But such was clearly not nature's design when she gave females a head almost too small for intellect but just big enough for love.[27]

In perhaps the most succinct of such androcentric, self-serving prescriptions for women, the French philosopher of anarchism and architect of decentralized, family-based labor organization, Proudhon, declared, "Housewife or harlot"; all women must be one or the other. In his name, generations of French working-class men voted resolutions to restrict the entrance of women into the paid labor force.[28]

The confusion of "nature" with men as arbiters of women's destiny was noted, with some irony, by the great philosopher of nineteenth-century liberalism, John Stuart Mill. If childbearing and wifehood were the "natural" employments of women, why close all others to them? Men, in fact, he pointed out, act as if women's alleged natural mission were the least attractive of occupations for the majority of them.[29]

Yet, short of universal anti-female armies, men could not have "monopolized all human activities, called them 'man's work' and managed them as such," as Gilman put it, had women in mass resisted. The acquiescence of women in an androcentric culture that allowed them such meager leavings from the men's table must be explained. There have always been women who, in words first read in 1848 at the Woman's Rights Convention in Seneca Falls, New York, "publish their degradation

by declaring themselves satisfied with their present position, [and] their ignorance, by asserting that they have all the rights they want."[30] The "fascinating woman," the "total woman," the "positive woman" created by contemporary apologists for androcentricity, have learned the psychology of powerlessness. Without authority, they gain their ends by well-turned deference and manipulation.[31] And, despite empirical evidence to the contrary, they declare their happiness with a social institution, marriage, that is in fact bad for women's health and good for men's.[32] That women don't rebel, that a collective consciousness of the injustices of our androcentric world has only lately developed, reflects the forces of both ideology and economics. John Stuart Mill, noting a difference between the oppression of classes of slaves and serfs and of women, suggested that if lords and masters had striven not only to gain their workers' labor power but also, as with women, their affections, slavery and absolute monarchy would reign supreme still. Mill pointed out that:

If it had been made the object of the life of every young plebeian to find personal favour in the eyes of some patrician, of every young serf with some seigneur; if domestication with him, and a share of his personal affections, had been held out as the prize which they all should look out for, the most gifted and aspiring being able to reckon on the most desirable prizes; and if, when this prize had been obtained, they had been shut out by a wall of brass from all interests not centering in him, all feelings and desires but those which he shared or inculcated; would not serfs and seigneurs, plebeians and patricians, have been as broadly distinguished at this day as men and women are? and would not all but a thinker here and there, have believed the distinction to be a fundamental and unalterable fact in human nature?[33]

To Gilman, however, it was less the power of affection than of bread—subsistence—that enabled men to dominate women. Coining the term "sexuo-economic" to describe the link between the sexual attractiveness of women and their ability to win a provider, she pointed out that human beings "are the only animal species in which the female depends on the male for food, the only animal species in which the sex-relation is also an economic relation."[34] Ending in the same place as Mill, the economic determinist says, "Whoever depends on another for her or his subsistence, is a slave."[35] Or at best, a bird in a gilded cage.[36]

None of this is new. Androcentric definitions of womanhood, of women's "nature" and women's "place," are, as the examples above attest, coeval with western civilization. Nor is protest by women against androcentricity of recent origin; its vintage dates from the same harvest. But leaving the history of feminism to students inclined to further research,[37] I want to conclude by raising questions about some of the consequences for intergender communication of confounding malekind with mankind. Beyond the omission of women from recorded history and canonized literature, from male ghettos of power in business, government, science, and religion;[38] beyond the perpetuation of distorting language, biased values, and incomplete interpretations, all documented by scholars in women's studies, lie barriers to interpersonal communication and human development. What are the effects on the consciousness of men, and on the consciousness of women, of thousands of years of androcentric thought and denial of female-centered experience? What are the ethics of a world designed to privilege one-half of its inhabitants? How would men and women relate to each other if the concept "opposite sex" were replaced with that of "neighboring sex?"[39] If power, authority, achievement, and reward followed individual merit without distinction by sex? If men and women stopped playing—and being—macho and kitten?

The list of potential changes in female behavior in language alone is long. Knowing themselves equally important and powerful as men, women might affect different speaking styles and conversational interactions. They might lose the "genderlect" that reflects and sustains their condition as not-male in an androcentric society.[40]

Linguists have shown that women and men speak different languages, and that "women's language" serves to keep them in "their place." According to the work of Robin Lakoff and others, girls typically learn to use speech filled with tag endings, question marks, meaningless particles, fence-hedging modifiers, euphemisms and hypercorrect grammar—speech that is deferential, exquisitely polite, and "lady-like." Women's speech is designed to seek approval, avoid conflict, and contain sexuality. Women demonstrate socially acceptable femininity, on the one hand, by avoidance of colorful, colloquial, vulgar words, and, on the other, by the employment of expressions suggesting refinement of taste in trivial matters: never "prick" but of course, "periwinkle."[41] Success in acquiring women's language, however, concomitantly assures failure in achieving social power:

The acquisition of this special style of speech will later be an excuse others use to keep her in a demeaning position, to refuse to take her seriously as a human being. Because of the way she speaks, the little girl—now grown to womanhood—will be accused of being unable to speak precisely or to express herself forcefully. . . . So a girl in this situation is damned if she does, damned if she doesn't. If she refuses to talk like a lady, she is ridiculed and subjected to criticism as unfeminine; if she does learn, she is ridiculed as unable to think clearly, unable to take part in a serious discussion: in some sense, as less than fully human.[42]

Women's secondary status in a "man's world" also affects their behavior in intergender communication. Studies of "conversational politics" show patterns of interruption that favor men over women. Power differences similarly influence the relative success of men and women in introducing and sustaining conversational topics: one study showed that topics introduced by men were further developed almost three times as often as those brought up by women.[43] Women constitute what anthropologists call a "muted group," not necessarily silent but forced to "encode" their thoughts in a language and to ground their actions in a definition of themselves derived from male reality.[44]

Today, however, some women are seeking a

new voice. Scholars and poets, they are exposing the pervasive androcentricity which has denied them full humanity, which has deprived their sex even of a name of its own. If language is, as Susan Sontag believes, "the most intense and stubborn fortress of sexist assumptions,"[45] then a new, feminist and woman-centered speech might create hairline fractures in the structural girdings of our androcentric world. New perceptions—of women and by women—might provoke new behavior patterns, and altered language might elicit revision of intergender communication. No longer muted, women, empowered to speak and to act, might create a new idiom and a new society.[46]

The nineteenth-century American feminist Elizabeth Cady Stanton once pointed out that all new ideas were once old. The "New Woman" is not a novel creature of the modern world. She is simply the age-old female of the human species, viewed without androcentric blinders. She is woman renaming herself. She envisages her own new self:

I will be neither a woman nor a man in the present historical meaning. I shall be some Person in the body of a woman.[47]

NOTES

1. Charlotte Perkins Gilman, "Our Androcentric Culture; or, The Man-made World" [hereafter OAC], *The Forerunner* I, no. 3 (Jan. 1910), p. 12; also *The Man-made World; or Our Androcentric Culture* (New York: Charlton Co., 1911). In her preface to the book, Gilman credits the American sociologist Lester F. Ward for his gynaecocentric theory of life, which along with his concepts of androcracy and androcentrism he developed in his treatise on social origins, *Pure Sociology* (New York: Macmillan, 1903). The term "androcentric" is commonly employed by contemporary American feminists, while English and continental feminists tend toward (often pejorative) use of the analogous word "phallocentric."

2. See Nancy Cott, "Passionlessness: An Interpretation of Victorian Sexual Ideology, 1790–1850," in Nancy F. Cott and Elizabeth H. Pleck, eds. *A Heri-*

tage of Her Own (New York: Simon & Schuster, 1979), pp. 162–181. Regarding the "cult of true womanhood" in the nineteenth-century United States, see Barbara Welter, "Cult of True Womanhood," *American Quarterly* XVIII (Summer 1966), pp. 151–174.

3. "OAC," in *The Forerunner* I, no. 1, p. 21, and no. 5, p. 18.

4. Edith A. Folb, "Who's Got the Room at the Top? Issues of Dominance and Nondominance in Intracultural Communication," pp. 119–127 in this volume. Folb lists women along with people of color among the nondominant groups made invisible and dehumanized by those in power (p. 123).

5. For a history and analysis of the development of women's studies, see Marilyn J. Boxer, "For and About Women: The Theory and Practice of Women's Studies in the United States," *Signs: A Journal of Women in Society and Culture* VII, no. 3 (Spring 1982), pp. 661–695.

6. According to August Bebel, the church council at Macon in the sixteenth century debated whether or not woman had a soul and decided in the affirmative by a majority of one vote. August Bebel, *Women Under Socialism*, 33rd ed., trans. Daniel De Leon (New York: New York Labor News Co., 1904), p. 52. See also Charlotte Perkins Gilman, "Are Women Human Beings?" *Harper's Weekly* (May 25, 1912).

7. On the development of feminist consciousness by the late medieval humanist writer, Christine de Pisan, see Joan Kelly, "Early Feminist Theory and the *Querelle des Femmes*, 1400–1789," *Signs: Journal of Women in Culture and Society* VIII, no. 1 (Autumn 1982), pp. 4–28. See also Susan Groag Bell, "Christine de Pisan: Humanism and the Problems of a Studious Woman," *Feminist Studies* III, nos. 3/4 (Spring/Summer 1976), pp. 173–184.

8. Refer, for example, to Martha Lee Osborne, *Women in Western Thought* (New York: Random House, 1979) and Barrie Thorne, Chris Kramarae, and Nancy Henley, *Language, Gender, and Society* (Rowley, Mass.: Newbury House, 1983).

9. Casey Miller and Kate Swift, *Words and Women: New Language in New Times* (Garden City, New York: Anchor Press, 1977), pp. 15–16.

10. Wendy Martyna, "Beyond the 'He/Man' Approach: The Case for Nonsexist Language," in *Signs: Journal of Women in Culture and Society* V, no. 3 (Spring 1980), pp. 482–493, especially p. 485.

11. Theodora Wells, "Woman—Which Includes Man, Of Course, An Experience in Awareness," first published in *Newsletter, Association for Humanistic Psychology* VII, no. 3 (December 1970).

12. Judith Shapiro, "Anthropology and the Study of Gender," *Soundings* LXIV, no. 4 (Winter 1981), pp. 446–465.

13. For an interesting analysis of the generic interpretation, see "Who Is Man?" in Miller and Swift, pp. 17–35.

14. Mary R. Beard, *Woman As Force in History: A Study in Traditions and Realities* (New York: Macmillan, 1946; Collier Books, 1962), p. 59.

15. Aristotle, *Generation of Animals*, trans. A. L. Peck (Loeb Classics, Harvard University Press, 1943), Book 1, pp. 101, 103, 109, 113; Book IV, pp. vi, 459f; cited in Julia O'Faolain and Lauro Martines, eds., *Not In God's Image* (New York: Harper & Row, 1973; Harper Torchbook, 1973), pp. 119–120.

16. St. Thomas Aquinas, *Summa Theologica*, trans. by Fathers of the English Dominican Province, 22 vols. (London, 1921–1932), Vol. IV, Pt. I. Quest. XCII, art. 1, 2; Quest. XCIII, art. 4; cited in O'Faolain and Martines, p. 131. These philosophers took care to turn a potential source of female superiority, girls' more rapid achievement of maturity, into a sign of inferiority: "After birth it [a female] quickly arrives at maturity and old age on account of weakness, for all inferior things come sooner to their perfection or end, and as this is true of works of art so it is of what is formed by nature." Aristotle, *On The Generation of Animals* IV 6 (775a18–23), quoted by Maryanne Cline Horowitz, "Aristotle and Woman," *Journal of the History of Biology* vol. 9, no. 2 (Fall 1976), p. 204.

17. Sigmund Freud, "Some Psychical Consequences of the Anatomical Distinction between the Sexes," in Freud, *Collected Papers*, ed. Ernest Jones, vol. 5, chapter XVII (New York: Basic Books, 1959), pp. 186–197.

18. Grant Allen, "Woman's Place in Nature," *The Forum* (May 1889), quoted by Gilman in *Women in Economics* (New York: Harper & Row, 1966), pp. 171–172.

19. See Susan Groag Bell and Karen M. Offen, *Woman, the Family, and Freedom: The Debate in Documents*, vol. 2 (Stanford, Calif.: Stanford University Press, 1983) and Kelly, "Early Feminist Theory."

20. Xenophon, "How Ischomachus Trained His Wife," *Oeconomicus,* trans. E. C. Marchant, in Nancy Reeves, *Womankind: Beyond the Stereotypes* (Chicago: Aldine–Atherson, 1971), pp. 156–160; Erik Erikson, "Inner and Outer Space: Reflections on Womanhood," *Daedalus* (Spring 1964), pp. 588–593. I owe to Reeves the recognition of the parallelisms in these two works. On Xenophon and his view of women's roles, see Stewart Irvin Oost, "Xenophon's Attitudes toward Women," *The Classical World* 71, no. 4 (December 1977–January 1978), pp. 225–236.

21. Inge K. Broverman et al., "Sex-Role Stereotypes: A Current Appraisal," *Journal of Social Issues* 28, no. 2 (1972), pp. 59–78.

22. Dorothy L. Sayers, "The Human-Not-Quite-Human," in Sheila Ruth, *Issues in Feminism: A First Course in Women's Studies* (Boston: Houghton Mifflin Co., 1980), p. 168.

23. I owe this idea to nineteenth-century feminists. See, for example, Sarah Grimke, *Letters on the Equality of the Sexes and the Condition of Woman* (New York: Burt Franklin, 1838; reprint, 1970), pp. 6–10; also see Lillie Devereaux Blake, "Comments on Genesis," in Elizabeth Cady Stanton, et al., *The Woman's Bible* (New York: European Publishing Co., 1898; reprint ed., Seattle: Coalition Task Force on Women and Religion, 1974), p. 26.

24. Jean Jacques Rousseau, *Emile*, trans. Barbara Foxley (New York: E. P. Dutton & Co., 1911; reprint ed., 1955), p. 324.

25. See Thomas Kuhn, *The Structure of Scientific Revolutions* (Chicago: University of Chicago Press, 1962), on the myth of scientific objectivity.

26. Angus McLaren, "Doctor in the House: Medicine and Private Morality in France, 1800–1850," *Feminist Studies* II, 2/3 (1975), pp. 39–54; Charles Rosenberg and Carroll Smith-Rosenberg, "The Female Animal: Medical and Biological Views of Woman and Her Role in Nineteenth-Century America," *Journal of American History* LX, no. 2 (September 1973), pp. 332–356; and Ruth Hubbard, "The Emperor Doesn't Wear Any Clothes: The Impact of Feminism on Biology," in Dale Spender, ed., *Men's Studies Modified: The Impact of Feminism on the Academic Disciplines* (Oxford: Pergamon Press, 1981), pp. 213–235.

27. C. D. Meigs, "Lecture," cited in Hubbard, p. 215.

28. J. P. Proudhon, *La Pornocratie ou les femmes dans les temps modernes* (Paris: A. Lacroix et Ce, 1875). For further discussion of Proudhon's views on women, see Marilyn J. Boxer, "Foyer or Factory: Working Class Women in 19th Century France," in Brison D. Gooch, ed., *Proceedings of the Second Annual Meeting, Western Society for French History* (College Station, Texas: Texas A & M University Press, 1975), pp. 193–203.

29. John Stuart Mill, *The Subjection of Women* (London: Longmans, Green, Reader, and Dyer, 1869; reprint ed., Cambridge: M.I.T. Press, 1970), p. 28.

30. "Declaration of Sentiments and Resolutions, Seneca Falls Convention, 1848," in Wendy Martin, ed., *The American Sisterhood* (New York: Harper & Row, 1972), pp. 42–46. Originally in Elizabeth Cady Stanton et al., eds., *History of Woman Suffrage* I (New York: Fowler & Wells, 1881–1922), pp. 70–73.

31. See, for example, Helen B. Andelin, *Fascinating Womanhood* (Santa Barbara, Calif.: Pacific Press, 1975); Marabel Morgan, *The Total Woman* (Old Tappan, N.J.: F. H. Revell, 1973); and Phyllis Schlafly, *The Power of the Positive Woman* (New Rochelle, N.Y.: Arlington House, 1977).

32. Walter R. Gove and Jeannette F. Tudor, "Adult Sex Roles and Mental Illness," *American Journal of Sociology* 78 (January 1973), pp. 50–69.

33. Mill, p. 17.

34. Gilman, *Women and Economics*, p. 5.

35. Nineteenth-century German feminist Louise Otto; quoted by Clara Zetkin, *Zur Geschichte der proletarischen Frauenbewegung* (Berlin: Dietz, 1958), pp. 74–75. Also Alexander Hamilton; quoted by Susan B. Anthony, "Social Purity, 1875," in Martin, ed., p. 91. Originally in Ida Husted Harper, *The Life and Work of Susan B. Anthony* II (Indianapolis, 1898), 1004–1012. Gilman felt that "no human creatures can be free whose bread is in other hands than theirs"; "Economic Basis of the Woman Question," *Woman's Journal*, Oct. 1, 1898.

36. George Bernard Shaw, cited in Betty Roszak and Theodore Roszak, eds., *Masculine/Feminine* (New York: Harper & Row, 1969; Harper Colophon, 1969), pp. 53–61. Also Gilman, "Economic Basis."

37. On feminism in modern history see, for example, Alice S. Rossi, ed., *The Feminist Papers: From Adams to de Beauvoir* (New York: Columbia University Press, 1973; Bantam Books, 1974).

38. For a striking visual image, see "The View from the Sexual Ghetto," in Reeves, pp. 135–152.

39. Sayers, p. 168.

40. Mary Brown Parlee, "Conversational Politics," in Laurel Richardson and Verta Taylor, eds., *Feminist Frontiers: Rethinking Sex, Gender, and Society* (Reading, Mass.: Addison-Wesley Publishing Co., 1983), pp. 7–10, especially p. 9.

41. Robin Lakoff, *Language and Woman's Place* (New York: Harper & Row, 1975).

42. Lakoff, cited in Miller and Swift, p. 99.

43. Parlee, p. 8. See also C. Kramarae, *Women and Men Speaking* (Rowley, Mass.: Newbury House, 1981).

44. The theory of muted groups, developed by British anthropologists Edwin and Shirley Ardener, is discussed in Shirley Ardener, ed., *Perceiving Women* (New York: John Wiley & Sons, 1975), pp. xxii–xvii and 21–25. On the silence of women, see also Tillie Olsen, *Silences* (New York: Dell, 1979).

45. Susan Sontag, "The Third World of Women," *Partisan Review* 40, no. 2 (1973), p. 186.

46. About the impact of language on perception, see Barbara Fried, "Boys Will Be Boys Will Be Boys: The Language of Sex and Gender," in Ruth Hubbard, Mary Sue Henifin, and Barbara Fried, eds., *Women Look at Biology Looking at Women* (Cambridge, Mass.: Schenkman, 1979), pp. 37–59.

47. From "Variations on Common Themes," *Questions féministes* no. 1 (November 1977), quoted in Elaine Marks and Isabelle de Courtivron, eds., *New French Feminisms: An Anthology*, trans. Yvonne Rochette-Ozzello (Amherst: University of Massachusetts Press, 1980), p. 226.

Sunday's Women: Lesbian Life Today

SASHA GREGORY LEWIS

In all the words about coming out, about lesbian revolution, about a brave new world, it seems like we're losing touch with the best of what we had: our tribes, our lesbian nation, our partisan underground if you want to call it that.

—Frances

The preliberation lesbian experience was primarily one of isolation, adaptation, and persecution. These were the roots of the "partisan underground" described by Frances. Two elements—isolation from one another, and adaptation to rapid change—are the supposed critical factors of future shock. They may, if society as a whole cannot cope with them, create the third element key to a partisan underground: persecution.

The lesbian subculture described by Frances, by virtue of the persecution it faced, was one of small groups of women who had come to trust each other implicitly. Though some might call them friendship cliques, they are, more realistically, extended families. Frances calls them tribes. When one or two tribeswomen would leave for new territory—because of persecution, job transfer, or hopes of greater economic opportunity—they would join or form another support group of trusted women. It was a process that continued until the contacts made by all of the individual women involved stretched, link by link, across the nation and sometimes into foreign lands. At a few points these links crossed both socioeconomic strata and race. This is what Frances calls her "lesbian nation." It was, and for the most part remains, a subculture in hiding.

Certain aspects of this subculture, particularly the trust and emotional support it provides, are reminiscent of another kind of group that flourished when communities were more stable and when moving to a different town was a major life event: the heterosexual women's community. Coexisting with the male community as a separate subculture, women formed tightly knit support groups in which they shared the familial love, lore, and wisdom of their lives. This heterosexual women's support network, now only a relic, broke down as America became a mobile society. The elements that bound this network had been time spent together, experiences shared over the years, and histories of generations of familial ties. As these disappeared, so did much of the strength of heterosexual female bonding.

The lesbian subculture has not had a history of generations of familial ties. It has also probably always tended toward greater mobility than the mainstream, in response either to persecution or to the hope of something new and better elsewhere. In many cases the time spent together by lesbians was months, not decades. Yet the warmth and support existing in the lesbian subculture in hiding was probably as strong, perhaps stronger, than that in the heterosexual female subcultures; and it developed a lore and wisdom of its own. The primary functions of the lesbian subculture in hiding have been to provide emotional support, both in a general and in a direct personal manner, to provide survival information and news, and to offer hospitality and help to migrating tribe members.

It is this subculture in hiding, much more than the bars or organizations generally described by the media, that is America's true lesbian underground. Bell and Weinberg commented on this briefly with regard to their attempt to recruit lesbians for their study. Their recruitment attempts were made in the San Francisco Bay Area, a region offering a wealth of public lesbian connections. Recruitment was done through public advertising, bars, organizations, mailing lists, in public contacts by research representatives to organizations, and through personal contacts. Of the 785 lesbians eventually located for the recruitment pool, 42 percent were found through personal contacts. In contrast, only 18 percent of the men in the recruitment pool were located this way.

ADAPTATION DURING THE McCARTHY ERA

Viv speaks of subculture's adaptation during the McCarthy era: "Things were getting pretty tough at the time. There we were, right in Manhattan, where everything was going on, where our friends were, where all the bars were. But during those McCarthy years people stopped going to bars. With all of the newspaper headlines people began to be afraid to be seen around someone who might be questioned. You know, the press ignores it now, but they were investigating homosexuals as well. More often than not the latest news you seemed to hear from your friends was of someone who had lost her job in one way or another just on suspicion, without any investigation. Everyone was scared.

"Then there was a big exposé in *Confidential* about some new gay organization that they said was a communist front, this was in 1954. By then you weren't only afraid if you worked in almost any kind of job, you were afraid just to be gay, that you would get called in or investigated or in some other way implicated.

"So most of our group stopped going to the bars. We started more visiting at each other's homes. One of the nicest things was when, I forget what year it was, maybe 1954 or 1955, Tallulah Bankhead had her radio program, ninety minutes every Sunday afternoon. Of course, everybody thought she was gay. [No evidence suggests that she was.] We had a group of thirty or forty of us that would get together at somebody's house, just sort of pot luck and bring your own liquor and a little food. We'd all sit around together and listen to the show. And that was a lot of fun. That went on for seven or eight months, so it kept the whole big bunch of us together. We didn't see each other all week, but we'd meet together on Sunday for the show and spend the rest of the day together. Sometimes a program brings you together like that. I think that's how we survived that terrible period."

Bev added, "Among the things we'd talk about, of course, was the purge. We'd pick up tips on what to do to protect ourselves and other gay people. I was just starting work as an intake counselor at the state hospital, and it was a real problem because a lot of people who came in there, or who were brought in, were obviously gay. You knew it would go against them if you wrote that in their record, so you wrote down anything you could think of. There was a lot of talk about what we could write. You'd put in anything, 'adult adjustment problem,' or whatever you could write in. Anything but 'homosexual.'

"I'm not in that line of work anymore, but I know counselors and psychologists who are gay and still to this day won't write in anything about homosexuality into their patients' records."

Viv comments, "That must have been about twenty-five years ago, and we still have friends from those days. Every once in a while, one of them that moved or something, will come back onto the scene. Those kind of ties just don't ever really end."

Viv also recalls the kind of practical assistance her group tried to offer, "One time, I remember, one of the group did lose her job, a teacher. You would never have suspected anything about her, I mean, she didn't 'look' like a butch or anything. She was one of the nicest people around. Apparently someone had just gone with some rumor to the head of the school and that was enough to get her out. Actually, the guy who fired her gave her the chance to resign so her record wouldn't be completely ruined. But still there were blacklists and she knew she couldn't get a job in the state ever again. She was on the verge of killing herself. That job of hers meant everything to her. We spent a lot of time with her, keeping an eye out for her. Finally she decided that she'd be better off if she left the state. Naturally, she didn't have any money, so we took up a collection. We got up a few hundred dollars, which was a lot in those days, and some-

body found a place where she could stay in Pennsylvania with one of someone's friends until she got back on her feet."

This type of personal assistance continues in the subculture today. Explains one woman, "I had just got a job offer in Washington. We had to get there in a couple of days and we were completely broke. We were so down we didn't know how we were going to make the next month's rent. So we called around and in just a couple of hours we had rounded up several hundred dollars from people, and they weren't that well off either. They really had to dig for the money, but they did. Three of them gave us the names and phone numbers of people to call when we got up there. Other people might be able to get that kind of help from their families, but ours had long ago written us off. In a way, our real family was that extended network of lesbians. We had straight friends who offered to help, but when it came right down to it, it was those lesbians who came up with the bucks."

Recalls another woman, "Someone had shot through our windows and broken into our house. The police came and went, saying they couldn't do much about it except take a report. We were afraid that whoever it was might come back. So we called one of our friends, and in about an hour eight people came to our place and arranged a schedule so there would always be someone staying with us. It was incredible!"

Once accepted into the extended family, the lesbian is likely to find herself with a host of friends ready to care for her in emotional as well as physical crises. Because of a history of isolation from mainstream society, lesbians have learned that when it comes down to the wire, their real support and defense comes only from that which they can muster up from among their peers. Their peers, knowing that they may need similar assistance at a later time, do double duty to help their sisters in trouble. Explains another woman, "One of our good friends had just broken up with her lover and was getting very depressed. We were afraid she might do something drastic, like kill herself, and we knew she needed a lot of emotional support right then. A group of us got together to look out for her. We arranged between ourselves to call and visit her often and made sure she had plenty of invitations to visit all of us. We nursed her along for about six months before her depression ended."

A practical function of the extended family is its pool of information about reliable attorneys, counselors, doctors, and other professionals, many of whom are gay themselves.

LORE, WISDOM, AND CUSTOM

As an important survival mechanism, the extended family has its own codes of behavior. The primary taboo of the lesbian subculture in hiding is against breaking the code of silence about members' affectional preference to outsiders—any outsiders, even other gay people not integrated into the prime unit of the subculture, the extended family. The lesbian who violates this taboo is excluded from the family. If she gets a reputation for indiscretion in one family, she may find, through the network of links connecting many such families, that her reputation has spread to other groups which will also exclude her.

Sexual indiscretions are also rapidly communicated in America's lesbian underground. One woman reports that while on a job assignment in Portland she spent an intimate weekend with a woman she had just met. By the time she got back home to Philadelphia, her lover had already learned of her affair—from a woman living in Phoenix!

It is through such networks that the members of the subculture learn (sometimes inaccurately, but often with great accuracy), which public figures are gay. This type of transmission, for a minority with few role models who have made it on the national scene, is important in sustaining the subculture's self-respect. Such transmissions have generally focused on political leaders, performers, and in the military, on upper-echelon officers. In recent years, as elements of the lesbian movement have become more politically conscious, transmissions about those involved in politics have become important in the voting behavior of some lesbians.

Explains one, "We know, on factual evidence, that one very high official in our state is as queer as a three-dollar bill. So we've kept an eye out for her career. Sometimes people like that will, maybe in an effort to hide their sexual orientation, go out of their way to go against gay people and gay rights. If that happens, you can bet they never get another lesbian vote in this state again." Even at this level, however, the code of silence is not broken. Continues the woman, "Sometimes I have fantasies about blowing her cover to the press. That would get rid of one problem. But it's just something you don't do." To date, it has not been done, so strong is the taboo against revealing another woman's lesbianism until she herself is prepared to do so.

Sexual indiscretions, perhaps communicated via the Portland-Phoenix-Philadelphia route, are likely to be tolerated within a lesbian's extended family. Explains Viv, "One thing you do is try not to take sides in fights between lovers. Now, if one of the two has been really rotten and they've broken up, you might tend to exclude the woman who's done something like taken all the property, or begun to spread lies, or whatever. Generally, even after partners have broken up, both are still welcomed. You just learn, after being around awhile, that those things happen, and so you say 'too bad,' but that doesn't mean that either one of them was wrong."

Each extended family of the subculture has different characteristics. Generally, there is little class or racial mixing within a single extended family, despite the fact that one or more of its members might have contact with other families in different racial or socioeconomic groups comprising the greater subculture. Also, different groups develop different patterns of sexual relations among their members. Some groups are comprised of primarily monogamous couples maintaining careful boundaries between friendship and sexual intimacy. Others, however, are somewhat promiscuous among themselves, as Rae describes: "Before we moved, we had a group of gay friends who'd been together for years. And it seemed as if every one of those women had had an affair with everyone else in that group at one time or another. You couldn't exactly call it wife-swapping, because these affairs and new relationships lasted for several years. And you wouldn't exactly call it promiscuity because in general, once a couple go together, they stayed monogamous for a while. I don't know what you'd call it and I can't explain why they stuck together. I guess there just wasn't very much sexual jealousy. In heterosexual society, sexual jealousy is a big thing. Probably it comes from the male trip of considering women property and from the woman's fears of losing the guy who's supporting her. What was important to these women, I think, was their emotional closeness. And, of course, no one had to worry about losing her income.

"It wasn't the way we chose to live, but for those women it seemed to work out pretty well, except every six months or so there'd be this whole emotional thing when someone began taking an interest in someone new. But they all hung together. They're probably still together doing just the same thing. Maybe because most of them had lived with each other at one time or another they became a tighter group, I don't know."

In general, this kind of tolerance for sexual indiscretion is fairly widespread within the subculture in hiding. Among some women, it is almost a point of personal ethics to try to maintain a friendship with a former lover. "After all," explains Jo Ann, "what is really important about a relationship isn't just that you had good sex. What's important is that you have come to love someone. It just doesn't make any sense that when your relationship ends you stop loving them."

From this vast diversity of styles among extended families or tribes, come only a few points of similarity in terms of shared wisdom. Viv summarizes, "Besides not finking on someone, about the only other things you could say as generalizations are that first relationships generally don't work out, and, whatever you do, stay away from so-called bisexual and heterosexual women. They'll leave you every time. A lot of kids now are trying to have relationships with bisexual women who've fallen

for them. I've watched it time after time. The bisexual leaves and the lesbian is left up a creek."

SUBCULTURE GAP

The subculture in hiding is extremely difficult to penetrate. A major criticism leveled at the extended family institutions of this subculture by some lesbian activities is their closed nature. Women in such groups are likely to have known each other for several years, and while new members are sometimes welcome, the least welcome of all are lesbians with ties to the gay rights movement. Part of the difficulty at first appears to be generational. A mainstay of today's subculture in hiding are women who have survived the McCarthy era. These women are likely to have developed careers and a reasonable amount of economic security. They are reticent to trust outsiders. Commented Viv, who consented to be interviewed only after several assurances from people she trusted in her own extended family, "I didn't want to give an interview. I still have a hard time trusting you. I've got it in the back of my mind that there's a chance that you might blow my cover, maybe not even on purpose, maybe by accident. And where does that leave me? I'd lose everything I've spent my life building. I'd be on welfare."

On further exploration, it turned out that the difficulty between women like Viv and critics of the subculture is not generational. Among Viv's network of trusted friends are women as young as twenty-five. The difficulty between the activist and the subculture in hiding, it turned out, is the activist's activism. Said Viv, "Look, Bev and I are about as closeted as you can get. So are our friends. That's a kind of security for us. When you do hear from these radical lesbians, they're always trying to get you to come out. I've lived my life in the closet and I'm going to stay there. And I certainly don't want to be around anyone who's going to start telling me to come out. I simply am afraid of them. I don't trust them."

On the other side of the subculture gap are lesbian activists trying to organize for civil rights.

Commented one, "Look, we need those women. They have the money. They have the experience. And there they are, sitting comfortably in their safe little closets as if the movement didn't exist at all. Sometimes I think they're our worst enemies."

AN EMERGING SYNERGY?

Said Viv, "You know what finally convinced me to do this interview? Anita Bryant. I thought McCarthy was dead. But Anita Bryant and the referendum they had in California showed me that it could all start over again. I thought about it a lot. Yes, I'm closeted and will remain that way. But if you get a McCarthy in there, even a closet won't help you. If they want you, they're going to get you. If you really think about it, they could probably find every one of us just by looking through some computer tapes—credit references, car registration, whatever. So maybe this is just my small way of fighting back."

Added Bev, "This gay rights stuff wasn't much of anything to us. We managed before it. We never had any hassle over the last twenty years. It just didn't seem necessary to make an issue out of it when you thought there wasn't any problem. But now, maybe it's time to do something."

The potential for a creative and valuable synergy between the subculture in hiding and the public lesbian subculture has been developing over the past two decades as women have emerged from their closets to struggle for civil rights. Some of these women, generally viewed as less radical than most gay activists, have, over more than two decades, built contacts and eventually bonds of trust with members of the subculture in hiding. The foundation laid by these early lesbian activists—women like San Francisco's Phyllis Lyon and Del Martin, and Philadelphia's Barbara Gittings and Kay Tobin—has set a precedent showing that it can be safe for closeted lesbians of the hidden subculture to retain their anonymity, yet still contribute to the movement for social change.

As a result, while there is still no merger between the two subcultures, they more and more frequently cooperate, making the experience and expertise of the subculture in hiding available when called upon.

And called upon they were when the 1977–1978 antigay backlash of Anita Bryant, California state senator John Briggs, and others provoked a fear so threatening that many of the subculture in hiding were forced to remember the repression of the McCarthy era, and rather than see its persecutions re-emerge, helped gay rights activities as best they could.

As the lesbian subcultures enter the 1980s, it appears that both the public one and the one in hiding are at least accessible to each other through trusted intermediaries. One of the greatest ironies of such accessibility, and of a future when lesbians may not need to face the degree of isolation that created the subculture in hiding, is that the subculture itself may disappear. As the lesbian is increasingly accepted by mainstream society, her need for such a tight trust-bound network of support may diminish. She may then face the world of future shock without the survival mechanism that might make her uniquely adaptable to it.

CONCEPTS AND QUESTIONS FOR CHAPTER 3

1. Can you think of any other subcultures that fall into Folb's category of nondominant groups?

2. How do you suppose someone from a foreign culture would respond to one of our subcultures? Be specific.

3. In terms of the development of an experiential background, what does it mean to be poor?

4. What does Carmichael mean when he suggests that integration of the elderly is not a cultural goal?

5. Do the poor and the elderly suffer from the same set of cultural problems? How would you compare them?

6. What does Boxer mean by "androcentric thinking"? How does it affect men's perceptions of women and women's perceptions of themselves?

7. What is "women's language" and how does it influence women's position in society?

8. What are some of the characteristics of the lesbian subculture? How does being lesbian affect one's views of oneself relative to the dominant culture?

9. What do you believe to be the great challenges facing communication between lesbians and non-lesbians? Be specific. Give examples.

10. Do you believe that subcultural groups seeking to practice their way of life ought to be permitted that freedom?

11. What is the relevance of the difference in which racial and ethnic minorities have been treated in the United States?

12. Why does the history of a culture or subculture offer us insight into its communication behaviors?

SUGGESTED READINGS

Bahr, H. M. *Skid Row: An Introduction to Disaffiliation*. New York: Oxford University Press, 1973. This book deals with homeless skid row dwellers as a subculture. It presents a detailed profile of the skid row individual and looks at the social organizations, both formal and informal, that are found on skid row.

Blubaugh, J. A., and D. L. Pennington. *Crossing Difference: Interracial Communication*. New York: Charles Merrill, 1976. This brief book is an introduction to the dynamics of interracial communication. The authors examine such topics as racism, power, language, nonverbal behavior, beliefs, and values.

Coles, R. *Eskimos, Chicanos, and Indians*. New York: Little, Brown, 1977. In this interesting and stimulating book, Coles looks at three cultures through the eyes of children. By talking to children and studying their drawings and paintings he is able to gather valuable insight into these three co-cultures living within the United States.

Eubanks, E. E. "A study of perceptions of Black and White teachers in de facto segregated high schools." *Education* 95 (1974), 51–57. Eubanks studied 97 teachers from six de facto segregated high schools, examining perceptions of job satisfaction, teacher-student relations, school status, attributes for success as a teacher, and opinions about the behavioral, emotional, and social characteristics of students.

Hess, B. "Stereotypes of the aged." *Journal of Communication* 24 (1974), 76–85. To better understand the myth and the reality of being old, Hess has reviewed the stereotypes of the aged and compared them to the real world. The factors that contribute to the stereotypes are also explained.

Kephart, W. M. *Extraordinary Groups: The Sociology of Unconventional Life-Styles*. New York: St. Martin's Press, 1982. This book is a collection of seven essays that focus on extraordinary groups. Kephart believes that a knowledge of these groups helps one understand subcultural diversity. The seven groups are gypsies, Old Order Amish, the Oneida Community, the Father Divine Movement, Shakers, Mormons, and Hutterites.

Kochman, T. *Black and White: Styles in Conflict*. Chicago: University of Chicago Press, 1981. This book presents points of misinterpretation between blacks and whites by examining differences in communicative style.

Lowney, J., R. W. Winslow, and V. Winslow. *Deviant Reality: Alternative World Views*. Boston: Allyn & Bacon, 1981. This collection of essays presents firsthand accounts of deviant subcultures such as nudists, alcoholics, prostitutes, and lesbians.

Luhman, R., and S. Gilman. *Race and Ethnic Relations: The Social and Political Experience of Minority Groups*. Belmont, Calif.: Wadsworth, 1980. This book gives an excellent view of minorities in the United States, detailing social and political experiences, social stratification, reactions to majority pressures, and the impact of pluralism.

Rosen, P. *The Neglected Dimension: Ethnicity in American Life*. Notre Dame: University of Notre Dame Press, 1980. This volume is designed to "afford students opportunities to learn more about the nature of their own heritage and to study the contributions of the cultural heritage of other ethnic groups." The rationale behind this book is that ethnicity is a neglected aspect of the study of American culture, and that to understand that culture one must study behavior associated with belonging to an ethnic group.

ADDITIONAL READINGS

Apaights, E. "Some dynamics of the Black family." *The Negro Educational Review* 24 (1973), 127–137.

Bell, A., and W. Weinberg. *Homosexualities: A Study of Diversity Among Men and Women*. New York: Simon & Schuster, 1978.

Briggs, N., and M. Pinola. "Contemporary American women: Conflict in roles and self concept." *The Journal of the Communication Association of the Pacific* 8 (1979), 165–174.

Clark, A. J., L. A. Weiman, and K. A. Paschall. "A preliminary report of an investigation of unwillingness to communicate among physically handicapped persons." *The Journal of the Communication Association of the Pacific* 12 (1983), 155–160.

Cogdell, R., and S. Wilson. *Black Communication in White Society*. Saratoga: Century 21, 1980.

Donaldson, J. "Changing attitudes toward handicapped persons: A review and analysis of research." *Exceptional Children* 46 (1980), 504–514.

Doyle, J. A. *The Male Experience*. Dubuque, Iowa: William C. Brown, 1983.

Ellis, D. "Ethnographic considerations in initial interaction." *Western Journal of Speech Communication* 44 (1980), 104–107.

Fletcher, P. "A comparison of adolescent sex-role perceptions among male and female Anglos and Chicanos." *The Journal of the Communication Association of the Pacific* 10 (1981), 87–115.

Freedman, M. *Homosexuality and Psychological Functioning*. Monterey, Calif.: Brooks/Cole, 1971.

Gentry, J., and M. Doering. "Sex role orientation and leisure." *Journal of Leisure Research* 11 (1979), 102–111.

Giallombardo, R. *The Social World of Imprisoned Girls: A Comparative Study of Institutions for Juvenile Delinquents*. New York: John Wiley, 1974.

Gordon, D. F. "The Jesus people: An identity synthesis." *Urban Life and Culture* 3 (1974), 159–178.

Hays, W. C., and C. H. Mindel. "Parental perceptions for children: A comparison of Black and White families." *Ethnic Groups* 1 (1977), 281–295.

Hur, K. K., and L. W. Jeffres. "A conceptual approach to the study of ethnicity, communication, and urban stratification." *The Journal of the Communication Association of the Pacific* 8 (1979), 67–87.

Jensen, G. F., J. H. Stauss, and V. W. Harris. "Crime, Delinquency, and the American Indian." *Human Organization* 36 (1977), 252–257.

Karon, B. P. *Black Scars*. New York: Spring Publishing Company, 1975.

Kitano, H. H. L. *Japanese Americans: The Evolution of a Subculture*. Englewood Cliffs, N.J.: Prentice-Hall, 1969.

Luhman, R., and S. Gilman. *Race and Ethnic Relations: The Social and Political Experience of Minority Groups*. Belmont, Calif.: Wadsworth, 1980.

McConnell-Ginet, S., R. Borker, and N. Furman, eds. *Women and Language in Literature and Society*. New York: Praeger, 1980.

Merry, S. E. "Racial integration in an urban neighborhood: The social organization of strangers." *Human Organization* 39 (1980), 59–69.

Mindel, C. H., and R. W. Habenstein, eds. *Ethnic Families in America: Patterns and Variations*. New York: Elsevier, 1976.

Mullen, R. W. *Black Communication*. University Press of America, 1982.

Nussbaum, J. F. "Relational closeness of elderly interaction: Implications for life satisfaction." *The Western Journal of Speech Communication* 47 (1983), 229–243.

Oyer, H., and J. Oyer. *Aging and Communication*. Baltimore: University Park Press, 1976.

Shanas, E., and M. B. Sussman. *Family, Bureaucracy, and the Elderly*. Durham, N.C.: Duke University Press, 1977.

Sherwood, R. *The Psychodynamics of Race: Vicious and Benign Spirals*. New Jersey: Humanities Press, 1980.

Shuter, R. "Initial interaction of American Blacks and Whites in interracial and intraracial dyads." *The Journal of Social Psychology* 117 (1982), 45–52.

Shuter, R., and J. Miller. "An exploratory study of pain expression styles among Blacks and Whites." *International Journal of Intercultural Relations* 6 (1982), 281–290.

Staiano, K. V. "Ethnicity as process: The creation of an Afro-American identity." *Ethnicity* 7 (1980), 27–33.

Tajfel, H., ed. *Social Identity and Intergroup Relations*. Cambridge: Cambridge University Press, 1982.

Thompson, T. L. "The development of communication skills in physically handicapped children." *Human Communication Research* 7 (1981), 312–324.

Thompson, T. L. "The development of listener-adapted communication in physically handicapped children: A cross-sectional study." *The Western Journal of Speech Communication* 46 (1982), 32–44.

Thompson, T. L. "You can't play marbles—you have a wooden hand: Communication with the handicapped." *Communication Quarterly* 30 (1982), 108–115.

4

Cultural Contexts

Communication does not occur in a vacuum. All communication takes place in a social setting or environment. We call this the context because the setting is never neutral; it always has some impact on the communication event by influencing how the participants behave. We have all learned culturally appropriate patterns of communicative behavior for the various social contexts in which we normally find ourselves. But, as in other aspects of intercultural communication, the patterns of behavior appropriate to various social contexts differ from culture to culture. Problems, therefore, sometimes arise when we find ourselves in strange contexts without an internalized set of rules to govern our behavior, or when we are interacting with someone who has internalized a different set of rules.

The classroom environment is one of these settings that specifically influences intercultural interaction. The rules, assumptions, values, customs, practices, and procedures of a given culture strongly affect the conduct of classroom activity. While many people naively believe that all classrooms are pretty much alike, Janis F. Andersen, in our first essay, takes the position that learning environments are different from culture to culture and that they alter the communication patterns of people within those environments. To support this assertion she highlights intercultural differences in classroom setting, teacher-student relationships, nonverbal behaviors, what is taught, and how it is taught.

A second cultural context in which intercultural communication frequently takes place, especially in domestic situations, is counseling. The relationship between counselor and client is an important one. An effective counselor understands his or her client and knows how to establish the relationship necessary to the counseling goals. These two tasks of understanding and knowing are made more difficult when the life experiences of the counselor are far removed from those of the client. Whether the difference is based on race, ethnicity, culture, or deviant values or behaviors, the counseling context is altered by the background of each of the participants. The

reasons for some of these alterations, in relation to nondominant cultural groups, is discussed in our next essay by Donald R. Atkinson, George Morten, and Derald Wing Sue.

They begin by examining some of the early attempts at minority counseling and point out how and why most of these programs failed. To better understand these failures the authors highlight some of the barriers often found in minority cross-cultural counseling and discuss those barriers that center around language differences, class-bound values, and culture-bound values. The authors also identify five "process manifestations of cultural differences" that are present to some extent in any counseling relationship that involves cultural differences. These are stereotyping, resistance, transference, countertransference, and client expectations. Being aware of the variables that influence the counseling setting helps conscientious communicators to better understand the messages of others, and to adapt to the specific client with whom they are working.

Our next article looks at the context of health care—yet another place where one's particular cultural experiences influence both the interaction and the outcome of the interaction. More specifically, the essay focuses on Hispanic women and health care. We have selected this particular culture both because Hispanics are the fastest growing nondominant population in the United States, and because it is a population that makes frequent use of the health care facilities in this country. Elizabeth Berry and Miriam Ojeda examine how the Mexican culture influences the way Hispanic women react to this communication context. They maintain that the prevailing image of the submissive Mexican-American woman is a stereotype derived from the use of completely misleading racist/sexist frames of reference. The authors propose an alternative image of Hispanic women that helps to explain their communicative behavior in health care settings.

The growth of international business during the last twenty years has been startling. Overseas transactions that were millions of dollars are now billions of dollars. In addition, the international business community has experienced a more pro-found change—business has become multination-al and organizational units include participants from a variety of cultures. In fact, the multination-al organization has become a subtopic of study within the fields of intercultural and organization-al communication. Successful businesspeople functioning in international business and world markets must learn about approaches to business practices that may be vastly different from their own or those they studied in school.

The Japanese approach to business and multi-national organizations is one of special interest, not only because of the financial impact the Japanese have had on the world economy, but also because of the unique ways in which they per-ceive the business context and the consequent implications for communication within multina-tional organizations. Lea P. Stewart, in her article "Japanese and American Management: Participa-tive Decision Making," examines Japanese and American management processes and their differ-ing styles of decision making and conferencing through an analysis and description of their nature and characteristics. She concludes with an observation that although Japanese companies are highly successful, we must first wonder whether we want to measure success in terms similar to those used by Japanese society before we start a wholesale application of Japanese management to U.S. corporations.

The final article, "Japanese Social Experiences and Concepts of Groups," focuses on the Far East. Dolores and Robert Cathcart explore how a cul-ture's view of a specific concept can influence be-havior. In this case, the concept is the Japanese view of groups. If one's experience with groups changes from culture to culture, then it follows that each culture might well bring a different way of acting to a group situation. The Cathcarts in-vestigate this issue when they compare Japanese concepts of groups with those found in the United States. Their essay clearly illustrates the impor-tance of what each of us brings to communication.

Educational Assumptions Highlighted from a Cross-Cultural Comparison

JANIS F. ANDERSEN

Nearly two decades ago, the anthropologist Edward Hall[1] argued that culture is a hidden dimension. He explained that culture penetrates our perceptual system, thus masking basic aspects of our existence which are immediately obvious to an outsider. Hall's position is now a basic tenet of intercultural communication,[2] but acknowledging this principle does little to reduce the size of the curtain of cul-ture. One context where the curtain obscures our vision is the classroom environment. The rules, assumptions, values, customs, practices, and proce-dures of a given culture strongly influence the con-duct of classroom activity.

Many people tend to think that all classrooms are pretty much alike. When asked to imagine a classroom interaction in central Illinois, southern California, northern New York, or even France, Brazil, or the Philippines, they basically picture an image of a classroom that they are most familiar with. They see different kinds of people in each of the various locations but their overall image of each classroom is quite similar. Maybe they picture wholesome looking, neatly scrubbed, conservative-ly dressed students sitting at desks in Illinois while they see blond-haired, informally dressed, sun-tanned individuals sitting in southern California classrooms, but the rest of the image reflects their

This essay was written especially for this volume. All rights reserved. Permission to reprint must be obtained from the publisher and the author. Dr. Andersen teaches at San Diego State University.

own educational experience. Probably the students are pictured sitting at desks that look the same—whatever location they are imagined to be in—and that are laid out in the same configuration. Probably even the classroom walls are visualized as the same color, perhaps a light institutional green or yellow gold.

The point is that people tend to think of the learning environment they are most familiar with as somehow representative of learning environments in general. Furthermore, even if these culturally based environmental images are not thought to be quite so generalizable, they are often held up as models for what is supposed to take place in a learning environment. If you were asked to create a classroom environment and to structure the interaction so that the most learning would occur, chances are you would create something very similar to the classroom you are now participating in. That may seem remarkable—you may not find your current situation ideal—but one's images of a proper learning environment are inextricably linked to one's familiarity and experience in learning environments. Teachers tend to teach the way they have been taught; parents treat their children the way they were treated. Culture's hidden dimensions influence our behavior.

Most Americans would not visualize a classroom with students naked from the waist up and would not have students snap their fingers and click their tongues to signal a desire to respond. Yet these are common behaviors in some other cultures and would seem normative to members of those cultures. The entire educational system, together with all the rules and procedures for proper classroom interaction, reflect a cultural dictate rather than a universal mandate.

The next section of this article highlights some intercultural differences in educational practices. These differences are interesting but not that informative; much more systematic, in-depth study of an individual culture, its institutions, and its people would be necessary to truly know another culture's educational system and to seriously improve our instructional encounters with someone from that culture. Instead, these intercultural anecdotes are more useful in enhancing understanding of our own educational system. Hall[3] believes that we can never really understand another's culture but our awareness of its diversity is a tremendous aid in better understanding our own culture. It is one way to see for ourselves what is so obvious to outsiders. By examining intercultural contrasts, this article highlights some assumptions of our culture about educational practices and instructional procedures.

If asked to describe a generic educational system, we might begin by talking about a classroom, a teacher, and some students. However, even these seemingly basic components reflect cultural assumptions. Classrooms are a relatively recent innovation that are still not used in schooling children in preliterate societies. Socrates, Plato, and Aristotle disseminated their teachings without the benefit of a blackboard and the comfort—or discomfort—of a classroom building. In the early 1970s the Metro School in Chicago was a complete high school without walls.[4] The classes met in museums, libraries, bookstores, and other interesting places. They taught a fascinating sociology class by having students walk the length of Halsted Street through numerous ethnic neighborhoods, where students dined in restaurants, visited with families, and observed street activity.

Teachers as we think of them also reflect a cultural bias. In the United States, it was not until around the Civil War period (1860s) that teachers became primarily female,[5] and many cultures still refuse to entrust the important process of educating their children to a stranger. One distinguishing characteristic of preliterate education is the kin responsibility for educating the young. Deciding which kin category will assume which responsibility is highly systematized; being a certain relative is a teaching credential for a specific content area. Instead of learning art from Mrs. Davis, home economics from Ms. Young, and woodworking from Mr. Smith, children learn pottery from their father's sister, cooking from their mother, and toolmaking from their mother's father.

Many of us think of teachers as being older than their students. Cultural anthropologist Margaret Mead states that this pattern reflects a culturally determined post-figurative learning paradigm.[6] In post-figurative societies, older people disseminate their knowledge to younger, less experienced and less knowledgeable individuals. Co-figurative cultures adopt primarily peer learning patterns, and pre-figurative societies learn from their younger members who are more up-to-date on changing knowledge. The one-room schoolhouses of the early 1900s relied more on co-figurative or peer instruction; and co-figurative patterns are more prevalent in preliterate and peasant societies. Pre-figurative learning patterns emerge in complex, industrial societies where rapid technological and scientific advances quickly outdate previously acquired knowledge. Thus, many successful fifty-year-old executives attend special seminars on computer technology that are taught by people twenty or thirty years younger than themselves.

Our acceptance of pre-figurative learning patterns permits and encourages younger students to inform or even to disagree with older teachers. In many cultures, particularly traditional Oriental ones, disagreeing with a teacher would not occur. In traditional Oriental societies, wisdom comes with age and all important learning is post-figurative. Furthermore, in some societies the teacher is a revered individual teaching sacred truth. Teachers in the United States have reported that rhetorical teaching devices like "You agree with that, don't you?" always receive a humble yes from young Vietnamese, Laotian and Cambodian immigrants, when they were intended to spark a lively discussion.

The teacher-student relationship is culturally mandated. The Israeli Kibbutz primary school system is highly informal, with close social relationships between teachers and students.[7] Students move from their desks at will to sharpen pencils, or to get a drink. They talk among themselves even during oral lessons, hum to themselves while writing, readily criticize teachers if they feel they are wrong, and address teachers by their first names. By our standards this may seem chaotic.

In sharp contrast to the warm social environment of the Kibbutz is the West African Bush School.[8] The head master of the school is the *da zo* "who is endowed with wisdom and mystic power in a superlative degree." In these schools the boys are grouped by age and aptitude, based on a series of tests, and then "all this training is tested in the laboratory of Bush school life. For example, instruction in warfare is accompanied by actual mock battles and skirmishes . . . entrance to the society is a symbolic death for the young, who must be reborn before returning to family and kin. Those who die from the strenuous life are considered simply not to have been reborn, and their mothers are expected not to weep or grieve for them."[9]

Classroom interaction rituals and patterns vary extensively from culture to culture. Even though we would obviously picture students in worldwide classrooms speaking their native languages in classroom interactions, we might picture all students raising their hands to begin an interaction. In Jamaica, however, primary school students flap or snap their fingers to signal they know the answer, and in Trinidad students put their index and middle fingers on their forehead with the inside facing out to ask permission to be excused.[10] Some cultures do not have a way for students to signal a desire to talk to the teacher since these students speak only after the teacher has spoken to them. There is virtually no classroom interaction in the Vietnamese culture, and in the Mexican culture all classroom interaction is tightly controlled and directed by the teacher.[11]

The Israeli Kibbutz is very noisy and interaction is spontaneous.[12] In sharp contrast, Chinese classrooms are so quiet that North Americans teaching there often find the silence unnerving.[13] Cultures reflecting a Buddhist tradition hold that knowledge, truth, and wisdom come to those whose quiet silence allows the spirit to enter. Our schools tend to reflect more of a Socratic, questioning, interactive search for truth.

Even within the U.S., subcultural differences create different interaction patterns. Children reared in middle-class home environments are generally taught an elaborate communication code, and their classroom answers tend to be long and involved. Lower-class children tend to learn more restrictive codes for interaction and are likely to answer questions with one-word answers.[14] Black children learn an interaction pattern that involves a lot of backchanneling. Backchanneling is a vocal listener response that is designed to reinforce and encourage the speaker in the black culture. Vocal utterances like "yeah," "right on," "go on," "amen," "ahuh," and "tell it" are examples of backchanneling phrases. White teachers not used to black interaction patterns are often offended by backchanneling and feel constantly interrupted rather than reinforced. Similarly, middle-class teachers often misinterpret short answers from lower-class children as indicating less knowledge rather than as reflecting a culturally learned interaction pattern.

Many nonverbal behaviors are culturally learned and the nonverbal literature is replete with examples of cross-cultural differences in interpreting these behaviors.[15] These nonverbal differences are also manifest in classroom environments. We show respect to teachers by looking at them when being spoken to, but in Jamaica looking is a sign of disrespect while not looking signifies respect.[16] Many West African cultures and black Americans also reflect the Jamaican pattern.[17] In Italian classrooms teachers and students touch each other frequently and children greet their teacher with a kiss on both cheeks while putting their arms around their teacher.[18] Chinese and Japanese children show complete emotional restraint in classrooms.[19] In short, our entire communication transaction, with its verbal and nonverbal messages, systematic patterns, and socialized rituals, is a reflection of our culture.

The use of time and our view of time reflects a cultural bias that alters our educational process. We value punctuality, often considering students who complete work more rapidly to be more intelligent, and designating certain time periods for certain curricular goals. Yet these clock-oriented values reflect a Western "monochronic" view of time.[20] The American Indian does things when the time is right, not when the calendar says it's a certain date. In many cultures, classes end when the subject matter has been thoroughly discussed rather than when the clock designates the end of the period. We measure education itself in time—

years spent in school—and it is only recently that we have allowed credit to be given for knowledge, rather than for investing a certain amount of time in a classroom focused on that knowledge. However, the entire notion of education as a timed process is a product of nineteenth-century thought.[21]

Finally, the central educational decisions about what is important to learn and how best to teach it are cultural decisions. Eskimo mothers exercise the arms of very young infants in the motions of paddling, and *Manu* children learn by one year of age to grasp their mothers firmly about the throat so they can ride in safety up and down rickety ladders while poised on the back of her neck.[22] In eighteenth-century Germany, noblemen's sons learned dancing, fencing, and riding while the bourgeoisie studied history, geography, physics, and chemistry.[23] High school curriculum planners today often consider art, music, and physical education frills while computer science, foreign language, and history are regarded as essential. One only need ask, Essential for what? to see the cultural bias.

Methods of teaching vary considerably. In a thorough outline of cross-cultural education, Jules Henry lists 55 different teaching methods.[24] Teaching by imitation, setting an example, using punishers or rewards, problem solving, guided recall, relevant association, irrelevant association, watching, doing, comparing, and student reports are only a few of Henry's categories. He reports a vivid example of teaching by watching from the writings of Chiang. Chiang says:

I do not remember that I ever had any proper lessons in painting from my father. He told me to watch him as closely as possible. . . . I remember that after watching my father painting a few times I thought I knew just how to paint, but when I actually began I found I was mistaken! . . . I asked my father to help, but he only smiled and told me to watch him again.[25]

The particular teaching method selected for instruction reflects cultural values more than it argues for the superiority of any one method. Cultures succeed in educating those they choose to educate, and who they choose to educate also reflects a cultural bias.

In an informative and interesting book on intercultural behavior, Geert Hofstede explores the differences in thinking and action among people from 40 different nations.[26] He argues that people have mental programs based on their cultural experiences that are both developed and reinforced by schools and other social organizations. Many of these patterns are so subtle that people fail to realize that things could be another way. By highlighting intercultural differences in classroom environments, we begin to realize that nothing about the educational process is absolute. Every component reflects a cultural choice, conscious or unconscious, about who to educate, how, when, in what subjects, for what purpose, and in what manner. Perhaps this realization will not only increase our tolerance for those educated in other systems, but will challenge us to improve our own educational processes.

NOTES

1. Edward T. Hall, *The Hidden Dimensions* (Garden City, N.Y.: Anchor Books, 1969).

2. Larry A. Samovar, Richard E. Porter, and Nemi C. Jain, *Understanding Intercultural Communication* (Belmont, Calif.: Wadsworth Publishing Co., 1981).

3. Hall.

4. *Chicago Sun Times*, December 6, 1972.

5. Jules Henry, "A cross cultural outline of education," in Joan I. Roberts and Sherrie C. Akinsanya, eds., *Educational Patterns and Cultural Configurations* (New York: David McKay Co., Inc., 1976).

6. Margaret Mead, *Culture and Commitment: A Study of the Generation Gap* (Garden City, N.Y.: Natural History Press, Doubleday & Company, Inc., 1970).

7. M. Spiro, *Children of the Kibbutz* (Cambridge, Mass.: Harvard University Press, 1958).

8. M. H. Watkins, "The West African 'Bush' School," *American Journal of Sociology* 48 (1943), 666–675.

9. Watkins, pp. 670–671.

10. Aaron Wolfgang, "The teacher and nonverbal behavior in the multicultural classroom," in Aaron Wolfgang, ed., *Nonverbal Behavior: Application and Cultural Implications* (New York: Academic Press, 1979).

11. Julie Becker, "A cross-cultural comparison of interaction patterns in the classroom" (Master's thesis, San Diego State University, 1983).

12. Spiro.

13. Wolfgang.

14. Philip S. Dale, *Language Development: Structure and Function* (New York: Holt, Rinehart & Winston, 1976), pp. 315–321.

15. See for example, Edward Hall, *The Silent Language* (Greenwich, Conn.: Fawcett Publications, 1959); Loretta Malandro and Larry Barker, *Nonverbal Communication* (Reading, Mass.: Addison-Wesley Publishing Co., 1983); Marianne LaFrance and Clara Mayo, *Moving Bodies: Nonverbal Communication in Social Relationships* (Monterey, Calif.: Brooks/Cole Publishing Co., 1978).

16. Wolfgang, p. 167.

17. Wolfgang, p. 167.

18. Wolfgang, p. 169.

19. Wolfgang, p. 170.

20. Malandro and Barker.

21. James J. Thompson, *Beyond Words: Nonverbal Communication in the Classroom* (New York: Citation Press, 1973).

22. Henry, p. 117.

23. Henry, p. 145.

24. Henry, pp. 100–170.

25. Henry, pp. 123–124.

26. Geert Hofstede, *Culture's Consequences: International Differences in Work-Related Values* (Beverly Hills, Calif.: Sage Publications, 1980).

Minority Group Counseling: An Overview

DONALD R. ATKINSON
GEORGE MORTEN
DERALD WING SUE

Until the mid 1960s, the counseling profession demonstrated little interest in or concern for the status of racial, ethnic, or other minority groups. Counseling and Guidance, with its traditional focus on the needs of the "average" student, tended to overlook the special needs of students who, by virtue of their skin color, physical characteristics, socioeconomic status, et cetera, found themselves disadvantaged in a world designed for White, middle class, physically able, "straight" people. Psychotherapy, with its development and practice limited primarily to middle and upper class individuals, also overlooked the needs of minority populations. By the late 1960s, however, "The winds of the American Revolution II . . . (were) . . . howling to be heard" (Lewis, Lewis & Dworkin, 1971, p. 689). And as Aubrey (1977) points out, the view that counseling and guidance dealt with the normal developmental concerns of individuals to the exclusion of special groups' concerns could no longer be accepted.

Events in the 1960s, however, would blur this simple dichotomy by suddenly expanding

potential guidance and counseling audiences to include minority groups, dissenters to the war in Viet Nam, alienated hippie and youth movements, experimenters and advocates of the drug culture, disenchanted students in high schools and universities, victims of urban and rural poverty and disenfranchised women (p. 293).

The forces that led to this voluminous, and often emotional, outcry in the professional counseling literature go far beyond the condition of social unrest existing in the United States in the late 1960s and early 1970s. The note of dissatisfaction was struck when the guidance movement first began and accepted, intentionally or unintentionally, the practically unfulfilled, idealistic promises of the Declaration of Independence as a guideline (Byrne, 1977). As Shertzer and Stone (1974) suggest, "The pervasive concept of individualism, the lack of rigid class lines, the incentive to exercise one's talents to the best of one's ability may have provided a philosophical base . . ." (p. 22) for the dramatic shift in emphasis the profession took almost 60 years after its inception. Fuel for the fire was added when the Civil Rights movement of the 1950s provided convincing evidence that the educational establishment had failed to make provision for equal educational opportunity to all and that the time had come to correct existing discrepancies. The fire of discontent was fanned into a bright flame as the political activism associated with the Viet Nam war touched almost all phases of American life.

Yet the promise of counseling and guidance for minority individuals remains, as yet, unfulfilled. Nor has counseling to date been able to bring much clarity to issues raised in the minority group literature. Central to all other considerations is the role of the profession itself vis-à-vis minorities. Should counselors work in the domain of "special" minority needs and experiences or should they continue to aim at serving the "middle American" population? While to some extent the question appears moot, one need only examine the curricula of major counselor training programs to deter-

From Donald R. Atkinson, George Morten, and Derald Wing Sue, *Counseling American Minorities*, 2nd ed. © 1979, 1983 Wm. C. Brown Publishers, Dubuque, Iowa. All rights reserved. Reprinted by permission of the publisher. Donald R. Atkinson teaches at the University of California, Santa Barbara. George Morten teaches at the University of Wisconsin, Milwaukee. Derald Wing Sue teaches at California State University, Hayward.

mine that the profession continues to train counselors for working with White, middle class, straight, mainstream clientele. Indeed, this has been a serious bone of contention for many minority professionals.

THE UNFULFILLED PROMISE OF COUNSELING FOR MINORITIES

Minority group authors, particularly those representing racial/ethnic minority groups, have been vociferous and unequivocal in their denunciations of the counseling profession since the mid 1960s. In a comprehensive review of counseling literature related to racial/ethnic minority groups, Pine (1972) found the following view of counseling to be representative of that held by most minority individuals:

. . . that it is a waste of time; that counselors are deliberately shunting minority students into dead end non-academic programs regardless of student potential, preferences, or ambitions; that counselors discourage students from applying to college; that counselors are insensitive to the needs of students and the community; that counselors do not give the same amount of energy and time in working with minority as they do with White middle-class students; that counselors do not accept, respect and understand cultural differences; that counselors are arrogant and contemptuous; and that counselors don't know themselves how to deal with their own hangups (p. 35)

Although Pine's article deals primarily with racial/ethnic minorities, similar views of counseling have been expressed by feminist, "gay," pacifist, and other activist minority groups ("Counseling and the Social Revolution," 1971).

To some extent minority group unhappiness with counseling reflects disillusionment with all the organized social sciences because of their poor performance as instruments for correcting social ills (Sanford, 1969). Psychology in particular has been criticized for its role as the "handmaiden of

the status quo" (Halleck, 1971, p. 30). Frequently minorities see psychology functioning to maintain and promote the status and power of the Establishment (Sue & Sue, 1972).

To a large degree, minority group dissatisfaction with the counseling profession can be explained as disenchantment with unfulfilled promises. As suggested earlier, counseling has at least covertly accepted such ideal rights as "equal access to opportunity," "pursuit of happiness," "fulfillment of personal destiny," and "freedom" as omnipresent, inherent goals in the counseling process (Adams, 1973; Belkin, 1975; Byrne, 1977). Although these lofty ideals may seem highly commendable and extremely appropriate goals for the counseling profession to promote, in reality they have often been translated in such a way as to justify support for the status quo (Adams, 1973).

While the validity of minority criticisms can and will be argued by professional counselors, there is little doubt that, for whatever reasons, counseling has failed to serve the needs of minorities, and in some cases, has proven counterproductive to their well-being. The fact that various minority groups are underrepresented in conventional counseling programs (Sue, 1973) suggests these groups see counseling as irrelevant to their needs.

There is evidence, for example, that ethnic minorities prefer to discuss emotional and educational/vocational problems with parents, friends, and relatives rather than professional counselors (Webster & Fretz, 1978). The lack of minority counselors in many counseling agencies may be a factor in underutilization and the preference for discussing personal concerns with friends and relatives. Thompson and Cimbolic (1978) found that Black college students were more likely to make use of counseling center services if Black counselors were available than if only White counselors could be seen for appointments. There is also substantial evidence that Asian Americans, Blacks, Chicanos, and Native Americans terminate counseling after an initial counseling session at a much higher rate than do Anglos (Sue, Allen & Conaway, 1978; Sue & McKinney, 1975; Sue, McKinney, Allen & Hall, 1974). Clearly, minorities see the counseling process, as currently implemented, as irrelevant to their own life experiences and inappropriate or insufficient for their felt needs.

When minorities do bother to seek treatment there is evidence that they are diagnosed differently and receive "less preferred" forms of treatment than do majority clients. In the area of diagnosis, Lee and Temerlin (1968) found that psychiatric residents were more likely to arrive at a diagnosis of mental illness when the individual's history suggested lower-class origin than when a high socioeconomic class was indicated. Haase (1956) demonstrated that clinical psychologists given identical sets of Rorschach test records made more negative prognostic statements and judgments of greater maladjustment when the records were identified as the products of lower-class individuals than when associated with middle-class persons. Broverman, Broverman, Clarkson, Rosenkrantz, and Vogel (1970) found sex also to be a factor in diagnosis, with less favorable judgments by clinical psychologists with respect to female clients than for male clients. In a related study, Thomas and Stewart (1971) presented counselors with taped interviews of a high school girl in counseling and found the girl's career choice rated more appropriate when identified as traditional than when identified as deviant (traditionally male attitude). Similar results have been cited by Schlossberg and Pietrofesa (1973). Mercado and Atkinson (in press) found that male counselors suggested sex-stereotypic occupations for exploration by a high school girl.

In the area of treatment, Garfield, Weiss, and Pollack (1973) gave two groups of counselors identical printed descriptions (except for social class) of a 9-year-old boy who engaged in maladaptive classroom behavior. The counselors indicated a greater willingness to become ego-involved when the child was identified as having upper-class status than when assigned lower-class status. Habermann and Thiry (1970) found that doctoral degree candidates in Counseling and Guidance more frequently programmed students from low-socioeconomic backgrounds into a noncollege bound track than a college preparation track. Research documentation of the inferior quality of mental health services pro-

vided to racial/ethnic minorities are commonplace (Clark, 1965; Cowen, Gardner & Zox, 1967; Guerney, 1969; Lerner, 1972; Thomas & Sillen, 1972; Torion, 1973; Yamamoto, James, Bloombaum & Hatten, 1967; Yamamoto, James & Palley, 1968).

Differential diagnoses and treatment of minorities is presumably a function of stereotypes held by counselors. Evidence that counselors do hold stereotypes of minorities is beginning to accumulate. Casas, Wampold, and Atkinson (1981) found that university counselors tend to group student characteristics into constellations reflective of common ethnic stereotypes. In a study employing an illusory correlation paradigm, Wampold, Casas and Atkinson (1981) found that nonminority counselor trainees are more likely to be influenced by stereotypes when assigning characteristics to ethnic groups than are minority counselor trainees. Finally, even when attempting to be sensitive to the needs of Mexican-American students, university counselors may base their counseling services on stereotypes that are not supported by research (Casas & Atkinson, 1981).

CRITICISM OF THE TRADITIONAL COUNSELING ROLE

Due in part to the unfulfilled promise of counseling for minorities, a great deal of criticism has been directed at the traditional counseling role in which an office-bound counselor engages the client in verbal interaction with the intention of resolving the client's psychological problems. For the most part, this criticism can be summarized as three interrelated concerns: criticism of the intrapsychic counseling model, criticism of how counseling approaches have developed, and criticism related to counseling process variables.

Criticism of Intrapsychic Counseling Model

Perhaps the strongest, most cogent indictment of the traditional counseling role has been criticism of the intrapsychic view of client problems inherent to some degree in all current counseling approaches. The intrapsychic model assumes client problems are the result of personal disorganization rather than institutional or societal dysfunctioning (Bryson & Bardo, 1975). Counselors, these critics argue, should view minority clients as victims of a repressive society and rather than intervene with the victim, counselors should attempt to change the offending portion of the client's environment (Banks, 1972; Williams & Kirkland, 1971).

The issue of whether one focuses on the *person* or *system* is an important one. Counseling in this country has grown out of a philosophy of "rugged individualism" in which people are assumed to be responsible for their own lot in life. Success in society is attributed to outstanding abilities or great effort. Likewise, failures or problems encountered by the person may be attributed to some inner deficiency (lack of effort, poor abilities, et cetera). For the minority individual who is the victim of oppression, the person-blame approach tends to deny the existence of external injustices (racism, sexism, age, bias, and so on).

Pedersen (1976) has suggested that the counselor can help the minority client either adopt, or adapt to the dominant culture. Vexliard (1968) has coined the terms autoplastic and alloplastic to define two levels of adaption; the first, "... involves accommodating oneself to the givens of a social setting and structure and the latter involves shaping the external reality to suit one's needs" (Draguns, 1976, p. 6). Thus, critics of the traditional counseling role see cultural adoption and the autoplastic model of adaption as repressive but predictable outcomes of the intrapsychic counseling model. The counseling roles they advocate can be viewed as directed toward the alloplastic end of the auto-alloplastic adaption continuum. . . .

Criticism of How Counseling Approaches Have Developed

Minority intellectuals have criticized contemporary counseling approaches which they contend have been developed by and for the White, middle class person (Bell, 1971; Gunnings, 1971; Mitchell, 1971). Little or no attention has been directed to the need to develop counseling procedures that are compatible with minority cultural values. Unimodal counseling approaches are perpetuated by graduate programs in counseling that give inadequate treatment to the mental health issues of minorities. Cultural influences affecting personality, identity formation, and behavior manifestations frequently are not a part of training programs. When minority group experiences are discussed, they are generally seen and analyzed from the "White, middle-class perspective." As a result, counselors who deal with the mental health problems of minorities often lack understanding and knowledge about cultural differences and their consequent interaction with an oppressive society.

Majority counselors who do not have firsthand experience with the minority client's specific cultural milieu may overlook the fact that the client's behavior patterns have different interpretations in the two cultures represented. Behavior that is diagnosed as pathological in one culture may be viewed as adaptive in another (Wilson & Calhoun, 1974). Grier and Cobbs (1968) in their depiction of Black cultural paranoia as a "healthy" development make reference to the potential for inappropriate diagnoses. Thus, the determination of normality or abnormality tends to be intimately associated with a White, middle class standard.

Furthermore, counseling techniques which are a product of the White middle class culture are frequently applied indiscriminately to the minority population (Bell, 1971). In addition, counselors themselves are often culturally encapsulated (Wrenn, 1962), measuring reality against their own set of monocultural assumptions and values, and demonstrating insensitivity to cultural variations in clients (Pedersen, 1976). New counseling techniques and approaches are needed, it is argued, that take into account the minority experience (Gunnings, 1971).

The issue is perhaps best represented semantically by the emic-etic dichotomy, which was first presented by the linguist, Pike (1954). Draguns

(1976) offers the following definition of these two terms:

Emic refers to the viewing of data in terms indigenous or unique to the culture in question, and etic, to viewing them in light of categories and concepts external to the culture but universal in their applicability (p. 2).

The criticisms relevant to the current discussion, then, focus on what can be called the "pseudoetic" approach to cross-cultural counseling (Triandis, Malpass, & Davidson, 1973); culturally encapsulated counselors assume that their own approach and associated techniques can be culturally generalized and are robust enough to cope with cultural variations. In reality, minority critics argue, we have developed emic approaches to counseling that are designed by and for White, middle class individuals.

Criticisms Related to Counseling Process Variables— Barriers to Minority Group/ Cross-Cultural Counseling

Much of the criticism related to minority group counseling focuses upon the interactions that occur between counselor and client. Counseling is seen as a process of interpersonal interaction and communication which requires accurate sending and receiving of both verbal and nonverbal messages. When the counselor and client come from different cultural backgrounds, barriers to communication are likely to develop, leading to misunderstandings that destroy rapport and render counseling ineffective. Thus, process manifestations of cultural barriers pose a serious problem in minority group/cross-cultural counseling.

Most of the writing on barriers to minority group/cross-cultural counseling has focused on racial/ethnic minorities as clientele with a major portion of these studies examining the White counselor–Black client relationship. It is evident, however, that many of the concepts developed by these authors have relevance to any counseling situation involving an individual from a minority (i.e.,

oppressed) group. It is equally clear that although presented from a majority counselor–minority client perspective, many of the same barriers may exist between a counselor and client who represent two different minority groups (i.e., two different cultures).

In the present discussion, we make a distinction between cultural barriers that are unique to a minority group/cross-cultural counseling situation (for example, language differences) and those that are process barriers present in every counseling relationship but are particularly thorny and more likely to occur in a cross-cultural situation (for example, transference).

Barriers Indigenous to Cultural Differences

In discussing barriers and hazards in the counseling process, Johnson and Vestermark (1970) define barriers as "... real obstacles of varying degrees of seriousness ..." (p. 5). They go on to describe cultural encapsulation as one of the most serious barriers that can affect the counseling relationship. Padilla, Ruiz, and Alvarez (1975) have identified three major impediments to counseling that a non-Latino counselor may encounter when working with a Latino client. Sue and Sue (1977) have generalized these barriers as relevant to all Third World people. We expand the concept further and attempt to relate the three barriers to all minority group/cross-cultural counseling situations. The three barriers are: (a) language differences; (b) class-bound values; and (c) culture-bound values. These three categories are used to facilitate the present discussion; it should be pointed out, however, that all three categories are recognized as functions of culture broadly defined.

Language Differences. Much of the criticism related to the traditional counseling role has focused on the central importance of verbal interaction and rapport in the counseling relationship. This heavy reliance by counselors on verbal interaction to build rapport presupposes that the participants in a counseling dialogue are capable of understanding each other. Yet many counselors fail to understand the client's language and its nuances sufficiently so as to make rapport building possible (Vontress, 1973). Furthermore, educationally and economically disadvantaged clients may lack the prerequisite verbal skills required to benefit from "talk therapy" (Calia, 1966; Tyler, 1964), especially when confronted by a counselor who relies on complex cognitive and conative concepts to generate client insight.

Sue and Sue (1977) have pointed out that the use of standard English with a lower class or bilingual client may result in misperceptions of the client's strengths and weaknesses. Certainly the counselor who is unfamiliar with a client's dialect or language system will be unlikely to succeed in establishing rapport (Wilson & Calhoun, 1974). Furthermore, Vontress (1973) suggests that counselors need to be familiar with minority group body language lest they misinterpret the meaning of postures, gestures, and inflections. For example, differences in nonverbal behavior are frequently seen in the comparison of Blacks and Whites. When speaking to another person, Anglos tend to look away from the person (avoid eye contact) more often than do Black individuals. When listening to another person speak, however, Blacks tend to avoid eye contact while Anglos make eye contact. This may account for statements from teachers who feel that Black pupils are inattentive (they make less eye contact when spoken to) or feel that Blacks are more angry (intense stare) when speaking.

Similar observations can be made regarding cross-cultural counseling with other, nonracially-identified minority groups. For instance, prison inmates have developed a language system that tends to change over a period of time. The naive counselor who enters the prison environment for the first time may find that his/her use of standard English may elicit smiles or even guffaws from clients, to say nothing of what this does to the counselor's credibility. Gays, too, have developed a vocabulary that may be entirely foreign to a "straight" counselor. Anyone who doubts this statement need only visit a gay bar in San Francisco or elsewhere and listen to the public dialogue. Any counselor un-

familiar with gay vocabulary is likely to be perceived as too straight by a gay client to be of any help. Gays, like other minority groups, rely heavily upon their own vernacular to convey emotions and, understandably, they prefer a counselor who can grasp these emotions without further translation into standard English.

Unique language patterns can also be associated with poor Appalachian Whites, drug users, the handicapped, and to some extent, almost any category that qualifies as a minority group.... Often with political activism, minority groups will develop expressive language that is not common to, or has a different connotation than, standard English. Inability to communicate effectively in the client's language may contribute significantly to the poor acceptance which counseling has received from minorities.

Class-bound Values. Differences in values between counselor and client that are basically due to class differences are relevant to minority group/cross-cultural counseling since, almost by definition, many minority group members are also of a lower socioeconomic class. Furthermore, for the purposes of this [reading], differences in attitudes, behaviors, beliefs, and values among the various socioeconomic groups constitute cultural differences. The interaction of social class and behavior has been well documented by Hollingshead (1949). The importance of social class for school counseling has been discussed by Bernard (1963). Combining the results of several studies, Havighurst and Neugarten (1962) concluded that at least fifty percent of the American population falls into either the upper lower or lower lower socioeconomic classes, suggesting that a large portion of the counselor's potential clientele may be from these socioeconomic classes. The impact of social class differences on counseling in general acquires added significance if one accepts the statement . . . that existing counseling techniques are middle and upper class based.

One of the first and most obvious value differences encountered by the middle class counselor and the lower class client involves the willingness to make and keep counseling appointments. As Sue and Sue (1977) point out, "... lower-class clients who are concerned with 'survival' or making it through on a day-to-day basis expect advice and suggestions from the counselor... (and)... appointments made weeks in advance with short weekly 50 minute contacts are not consistent with the need to seek immediate solutions" (p. 424). Vontress (1973) states that Appalachian Whites refuse to be enslaved by the clock and not only do they refuse to adhere to values of promptness, planning, and protocol, but they suspect people who do adhere to these values.

Differences in attitudes toward sexual behavior often enter the counseling relationship between a counselor and client representing different socioeconomic classes. For the most part, open acceptance of sexual promiscuity differs from one socioeconomic level to another, although other factors (such as religious beliefs) play heavy roles. Middle class counselors, whether consciously or unconsciously, often attempt to impose middle class sexual mores on lower and upper class clients.

The fact that the clients' socioeconomic status affects the kind of therapeutic treatment clients receive has been well documented. Ryan and Gaier (1968), for instance, found that students from upper socioeconomic backgrounds have more exploratory interviews with counselors than do students representing other social classes. Middle class patients in a veterans administration clinic tend to remain in treatment longer than do lower class patients. And Hollingshead and Redlich (1958) found that the level of therapeutic intensiveness varies directly with socioeconomic background.

Culture-bound Values. Culture, as broadly defined for the purposes of this [reading], consists of behavior patterns shared and transmitted by a group of individuals. In addition to language and class-bound values already discussed, culture-bound values obviously involve such elements as attitudes, beliefs, customs, and institutions identified as integral parts of a group's social structure.

Counselors frequently impose their own cultural values upon minority clients in ignorance, reflecting an insensitivity to the clients' values. Referring to clients from racial/ethnic minorities as "culturally deprived" is an example of this imposition. "Straight," male counselors sometimes make sexual remarks about females in front of a male client that may be repugnant to the client if he is gay (to say nothing about how it would affect females who overheard it). Nor is the experience reported by Granberg (1967) in which he found himself incorrectly assuming his homosexual client wanted to become "straight" an unusual example of the counselor's cultural values interfering with the counseling relationship. Drug and prison "counselors" often fulfill roles of instilling the values of the larger society upon their clientele without full awareness of their impact.

The role of the counselor's values in the counseling relationship has been a thorny professional issue for some time. The issue becomes even more poignant when a majority counselor and minority client are involved. In this case, "... the values inherent in (the) two different subcultures may be realistically as diverse as those of two countries" (Wilson & Calhoun, 1974). While the major concern with this issue, in the broader context, centers on the counselor's influence upon the client, class- and culture-bound value differences can impede further rapport building.

For example, one of the most highly valued aspects of counseling entails self-disclosure, a client's willingness to let the counselor know what he or she thinks or feels. Many professionals argue that self-disclosure is a necessary condition for effective counseling. Jourard (1964) suggests that people are more likely to disclose themselves to others who will react as they do, implying that cultural similarity is an important factor in self-disclosure. Furthermore, self-disclosure may be contrary to basic cultural values for some minorities. Sue and Sue (1972) have pointed out that Chinese American clients, who are taught at an early age to restrain from emotional expression, find the direct and subtle demands by the counselor to self-disclosure very threatening. Similar conflicts have been reported for Chicano (Cross & Maldonado, 1971) and Native American (Trimble, 1976) clients. Poor clients, of whatever racial or ethnic background, frequently resist attempts by the counselor to encourage client self-exploration and prefer to ascribe their problems, often justifiably, to forces beyond their control (Calia, 1966). In addition, many racial minorities have learned to distrust Whites in general and may "shine on" a majority counselor, since this has proven to be adaptive behavior with Whites in the past. Sue and Sue (1977) suggest that self-disclosure is itself a cultural value and counselors who, ". . . value verbal, emotional and behavioral expressiveness as goals in counseling are transmitting their own cultural values" (p. 425).

Related to this last point is the lack of structure frequently provided by the counselor in the counseling relationship. Often, in order to encourage self-disclosure, the counseling situation is intentionally designed to be an ambiguous one, one in which the counselor listens empathically and responds only to encourage the client to continue talking (Sue & Sue, 1972). Minority clients frequently find the lack of structure confusing, frustrating, and even threatening (Haettenschwiller, 1971). Atkinson, Maruyama, and Matsui (1978) found that Asian Americans prefer a directive counseling style to a nondirective one, suggesting the directive approach is more compatible with their cultural values.

Similar results were found in a replication of the Atkinson et al. (1978) study with American Indian high school students (Dauphinais, Dauphinais, & Rowe, 1981). Black students also were found to prefer a more active counseling role over a passive one (Peoples & Dell, 1975).

Process Manifestations of Cultural Differences

Many of the problems encountered in minority group/cross-cultural counseling which have been identified as cultural barriers might better be conceived of as process manifestations of cultural differences, since they may be present to some extent in any counseling relationship but are aggravated by cultural differences. We will briefly discuss five

of them: stereotyping, resistance, transference, countertransference, and client expectations.

Stereotyping. Stereotyping is a major problem for all forms of counseling. It may broadly be defined as rigid preconceptions which are applied to all members of a group or to an individual over a period of time, regardless of individual variations. The key word in this definition is *rigidity*, an inflexibility to change. Thus, a counselor who believes that Blacks are "lazy," "musical," "rhythmic," and "unintelligent"; Asians are "sneaky," "sly," "good with numbers," and "poor with words"; or that Jews are "stingy," "shrewd," and "intellectual" will behave toward representatives of these groups as if they possessed these traits. The detrimental effects of stereotyping have been well documented in professional literature (Rosenthal & Jacobson, 1968; Smith, 1977; Sue, 1973). First, counselors who have preconceived notions about minority group members may unwittingly act upon these beliefs. If Black students are seen as possessing limited intellectual potential, they may be counseled into terminal vocational trade schools. Likewise, if Asian Americans are perceived as being only good in the physical sciences but poor in verbal-people professions, counselors may direct them toward a predominance of science courses. The second and even more damaging effect is that many minorities may eventually come to believe these stereotypes about themselves. Thus, since the majority of stereotypes about minorities are negative, an inferior sense of self-esteem may develop.

Due to stereotyping or attempts to avoid stereotyping by the counselor, majority counselors frequently have difficulty adjusting to a relationship with a minority client. The most obvious difficulty in this area occurs when the counselor fails to recognize the client as an individual and assigns to the client culturally stereotypic characteristics that are totally invalid for this individual (Smith, 1977). In an effort to treat the client as just another client, on the other hand, the counselor may demonstrate "color or culture blindness" (Wilson & Calhoun, 1974). In this case the counselor may avoid altogether discussing the differences between the two participants, thus implying that the client's attitudes and behaviors will be assessed against majority norms. The content of the counseling dialogue may also be restricted by the preoccupation of the majority counselor with fear that the client will detect conscious or unconscious stereotyping on the part of the counselor (Gardner, 1971).

Resistance. Resistance is usually defined as client opposition to the goals of counseling and may manifest itself as self-devaluation, intellectualization, and overt hostility (Vontress, 1976). While it is a potential difficulty in any counseling encounter, the problem becomes particularly acute when the counselor and client are culturally different, since the counselor may misinterpret the resistance as a dynamic of the client's culture.

Transference. Transference occurs when the client responds to the counselor in a manner similar to the way he or she responded to someone else in the past (Greenson, 1964, pp. 151–152), and this may manifest itself as either a liking or disliking of the counselor. Clients may or may not be aware of the transference effect themselves. This phenomena is particular problematic in the majority counselor–minority client dyad, ". . . because minority group members bring to the relationship intense emotions derived from experiences with and feelings toward the majority group" (Vontress, 1976, p. 49). Minority clients for instance, due to their experiences with an oppressive, majority-controlled society, are likely to anticipate authoritarian behavior from the counselor.

Countertransference. Countertransference occurs when the counselor responds to a client as he or she responded to someone in the past (Wilson & Calhoun, 1974, p. 318). Countertransference is particularly difficult for the counselor to recognize and accept since counselors typically view themselves as objective, although empathic, participants in the counseling relationship. It seems highly unlikely, however, that majority counselors in this society are entirely free of the stereotypic attitudes toward minority peoples (Jackson, 1973). An argument can be made that counselors, like everyone else, carry with them conscious and unconscious attitudes, feelings, and beliefs about culturally different people and that these will manifest themselves as countertransference (Vontress, 1976).

Client Expectation. Closely related to countertransference, client expectations for success in the counseling relationship can directly affect counseling outcome. When the minority client finds him/herself assigned to a majority counselor, the client's prognostic expectations may be reduced (Wilson & Calhoun, 1974). Prior to the initial counseling session the client may experience feelings of distrust, futility, and anger which generate an expectation that counseling will not succeed. Such an expectation usually dooms the counseling relationship to failure.

BARRIERS TO MINORITY COUNSELOR–MINORITY OR MAJORITY CLIENT COUNSELING

As used in the counseling literature, minority group counseling frequently implies that the counselor is a member of the dominant culture and the client a minority group member, suggesting that this combination is of greatest threat to effective counseling. A few authors have referred to the problems encountered in counseling when the client and counselor are from the same minority group. Virtually none have discussed the difficulties experienced when the counselor is from a different minority group than the client. Lest the impression be given that culturally related barriers only exist for the majority counselor–minority client dyad, we now turn briefly to difficulties experienced by minority counselors and their clients.

Intra-Minority Group Counseling

Several authors have identified problems that the minority counselor may encounter when working with a client from a cultural background similar to that of the counselor. Jackson (1973) points out that the minority client may respond with anger when confronted by a minority counselor. The anger may result from finding a minority person associated with a majority controlled institution. Some clients may experience anger, on the other hand, because they feel a majority counselor would be more competent, thus enhancing the probability of problem resolution. Or the client's anger may reflect jealousy that the counselor has succeeded through personal efforts in breaking out of a repressive environment. In the case of a Third World counselor, the counselor may also be seen as:

... too white in orientation to be interested in helping, as less competent than his colleagues, as too far removed from problems that face the patient, or as intolerant and impatient with the patient's lack of success in dealing with problems (Jackson, 1973, p. 277).

The minority counselor may respond to minority client anger by becoming defensive (Jackson, 1973), thus impeding the counseling process. Minority counselors may also either deny identification with or over-identify with the client (Gardner, 1971). Sattler (1970) has suggested that minority counselors may have less tolerance and understanding of minority clients and view the contact as low status work compared to counseling a majority client.

Calnek (1970) points out the danger that Third World counselors too often adopt stereotypes which Whites have developed, concerning how minority clients think, feel, and act. The counselor may deny that the client is also a minority person, for fear the common identification will result in a loss of professional image for the counselor. Over-identification, on the other hand, may cause the counseling experience to degenerate into a gripe session. Calnek also refers to the danger of the counselor projecting his/her own self image into the client because they are culturally similar.

While the foregoing comments are, for the most part, directed at the Black counselor–Black client dyad, it is easy to see that the problem could be generalized to include other intra-minority group situations.

Inter-Minority Group Counseling

Counselors representing one minority group who find themselves working with a client representing a different minority group often face the problems associated with both the majority counselor–minority client and the intra-minority group counseling situations. Although the camaraderie of Third World peoples that results from awareness of shared oppression helps to bridge cultural differences on college and university campuses, in the nonacademic world these differences are often as intense or more intense than those between the dominant and minority cultures. One need only observe Chicano students and parents in East Los Angeles or Black students and parents in Bedford-Stuyvesant to gain an appreciation of ethnocentrism and the difficulty which culturally different minority counselors can perceive in these situations. Furthermore, the counselor representing a different minority than the client may be suspect to the client, for the same reasons counselors of similar minority backgrounds would be suspect.

POTENTIAL BENEFITS IN CROSS-CULTURAL COUNSELING

Almost no attention has been given in the counseling literature to identifying the benefits of cross-cultural counseling. In reference to the minority counselor–majority client dyad, Jackson (1973) suggests that the client may find it easier to "... share information that is looked on as socially unacceptable without censor from the therapist" (p. 275), suggesting self-disclosure, at least of some materials, may be enhanced. Students who are rebelling against the Establishment, for instance, may prefer a minority counselor, feeling that the counselor's experience with oppression qualifies him/her to acquire empathy with the client (Gardner, 1971). Gardner (1971) also suggests majority clients may prefer minority counselors if they are dealing with material that would be embarrassing to share with a majority counselor. Jackson (1973) points out that there is a tendency in this situation to perceive the counselor more as another person than as a super-human, notwithstanding those cases where the counselor is perceived as a "super-minority." In the latter case, the client may view the minority counselor as more capable than his/her majority counterpart, owing to the obstacles the counselor had to overcome. The net effect in this case may be a positive expectation. The possibility that minority counselors are less likely to let secrets filter back into the client's community is also cited by Gardner (1971) as a positive variable in cross-cultural counseling. Several authors (Draguns, 1975, 1976; Trimble, 1976), while referring in part to national cultures, have suggested that cross-cultural counseling is a learning experience to be valued in and of itself. The counseling process, with its intentional provision for self-disclosure of attitudes, values, and intense emotional feelings, can help the counselor and client gain a perspective on each other's culture, frequently in a way never experienced outside of counseling. Cross-cultural counseling also offers an opportunity to both counselor and client to expand their modes of communication, to learn new ways of interacting. Rather than being viewed as a deficit, client (and counselor) bilingualism should be viewed and treated as a strength.

Again it seems apparent that much of the foregoing can be generalized to apply to nonracially or ethnically identified minorities. It also seems evident that further research and discussion are needed regarding both the barriers and benefits of cross-cultural counseling. Those discussed above, along with several proposed by the current authors, are outlined in Table 1. In addition to citing positive and negative aspects of cross-cultural situations, the authors have attempted, as shown in Table 1, to identify their counterparts when counselor and client are culturally similar.

EDITORS' VIEW

The editors of *Counseling American Minorities* are in agreement with those earlier writers who have suggested that cross-cultural counseling can not only be effective for resolving client difficulties, but can also serve as a forum for a unique learning experience. That barriers to cross-cultural counseling exist is not at issue here. Clearly, cultural differences between counselor and client can result in barriers that are, in some instances, insurmountable. As suggested earlier, however, cross-cultural counseling can involve benefits to both client and counselor that may not be possible in intra-cultural counseling.

Furthermore, it is our contention that the primary barrier to effective counseling and one which underlies many other barriers is the traditional counseling role itself. No one has yet offered conclusive evidence that differences in status variables (for example, race, ethnicity, sex, sexual orientation) alone create barriers to counseling. The fact that one person in a counseling dyad is born Black and one White, for instance, should not negate the possibility of their working together effectively. From our perspective, it is how we perceive and experience our and our client's Blackness and Whiteness that creates barriers to constructive communication. For the most part, our perceptions and experiences are shaped by a socialization process that begins at birth. We feel that the traditional counseling role (nonequalitarian, intrapsychic model, office-bound, and so on) often helps to perpetuate the very socialization process that creates a barrier between culturally different individuals.

Some critics will argue that differences in experiences are paramount, that a counselor who experiences being Black will understand the Black client's perspective better than any White counselor ever can. We agree up to a point. There is simply no conclusive evidence, however, that a counselor must experience everything his/her client does. Carried to the extreme, the similarity of experience argument suggests that all counseling is doomed to failure since no two individuals can ever fully share the same life experiences. Furthermore, while cultural differences do result in unique experiences for both the client and the counselor, our experiences as human beings are remarkably similar. This view—that we are more alike than different—is perhaps best expressed by the sociobiologist De Vore (1977):

Table 1 Culturally Relevant Barriers and Benefits in Inter- and Intra-Cultural Counseling

Inter-Cultural Counseling	
Barriers	*Benefits*
Client resistance	Client's willingness to self-disclose some material
Client transference	Client less likely to view counselor as omniscient
Client cultural restraints on self-disclosure	Client expectation for success may be enhanced
Client expectations	Potential for considerable cultural learning by both client and counselor
Counselor countertransference	
Counselor maladjustment to the relationship	Increased need for counselor and client to focus on their own processing
Counselor misdirected diagnosis	
Counselor patronization of client's culture	Potential for dealing with culturally dissonant component of client problem
Counselor denial of culturally dissonant component of client problem	
Counselor "missionary zeal"	
Language differences	
Value conflicts	

Intra-Cultural Counseling	
Barriers	*Benefits*
Unjustified assumption of shared feelings	Shared experience may enhance rapport
Client transference	Client willingness to self-disclose some materials
Counselor countertransference	Common mode of communication may enhance process

Anthropologists always talk about crosscultural diversity, but that's icing on the cake. The cake itself is remarkably panhuman. Different cultures turn out only minor variations on the theme of the species—human courtship, our mating systems, child care, fatherhood, the treatment of the sexes, love, jealousy, sharing. Almost everything that's importantly human—including behavior flexibility—is universal, and developed in the context of our shared genetic background (p. 88).

[We can] propose an identity development model that assumes a pan human response *across* minority groups to the experience of oppression. A primary purpose of the model, however, is to suggest that attitudes and behaviors vary greatly *within* the various minority groups and are reflective of stages in identity development. One of the great dangers of attempting to study minority groups, despite the best of intentions, is that old stereotypes are replaced by new ones. The Minority Identity Development model . . . minimize[s] the development of new stereotypes by suggesting that, even within cultural groups, attitudes and behaviors vary greatly.

REFERENCES

Adams, H. J. The progressive heritage of guidance: A view from the left. *Personnel and Guidance Journal*, 1973, *51*, 531–538.

Atkinson, D. R., Maruyama, M., & Matsui, S. The effects of counselor race and counseling approach on Asian Americans' perceptions of counselor credibility and utility. *Journal of Counseling Psychology*, 1978, *25*, 76–83.

Aubrey, R. F. Historical development of guidance and counseling and implications for the future. *Personnel and Guidance Journal*, 1977, *55*, 288–295.

Banks, W. The Black client and the helping professionals. In R. I. Jones (Ed.) *Black Psychology*. New York: Harper & Row, 1972.

Belkin, G. S. *Practical Counseling in the Schools*. Dubuque, Iowa: William C. Brown, 1975.

Bell, R. L. The culturally deprived psychologist. *Counseling Psychologist*, 1971, *2*, 104–107.

Bernard, H. W. Socioeconomic class and the school counselor. *Theory into practice*, 1963, *2*, 17–23.

Broverman, I., Broverman, D. M., Clarkson, F. E., Rosenkrantz, P. S., & Vogel, S. Sex role stereotype and clinical judgments of mental health. *Journal of Consulting and Clinical Psychology*, 1970, *34*, 1–7.

Bryne, R. H. *Guidance: A behavioral approach*. Englewood Cliffs, N.J.: Prentice-Hall, 1977.

Bryson, S., & Bardo, H. Race and the counseling process: An overview. *Journal of Non-White Concerns in Personnel and Guidance*, 1975, *4*, 5–15.

Calia, V. F. The culturally deprived client: A reformulation of the counselor's role. *Journal of Counseling Psychology*, 1966, *13*, 100–105.

Calnek, M. Racial factors in the countertransference: The Black therapist and the Black client. *American Journal of Orthopsychiatry*, 1970, *40*, 39–46.

Casas, J. M., & Atkinson, D. R. The Mexican American in higher education: An example of subtle stereotyping. *Personnel and Guidance Journal*, 1981, *59*, 473–476.

Casas, J. M., Wampold, B. E., & Atkinson, D. R. The categorization of ethnic stereotypes by university counselors. *Hispanic Journal of Behavioral Sciences*, 1981, *3*, 75–82.

Clark, K. B. *Dark Ghetto: Dilemmas of Social Power*. New York: Harper and Row, 1965.

Counseling and the Social Revolution. *Personnel and Guidance Journal*, 1971, *49* (9).

Cowen, E. L., Gardner, E. A., & Zox, M. (Eds.) *Emergent approaches to mental health problems*. New York: Appleton-Century-Crofts, 1967.

Cross, W. C., & Maldonado, B. The counselor, the Mexican American, and the stereotype. *Elementary School Guidance and Counseling*, 1971, *6*, 27–31.

Dauphinais, P., Dauphinais, L., & Rowe, W. Effects of race and communication style on Indian perceptions of counselor effectiveness. *Counselor Education and Supervision*, 1981, *21*, 72–80.

De Vore, I. The new science of genetic self-interest. *Psychology Today*, 1977, *10* (9), 42–51, 84–88.

Draguns, J. G. Counseling across cultures: Common themes and distinct approaches. In P. Pedersen, W. J. Lonner, & J. G. Draguns (Eds.), *Counseling across cultures*. Honolulu: The University of Hawaii Press, 1976.

Draguns, J. G. Resocialization into culture: The complexities of taking a worldwide view of psychotherapy. In R. W. Brislin, S. Bochner, & W. J. Lonner (Eds.), *Cross-cultural perspectives in learning*. New York: John Wiley & Sons, Halsted, 1975.

Gardner, L. H. The therapeutic relationship under varying conditions of race. *Psychotherapy: Theory, Research and Practice*, 1971, *8* (1), 78–87.

Garfield, J. C., Weiss, S. L., & Pollack, E. A. Effects of the child's social class on school counselor's decision making. *Journal of Counseling Psychology*, 1973, *20*, 166–168.

Granberg, L. I. What I've learned in counseling. *Christianity Today*, 1967, *2*, 891–894.

Greenson, R. R. *The technique and practice of psychoanalysis* (Vol. 1). New York: International Universities Press, 1964.

Grier, W. H. & Cobbs, P. M. *Black Rage*. New York: Bantam Books, Inc., 1968.

Guerney, B. G. (Ed.) *Psychotherapeutic agents: New roles for nonprofessionals, parents, and teachers*. New York: Holt, Rinehart & Winston, 1969.

Gunnings, T. S. Preparing the new counselor. *The Counseling Psychologist*, 1971, *2* (4), 100–101.

Haase, W. *Rorschach diagnosis, socio-economic class and examiner bias*. Unpublished doctoral dissertation, New York University, 1956.

Habermann, L., & Thiry, S. *The effect of socio-economic status variables on counselor perception and behavior*. Unpublished master's thesis, University of Wisconsin, 1970.

Haettenschwiller, D. L. Counseling black college students in special programs, *Personnel and Guidance Journal*, 1971, *50*, 29–35.

Halleck, S. L. Therapy is the handmaiden of the status quo. *Psychology Today*, 1971, *4*, 30–34, 98–100.

Havighurst, R. J., & Neugarten, B. L. *Society and Education* (Second edition). Boston: Allyn & Bacon, Inc., 1962.

Hollingshead, A. B. *Elmtown's youth: The impact of social classes on adolescents*. New York: John Wiley and Sons, Inc., 1949.

Hollingshead, A. B. & Redlich, F. C. *Social class and mental health*. New York: John Wiley & Sons, Inc., 1958.

Jackson, A. M. Psychotherapy: Factors associated with the race of the therapist. *Psychotherapy: Theory, Research and Practice*, 1973, *10*, 273–277.

Johnson, D. E., & Vestermark, M. J. *Barriers and hazards in counseling*. Boston: Houghton Mifflin Co., 1970.

Jourard, S. M. *The transparent self*. Princeton, N. J.: D. Van Nostrand Co., 1964.

Lee, S., & Temerlin, M. K. *Social class status and mental illness*. Unpublished doctoral dissertation, University of Oklahoma, 1968.

Lerner, B. *Therapy in the ghetto: Political impotence and personal disintegration*. Baltimore: Johns Hopkins University Press, 1972.

Lewis, M. D., Lewis, J. A., & Dworkin, E. P. Editorial: Counseling and the social revolution. *The Personnel and Guidance Journal*, 1971, *49*, 689.

Mercado, P., & Atkinson, D. R. Effects of counselor sex, student sex, and student attractiveness on counselor's judgments. *Journal of Vocational Behavior*, in press.

Mitchell, H. Counseling black students: A model in response to the need for relevant counselor training programs. *The Counseling Psychologist*, 1971, *2* (4), 117–122.

Padilla, A. M., Ruiz, R. A., & Alvarez, R. Community mental health services for the Spanish-speaking/ surnamed population. *American Pscyhologist*, 1975, *30*, 892–905.

Pedersen, P. B. The field of intercultural counseling. In P. B. Pedersen, W. J. Lonner & J. G. Draguns (Eds.), *Counseling across cultures*. Honolulu: The University of Hawaii Press, 1976.

Peoples, V. Y., & Dell, D. M. Black and white student preferences for counselor roles. *Journal of Counseling Psychology*, 1975, *22*, 529–534.

Pike, K. L. *Language in relation to a unified theory of the structure of human behavior*. Part 1: Preliminary edition. Summer Institute of Linguistics, 1954.

Pine, G. J. Counseling minority groups: A review of the literature. *Counseling and Values*, 1972, *17*, 35–44.

Rosenthal, R., & Jacobson, L. *Pygmalion in the classroom: Teacher expectation and pupils' intellectual development*. New York: Holt, Rinehart & Winston, 1968.

Ryan, D. W., & Gaier, E. L. Student socio-economic status and counselor contact in junior high school. *Personnel and Guidance Journal*, 1968, *46*, 466–472.

Sanford, N. Research with students as action and education. *American Psychologist*, 1969, *24*, 544–546.

Sattler, J. M. Racial "Experimenter Effects" in experimentation, testing, interviewing and psychotherapy. *Psychological Bulletin*, 1970, *73*, 137–160.

Schlossberg, N. K., & Pietrofesa, J. J. Perspectives on counseling bias: Implications for counselor education. *The Counseling Psychologist*, 1973, *4*, 44–54.

Shertzer, B., & Stone, S. C. *Fundamentals of*

Counseling (2nd ed.) Boston: Houghton Mifflin, 1974.

Smith, E. J. Counseling Black individuals: Some stereotypes. *Personnel and Guidance Journal*, 1977, *55*, 390–396.

Sue, D. W. Ethnic identity: The impact of two cultures on the psychological development of Asians in America. In S. Sue & Wagner (Eds.), *Asian Americans: Psychological perspectives.* Ben Lomond, California: Science and Behavior Books, Inc., 1973, 140–149.

Sue, D. W. & Sue, D. Barriers to effective cross-cultural counseling. *Journal of Counseling Psychology*, 1977, *24*, 420–429.

Sue, D. W., & Sue, S. Counseling Chinese-Americans. *Personnel and Guidance Journal*, 1972, *50*, 637–644.

Sue, S., Allen, D., & Conaway, L. The responsiveness and equality of mental health care to Chicanos and Native Americans. *American Journal of Community Psychology.* 1978, *6,* 137–146.

Sue, S., & McKinney, H. Asian Americans in the community mental health care system. *American Journal of Orthopsychiatry.* 1975, *45*, 111–118.

Sue, S., McKinney, H., Allen, D., & Hall, J. Delivery of community health services to Black and White clients. *Journal of Consulting Psychology*, 1974, *42*, 794–801.

Thomas, A., & Sillen, S. *Racism and psychiatry.* New York: Brunney Mazel, 1972.

Thomas, A. H. & Stewart, N. R. Counselor response to female clients with deviate and conforming career goals. *Journal of Counseling Psychology*, 1971, *18*, 352–357.

Thompson, R. A., & Cimbolic, P. Black students' counselor preference and attitudes toward counseling center use. *Journal of Counseling Psychology*, 1978, *25*, 570–575.

Torion, R. P. Socioeconomic status and traditional treatment approaches reconsidered. *Psychological Bulletin*, 1973, *79*, 263–270.

Triandis, H. C., Malpass, R. S., & Davidson, A. R. Psychology and Culture. *Annual Review of Psychology*, 1973, *24*, 355–378.

Trimble, J. E. Value differences among American Indians: Concern for the concerned counselor. In P. Pedersen, W. J. Lonner, & J. G. Draguns (Eds.), *Counseling across cultures.* Honolulu: The University of Hawaii Press, 1976.

Tyler, L. The methods and processes of appraisal and counseling. In A. S. Thompson and D. E. Super (Eds.), *The professional preparation of counseling psychologists.* New York: Bureau of Publications, Teachers College, Columbia University, 1964.

Vexliard, A. Tempérament et modalités d'adaptation. *Bulletin de Psychologie*, 1968, *21*, 1–15.

Vontress, C. E. Counseling: Racial and ethnic factors. *Focus on Guidance*, 1973, *5*, 1–10.

Vontress, C. E. Racial and ethnic barriers in counseling. In P. Pederson, W. J. Lonner, & J. G. Draguns (Eds.), *Counseling across cultures.* Honolulu: The University of Hawaii Press, 1976.

Wampold, B. E., Casas, J. M., & Atkinson, D. R. Ethnic bias in counseling: An information processing approach. *Journal of Counseling Psychology*, 1981, *28*, 498–503.

Webster, D. W., & Fretz, B. R. Asian American, Black, and White college students' preferences for help-giving sources. *Journal of Counseling Psychology*, 1978, *25*, 124–130.

Williams, R. L., & Kirkland, J. The white counselor and the black client. *Counseling Psychologist*, 1971, *2*, 114–117.

Wilson, W., & Calhoun, J. F. Behavior therapy and the minority client. *Psychotherapy: Theory, Research and Practice*, 1974, *11*, 317–325.

Wrenn, C. G. The culturally encapsulated counselor. *Harvard Educational Review*, 1962, *32*, 444–449.

Yamamoto, J., James, Q. C., Bloombaum, M., & Hatten, J. Racial factors in patient selection. *American Journal of Psychiatry*, 1967, *124*, 630–636.

Yamamoto, J., James, Q. C., & Palley, N. Cultural problems in psychiatric therapy. *Archives of General Psychiatry*, 1968, *19*, 45–49.

Hispanic Women and Health Care: Bridging a Cultural Gap

ELIZABETH BERRY
MIRIAM OJEDA

The difficulty with cultural explanations for the underutilization of health care is that they tend to blame the victim and suggest that if Hispanics were more like middle class Anglos, they would be able to receive all of the health care that was needed.[1]

I. INTRODUCTION

Cultural barriers between Hispanics and Anglos present numerous communication problems that are especially evident in attempts to provide health care.[2] These communication problems vary, as do the backgrounds of the population receiving health care. The traditional Mexican immigrant is quite different from the assimilated Mexican-American (born in the U.S.), and yet both can encounter problems when communicating with the modern Anglo health care system.

Because the Hispanic population is the fastest growing minority population in the United States, those who provide health care to the public must have accurate information about the needs and values of this particular group. In addition to having an understanding of and a sensitivity to the

This original essay appears here in print for the first time. All rights reserved. Permission to reprint must be obtained from the publisher and the authors. Elizabeth Berry is President of the Faculty at California State University, Northridge, and Miriam Ojeda is Director, Corporate Scholars Program, School of Business Administration and Economics, California State University, Northridge.

Hispanic in general, non-Hispanics attempting to provide health care to the Hispanic population must be aware of the role of the female in the family and of her importance in serving as a vital link to health care facilities. Health workers must also recognize the diversity among Hispanic women and they must avoid stereotypical analyses that lead to ineffective programs. Some guarded generalizations can be made about Hispanic women, but one must always bear in mind the dangers of any stereotype.

In an effort to provide health care personnel with a more enlightened view of the Hispanic female and of her relationship to effective health care programs, this paper will briefly examine the traditional stereotypes of Hispanic women and critique them in light of recent studies. We will then summarize research about the underutilization of health care programs by Hispanics.

II. STEREOTYPE OF HISPANIC WOMEN

The ideal Hispanic woman, as defined by a long-standing social science stereotype, is primarily a mother whose life is devoted to her family. Family, in the Hispanic culture, is defined as those persons related by blood, marriage, or choice (through religious ceremonies such as baptisms).[3]

In this role, a woman takes on the responsibility of homemaker, healer, and mother; she is the focus of all emotional and physical support for her family. Her social life, if permitted by her husband, centers around the church. By tradition, this is the only appropriate social endeavor in which she may participate without damaging her honor and that of her family. This woman has been described by many sociologists as submissive, passive, and isolated. Her world is her family. Her sphere of influence extends only to her children and then only for a very limited time.[4] The ideal Hispanic woman lives not for herself but for others. She is taught to be ashamed of her body. Sex is a taboo topic about which she should know nothing.

Much of the stereotypical description of Hispanic women is based on the dichotomy between virgin and whore. The Hispanic female has been described in the literature on one hand as a loose prostitute and on the other as a sweet and glorious virgin.[5] The literature has underscored the image of the loose prostitute by describing women who work outside the home as "widows or older unmarried women who had 'no man to control them.' Many of these women were known for their promiscuity, and they and their occupation have little status."[6] This woman is the object of men's pleasures, the seducer with eyes that are said to set men on fire. Moreover, she is unruly, domineering, and vicious. According to H. L. Foster, the "señorita has always been portrayed in our fiction as a wild vampire."[7] In 1943, during the zoot-suit riots of Los Angeles, the Los Angeles newspaper published a story to the effect that "cholitas and pachucas are merely cheap prostitutes, infected with venereal disease and addicted to the use of marihuana."[8]

This image lives on in contemporary society. In a recent article advising health workers about the need for sensitivity to cultural factors when providing treatment, the author states:

The wife-mother role tends to be a conservative one. As keeper of tradition and homemaker, the woman resists changes and new ways. What she knows, and has tested and proven by experience, has to be better.[9]

The Virgin in the Catholic religion is the female side of the Church. The Virgin—whether it be the Virgin Mary, the Virgin of Guadalupe, the Virgin of el Perpetuo Socorro, or one of many others—is the forgiving one. She serves as an intermediary between the parishioner and God. Religious Hispanic women revere their religion's virgins; their culture, perhaps more than any other, places the Virgin in the highest regard.

According to the stereotype, the ideal Hispanic woman models herself and her behavior after one of the Virgins, submitting to authority as the Virgin is said to submit to the word of God. She is taught never to question authority, and the authority she

acknowledges is personified in the male. More importantly, she is taught the virtue of silence. Her opinion is not often sought, regardless of the topic at hand.

An Hispanic woman becomes "complete" (a real woman) within the bonds of "holy matrimony." Of course, she may have had no voice in choosing her husband. In fact, according to Madsen, the role of wife is like that of a sacrificial lamb:

The wife is expected to give comfort and pleasure to her husband. She must acknowledge his authority and superiority and think of his needs before her own. She is supposed to accept abuse without complaint and avoid resentment of his pastimes and extramarital affairs. Her in-laws may criticize her and her husband may beat her for demanding that he spend too much time at home. She sets the tone of the home atmosphere, ideally by radiating love and understanding. In her role as wife and mother, she is frequently compared to the Virgin of Guadalupe.... By extension but rarely by direct comparison, the husband and father is seen as a human image of God.[10]

The Hispanic woman's social sphere revolves around other females of her family. In fact, she is often forbidden to have social relationships outside that sphere.[11] Her world is her home, where she is responsible for carrying out all the menial work required to care for her husband and children. Though she is also the educator of her children, it is believed by her "keepers" that no formal education is required for this effort.[12]

The purity of this sanctified Virgin is questioned by Madsen, although he presents an alternative negative stereotype:

The conservative Latin wife is, in fact, a skilled manipulator of her Lord and master. The weapons she uses in disguised form are his own self-esteem, his machismo and his role as provider and protector.[13]

Madsen also suggests that she is not always as understanding as she might be. He describes the following scenario, which also presents a negative picture of the Hispanic female:

Josefina, a high school student, asked her mother to obtain her father's permission for her to go to a movie with a date; the mother slapped her repeatedly while asking God if her own daughter was destined to be a whore.[14]

The ideal Hispanic woman is locked into following the path of the Virgin. Any deviation leads to the dark side of life; this must be avoided for survival in the family and in the society. These denigrating descriptions of the Hispanic female are pernicious to the Hispanic women's self concept.

III. CRITIQUE OF STEREOTYPE—WHAT'S WRONG WITH THIS PICTURE?

There are many who contend that the concept of the submissive Mexican-American woman is a stereotype derived from the use of racist/sexist frames of reference, and that alternative frames of reference should be examined. According to Baca-Zinn:

The common social science presentation of the submissive Chicana tells us more about the social science view of women of color than it does about their identity.[15]
Social scientists have correctly analyzed Chicano organizations in terms of patriarchal-authoritarian principles, but they have incorrectly assumed this to mean that women are insignificant, and that they exert power only by manipulation.[16]

An alternative frame of reference criticizes the methods and models used by social science researchers. In his analysis of social science research, Miguel Monteil criticizes the methodological procedures used in previous studies. He asserts that such studies lack sound operational definitions and are filled with value-laden concepts that lack empirical referents. As a result, the theories postulated about Chicano male supremacy and the absolute self-sacrifice of the mother lack validity.[17] So-

cial scientists have assumed similarities between the Mexican family and the Mexican-American family and have based their conclusions on an incomplete understanding of the Hispanic culture:

Specifically, they have relied almost totally upon a psychoanalytical model in which there is uncritical use of concepts like machismo. *However, as used, this approach has relegated all explanation of Mexican family life to a pathological perspective.*[18]

Other authors also criticize the "pathological model" perpetuated by social scientists. Contrary to the view that the Mexican family role structure causes problems, authors such as Mirandé and Enríquez suggest that the family is a source of strength and perhaps the single most important unit in life. The warm, nurturing, and supportive unit of reality contrasts sharply with the social science depiction of the Mexican-American family.[19] By questioning the social science descriptions of the Mexican-American family, critics also question the role of the female in the family. Although the mother is expected to be devoted to the family and to minister to its needs, the mother's status is not without influence. This influence has been underplayed by social science researchers:

Anyone who has grown up in a Chicano family would scoff at the notion that the woman is weak, quiet, or submissive. If there is a persistent image of the woman in Chicano culture, it is that she is a strong and enduring figure. The family is undoubtedly the most important institution for Chicanos, and the woman in turn is the backbone of the culture. Although the woman is largely relegated to the home, her domestic role is not passive. She is charged with essential familial functions: reproduction of the species, transmission of cultural values and beliefs to the next generation, and provision of needed warmth, support, and affection for family members who must survive in a hostile environment.[20]

García-Bahne not only criticizes current interpretation of the Chicano family but also suggests a more dynamic, complex set of factors that determine how the family functions and the woman's role in the family. She suggests that class position, income level, adequacy of diet, and standards of schooling are crucial determinants to the analysis of the Chicano family.[21] She analyzes the socioeconomic limits placed on the Chicano family, and notes that, even though the family structure is changing as a result of the post-industrial period in the United States (with more women working), "there is still a clear division of labor within the home, with Chicanas continuing to carry major responsibility for organizing and completing domestic tasks."[22] She also notes the relationship between the form the family takes and the stratum of society it inhabits.[23] She indicates that although the differences may be subtle, they are very real:

Families of different social strata handle the issues of authority and decision-making quite differently. This suggests that although manifested and recognizable behavior may be the same in upper, middle, and lower class families, the dynamics and meaning of behaviors may be totally distinctive to each respective class because of differing histories and conditions.[24]

García-Bahne contends that the low-income Chicana mother and wife (who represents the majority of Chicanas) usually lives in a situation where the male makes the decisions and expects cooperation and unity from her. She sees the Chicano family as a "vehicle which incorporates those strengthening qualities that are necessary for social units to survive under exploitive conditions and paradoxically embodies those values which mitigate against the development and exercise of self-determination."[25] Thus the role of the female in the Chicano family serves both as a strengthening force for others and as a self-denying force for herself.

Baca-Zinn also criticizes the "simplistic patriarchal-authoritarian model of family life" and distinguishes between generalized male authority and women's control of specific domestic activities.[26] She asserts that women control family activities despite the patriarchal orientation of Chicano life,

that Chicano families are mother-centered not patrifocal,[27] and that Chicanas develop alignments with other women that nurture a collective sense of their own worth.[28] Her conclusions vary sharply from the stereotype:

By recognizing Chicanas' informal power and influence in the domestic sphere, we may begin to reconstruct sociologically, Chicanas' roles. The Chicano family, as an institution, has operated to maximize security by maintaining solidarity, support in an Anglo dominated society. In this process, it has been women who have kept families together as men have gone about the duties of supporting their families by working in institutions of the public sphere. . . . Those characteristics of Chicanas which social scientists have interpreted as passivity, dependence, and submissiveness have been part of a process to preserve the stability of the family. It has been the women's role to mediate between family members, to see to it that there is a minimal amount of conflict. Deference to males, and the "giving in" whereby women temporarily relinquish their control of domestic sphere matters, when males exercise their generalized authority, has not been submissiveness, but a mechanism for safeguarding the internal solidarity of the family.[29]

Clearly, anyone interested in understanding the role of the female in the Hispanic family must consider the many interacting factors that influence her life and must not accept the stereotypical notions perpetrated by social scientists with limited vision.

IV. UTILIZATION OF HEALTH CARE SERVICES BY HISPANICS

The role of the Hispanic woman may be a key factor in planning successful health care programs, but in examining the utilization of health care by Hispanic women one must not oversimplify and generalize. Underutilization of health care by Hispanics is well-documented,[30] but too often we assume that specific cultural barriers limit the use of health care facilities when there are numerous complex causes. For example, one common explanation for Mexican-Americans underutilizing health care facilities is that familism acts as a deterrent.[31] According to Hoppe and Hiller, however, familism does not preclude the acceptance of modern medical services by Mexican-Americans and, in fact, may even encourage the use of such services.[32]

Other explanations of health service utilization include acculturation, social class, and social isolation. The results of a study by Chesney et al. suggest that acculturation has a direct effect, while social class and social isolation interact to have a weak effect, independent of acculturation. Moreover, the results confirm the importance of understanding all three variables in planning and implementing health programs in Mexican-American communities.[33]

Marín et al. provide an excellent summary of possible explanations for underutilization of health care services. They distinguish among economic factors, cultural barriers, and system barriers. Economic factors that affect use of health care facilities include low income compounded by lack of medical insurance. According to the California Raza Health Alliance, fully 35% of Mexican-Americans in California are without any source of health insurance.[34] Cultural barriers commonly thought to deter use of health facilities include familism, ethnocentricity, machismo, and sensitivity to nudity, although many of these explanations have not been carefully researched. Another frequently cited reason for underutilization of health services by Hispanics is the use of folk medicine. There is mixed evidence about folk health beliefs and practices among Hispanics, but the use of folk healers has probably been exaggerated.

More useful in explaining underutilization of health services are system barriers,[35] the most obvious of which is language. Many times an Hispanic cannot even gain telephone access to health care because there are serious shortages of Spanish-speaking operators and bilingual health care providers. Yet another barrier to the use of health care

is undocumented immigration status and the fear of deportation.[36]

Results of an investigation showed that patients usually sought care for relief of symptoms rather than for prevention of illness.[37] They underutilized most sources of medical care, with the possible exception of the emergency room; they were not using folk healers as sources of care; and they were not seeking enough preventive care. The study also explained salient reasons given by Hispanics for underutilization of health care:

System barriers such as language difficulties, undocumented status, long wait, and lack of child care are perceived as being significant reasons for not receiving needed medical care. These system barriers are seriously complicated by the economic difficulties and lack of medical insurance that characterize the respondents in this study. The problem of underutilization of medical care can be solved by lowering both the economic and system barriers to care that are presently experienced by poor Hispanics.[38]

Research about the Hispanics' use of health services shows discrepant explanations, a result, no doubt, of the varying perspectives of researchers. It does seem, however, that when planning health programs, greater emphasis must be placed on system barriers and on improved accommodation to patients' needs.

V. IMPLICATIONS

We can see that although social science research has provided stereotypical explanations of the role and behavior of the Hispanic woman, recently a number of questions have been raised about the Hispanic woman's role and her important influence on others. Health care researchers seem to have taken little notice of the woman as an influential agent in seeking health services. Few studies focus on the woman's role in seeking health care. Admittedly, economic and system barriers affect the woman as well as the man in the family, but one wonders what effect preventive health care programs (aimed primarily at women) would have if developed with an enlightened, non-stereotypical view of the Hispanic female. Although it might appear that the barriers to the use of health services by Hispanics are insurmountable, especially in this period of health care cutbacks, the role of the woman as the foundation of the family deserves consideration when planning outreach programs in the Hispanic community.

NOTES

1. Barbara Vanoss Marín, Geraldo Marín, Amado Padilla, and Castulo de la Rocha, *Utilization of Traditional and Non-traditional Sources of Health Care Among Hispanics*, Occasional Paper, 14 (Spanish Speaking Mental Health Research Center, 1982), p. 4.

2. The problem of naming is apparent when dealing with a large group. The terms used to describe the population we discuss in this paper include *Mexican, Mexican-American, Latino, Hispanic,* and *Chicano.* In general we will use the term *Hispanic,* but when quoting from an article, we will use the term used by the author. This paper focuses on urban women of Mexican descent.

3. Margarita Melville, *Twice a Minority: Mexican American Women* (St. Louis: V. Mosby, 1980), p. 53.

4. See, for example, Madsen, Rubel, Lewis, McWilliams, and Foster.

5. Harry L. Foster, *A Gringo in Mañana Land* (New York: Dodd, Mead and Company, 1925), pp. 80–81.

6. Oscar Lewis, *Life in a Mexican Village* (Urbana: University of Illinois Press, 1951), p. 103.

7. Foster, p. 80.

8. Carey McWilliams, *North from Mexico* (New York: Greenwood Press Publishers, 1968), p. 257.

9. Pedro A. Poma, "Impact of Culture on Health Care," *Illinois Medical Journal* 156 (December 1979), p. 453.

10. William Madsen, *Mexican Americans of South Texas* (New York: Holt, Rinehart and Winston, 1964), p. 48.

11. Arthur J. Rubel, *Across the Tracks* (Austin: University of Texas Press, 1966), pp. 84–85.

12. Madsen, p. 21.

13. Madsen, p. 51.

14. Madsen, p. 53.

15. Maxine Baca-Zinn, "Chicanas' Power and Control in the Domestic Sphere," *De Colores, Journal of Emerging Raza Philosophies* 2 (No. 3, 1975), 29; hereafter cited as *De Colores.*

16. Maxine Baca-Zinn, "Gender and Ethnic Identity Among Chicanos," *Frontiers* V (No. 2, 1980), 19.

17. Miguel Monteil, "The Social Science Myth of the Mexican-American Family," *Voices: Readings from El Grito,* ed. Octavio Romano (Berkeley: Quinto Sol Publications, 1971), p. 62.

18. Monteil, p. 57.

19. Alfredo Mirandé and Evangelina Enríquez, *La Chicana, the Mexican-American Woman* (Chicago: University of Chicago Press, 1979).

20. Mirandé and Enríquez, p. 116.

21. Betty García-Bahne, "La Chicana and the Chicano Family," in *Essays on La Mujer* by Rosanna Sanchez and Rosa Martin Cruz (Los Angeles: University of California Press, 1977), p. 32.

22. García-Bahne, p. 34.

23. García-Bahne, p. 35.

24. García-Bahne, p. 36.

25. García-Bahne, p. 43.

26. *De Colores,* p. 24.

27. Baca-Zinn believes that the concept of matrifocality needs further research and that although Hispanics exhibit some structural centrality, it is limited to the family.

28. *De Colores,* p. 29.

29. *De Colores,* pp. 28–29.

30. See Marín et al.

31. See, for example, Leo Grebber, Joan W. Moore, and Ralph C. Guzman, *The Mexican American People* (New York: Free Press, 1970).

32. Sue Reis Hoppe and Peter L. Hiller, "Alienation, Familism, and Utilization of Health Services by Mexican Americans," *Journal of Health and Social Behavior* 16 (1975), p. 311.

33. S. A. P. Chesney, J. A. Chavira, R. P. Hall, and H. E. Gary, Jr., "Barriers to Medical Care of Mexican-Americans: The Role of Social Class, Acculturation and Social Isolation," *Medical Care* (September 1982), pp. 883–891.

34. *The California Raza Health Plan: An Action Guide for the Promotion of Raza Health in California* (Berkeley: Chicano Health Institute of Students, Professors, and Alumni, 1979), quoted in Marín et al., p. 2.

35. Marín et al., p. 4.

36. Marín et al., p. 6.

37. Marín et al., p. 11.

38. Marín et al., p. 18.

Japanese and American Management: Participative Decision Making

LEA P. STEWART

In recent years, Japanese management techniques have been proclaimed by both scholars and lay authors as the salvation of American business. Perhaps because of popular books such as *Theory Z* by William Ouchi (1981) and *The Art of Japanese Management* by Richard Tanner Pascale and Anthony G. Athos (1981), it seems that everyone has heard of the wonders of Japanese management. According to Ouchi, corporations such as Hewlett-Packard, Eli Lilly, and Dayton-Hudson are using his Theory Z approach to management. Given the glowing success stories described by Ouchi and others, it would seem that American industry could profit from the widespread application of these techniques. This may or may not be true. The danger lies in applying techniques based on Japanese management without critically examining them. This is easy to do because, as one searches for information on this approach, one finds that the vast majority of articles portray the Japanese system in a favorable light. Yet, there are some authors who criticize, or at least express concern about, Japanese management techniques. This paper will review some of these articles to provide a more balanced look at an approach to management that everyone seems to be talking about.

The differences between U.S. and Japanese man-

This original essay appears here in print for the first time. All rights reserved. Permission to reprint must be obtained from the publisher and the author. Professor Stewart teaches at Rutgers University.

Table 1

	United States	Japan
Employment	Short term, market oriented	Long term, career oriented
Management values	Openness and accountability	Harmony and consensus
Management style	Action oriented, short term horizons	Perfectionism in long term, paralysis in short term
Work values	Individual responsibility	Collective responsibility
Control processes	Formalized and explicit	Not formalized, implicit
Learning systems	External consultants and universities	Internal consultants and company training

agement are summarized in Table 1 adapted from McMillan (1980).

Americans and Japanese live in quite different conceptual worlds. Whereas Americans regard responsible individuality as a virtue and view lack of autonomy as a constraint, the Japanese regard individuality as evidence of immaturity, and autonomy as the freedom to comply with one's obligations and duties (Fox 1977). According to Fox, the "traditional Japanese male employee is born into an intricate web of obligations and relationships" in which ridicule is unbearable and the ideal is to "blend selflessly into a system of 'other-directedness'" (p. 77). This socially committed male is chosen from the graduating class of one of the best universities to become a manager in a Japanese company for life. As a Japanese manager who abhors unpleasant face-to-face confrontations and discord, he will manage through a system of apparent consensus building (Tsurumi 1978).

This consensus building system, the *ringi* system, is one of the most talked about virtues of the Japanese system. There is evidence, however, that this system is not dedicated to true consensus. Fox (1977) describes the *ringi* system as a process in which a proposal prepared by middle management is circulated to affected units of the organization for review, revision, and approval. When each unit has attached its approval seal to the proposal, it goes to the appropriate higher level authority for final approval and implementation. Although the system

involves numerous group meetings and much delay, once final approval is granted, the organization moves surprisingly quickly to implement it. Fox claims that this system should be labeled "consensual understanding" instead of decision making by consensus. According to Fox:

It is not uncommon for the ringisho *to be merely the formalization of a suggestion from higher management which has had the benefit of considerable prior discussion before being drafted. Apparently, not many* ringisho *are drastically revised en route to the top or vetoed when they get there. And considerable discretion is retained by management to prescribe in detail when and by whom they will be implemented.* (pp. 79–80)

Although Fox believes the *ringi* system is not true decision making by consensus, he does believe the system nurtures commitment and, thus, "recalls the work of Lewin, Maier, Coch and French, and Likert who demonstrated the effectiveness of participative decision making in American organizations long ago" (p. 85). Krauss (1973) sees many parallels between the management styles of successful U.S. companies dedicated to participative decision making and the Japanese system. Tsurumi (1978) takes a more critical view and characterizes the decision-making process inside Japanese corporations as "personality-based." He claims that "the art of consensus-building is to sell ideas and decisions to others" (p. 60). This criticism echoes the claims of American critics who have challenged participative decision making. Often American employees are allowed only limited participation (see French et al. for a classic application of participation in a manufacturing plant), or are allowed to participate in making only insignificant decisions. Participation is often used to make an employee *feel* that he or she is taking part in the decision-making process even if the employee's input does not actually have an effect on the process.

Pascale (1978) reinforces the similarity in decision-making style between American and Japanese managers in an extensive study of communication practices in U.S. and Japanese corporations. Pascale found that managers in Japanese firms engage in over 30 percent more face-to-face contacts each day than do managers in U.S. firms. In addition, compared to U.S. managers, Japanese managers score themselves higher on decision quality and substantially higher on implementation quality. Yet, there is no significant difference in the style of decision making used by Japanese and U.S. managers. Japanese managers do not use a consultative decision-making process more often than do American managers. Pascale argues that the Japanese manager's tendency to use more face-to-face contacts is more efficient because the Japanese language does not lend itself to mechanical word processing and most written communication has to be done by hand, which is a lengthy process. In addition, face-to-face communication is encouraged by the crowded Japanese work setting in which many levels of the hierarchy are located in the same open work space. Thus, the nature of the Japanese language and of the work setting may be the major determinants of the Japanese manager's communication style. This face-to-face style, in turn, leads to higher perceived decision quality and higher perceived implementation quality.

The dominance of face-to-face communication may account for the perception that there is more openness about major decisions in Japanese firms and "more desire to explore and learn together" (McMillan 1980). While Japanese managers are not actually using a consultative decision-making style, they are talking to their workers a great deal. This increased face-to-face contact is interpreted by observers of the system as openness. Systematic research into the content of these face-to-face interactions is needed to determine if Japanese managers are being "open" with their subordinates or merely answering questions and giving advice.

No matter how decisions are actually made within Japanese corporations, there is no doubt that Japanese companies are highly successful. McMillan attributes the phenomenal success of Japanese industry to high productivity due to the "best technology-oriented hardware, which combines the newest processes available, an emphasis on quality control and cost-volume relationships, and, where necessary, automation and robot technology" (p. 28)—in essence, machines. McMillan argues that the Japanese have invested a great deal in developing and maintaining advanced hardware systems and are reaping the benefits of this technology. Fox (1977), on the other hand, takes a more human approach to the success of the Japanese system. He claims that the Japanese system has accomplished so much due to "dedicated, self-sacrificing workers, spurred by a sense of urgency" (p. 80). Supposedly these workers are rewarded by lifetime employment, but this is not actually the case.

Permanent employment (the *nenko* system) operates mainly in the larger Japanese firms and applies to a minority of Japanese workers (Oh 1976). It is reserved for male employees in government and large businesses (Drucker 1978). The limitation of the *nenko* system and its benefits to perhaps 30 percent of the nonagricultural Japanese labor force, according to Oh, "appears to be essential to the continued survival of the *nenko* system, and is probably its greatest cost to Japanese society" (p. 15). The benefits of the *nenko* system, however, are not limitless for those who are covered by it. Although a manager can expect yearly raises and bonuses since wages are based at least partly upon seniority, lifetime employment for most managers ends at age 55, pensions rarely exceed two or three years of salary, and government social security benefits are nominal (Fox 1977). To keep this system in operation and to assure a flexible supply of workers, the Japanese system considers 20 to 30 percent of its workers as "temporary" (Fox 1977). Women, by definition, are temporary employees (Drucker 1978) and are "consistently discriminated against with regard to pay, benefits, and opportunity for advancement" (Fox 1977, p. 79). Even Ouchi (1981) admits that "Type Z organizations have a tendency to be sexist and racist" (p. 77).

To avoid the stigma of becoming a temporary worker or a manual laborer, Japanese children are pressured at increasingly younger and younger ages to learn enough to be admitted to the most prestigious schools. According to Drucker (1978), since "career opportunities are dependent almost entirely on educational attainment" (p. 33), the pressure starts with the child's application to nursery school. As the pressure is becoming more intense, Drucker notes, the suicide rate among teenagers and even preteens is reaching alarming proportions. Perhaps partly because of this pressure, young people in Japan are starting to defect from the traditional values (Fox 1977). Although McMillan (1980) discounts its effect, he notes that "a growing minority of young people are impatient with the career employment system and the age-related wage practice" (p. 29). Oh (1976) claims that management tends to cultivate these grievances among younger workers to keep them from unifying with older workers to oppose management. Whether or not these grievances will become strong enough to challenge traditional management practices remains to be seen.

After careful examination, Japanese management appears to be a system of contradictions. Managers spend a great deal of time in face-to-face communication with workers, but they do not use consultative decision making more than American managers. The *ringi* system gives the appearance of consensus-seeking, but it is actually more of an information dissemination system. The Japanese are rewarded for their educational attainments, so they are pressured into starting on the path toward the best schools at increasingly earlier ages.

"Permanent" employment ends at age 55. Undoubtedly, the Japanese system has produced successful corporations, but, as Sethi (1973) notes, "Do we want to measure success in terms similar to those used by the Japanese society?" (p. 14). This question must be answered before we start the wholesale application of Japanese management to U.S. corporations.

REFERENCES

Drucker, P. F. "The price of success: Japan revisited." *Across the Board*, 1978, 15 (8), 28–35.

Fox, W. M. "Japanese management: Tradition under strain." *Business Horizons*, 1977, 20 (4), 76–85.

French, J. R. P.; Ross, I. C.; Kirby, S.; Nelson, J. R.; and Smyth, P. "Employee participation in a program of industrial change." *Personnel*, 1958, 35 (6), 16–29. Reprinted in Redding, W. C., and Sanborn, G. A. (eds.), *Business and Industrial Communication*. New York: Harper & Row, 1964, 372–387.

Krauss, W. P. "Will success spoil Japanese management?" *Columbia Journal of World Business*, 1973, 8 (4), 26–30.

McMillan, C. "Is Japanese management really so different?" *Business Quarterly*, 1980, 45 (3), 26–31.

Oh, T. K. "Japanese management—A critical review." *Academy of Management Review*, 1976, 1, 14–25.

Ouchi, W. G. *Theory Z*. New York: Avon Books, 1981.

Pascale, R. T. "Communication and decision making across cultures: Japanese and American comparisons." *Administrative Science Quarterly*, 1978, 23, 91–110.

Pascale, R. T., and Athos, A. G. *The Art of Japanese Management*. New York: Warner Books, 1981.

Sethi, S. P. "Drawbacks of Japanese management." *Business Week*, November 24, 1973, 12–13.

"The profit in breaking Japanese traditions." *Business Week*, February 14, 1977, 51.

Tsurumi, Y. "The best of times and the worst of times: Japanese management in America." *Columbia Journal of World Business*, 1978, 13 (2), 56–61.

Japanese Social Experience and Concept of Groups

DOLORES CATHCART
ROBERT CATHCART

Deru kugi wa utareru ("the nail that sticks up is hit") is a well-known saying in Japan. Japanese children hear it continually from parents and teachers. It reflects an important cultural attitude. Japanese are fond of the saying because it suggests their abhorrence of egocentricity and their wish to avoid being singled out for praise or blame. More importantly, this saying reminds them of the pain experienced when one fails to blend harmoniously into a group. It is this great desire to lose oneself within the confines of a group that is most characteristic of the Japanese.

If we were to place Japanese concepts of self and group at one end of a continuum it would be possible to produce an almost perfect paradigm by placing American concepts at the other. This remarkable polarity in cultural variation makes the study of Japanese groups useful to those interested in intercultural communication.[1] In both cultures we find a similar social phenomenon, highly developed group activity, but the contrasting perceptions of group dynamics are so disparate they bring into sharp focus the divergent social values of Japanese and Americans. Understanding these cultural variances in perception and values can help us cross communication barriers, and more

This original essay appeared in print for the first time in the second edition. All rights reserved. Permission to reprint must be obtained from the publisher and the authors. Dolores Cathcart is a freelance writer. Robert Cathcart teaches at Queens College of the City of New York. This joint project grew out of a research sabbatical spent in Japan.

importantly, help us understand how our American concepts of group are cultural variants rather than universal theories. In other words, the ethnocentrism of American theories of group dynamics may emerge more clearly as we examine Japanese concepts standing in polar opposition to our own.

I

An American would most likely begin the examination of "group" by defining or categorizing groups. Questions would be asked like, "What is a group?" "Can two persons be a group?" "What are the main differences between a small group and a large group?" These questions reflect Western thought patterns and would represent one end of the cultural continuum. The Japanese would not begin in this manner. Groups are not defined, they simply "are." They are the "natural" or normal milieu in which human interaction takes place. There is no counterpart in Japan to that American thought process which produces long essays and collections of experimental data on "how best to define a group." Such attempts at defining and categorizing are typical of Western attitudes and values.

Another American approach to groups is to consider *the role of the individual* in the group. On this continuum the American position is represented by the attitude that the individual is the more important part of the group. In American culture each person is perceived of as having a unique identity, a "self" separate from but influenced by the other members of a group and by group norms. This leads to the view that a group is a *collection* of individuals in which a person has a great deal of freedom to choose individual roles or even to remain apart from the group if he so chooses. This belief carries with it the assumption that the individual can function, in theory at least, independent of the group, guided by a duty to self and obligated to do that which he sees as morally right no matter what course the group follows.

The Japanese view of "no-self" stands in opposition to this. In Japan it is believed society is composed of on-going groups in which individual identity is submerged. The Japanese approach to the group role is to perceive of oneself as an integral part of the whole. Sociologist Yoshiharu Matsumoto explains:

The individual does not interact as an individual but as a son in a parent-child relationship, as an apprentice in a master-apprentice relationship, or as a worker in an employer-employee relationship. Furthermore, the playing of the role of son, apprentice, student, or worker persists twenty-four hours a day. There is no clear-cut demarcation between work and home life.[2]

The identification through group rather than self can be observed in ordinary interactions. When Japanese family members converse, they address one another not by using their given names but by using names that denote the person's group functions. A daughter-in-law named Reiko will be called by a name that denotes her place in the family rather than "Reiko," which designates her individually. Should a father in a family die and be replaced by the eldest son as head of the family, the son would then be called "father" even by his own mother.

Groups in Japan are permanent and determinate. Individuals are temporary and have no existence, in theory, outside the group. This outlook does not negate the important functions and contributions of individuals within groups but it does subordinate the "self" to the group. Individual fulfillment of self is attained through finding and maintaining one's place within the group. If the group is successful, so is each part of it.

The American concept of individual responsibility based on a belief in individual morality stands in sharp contrast to the Japanese concept of *group* morality and ultimate group responsibility. The Japanese see all decisions and actions as the product of group consensus. The individual is not held morally responsible for such decisions. When a person commits a wrongful act, it is the group that is embarrassed and, in the final analysis, responsible for the misdeed. It is commonly accepted in Japanese law and practice that the group should make amends and pay damages resulting from individual misconduct. This embodiment of group can be carried to the point where, in extreme circumstances, those persons at the top of the group hierarchy feel constrained to answer for the misdeeds of individual group members by committing *hara-kiri* (suicide) in order to erase the blot on the group's honor. This act of *hara-kiri* reflects a total denial of self and a complete loyalty to the group.

The Japanese is relieved of the typical American moral struggle wherein each person must continually weigh the duty to self and individual rights against obligations to the group. On the other hand, the Japanese cannot escape tremendous anxiety produced by having to ensure that every thought and act enhances the group. As Kawashima Takeoyoshi states it,

There is no place for the concept of the individual as an independent entity equal to other individuals. In (Japanese) culture, the social order consists of social obligations, which are defined not in specific determinate terms, but in diffuse, indeterminate terms. . . . The indeterminateness of social obligations—hence the lack of concepts of equality and independent individual—does not allow the existence of [individual] "right" as the counterpart of social obligations.[3]

Americans seldom feel an all-consuming loyalty to one group. As a result, America has been called a nation of "joiners." There is a tendency to be on the lookout for new groups to join which can fulfill one's personal desires as well as provide a place for meeting social obligations. Americans readily form groups, dissolve them, and go on to form new groups. The motivation is the individual search for identity.

Japanese cannot imagine this kind of "joining." A person in Japan is part of particular groups because that is the way society is structured, and the individual does not believe he can "go it alone." To leave a group in Japan is to lose one's identity, and it decreases the chances of finding fulfillment. Leaving a group is not a matter of individual choice just as joining a group is not. In Japan necessary group transitions such as leaving the university to join a company are circumscribed by elaborate rituals constructed to serve group needs rather than individual desires.

II

The perceptual patterns and value systems that produce this extreme identification with group rather than self can be traced to the central role of family as a model for all Japanese interpersonal relationships. As in the West, the family is the primary group and is the place where most attitudes and values are learned. Unlike the nuclear family of the West, which functions primarily to protect the offspring while preparing them to leave and assume a role in the larger society (where it is expected they will replicate the family with another nuclear family), "the Japanese family is conceived of as existing from the past and into the future, unceasingly, independent of birth and death of its members."[4]

In Japan, the family does not prepare the child to leave it and enter the social order; the family, itself, is perceived as the *basis of all social order.* Within the family the child learns the intricate rituals and linguistic nuances that influence the Japanese personality and that are operative in all relationships in and outside the family. That is, the Japanese *replicate* the family group structure and process throughout their society.

The Japanese word for family is *ie*, which literally means "the house" or "the household." The use of the term *ie* emphasizes the organizational and functional aspects of family. Each household consists of the head of the house and all persons, whether related by blood or not, who share in the social and economic life of the family. This relationship is designated *keifu*, which means "bond" and which refers to the maintenance and continuance of the family as an institution. This is in contrast to the kinship that binds the Western family through blood and inheritance. Although strictly patrilinear in structure, the Japanese family can be headed by a member with no blood relationship to the other family members. This is possible through the traditional practice of "adoption." For example, if there is no son to take over as the head of the house, a family adopts a suitable "son" and he immediately takes on the role of the eldest son, with all the rights and privileges entailed and with all the duties and obligations that a son born to the position would have. After adoption, he would no longer "exist" as a son in the family he left and he could never return to or make claims in his blood family. His name is literally erased from that family's records. He takes a new name and his former name and "self" disappear.

The ancient feudal household consisting of a lord and all his retainers, peasants, warriors, and craftsmen was considered *ie*, or family. In this arrangement the line between kin and non-kin is blurred, and loyalty and contribution to the group becomes the bond (*keifu*) that unifies and distinguishes the family. In modern Japan, this concept of *ritual kinship* prepares a person to enter a group outside the family or household. When a Japanese is chosen to work for a company or organization he sees himself as being *adopted into a family* and he carries with him the same kinds of loyalties and methods of interpersonal relationships that he has learned in his (*ie*) family.

An important characteristic of the Japanese family is the way in which it fosters and perpetuates *dependency.* This dependency produces "indebtedness" or *on*, which in turn governs interpersonal relationships. A Japanese child, like an American one, learns at a very young age that he must rely on others. Unlike American families, the Japanese family purposefully *fosters* dependency as the child matures. Dependency, in Japan, is considered a natural and desirable trait capable of producing warm human relationships. (See the following discussion of *amae.*) In America, on the other hand, dependency is considered a limitation on individual growth and fulfillment, and so the family and school teach the child to become *self-reliant.*

A Japanese, even as an adult, never escapes dependency. All his life he depends on others, and all his life he must seek to repay his indebtedness to those who have cared for him by providing for those beneath him. This is what is meant by *on*.

On should be viewed as part of group structure and not as a relationship between two persons only. Everyone in a group *is at the same time* an *on*-receiver and an *on*-giver. Each member of the group is indebted to all those above him on whom he has had to depend, and in turn he must repay this indebtedness by giving assistance to all those below him who are dependent on him. *On* works to bind persons to the group, for if they left the group they would have no way of repaying the indebtedness incurred while a member of the group. It also functions as a means of linking all persons in the group in an unending chain of indebtedness and obligation.

While the *on* relationship might appear to be a typical pecking order hierarchy to the Westerner, it is a hierarchy of a very different quality. It is based on the natural dependency inherent in human relationships rather than on inherent individual qualities or attributes that enable some human beings to assume superior positions to others. *On* requires that the Japanese see himself as fitting into a hierarchy—a hierarchy that exists in every group of which he is a member.

The very strong personal relationships characteristic of this vertical dyadic order are fostered by the *oyabun-kobun* relationship, a companion dimension that exists along with *on*. The *oyabun* is a father, boss, or patron who protects and provides for the son, employee, or student in return for his service and loyalty. Again, this is a part of the two-way dependency relationship. Every boss or group leader recognizes his dependence on those below him. Without their undivided loyalty he could not function. He is acutely aware of the double dimension of this dependency because he has had to serve a long period as a follower or *kobun*, working his way up the hierarchy. He has reached his position at the top by faithfully serving his *oyabun* who in turn has protected him and provided for him. Each *oyabun* has one or more *kobun* whom he looks after much as a father looks after his chil-

dren. The more loyal and devoted the "children," the more he succeeds and the better he can care for them. In the Japanese business world the *oyabun* finds work for his *kobun*, places them where they are best suited, provides for them when they are out of work, and accepts responsibility for personal problems they have on and off the job. In turn, *kobun* must heed his advice, defend him, and depend on him for help. "Everyone gets some sort of reward for submitting to an *oyabun*; consequently followers remain faithful to their *oyabun* during difficult times in a way they never would for a man who has used sheer power to subordinate them."[5]

The *oyabun-kobun* relationship makes for a unique structure in Japanese groups, one not found in American groups, where relationships are dependent on changing role functions and where the ideal group is one in which every person is considered equal to every other, free to participate as he chooses. Relationships with a Japanese group are vertical: something like a chain, each person being a link in the chain. Each member has a direct relationship with the person above (one's *oyabun*) and the person or several persons directly below (one's *kobun*). Interaction is usually with one person at a time and never with more than one above. The *kobun* does not go over the head of his superior or *oyabun*. Indeed, it would be unnecessary ever to do so, because the *oyabun* would never make a decision without considering the needs, interests, and desires of the *kobun*.

On and *oyabun-kobun* stress dependency and loyalty of superior and inferior in the vertical hierarchy of Japanese society. Without some balance, however, these concepts would produce a highly factionalized system with little or no regard for the interests of the whole. The group or collective, to be strongly united, must demand a mutual regard or loyalty to something larger than one's faction or *oyabun-kobun* link. In Western societies the normal tendency toward factionalism is counterbalanced by individualism and by the individual's acceptance of a universalist ethic. An American, for example, might be a Republican or

Democrat but he has a duty to all other American citizens that supersedes or at least holds in check excessive loyalty to his chosen party. Oftentimes this is stated as one's duty to be a "good neighbor" or a "good Christian" and this requires the American to be helpful or understanding of others even though they may be members of competing organizations or factions.

Japanese adhere to no such universalist ethic. Instead, the Japanese have internalized the concept of *giri*, which serves a similar function in checking factionalism. *Giri* controls the horizontal relationships in this vertically organized society.

It is difficult to produce an easily understood translation of or definition of *giri*. The term is widely used in Japan and can be found in almost every discussion of Japanese behavior. John W. Hall and Richard K. Beardsley, in their book, *Twelve Doors to Japan*, offer the following explanation of *giri*:

To some Japanese, giri *is the blanket term for obligation between persons in actual situations as contrasted with a universalistic ethic of duty. Others see* giri *as the form of obligation to the group without superiority on one side and inferiority on the other as in the* on *relationship. In either case,* giri *connotes obligation and as such sets the tone of relationship toward specifiable other persons. . . . One can recognize the inevitable tensions between* giri *and* ninjo*. . . .* Ninjo *refers to what one would like to do as a human being and equally to what one finds distasteful or abhorrent out of personal sentiment;* giri *pertains to what one must do or avoid doing because of status or group membership.*[6]

Giri implies the self-discipline that must be used to repress or channel personal desires and feelings. One may not like, personally, the older members of the group or think they are particularly wise or competent, but one must show affection and humbleness toward them for the sake of the group. In this way the selfish impulses of an individual or faction are held in check, not out of a desire to be polite or to avoid confrontation but rather through

an obligation not to embarrass the group by causing any member to lose face.

Giri is well-suited to this society, which produces lifelong relationships. Japanese spend most of every day in close proximity with the other members of their group, and without *giri* such an intense interaction over such an extended period of time would be impossible to bear. The highly ritualized mode of interpersonal relationships developed to accommodate *giri* prevents incidences that could produce hostility. It is not difficult to understand that American notions of group participation, such as "group communication should be characterized by frank, open, and candid statements expressing individual personal feelings, wishes, and dislikes," would be the antithesis of the Japanese concept of *giri*.

Family traditions, the concepts of *on, oyabun-kobun*, and *giri* confine the individual Japanese within a fixed group, keeping him there all his life, and effectively cut him off from other groups. He naturally grows more and more dependent on his group and more distrustful of anyone "outside." In fact, the Japanese are often callously indifferent (although always polite) to anyone outside their own group.

It is difficult for a Westerner to imagine a culture that so totally submerges the individual within the group. There is a tendency for Westerners to account for what they see by attributing subjugation of self to political and economic pressures that force or coerce submission to authority. Such an explanation does not fit Japanese culture nor can it account for the widespread satisfaction the Japanese feel for their way of life. A *Japanese* explanation of this behavior is offered by the psychiatrist, L. Takeo Doi. He maintains that the Japanese desire for group identity can be found in the concept of *amae*. There is no English equivalent of the word *amae* or *ameru* (the verb form), but it can be translated to mean to depend on or presume upon another's love, or it can mean lovable, or it can even mean "spoiled" as in the case of a child spoiled by too much affection. It can also mean "sweet" as in the sweet warmth of a mother's love.

According to Doi, "it (*amae*) carries a positive connotation related to the sweet and warm dependency that a child feels when surrounded by his parents and other loving kin."[7] Doi believes that the Japanese carry this notion with them both consciously and unconsciously throughout life, continually seeking this dependency status in all activities. This, he feels, would account for their desire to constantly subordinate themselves in a group. Each Japanese is attempting to recreate in each group that state of sweet bliss he first experienced in his family. Doi finds the concept of *amae* so pervasive, he claims that "*Amae* might be the very factor that distinguishes Japanese people from other nations. . . ."[8]

III

The ability of the Japanese people to maintain their basic value system and to readily adapt their cultural concepts to new and changing situations is one of the more intriguing aspects of Japanese studies. Nowhere is this more apparent than in the Japanese re-creation of the Western industrial corporation as the twentieth-century counterpart of the feudal system family.

Today, Japan is a modern industrial giant absorbed in a technological race with other industrial nations. Her cities are overcrowded, polluted, fast-paced, and impersonal. To the casual observer, a Japanese city is like any other "big city" in the world: surrounded with huge factories populated by persons isolated from the rural regions, living in an impersonal atmosphere, bent on material acquisition. But anyone who lives in Japan knows how persistently the concepts of *on, giri,* and *amae* remain central to Japanese life. For example, the big corporation occupies a central position in modern Japan, not only as a producer of economic strength and goods, but as the system in which the Japanese maintain their traditional values. Chie Nakane, in an excellent sociological study called *Japanese Society*, argues that the corporate group is the unit that forms the basis for modern Japanese society.[9] Suzuki and Mitsubishi have replaced the feudal family, but the structure has remained the same.

In feudal Japan, and it is important to recall that the Japanese feudal era extended well into the nineteenth century, the family household—composed of the lord and his retainers, warriors, peasants, and craftsmen—was the basic social unit or group. The codes of behavior, loyalty, and honor that served the household then have been transformed in essentially the same form to the modern version of the *ie*, the corporate group. It also is organized in a strict hierarchical order. Seniority determines rank, and merit plays an insignificant part in the advancement of an employee. The *oyabun-kobun* concept governs company-employee interaction. Once a person enters employment with a company he becomes an integral part of that corporate community and usually remains with it the rest of his life. The new employee is indebted to all those above him and he repays *on* through his obligation to all those who come after him or are below him. He is totally dependent on his company and he finds pleasure and satisfaction in this institutionalization of *amae*. Unlike the American company, which is considered primarily a place of employment *apart* from one's family, religious, and social groups, the company in Japan is intimately involved in each member's life. It is the center of the individual's social and economic life. Off-work hours are spent with one's fellow employees, vacations are taken at the company-owned retreat, health services and counseling are provided, even family matters like marriage and divorce are the concern of the company. The worker becomes emotionally involved with the company group, and group duty or *giri* governs his life.

Kaisha, meaning "company" or "enterprise," has become a familiar word in modern Japan. *Kaisha*, superimposed on *ie*, has become the symbol of group consciousness. Nakane describes the importance of his "new" group:

Kaisha *does not mean that individuals are bound by contractual relationships into a corporate enterprise, while still thinking of* themselves as separate entities; rather kaisha is "my" or "our" company, the community to which one belongs primarily, and which is all-important in one's life. Thus in most cases the company provides the whole social existence of a person, has authority over all aspects of his life; he is deeply involved in the association.[10]

In less than one hundred years Japan has moved from a feudal, agrarian society to become a major industrial power. The startling changes necessitated by this quick transition have come about without markedly disrupting the basic patterns of human interactions or altering the fundamental group value orientations. The Japanese have had the ability to accept and absorb methods and ideas from Western culture and yet keep their traditional ritual and ethic. It is clear that the concept binding each Japanese to his group has served to preserve these ancient patterns.

NOTES

1. See Richard E. Porter and Larry A. Samovar, "Approaching Intercultural Communication," in *Intercultural Communication: A Reader*, 3rd. ed., ed. Larry A. Samovar and Richard E. Porter (Belmont, Calif.: Wadsworth, 1982), p. 35.

2. Yoshiharu Matsumoto, "Contemporary Japan: The Individual and the Group," *Transactions of the American Philosophical Society*, 50:1 (January 1960), p. 60.

3. Kawashima Takeoyoshi, "The Status of the Individual in the Notion of the Law, Right, and Social Order in Japan," in *The Japanese Mind*, ed. Charles A. Moore (Honolulu: University Press of Hawaii, 1967), p. 274.

4. Kizaemon Ariga, "The Family in Japan," *Marriage and Family Living*, 16:4 (1954), p. 362.

5. John W. Hall and Richard K. Beardsley, *Twelve Doors to Japan* (New York: McGraw-Hill, 1965), p. 84.

6. Ibid., p. 94.

7. L. Takeo Doi, "Amae: A Key Concept for Understanding Japanese Culture," in *Japanese Culture: Its Development and Characteristics*, ed. Robert J. Smith and Richard K. Beardsley (New York: Aldine, 1962), p. 132.

8. Ibid, p. 133.

9. Chie Nakane, *Japanese Society* (Berkeley: Center for Japanese and Korean Studies, 1970).

10. Ibid., pp. 3–4.

CONCEPTS AND QUESTIONS FOR CHAPTER 4

1. What influences does culture have on the context of the classroom?

2. How does the culturally defined role of the teacher affect the classroom context? Be specific and give examples.

3. Can you think of ways in which your culture has shaped the expectations for classroom behavior? Be specific and give examples.

4. What influences does culture have on the context of the counseling environment? How might expectations differ when counselor and counselee are from different cultures?

5. What criticism of the counseling process (as it involves minorities) has arisen recently? Give examples.

6. How do class-bound values influence the counseling context?

7. What problems might arise in health care counseling if the counselor were influenced by stereotypic notions about Hispanic women?

8. What might health care counselors or practitioners do to improve their ability to serve the Hispanic community?

9. What does Stewart mean when she refers to *ringi*?

10. How do imported Japanese management techniques affect communication in the conduct of the multinational business organization in the United States?

11. Does the Japanese concept of *amae* have any equivalent in the United States?

12. How would knowing about *amae* aid you in understanding intercultural communication contexts?

SUGGESTED READINGS

Chao, K., and W. I. Gorden. "Culture and communication in the modern Japanese corporate organization." *International and Intercultural Annual* 4 (1977), 23–36. This excellent article concentrates on how to improve communication within the context of the Japanese organization. The authors maintain that we must understand the norms of harmony and group cooperation. These concerns of the Japanese are reflected in "the ambiguities of the Japanese language, the use of face-to-face over written communication, the open-space office setting, the concept of shared leadership and responsibility and the *ringi* system through which consensus is sought."

Condon, E. C. "Cross-cultural interferences affecting teacher-pupil communication in American schools." *International and Intercultural Annual* 3 (1976), 108–120. This essay looks at the influence of culture on the classroom setting. Specifically Condon examines: (1) the use of language (vocabulary and grammatical structure), (2) language auxiliaries (paralinguistic and kinesic signals), (3) norms of classroom interaction (modes of address, learning style, and classroom roles), and (4) the general context of human interaction (time and space).

Gould, J. W., P. T. McGuire, and C. Tsang Sing. "Adequacy of Hong Kong–California business communication methods." *The Journal of Business Communication* 20 (1983), 33–40. Companies communicating between Hong Kong and California employ seven basic methods: telex, letter, telephone, visit, courier, computer, and telegram. The main advantages and disadvantages of these methods and recommended safeguards against their misuse are discussed.

Halpern, J. W. "Business communication in China: A second perspective." *The Journal of Business Communication* 20 (1983), 43–56. "To understand the teaching of business communication in China, it is important to have a broad view of the political and educational context in which instruction occurs." The article discusses these areas as observed in China and offers a perspective on English business communication courses in China.

Hofstede, G. *Culture's Consequences: International Differences in Work-Related Values.* Beverly Hills, Calif.: Sage Publications, 1980. Hofstede demonstrates the effects of national culture by analyzing such countries as France, Belgium, Germany, Japan, and India in terms of organizational behavior and theory.

Hornik, J. "Comparative evaluation of international vs. national advertising strategies." *Columbia Journal of World Business* 15 (1980), 36–48. In this paper the author investigates the "standardization dilemma" in international advertising, that is, whether a given concept means to the people of other cultures what it means to the people of the culture in which it was originally developed.

Krarr, L. "The Japanese are coming—with their own style of management." *Fortune* 91 (March 1978), 116–121, 160–161, 164. Krarr, a staff writer for *Fortune*, has written an excellent account of Japanese management techniques in manufacturing plants opened in the United States. This article describes the stark differences between the roles of management in the United States and in Japan and the effect of the Japanese management concepts as applied to American workers.

Lin, E. H. "Intraethnic characteristics and the patient-physician interaction: 'Cultural blind spot syndrome.'" *Journal of Family Practice* 16

(1983), 91–98. This article uses the case method and a literature review to present a conceptual framework for analyzing patient-physician interaction in any cultural context. The author concludes that a good match of intraethnic factors between patient and physician enhances communication.

Montague, A., ed. *Learning Non-Aggression: The Experience of Non-Literate Societies*. New York: Oxford University Press, 1978. This interesting collection explores the impact of child rearing and other cultural inputs on aggression. The authors are concerned with why some cultures are aggressive and others gentle, why some seek violence and others strive to avoid it.

Terpstra, V. *The Cultural Environment of International Business*. Cincinnati: South-Western, 1978. Although this book takes an international business perspective, it nevertheless touches on ideas that are applicable to any intercultural context. Terpstra examines language, religion, values, attitudes toward time, work, change, social organizations, education, and technology, as well as political and legal environments.

Westwood, M. J., A. Bernadelli, and J. Destefano. "Counseling in the culturally diverse society: Some neglected variables in research." *International Journal for the Advancement of Counseling* 4 (1981), 131–137. This paper discusses some of the cultural factors that are relevant to the cross-cultural counseling process, such as differences in perception toward seeking help in a psychological context, perceptions of which type of client-counselor relation is most helpful, perceptions of counseling as a profession, and expectations of different groups.

Zong, B., and H. W. Hildebrandt. "Business communication in the People's Republic of China." *The Journal of Business Communication* 20 (1983), 25–32. The authors discuss the preeminent position held by business communication in China, as well as historical backgrounds, a review of three courses in business communication and their methods of instruc-tion, and conclusions describing opportunities for closer academic ties with China.

ADDITIONAL READINGS

Althen, G., ed. *Learning Across Cultures: Intercultural Communication and International Education Exchange*. Washington, D.C.: National Association for Foreign Student Affairs, 1981.

Arredondo-Dowd, P. M., and J. Gonsalves. "Preparing culturally effective counselors." *Personnel and Guidance Journal* (1980), 657–661.

Ayman, R., and M. M. Chemers. "Relationship of supervisory behavior rating to work group effectiveness and subordinate satisfaction among Iranian managers." *Journal of Applied Psychology* 68 (1983), 338–341.

Barker, L. L., ed. *Communication in the Classroom: Original Essays*. Englewood Cliffs, N.J.: Prentice-Hall, 1982.

Baseman, G. E., and J. L. Simonelli. "Management policy toward task environment agents: A cross-cultural study." *Management International Report* (June 1973), 121–126.

Bass, B., and F. Burger. *Assessment of Managers: An International Comparison*. New York: Macmillan, 1979.

Clark, R. R. "African healing and western psychotherapy." *International Journal of Intercultural Relations* 6 (1982), 5–15.

Dadfar, S., and M. L. Fried-Lander. "Differential attitudes of international students toward seeking professional psychological help." *Journal of Counseling Psychology* 29 (1982), 335–338.

Delgado, M. "Cultural consultation: Implications for Hispanic mental health services in the United States." *International Journal of Intercultural Relations* 6 (1982), 227–250.

Delgado, M. "Hispanic cultural values: Implications for groups." *Small Group Behavior* 12 (1981), 69–80.

Dyol, J. A., and R. Y. Dyol. "Acculturation, stress and coping: Some implications for research and education." *International Journal of Intercultural Relations* 5 (1981), 301–327.

Endicott, C. "Doing business in Spain." *The Bridge: A Review of Cross-Cultural Affairs and International Training* (Summer 1981), 21–28.

Fishman, R. G. "A note on culture as a variable in providing human services in social service agencies." *Human Organization* 38 (1979), 189–192.

Gritzmacher, K. J. "Multinational companies: Exploring the challenges facing consultants." *The Journal of the Communication Association of the Pacific* 9 (1980), 18–23.

Harris, P. R., and D. L. Harris. "Intercultural education for multinational managers." *International and Intercultural Communication Annual* 3 (1976), 70–85.

Hornik, J. "Contemparative evaluation of international vs. national advertising strategies." *Columbia Journal of World Business* (1980), 36–48.

Kleinman, A. *Patients and Healers in the Context of Culture*. Berkeley: University of California Press, 1979.

Musgrove, F. *Education and Anthropology: Other Cultures and the Teacher*. New York: John Wiley, 1982.

Natharius, D. "The minority or other cultural student in the interpersonal communication classroom: Some teaching strategies." *The Journal of the Communication Association of the Pacific* 8 (1979), 100–104.

Nguyen, S. D. "Psychiatric and psychosomatic problems among Southeast Asian refugees." *Psychiatric: Journal of the University of Ottawa* 7 (1982), 163–172.

Nishiyama, K. "Intercultural communication problems in Japanese multinationals." *Communication: The Journal of the Communication Association of the Pacific* 12 (1983), 50–60.

Pedersen, P., W. J. Lonner, and J. G. Draguns, eds. *Counseling Across Cultures*. Honolulu: University Press of Hawaii, 1976.

Philips, S. V. *The Invisible Culture: Communication and Community on the Warm Springs Indian Reservation*. New York: Longman, 1983.

Pusch, M., ed. *Multicultural Education: A Cross-Cultural Training Approach*. La Grange, Ill.: Intercultural Network, 1980.

Rome, D. "International training: What is it?" *The Bridge: A Review of Cross-Cultural Affairs and Training* (Spring 1981), 23–28.

Seelye, H. *Teaching Culture: Strategies for Foreign Language Educators*. Skokie, Ill.: National Textbook Company, 1974.

Segal, M. H. "On teaching cross-cultural psychology." *Journal of Cross-Cultural Psychology* 11 (1980), 89–99.

Simpkin, R., and R. Jones. *Business and the Language Barrier*. London: Business Books, Ltd., 1976.

Sue, D. W., and D. Sue. "Barriers to effective cross-cultural counseling." *Journal of Counseling Psychology* 24 (1977), 420–429.

Part Three

Intercultural Interaction: Taking Part in Intercultural Communication

If we seek to understand a people we have to put ourselves, as far as we can, in that particular historical and cultural background.... One has to recognize that countries and people differ in their approach and their ways, in their approach to life and their ways of living and thinking. In order to understand them we have to understand their way of life and approach. If we wish to convince them, we have to use their language as far as we can, not language in the narrow sense of the word, but the language of the mind.

—Jawaharlal Nehru

In this part we are concerned with taking part in intercultural communication. Our interest focuses on both verbal and nonverbal forms of symbolic interaction. As we pointed out in introducing Part Two, meanings reside within people, and symbols serve as stimuli to which these meanings are attributed. Meaning-evoking stimuli consist of both verbal and nonverbal behaviors. Although we consider these forms of symbolic interaction separately for convenience, we hasten to point out their interrelatedness. As nonverbal behavior accompanies verbal behavior, it becomes a unique part of the total symbolic interaction. Verbal messages often rely on their nonverbal accompaniment for cues that aid the receiver in decoding the verbal symbols. Nonverbal behaviors not only serve to amplify and clarify verbal messages but can also serve as forms of symbolic interaction without verbal counterparts.

When we communicate verbally, we use words with seeming ease, because there is a high consensus of agreement about the meanings our words evoke. Our experiential backgrounds are similar enough that we share essentially the same meanings for most of the word symbols we use in everyday communication. But, even within our culture we disagree over the meanings of many word symbols. As words move farther from sense data reality they become more abstract, and there is far less agreement about appropriate meanings. What do highly abstract words such as *love, freedom, equality, democracy,* or *good time* mean to you? Do they mean the same things to everyone? If you are in doubt, ask some friends; take a poll. You will surely find that people have different notions of these concepts and consequently different meanings for these words. Their experiences have been different, and they hold different beliefs, attitudes, values, concepts, and expectations. Yet all, or perhaps most, are from the same culture. Their backgrounds, experiences, and concepts of the universe are really quite uniform. When cultures begin to vary, much larger differences are found.

Culture exerts no small influence over our use of language. In fact, it strongly determines just what our language is and how we use it. In the narrowest sense, language is a set of symbols (vocabulary) that evoke more or less uniform meanings among a particular population and a set of rules (grammar and syntax) for using the symbols. In the broadest sense, language is the symbolic representation of a people, and it includes their historical and cultural backgrounds as well as their approach to life and their ways of living and thinking.

What comes to be symbolized and what the symbols represent are very much functions of culture. Similarly, how we use our verbal symbols is also a function of culture. What we think about or speak with others about must be capable of symbolization, and how we speak or think about things must follow the rules we have for using our language. Because the symbols and rules are culturally determined, how and what we think or talk about are, in effect, a function of our culture. This relation between language and culture is not unidirectional, however. There is an interaction between them—what we think about and how we think about it also affect our culture.

As we can see, language and culture are inseparable. To be effective intercultural communicators requires that we be aware of the relationship between culture and language. It further requires that we learn and know about the culture of the person with whom we communicate so that we can better understand how his or her language represents that person.

Another important aspect of verbal symbols or words is that they can evoke two kinds of meaning: *denotative* and *connotative*. A denotative meaning indicates the referent or the "thing" to which the symbol refers. For example, the denotative meaning of the word *book* is the physical object to which it refers; or, in the case of the set of symbols *"Intercultural Communication: A Reader,"* the referent is the book you are now reading. Not all denotations have a physical correspondence. As we move to higher levels of abstraction, we often deal with words that represent ideas or concepts, which exist only in the mind and do not necessarily have a physical basis. For example, much communication research is directed toward changes in attitude. Yet attitude is only a hypothetical construct used to explain behavior; there is no evidence of any physical correspondence between some group of brain cells and a person's attitudes.

The second type of meaning—connotative—indicates an evaluative dimension. Not only do we identify referents (denotative meaning), we place them along an evaluative dimension that can be described as positive-neutral-negative. Where we place a word on the dimension depends on our prior experiences and how we "feel" about the referent. If we like books, we might place *Intercultural Communication: A Reader* near the positive end of the dimension. When we are dealing with more abstract symbols, we do the same thing. In fact, as the level of abstraction increases, so does our tendency to place more emphasis on connotative meanings. Most will agree that a book is the object you are holding in your hand, but whether books are good or bad or whether this particular book is good or bad or in between is an individual judgment based on prior experience.

Culture affects both denotative and connotative meanings. Consequently, a knowledge of how these meanings vary culturally is essential to effective intercultural communication. To make the assumption that everyone uses the same meanings is to invite communication disaster.

There are other ways in which culture affects language and language use. We tend to believe that our way of using language is both correct and universal and that any deviation is wrong or substandard. This belief can and does elicit many negative responses and judgments when we encounter someone from another culture whose use of language deviates from our own specifications.

What all of these examples are trying to point out should be quite obvious—language and culture are inseparable. In fact, it would be difficult to determine which is the voice and which is the echo. How we learn, employ, and respond to symbols is culturally based. In addition, the sending and the receiving of these culturally grounded symbols are what enable us to interact with people from other cultures. Hence, it is the purpose of this part of the book to highlight these verbal and nonverbal symbols to help you understand some of the complexities, subtleties, and nuances of language.

5

Verbal Interaction

This chapter begins with a general look at the study of language and culture. Stephen W. King in "A Taxonomy for the Classification of Language Studies in Intercultural Communication" brings together and summarizes various approaches to the role of language in intercultural communication. He sets forth a classification scheme that accomplishes two purposes. First, it indicates what is already known about language in intercultural communication. Second, King's taxonomy isolates those issues that scholars have left still unresolved. His overview highlights studies that search for universals (*etic*) as well as those that deal with specific cultural attributes (*emic*). In addition, phonemic, semantic-lexical, syntactic, and pragmatic approaches are reviewed. Although these issues are not examined in detail, they do provide an excellent introduction to the topic of intercultural language.

The second selection, "The Sapir-Whorf Hypothesis" by Harry Hoijer, introduces us to Benjamin Whorf's hypothesis of "linguistic relativity." This classic and sometimes controversial idea postulates that each language both embodies and imposes upon its users and their culture a particular world view that functions not only as a device for reporting experience but also, and more significantly, as a way of defining experience. To help understand this point of view and its ramifications, Hoijer looks at the basic assumptions, usability, and plausibility of "linguistic relativity."

As we noted in the introduction to this part, language involves attaching meanings to word symbols. If those symbols have to be translated, as when a foreign language is dealt with, numerous problems arise. Without accurate translations those trying to communicate often end up simply exchanging noise or meaningless sounds. What usually happens is that the interpretations lack a common vocabulary and familiar referents. For mutual understanding, equivalencies in each culture are needed. A search for this common ground is the main focus of Lee Sechrest, Todd L. Fay, and S. M. Zaidi in their article, "Problems of Translation in Cross-Cultural Communication." They maintain that while equivalence in idiom, grammar, and syntax may be important, equivalence of experience and concepts is probably most important. With this notion as their central thesis, they attempt to point out some of the inherent problems of translation and also suggest some ways for overcoming these problems.

The first three articles in this chapter explore problems that basically are related to foreign languages. The next three selections examine language and culture from a slightly different perspective. These articles concentrate on language and *intra*cultural communication—communication between members of a dominant culture and members of nondominant subcultures. These three articles are concerned with what happens when people seem to "speak the same language" in a literal sense, yet in reality come from divergent backgrounds.

First, Edith A. Folb's "Vernacular Vocabulary: A View of Interracial Perceptions and Experiences" is important for a number of reasons. First, as the title indicates, she extends her analysis to include perception, experience, and language. For her, the three issues are inseparable. She notes, "What we think about and how we think about it are direct functions of our language; and what we think about and how we think about it in part determine the nature of our culture." To document this particular point of view, Folb examines various terms that were used by black and white youths who, although not interacting with each other, were sharing the same experiences. This comparison demonstrates the interdependence of background and language. Second, this essay is important because it shows the influence subcultures often have on the majority culture. For example, a careful reading of this article will give credence to the contention that black vernacular is a chief source of new words for the white community. Note how many of the expressions in this essay have found their way into the vocabularies of many white Americans.

Understanding how the members of another culture or subculture "talk" can be beneficial to anyone who seeks to improve his or her communication abilities. Knowing a group's specialized forms of speech is even more important when the people involved come from diverse cultures—cultures that often are identified as non-dominant or subordinate. Because of the potential for conflict when the interaction is between members of the dominant culture and members of subordinate subcultures, these types of encounters are often characterized by unique communication strategies—particularly on the part of the "subordinate" group. Stanback and Pearce look at four of these language strategies from the perspective of a member of a lower-status group interacting with a higher-status person. These four strategies are "tomming," "passing," "shucking," and "dissembling." Knowledge of these strategies can often ease some of the conflict and misunderstanding that can arise when interaction takes place between members of these groups.

One of the basic purposes of this book has been to help you learn to appreciate the communication behavior of people from cultures different from your own. The assumption behind this goal is that if you know something about the way other people communicate you can improve the quality of your communication with them. One crucial element in understanding people's communication behavior is understanding how they use language. This study of language is important because one's language is a model of one's culture; language functions as a reflection of a culture's unique experiences. In no instance is this point more vivid than in the black community. Here the study of language not only reveals something about that group's view of the world, but in the case of blacks it is also an examination of the African people and their adjustment to the conditions of American slavery. Our final essay by Shirley N. Weber offers an examination of five important aspects of black language: (1) the dynamic quality of the communication environment, (2) rhythmic quality, (3) "rappin'," (4) "dozens," and (5) proverbial wisdom.

A Taxonomy for the Classification of Language Studies in Intercultural Communication

STEPHEN W. KING

The emerging field of intercultural communication has, apparently, reached consensus on two fundamental propositions:

1. "Intercultural communication occurs whenever a message producer is a member of one culture and a message receiver is a member of another."[1] (Emphasis deleted.)

2. "Culture and language are inseparably intertwined."[2]

These propositions, or ones similar to them, have led researchers from such widely diverse disciplines as cultural anthropology, linguistics, speech communication, and sociology to investigate the complex interrelationships among culture, language, and intercultural communication. However, that research has not been aggregated into a coordinated body of knowledge about the role and nature of language in intercultural communication. Rather, there exists today a variety of disconnected observations, research conclusions, anecdotes, and theoretic speculations on the topic. Two of the causes of the current incoherent situation are (1) the diversity of topics and phenomena justifiably

This original essay appeared in print for the first time in the third edition. All rights reserved. Permission to reprint must be obtained from the publisher and the author. Professor King teaches in the Speech Communication Department at San Diego State University.

included in the topic of language and intercultural communication and (2) the numerous objectives and perspectives of the researchers undertaking these studies.

In this article I propose a taxonomy or classification scheme for sorting language studies in intercultural communication into sensible and usable categories. My hope is that this taxonomy will assist both students and scholars in understanding what is currently known about language in intercultural communication and in identifying those areas most in need of additional research. Simply, the taxonomy described in this article is one way to impose coherence on what is now incoherent and to provide direction for research efforts that are currently uncoordinated.

Language studies in intercultural communication can be divided or sorted on three broad dimensions: (1) the type or level of research objective, (2) the level of language investigated, and (3) the level of language community studied. That is, studies can be usefully viewed (1) as searching for language differences or language similarities, (2) by investigating the sounds, words, grammar, or uses of language, (3) within culture(s), subculture(s), or a given group over time. Each of these dimensions, which I will ultimately combine to create an analytic matrix, is discussed in the following pages.

LEVEL OF RESEARCH OBJECTIVE

Studies of language are undertaken, generally, to accomplish one of two broad and very different objectives: Research aims at either establishing similarities or discovering differences. Both types of studies are needed for a comprehensive understanding of intercultural communication. As Prosser said, "Central to the study of communication between members of different cultures is the importance of similarities and differences as they affect all intercultural and cross-cultural communication."[3] Clark and Clark echoed the importance of both research objectives when they noted

that "if languages are molded in part by the ideas, processing capacities, and social factors all people have in common, they should have certain features in common—linguistic universals. But to the extent that languages are molded by accidental properties of thought, technology, and culture, features will also differ from language to language."[4] Clearly, both objectives will need to be met for a comprehensive understanding of language in intercultural communication.

Studies that search for universal, *etic*, aspects of language take a variety of forms. For example, Osgood and his colleagues established that every one of the 26 languages they investigated employed the dimensions of activity, evaluation, and potency in determining the connotative or affective dimension of meaning.[5] Similarly, Clark and Clark reported that "all languages distinguish at least three characteristics in relatives—generation, blood relationship, and sex."[6] Findings of this type, Prosser argued, cut across cultures and "serve as a primary linkage between communication and culture, and as a base for intercultural communication."[7]

The search for culturally specific, *emic*, attributes of language promotes understanding of the unique relationship between a particular culture and its particular language. For example, Doi's demonstration of "how the psychology of *amae* pervades and actually makes the Japanese patterns of communication" illustrates the connection between Japanese culture and language.[8] On a more particularist level, Folb revealed that for white youth the word *punk* is someone who is disliked, while for black youth *punk* is a male homosexual.[9] Studies of this type highlight the differences between and among language communities and describe the intercultural communication practices involving persons of those communities.

LEVEL OF LANGUAGE

Language studies in intercultural communication do not, indeed cannot, simultaneously investigate all aspects of language. Rather, researchers must focus attention on one aspect or level of language. A language is, in the simplest terms, a system "of sounds and combinations of sounds in commonly established patterns (words) arranged in commonly understood sequences (word orders, sentences) to communicate."[10] Accordingly, each language is composed of sounds, words, sequences of words, and communicative uses. Studies emphasizing each of these dimensions of a language can be called phonemic, semantic, syntactic, and pragmatic, respectively. To understand the contribution of a given study of language in intercultural communication it is essential that we correctly identify the level of language being investigated.

Phonemic

Not all languages of the world contain the same set of acceptable or meaningful sounds. The smallest relevant speech sound of a language is a phoneme; for example, in English the phoneme /k/ is common in the words *key* and *cow*. In English there are approximately 45 phonemes.[11] Phonemic theory and research are necessary in intercultural communication because "if we approach other languages naively we will only respond to those cues as different which are significant in our own language. On the other hand, we will attribute significance, and consider as indicative of separate elements, those differences which have a function in our own language, although they may not have such a function, in [another language]."[12] For example, "speakers of English have usually never noticed that the sound spelled *t* in 'stop' is unaspirated as contrasted with the *t* in 'top'. Yet this difference is sufficient to differentiate forms in Chinese, Hindustani, and many other languages."[13] Comprehensive understanding of and effective practice in intercultural communication require knowledge of phonemic differences and similarities.

Semantic/Lexical

Many studies of language in intercultural communication investigate language at the word level. A semantic analysis investigates the nature and evolution of meanings attached to the words of a language. A lexical assessment of a language explores the total stock of words in a language. Numerous lexical and semantic language studies have been undertaken in intercultural communication research. Obviously, questions of semantics and lexicon are critical to the entire issue of translation.[14] Other general questions at this level of language analysis include investigation of how different cultures have different words with the same meaning, have the same words with different meanings, or have the same words with the same meaning. Less significant is the obvious observation that different cultures have different words with different meanings. Research illustrative of the semantic/lexical type of language study includes the previously mentioned study establishing that connotative meaning is similar in 26 language communities,[15] Clark and Clark's observation that Garo has more names for rice than does Russian,[16] Boas's classic observation that Eskimo has four words for snow while English has only one,[17] and Berlin and Kay's research establishing that every language gets its basic color words from only 11 color names and that those 11 terms are hierarchically arranged.[18] Some languages have as few as only two color terms, but "if a language acquires a new basic color term, it always acquires the next one (in the hierarchy) to the ones it already has."[19] Obviously, intercultural communication, understanding and practice must be based on a solid grounding in the ways languages are different and similar with respect to the total stock of words in a language and the ways meanings are attached to words.

Syntactic

All languages have rules governing the arrangement of words as elements in sentences; those rules constitute the syntax or grammar of the language. Fundamental issues at the syntactic level of intercultural language analysis include such questions as: How do languages resemble or differ from each other with respect to the organization of sentences? How do languages express possession? For instance, by simply analyzing a sentence as containing a subject (S), a verb (V), and an object (O), we know that English is predominantly an SVO language—for example, George hit the ball. Of the six possible orders for S, V, and O, the world's languages are distributed as follows:[20]

SVO—35 percent
VSO—19 percent
VOS—2 percent
SOV—44 percent
OVS—0 percent
OSV—0 percent

Other illustrative syntactic level studies have reported that the Japanese have a grammatical form, adversative passive, that disclaims responsibility for the reported, and usually unpleasant, event or action.[21] In this case the cultural sensitivity to responsibility among the Japanese apparently resulted in or reflects itself in a grammatical form to avoid responsibility. Price-Williams reported that the Hopi language has no tense system reflecting present, past, and future, as does English.[22]

Knowledge about the syntax of a language and, therefore, the way in which a language community organizes its thought is critical to understanding intercultural communication. The need for syntactic level knowledge for the practice of intercultural communication is self-evident.

Pragmatic

The pragmatics of a language concern the rules for and consequences of language usage. Questions of interest at this level of analysis include the following: How do users of a language accomplish communicative objectives, such as insulting and paying deference? What are the effects of particular language use patterns? On what basis do language users decide among semantically equivalent utterances? Two research samples will be briefly described here to illustrate studies of the pragmatics of language usage.

Brown and Levinson have comprehensively investigated the ways that various cultures linguistically create and enforce social relationships and accomplish socially defined objectives such as paying respect, thanking, insulting, and complaining.[23] They indicate, among literally hundreds of such conclusions, that persons in especially debt-sensitive cultures, such as India, express thanks by saying something like "I am humiliated, so awful is my debt," which would be heard as anomalous in other cultures.[24] Further, Tzeltal-speakers use creaking voice to express commiseration and complaint."[25] These conclusions obviously relate not to the structure or phonemics of a language *per se*, but to the use to which language can be put to accomplish particular communicative objectives. Further, knowledge of such conclusions is absolutely essential for understanding and practicing intercultural communication.

Another illustrative area of pragmatics is the extensive research now being conducted on the fact that "the way English is used to make the simplest points can either acknowledge woman's full humanity or relegate the female half of the species to secondary status."[26] Clark and Clark suggested that among the world's languages the bias of male over female is widespread, though not universal.[27] This fact of language in use both reflects and affects society. Repression of women, socially disadvantaged persons, blacks, Indians, and other minorities occurs, in part, linguistically.

Knowledge of a culture's language use norms, the consequences of alternative language use patterns, and the ways language can be exploited to accomplish various social objectives are all essential for comprehensive understanding of intercultural communication.

LEVEL OF COMMUNITY

As has been illustrated throughout this essay, studies of language in intercultural communication have taken as their language population both cultures and subcultures. In addition, several language studies have investigated the changes in language use within a particular culture or subculture over time. It is useful to distinguish among research conducted on cultures, subcultures, and language change.

Many studies are predominantly concerned with the relationship between a culture and a language. Porter and Samovar suggested both directions of influence when they observed that "to a very great extent our language is a product of our culture. At the same time, our culture is very much a product of our language."[28] Indeed, these authors include language as a defining characteristic of a culture. Other researchers, however, focus on identifiable groups within a culture who ostensibly share a language but are identifiable on the basis of values, experience, socio-economic standing or even linguistic idiosyncrasy. Studies have investigated such subgroups as the socially disadvantaged, homosexuals, and black youth. Finally, some intercultural language studies include a comparison of the same language community at various points of time. For example, as Salus explained, "Given that German, English, Latin, Greek, Russian and Armenian have a common ancestor, how long ago were English and German mutually comprehensible dialects?"[29] The previously cited research on the ways in which a language acquires color terms is also illustrative of the type of research that looks longitudinally at some aspect of a language evolution.

THE TAXONOMY

The three dimensions described in this essay (level of objective, level of language, and level of community) combine to create a useful matrix for understanding and classifying language studies in intercultural communication. The aggregate analytic grid is presented in Figure 1.

The development of knowledge of the nature and role of language in intercultural communication will be facilitated by the use of this, or a similar, taxonomy. The use of this classification scheme

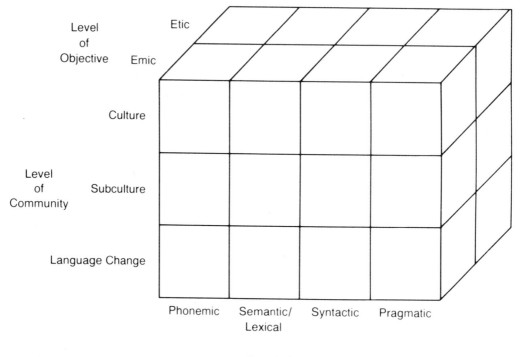

Figure 1 Analytic Taxonomy

assists in (1) understanding what sort of knowledge about language and intercultural communication we now have and (2) identifying areas of needed research.

NOTES

1. Richard E. Porter and Larry A. Samovar, "Approaching Intercultural Communication," in Larry A. Samovar and Richard E. Porter, eds., *Intercultural Communication: A Reader*, 4th ed. (Belmont, Calif.: Wadsworth, 1982), p. 15.

2. Richard E. Porter and Larry A. Samovar, "Communicating Interculturally," in Larry A. Samovar and Richard E. Porter, eds., *Intercultural Communication: A Reader*, 2nd ed. (Belmont, Calif.: Wadsworth, 1976), p. 18.

3. Michael H. Prosser, "Intercultural Communication Theory and Research: An Overview of Major Constructs," in Brent D. Ruben, ed., *Communication Yearbook 2* (New Brunswick, N.J.: Transaction Books, 1978), p. 336.

4. Eve V. Clark and Herbert H. Clark, "Universals, Relativity, and Language Processing," in Joseph H. Greenberg, ed., *Universals of Human Language*, Vol. 1 (Stanford, Calif.: Stanford University Press, 1978), p. 227.

5. Charles E. Osgood, W. May, and M. Miron, *Cross-Cultural Universals of Affective Meaning* (Urbana: University of Illinois Press, 1975).

6. Clark and Clark, p. 252.

7. Prosser, p. 340.

8. L. Takeo Doi, "The Japanese Patterns of Communication and the Concept of *Amae*," in Samovar and Porter, 3rd ed., p. 218.

9. Edith A. Folb, "Vernacular Vocabulary: A View of Interracial Perceptions and Experiences," in Samovar and Porter, 4th ed., p. 232.

10. Thomas Elliott Berry, *The Study of Language* (Encino, Calif.: Dickerson Publishing Co., 1971), pp. 3–4.

11. Berry, p. 224.

12. Joseph H. Greenberg, *Language Universals* (The Hague: Mouton, 1966), p. 123.

13. Ibid.

14. Lee Sechrest, Todd L. Fay, and S. M. Zaidi, "Problems of Translation in Cross-Cultural Communication," in Samovar and Porter, 3rd ed., p. 223.

15. Osgood, May, and Miron.

16. Clark and Clark, p. 228.

17. Franz Boas, "Interaction," in Franz Boas, ed., *Handbook of American Indian Languages, Part 1* (Washington, D.C.: U.S. Government Printing Office, 1911), pp. 1–84.

18. B. Berlin and P. Kay, *Basic Color Terms: Their Universality and Evolution* (Berkeley, Calif.: University of California Press, 1969).

19. Clark and Clark, p. 232.

20. Clark and Clark, p. 257.

21. A. M. Niyekawa, *A Study of Second Language Learning* (Washington, D.C.: Department of Health, Education and Welfare, 1968), cited by Tulsi B. Saral, "Intercultural Communication Theory and Research: An Overview," in Brent D. Ruben, ed., *Communication Yearbook I* (New Brunswick, N.J.: Transaction Books, 1977), pp. 389–396.

22. D. Price-Williams, "Cross-Cultural Studies," in Samovar and Porter, 3rd ed., p. 78.

23. Penelope Brown and Stephen Levinson, "Universals in Language Usage: Politeness Phenomena," in Ester N. Goody, ed., *Questions and Politeness: Strategies in Social Interaction* (Cambridge: Cambridge University Press, 1978), pp. 56–289.

24. Brown and Levinson, p. 252.

25. Brown and Levinson, p. 272.

26. Casey Miller and Kate Swift, *Words and Women* (Garden City, N.Y.: Anchor Books, 1977), p. "x."

27. Clark and Clark, p. 253.

28. Porter and Samovar, "Communicating Interculturally," in Samovar and Porter, 2nd ed., p. 18.

29. Peter H. Salus, *Linguistics* (Indianapolis: Bobbs-Merrill, 1969), p. 49.

The Sapir-Whorf Hypothesis

HARRY HOIJER

The Sapir-Whorf hypothesis appears to have had its initial formulation in the following two paragraphs, taken from an article of Sapir's, first published in 1929.

Language is a guide to "social reality." Though language is not ordinarily thought of as of essential interest to the students of social science, it powerfully conditions all of our thinking about social problems and processes. Human beings do not live in the objective world alone, nor alone in the world of social activity as ordinarily understood, but are very much at the mercy of the particular language which has become the medium of expression for their society. It is quite an illusion to imagine that one adjusts to reality essentially without the use of language and that language is merely an incidental means of solving specific problems of communication or reflection. The fact of the matter is that the "real world" is to a large extent unconsciously built up on the language habits of the group. No two languages are ever sufficiently similar to be considered as representing the same social reality. The worlds in which different societies live are distinct worlds, not merely the same world with different labels attached.

From *Language in Culture*, edited by Harry Hoijer, Copyright 1954 by The University of Chicago. Reprinted by permission of the publisher and the author. Professor Hoijer teaches in the Department of Anthropology, University of California at Los Angeles.

The understanding of a simple poem, for instance, involves not merely an understanding of the single words in their average significance, but a full comprehension of the whole life of the community as it is mirrored in the words, or as it is suggested by their overtones. Even comparatively simple acts of perception are very much more at the mercy of the social patterns called words than we might suppose. If one draws some dozen lines, for instance, of different shapes, one perceives them as divisible into such categories as "straight," "crooked," "curved," "zigzag" because of the classificatory suggestiveness of the linguistic terms themselves. We see and hear and otherwise experience very largely as we do because the language habits of our community predispose certain choices of interpretation. [In Mandelbaum 1949: 162]

The notion of language as a "guide to social reality" is not entirely original with Sapir. Somewhat similar ideas, though far less adequately stated, may be found in Boas' writings, at least as early as 1911. Thus we find in Boas' introduction to the *Handbook of American Indian Languages* a number of provocative passages on this theme, to wit:

It seems, however, that a theoretical study of Indian languages is not less important than a practical knowledge of them; that the purely linguistic inquiry is part and parcel of a thorough investigation of the psychology of the peoples of the world [p. 63].

. . . language seems to be one of the most instructive fields of inquiry in an investigation of the formation of the fundamental ethnic ideas. The great advantage that linguistics offer in this respect is the fact that, on the whole, the categories which are formed always remain unconscious, and that for this reason the processes which lead to their formation can be followed without the misleading and disturbing factors of secondary explanation, which are so common in ethnology, so much so that they generally obscure the real history of the development of ideas entirely [pp. 70–71].

The Sapir-Whorf hypothesis, however, gains especial significance by virtue of the fact that both these scholars had a major interest in American Indian languages, idioms far removed from any in the Indo-European family and so ideally suited to contrastive studies. It is in the attempt to properly interpret the grammatical categories of an American Indian language, Hopi, that Whorf best illustrates his principle of linguistic relativity, the notion that "users of markedly different grammars are pointed by their grammars toward different types of observations and different evaluations of externally similar acts of observations, and hence are not equivalent as observers but must arrive at somewhat different views of the world" (1952: 11).

The purpose of this paper is twofold: (1) to review and clarify the Sapir-Whorf hypothesis, (2) to illustrate and perhaps add to it by reference to my own work on the Navajo language. . . .

The central idea of the Sapir-Whorf hypothesis is that language functions, not simply as a device for reporting experience, but also, and more significantly, as a way of defining experience for its speakers. Sapir says (1931: 578), for example:

Language is not merely a more or less systematic inventory of the various items of experience which seem relevant to the individual, as is so often naively assumed, but is also a self-contained, creative symbolic organization, which not only refers to experience largely acquired without its help but actually defines experience for us by reason of its formal completeness and because of our unconscious projection of its implicit expectations into the field of experience. In this respect language is very much like a mathematical system which, also, records experience in the truest sense of the word, only in its crudest beginnings, but, as time goes on, becomes elaborated into a self-contained conceptual system which previsages all possible experience in accordance with certain accepted formal limitations. . . . [Meanings are] not so much discovered in experience as imposed upon it, because of the tyrannical hold that linguistic form has upon our orientation in the world.

Whorf develops the same thesis when he says (1952: 5):

... the linguistic system (in other words, the grammar) of each language is not merely a reproducing instrument for voicing ideas but rather is itself the shaper of ideas, the program and guide for the individual's mental activity, for his analysis of impressions, for his synthesis of his mental stock in trade.... We dissect nature along lines laid down by our native languages. The categories and types that we isolate from the world of phenomena we do not find there because they stare every observer in the face; on the contrary, the world is presented in a kaleidoscopic flux of impressions which has to be organized by our minds—and this means largely by the linguistic systems in our minds.

It is evident from these statements, if they are valid, that language plays a large and significant role in the totality of culture. Far from being simply a technique of communication, it is itself a way of directing the perceptions of its speakers and it provides for them habitual modes of analyzing experience into significant categories. And to the extent that languages differ markedly from each other, so should we expect to find significant and formidable barriers to cross-cultural communication and understanding. These barriers take on even greater importance when it is realized that "the phenomena of a language are to its own speakers largely of a background character and so are outside the critical consciousness and control of the speaker" (Whorf 1952: 4).

It is, however, easy to exaggerate linguistic differences of this nature and the consequent barriers to intercultural understanding. No culture is wholly isolated, self-contained, and unique. There are important resemblances between all known cultures—resemblances that stem in part from diffusion (itself an evidence of successful intercultural communication) and in part from the fact that all cultures are built around biological, psychological, and social characteristics common to all mankind.

The languages of human beings do not so much determine the perceptual and other faculties of their speakers vis-à-vis experience as they influence and direct these faculties into prescribed channels. Intercultural communication, however wide the difference between cultures may be, is not impossible. It is simply more or less difficult, depending on the degree of difference between the cultures concerned.

Some measure of these difficulties is encountered in the process of translating from one language into another language that is divergent and unrelated. Each language has its own peculiar and favorite devices, lexical and grammatical, which are employed in the reporting, analysis, and categorizing of experience. To translate from English into Navaho, or vice versa, frequently involves much circumlocution, since what is easy to express in one language, by virtue of its lexical and grammatical techniques, is often difficult to phrase in the other. A simple illustration is found when we try to translate the English phrases *his horse* and *his horses* into Navaho, which not only lacks a plural category for nouns (Navaho lí? translates equally English *horse* and *horses*) but lacks as well the English distinction between *his, her, its,* and *their* (Navaho bìlí? may be translated, according to context, *his horse* or *horses, her horse* or *horses, its horse* or *horses,* and *their horse* or *horses.*) These Navaho forms lí?, bìlí? make difficulties in English also because Navaho makes a distinction between a third person (the bì- in bìlí·?) psychologically close to the speaker (e.g., *his* [that is, a Navajo's] *horse*) as opposed to a third person (the hà- of hàlí?) psychologically remote (e.g., *his* [that is, a non-Navaho's] *horse*).

Differences of this order, which reflect a people's habitual and favorite modes of reporting, analyzing, and categorizing experience, form the essential data of the Sapir-Whorf hypothesis. According to Whorf (1952: 27), it is in these "constant ways of arranging data and its most ordinary everyday analysis of phenomena that we need to recognize the influence ... [language] has on other activities, cultural and personal."

The Sapir-Whorf hypothesis, it is evident, includes in language both its structural and its semantic aspects. These are held to be inseparable, though it is obvious that we can and do study each more or less independently of the other. The structural aspect of language, which is that most easily analyzed and described, includes its phonology, morphology, and syntax, the numerous but limited frames into which utterances are cast. The semantic aspect consists of a self-contained system of meanings, inextricably bound to the structure but much more difficult to analyze and describe. Meanings, to reiterate, are not in actual fact separable from structure, nor are they, as some have maintained (notably Voegelin 1949: 36), to be equated to the nonlinguistic culture. Our interest lies, not in questions such as "What does this form, or form class, mean?" but, instead, in the question, "In what manner does a language organize, through its structural semantic system, the world of experience in which its speakers live?" The advantage of this approach to the problem of meaning is clear. As Bloomfield long ago pointed out, it appears quite impossible, short of omniscience, to determine precisely the meaning of any single form or form class in a language. But it should be possible to determine the limits of any self-contained structural-semantic system and the ways in which it previsages the experiences of its users.

To illustrate this procedure in brief, let us turn again to Navaho and one of the ways in which it differs from English. The Navaho color vocabulary includes, among others, five terms: lìgài, dìlxìl, lizìn, lìčí?, and dòʌ̀ìž, to be taken as one way of categorizing certain color impressions. lìgài is roughly equivalent to English *white*, dìlxìl and lizìn to English *black*, lìčí? to English *red* and dòʌ̀ìž to English *blue* or *green*. Clearly then, the Navaho five-point system is not the same as English white-black-red-blue-green, which also has five categories. English *black* is divided into two categories in Navaho (dìlxìl and lizìn), while Navaho has but one category (dòʌ̀ìž) for the English *blue* and *green*. We do not, it should be noted, claim either that English speakers cannot perceive the difference between the two "blacks" of Navaho, or that Navaho speakers are unable to differentiate "blue" and

"green." The difference between the two systems lies simply in the color categories recognized in ordinary speech, that is, in the ordinary everyday ways in which speakers of English and Navaho analyze color phenomena.

Every language is made up of a large number of such structural-semantic patterns, some of which pertain to lexical sets, as in the case of the Navaho and English color terms, and others of which pertain to sets of grammatical categories, such as the distinction between the singular and plural noun in English. A monolingual speaker, if his reports are to be understood by others in his speech community, is bound to use this apparatus, with all its implications for the analysis and categorization of experience, though he may of course quite often select from a number of alternative expressions in making his report. To quote Sapir again (Mandelbaum 1949: 10–11):

. . . as our scientific experience grows we must learn to fight the implications of language. "The grass waves in the wind" is shown by its linguistic form to be a member of the same relational class of experiences as "The man works in the house." As an interim solution of the problem of expressing the experience referred to in this sentence it is clear that the language has proved useful, for it has made significant use of certain symbols of conceptual relation, such as agency and location. If we feel the sentence to be poetic or metaphorical, it is largely because other more complex types of experience with their appropriate symbolisms of reference enable us to reinterpret the situation and to say, for instance, "The grass is waved by the wind" or "The wind causes the grass to wave." The point is that no matter how sophisticated our modes of interpretation become, we never really get beyond the projection and continuous transfer of relations suggested by the forms of our speech. . . . Language is at one and the same time helping and retarding us in our exploration of experience, and the details of these processes of help and hindrance are deposited in the subtler meanings of different cultures.

It does not necessarily follow that all the structural-semantic patterns of a language are equally important to its speakers in their observation, analysis, and categorizing of experience. In describing a language, we seek to uncover all its structural-semantic patterns, even though many of these exist more as potentialities of the system than in actual usage. For ethnolinguistic analysis we need to know, not only that a particular linguistic pattern exists, but also how frequently it occurs in everyday speech. We also need to know something of the degree of complexity of the pattern of expression. There are numerous patterns of speech, particularly among peoples who have well-developed arts of oratory and writing, that are little used by any except specialists in these pursuits. The patterns of speech significant to ethnolinguistic research fall clearly into the category of habitual, frequently used, and relatively simple structural-semantic devices; those, in short, which are common to the adult speech community as a whole, and are used by its members with the greatest of ease.

Not all the structural patterns of the common speech have the same degree of semantic importance. In English, for example, it is not difficult to ascertain the semantic correlates of the structural distinction between singular and plural nouns; in most cases this is simply a division into the categories of "one" versus "more than one." Similarly, the gender distinction of the English third-person singular pronouns, as between "he," "she," and "it," correlates fairly frequently with the recognition of personality and sex.

In contrast to these, there are structural patterns like that which, in many Indo-European languages, divides nouns into three great classes: masculine, feminine, and neuter. This structural pattern has no discernible semantic correlate; we do not confuse the grammatical terms "masculine," "feminine," and "neuter" with the biological distinctions among male, female, and neuter. Whatever the semantic implications of this structural pattern may have been in origin, and this remains undetermined, it is now quite apparent that the pattern survives only as a grammatical device, important in that function but lacking in semantic value. And it is

perhaps significant that the pattern is an old one, going back to the earliest history of the Indo-European languages and, moreover, that it has disappeared almost completely in some of the modern languages of this family, notably, of course, in English.

In ethnolinguistic research, then, it is necessary to concentrate on those structural patterns of a language which have definable semantic correlates, and to omit those, like the Indo-European gender system, which survive only in a purely grammatical function. The assumption behind this procedure is as follows: every language includes a number of active structural-semantic categories, lexical and grammatical, which by virtue of their active status serve a function in the everyday (nonscientific) analysis and categorizing of experience. It is the study of these categories, distinctive when taken as a whole for each language, that yields, or may yield, significant information concerning the thought world of the speakers of the language.

One further point requires emphasis. Neither Sapir nor Whorf attempted to draw inferences as to the thought world of a people simply from the fact of the presence or absence of specific grammatical categories (e.g., tense, gender, number) in a given language. To quote Whorf (1952: 44) on this point: the concepts of time and matter which he reports for the Hopi

do not depend so much upon any one system (e.g., tense, or nouns) within the grammar as upon the ways of analyzing and reporting experience which have become fixed in the language as integrated "fashions of speaking" and which cut across the typical grammatical classifications, so that such a "fashion" may include lexical, morphological, syntactic, and otherwise systematically diverse means coordinated in a certain frame of consistency.

To summarize, ethnolinguistic research requires the investigator to perform, it seems to me, the following steps:

1. To determine the structural patterns of a langauge (that is, its grammar) as completely as pos-

sible. Such determination should include not only a statement of the modes of utterance but as well a careful indication of the frequency of occurrence of these modes, lexical and grammatical, in the common speech.

2. To determine, as accurately as possible, the semantic patterns, if any, that attach to structural patterns. This is a task neglected by most structural linguists who, as is repeatedly mentioned in the discussions that follow, are frequently content simply to label rather than to define both lexical units and grammatical categories. In this connection it is important to emphasize that the analyst must not be taken in by his own labels; he is to discover, where possible, just how the form, or form class, or grammatical category functions in the utterances available to him.

3. To distinguish between structural categories that are active in the language, and therefore have definable semantic correlates, and those that are not. It goes without saying that such distinction requires a profound knowledge of the language, and possibly even the ability to speak and understand it well. Mark Twain's amusing translation of a German folktale into English, where he regularly translates the gender of German nouns by the English forms "he," "she," and "it," illustrates, though in caricature, the pitfalls of labeling the grammatical categories of one language (in this case, German gender) by terms belonging to an active structural-semantic pattern in another.

4. To examine and compare the active structural-semantic patterns of the language and draw from them the fashions of speaking there evidenced. As in Whorf's analysis of Hopi (1952: 25–45), while clues to a fashion of speaking may be discovered in a particular grammatical category or set of lexical items, its validity and importance cannot be determined until its range and scope within the language as a whole is also known. Whorf's conclusions as to the nature of the concept of time among speakers of English rest not alone on the tense distinctions of the English verb (mixed as these are with many other and diverse distinctions of voice,

mode, and aspect) but as well on techniques of numeration, the treatment of nouns denoting physical quantity and phases of cycles, and a host of other terms and locutions relating to time. He says (1952: 33):

The three-tense system of SAE verbs colors all our thinking about time. This system is amalgamated with that larger scheme of objectification of the subjective experience of duration already noted in other patterns—in the binomial formula applicable to nouns in general, in temporal nouns, in plurality and numeration.

5. Taken together, the fashions of speaking found in a language comprise a partial description of the thought world of its speakers. But by the term "thought world" Whorf means

more than simply language, i.e., than the linguistic patterns themselves. [He includes] . . . all the analogical and suggestive value of the patterns . . . and all the give-and-take between language and the culture as a whole, wherein is a vast amount that is not linguistic yet shows the shaping influence of language. In brief, this "thought world" is the microcosm that each man carries about within himself, by which he measures and understands what he can of the macrocosm [1952: 36].

It follows then that the thought world, as derived from ethnolinguistic studies, is found reflected as well, though perhaps not as fully, in other aspects of the culture. It is here that we may search for connections between language and the rest of culture. These connections are not direct; we see, instead, in certain patterns of nonlinguistic behavior the same meaningful fashions that are evidenced in the patterns of the language. Whorf summarizes this facet of his researches in a discussion of "Habitual Behavior Features of Hopi Culture and Some Impressions of Linguistic Habit in Western Civilization" (1952: 37–52).

It may be helpful to outline briefly some aspects of Navaho culture, including the language, as illustration of the Sapir-Whorf hypothesis. In particular, I shall describe first some of the basic postulates of

Navaho religious behavior and attempt to show how these fit in a frame of consistency with certain fashions of speaking evidenced primarily in the morphological patterns of the Navaho verb.

A review of Navaho religious practices, as described by Washington Matthews, Father Berard Haile, and many others, reveals that the Navaho conceive of themselves as in a particular relationship with the environment—physical, social, and supernatural—in which they live. Navaho man lives in a universe of eternal and unchanging forces with which he attempts to maintain an equilibrium, a kind of balancing of powers. The mere fact of living is, however, likely to disturb this balance and throw it out of gear. Any such disturbance, which may result from failure to observe a set rule of behavior or ritual or from the accidental or deliberate committal of some other fault in ritual or the conduct of daily activities, will, the Navaho believe, be revealed in the illness or unexplained death of an individual, in some other personal misfortune or bad luck to an enterprise, or in some community disaster such as a food shortage or an epidemic. Whereupon, a diviner must be consulted, who determines by ritual means the cause of the disturbance and prescribes, in accordance with this knowledge, the appropriate counteracting religious ceremony or ritual.

The underlying purpose of the curing ceremony is to put the maladjusted individual or the community as a whole back into harmony with the universe. Significantly, this is done, not by the shaman or priest acting upon the individual and changing him, nor by any action, by shaman or priest, designed to alter the forces of the universe. It is done by re-enacting one of a complex series of religious dramas which represent, in highly abstract terms, the events, far back in Navaho history, whereby the culture heroes first established harmony between man and nature and so made the world fit for human occupation. By re-enacting these events, or some portion of them, the present disturbance, by a kind of sympathetic magic, is compensated and harmony between man and universe restored. The ill person then gets well, or the community disaster is alleviated, since these misfortunes were but symptoms of a disturbed relation to nature.

From these numerous and very important patterns of Navaho religious behavior, it seems to me we can abstract a dominant motif belonging to the Navaho thought world. The motif has been well put by Kluckhohn and Leighton, who also illustrate it in many other aspects of Navaho culture. They call it, "Nature is more powerful than man," and amplify this in part by the Navaho premise "that nature will take care of them if they behave as they should and do as she directs" (1946: 227–28). In short, to the Navaho, the way to the good life lies not in modifying nature to man's needs or in changing man's nature but rather in discovering the proper relation of nature to man and in maintaining that relationship intact.

Turning now to the Navaho language, let us look at some aspects of the verb structure, illustrated in the following two forms:

nìńtį́ *you have lain down*

nìšínłtį́ *you have put, laid me down*

Both these verbs are in the second person of the perfective mode (Hoijer 1946); the ń- marks this inflection. Both also have a prefix nì-, not the same but subtly different in meaning. The nì- of the first means [*movement*] *terminating in a position of rest*, that of the second [*movement*] *ending at a given point*. The second form has the causative prefix ł- and incorporates the first person object, expressed in this form by ši-. The stem -tį́, common to both forms, is defined *one animate being moves*.

The theme of the first verb, composed of nì- . . . -tį́, means *one animate being moves to a position of rest*, that is, *one animate being lies down*. In the second verb the meaning of the theme, nì- . . . -ł-tį́, is *cause movement of one animate being to end at a given point* and so, by extension, *put an animate being down* or *lay an animate being down*.

Note now that the first theme includes in its meaning what in English we should call both the actor and the action; these are not, in Navaho, expressed by separate morphemes. The subject pronoun prefix ń- serves then simply to identify a particular being with the class of possible beings already delimited by the theme. It functions, in short, to individuate one belonging to the class *animate being in motion to a position of rest*. The theme of the second verb, by reason of the causative ł-, includes in its meaning what in English would be called action and goal. Again the pronoun ši-, as a consequence, simply identifies or individuates one of a class of possible beings defined already in the theme itself. It should be emphasized that the forms used here as illustration are in no sense unusual; this is the regular pattern of the Navaho verb, repeated over and over again in my data.

We are now ready to isolate, from this necessarily brief analysis, a possible fashion of speaking peculiar to Navaho. The Navaho speaks of "actors" and "goals" (the terms are inappropriate to Navaho), not as performers of actions or as ones upon whom actions are performed, as in English, but as entities linked to actions already defined in part as pertaining especially to classes of beings. The form which is glossed *you have lain down* is better understood you [*belong to, equal one of*] *a class of animate beings which has moved to rest*. Similarly the second form, glossed *you have put, laid me down* should read *you, as agent, have set a class of animate beings, to which I belong, in motion to a given point*.

This fashion of speaking, it seems to me, is wholly consistent with the dominant motif we saw in Navaho religious practices. Just as in his religious-curing activities the Navaho sees himself as adjusting to a universe that is given, so in his habits of speaking does he link individuals to actions and movements distinguished, not only as actions and movements, but as well in terms of the entities in action or movement. This division of nature into classes of entity in action or movement is the universe that is given; the behavior of human beings or of any being individuated from the mass is customarily reported by assignment to one or other of these given divisions. . . .

REFERENCES

Boas, Franz (ed.) (1911). "Introduction," *Handbook of American Indian Languages*, Part 1. Washington, D.C.

Hoijer, Harry (1946). "The Apachean Verb, Part III: The Prefixes for Mode and Tense," *International Journal of American Linguistics* 12:1–13— (1953). "The Relation of Language to Culture." In *Anthropology Today* (by A. L. Kroeber and others), pp. 554–73. Chicago, University of Chicago Press.

Kluckhohn, Clyde, and Dorothea Leighton (1946). *The Navaho*. Cambridge, Harvard University Press.

Mandelbaum, David G. (ed.) (1949). *Selected Writings of Edward Sapir*. Berkeley and Los Angeles, University of California Press.

Sapir, Edward (1931). "Conceptual Categories in Primitive Languages," *Science* 74:578.

Voegelin, C. F. (1949) "Linguistics without Meaning and Culture without Words," *Word* 5:36–42.

Whorf, Benjamin L. (1952). *Collected Papers on Metalinguistics*. Washington, D.C., Department of State, Foreign Service Institute.

Problems of Translation in Cross-Cultural Communication

LEE SECHREST
TODD L. FAY
S. M. ZAIDI

To at least some degree every cross-cultural research project must involve the use of language, if only to convey the instructions for a "non-verbal" procedure of some sort. Of course, some projects are far more dependent on linguistic communication than others, and some are exclusively verbal, or linguistic, in nature. We think that there are at least potential communication problems in *all* cross-cultural research, e.g., can one be *sure* that a Pashtun version of "Please do this as quickly as you can" is the same in its meaning as the English? Nonetheless, the problems do vary, and it is worthwhile to note the kinds of problems that are involved and the errors they may produce. We hope in this paper to achieve some clarification of the process of translating from one language into another for purposes of cross-cultural research. We will begin with a discussion of the types of materials which cause translation difficulties, go on to a discussion of the kinds of equivalences which are necessary, and then describe attempts which have

From *Journal of Cross-Cultural Psychology*, Vol. 3, No. 1 (March 1972), pp. 41–56 Copyright © 1972. Reprinted by permission of Sage Publications, Inc. Professor Sechrest is in the Psychology Department, Northwestern University; Professor Fay is in the Psychology Department, University of Western Ontario; and Professor Zaidi teaches at Karachi University. The preparation of this article was supported in part by the Ateneo-Penn State Basic Research Program, sponsored by the United States Office of Naval Research, with the Pennsylvania State University as prime contractor (Nonr-656 37).

been made to overcome translation difficulties. Along the way we will refer to our own work in connection with a comparative study to be carried out in several cultures. It will be evident that we have relied heavily on the work of Werner and Campbell (1970) and Brislin (1970).

TYPES OF TRANSLATION PROBLEMS IN CROSS-CULTURAL RESEARCH

There are, generally speaking, four types of translation problems in cross-cultural studies although little attention has been paid to but one of them. First, nearly all instances of cross-cultural work require that some orientation to the research be given. Ordinarily those persons who are research subjects or informants must be given some rationale for the tasks set for them, and it would seem obvious that some attention would be paid to the equivalence of such introductions as made in different cultures. However, there are no instances known to us in which an investigator specifically mentions such a problem, let alone a solution to it. In any case, there often will be instances in which an investigator must "explain himself" to members of different language groups, and when that necessity arises, its companion necessity is for precision in translation.

The second type of translation problem involves the translation of instructions specific to different types of tasks or measures being used. Even though the response of a subject may require no verbal component, it is almost always necessary that the nature of the task and of his response be explained in words (Anderson, 1967). And those words must be translated from one language to another when one crosses linguistic boundaries. Again, very few investigators seem to have paid much attention to this problem. It seems usually to be *assumed* that translations are adequate. Very few investigators can be described as having been sufficiently wary to make us totally confident in their findings. Rather paradoxically, it is probably the case that the briefer the instructions are, the greater the tendency to assume similarity. However, as Werner and Campbell (1970) make clear, it is, in fact, more difficult to get and to be sure one has gotten a satisfactory translation of a short passage than a longer one. Such phrases as "Do your best," "Guess if you want to," "Take the one you like best," and "Make A the same as B" involve many translational pitfalls for the unwary. It is the lack of context in short phrases and sentences that makes the problem so difficult. Or, viewed in another way, the redundancy in short messages may be very limited. Recently we have been using the Rod-and-Frame Test to measure field dependence-independence in different cultures, and two of the most difficult problems we encountered were in finding a Tagalog (Philippine) word or phrase for "upright" or an Urdu word for "rod."

The third type of translation problem is the obvious one of phrasing questions or the other verbal stimuli in ways that are comparable in two or more languages. Interview questions, statements on personality inventories or attitude questionnaires, and verbal stimuli on projective tests such as incomplete sentences are all examples of the third type of translation problem. This is a problem to which many investigators have addressed themselves. In fact, the problem is so obvious that it is inescapable, and unlike the first two problems, there are almost no investigators unaware of the problem. However, we might point out that translation problems can and do arise even within cultures when different subcultures are being examined, and many investigators have ignored the likelihood that a particular verbal stimulus may not mean the same to a person in one subculture as to a person in another. Dialect differences, use of scholarly rather than vernacular language, and regional differences in colloquial speech and idiom all contribute to potential subcultural research problems. Odd as it may seem, English may at times need to be translated into English, and Urdu into Urdu.

The fourth type of translation problem involves translation of *responses* from one language or dialect to another so that comparisons may be made. Many questionnaires have limited response alternatives, e.g., true-false, agree-disagree, and the translation is made prior to the response. However,

for open-ended questions, interviews, projective tests, and the like, it may be necessary to translate the responses. When responses must be translated, the same problems exist as in translating other material. In many cases translation and its attendant expense and difficulties can be avoided by coding, categorizing, or scoring responses in the language in which they are given. If the coding system is easily communicated and relatively unambiguous, many difficulties can be obviated. To be sure, the coding system itself must be translated, but that is a decidedly simple task when compared to translation of responses, and especially when one has access to bilingual coders. It should be noted, though, that Ervin (1964) found that language of response could make a difference in the responses of bilinguals, and bilingual coders need to be checked for their consistency also.

PROBLEMS OF EQUIVALENCE IN TRANSLATION

As we stated earlier the major problem in translation is to determine that the translation is equivalent to the original language. There are, however, a number of different kinds of equivalence that have somewhat different effects and implications. We propose here to discuss several different aspects of equivalence which must be considered in transporting a research instrument from one linguistic area to another. While the problems vary somewhat in importance and are most serious when language and cultures are maximally different, we think that all the problems exist in some measure even within cultures; they merely become increasingly troublesome with increasing-decreasing linguistic and cultural similarity.

Vocabulary Equivalence

Perhaps the most obvious kind of equivalence is in vocabulary, in the words used in two or more translations. For example, an item such as "I am happy most of the time" could be translated rather directly into another language than English with the major vocabulary problem being, in most instances, finding an equivalent term for "happy." Or, in using a Semantic Differential (Osgood, Suci & Tannenbaum, 1957), one would need to find comparable terms for such items as strong-weak, rich-poor, and fast-slow.

While it might seem that vocabulary problems could be solved with a good dictionary, and indeed, that is a valuable resource, the fact of the matter is that the problems are not by any means so simple. In the first place, dictionary language is often not the language of the people. In fact, we could make a parallel comment about the use of translators, who are often chosen from a population of highly educated persons who speak and write somewhat pedantically in both their languages. We have numerous instances of translations made with either dictionary or translator that proved unworkable because they did not have the right meaning to persons for whom the test was intended. Thus, a good first rule in translating is to use translators who have good acquaintance with the language *as used by the prospective test respondents*.

A second aspect of the problem of vocabulary equivalence in relation to dictionary translations is that most words in the dictionary are defined in a number of ways or by a number of terms. It is not easy to know which terms to select for the translation. The problem is to reflect in the term chosen the obvious meaning and the important nuances of the original term. Such terms as *responsible, suggestible, aloof,* and *tough* are all English terms with nuances that make it difficult to find just the right equivalent in other languages. On the other hand such Urdu terms as *sanjida, pakbaz, ameen* and *ghairat* (all indicating good and desirable personality traits in Pakistan) are also expressive of delicacies of thought that make the discovery of a vocabulary equivalent difficult.

There may, in fact, be terms in one language for which it is almost impossible to find an equivalent in another language. For example, we found that there is no really good Tagalog term for *feminine*, i.e., a term that makes it possible to say "Maria is more *feminine* than Elena." Similarly, there was no Tagalog equivalent for *domestic* that we might ap-

ply in describing people, so as to say, "Mr. Santos is very *domestic* in his interests." On the other hand, *hiya* (related to shyness, embarrassment, shame, and deference) and *pakikisama* (related to getting along with others, acceding to wishes of one's peer group, and conformity) are Tagalog words difficult to translate into English because there just are not any equivalents. We found it somewhat difficult to find good counterparts for *orderly, conforming,* and *polite* in Urdu, and *moonis, humdum,* and *habeeb* (all indicating differences in degree of friendship and closeness) are Urdu words without ready English equivalents.

A frequent attempted solution to problems of nonequivalence of terms, one recommended by Werner and Campbell (1970), is the use of several words in the target language to try to convey an idea expressible in one word in the source language. Although such a procedure will be discussed later in this paper, we would note here that differences in length of materials should be kept within fairly close limits.

Vocabulary equivalence is not necessarily equally difficult to achieve between all pairs of languages. We have no data on this but there are many reasons such as cultural differences, as well as linguistic traditions, for incomparability between two languages. To illustrate, however, we have been involved in considerable translation from English to Tagalog and back, and from English to Urdu and back. It is our distinct impression that it is easier to translate between English and Urdu than between English and Tagalog. At least a part of the difference in difficulty we attribute to the differential availability of words in the two languages which are comparable to English words. Tagalog does not seem to have very good words for a lot of English terms and vice versa. While there are obvious problems translating from English into Urdu, it seems to be richer in the kinds of words which are used in English texts. Brislin (1970) found substantial differences between languages in translation error rates (while he found Tagalog-English to be relatively easy, it is almost certainly the case that his Tagalogs were more nearly bilingual than his other linguistic assistants).

To the extent that words do not mean the same thing to respondents in different cultures, the responses are uninterpretable with respect to cultural similarities or differences. But, vocabulary equivalence is only part of the problem.

Idiomatic Equivalence

Frequently in translating one encounters problems that arise because idiomatic speech is employed in one language, and idioms never translate properly, if at all. In fact, one often becomes aware of idiomatic language only when one attempts to translate and realizes that a direct translation would not make sense at all. For example, the direct translation of the Tagalog adjectival expression *hipong-tulog* is "fish sleeping"; yet a more meaningful equivalent in English might be conforming, indecisive, or "following the present current of thought or action."

Although it might seem that one should avoid use of idioms in producing technical research material, and that is what Werner and Campbell recommend, idioms are so firmly embedded in our speech patterns that under most circumstances we are scarcely aware of them. Moreover, to attempt to avoid idioms completely in, for example, writing instructions or writing items, would probably produce a highly stilted, pedantic form of discourse which would be utterly unsuitable for research efforts with the general population in any culture. And, of course, if one is translating the responses of an informant or subject, idiom cannot be avoided. Therefore, the best that can be done is to attempt to ensure that when idioms are used in a translation they are equivalent in meaning to the idioms used in the original, and that the general level of idiomatic speech in the two languages is approximately equivalent so that one does not seem more scholarly, more stilted, or in some other way different from the other. For example, the Tagalog idiom *galit-bulkan* is literally translated "angry volcano" and is interpreted to mean a sudden expression of anger. One might be able to use the English slang term "blow up" as an idiomatic equivalent. To "keep your mouth shut" can

be translated into Urdu, but a better equivalent in terms of usage would be *tum chup raho*, which back translates as "you keep quiet."

Grammatical-Syntactical Equivalence

Still another equivalence problem arises from the fact that languages differ widely in their grammars and syntaxes and these differences are often critical to the meanings in various translations. While these problems are probably of somewhat greater importance with longer passages, they do occur even in relation to very short passages, perhaps even for single words. One of the reasons for a grammatical equivalence problem involving single words is that two languages may not have equivalent parts of speech. Thus, for example, if there is no gerund in a particular language there may be some problems in achieving good equivalence for the commonly used gerunds in English. (Urdu has no gerund quite like English.) A fairly ordinary type of test item consists of asking an individual which of a list of activities he enjoys and the list is often couched in terms of such gerunds as singing, dancing, eating, playing, writing, and the like. While it is most certainly possible to develop an equivalent form for such items in most languages, there do arise some difficulties in specifying the exact linguistic form which is to be used in a language which lacks the gerund. Other parts of speech such as adjectives, adverbs, and the like, may be missing in particular languages and may pose some problems for translators.

Nonetheless, the more important problems in attaining grammatical syntactical equivalence involve longer passages. Probably one of the more common grammatical problems in achieving equivalence is in dealing with verb forms. Not all languages deal with the problems of verb mood, voice, or tense in the same way by any means, and it is sometimes very difficult in a given language to put expressions which have the same verb form or meaning in English. For example, in the Tagalog dialect there is no subjunctive mood. As a result, it becomes impossible to find literal equivalents and difficult to find conceptual equivalents for English conditional subjunctive expressions. The English sentence, "If I had had the money, I would have bought the dress," can be translated in Tagalog to *Kung mayroon sana akong pera, nabili ko sana ang baro.* The literal translation of this Tagalog sentence into English would be "If I have the money (understood I have not), I bought the dress (understood I did not)." Needless to say, the tense and the conditional sense seem not to be the same as the original English.

The whole area of translation has been so little studied in the context of the field of psychology that it is difficult to cite specific instances of syntactic nonequivalence, although there is no question that they abound and that they can affect the meaning of translations.

The work of Whorf (1956) contains many examples such as the Hopi utilization of what we think of as nouns as verb or action forms. Thus *chair* is *chairing* or the act of sitting. Or, looking elsewhere one finds that in English it is obligatory to specify number in relation to nouns, nearly all of which are either singular or plural. However, in Yoruba (Nigeria) it is not at all obligatory that number be specified. And Arabic obliges that number be specified as singular, dual, or plural. Obviously such syntactical variations can very much affect meaning and the problems of translation.

Experiential Equivalence

There are two remaining equivalence problems that are of a somewhat different order from the ones we have discussed above, since the remaining two do not involve purely linguistic considerations. Nonetheless, they are important for translators to keep in mind and may constitute severe impediments to the development of adequate materials for studies in societies with different languages. The first of these is experiential equivalence, the second is conceptual equivalence.

By experiential equivalence we mean that in order for translations to be successful from one culture to another they must utilize terms referring to real things and real experiences which are famil-

iar in both cultures, if not exactly equally familiar. Werner and Campbell call this "*cultural* translation" as distinguished from *linguistic* translation. If two cultures differ so greatly in the nature of their objects, in the nature of their social arrangements, in their overall ways of life, or that objects or experiences which are familiar to members of one culture are unfamiliar to members of another, it will be difficult to achieve equivalence in meaning of a variety of linguistic statements no matter how carefully the translation is done from the standpoint of the language involved. Let us take a perhaps trivial, but very obvious example. If the item "I would like to be a florist" appeared on a personality or interest measure for use with Americans it would probably be understood by most of them. That same item, however, would be incomprehensible to most people around the world, no matter how carefully it was explained to them. Flower shops simply are not found in most parts of the world and, in many cases, the idea of a flower shop where one has flowers made into fancy arrangements and the like would be totally foreign to the experience of most people. Consequently, if one wished to achieve experiential equivalence one would have to think about why the item involving doing the work of a florist is used in an American sample and then find an equivalent that is in terms of a local experience type of activity in the other culture being studied. Thus, if in an American test the item is scored for femininity because it is thought to reflect an interest in feminine kinds of activities, then in another culture in which flower shops were missing one would have to look for a similar kind of economic activity primarily identified with females and thought to reflect an effeminate outlook even when it occurred among males. That might not be easy to do but, for example, in the Philippines most market vendors are women, and it is possible that Filipinos might think a male effeminate if he were a market vendor. In that case one could use the item "I would like to be a market vendor" as an experiential equivalent to "I would like to be a florist."

In some cases there may be no alternative but to eliminate items because a counterpart does not exist or would be of too uncertain equivalence in another culture. Animals, household objects, architectural features, terrain features, biological specimens, etc. are all examples of categories of concrete objects where cultures may differ so much in experience that the problem of attaining equivalence is difficult. No translation of "department store" into Urdu is possible because they are unknown in Pakistan, and the closest one could get would be "large shop."

However, it should not be thought that the problems of equivalence pertain only to such concrete aspects of cultures. They may also stem from differences between other cultural arrangments. One good example lies in the kinship patterns and social relations that differ so widely from one culture to another. The term "cousin," for example, means something very different in the Philippines than it means in the United States, and it means something else again in Pakistani culture. Or, to take another example, the typical school classroom or even university classroom is so very different in its meaning, in the way it is conducted, in the relationship among the students or in the relationship between the students and professors, that it is very difficult to ensure that any items or statements about the university classroom as an experience can possibly be equivalent for members of cultures as diverse as, let us say, Pakistani and American. Such an item as "I seldom speak up in class" would undoubtedly have a very different meaning for American and Pakistani students because the experience of being in a class is so very different for the two groups. Again, achieving an adequate translation of the item would involve figuring out what the item was supposed to reflect in the way of a trait or response disposition in an American culture and then finding an equivalent lying within the experience of typical Pakistani students.

The position taken here is much akin to that of Przeworski and Teune (1970), who suggest that in most instances of the kind at issue here the important question concerns the *equivalence of inferences* rather than of stimuli. They indicate that inferences must be validated within rather than across social systems. "An instrument is equivalent across systems to the extent that the *results* provided by the instrument reliably describe with (nearly) the same validity a particular phenomenon in different social systems" (opus cited, p. 108). While we are perhaps somewhat more interested in and sanguine about achieving linguistic equivalence than Przeworski and Teune, and while we have some reservations about using similarity of factorial structure as the sole criterion of equivalence, we are in general agreement with their propositions.

Conceptual Equivalence

The final problem in achieving equivalence between measures to be used in two or more cultures is the problem of ensuring that the concepts used in the measures, interview, or other translated materials are equivalent in the two cultures. This is somewhat apart from the previous kinds of equivalence problems for it may very well be that one has in two cultures a word that, when translated, mutually yields high agreement and yet it may not be that the concepts implied by the two words are, in fact, identical or particularly close in nature. For example, the item "I love a parade" might be quite easy to translate into other languages than English and, at least on a word-for-word basis, there would be no problem in equivalence in such things as vocabulary and experience. Nonetheless, the concept "love" as used in that English item is far different in its implications from the concept which might be implicit in words used in other languages. English is, perhaps, not an especially rich language for expressing positive feelings about things and, consequently, the word "love" is used to mean several different things, or at least to connote varying degrees of positive affect toward some object.

A second aspect of the problem of conceptual equivalence is that a concept well understood and frequently employed in one culture may be lacking altogether in another culture, or it may appear at least in such varied different fragmented forms that it is very difficult to construct materials that treat the true concepts equivalently. For example in the

Philippines it proved to be very difficult to find even a concept, let alone words, which had the same connotations as the common American concept of homosexual. The available Philippine words are used in a variety of ways which suggests that the concept simply does not exist in the same highly developed form as it does in the American culture (Sechrest & Flores, 1969). In fact, it is our feeling that doing translations in both directions in two or more cultures is an excellent way of coming to understand the divergent ways of thinking about problem areas in different cultures.

The Paradox of Equivalence

We have gone into some detail concerning the problems of achieving equivalence across two or more languages as if equivalences were the fundamental problem. Actually, in certain respects it is not, for there may be a distinct paradox involved in translation for the sake of achieving equivalence. The paradox is that if one demands that a form of a test or other measure yield comparable results in two cultures in order to demonstrate equivalence, then the more equivalent two forms become the less the probability of finding cultural differences. On the other hand, if one looks predominantly for cultural differences and ignores the problem of equivalence, then the less attention that is paid to the problem of equivalence the greater the probability of finding cultural differences. For example, in his work on the comparison of Japanese and American college students' responses to the Edwards Personal Preference Schedule, Barrien (1966) argued that differences found between the two samples stemmed from different concepts of social desirability for the two cultures. If that were done, however, it is entirely possible that important cultural differences would be obliterated, or at least obscured, by the attempt to achieve what is a rather misleading form of equivalence. Obviously, we are not thinking here of the kinds of questions for which prior knowledge can be used to justify expectations either of differences or similarities between cultures, e.g., proportion of Roman Catholics in a culture. The paradox is troublesome for more complex issues for which prior expectations are uncertain or a poor guide, e.g., "What is the true cause of personal misfortune?"

The resolution of the equivalence paradox is not a simple one, but our feeling is that it probably lies in some method of triangulation whereby measures are subjected to increasingly more severe tests of equivalence, and we determine what sort of convergence in the responses of two cultures we may be able to obtain. The more rapidly the findings from two cultures converge in terms of the degree of effort required to achieve equivalence, the smaller the differences between the two cultures probably are. In any case, we can never know for sure what the absolute differences between cultures are and can probably only guess at their relative magnitude. Thus, we may be able to say that the members of two cultures are more similar with respect to one area of functioning than with respect to another, or that they are more or less similar to each other than they are to members of some third culture. There are, of course, some measures for which diminishing returns of equivalence manipulations are likely to be achieved at a very rapid rate. For example, in the case of the Rod-and-Frame Test it seems scarcely likely that any real differences, for example between men and women, are simply a function of equivalence of instructions to the two groups.

Obviously in research the aim of producing versions of some communication which are equivalent in two or more languages has a pragmatic justification. One does not labor over translations for the sake of art. The aim of equivalence is that the specific influence of language on responses may be removed. It is, as we have suggested, difficult to know when equivalence has been achieved, but Werner and Campbell and Brislin have proposed several very useful criteria. However, in his empirical study of translation equivalence Brislin had monolingual raters examine an original English version and one translated back into English in order to detect "errors that might make differences in the meaning people would infer." That process when followed by correction of the errors produced reasonably good translations although pretesting of instruments revealed some additional errors.

Direct Translation

The most common procedure by which an attempt to achieve equivalent forms of questionnaires, interview, and the like for cross-cultural research has been the direct translation. That is, a translator or translators who are bilingual attempt to translate as best they can from one language into the other. This translation procedure, as a matter of fact, is still characteristic of a great deal of work of a cross-cultural nature and it is particularly likely to be used in relation to brief sets of materials, orientation, instructions, and the like. The method has also been used for the development of adjective check lists and similar materials. However, as Werner and Campbell have pointed out it is exactly for such brief materials that a method of direct translation is likely to be most inadequate. To be sure, it is probably rare that a translator works without any check at all on the adequacies of his efforts, but in a great many instances the checking is likely to be unsystematic and inadequate.

There are several problems with direct translation, the most important of which is that idiosyncracies may be introduced by the translator himself. The translator himself may not be sufficiently skilled on one or the other of the languages in which he is working, he may not be culturally representative of the group for which the materials are to be used, and he may, by reason of his own experience, have peculiarities of word understanding or word use which will not be shared by persons for whom the materials are intended.

Obviously, it would be going beyond the realm of reason to assert that all translations made by a single translator are inadequate, but we feel that the probability of inadequacies of translations may go undetected. Therefore, we believe that the method should be rejected out of hand, particularly when in nearly all instances there are better, if

not perfect, alternatives. We would, however, point out that the method of direct translation is still quite common and, in fact, it is probably still characteristic of the large bulk of all anthropological translation.

Back Translation

Werner and Campbell have described a method of translation which is distinctly superior to the method of direct translation even though it may not be the ideal solution in many instances. In the method of back translation a translation is first made from one language to another, for example, from English to Urdu, by one or more translators. The translated material is then back translated, for example, from Urdu to English, by another translator or set of translators. The two versions of the original can then be checked for the adequacy of the translation. For example, if a statement in English such as "I get tense before examinations," is translated into Urdu and then comes back into English translated from the Urdu as "I get excited before examinations,"[1] the discrepancy between the two versions would suggest to the experimenter that further translation is required. Presumably, by successive translations and back translation a better and better approximation to the original can be obtained, and the final version of the translated material should be satisfactory.

However, we would suggest that not all problems in translation are quite so easily solved as might be suggested by the foregoing. For one thing, when a back translation is accomplished there are almost inevitably some discrepancies between the original English version and the back-translated version. It then requires a judgment on the part of someone whether the two versions are, in fact, equivalent. There may be a number of reasons for nonequivalence which have to be treated quite differently in the process of developing a satisfactory research instrument. For one thing discrepancies may occur because the original translation was inadequate, and if that is true the only solution is improvement of the translation.

However, the inadequacy may have stemmed from different sources. It may have been the result of an idiosyncratic translation by the translator. For example, a translator may himself not know the difference between the words "tense" and "excited," or may not regard the distinction as important. A second possibility is that since the translation and back translation are done by different people, the two separate English versions may be more equivalent than they seem because of idiosyncratic habits in the use of English words. Thus, if the word "annoyance" is translated into Urdu and then comes back translated into English as "pain" it is entirely possible that the discrepancy is attributable to faulty knowledge of English rather than to any inadequacies in Urdu. In any case, in such an instance the experimenter would have to make a decision as to whether the translation was inadequate or not, that is, whether "pain" is a reasonable English synonym for "annoyance," e.g., as in "waiting in line is a pain."

A second source of difficulty in producing equivalent back translations is that the lack of equivalence may in fact stem from the absence of a satisfactory word, or at least from the lack of equivalence of concepts in the two languages. Thus, the word "homosexual" when translated into Tagalog usually becomes "bakla" which, when translated back into English might come out as "sissy" or something of that sort. The problem lies not in the idiosyncracy of the translator or in the failure to use the best term, but simply in the fact that there is no equivalent in Tagalog for the English term "homosexual." Such problems of nonequivalence can only be resolved by having available a number of bilingual speakers who can be consulted with respect to the problems involved. Preferably the bilingual speakers should come from different backgrounds of the subjects who are to respond to the instrument being developed. For example, we have found that many of the persons who are most readily available as translators are persons who are considerably higher in education than the subjects who will be using the instrumental and they therefore produce stilted, academic versions of a questionnaire which are not

readily understood by the subjects. In fact, an additional problem arose in the Philippines where, since there are many different dialects, many potential translators were not in fact native speakers of the dialect into which they were making translations. Because of the movement toward development of a national language in the Philippines there has been a considerable increase in the number of students who are studying the national language, Pilipino, in school. Such speakers of Pilipino may actually be superior in terms of grammatical knowledge and in terms of formal linguistic knowledge of Pilipino or Tagalog to native speakers, but in fact their language is different from that of the native speaker of Tagalog, and if one is to use a questionnaire with native speakers then the versions produced by the academically trained persons may be quite inadequate. For example, the Tagalog word for science, *agham*, is not familiar to many native speakers who do use the English word. We believe that the only solution is to have available as translators, or at least as informants, persons who are native speakers of the language into which the translation is to be done.

Actually the process of back translation, when properly done, is literative, i.e., an initial translation is made, back translated, examined for errors, corrected, again back translated, etc. At every stage improvement depends upon a rather critical set being taken by the translator working at that stage. Brislin has shown that the pretesting is an important addendum to the back translation process, for he found a number of meaning errors that had previously gone undetected. Errors may well go undetected for any of a number of reasons mentioned above, e.g., translators of different subculture than subjects, conventions in translating that are not completely legitimate (*bakla* = homosexuality), etc. Fortunately, despite the problems with back translation as a technique, Brislin has shown that very good results may be obtained when it is carefully done.

The major advantage of back translation is that it operates as a filter through which nonequivalent terms will not readily pass. If there is not an appropriate word or phrase in a target language for one in the source language, that fact has a high probability of being discovered. For example, if there is no equivalent in a target language for the American expression "take advantage of someone," it will probably be back translated as "boss someone around," "cheat someone," etc. The investigator will be able to decide fairly accurately just what concepts he can employ in the two languages. He need not speculate; he can act on the basis of the back translation results.

NOTE

1. There is no good Urdu equivalent for *tense*, and the likely substitute, *Tanao*, might be back translated as *excited*, *upset*, or even *embarrassed*.

REFERENCES

Anderson, R. B. W. On the comparability of meaningful stimuli in cross-cultural research. *Sociometry*, 1967, *30*, 124–136.

Berrien, F. K. Japanese and American values. *International Journal of Psychology*, 1966, *1*, 129–141.

Brislin, R. W. Back-translation for cross-cultural research. *Journal of Cross-Cultural Psychology*, 1970, *1*, 185–216.

Ervin, S. M. Language and TAT content in bilinguals. *Journal of Abnormal and Social Psychology*, 1964, *68*, 500–507.

Osgood, C. E., Suci, G. J., & Tannenbaum, P. H. *The Measurement of meaning*. Urbana, Ill.: Univ. of Illinois Press, 1957.

Sechrest, L., & Flores, L. Homosexuality in the Philippines and the United States: The handwriting on the wall. *Journal of Social Psychology*, 1969, *79*, 3–12.

Werner, O., & Campbell, D. T. Translating, working through interpreters, and the problem of decentering. In R. Naroll & R. Cohen (eds.) *A handbook of method in cultural anthropology*. New York: The Natural History Press, 1970, pp. 398–420.

Whorf, B. L. *Language, thought, and reality*. New York: John Wiley & Sons, 1956.

Vernacular Vocabulary: A View of Interracial Perceptions and Experiences

EDITH A. FOLB

Students of intercultural communication are aware of the intimate reciprocity of language with cultural perceptions and experiences. As Porter and Samovar have observed, "Culture and language are inseparably intertwined. What we think about and how we think about it are direct functions of our language; and what we think about and how we think about it in part determine the nature of our culture" (p. 18). However, when two groups of people—even within the same culture—share a language, this does not necessarily mean that vocabulary is used to characterize similar or identical experiences. One of the greatest barriers to effective communication, whether it be intracultural or intercultural, is the lack of shared experiences and a common vocabulary to define them. In American society, this sociolinguistic chasm between racial and ethnic subcultures and the dominant culture is still apparent. In his discussion of linguistic hostility as a factor in intracultural conflict, Maurer (1969) pointed out that "the so-called ghettos constitute sub-cultures within sub-cultures in many parts of the United States. . . . In these areas the break with the mores and the language of the dominant culture is of such proportions that several generations will be required to bring them together" (p. 606).

This original essay appeared in print for the first time in the second edition. All rights reserved. Permission to reprint must be obtained from the publisher and the author. Dr. Folb teaches at San Francisco State University.

If we are to understand how intracultural and intercultural tensions can be reduced, we must look at the kinds of cultural experiences that are designated as important within and between groups of people. Because vocabulary is the part of language that is most immediately under the conscious manipulation and control of its users, it provides the most accessible place to begin exploration of shared and disparate experiences.

This paper focuses on a subset of the American lexicon, here referred to as *vernacular vocabulary* (nonstandard, unconventional, and so-called deviant words and phrases that have been variously labeled slang, argot, lingo, and jargon). The discussion deals with a selected body of vernacular expressions that were elicited from a cross section of black youths living in the greater Los Angeles area, and subsequently presented to a cross section of white youths also living in Los Angeles. The paper explores how those terms were defined, used, and talked about by the black and white youths interviewed.

BACKGROUND

The findings presented here are drawn from my continuing work on intracultural and intercultural vernacular vocabulary use (see Folb, 1972, 1973a, 1973b). Over the past six years, I have participated in some 200 taped interviews and numerous informal conversations with black and white youths from low- and middle-income backgrounds, living in diverse residential areas of Los Angeles. All youths were 15 to 20 years old. A background questionnaire and a glossary of vernacular vocabulary items were administered in the taped interviews in order to compare informant responses. During informal conversations, the same format was essentially used. As additional lexical items were elicited from black youths, they were presented to white youths for their definition and response.[1] All interviews were oral and personally conducted in a face-to-face informal context. The interview itself usually took place in the youth's neighborhood.

The lexicon covered a wide range of topics that labeled and identified important areas of youthful black interest and concern. These "interest categories" dealt with such matters as covert and overt forms of verbal and physical manipulation; male-female relations; sex; the care, maintenance, and display of one's car; drugs; and so on.[2]

THE DRUG EXPERIENCE

Shared Drug Experiences

Though there were several interest categories represented in the lexicon, only one area clearly linked youths from different racial, economic, and residential backgrounds—namely, drugs and drug-related activities. Fully 50 percent of the drug terms elicited from black informants were known by some portion of the white population.[3] Aside from this one area of interracial usage, virtually none of the other terms were shared by blacks and whites.

The drug lexicon can be divided into subsections that relate to specific kinds of drugs and drug behavior. Shared informant knowledge of these subsets of drug terms is of particular significance, since it tells us what aspects of the drug experience were most consistently perceived as important to both black and white youths.

The largest body of shared drug vernacular revolved around the use of pills, such as barbiturates and amphetamines, and marijuana. The number of synonyms known and used by black and white youths to describe each of these drugs was extremely elaborate and reflected the attention and importance assigned to them.

Barbiturates, known in the vernacular as *downs, downers, stums,* and *stumblers,* are commercially distributed under various trade names. The most popularly used barbiturates were sometimes called by the name of their manufacturer or by their commercial identification number, but most often by their color. For example, Amytal (amabarbital marketed by Eli Lilly and Company) was called *blue, blue angel, blue heaven;* Nembutal (pentobarbital, Abbott Laboratories), *yellow, yellow jack, yellow jacket;* and Tuinal (amobarbital and secobarbital, Eli Lilly and Company), *rainbow, Christmas tree.*

By far the most commonly used commercial barbiturate,[4] among both black and white informants, was secobarbital, known by the trade name Seconal (Eli Lilly and Company). Its popularity was attested to by the proliferation of vernacular expressions identifying it—*r.d., red, red devil, Lilly, Lilly F40* (manufacturer and commercial identification number), *F40, bullet,* and *bullethead.*

Though a number of commercially prepared amphetamines (known in the vernacular as *ups, uppers,* and *pep-'em-ups*) were used by both black and white informants, the one that was most often referred to was the compound Benzedrine, variously labeled *white, benny, chalk,* or *wake-up.* Interestingly, the amphetamine Methedrine, which was extremely popular among white youths, proved to have limited appeal among blacks. Only two vernacular terms—*speed* and *meth*—were elicited from black informants to describe the drug. Though some black youths had taken *speed,* Methedrine was generally considered to be a "white trip."

Shared vernacular was used to identify not only pills but the quantity or unit of measurement in which they could be gotten. For example, a single pill was referred to as an *ace;* two pills, a *deuce;* three to ten pills of varying or similar strength or type, a *roll;* and a bottle of 500 to 1,000 pills, a *jar.* A common way of asking for a given quantity of pills was *throw me out an* (*ace, deuce, roll,* and so on).

Without question, the most popular and widely used substance among both black and white informants was marijuana. Its immense popularity was reflected in the striking number of terms used to identify it—*grass, gani, weed, gauge, maryjane, juana, boo, shit, bush, tea, pot, smoke*—to name a few. Furthermore, youthful "connoisseurs" of marijuana further classified it according to assumed place of origin and degree of potency. So, for example, informant discussion would often move from general terms for marijuana to detailed comparisons of the various types available, like *Acapulco gold, Chicago green, Mexican green,* or *Panama red.*

Corollary to this intense interest in marijuana was the detailed vernacular attention given to the quantity or unit of measurement in which it could be obtained. Again, marijuana connoisseurs demonstrated detailed knowledge of such matters. The following conversation between a black and a white youth illustrates some of the fine points (and particularized vernacular) surrounding a purchase.

B: Man, in them olden days you could *score* (purchase) a *match* (matchbox full of marijuana). No more. Don't even see no more *cans* (one ounce container of marijuana) or *lids* (one ounce container of marijuana)! It be *baggies* (plastic food bags used to hold various quantities of marijuana) now!

W: Yeah, me and my partner tried to *cop* (purchase) a *five cent bag* (five dollars worth of marijuana) last night. Dude told us he don't sell no more five cent bags. "Inflation, man"—that's what he told us. It's *ten cent* (ten dollar) or *quarter* (twenty-five dollar) bags nowadays. And shit, you're not getting any more weed than before! I'm gonna start *dealing* (selling drugs) myself! I have this friend who deals and he said he'd turn me on to his *connection* (source of drugs). Make some bread.

B: I hear ya, man. Next time, Ima get me a whole fuckin' *key* (approximately two pounds of marijuana)! Me an' some brothers gon' trip on down to *T.J.* (Tijuana) and score a righteous *brick o' shit* (approximately two pounds of marijuana). Yeah, then I'm gonna have a righteous *stash* (supply) *for days* (for a long time)! Can you dig it! (Mutual laughter.)

Finally, the ritual surrounding the preparation, paraphernalia, and act of smoking a marijuana cigarette (*J, joint, dubee, stick, smoke, number*) carried its own extended vernacular description. When I asked a white middle-class informant to describe the ritual, he provided the following narrative:

Well, man, I get high every day, so I guess I'm an expert in that field. First, I get out my stash and my papers (cigarette papers used to roll a marijuana cigarette)*—usually me and my partner* light up (light up a marijuana cigarette) *after school—then I roll two or three* numbers. *It* *depends on how good the shit is, you know. Like with gold (Acapulco gold), you take four or five hits (puffs) and you can get loaded pretty fast. That is some fine grass! Anyway, I roll some numbers. (What kind of papers do you use?)* Zig-Zag whites *(a particular brand of cigarette papers used to roll a marijuana cigarette; they come in brown and white). But this dude turned me on to some licorice papers—you know they come in all flavors and colors now. They're okay. Anyway, depending on my mood and how much grass I've got, I may roll a regular j or a couple of* bombers *(fat marijuana cigarettes). So then, anyway, we* fire up *(light up) and just sit back—get some wine—listen to some music maybe and just get stoned! (How many terms can you think of that describe being under the influence of marijuana or pills?) Shit, there's so many of them*—stoned, loaded, high, wired, ripped, wasted, ruined. *If you really get loaded, like you're* really fucked up *(profoundly under the influence), you just* flake out *(fall asleep).*

Though the interracial drug vocabulary indicated a keen awareness of an interest in barbiturates, amphetamines, marijuana, and the behavior surrounding their use, the same was not true for the so-called hard drugs—opium and its derivatives (morphine, codeine, and heroin) or cocaine. Only the most common vernacular terms for heroin (*H, smack, boy, stuff, skag*) and cocaine (*coke, girl, snow*) were elicited from black informants. No vernacular terms were offered for either codeine or morphine. Though white informants were encouraged to provide additional vernacular to describe hard drugs, none contributed any items other than those elicited from blacks. Similarly, terms describing the preparation, handling, and effects of hard drugs were infrequently brought up in conversation. When statements were made about the effects of getting high, they invariably centered on pill- or marijuana-induced behavior. Though some youths had *chipped* (occasionally used one or another of the hard drugs), they were not habitual users. Of the total informant population, less than 5 percent admitted to frequent or habitual use of hard drugs.

A variety of reasons were offered for an informant's lack of involvement with these drugs—lack of opportunity, lack of money, lack of accessibility, lack of interest, fear of becoming hooked. One black youth, who lived in Watts, provided a graphic statement about why he did not use hard drugs that rather clearly summarizes informant feelings:

Pills and weed—*da's fo' me. Nice high, cheap high. I kin git 'em—one way or d'other.* Irvine *(police) ain' gon'* swoop *(suddenly appear) and bust me fo' none o' dem* tracks *(needle marks) on my arms. Don' need that shit.* Green ain't never gonna be long enough *(money is never going to be sufficient)* to support *dat habit. Ain' gon' break my momma's heart wid a few little ole pills and shit. Junkie he a fool, a sucker! He got a hunger he ain't* never *gonna fill—til he* dead!

Whether as the result of circumstance or choice, hard drugs did not figure importantly in informant conversations or the vocabulary they shared.

Divergent Drug Experiences

Thus far, no mention has been made about the whole class of consciousness-altering drugs popularly known as *psychedelics* or *hallucinogens*. Popularized vernacular terms for the most commonly known psychedelic drugs—lysergic acid diethylamide (*acid, LSD*), mescaline (*cactus*), peyote (*button*), and psilocybin (*magic mushroom*)—were virtually nonexistent in the vocabulary elicited from black informants. Fewer than ten terms referred to this whole area of drug use and related behavior; and then only *LSD, acid, to trip* (when used specifically to refer to the effects of hallucinogens) and *psychedelic* (of or pertaining to the psychedelic experience) were used with any frequency.

Yet, if one were to glance through Landy's *The Underground Dictionary* (1971), which deals extensively with contemporary drug terms and their use, one will find a substantial number of entries describing and defining psychedelic drugs and related behavior. Why? Simply put, hallucinogenic drugs were not a viable part of the black drug experience. The psychedelic experience that fueled so many anti-Establishment actions and attitudes on the part of the so-called *flower children, hippies, long hairs,* and countercultural *drop-outs* of the sixties was preeminently a white middle-class phenomenon.[5]

Black informant response to the use of psychedelics was overwhelmingly negative. Their use was seen as part of "whitey's trip," and provoked responses of disdain, outright dismissal, and most significantly, apprehension and fear. Less than a dozen blacks had experimented with any of the psychedelic drugs. The experiences of two black youths who had *dropped acid* (taken LSD) are worth recounting. They provide some insight into possible cultural reasons for the aversion to these drugs. One young woman told the following story about her experience with acid:

I've taken one acid trip, you know, to see what it was like, but I didn't like it. I was at home, there was this party going on, and me and my old man dropped some acid. It was a real bad scene. I started talking a whole lotta trash *(nonsense) and then I started crying because my brother wouldn't be my friend.... He got mad at me. And, I said, "Just say that you'll be my friend!" And he wouldn't. He just looked at me like I was crazy. Kept telling me, "C., be cool, you ain't acting right, be cool! Your* mind is weak *(not in control of yourself). You talkin' like one o' them crazy hippies! Get yourself together, girl!" Then, I started crying. I really started crying.*

Another story was told by a young man who lived in South Central Los Angeles:

Me an' my partner we was trippin' *on some acid (feeling the effects of* LSD*). Went over to the* projects *(Hacienda housing project in Watts) lookin' for a party. But my head wasn't right. Started seein' things—polices everywhere. Heard sirens, and man, I* freaked *(lost control)! Started runnin' through the projects, yellin', "Pigs after me! They after me! Gon'* jack me up *(beat me up)! They gonna* blow me away *(kill me)!" Spent the whole fuckin' night hidin' from the police an' "Bear" (a member of a rival gang who had*

threatened him), hidin' from everybody! ... Acid jus' ain't my bag. Mind gets crazy with that stuff! Gimme some reds! *Gimme some* weed! *Gimme some* pluck (wine)! *Now, da's a nice high. Relax you, make you feel mellow. World look good den.*

Generally, black informant response gave support to two important cultural factors, implicit in the narratives, that mitigated against the use of psychedelics. One was the possibility of losing one's "cool" (losing control over one's environment and personal behavior, a negatively valued psychological stance in black culture). Another was the accompanying fear and paranoia brought on by becoming physically and psychologically vulnerable to a world which, for many black youths, is already sufficiently distressful and dangerous without its being exacerbated by mind-altering drugs.

When black experiences are compared with white responses to taking psychedelics, we begin to see where culture-specific experiences and perceptions determine not only what drugs one uses and enjoys, but why one enjoys them. The experience of one white youth may highlight this point.

Yeh, I drop reds and I smoke grass. It's alright, if you wanna kick back *(relax) and do some lightweight* tripping *(mild consciousness expansion). But mostly my bag is acid and mescaline. I dropped some acid this weekend—some* Sunshine *(a particular type of LSD that comes in yellow or orange tablets). Me and some friends went over to the park back of my house and really got into nature. Cops came by, we just waved. No hassle, just went on. We spent the day there, just trippin'. No cares, no hassles, just trippin'.*

Nathan Kantrowitz (1969), in his discussion of the vocabulary of race relations used by prisoners to characterize fellow inmates, observed that "if a phenomenon is important, it is perceived, and, being perceived, it is named" (p. 24). As I have noted elsewhere (Folb 1972), that supposition can be carried one step further:

It may be said that those who have identified the phenomenon as important, and consequently, have named it, will come to share that name with others whom they [may] encounter and with whom they [may] interact in the pursuit of shared activities of which the phenomenon is a part (p. 13).

There is no doubt that most informants, whether black or white, perceived drugs to be an important phenomenon—whether in their own lives, the lives of their peers, or in both. The heavy drug users[6] among black and white youths, regardless of socioeconomic background, knew the greatest number of terms related to drugs and their use. Their superior knowledge of the drug lexicon was understandable, given their self-admitted, deep involvement in the drug experience. But the influence of the so-called drug culture was so far-reaching (and still is), that even the *lame* (socially inexperienced or naive person) knew many of the vernacular terms used by his or her drug-savvy peers. The profundity of the drug experience was so keenly felt across barriers of race, economics, and geography, that significant portions of informant conversations were given over to discussing this phenomenon. If youths took drugs, they talked at length about their experiences; if they didn't take drugs, they rationalized about why they didn't; if they were undecided, they weighed the alternatives in light of the experiences of others. And consistently, they talked about drugs in the vernacular vocabulary used by their friends and acquaintances—a drug vocabulary that, as this paper points out, was shared in some significant measure interracially.

SEMANTICALLY DIFFERENTIATED LEXICAL ITEMS AND INTERRACIAL CONCERNS

The following conversation took place at a bus stop, where two young men—one white, the other black—were "hanging out."

Young white man: Hey, man, see that dude over there (points across the street), he a real *punk*!

Young black man: I hear ya. Don't be messin' with me, 'lessen he wanna be *blowed away* (killed)!

Young white man: Yeh, dude tried to hustle my old lady—right in front of me too!

Young black man: What you talkin' 'bout, man? Thought you said he a *punk*. No punk gon' hustle a young lady.

Young white man: Whadda you mean? I *saw* him *do* it, man. (Two look at each other with puzzled expressions.)

Despite the proprietary tone of the conversation, the exchange points up an important feature of vocabulary use. Though a word or phrase may be phonetically realized as, for example, *punk*, the semantic reading assigned to that expression may be primarily or totally different for two people. The fact that in the white youth's vernacular *punk* meant someone you dislike or have little regard for, while in the black youth's vocabulary, it referred to a male homosexual, indicates that we are dealing with semantically different lexical items that happen to take an identical phonetic form. It is apparent from the preceding example that if two people—or two cultures—do not share the same experiential referent for a given expression, communicative confusion is inevitable.

As already suggested, one of the primary functions served by vernacular vocabulary is to provide nonstandard or unconventional words and phrases to characterize new or important experiences in our lives. More often than not, these words and phrases are not newly coined, but are borrowed, directly or circuitously, from various subcultures within the larger culture, where they may be used to label significantly different phenomena. Therefore, the potential for interracial miscommunication, for example, is likely to be magnified.

In the present context, the potential for miscommunication becomes apparent if we look at the number of phonetically identical lexical items that were assigned different semantic readings by black and white youths. They are of particular importance, since they point up divergent interracial experiences. In white usage, these expressions were invariably associated with drugs; among black youths, they identified with a whole range of cultural experiences, many of which were specifically tied to being black.

A number of verbs and verb phrases differentiated black nondrug from white drug usage. The expression *to bogart* meant to smoke more than one's share of a marijuana cigarette in the white vernacular;[7] among blacks, its primary meanings were more generalized: to physically assert one's presence or to physically accost another. The phrase *to burn someone* also had a drug-specific meaning for the white youths who knew it: It meant either to accept money for drugs that were never delivered or to sell diluted or "phony" drugs. Within the black vernacular, the primary meaning was to "steal" the affections of another's spouse or lover. The expressions *to be clean* and *to kick* had drug-related meanings among white youths. *To kick* was an abbreviated version of *to kick the habit*, to stop using drugs. *To be clean* meant the same thing, but had an additional semantic reading—to be free of drugs on one's person. In black vernacular, *to kick* meant to depart from somewhere, while *to be clean* referred to the state of being well-dressed.

To bust a cap and *to flash* both related to the psychedelic experience in the white vernacular. *To bust a cap* meant either to ingest a capsule containing *LSD* or to share a capsule of *LSD* with a friend. *To flash* has two primary meanings: to experience the first effects of a drug—especially a psychedelic—and to hallucinate. For some white informants, it had a third meaning: to vomit. In the black vernacular, the expressions were totally unconnected with drug use. *To bust a cap* meant to shoot a gun, and *to flash* meant to show off what one possessed—one's clothes, car, lover, money, and so forth.

A number of black vernacular nouns were used to positively or negatively characterize or classify a person's manner, appearance, or behavior. One such set of these black "classification names" related to the evaluation of women. In the white ver-

nacular they again related to drugs. For example, the white semantic reading for *stuff* was drugs—often heroin. Though the term has long been used by blacks to refer to heroin, the primary black definition here connoted a sexually desirable woman. In a similar vein, the expression *main stuff*, among whites, referred to the principal drug one used; among blacks, the phrase identified one's number-one woman, one's woman friend, or the woman with whom one regularly had sex. Again, the black pejoratives *chippy* (prostitute or sexually promiscuous woman), *dog food* or *skag* (an unattractive woman), and *peach* (a woman with extremely short hair, an unkempt woman) meant, respectively, an occasional drug user; heroin; and an amphetamine in the white vernacular.

A number of classification names in the black vernacular characterized black people from a decidedly intraracial perspective. Such terms as *cotton* (a black person who has recently arrived from the South); *monkey* (an obsequious black person who curries favor with whites); *Sam* (abbreviation for *Sambo*—a "country hick," or an obsequious black person); and *head* (black male—usually one who makes trouble or is unruly) all reflect culture-specific usage. In the white vernacular these expressions all revolved around the drug experience. *Cotton* referred to the wad of cotton used to absorb a liquefied drug; a hypodermic needle is then stuck into the drug-soaked cotton, and the drug is drawn into the syringe in preparation for *shooting up* (injecting the drug). *Monkey*, an abbreviation for *monkey on one's back*, referred to a drug habit—usually an addiction to heroin. *Sam* identified a federal narcotics agent. Finally, *head* referred to someone who frequently uses a particular drug, such as *acidhead* (a habitual user of LSD), *pothead* (a habitual user of marijuana), *pillhead* (a habitual user of pills), and so on.

The terms *hippy* and *freak* were used by both blacks and whites to characterize a given person, but the respective characterizations were decidedly different. In the white vernacular, the terms carried a positive connotation; in black usage, the connotation was unquestionably negative.

Hippy acutally had a number of meanings in the black vernacular. It referred to a black person who was uninformed, naïve, or dated in dress or manner. It also meant a black person who emulated whites in various ways. Finally, the term referred to a trouble-maker, particularly someone who provoked fights. On the other hand, the *hippy* was embraced by white informants as a counter-culture ideal, and was predominantly characterized as a white middle-class youth who had dropped out of mainstream society. That is, he or she seldom worked, invariably took drugs, grew long hair, dressed unconventionally, and often lived in a communal environment.

Similarly, the term *freak* had a generally positive association in the minds of white informants. Like *hippy*, *freak* designated one who had rejected mainstream American values and defied the Establishment by his or her shocking appearance and/or behavior. In addition, the term means one who demonstrated a strong preference for a particular drug, for example, *acid freak*. For the majority of blacks interviewed, a *freak* was one who engaged in so-called deviant sexual activity. Most often, the reference was to homosexuality, a sexual preference that was viewed with particular repugnance—especially among black males.

OBSERVATIONS

The comparative vernacular vocabulary data suggest that interest in drugs and drug use was the single most important experiential bridge between the black and white youths interviewed. This preoccupation with drugs was particularly apparent among white informants—especially those from middle-class backgrounds. As a group, middle-class whites provided the greatest number of drug-related semantic readings for nondrug black vernacular expressions.

Conversations with informants indicated that a variety of drugs had long been available in the black community. But, the widespread smoking of *dope* (marijuana) and the taking of various pills for "kicks" was a phenomenon that developed during the sixties among white youths—particularly among affluent white youths living in Los Angeles County.[8] Therefore, it is congruent with their keen and new-found interest in drugs that they should not only use more drug terms in the course of the interviews, but provide the greatest number of drug-related semantic readings for nondrug stimulus terms.

The fact that a negligible number of terms elicited from black informants were known by whites or assigned the same semantic readings by them suggests that a well-formed black vernacular vocabulary exists that is largely a private part of the black experience. As Kochman (1972) has noted: "That black people in general should possess and use a different vocabulary from whites is understandable, given the respectively different nature of the black and white experiences in this country" (p. 140).

In this paper, I have explored only one aspect of interracial vocabulary use and its relationship to shared and disparate life experiences. Much additional comparative information is needed to provide answers to questions about the origin, nature, and function of vernacular vocabulary in intercultural contexts. Certainly, the study of vernacular usage promises to provide a rich and relatively unmined source of data about social interaction. As Kochman (1972) has stated:

one of the best ways to get to know a group is to identify and examine the vocabulary (names, terms and expressions) habitually used within the group. . . . It is this "other" world, oral, vernacular, induced and unsanctioned, that is the antithesis (and at times the antidote) to the formalized, academic, imposed, and legitimated world of adults and institutions, one from which adults can learn a great deal about culture, learning, and life." (p. 109)

NOTES

1. To date, the lexicon includes over 2,000 entries. It forms part of a larger work on black vernacular vocabulary that I am presently engaged in writing.

2. See Folb (1972), Chapter Six, "A Comparative Study of Urban Black Argot," for a full explanation and discussion of these interest categories.

3. The total number of drug-related entries was 280.

4. Not all pills were commercially prepared compounds. In the case of barbiturates, some were secured through prescriptions; many others were purchased from drug dealers who, in turn, got the barbiturates through black market contacts in Mexico and Canada. Though these illegally secured pills were often from commercial drug companies, they were extracted from their original capsules and mixed with a variety of substances, such as baking soda or sugar, to dilute them before they reached the streets. Knowledgeable informants, in fact, made a vernacular distinction between commercially prepared barbiturates, such as secobarbital, and dealer compounds. The former were called *prescription reds*; the latter, *border reds*.

5. The power and mystique of psychedelics gave birth to a whole generation of middle-class white rebels who—along with Timothy Leary, the guru of mind expansion—"turned on, tuned in, and dropped out." However, blacks did not "tune in" to the white drug prophets, nor did they "turn on" to psychedelics. As far as "dropping out," many of them had been forced or chose to reject mainstream white values long before any of the psychedelic savants appeared on the scene. If anything, blacks during the sixties were marching to the tune of different drummers—Huey Newton, Rap Brown, Stokely Carmichael, and Malcolm X.

6. The designation "heavy drug user" was applied to youths who (1) admitted to repeated use of drugs, (2) used a variety of drug terms not represented in the glossary, (3) displayed intimate knowledge of the ritual activities surrounding the taking of drugs, as well as knowledge of the effects these drugs produced, and/or (4) had school or police records (or both) of extensive drug use.

7. In fact, the expression *to bogart* was part of the opening line of a popular song of the late sixties that was often aired on white rock radio stations: "Don't bogart that joint, my friend, pass it over to me."

8. "The Incidence of Drug Use among Los Angeles County Youth: A Profile," Department of Probation, County of Los Angeles (1968).

REFERENCES

Folb, Edith A. (March 1972). "A Comparative Study of Urban Black Argot." *Occasional Papers in Linguistics* No. 1. Los Angeles: UCLA.

Folb, Edith A. (1973a). "Black Vernacular Vocabulary: A Study in Intra-Intercultural Concerns and Usage." *Afro-American Monograph Series*, No. 5. Los Angeles: Afro-American Studies Center, UCLA.

Folb, Edith A. (August 1973b). "Rappin' in the Black Vernacular." *Human Behavior*. Reprinted in Spain, ed. (1975). *The Human Experience: Readings in Sociocultural Anthropology*. Illinois: The Dorsey Press.

Kochman, Thomas, ed. (1972). *Rappin' and Stylin' Out: Communication in Urban Black America*. Urbana: University of Illinois Press.

Landy, Eugene E. (1971). *The Underground Dictionary*. New York: Simon and Schuster.

Maurer, David W. (1969). "Linguistic Hostility as a Factor in Intra-Cultural Conflict." *Papers of the Tenth International Congress of Linguistics*. Bucharest, Rumania.

Porter, Richard E. and Larry A. Samovar. (1976). "Communicating Interculturally." In Larry A. Samovar and Richard E. Porter, eds., *Intercultural Communication: A Reader*, 2nd. ed. Belmont Calif.: Wadsworth.

Talking to "the Man": Some Communication Strategies Used by Members of "Subordinate" Social Groups

MARSHA HOUSTON STANBACK
W. BARNETT PEARCE

The relations among different ethnic, cultural, political, or national groups that cohabit the same geographic space are seldom egalitarian. Even groups pledged to tolerate exotic customs and divergent beliefs usually form a hierarchical pecking order when they must interact regularly with other groups. If everyone involved "agrees" about which groups are dominant and which inferior, a stable social reality is created in which each individual knows how to communicate with persons from other groups. The interaction patterns may include recurrent "degradation rituals" involving public facilities, the back seats of busses, and pronominal address forms which are not pleasant or profitable to persons from either group, particularly the lower-statused persons. These forms of communication recur, however, because they provide a familiar way of avoiding potentially catastrophic uncertainty or conflict.

The asymmetrical relationship between a dominant and inferior group becomes real when the members of both define it as real.[1] These definitions are more importantly expressed in the patterns of ordinary communication between members of each group than in credos, party platforms, or philosophic manifestos. Objective indices of inequality—income, employment, education—are derivative rather than causal and are the results of patterned interactions between individuals who follow "scripts" dictated by their perceptions of social reality. An analysis of recurring forms of intergroup communication thus not only adds to the list of descriptors of social stratification, it provides an explanation of why the more tangible socioeconomic indicators vary as they do.[2]

All social realities impose performance demands on those who participate in them. There are particularly stringent demands on the performances by members of "inferior" groups when they communicate with persons from the dominant group. Somehow they must work within the constraints imposed by their own intentions and concepts of self and the "agreed-upon" script lines about how such communication should go. At first glance, it would appear that the second set of constraints—which reflect the prejudices of the dominant group and implement a status and power difference between the communicators—would obscure those deriving from intentions and self-concept: the members of the inferior group would define themselves consistently with the social reality of the dominant group and see to it that their communication behavior conforms to expected patterns. In fact, generations of social scientists have made precisely this assumption. Noting that American Blacks are less powerful, affluent, and numerous than Whites and for many years were subject to a variety of degradation rituals in daily interaction, predominantly White social scientists were puzzled when their data showed no average differences in self-esteem between Whites and Blacks.[3] Apparently American Blacks—and presumedly other minority/subordinate groups—have developed ways to interact with dominant groups without internalizing the low esteem in which they are held.

An examination of the communication strategies used by members of lower-statused groups is of

From *Quarterly Journal of Speech* 67 (February 1981), 21–30. Reprinted by permission of the Speech Communication Association and the authors. Ms. Stanback is a Danforth Fellow, and Mr. Pearce is Professor of Communication Studies at the University of Massachusetts, Amherst.

value in at least three ways. First, it is a celebration of human creativity. Confronted with the undeniable facts of oppression and denial of status, at least some ostensibly inferior groups have managed to avoid the invidious consequences of subordination. Second, an analysis of these communication strategies informs the development of communication theory. The concept of "concatenated coherence" was suggested by the analysis in this paper, and has considerable utility. Third, the characteristics of these communication strategies illuminate the relationships among socially unequal groups as perceived by members of the lower-statused group.

Four ways of "talking to 'the Man'" have been described in the literature: passing, tomming, shucking, and dissembling. These have in common the feature that they do *not* attempt to change the existing relationship among social groups. From the perspective of the dominant group, the behaviors in each form of communication are appropriate. However, the meaning of these behaviors to the members of the lower-statused group are quite different, making them different forms of communication with different implications for the relations among the groups.

PERCEPTIONS OF INTERGROUP RELATIONS

In the first paragraph of this paper, we referred to those situations in which persons from different groups "agree" that one dominates the other. The word "agree" was italicized to indicate deliberate equivocation. In the original statement, we meant "persons from each group *act as if* they agree about the hierarchical social order" without distinguishing, e.g., between a person who acts in a servile manner because s/he believes herself/himself inferior and one who acts in a servile manner in order to avoid punishment. However, differentiating behaviors on the basis of the actors' meanings is essential to understand the forms and effects of the strategies used in intergroup communication.[4]

"Action theorists" such as Burke[5] and Searle,[6]

insist on the necessity of distinguishing mere movement ("behavior") from interpreted movement ("action"). We agree. Since any movement in principle is susceptible to virtually any interpretation, the primary units of analyses in a description of communication are actors' meanings. We extend this argument with the claim that the structure and content of actors' meanings have implications: they constrain the actors' ability to assign particular interpretations to specific acts or to express particular meanings by specific actions. These constraints may be described as a "logic" in which some elements entail others.[7]

The meanings with which lower-statused persons interpret their intergroup communication patterns are closely related to their concept of the relation between the groups. There are at least three perspectives available to members of lower-statused groups. The "monocultural" perspective is a denial of the status inequality, in which the person treats the two groups as if they were the same. Communication patterns consistent with this perspective include attempts to integrate the groups, to eliminate defamation and other degrading practices, and to abolish discrimination on the basis of group identity. Since these communicative patterns deny the status hierarchy, we will not deal with them. The "other-cultural" perspective accepts the difference between the groups and is willing to maintain it. The "co-cultural" perspective accepts the difference between the groups, but strives to develop a culture which includes selected aspects of both.

Both "other-cultural" and "co-cultural" perspectives accept the existing hierarchical relation between groups, but they differ with respect to the perceived overlap between groups. If communicators' beliefs about intergroup relations comprise a logic which constrains communication behaviors, persons who endorse one of these perspectives should communicate differently than those who endorse the other. However, when we began to analyze passing, tomming, shucking, and dissembling, we found that a more precise set of conceptual distinctions was needed. For convenience—not because we think that it happens in this linear, rational way in real life—we ordered these conceptual distinctions as a series of three decision-points and treat them as if we could describe particular communicators on the basis of the answers they would give. Assuming that the members of the dominant group have a well-known set of expectations about the way members of the inferior groups should act when communicating:

1. Are these expectations (as perceived by a member of the "inferior" group) valid?
—if "yes," go to question #2.
—if "no," go to question #3.

2. Can I avoid complying with these expectations?
—if "yes," *passing* is an appropriate form of communication;
—if "no," *tomming* is an appropriate form of communication.

3. Are the meanings which the dominant group assigns to the behaviors they expect of me important to me?
—if "yes," *shucking* is an appropriate form of communication;
—if "no," *dissembling* is an appropriate form of communication.

The communication forms of tomming, passing, shucking, and dissembling are described below in some detail. Although we rely on the descriptive work of others, we will show that a comparison of these forms of communication and an assessment of their significance requires the analytical distinctions underlying the questions above. For example, the *behaviors* of tomming, shucking, and dissembling are identical—that is, in all three cases, the lower-statused person behaves just as the higher-statused person expects a social inferior to act.[8] These forms of communication function differently, though: tomming and dissembling are consistent with an other-cultural perspective; and shucking with a co-cultural perspective. Further, shucking and passing are very different behaviorally, but both are consistent with a co-cultural perspective. Finally, tomming is honest, while all the others involve a kind of deception which we describe below as "concatenated coherence."

FOUR FORMS OF COMMUNICATION

All of the forms of communication described in this section are performed by and seen from the perspective of a member of a lower-statused person communicating with a higher-statused person. We assume in all cases that the higher-statused person has a specific expectation about how the communicative experience should proceed, including some degree of degradation of the lower-statused person, and that both persons orient their performance around this model.

The descriptions of these forms of communication are based on data in the public domain which report extensive and intensive ethnographic and/or ethnomethodological research. In some cases, we wish the data included features which it does not. However, since our purpose is comparative and analytical[9] rather than empirical, we think the use of secondary data defensible.

Tomming

Tomming occurs when a member of a subordinate group accepts the way s/he is perceived and expected to act as valid, and communicates with members of the dominant group exactly as they expect him/her to do. Each instance of tomming reinforces the existing hierarchical relationship between the two groups.

As Kochman describes tomming,[10] it is a capitulation of the subordinate group to the values and expectations of the dominant group. For the purposes of comparison, it is useful to unpack this description in terms of the participants' meanings. Pearce and Cronen[11] described communication as jointly produced by two or more persons, each of whom monitors the emerging sequence of actions and compares it to what they expect. In tomming, both high- and low-statused persons have comparable expectations of how the communication should go, and the resulting patterns of communication are likely to be unproblematic and mutually coherent. Further, since the lower-statused person has internalized the stereotype of his/her group, s/he may feel that s/he shares control of the interaction and that s/he is the source of the meaning for the interaction.

Passing

Passing occurs when a member of a subordinate group acts as if s/he were actually a member of the dominant group. For example, some light-skinned, straight-haired blacks "pass" by pretending to be whites; some "mere M.A.'s" pass themselves off as having received a terminal degree; and an "in-place" spy pretends to be a citizen of the country in which s/he practices espionage. The most detailed analysis of passing in the literature is Garfinkle's study of an inter-sexed person who for many years pretended to be a normal female.[12]

A person who is passing knows the expectations for a member of the subordinate group, and avoids performing them without denying their legitimacy. The degree to which the person is able to communicate successfully as if s/he were a member of the dominant group depends on his/her knowledge of the communicative responsibilities of that role. Much humor in films and television is based on persons trying to pass who exceed the tolerance limits for the role they have assumed.

Passing involves a particular kind of deception which we call concatenated coherence. Assume that the person is passing successfully: both the passer and the higher-statused person are monitoring the emerging sequence of communicative acts, comparing it to their expectations, and finding it interpretable. However, the person passing frames this mutually coherent communicative event within a perspective in which s/he knows his/her role to be fraudulent and the other person to be deceived.

Even though the behaviors of passing and tomming are different—that is, one enacts the dominant groups' expectations for a lower-statused person and the other those for a higher-statused person—both forms of communication reinforce the existing hierarchical relationship between groups. The tomming person reinforces the expectations for the subordinate group by exemplifying them; the passing person by avoiding them. A person passing must accept the meanings of a group which s/he knows is not his/her own and which— if the deception fails—would disavow him/her.

Shucking

"Shucking" is a term used by American Blacks to identify a form of communication in which they behaviorally conform to racial stereotypes while cognitively rejecting the meanings associated with those behaviors and stereotypes. Shucking is "the talk and accompanying physical movements . . . that are appropriate to some *momentary* guise, posture or facade [designed] to accommodate the Man . . . to produce whatever appearance would be acceptable."[13]

In any given instance, the behaviors for shucking and tomming may be identical: both conform to the expectations of the dominant culture. However, the differences between these forms of communication are important both analytically and within the subordinate group.

At the behavioral level, those who "tom" do so consistently; those who use shucking do so only when they must. These behavioral differences derive from differences in meanings, particularly the mutual coherence of the person tomming as it differs from the concatenated coherence of the person shucking. The person shucking must produce a mutually coherent interaction (conforming to the dominant group's expectations) and then frame it in a context not shared by the other person in which the stereotypical behaviors do not mean what the other thinks they mean.

The distinctive feature of shucking is the split in perceived source of meaning and the locus of control. The behaviors of the person shucking are controlled by the expectations of the dominant group, but s/he reserves the source of meaning for him/ herself by achieving concatenated coherence. This split explains the rage often associated with shucking. The stereotypical acts are disliked and the person resents doing them, but feels that s/he must in order to accomplish particular goals.

Dissembling

Dissembling occurs when a person of a lower-statused group conforms to the behaviorial expectations but disregards the meanings associated with those behaviors by the higher-statused group. The most detailed description of dissembling is Turnbull's study of the relationship between the Pygmies of the Ituri forest and the Bantu villagers who live at the forest's edge.[14] Not only do the Pygmies perform as expected when forced to interact with the Bantu, they embellish their role as "slaves" and use it to exploit the ostensibly dominant culture. For example, the Pygmy Cephu told his "master" a story (invented for the purpose) of being attacked by evil spirits and threw himself on the benevolence of the "master." Cephu later recounted this story to the delight of the other Pygmies, most of whom—from Turnbull's data—seem to have developed dissembling into an art form and a major means of obtaining goods and services from the Bantu.

Like tomming and shucking, dissembling involves acting consistently with the expectations of the higher-statused group. Unlike tomming, dissembling proceeds by concatenated coherence: the dissembler does not accept as "true" the stereotypes of his group but maintains the pretense that s/he does. Unlike shucking, the negative values which the dominant culture associates with those behaviors are irrelevant to the dissembler. For example, the Pygmies differentiate between events which occur in the forest and in the village: nothing which they do outside the forest while interacting with the Bantu is "real," so whatever they do in these contexts is unimportant to them.

The distinctive feature of dissembling is that the locus of meaning and control is in the lower-statused person. Even though the behaviors which the lower-statused person performs are selected to match the expectations of the dominant group, the dissembler chooses to perform them and defines them as a strategem to accomplish particular purposes, not as an involuntary participation in a degrading act. This feature accounts for the difference in valence between dissembling and shucking. Kochman described those who use shucking in terms of shame or rage, betraying their self-concepts and pride because of the necessity to placate those in power. However, Turnbull described the dissembling Pygmies as joyfully content in the forest and hilariously amused by their interactions with the Bantu villagers.

Dissembling is a communication strategy consistent with the "other cultural" perspective. If a dissembler accepted the meanings of the dominant culture as either correct or relevant, the conformity to their expectations would be conflict-producing and appropriately understood as shucking. Only by maintaining a profound disinterest in the other culture can dissembling occur.

DISCUSSION

The descriptions in the literature of passing, tomming, shucking, and dissembling are based on ethnographic and/or ethnomethodological research. These methods produce results rich in detail and faithful to the subjects' own meanings, but, to say the least, they are difficult to summarize and compare with other studies. By drawing from a consistent theoretical perspective, we were able to sort through the original reports and impose a conceptual structure which allowed us to demonstrate nonobvious similarities and differences among these four forms of communication.

It was never our purpose to identify forms of communication not previously introduced to the literature or to quarrel about the accuracy of existing descriptions. Rather, we intended to say something new about already well-known forms of communication. Our procedure was to focus on the behaviors and meanings of the lower-statused communicator, defining each in terms of the expectations held by the higher-statused group. This procedure showed that behavioral compliance with expectations of the higher-statused group is common to three forms of communication (tomming, shucking, and dissembling) which imply very different perceptions on the relationships between the groups, are associated with different concepts of the self, and have different values for the communicators. Further, tomming and passing differ in terms of compliance with the behavioral expectations of the higher-statused group but are characteristic of persons whose perceptions of the relationship between the groups are more similar than either is to persons using shucking or dissembling.

Our selection of a theory from which to draw concepts was not, of course, entirely capricious. Our interest in the communicative performance of lower-statused persons in hierarchical social structures was aroused by reading Turnbull's descriptions of dissembling Pygmies. We realized that the concepts then in the theory of the "coordinated management of meaning" could not account for their gleeful deception of Bantu villagers, who, from Turnbull's description, solidly labored under what might be characterized as the "tall man's burden." The theory had described communicators' perception of the emerging sequence of acts in terms of "coherence"; but to account for dissembling, the concept of "concatenated coherence" was necessary, and this proved a useful way to distinguish various forms of communication. Believing as we do in the potential for complexity in human communication, we expect data from studies yet undone to force theorists to develop even less straightforward concepts in their attempt to describe and explain the convolutions of social action.

Careful readers may have noted our awkwardness in describing the relation between the beliefs/perspectives of the lower-statused persons and the form of communication which they perform. Using terms such as "appropriate," we shied away from saying that if the person has a particular pattern of meanings, s/he *must* use a specified form of communication. Our caution here is based on the nature of the available evidence. The data on which the accounts of these communication forms were based are not sufficient to demonstrate any sort of "causality"; at best they support the claim that there is a correlation between certain beliefs and actions. Given other forms of data in other projects, our colleagues and we have not needed to be so reticent. When the subjects' rules for meaning and action were manipulated in a simulated conversation, predicted forms of communication occurred;[15] and when particular forms of communication were elicited in an interview, predicted structures of subjects' rules for meaning and action were observed.[16] These and other studies support the claim that the structure and content of subjects' meanings comprise a logic which impels a person with measurable force toward specified lines of action.[17]

Based on the support for "logical force" as a form of necessity in social action, we can extrapolate beyond the data available in the ethnographic/ethnomethodological studies cited to make this claim: given the meanings identified by the answers to the three questions on page 238, the lower-statused persons *must* use the form of communication specified as "appropriate." This claim is empirically testable and constitutes the mandatory call for "more research" to be done. More importantly, it implies that persons in lower-statused groups do not and cannot have unfettered volition in selecting how to communicate with members of the higher-statused group. As long as their meanings are constant, only one of these forms is possible: one cannot, for example, use dissembling if s/he defines the dominant group's meanings as important.

The claim of a necessary relation between the structure and content of a person's rules for meaning and action and the form of communication which s/he performs appears to lead to a simple mechanical, predictive model from which human will and creativity are excluded. However, it does not. The conditional clause of the last sentence of the preceding paragraph is crucial, for human meanings are not fixed; they fluctuate as a result of experience and deliberate choice. Members of lower-statused group have at least some ability to alter their meanings and thus their communication behavior or to alter their communication behavior and thus their meanings.[18] Confronted by the social reality of inequitable relations among groups, some have sought to change the overt conditions; others have developed a variety of ways to escape the apparently inexorable degradation of being identified with the subordinate group. Passing, tomming, shucking, and dissembling represent different ways of "talking with the Man," but the choice among them is based on the structure of the lower-statused person's perspective on the relationship between the groups, and becomes a causal factor in perpetuating that relationship. There are reasons to choose, e.g., between shucking and dissembling. Dissembling is a sometimes gleeful communication pattern which can only be used by persons content for the groups to remain separate; shucking is a sometimes stressful communication pattern which can only be used by persons who have accepted at least some of the dominant groups' values, and thus shucking is the perhaps necessary if lamented consequent of a co-cultural perspective.[19]

Rather than denying human creativity, the claim of a necessary relationship between communicators' meanings and forms of communication—combined with the demonstrable facts of cognitive and social change—indicate that creativity operates at a level which includes both meanings and patterns of behaviors. The co-cultural perspective on intergroup relations is probably the most difficult to achieve, necessitating a differentiated communication strategy. There are some portions of the dominant culture which the subordinate group will assimilate, in effect adopting a limited monocultural perspective. Other portions of the dominant culture will be perceived as alien and unwanted, leading to passing if they can get away with it and shucking if they cannot.

A subordinate group with a co-cultural perspective faces major problems coordinating with each other about the meaning of their acts and the boundaries between the two cultures which they are fusing. How can the group select among the dominant culture's values and beliefs without group-shattering disagreements about what to adopt and without becoming so enmeshed in the logic of that culture that they are assimilated at the price of their uniqueness? Behaviorally, this question takes the form of asking when compliance to the dominant group's expectations is tomming and when it is shucking. Since the behaviors are the same, we expect that subordinate groups with a co-cultural perspective will require their members to display rage or disgust when complying with expectations as a signal that they are shucking. Further, when is acting like a member of the dominant culture assimilation nd when is it passing? On the behavioral level, there are no differences, so again we expect some meta-communication or facework which signals to other members of the group which [form of communication] is occurring. We suspect that much of the communication among members of the group may be interpreted as defining partitions between these forms of communication and as providing mechanisms for extricating themselves from too-great enmeshment in the logic of either culture. Further, we suspect that these activities will frequently be misunderstood and perhaps resented by members of the dominant group and by members of the subordinate group who endorse as "other culture's" perspective.

The problem in differentiating which form of communication members of subordinate groups are using legitimates our equivocal use of the verb "agree" in the opening paragraph. Rather than resulting from our deficiencies in developing definitions, the apparent "agreement" which occurs when members of subordinate groups conform to the dominant group's expectations is inherent in the phenomena. Paraphrasing an old adage from a somewhat different context, some members of inferior groups are born "agreeing" with the expectations for them by the dominant group; some achieve "agreement" as the result of hard work maintaining separation between groups; and others have "agreement" thrust upon them by the requirements of creating a culture combining selected characteristics of both groups.

NOTES

1. Pearce and Cronen somewhat cavalierly defined "social reality" as that which people believe that people believe." See W. Barnett Pearce and Vernon E. Cronen, *Communication, Action and Meaning: Constructing Social Realities* (New York: Praeger, 1980), p. 21.

2. This argument is consistent with the "action theory" principle that communication is culturally morphogenic. For a review of this literature, see Pearce and Cronen, *Communication, Action and Meaning*, Chapters 2 and 3.

3. Ruth Simons, "Blacks and High Self Esteem: A Puzzle," *Social Psychological Quarterly* 41 (1978), 54–57.

4. Such is the state of communication theory that these attributes of our perspective are controversial and require special notation!

5. Kenneth Burke, *A Rhetoric of Motives* (Berkeley: University of California Press, 1969).

6. John Searle, *Speech Acts* (London: Cambridge University Press, 1969).

7. This logic of meaning and action is hierarchical and deontic rather than a traditional alethic logic. As such, the entailments are the person's perceptions that particular acts *ought* to happen or that particular events *ought* to have specified meanings. The "force" of these entailments can be quantified and is perceived by individuals as a variable amount of necessity to act or interpret actions in particular ways. See Pearce and Cronen, *Communication, Action and Meaning*, pp. 144–148, 176–184.

8. Our focus on the *form* rather than the *content* of particular communicative events leads to an unusual definition of similarity between events. For present purposes, we describe the meaning of a communication event as the *relationship* between the behaviors of the lower-statused person and the expectations for those behaviors by the dominant group. This definitional strategy means that the identical behavior performed in two intergroup relationships may differ in meaning: conforming to the expectations in one context but violating expectations in the other. Further, quite dissimilar behaviors by persons in different groups may be considered to have the same form because each has the same relationship to the expectations of the dominant group.

9. A 5×4 matrix is embedded without enumeration in the following sections. One axis consists of the four forms of communication used by lower-statused persons which do not challenge the hierarchical social order; the other defines five points of comparison among these forms.

10. Thomas Kochman, "Toward an Ethnography of Black American Speech Behavior," ed. Thomas Kochman *Rappin' and Stylin Out: Communication in Urban Black America* (Urbana, Ill.: University of Illinois Press, 1972), pp. 246–253.

11. Pearce and Cronen, *Communication, Action and Meaning*.

12. Harold Garfinkel, *Studies in Ethnomethodology* (Englewood Cliffs, N.J.: Prentice-Hall, 1967), pp. 116–185.

13. Kochman, pp. 246–247.

14. Colin Turnbull, *The Forest People: A Study of the Pygmies of the Congo* (New York: Simon and Schuster, 1961).

15. Kenneth Johnson, "The Effects of the Structure of Communication Rules on Persons' Simulated Conversations," a paper presented to the Annual Conference of the International Communication Association, Philadelphia, 1979.

16. Vernon E. Cronen, W. Barnett Pearce, and Lonna Snavely, "A Theory of Rule-Structure and Types of Episodes, and a Study of Perceived Enmeshment in Undesired Repetitive Patterns (URP's)" in *Communication Yearbook III*, ed. D. Nimmo (New Brunswick, N.J.: Transaction, 1979).

17. Cf. Vernon E. Cronen and W. Barnett Pearce, "The Logic of the Coordinated Management of Meaning: An Open Systems Model of Interpersonal

Communication," paper presented to the Annual Conference of the International Communication Association, Chicago, 1978; and "Toward a Logic of Interactional Rules," a paper presented to Human Communication for an Interactional View, Asilomar, California, 1979.

18. Cognitively-oriented social scientists have generally agreed that there is a "strain toward consistency" between persons' actions and meanings, but they disagree about the strength of the strain produced by inconsistency and about whether behaviors reflect prior cognitions or cognitions are retrospective accounts of the persons' behaviors. Professional careers, if not fortunes, have been made by partisans in these disputes, but the finer points of the controversies are irrelevant to our concerns.

19. Our stress on the necessary relationships between meanings and forms of communication does not imply that other factors are not also involved. For example, the Pygmy treat the Ituri forest as deity, provider, and refuge, and this facilitates their "other cultural" perspective toward the villagers. Since the Bantu fear the forest—a fear deliberately augmented by Pygmy tales of superstitious horror—they seldom enter it, thus giving the Pygmies a convenient place where the dominant groups' expectations for their behaviors are irrelevant and they can find a social referent group for their own cultures. No such refuge from the dominant culture is available for American Blacks, and most have lost contact with much of their own ethnic history. Given these conditions, dissembling seems an extraordinarily difficult communication strategy for American Blacks, and many have opted for a co-cultural perspective as indicated by the term "Afro-American." There are now at least three self-defined co-cultural groups within the United States: Afro-Americans, Chicanos, and Nisei. To compare the communication patterns of these groups as a function of their development is an intriguing direction for future research, as is a contrast between these groups and British colonists in Africa and Asia who were intent on *not* "going native."

The Need to Be: The Socio-Cultural Significance of Black Language

SHIRLEY N. WEBER

"Hey blood, what it is? Ah, Man, ain't notin to it but to do it."
"Huney, I done told ya', God, he don't lak ugly."
"Look-a-there. I ain't seen nothin like these economic indicators."

From the street corners to the church pew to the board room, black language is used in varying degrees. It is estimated that 80 to 90 percent of all black Americans use the black dialect at least some of the time.[1] However, despite its widespread use among blacks at all social and economic levels, there continues to be concern over its validity and continued use. Many of the concerns arise from a lack of knowledge and appreciation for the history of black language and the philosophy behind its use.

Since the publication of J. L. Dillard's book *Black English* in 1972, much has been written on the subject of black language. Generally, the research focuses on the historical and linguistic validity of black English, and very little has been devoted to the communications and cultural functions black language serves in the black community. It seems obvious that given the fact that black English is not "formally" taught in schools to black children and, yet, has widespread use among

This essay was written especially for this volume. All rights reserved. Permission to reprint must be obtained from the publisher and the author. Dr. Weber teaches in the Afro-American Studies Department at San Diego State University.

blacks, it must serve some important functions in the black community that represents the blacks' unique experience in America. If black language served no important function, it would become extinct like other cultural relics because all languages are functional tools that change and adapt to cultural and technological demands. If they cease to do this, they cease to exist as a living language. (The study of the English language's evolution and expansion over the last hundred years, to accommodate changing values and technological advancements, is a good example.) This article looks at the "need to be," the significance of black language to black people.

One's language is a model of his or her culture and of that culture's adjustment to the world. All cultures have some form of linguistic communications; without language, the community would cease to exist. To deny that a people has a language to express its unique perspective of the world is to deny its humanity. Furthermore, the study of language is a study of the people who speak that language and of the way they bring order to the chaos of the world. Consequently, the study of black language is really an examination of African people and of their adjustment to the conditions of American slavery. Smitherman says that black English (dialect) is

an Africanized form of English reflecting Black America's linguistic-cultural African heritage and the conditions of servitude, oppression and life in America. . . .

(It) is a language mixture, adapted to the conditions of slavery and discrimination, a combination of language and style interwoven with and inextricable from Afro-American culture.[2]

Much has been written about the origins of black language, and even though the issue seems to be resolved for linguists, the rest of the world is still lingering under false assumptions about it. Basically, there are two opposing views: one that says there was African influence in the development of the language and the other that says there was not. Those who reject African influence believe

that the African arrived in the United States and tried to speak English. And, because he lacked certain intellectual and physical attributes, he failed. This hypothesis makes no attempt to examine the phonological and grammatical structures of West African languages to see if there are any similarities. It places the African in a unique position unlike any other immigrant to America. Linguistic rationales and analyses are given for every other group that entered America pronouncing words differently and/or structuring their sentences in a unique way. Therefore, when the German said *zis* instead of *this*, America understood. But, when the African said *dis*, no one considered the fact that consonant combinations such as *th* may not exist in African languages.

Countering this dialectical hypothesis is the creole hypothesis that, as a result of contact between Africans and Europeans, a new language formed that was influenced by both languages. This language took a variety of forms, depending on whether there was French, Portuguese, or English influence. There is evidence that these languages were spoken on the west coast of Africa as early as the sixteenth century (before the slave trade). This hypothesis is further supported by studies of African languages that demonstrate the grammatical, phonological, and rhythmic similarities between them and black English. Thus, the creole hypothesis says that the African responded to the English language as do all other non-English speakers: from the phonological and grammatical constructs of the native language.

The acceptance of the creole hypothesis is the first step toward improving communications with blacks. However, to fully understand and appreciate black language and its function in the black community, it is essential to understand some general African philosophies about language and communications, and then to see how they are applied in the various styles and forms of black communications.

In Janheinz Jahn's *Muntu*, basic African philosophies are examined to give a general overview of African culture. It is important to understand that while philosophies that govern the different groups in Africa vary, some general concepts are found throughout African cultures. One of the primary principles is the belief that everything has a reason for being. Nothing simply exists without purpose or consequences. This is the basis of Jahn's explanation of the four basic elements of life, which are Muntu, mankind; Kintu, things; Hantu, place and time; and Kuntu, modality. These four elements do not exist as static objects, but as forces that have consequences and influence. For instance, in Hantu, the west is not merely a place defined by geographic location, but a force that influences the east, north, and south. Thus, the term "western world" connotes a way of life that either complements or challenges other ways of life. The western world is seen as a force and not a place. (This is applicable to the other three elements also.)

Muntu, or man, is distinguished from the other three elements by his possession of Nommo, the magical power of the word. Without Nommo, nothing exists. Consequently, mankind, the possessor of Nommo, becomes the master of all things.

All magic is word magic, incantations and exorcism, blessings and curse. Through Nommo, the word, man establishes his mastery over things. . . .

If there were no word all forces would be frozen, there would be no procreation, no changes, no life. . . . For the word holds the course of things in train and changes and transforms them. And since the word has this power every word is an effective word, every word is binding. And the muntu is responsible for his word.[3]

Nommo is so powerful and respected in the black community that only those who are skillful users of the word become leaders. One of the main qualifications of leaders of black people is that they must be able to articulate the needs of the people in a most eloquent manner. And because Muntu is a force who controls Nommo, which has power and consequences, the speaker must generate and create movement and power within his listeners. One of the ways this is done is through the use of imaginative and vivid language. Of the five canons of speech, it is said that Inventio or invention is the most utilized in black American. Molefi Asante called it the "coming to be of the novel," or the making of the new. So that while the message might be the same, the analogies, stories, images, and so forth must be fresh, new, and alive.

Because nothing exists without Nommo, it, too, is the force that creates a sense of community among communicators, so much so that the speaker and audience become one as senders and receivers of the message. Thus, an audience listening and responding to a message is just as important as the speaker, because without their "amens" and "right-ons" the speaker may not be successful. This interplay between speaker and listeners is called "call and response" and is a part of the African world view, which holds that all elements and forces are interrelated and indistinguishable because they work together to accomplish a common goal and to create a sense of community between the speaker and the listeners.

This difference between blacks and whites was evident, recently, in a class where I lectured on Afro-American history. During the lecture, one of my more vocal black students began to respond to the message with some encouraging remarks like "all right," "make it plain," "that all right," and "teach." She was soon joined by a few more black students who gave similar comments. I noticed that this surprised and confused some of the white students. When questioned later about this, their response was that they were not used to having more than one person talk at a time, and they really could not talk and listen at the same time. They found the comments annoying and disruptive. As the lecturer, I found the comments refreshing and inspiring. The black student who initiated the responses had no difficulty understanding what I was saying while she was reacting to it, and did not consider herself "rude."

In addition to the speaker's verbal creativity and the dynamic quality of the communication environment, black speech is very rhythmic. It flows like African languages in a consonant-vowel-consonant-vowel pattern. To achieve this rhythmic effect, some syllables are held longer, and are accented stronger and differently from standard English, such as DE-troit. This rhythmic pattern is learned early by young blacks and is reinforced by the various styles it complements.

With this brief background into the historical and philosophical foundation of black language, we can examine some of the styles commonly employed and their role in African American life. Among the secular styles, the most common is *rappin'*. Although the term *rappin'* is currently used by whites to mean simply talking (as in *rap sessions*), it originally described the dialogue between a man and a woman where the main intention is to win the admiration of the woman. A man's success in rappin' depends on his ability to make creative and imaginative statements that generate interest on the part of the woman to hear more of the rap. And, although she already knows his intentions, the ritual is still played out; and, if the rap is weak, he will probably lose the woman.

To outsiders, rappin' might not appear to be an important style in the black community, but it is very important and affects the majority of black people because at some time in a black person's life, he or she will be involved in a situation where rappin' will take place. For, in the black community, it is the mating call, the introduction of the male to the female, and it is ritualistically expected by black women. So that while it is reasonable to assume that all black males will not rise to the level of "leader" in the black community because only a few will possess the unique oral skills necessary, it can be predicted that black men will have to learn how to "rap" to a woman.

Like other forms of black speech, the rap is rhythmic and has consequences. It is the good *rapper* who *gets over* (scores). And, as the master of Nommo, the rapper creates, motivates, and changes conditions through his language. It requires him to be imaginative and capable of responding to positive and negative stimuli immediately. For instance:

R: Hey Mama, how you doing?

L: Fine.

R: Yeah, I can see! (looking her up and down) Say, you married?

L: Yes.

R: Is your husband married? (bringing humor and doubt)

The rap requires participation by the listener. Thus, the speaker will ask for confirmation that the listener is following his line of progression. The rap is an old style that is taught to young men early. And, while each male will have his own style of rappin' that will adapt to the type of woman he is rappin' to, a poor, unimaginative rap is distasteful and often repulsive to black women.

Runnin' it down is a form of rappin' without sexual overtones. It is simply explaining something in great detail. The speaker's responsibility is to vividly recreate the event or concept for the listener so that there is complete agreement and understanding concerning the event. The speaker gives accurate descriptions of the individuals involved, describing them from head to toe. Every object and step of action is minutely described. To an outsider this might sound boring and tedious. However, it is the responsibility of the speaker to use figurative language to keep the listener's attention. In a narrative of a former slave from Tennessee, the following brief excerpt demonstrates the vivid language used in runnin' it down:

I remember Mammy told me about one master who almost starved his slaves. Mighty stingy I reckon he was.

Some of them slaves was so poorly thin they ribs would kinda rustle against each other like corn stalks a-drying in the hot winds. But they gets even one hog killing time, and it was funny, too, Mammy said.[4]

Runnin' it down is not confined to secular styles. In C.L. Franklin's sermon, "The Eagle Stirreth Her Nest"—the simple story of an eagle, mistaken for a chicken, that grows up and is eventually set free—the story becomes a drama that vividly takes the listener though each stage of the eagle's development. And even when the eagle is set free because she can no longer live in a cage, she does not simply fly away. Instead, she flies from one height to the other, surveying the surroundings, and then flies away. The details are so vivid that the listener can "see" and "feel" the events. Such is the style and the effect of runnin' it down.

Another common style of black language is *the dozens*. The dozens is a verbal battle of insults between speakers. The terms dozens was used during slavery to refer to a selling technique used by slavers. If an individual had a disability, he was considered "damaged goods" and was sold with eleven other "damaged" slaves at a discount rate. The term dozens refers to negative physical characteristics. To an outsider, the dozens might appear cruel and harsh. But to members of the black community, it is the highest form of verbal warfare and impromptu speaking. The game is often played in jest.

When the dozens is played, there is usually a group of listeners that serves as judge and jury over the originality, creativity, and humor of the comments. The listeners encourage continuation of the contest by giving comments like "Ou, I wouldn't take that," "Cold," "Rough," "Stale," or any statement that assesses the quality of the comments and encourages response. The battle continues until someone wins. This is determined by the loser giving up and walking away, or losing his cool and wanting to fight. When a physical confrontation occurs, the winner is not determined by the fight, but by the verbal confrontation. The dozens is so popular that a rock 'n' roll group made a humorous recording of insults between friends. Some of the exchanges were:

Say Man, your girlfriend so ugly, she had to sneak up on a glass to get a drink of water.

Man, you so ugly, yo mama had to put a sheet over your head so sleep could sneak up on you.

The dozens, like other forms of black language, calls on the speaker to use words to create moods. More than any other form, it pits wit against wit, and honors the skillful user of Nommo.

The final secular style to be discussed is proverbial wisdom. Sayings are used in the black community as teaching tools to impart values and truths. Their use demonstrates the African-American's respect for the oral tradition in teaching and socializing the young. Popular phrases, such as "what goes around comes around," "if you make you bed hard you gon lay in it," "God don't like ugly," and "a hard head make a soft behind," are used in everyday conversation by blacks from all social, economic, and educational strata. At some time in a black child's life, the sayings are used to teach them what life expects of them and what they can expect in return. It is also used to expose the truth in an artful and less offensive manner, such as "you don't believe fat meat is greasy." In this saying the listener is being put down for having a narrow or inaccurate view of things. And while it might appear that proverbial wisdoms are static, they are constantly changing and new ones are being created. One of the latest is said when you believe someone is lying to you or "putting you on." It is, "pee on my head and tell me it's raining." Or, if someone is talking bad about you, you might say, "don't let your mouth write a check your ass can't cash." Proverbial wisdom can be found on every socioeconomic level in the black community, and it is transmitted from generation to generation. Listening to speech that is peppered with proverbial sayings might seem strange to non-blacks. But, because proverbial sayings are generally accepted as "truths" because they are taught to children at a very early age, they effectively sum up events and predict outcome.

Like the secular, the nonsecular realm places a tremendous emphasis on the creative abilities of the speaker. The speaker (preacher) creates experiences for his listeners, who are participants in the communication event. The minister calls and his audience responds, and at some point they become one. The minister actively seeks his audience's involvement and when he does not receive it, he chides and scolds them. The audience also believes that the delivery of a good sermon is dependent upon them encouraging the minister with their "amens" and "right-ons." And if the minister preaches false doctrine, the audience also feels obliged to tell him, "Uh, oh Reb, you done gone too far now!"

The language used by the minister, who is probably very fluent in standard English, is generally seasoned with black English. Seldom will you hear the term *Lord* used, but you will head *Lawd* because the *Lord* is the man in the big house who is an overseer, but the *Lawd* is a friend who walks, talks, and comforts you. The relationship between the *Lawd* and his people is more personal than the *Lord*'s.

Also, the speaker may overaccent a word for black emphasis. In C. L. Franklin's sermon, he said, "*extra*-ordinary sight." He then came right back and said *extraordinary*, to demonstrate that he knew how to "correctly" enunciate the word. The nonsecular style of speech is generally the most dramatic of all forms and has the highest degree of audience participation. It encompasses all the elements of black language, and of all the styles it is the most African in form.

Black language and the numerous styles that have been developed are indications of the African American's respect for the spoken word. The language has often been called a hieroglyphic language because of the vivid picture created by the speaker for the listener about the activities or feelings taking place. To say someone is "all jawed up," or "smacking on some barnyard pimp," or "ready to hat," is more imaginative and creative than saying they had "nothin to say," or "eating chicken," or "ready to leave." The responsibility of the speaker and the listener to participate in the communication event also emphasizes the African world view, which stresses the interrelatedness of all things to each other. And finally, the dynamics of the communication, and the responsibility of man as the user of Nommo, places communication and the spoken word in the arena of forces and not static objects. The rhythm and flow of the language approximates the style and flow and unity of African life.

Despite all of the explanation of the Africanness found in black language, many continue to ask, why use it? Why do blacks who have lived in America for hundreds of years continue to speak "black"? Why do those who possess degrees of higher learn-ing and even write scholarly articles and books in standard English continue to talk "black"?

There are many reasons for the continued use of black language. A language expresses an experience. If the experiences of a group are culturally unique, the group will need a different vocabulary to express them. If white folks in white churches don't *get happy* because they have been socialized to be quiet listeners in church, then they don't have the vocabulary that blacks have to describe levels of spiritual possession. And if they do not have curly hair, they probably do not *press* their hair or worry about *catching up* their *kitchins*. Thus, because blacks experience the world differently from other groups in America, there is a need for a language that communicates that experience.

Secondly, black language reaches across the superficial barriers of education and social position. It is the language that binds, that creates community for blacks, so that the brother in the three-piece Brooks Brothers suit can go to the local corner where folks "hang out" and say, "hey, blood, what it is?", and be one with them. Additionally, the minister's use of black language reminds the listeners of their common experiences and struggles (for example, "I been thur the storm"). Through black language, barriers that separate blacks are lowered and they are finally "home" with each other. So, for cultural identity, the code is essential to define the common elements among them.

Finally, black language usage stands as a political statement that black people are African people who have not given up a vital part of themselves in slavery: their language. They have retained the cultural link that allows them to think and to express themselves in a non-European form. As an old adage says, The namer of names is the father of things. Thus, the ability of blacks to maintain and sustain a living language shows their control over that aspect of their lives, and their determination to preserve the culture. The use of black language is the black man's defiance of white America's total indoctrination. The use of black language by choice is a reflection not of a lack of intelligence, but of a desire to retain and preserve black life styles.

The purpose of this discussion is to help others understand and appreciate black language styles and the reasons blacks speak the way they do, in hopes of building respect for cultural difference. Now the question may be asked, what does the general society do about it? Some might ask, should whites learn black english? To that question comes a resounding *no*! Black language is, first of all, not a laboratory language and it cannot be learned in a classroom. And even if you could learn definition and grammar, you would not learn the art of creative expression that is taught when you're "knee high to a duck." Thus, you would miss the elements of rhythm and style, and you would sound like invaders or foreigners.

What one should do about the language is be open-minded and not judge the speaker by European standards of expression. If you're in a class-room and the teacher is *gettin down*, don't *wig out* because the black student says "teach." Simply realize that you must become listening participants. If some *bloods* decide to use a double negative or play *the dozens*, don't assume some social theory about how they lack a father image in the home and are therefore culturally and linguistically deprived. You just might discover that they are the authors of your college English text.

The use of black language does not represent any pathology in blacks. It simply says that, as African people transplanted to America, they are a different flower whose aroma is just as sweet as other flowers. The beginning of racial understanding is the acceptance that difference is just what it is: different, not inferior. And equality does not mean sameness.

NOTES

1. Geneva Smitherman, *Talkin' and Testifyin'* (Boston: Houghton Mifflin Company, 1972), p. 2.

2. Ibid, p. 3.

3. Janheinz Jahn, *Muntu* (New York: Grove Press, Inc., 1961), pp. 132–133.

4. Smitherman, *Talkin' and Testifyin'*, p. 156.

CONCEPTS AND QUESTIONS FOR CHAPTER 5

1. Can you think of examples that would demonstrate the validity of linguistic relativity?

2. What is meant by the phrase "Language is a guide to social reality"?

3. Can you think of some arguments that would tend to disprove the concept of linguistic relativity?

4. How do the types of translation problems discussed by Sechrest, Fay, and Zaidi apply to everyday intercultural encounters?

5. Some people have suggested that the problems associated with translation could be solved if everyone spoke the same universal language. Evaluate this view in light of the influence culture has on language?

6. Does Folb's essay offer support for the Sapir-Whorf hypothesis? If so, in what ways?

7. What groups, in addition to blacks, have developed a subset of words and phrases? Can you think of some examples that would represent that group's vernacular vocabulary?

8. What forms of vernacular language are common among you and your friends? How does this usage differ from that of your parents or other members of the dominant community?

9. Suggest ways that people might learn about the experiential aspects of other cultures that lead to unique language differences.

10. What are the advantages of having an interpreter who is aware of nonverbal behaviors as well as verbal behaviors?

11. How do nondominant cultures use language strategies as a way of coping with dominant cultures?

12. What is meant by the act of "tomming"?

13. What is black language and how does it function within the black community?

14. What are the "dozens" and what purpose does it play in black language?

SUGGESTED READINGS

Bosmajian, H. A. "Defining the 'American Indian': A case study in the language of suppression." *The Speech Teacher* 21 (1973), 89–99. Bosmajian shows how language has functioned as a force in suppressing the American Indian. He asserts that the first act an oppressor does linguistically is to redefine the suppressed victims he intends to jail or to eradicate, so that they will be seen as deserving suppression.

The Florida FL Reporter (Spring/Summer 1969). This special issue is devoted to the problems of cultural differences in language and language use in the United States. Emphasis is placed on teaching problems and practical methods for improving intercultural understanding.

Folb, E. A. *Runnin' Down Some Lines: The Language and Culture of Black Teenagers*. Cambridge, Mass.: Harvard University Press, 1980. Folb focuses on the special vocabulary, idiomatic usages, and culture of black teenagers who live in the inner city of South Central Los Angeles. Through her study of language, she enables the reader to gain insight into beliefs, world view, attitudes, and values of this particular group.

Kramer, C. "Women's speech: Separate, but unequal?" *Quarterly Journal of Speech* 60 (1974), 14–24. In this very interesting article, Kramer seeks to discover differences in the ways men and women use the English language. She maintains that "sex roles are important to our culture." Specifically she focuses on differences in verbal skills, instrumental uses of language, and the relationship between verbal and nonverbal dimensions.

Lambert, W. E., and R. G. Tucker. *Tu, Vous, Usted: A Social-Psychological Study of Address Patterns*. Rowley, Mass.: Newbury House, 1976. In this book the authors examine the ways people from different cultures address each other. Lambert and Tucker look at the patterns of distancing relationships through language. A major area of research was the influence of nonreciprocal language patterns.

Lewis, I., ed. *Symbols and Sentiments: Cross-Cultural Studies in Symbolism*. New York: Academic Press, 1977. This collection grew out of an interdisciplinary seminar that focused on problems of language in a cross-cultural setting. The authors are concerned with the emotional aspects of meaning as well as with the cognitive dimensions of symbols.

Munroe, R. L., and R. H. Munroe. *Cross-Cultural Human Development*. Monterey, Calif.: Brooks/Cole, 1975, Chapter 4. The authors begin with this true and important concept: "Language is, uniquely, a part of man's culture as well as the chief tool for transmitting culture to each succeeding generation." They then look at issues such as language acquisition, lexical distinctions, grammatical classifications, sound development, and environmental effects. Each of these concepts is placed within an intercultural context.

Nist, J. *Handicapped English: The Language of the Socially Disadvantaged*. Springfield, Ill.: Charles C. Thomas, 1974. Nist examines the concept of speech and prestige from the perspective of social class as a subculture. He explains how the language and dialect of a subculture can give information about the characteristics of that group. He concentrates on three types of speech, to determine the extent to which differences are found as one moves in and out of various social classes.

Sapir, E. *Language*. New York: Harcourt Brace Jovanovich, 1949. The author's main purpose is to show what he conceives language to be rather than to assemble facts about it. A complete coverage of various aspects of language is included with sections dealing with interaction between languages and the relationship of language, race, and culture.

Thorne, B., and N. Henley. *Language and Sex: Difference and Dominance*. Rowley, Mass.: Newbury House, 1975. This collection of twelve essays examines the relationship between language and sex. Topics such as sexism in language, sex differences in word choice, sex differences in intonation patterns, sex differences in choice of phonetic variants, conversational patterns between the sexes, and the effect of sex on the verbal interaction between teachers and children are covered in this text.

ADDITIONAL READINGS

Abdulaziz, M. H. "Patterns of language acquisition and use in Kenya: Rural-urban differences." *International Journal of the Sociology of Language* 34 (1982), 95–120.

Abrahams, R. D., and R. C. Troike, eds. *Language and Cultural Diversity in American Education*. Englewood Cliffs, N.J.: Prentice-Hall, 1972.

Angle, J. "Mutual language group accommodation: Can the privileged language group respond to economic incentives too?" *Western Sociological Review* 12 (1981), 71–89.

Beaujot, R. P. "The decline of official language minorities in Quebec and English Canada." *Canadian Journal of Sociology* 7 (1982), 367–389.

Bond, M. H., and K. Yang. "Ethnic affirmation versus cross-cultural accommodation: The variable impact of questionnaire language on Chinese bilinguals from Hong Kong." *Journal of Cross-Cultural Psychology* 13 (1982), 169–185.

Brasch, W. M. *Black English and the Mass Media*. Amherst, Mass.: University of Massachusetts Press, 1981.

Brislin, R. W., ed. *Translations: Applications and Research*. New York: Halsted, 1976.

Burke, S. M., S. W. Pflaum, and J. D. Knafle. "The influence of black English on diagnosis of reading in learning disabled and normal readers." *Journal of Learning Disabilities* 18 (1982), 19–22.

Cogdell, R., and S. Wilson. *Black Communication in White Society*. Saratoga, Calif.: Century 21, 1980.

Cohen, R. "The language of the hard-core poor: Implications for culture conflict." *The Sociological Quarterly* 9 (1968), 19–28.

Edwards, W. F. "Some linguistic and behavioral links in the African diaspora." *International Journal of Intercultural Relations* 6 (1982), 169–184.

Fisherman, J. A. "Whorfianism of the third kind: Ethnolinguistic diversity as a worldwide social asset." *Language in Society* 11 (1982), 1–14.

Foster, H. L. *Ribbin', Jivin', and Playin' in the Dozens*. Cambridge, Mass.: Ballinger, 1974.

Grayshon, M. C. "The possible contribution of social grammar of language analysis to intercultural communication and the avoidance of misunderstanding" in D. Nimmo, ed. *Communication Yearbook* 4. New Brunswick, N.J.: Transaction Books, 1980, pp. 437–445.

Haas, M. *Language, Culture, and History*. Stanford, Calif.: Stanford University Press, 1978.

Hawana, S. A., and J. K. Smith. "Can philosophical meaning cross linguistic/cultural barriers?" *International Journal of Intercultural Relations* 3 (1979), 119–210.

Hawkes, G. R., J. Smith, and C. Acredolo. "English language use among Mexican immigrants: A causative analysis." *Hispanic Journal of Behavioral Sciences* 2 (1980), 161–176.

Hoppe, R. A., and J. F. Kess. "Differential detection of ambiguity in Japanese." *Journal of Psycholinguistic Research* 3 (1980), 303–318.

Kantrowitz, M. "The vocabulary of race relations in prison." *Pads* 51 (1969), 23–34.

Katzner, K. *The Languages of the World*. New York: Funk and Wagnalls, 1975.

Kirch, M. "Language, communication, and culture." *Modern Language Journal* 57 (1973), 340–343.

Labov, W. *Language in the Inner City*. Philadelphia: University of Pennsylvania Press, 1972.

Lambert, W. E., ed. *Language, Psychology and Culture*. Stanford, Calif.: Stanford University Press, 1972.

Levine, D. R., and M. B. Adelman. *Beyond Language: Intercultural Communication for English as a Second Language*. Englewood Cliffs, N.J.: Prentice-Hall, 1982.

Lewis, I., ed. *Symbols and Sentiments: Cross-Cultural Studies in Symbolism*. New York: Academic Press, 1977.

Lukens, J. G. "Ethnocentric speech: Its nature and implications." *Ethnic Groups* 2 (1978), 35–53.

Miller, R. A. *The Japanese Language*. Chicago: University of Chicago Press, 1967.

Osgood, C. E., et al. *Cross-Cultural Universals of Affective Meaning*. Urbana: University of Illinois Press, 1975.

Pettersen, D. D. "Language and information processing: An approach to intercultural communication." *International and Intercultural Communication Annual* 3 (1976), 1–10.

Philipsen, G. "Speaking 'like a man' in Teamsterville: Cultural patterns of role enactment in an urban neighborhood." *Quarterly Journal of Speech* 61 (1975), 13–22.

Sedano, M. V. "Chicanism: A rhetorical analysis of themes and images of selected poetry from the Chicano movement." *Western Journal of Speech Communication* 44 (1980), 177–190.

Simard, L. M. "Cross-cultural interaction: Potential invisible barriers." *Journal of Social Psychology* 2 (1981), 171–192.

Smith, A. L. *Language, Communication and Rhetoric in Black America*. New York: Harper & Row, 1972.

Snow, C. E., R. Van Eeden, and P. Muysken. "The interactional origins of foreigner talk: Municipal employees and foreign workers." *International Journal of the Sociology of Language* 28 (1981), 81–91.

Sossman, N. M., and H. M. Rosenfeld. "Influence of culture, language, and sex on conversational distance." *Journal of Personality and Social Psychology* 1 (1982), 66–74.

Stanley, J. P. "Homosexual slang." *American Speech* 45 (1970), 45–59.

Turner, P. R. "Why Johnny doesn't want to learn a foreign language." *The Modern Language Journal* 58 (1974), 191–196.

Tzeng, O. C., R. Neel, and D. Landis. "[...] cultures and languages on self conc[...] *International Journal of Psycholog[...]* (1981), 95–109.

Valdman, A. "Sociolinguistic aspects of foreign[...] talk." *International Journal of the Sociology of Language* 28 (1981), 41–52.

Vetter, H. J. "Special language: The psychedelic subculture" in *Language and Behavior*. Itasca, Ill.: F. E. Peacock, 1969, Chapter 11.

6

Nonverbal Interaction

Successful participation in intercultural communication requires that we recognize and understand culture's influence not only on verbal interaction but on *nonverbal* interaction as well. Nonverbal behaviors constitute messages to which people attach meaning just as do verbal behaviors. Because nonverbal symbols are derived from such diverse behaviors as body movements, postures, facial expressions, gestures, eye movements, physical appearance, the use and organization of space, and the structuralization of time, these symbolic behaviors often vary from culture to culture. An awareness of the role of nonverbal behaviors is crucial, therefore, if we are to appreciate all aspects of intercultural interaction.

Nonverbal behavior is largely unconscious. We use nonverbal symbols spontaneously, without thinking about what posture, what gesture, or what interpersonal distance is appropriate to the situation. These factors are critically important in intercultural communication because, as with other aspects of the communication process, nonverbal behaviors are subject to cultural variation. These nonverbal behaviors can be categorized in two ways.

In the first, culture tends to determine the specific nonverbal behaviors that represent or symbolize specific thoughts, feelings, or states of the communicator. Thus, what might be a sign of greeting in one culture could very well be an obscene gesture in another. Or what might be a symbol of affirmation in one culture could be meaningless or even signify negation in another. In the second, culture determines when it is appropriate to display or communicate various thoughts, feelings, or internal states; this is particularly evident in the display of emotions. Although there seems to be little cross-cultural difference in the behaviors that represent emotional states, there are great cultural differences in which emotions may be displayed, by whom, and when or where they may be displayed.

As important as verbal language is to a communication event, nonverbal communication is just as, if not more, important. Nonverbal messages tell us how other messages are to be interpreted. They indicate whether verbal messages are true, joking, serious, threatening, and so on. Gregory Bateson has described these "second-order messages" as meta communication, which we use as frames around messages to designate how they are to be interpreted.* The importance of meta communication can be seen from communication research indicating that as much as 90 percent of the social content of a message is transmitted paralinguistically or nonverbally.†

Chapter 6 deals with nonverbal interaction. The readings examine the influence of culture on various aspects of nonverbal behavior in order to demonstrate the variety of culturally derived nonverbal behaviors and the underlying value structures that produce these behaviors.

As in the last chapter, the first article here is an overview. "Perspective on Nonverbal Intercultural Communication" by J. Vernon Jensen recounts the ways in which culture influences nonverbal messages. Jensen, after discussing the importance of nonverbal communication, examines body motion and gesture, use of the eyes, and attitudes toward time and space as they are reflected in different cultures. In addition, intimacy of address, degree of emotion and animation, frankness, intensity, persistency, and volume are related to culture and communication.

Weston LaBarre in "Paralinguistics, Kinesics, and Cultural Anthropology" provides us with a second overview. He introduces the concept of nonverbal communication by pointing out cultural differences in the use of bodies, limbs, and eyes. As a means of demonstrating cultural kinesics, LaBarre explains how various cultures engage in greeting, kissing, gestures of contempt, politeness, and beckoning. For example, kissing in the Orient is an act of private lovemaking and often arouses disgust when performed publicly. This and many other examples show that simple movements can elicit entirely different meanings from culture to culture. Awareness of these cultural differences is one sign of successful intercultural communicators.

Tom Bruneau in "The Time Dimension in Intercultural Communication" looks at the conscious and unconscious ways different cultures treat the concept of time. He examines such topics as futurism, timing and timekeeping, the pace of life, and cultural tempo.

In Chapter 3 we noted that the experiences of men and women often produce some significant differences in values, attitudes, and communication patterns. One of these major differences is found in the area of nonverbal communication. More specifically, researchers have found sex differences in all the categories normally associated with nonverbal behavior. In our next selection, Barbara Westbrook Eakins and R. Gene Eakins review these research findings. Male-female comparisons are made for eye contact, facial expressions, posture and bearing, gestures, clothing, grooming and physical appearance, use of space, and touch. Being aware of and knowing how these sex differences in nonverbal behavior operate during interaction should be helpful to both women and men as they attempt to exchange ideas, information, and feelings with one another.

In the final article, "To Hear One and Understand Ten: Nonverbal Behavior in Japan," Sheila Ramsey provides us with a functional awareness about the role of nonverbal behavior in Japan. She shows how this awareness can facilitate effective interaction with the Japanese. Ramsey also offers suggestions about how to learn about nonverbal behavior in Japan.

---

*Gregory Bateson, "A Theory of Play and Fantasy," *Psychiatric Research* 2 (1955), 39–51.

†Albert Mehrabian and Morton Wiener, "Decoding in Inconsistent Messages," *Journal of Personality and Social Psychology* 6 (1967), 109–114.

Perspective on Nonverbal Intercultural Communication

J. VERNON JENSEN

There is a great need to revise and broaden our view of the human situation, a need to be both more comprehensive and more realistic, not only about others, but about ourselves as well. It is essential that we learn to read the silent communications as easily as the printed and spoken ones. Only by doing so can we also reach other people, both inside and outside our national boundaries, as we are increasingly required to do.

—Edward Hall[1]

The assertion that the world is getting smaller has become commonplace and trite. The advent of the jet age has dazzlingly reduced time of travel to hours whereas only a short time ago it was measured in days or weeks. The United States is linked intimately with all other parts of the world. Many of its citizens are coming in contact with peoples of other languages and cultures. Expanding international business and industrial networks, increasing international educational exchange programs, and mushrooming tourism are bringing more and more of the world's inhabitants into contact with each other. So are military and foreign aid commitments and international programs such as the Peace Corps. The promise that super jets will in the very near future carry a vastly larger passenger load, at a greater speed, and at a lower cost to most major population centers of the globe staggers the imagination. We are indeed, in the words of Buckminster Fuller, witnessing "a swiftly emerging spherical world city."[2]

INTRODUCTION

Importance of Nonverbal Cues in Intercultural Communication

What will this increased intercultural contact bring forth? The superficial assumption that "the more we get together the happier we'll be" is hardly substantiated, even in many of our small family circles. It must be frankly recognized that increased contact may bring additional misunderstanding, friction, and tension. Why? Among many possible causes is the virtually unrecognized factor of nonverbal cues in communication across cultures and subcultures. Edward Hall, a leading cultural anthropologist who is a pioneer in this field of intercultural communication, has stated it well:

I am convinced that much of our difficulty with people in other countries stems from the fact that so little is known about cross-cultural communication. . . . Formal training in the language, history, government, and customs of another nation is only the first step in a comprehensive program. Of equal importance is an introduction to the nonverbal language which exists in every country of the world and among the various groups within each country. Most Americans are only dimly aware of this silent language even though they use it every day.[3]

During the last decade, anthropologists, linguists, psychiatrists, sociologists, language teachers, and communication specialists have begun to awaken us to the urgent need of understanding this "silent language." That is, these scholars have demonstrated how gestures, body motions, practices due to attitudes toward time and space, and general social behavior all communicate a great deal. "It is certain," write two contemporary scholars, "that [these] 'silent languages' . . . are as important—often more so—as the verbal matter we are accustomed to regard as the essence of communication."[4] Rooted deeply in cultural conventions, a virtual "hidden dimension" in communication between people of different countries—these nonverbal cues must be exposed and appreciated more than they now are.

Fortunately, an increasing amount of research findings in this area is beginning to appear in scholarly journals and treatises. The Institute for the Study of National Behavior in Princeton, New Jersey, is doing pioneering work in this field. Some colleges and universities are including intercultural communication in their curricula. Some, like the University of Minnesota under the leadership of William S. Howell, are creating centers of intercultural communication to promote faculty and student research. Language teachers are beginning to include some teaching of gesturing together with the written and spoken dimensions of that language.

But as yet, textbooks in communication have not devoted much space to discussing these nonverbal cues so important in intercultural communication. It is hoped that this [article], then, will meet an urgent and growing contemporary need. The urgency is certainly greater than it was two decades ago when one writer pleaded: "We must train many young Americans, quickly, to communicate with the peoples of the world."[5]

Hazards of Superficial Study of Nonverbal Intercultural Communication

Some potential hazards need to be explicitly enunciated before we enter into a discussion of the intricacies and subtleties of nonverbal intercultural communication. You are urged to keep these in mind as you read the [article] in order to interpret more accurately and clearly the assertions made.

Overgeneralization. The danger of overgeneralizing about a geographical area (e.g., "the Middle East," "the Orient," or "Latin America"), a religious group (e.g., "Catholics," "Moslems," or "Buddhists"), or a nation (Japan, Italy, or the United States) is obviously very great indeed. The enormous number of subcultures within any of the above groupings cannot be stressed enough. Many variations will exist within any grouping, depending upon education, social class, occupation, economic level, sex, religion, or geographical location. Coastal areas, for instance, in touch with the outside world, may differ considerably from the isolated interior. Large urban centers may have more in common with cities in other countries than with their own countryside.

Many of us are unaware of, or insensitive to, the nonverbal cues of those subgroups in our own culture. For instance, how many non-Catholics *really* understand the significance of the various body motions and gestures employed during a worship service by a devout Catholic? How many whites recognize that some blacks establish eye contact only when angry, or that many black school children need to be touched to sense fully the teacher's approval?

The educated in any society may be totally ignorant of the meaning of gestures employed by uneducated segments of the population. This is frequently illustrated when some foreign students on university campuses are surprised, and tend to deny, that certain gestures are used in their homeland. They may come from urban, upper class, educated circles, whereas the gestures may have been observed in the country market place among uneducated segments of the population, which the student himself may have never observed. Americans are prone to be particularly insensitive to geographical variations, since in the United States the regional variations in nonverbal cues, like in spoken dialects, vary slightly compared to regional variations within most other countries.

Having expressed the need to be highly sensitive to subcultural considerations, I now have to confess that in a textbook such as this, simplicity and coherence necessitate the use of generalizations. The names of tribes and places known only to the specialist in anthropology and geography would merely confuse the reader. Hence, of necessity I will be speaking of "the Arabs," the "Latin Americans," and so on. Also, the term "American" will refer to people living in the United States even though this is a usurpation of a label belonging to all in the Western Hemisphere. But I feel I can use these labels with safety now that you have been alerted.

Mythical "Average Person." Many of the characterizations will be in the form of cultural norms. But it should be recognized that this mythical "average person" may not exist in quite the precise form depicted.

All Cues Are Created Equal. Some of the nonverbal cues occur much more frequently than others. Some may be rather rare, at least in some subgroups. Also, some cues are more significant than others in the social process of communication. Hence, all of these nonverbal cues are not to be considered as occurring with equal frequency or with equal impact.

Exaggeration of Differences. Since the very objective of the present chapter is to ascertain and discuss the *differences* between cultures, the danger exists that these contracts in cues or their interpretation will loom disproportionately large. Thus, with proper perspective it must be recognized that many nonverbal cues and the interpretation of them are not appreciably different in different countries. But, by definition, discussion of such similarities is omitted from this [article].

Exaggeration of Effects. The seriousness of the misunderstandings stemming from these varying nonverbal cues ought not to be exaggerated. It is common for anyone, including textbook writers, to overstate a case that has not had much previous publicity. To catalog the dire results that will occur if certain information is not understood and ap-

plied is a familiar lamentation. But we all have often experienced how apparently minor misunderstandings have become major irritants. The modern world surely needs to eliminate as many sources of friction as possible, be they small or large, many or few.

Distortion of Primary Cause. It should also be recognized that many of the ill effects attributed to lack of understanding of these nonverbal intercultural cues may be more accurately laid to antisocial personality factors. After all, an arrogant, insensitive individual is likely to act in an arrogant, insensitive manner until he has had some fundamental alteration in his values. But hopefully, even he—perhaps especially he—with fuller knowledge of these silent languages will modify his relationships with peoples of other cultures, and at least reduce unintentional offensiveness.

Prejudice. We need to assess carefully and honestly whatever preconceptions about, and prejudices toward, cultures other than our own we may possess. Likewise, our current attitudes toward certain body motions, gestures, or social mannerisms as inherently bad, improper, or uncivilized, need to be re-examined. So do any notions that these nonverbal cues with which we are accustomed are necessarily good and proper. Thus, a considerable amount of intellectual self-introspection and a sizable amount of tolerance for differences are needed. This applies to the various subcultures within our own nation as well, for we may actually be less tolerant of them than of foreigners, whom we expect to be different.

Viewing Culture as Static. We need to realize that culture is not static, that it cannot be stereotyped once and for all. Just as culture is molding humans, so are humans, unlike animals, changing and modifying their culture. Admittedly, basic cultural patterns shift slowly, but some change is usually present, just as spoken and written languages change slowly and often imperceptibly through the years. Cultural changes are occurring more rapidly in this modern interrelated world, and what may have been true a generation ago, to say nothing of a century ago, may not be true today.

It is important to keep these hazards in mind, then, as we now look at nonverbal cues (1) expressed in body motion and gestures, (2) stemming from attitudes toward time, (3) stemming from attitudes toward space, and (4) stemming from general habits in communicating.

NONVERBAL CUES EXPRESSED IN BODY MOTION AND GESTURE

At the outset it should be clearly understood that modern research has strongly emphasized that body motions and gestures are *learned*. That is, they are *culturally determined*. Most studies prior to World War II were based on a single culture, and they assumed that the same gestures were present, with the same meaning, in other cultures as well. The studies assumed that gestures were "natural," especially in the expression of certain emotions. If natural, then of course they would be universal. But contemporary scholars have concluded that "there is no 'natural' language of emotional gesture,"[6] and that our "gesture language which is meaningful to us is as unintelligible to another culture as our verbal language is."[7] Earlier studies also asserted or implied that body movements and gestures were biological, instinctive, and inherent characteristics of a certain race or nationality. These traits would thus not be subject to modification and change. But this has been disproven. Studies of immigrants have revealed how gestures are modified and changed to conform to the gestural patterns of the new homeland, just as the spoken language is changed. Just as they exhibit "foreign accents" in their speech, first and second generation immigrants usually retain some vestiges of past gestural habits and thus develop what is called "hybrid gestures." Following generations, however, thoroughly adopt the new gestural habits just as foreign accents disappear.

Body Postures

Mankind's body postures are legion. One authority has asserted that the human body is capable of adopting about one thousand different "steady postures," that is, "a static position which can be maintained comfortably for some time."[8] These are to a large degree culturally determined, learned behavior. For instance, although you are accustomed to sitting in a chair when resting, about one-fourth of the world population has learned to rest in a squatting position. Most Westerners look on this as a rather improper, primitive, and childish position. Our children squat very naturally, but through verbal admonishment and constant example we teach them to forgo this highly comfortable position for the sitting posture. Furthermore, many people in other lands do most of their sitting on the ground and floor (frequently on mats), and hence when they sit in chairs they tend to curl one or both legs under them, which to some Westerners seems strange and perhaps primitive. Sitting on one's heels with knees resting on the floor is a formal sitting position of Japan, and is one position of prayer for the Moslem.

Positions of prayer have vastly differing connotations depending upon whether one is a member of the "in-group" or not. When a devout Moslem prostrates himself and a devout Christian kneels, they feel they are engaging in acts symbolizing humility and appropriate submission to a deity. But to a person outside of these religious frameworks, such motions may connote a primitive and even pagan gesture of appeasement to some wrathful God, and thus an affront to the dignity of man.

Westerners stand up to show respect, which they say is the "natural" thing to do. But some Polynesians sit down. The erect, stiff Prussian posture connotes arrogance to many people, but to a German it conveys respect.

When an American puts his feet up on his desk, it signifies a relaxed, informal attitude, many times a sort of tribute to the person with whom he is conversing. But to some Latin Americans and Asians, this connotes rudeness and perhaps arrogance.

Movements of the Body or Torso

Movements of the whole body or parts of the torso can communicate different messages in different cultures. The impression we may receive from vigorous African dance movements or intricate Oriental dance gestures may be quite different from the impressions received by members of those cultures.

The slow saunter of the American cowboy and the small rapid steps of a Chinese woman quickly illustrate that people walk differently, and that the type of walk may connote different things to different people. In England and parts of South America a male commonly clasps his hands behind his back when he walks, but to Americans this may connote an aristocratic, haughty attitude. Male friends in parts of the Middle East, Asia, and South America commonly walk arm in arm or holding hands, which to an American may connote effeminate behavior.

In parts of South America a slight bow is a common courteous gesture of greeting, especially when one does not stop to converse. An Oriental who has to leave a gathering will usually bow before departing, which communicates his apology. Similarly, members of the British House of Commons when entering or leaving the chamber will stop and bow toward the Speaker, thus communicating not only an apology for interrupting the proceedings but also a general respect for the Crown. Some in the Middle East bow to show respect for someone. To an American, the bowing gesture connotes formal, aristocratic, quaint movement that he considers rather irksome, fastidious, and undemocratic.

Some Mediterranean, Middle East, and South American males embrace as a common form of greeting by placing the head over the other person's right shoulder and then over the left, together with gentle pats on the back. Most Northern Europeans and Americans think this to be too emotional and possibly effeminate. Kissing in public is rather common in America, whereas in Asia it is considered highly indecent. Furthermore, instead of bringing the lips into contact to show mutual affection, some people, like the Eskimos and Polynesians, rub noses.

Movements of the Head and Facial Expression

Movements of the head and facial expressions may communicate different messages in different cultures. For instance, an educated Englishman may lift the chin slightly when conversing, as a poised, polite gesture. But to an American it may connote arrogance or snobbery. "Turning up his nose" has become a meaningful American idiom.

We may think that nodding the head up and down for affirming something, and shaking it from side to side for negation, is the "natural" thing to do. But other cultures employ other gestures to say "yes" or "no." A Malayan tribe says "yes" by thrusting the head forward, whereas Ethiopians say "yes" by throwing the head back, and "no" by jerking the head to the right. Some Arabs and Italians indicate the negative by lifting the chin, whereas this means "yes" to the Maori in New Zealand. The Arab communicates a minimal negative by merely raising the eyebrows, whereas that means "yes" in some Borneo tribes, who would lower them to indicate negation. In different parts of India and Ceylon, affirmation may be communicated by throwing the head backward and slightly turning the neck, by bending the head down and to the right, or by turning the head rapidly in a circular motion. Some inhabitants of northern Japan communicate negation by passing the right hand back and forth in front of the chest, and indicate affirmation by bringing both hands up to the chest, and then waving them downwards with palms up.

Many times an American in some tropical land will erroneously interpret an expressionless face and a slight frown as meaning the person is uninterested or even somewhat hostile. But the individual probably is shy and is unconsciously frowning because of years in a hot sun. Americans are thus taken by surprise when this face suddenly bursts forth with a huge smile once the shyness is broken.

The Japanese smile and laugh does not necessarily mean happiness or friendship. As a carefully cultivated act of social duty and etiquette, it is employed in a large number of circumstances and may, among other things, suggest shyness, embarrassment, discomfort, wonder, or surprise. In some areas of Asia and Africa laughing or smiling suggests weakness. Hence, teachers never smile in the classroom lest it impair discipline.

Use of the Eyes

Different cultures have developed a variety of uses for the eyes in the communicative process. We are familiar with the American admonition to maintain good eye contact with one's audience. But some cultures teach their young people, especially girls, that to look someone in the eye, especially an older or more important person, is disrespectful and highly improper. Hence, one should lower one's gaze accordingly. For example, recently a very expressive girl from Indonesia, studying at an American university, told me that because of this emphasis in her culture, the most difficult thing for her in American public speaking classes was to learn to look at her audience.

On the other hand, in a conversational situation, Americans do not practice such rigorous eye contact as do Britons and Arabs. The educated Briton considers it part of good listening behavior to stare at his conversationalist and to indicate his understanding by blinking his eyes, whereas we Americans nod our head or emit some sort of grunt, and are from childhood taught not to stare at people. One writer has asserted that the "Arabs look each other in the eye when talking with an intensity that makes most Americans highly uncomfortable."[9] Furthermore, the Arab has grown so accustomed to facing the person with whom he is conversing, that he finds it awkward and feels it is impolite, for instance, to talk when walking side by side. Thus he may dance ahead in order to achieve eye contact. Americans make more use of eye movements in general, while other cultures make more use of hand and arm motions.

Hand and Arm Motions

The use of hand and arm motions for communicative purposes varies to a remarkable degree between cultures. The following contrasts have been suggested:

Gesture among the Americans is largely oriented toward activity; among the Italians it serves the purposes of illustration and display; among the Jews it is a device of emphasis; among the Germans it specifies both attitude and commitment; and among the French it is an expression of style and containment.[10]

Some, like Americans and northern Europeans, look on frequent and vigorous gesturing as too emotional, immature, and rather vulgar, and thus use them rather sparingly and with restraint. On the other hand, those inhabitants of Southern Europe, the Middle East, and South America, view gestures differently and use them much more frequently and with much more energy. The familiar adage that if an Italian had his arms amputated, he would be speechless, rather meaningfully depicts his reliance on gesture. Recently when judging twenty-five contestants in a high school oratory contest, I noted that only one student used arm and hand movements with grace and ease and meaningful reinforcement of the verbal message. He proved to be an exchange student from Italy! The Arabs, writes one observer, "have obtained such an eloquence of gesture that often words seem superfluous in conversation."[11] At the other extreme would be those who use hand and arm gestures very sparingly, like some Indian tribes in Bolivia. Because of the cool climate, they keep their hands under shawls or blankets most of the time, and hence rely more on facial and eye expressions.

When an American clasps his hands over his head, it signifies, usually with pride and occasionally a touch of arrogance, that victory over some foe has been achieved. A prize fighter, for instance, so signals after having been designated the victor. But to the Russians this is a symbol of friendship. Thus, when Khrushchev came to the United States a few years ago and was photographed making that gesture, millions of Americans were irritated at what they interpreted to be an arrogant signal of confidence in eventual victory of Communism over America and capitalism. But the gesture was meant to communicate a spirit of friendship. In Colombia, a similar gesture but with clasped hands level with the face means "I agree with you." To clap the hands together is a familiar Western habit to communicate approval, but to many in the Orient it is used primarily to summon an inferior person, such as a servant.

Shaking hands is a gesture of friendship widely used in many cultures, but some Indian tribes in Bolivia have taken it as a challenge to wrestle and have obliged accordingly! Latin Americans shake hands more frequently, more vigorously, and continue it longer than do North Americans. The latter omit it occasionally as a sign of informality, but Latin Americans may interpret its omission as discourtesy. Of course, shaking hands is done with the right, not the left hand. One origin of such a practice is that it symbolized a peaceful gesture, in that the right hand was the hand which held weapons, and these would have to be set aside in order to shake hands.

But the right hand has been glorified throughout the centuries for other reasons as well. In Moslem countries and some other Oriental countries, to touch anybody with the left hand is an obscenity, for a main function of the left hand is to aid in the process of elimination of body wastes, whereas the right hand is used for the intake of food. Hence, the left hand is unclean and the right is clean. To offer something in the left hand to a Moslem would be an insult of the most serious type.

This pragmatic origin of the prestige of the right hand has been buttressed by religious literature and practices. In the Old Testament, the right hand has always held more favor. It is with His right hand that Jehovah slays foes and protects followers. The right hand is associated with strength, goodness, honor, guidance, sustenance, safety, pleasure, and salvation. The New Testament has of course retained this glorification of the right hand, for on the Judgment Day the saved shall be on the right hand of God and the damned on the left. The ascended Christ is metaphorically seated on the right hand of God. This image is repeated in basic liturgical statements of faith of the institutional church, such as The Apostle's Creed and the Gloria in Excelsis. In a Christian marriage ceremony the participants are instructed to join, not their left, but their right hands. The Koran, the Moslem holy book, likewise associates the right hand with favorable connotations. The Buddhists also glorify the right hand.

In addition, the terms for "left" in Latin ("sinister") and French ("sinistre") carry negative connotations. In contrast, "dextrous," meaning "right," has favorable connotations. "Right" has multiple meanings, all of which carry highly favorable connotations, such as being the "accurate" answer, the "proper" behavior, or the "appropriate" garment. When we correct an error, we "right" the situation. Our most trusted associate is our "right-hand man." We salute and take an oath with the right hand. Furthermore, we all have certain "rights," and "righteousness" is a basic virtue.

One only needs to observe the shape of school desks, the contours of handles of kitchen utensils, and the placement of levers on machines to realize how completely dominant right-handedness is in our own Western culture. Thus, it is not surprising that the right hand has been so prestigious that it is only in the last generation or so that parents in the Western world have finally ceased the cruel and laborious practice of forcing their left-handed children to eat and write with their right hands. According to some theorists, this forced shifting of handedness has been a contributory cause of stuttering and other nervous insecurities.

A number of other gestures with hands and arms vary considerably between different cultures. In some parts of the world, members of the same sex greet each other by grasping forearms. In many parts of the world a slap on the back is a familiar form of greeting, although this may be interpreted by some people as too informal, aggressive, and even discourteous. In parts of the Middle East males may greet each other by grasping, raising, and kissing right hands. We may greet someone by a boisterous wave of the arm, but Hindus and Buddhists do so with a graceful and dainty placing of the palms together with fingers pointing skyward, which communicates not only a "hello" but also a sort of "peace be with you."

Americans beckon for someone to come by extending the arm, palm up, and moving the index finger or all fingers upward and toward the summoner. This, we say, is the natural way to beckon to someone. But in many parts of the Mediterranean area, the Middle East, the Orient, and South America the same request is communicated with palm down and the fingers and hand curving downward and toward the summoner. Many a North American has been initially puzzled by such a motion, for it approximates the gesture we would use to tell someone to go away.

When departing or when refusing some food or drink, some Arabs will place their right hand over their heart to indicate sincere regret. In parts of Asia, an individual gives an article with both hands, not just one, and receives an article in the right hand, with the left hand supporting the right elbow to demonstrate proper respect and gratitude. Raising the thumb to the nose is a recognized disrespectful vulgarism in the Western world, but in South India a similar gesture with the thumb higher on the bridge of the nose is a sign of respect. The American thumb gesture in hitchhiking is absent from many cultures, for as one source contends, it would originate only "in a country where total strangers are welcomed as passengers."[12] Latin Americans customarily call a waiter by sharply tapping on the table or striking a glass with a ring or a utensil. North Americans would consider this somewhat aggressive and rude and would call the waiter by raising the hand slightly or "catching his eye." A Portuguese will communicate his approval of something by tugging at an ear, whereas in Colombia, a similar motion indicates anticipation of some punishment, such as a child expecting a parental scolding. American male teachers who serve in the Orient are cautioned not to touch the girl students, for it is considered a virtual obscenity for a man to touch a woman.

In parts of South America one would indicate the size of an animal by extending the arm, palm down, but to indicate the height of a human, one would keep the palm vertical. Not to distinguish between these gestures for animal and human would be a grave error, one which North Americans customarily commit since they have no such separate gestures. Likewise, we frequently point at humans and animals with the same kind of hand and index finger gesture, but in parts of Asia it would be extremely rude to point at people, for this is only done toward animals. This involves another adjustment for American teachers abroad who are accustomed to calling on students by pointing at them.

The specific use of fingers has a variety of messages in different cultures. Some Arabs will demonstrate friendship by placing index fingers side by side. In Jordan, friendship may also be symbolized by locking little fingers, and enmity is demonstrated by extending the second finger and inviting to lock. But in neighboring Syria and Lebanon, according to some observers, the meaning of those symbols seem to be reversed. The familiar Roman thumbs-up gesture still symbolizes in Britain good fortune or success, but in parts of India "the same gesture is so offensive that to make it could actually cause a fight."[13] In the United States we admonish a small child not to do something by shaking the index finger forward and backward, whereas in South America the finger would move from side to side. In America we indicate in jest that someone is mentally unstable by making a circular motion with an index finger near the temple, whereas in France the same message is conveyed by a similar motion in front of the forehead.

NONVERBAL CUES STEMMING FROM ATTITUDES TOWARD TIME

The varying attitudes toward time and its utilization held by the various cultures in the world means that serious misunderstandings may arise in intercultural communication unless those individuals involved are aware of, and sensitive to, a number of basic considerations. Relative to the dimension of time, different cultures train their peoples to have significantly varying habits in (1) preparation for communication, (2) commencement of communication, (3) use of the communicating period, and (4) termination of the communication.

Preparation for Communication

Approaches to preparation for communication vary greatly. Americans and others in the Western world are said to live in the present and the near future and hence plan carefully. Other cultures, such as in the Middle East or Asia, live in their ancient pasts or in the far distant future and hence do not plan so assiduously. To the Hindu and Buddhist this life is only one among countless lives yet to come, merely one dot in an endless series of dots, so why plan? To the Moslem, the future belongs to Allah, not to man, so to plan would be to infringe on Allah's prerogative. To some cultures only a fool plans. Thus, to some people, planning can be unwise, disrespectful, unnecessary, and superfluous.

Americans look upon time as a present, tangible commodity, something to be used, something to be held accountable for. We spend it, waste it, save it, divide it, and are stewards of it, just as if we were handling some tangible object. In order to use time well, we schedule the day and week and month carefully, set up timetables, and establish precise priorities. We prepare carefully for business conferences, for personal interviews, for group meetings of all types. This we assume to be an elementary aspect of efficiency. But some Arabs, Asians and others look on this as obsessiveness, and aggressiveness. Their lack of planning communicates to Westerners laziness, inefficiency, and untrustworthiness.

Americans expect an invitation to a dinner or a request for a date or for any other social event to be proffered reasonably far in advance. This shows evidence that the inviter really wanted to have the guests, and that it was not some last minute decision on his part dictated by factors other than his honest desire. To do otherwise would be considered an insult. In fact, often such last minute invitations, no matter how enticing, will be turned down basically because the recipient refuses to permit himself to be "secured" at the last minute. But in the Arab and Asian world, many simply forget appointments and arrangements if they are planned too far in advance, and their last minute invitations are sincere, and certainly not to be interpreted as insults.

Furthermore, Westerners expect specific, definite invitations, so they can plan accordingly. Thus, "come see us sometime," or "come anytime," are looked upon merely as general good will verbalisms upon parting, and are not necessarily meant to be acted on. But to persons from Asia and other parts of the world such a general invitation is meant to be acted on, and they are disappointed when Westerners so invited do not show up. Likewise, foreign students in the United States have often been hurt when some fellow student or local host at the beginning of the school year says "see you later," but, then, are never seen later! Some peoples, the Filipinos, for instance, are much more casual than Americans about bringing uninvited friends with them to a party without notifying the hostess. In America that would generally be an improper thing to do unless the gathering were an unusually informal one.

Americans place great stress on carefully planned and prepared speeches, and tend to distrust impromptu speeches as reflecting laziness, lack of substance and coherence, and lack of respect for the auditors. But in South America, Asia, and the Middle East, much more value is placed on the impromptu speech, and the person who can speak on the spur of the moment is much more highly praised than in the United States.

The American divides up the day very precisely and communicates only during certain hours. He withholds communication during other hours, such as late at night or early in the morning, at which times only some emergency would initiate a telephone call, or a visit, to someone. But people of some other cultures do not divide the day so rigidly and are more liable to call at any time without being prompted by an emergency.

Commencement of Communication

Sharply divergent habits exist in varying cultures regarding the commencement of any communicative event. Americans place great stress on punctuality. Any consistently tardy person is taken to be undependable, untrustworthy, and disrespectful *vis-à-vis* the audience, message, or occasion. He is likely to suffer whatever ill consequences the person affected has the power to inflict.

For many situations Americans would consider a tardiness of five minutes to be relatively serious and improper, but other cultures would consider such an attitude to be a rather neurotic slavery to time. Many Americans abroad would avoid much frustration if they realized that someone in another culture would have to be fifteen or even as much as forty-five minutes tardy if he were to be as late in his time framework as five minutes is in ours. In some cultures it is assumed that a busy, important person should come late. Hence, coming on time would only lower his prestige. Americans serving abroad have to clarify whether the beginning time of a scheduled meeting is to be "American" or "local" time. When I was teaching in a college in Burma and applying my customary American obsession with being right on time for classes and meetings, my students gave me the nickname of "the diesel," for the diesel train running between Mandalay and Rangoon was a national symbol of punctuality.

Use of the Communication Period

Different cultures have developed varying attitudes and practices relative to the period of communication itself, which often create obstacles to intercultural understanding. Americans, Britons, and other Europeans place high value on the conservation of time, on the principle of economy. To them, to be brief, succinct, and to the point is an important virtue in any communication situation. Not to do so is interpreted as lack of preparation, lack of command of the message, longwindedness, inefficiency, and even charlatanism, for the person is suspected of covering up his weaknesses by time-consuming wordage. But Arabs, Latin Americans, and other cultures do not worship economy of expression quite so much, and they interpret Western brevity to be "coldness" and haughtiness.

American businessmen in international conferences are said to like to come quickly to, and settle, the main issues and leave the details for subordinates to work out. To deal with minute details is to waste valuable conference time. But to the Arab and Greek, among others, this raises suspicions that something is being hidden, omitted, glossed over and that some form of cheating is taking place. Furthermore, the American expects to separate business discussion from social discussion, whereas the Latin American, for instance, enjoys to combine the two, thus lengthening and perhaps confusing any conference or interview considerably. The American prefers to take care of one thing at a time in a discussion. On the other hand, the Latin American prefers to discuss a number of varying issues, germane and not so germane, business or social, all in one period of communication. To do otherwise reduces the warm human element that he feels should be present when individuals communicate. The American interprets this as evidence of immaturity, ineffectiveness, and lack of discipline.

The American feels that the length of a duty visit to a home or office should be approximately forty-five minutes, and a social visit in one's home should be about three or four hours. To stay longer suggests a lack of respect for the host's time. But Arabs and others would consider these time periods very short indeed, and to them such brief visitations would suggest "coldness," and a lack of genuine desire to visit and discuss.

The Asian and Arab like to bargain at the open market. This is part of the fun of buying and selling, and it is considered as using time in an enjoyable and profitable way. To the American, however, with his background of set prices clearly marked on visible tags, to spend time haggling over prices is an irritating and unnecessary waste of time and suggests that the seller is attempting to cheat by not being open and constant about the price.

It has been said that businessmen and government officials from India like to discuss abstract ideas and plans, but do not push these to final form in conferences. To them, to think and to talk are more prestigious than to *do* something.

Termination of Communication

Finally, different cultures vary considerably in their attitude toward the termination of communication events. The American is concerned with deadlines, with a definite set time at which the task is supposed to be completed. He likes to see the discussion move along step by step and the designated goal reached at the appointed time. The Taoist and Buddhist is content to wait passively for truth to emerge in a discussion, whereas the American is anxious to analyze the issue and discover the truth quickly and actively. Our attitude communicates to them impatience and aggressiveness. Their attitude suggests to us inefficiency, laziness, fatalism.

The American is task oriented, whereas representatives of other cultures would consider that the completion of the task is secondary to the happiness and well being of the participants involved. They would consider the American attitude as being too concerned for the material things in life rather than the human or spiritual. Peace Corps volunteers are discovering American impatience to be a major problem. One official with experience in Latin America has concluded that "one must be willing to spend considerable time in rapport-building activities such as fiestas, or in just passing the time of day with one's neighbors."[14]

The American is driven by a competitive spirit, a desire to get the jump on someone, to be "first," to out-do someone. He is anxious to see fruits of his labor, and takes pride in accomplishments, in workmanship, in *doing* something. Other cultures not imbued with this competitive spirit are more content with subsistence and with a communitarian organization to society and its activites. For example, when an American brings a radio to be repaired, he expects to find it ready, the task completed at the agreed upon time. But in the Arab world such deadlines are not so sacred, and the workman proceeds at a pace suited to his well-being. It may be necessary to pay frequent trips to the shop, "needling" the repairman in order to make sure he has it finished on time. This kind of constant reminder would to the American seem to be unkind, inappropriate, and in itself a waste of valuable time.

Some Arabs and Latin Americans, among others, would have a strong strain of procrastination, to do it tomorrow rather than today. They can wait, the American cannot.

In an American speech class, the length of the speech is clearly indicated. That is, it is to be, for instance, a "five minute speech," defined by a time limitation. Speeches are carefully timed and if the student runs overtime he is looked upon as being inefficient and unscholarly and is penalized accordingly. In the United States, public speakers quickly lose their appeal if they continue longer than they are expected to. On the other hand, in Latin America and in Asia, a public speaker gains momentum and appeal as he rambles on hour after hour.

It has been said that time is "an inexplicable dimension in which we all participate but of which no one is master."[15] But many have earnestly tried to master it, and many Westerners think they have corralled and harnessed it rather well. In reply, other cultures seem to be saying, "Thou fool, don't you know that when you have done these things you have merely demonstrated that you are the slave, not the master, of time?" Perhaps some middle road is desirable. Surely a deeper understanding of the varying cultural approaches to the dimension of time is urgently needed if man on this shrunken globe is to communicate with people of other cultures clearly and harmoniously.

NONVERBAL CUES STEMMING FROM ATTITUDES TOWARD SPACE

Man's use of space, the study of which is called "proxemics," is another silent language about which we all need to know more if we are to achieve clear communication and harmonious relations with people of varying cultural backgrounds. We need to be sensitive to the nonverbal cues stemming from (1) varying definitions of comfortable distances between conversants, (2) the use of space in public places, (3) the use of space in offices, and (4) the use of space in homes.

Distances in Interpersonal Communication

The various cultures have accustomed their peoples to feel comfortable at different distances in personal conversation situations. It is estimated, for instance, that American males prefer to be approximately 18 to 20 inches away from their conversationalists if they are not known too well, and about 22 to 24 inches if they are conversing with a woman. These distances become less if the people are close friends. The Arabs, South Americans, French and others, on the other hand, do not feel comfortable in conversation unless they are much closer to each other. To the American this communicates pushiness and aggressiveness. It suggests a personal relationship reserved only for members of the opposite sex between whom there is mutual affection. On the other hand, the American's greater distance communicates to members of these other cultures a sort of reserve, coldness, haughtiness and a sense of superiority. Many an American has experienced himself moving backward as his foreign acquaintance moves in on him in a conversation, until (the American) has back-pedaled clear across the room and literally has his back against a wall. Both participants are simply attempting to create the spatial dimension with which their respective cultures have conditioned them to be comfortable. The more they each understand this, the fewer will be the unnecessary misunderstandings.

Closely related to this factor of comfortable distances in conversation is the different cultural attitudes toward the olfactory dimension. Americans are admonished from childhood "not to breathe on people." This social sin can of course be averted or reduced if one stands further away from the individual with whom one is talking. On the other hand, the Arabs, for instance, by habit do breathe

on people when they talk. As an observer has put it, to the Arab "to smell one's friend is not only nice but desirable, for to deny him your breath is to act ashamed."[16] Americans are taught to be ashamed if they do breathe on someone, and a huge commercial industry has made Americans highly prejudiced against not only mouth and body odors but all kinds of unique smells. Americans have deodorized everything, so that, as Hall says, we have become "culturally underdeveloped" in the "use of olfactory apparatus."[17] Americans, then, should not think of others as necessarily unsanitary, uncouth, or primitive in this regard; and others should not interpret the American's greater distance and deodorized breath as coldness or haughtiness.

Use of Space in Public Places

How varying cultures differently approach the use of space in public places needs to be understood if communication is not to be unnecessarily strained. The English and Germans, for instance, are conditioned to standing in line and "waiting their turn," be it at a theatre ticket office or in a bus queue. In this way they feel they are expressing maturity and a concern for individual rights and equality of treatment. But the Arabs, Mediterranean peoples, and South Americans look on a public place as where everyone has a right to push and shove in order to assert his individual rights. This behavior is looked on by other cultures as rude, aggressive, thoughtless, and immature, much as undisciplined children push and shove before they have learned better. Americans and Englishmen feel much more ill at ease in crowded buses or trains than do some of the people from Asian or Mediterranean lands, where public conveyances are often not only bulging with humanity on the inside but also covered with people hanging on to the outside like barnacles.

Americans and others who drive their cars on the right-hand side of the road also veer to the right side of the sidewalk or anywhere else in a public place, and the English, who drive cars on the left side of the road, walk to the left. Thus, American tourists in England, for instance, and the local people tend to bump into each other and each thinks the other is being thoughtless. Now that the Swedes have changed from driving on the left side to the right, it will be interesting to see if they gradually shift habits in walking as well.

Use of Space in Offices

Varying use of space in places of work may also lead to misunderstandings between cultures. Some Americans like to keep the desk between them and the other person. But to the Latin American the desk is a sort of barrier that keeps the distance too great for him to feel comfortable, and he may crowd in to the point where it seems too "pushy" to the North American. In the United States people are likely to keep the office door open. If it is shut, it means that a special conference, private conversation, or other special occasion is altering the usual habit. On the other hand, Germans, for instance, are more likely to keep the office door closed all the time, and to open the door or enter without express permission is the height of rudeness and intrusion. The English and others do not have the carefully walled off private offices that Americans do and are more accustomed to working in a larger, unenclosed, more public atmosphere. Even Members of Parliament have to dictate letters and hold important conferences in the public lobbies of Parliament. Thus, English learn to erect walls, as it were, by talking in subdued tones so that others will not hear or be disturbed. An American, accustomed to the luxury of louder volume than his enclosed, private office permits, may interpret this kind of behavior as somewhat suspicious and secretive.

The English, Arabs, and others in like situations of not being accustomed to private, enclosed offices, also have become accustomed to building invisible walls of silence, thus retaining a sense of privacy even though surrounded by people. This habit the American may misinterpret as the "silent treatment" given to someone when ill feelings have been aroused. Foreign students have had to assure their American friends that they are not angry at anything or anybody merely because they are silent.

Use of Space in Homes

The use of space in the home setting can also create nonverbal messages that may breed misunderstanding between people of different cultures. Most Asians and some Europeans feel that their small and crowded houses are not worthy of entertaining their American acquaintances (all of whom are, mistakenly, assumed to be rich!), and hence would entertain them at a café or restaurant. The American may erroneously interpret this as not being willing to share the intimacy of the home, of being too formal, distant, and unfriendly. The American usually would entertain in his own home as a sign of bringing the guest into the intimacy of the family setting—a supreme symbol of friendliness. Furthermore, as a symbol of friendship and openness the American is accustomed to sharing his home rather freely with his neighbors (at least their children!). But to the English and Germans, for instance, physical proximity of houses does not entitle this freedom of access. Being much more class oriented, they would not permit the factor of spatial proximity to dictate who should be free to gain entrance to their home. To Americans abroad, this lack of communication with people in neighboring houses seems to be unfriendly, snobbish, and undemocratic. To the English and others, the American habit seems too nosey and too much an infringement of individual privacy. In Germany, for a person to open the door of the house or enter into the yard without permission would be considered an extremely rude intrusion.

NONVERBAL CUES STEMMING FROM GENERAL HABITS IN COMMUNICATING

The general manner of communicating orally in intercultural communication situations can lead to unfortunate misunderstandings. If unclear communication and needless friction are to be avoided or reduced, members of different cultures need to understand the varying habits and manners of others, and what these practices mean and do not mean.

Degree of Expressiveness

Different cultures have considerably differing habits in the amount of expressiveness. This is rooted in the varying habits of child rearing and in varying attitudes toward people of different ages, classes, and stations in life. In the family setting, for instance, most Americans encourage their children to enter freely into dinner table conversation and other family discussions and to participate early in decision making. By contrast, in Asia and elsewhere, children are taught to be silent in the presence of elders and, for instance, are usually separated from them when eating. The children certainly are never to disagree verbally with the parent, or with older brothers and sisters, for that matter. In parts of India, even an adult would not enter into the decision-making discussions if his aged parents were still in the family circle. It is not surprising therefore, that many foreigners look upon American young people as brash, immodest, and rude, possessing no proper respect for parents or older siblings. On the other hand, Americans may look upon young people of other cultures as being too reticent, too quiet, too unresponsive, too lacking in self-confidence, which may be interpreted erroneously as inferiority.

In many countries a student would very seldom ask a question in class, for to do so would not only suggest that he is uninformed but that he is implying that the teacher has been unclear, which would be highly disrespectful. In America most teachers encourage the student to ask all kinds of questions. It is a mark of a good teacher to draw out questions and a mark of a good student to ask numerous, meaningful questions. American teachers abroad thus have to realize the lack of questions or lack of recitation from their students does not mean that the teacher is being ineffective or

that the students are ignorant and lethargic, for they are merely being respectful.

Degree of Intimacy of Address

In parts of Asia or in other lands where strict social hierarchies are firmly entrenched, a person younger than, or in a lower class than, the person with whom he is communicating should manifest an appropriate humbleness and choose language appropriately. Specific labels should precede the person's name to indicate the appropriate status of the person spoken to and relationship between the conversants. Titles and educational degrees should be carefully acknowledged. In order to ascertain the proper relationship, an Asian, for instance, is likely to ask a foreigner a number of questions, such as how old he is, what is his occupation, how much does he earn, or is he married. To an American these questions seem much too personal and inappropriate. But they are meant to be a respectful endeavor to determine how to address the visitor.

Americans are quick to get on a first name basis with everyone. But to the British and others this is considered too personal, too pushy, too rude. They are offended and irritated with what they feel is aggressive egalitarianism. The British would use the first name only when speaking to a servant, gardener, or others lower on the social ladder, but not for a person of equal rank, until they became very intimate friends. Americans misinterpret the reticence to adopt first name labels as unfriendliness.

Degree of Emotion and Animation

Different cultures have decidedly varying attitudes and practices in relation to how much emotion and animation an individual should display in a communication situation. As noted earlier in the chapter when discussing gesturing, the northern European and North American attempt to control and suppress their emotions greatly. This is based on the cultural premise that this demonstrates maturity, disciplined behavior, and emotional stability. On the other hand, this behavior is viewed by others, such as the Russians, Mediterranean peoples, and Latin Americans, as lacking in frankness, friendliness, and sincerity, as hiding something and as suggesting an air of superiority. Many foreigners misinterpret American lack of excitement in conversation or public speaking as a lack of interest or concern.

However, quite the reverse is true in a gift exchanging situation. Some Asians and South Americans do not normally show gratitude for a gift and do not open it in the presence of the giver, whereas Americans tend to express gratitude profusely and usually open the gift immediately in the presence of the giver. This communicates that the recipient is so grateful that he can hardly wait to open it. The American interprets the other practice as showing lack of enthusiastic appreciation.

Women speak more excitedly than men in America. But in many cultures it is just the reverse. For instance, in Arab societies, the men manifest more animation than the women.

Degree of Frankness

Cultures vary considerably in the degree of frankness expected. The English, for instance, with their long heritage of open, direct, and frank confrontation in parliamentary debating and in the heckling of public speakers, are more likely to be more sharp and blunt than most people, including the Americans. Britons hit hard and expect to be hit hard in return. This was freshly illustrated for me recently when a British colleague in a faculty committee meeting stirred considerable animosity by his frank, sharp, and unambiguous statement of his views on the topic under consideration. When told later of the reactions of some of the committee members, he was shocked, for he thought he had expressed himself rather mildly and circumspectly.

Most Asians would be far more reticent than Americans to engage in a sharp exchange, and tend to couch their remarks very carefully so as not to hurt the feelings of, or embarrass, the other person. This results in rather heavy use of euphemisms and ambiguity. It has also been asserted that some Asians are less able than some Westerners to separate the criticism of issues and the criticism of the person holding those views. Thus, criticizing their views means you are really criticizing the person. Peace Corps volunteers are learning that the common American frankness and open criticism creates in the recipient a strong embarrassment, loss of face, and possible hostility.

Degree of Intensity and Persistency

Different cultures have developed varying habits in relation to the use of intensity and persistency in certain communicative situations. For instance, a normal unstressed English "no" may be interpreted by an Arab to mean "yes," for a *real* negation, to the Arab's way of thinking, would be emphasized much more. Likewise, in some cultures a mild, hesitant "yes" is interpreted as a polite refusal. A Filipino expects to be asked more than once when invited to a dinner, until he "reluctantly" accepts. A single invitation would be considered an affront, being interpreted to mean that he really is not sincerely invited. Likewise, he will usually wait until the hostess has asked him two or three times before he will approach the prepared feast. An Arab likewise considers it polite to refuse some proferred food several times and then finally to accept it. But when an American says "no thank you" to the hostess's offer of food, he usually means it, and that ends it.

Degree of Volume

Different habits between cultures regarding the degree of volume in communication situations need to be understood. Some, like the Arabs, like to be bathed in sound, as it were. Thus, conversation tends to be loud, and the volume on the radio and phonograph is turned up. Some foreign students in American college dormitories cause some unintentional ill feeling by keeping their radios very loud. In many countries where radios are not so plentiful, and where warmer climate permits open houses, it is an act of thoughtful and kind neighborliness to keep the volume high in order to permit neighbors to listen. To Americans, such loud volume is interpreted as thoughtless imposition on another's privacy. In interpersonal conversation, on the other hand, many in the Orient and elsewhere speak more softly than Americans, and would interpret the loud volume of an excited American as connoting aggressiveness, loss of self-control, or even anger.

SUMMARY

In today's jet dominated world, it is becoming increasingly urgent that the peoples of the earth learn not only each other's languages but also each other's nonverbal habits in communication. Many nonverbal cues are transmitted by body motion and gesture. In different cultures many similar gestures transmit different messages. In other instances the same message is sent by different motions and gestures, thus creating unfortunate misunderstanding. Different nonverbal cues stem from different attitudes toward time, which results in varying practices prior to, at the beginning of, during, and at the end of communication situations. Nonverbal cues also emanate from attitudes toward space. As a result, different habits develop regarding distances involved in interpersonal communication, and in the use of space in public places, in the office, and in the home. Furthermore, nonverbal cues stem from general habits in communicating, which may differ considerably between cultures. Varying degrees of expressiveness, intimacy of address, animation, frankness, persistence, and volume in different cultures need to be recognized.

It is clearly apparent that man on this shrunken globe must become aware of these culturally determined differences, and accordingly act with greater enlightenment. But this, of course, will not solve all problems in human relations. That all cultures have cues for expressing animosity as well as affection only demonstrates that animosity exists to be expressed. But through greater clarity of communication we can surely hope for, and confidently expect, a reduction of unintentional offensiveness and an increase in mutual understanding.

NOTES

1. Edward T. Hall, *The Hidden Dimension* (Garden City, N.Y.: Doubleday & Company, Inc., 1966), p. 6.

2. Buckminster Fuller, "Man With a Chronofile," *Saturday Review* (April 1, 1967), p. 15.

3. Edward T. Hall, *The Silent Language* (Greenwich, Conn.: Fawcett Publications, Inc., 1959), p. 10.

4. Robert L. Saitz and Edward J. Cervenka, *Colombian and North American Gestures* (Bogota: Centro Colombo Americano, 1962), p. 10.

5. Douglas Haring, "Cultural Contexts of Thought and Communication," *The Quarterly Journal of Speech*, XXXVII (April 1951), p. 172.

6. Weston LaBarre, "The Cultural Basis of Emotions and Gestures," *Journal of Personality*, XVI (September 1947), p. 55.

7. Mary Key, "Gestures and Responses: A Preliminary Study Among Some Indian Tribes of Bolivia," *Studies in Linguistics*, XVI (1962), p. 98.

8. Gordon W. Hewes, "The Anthropology of Posture," *Scientific American*, CXCVI (February, 1957), p. 123.

9. Hall, *The Hidden Dimension*, p. 151.

10. Jurgen Ruesch and Weldon Kees, *Nonverbal Communication: Notes on the Visual Perception of Human Relations* (Berkeley: University of California Press, 1964), p. 22.

11. Lee Hamalian, "Communication by Gesture in the Middle East," *ETC.*, XXII (March 1965), p. 43.

12. Ruesch and Kees, *Nonverbal Communciation*, p. 23.

13. Alec Laurie, "Visual Communication," in *Communication and Language: Networks of Thought and Action*, eds. Sir Gerald Barry, et al. (London: Macdonald, 1965), p. 84.

ghty, "Pitfalls and Progress in the
in *Cultural Frontiers of the Peace*
B. Textor (Cambridge, Mass.: Mas-
ite of Technology Press, 1966),

15. Hal Borland, *Countryman: A Summary of Belief* (Philadelphia: J. B. Lippincott Company, 1965), p. 80.

16. Hall, *The Hidden Dimension,* p. 49.

17. Hall, *The Hidden Dimension,* p. 43.

Paralinguistics, Kinesics, and Cultural Anthropology

WESTON LABARRE

Though man is everywhere a notably "handed" animal, pointing with the forefinger and other fingers curled palmward is a limitedly cultural phenomenon, probably of Old World origin and dispersion (American Indians, on both New World continents, point with the lips, as also do Shans and other Mongoloid peoples; in other groups, pointing is done with eye-movements, or nose-chin-and-head movements, or head-movements alone). As for negation and affirmation kinemes, behaviorists and other psychologists have sought to explain our "yes" nod as the movement of the infant seeking the breast, the "no" as avoiding it. But here the psychologists have reckoned without their cultural hosts: they have an elegantly universalistic explanation for a phenomenon which is not humanly universal, a common pitfall for any social scientist who ignores culture. Cultural anthropologists can supply us with many alternative kinemes for "yes" and "no" in various cultures.[1] For example, shaking the hand in front of the face with the forefinger extended is the Ovimbundu sign of negation, while Malayan Negritos express negation by casting down the eyes. The Semang thrust the head forward in affirmation. In fact, there are even regional "dialects" of affirmation in the Indic area: crown of the head following an arc from shoulder to shoulder, four times, in Bengal; throwing the head back in an oblique arc to the left shoulder, one time, some-

From *Approaches to Semiotics,* ed. Thomas Sebeok (The Hague: Mouton Publishers, 1964), pp. 198–202, 216–220. Reprinted by permission of the publisher and the author. Weston LaBarre holds the chair of James B. Duke Professor of Anthropology at Duke University.

what "curtly" and "disrespectfully" to our taste, in the Punjab and Sind; curving the chin in a downward leftward arc in Ceylon, often accompanied by an indescribably beautiful parakineme of back-of-right-hand cupped in upward-facing-palm of the left hand, plus-or-minus the additional kineme of a crossed-ankle curtsey.

Greeting kinemes vary greatly from culture to culture. In fact, many of those motor habits in one culture are open to grave misunderstanding in another. For example, the Copper Eskimo welcome strangers with a buffet on the head or shoulders with the fist, while the northwest Amazonians slap one another on the back in greeting. Polynesian men greet one another by embracing and rubbing each other's back; Spanish-American males greet one another by a stereotyped embrace, head over the right shoulder of the partner, three pats on the back, head over reciprocal left shoulder, three more pats. In the Torres Straits, the old form of greeting was to bend the right hand into a hook, then mutually scratching palms by drawing away the right hand, repeating this several times. An Ainu, meeting his sister, grasped her hands in his for a few seconds, suddenly released his hold, grasped her by both ears and gave the peculiar Ainu greeting cry: then they stroked one another down the face and shoulders. Kayan males in Borneo grasp each other by the forearm, while a host throws his arm over the shoulder of a guest and strokes him endearingly with the palm of his hand. When two Kurd males meet, they grasp one another's right hand, raise them both, and alternately kiss the other's hand. Andamanese greet one another by one sitting down in the lap of the other, arms around each other's necks and weeping for a while; two brothers, father and son, mother and daughter, and husband and wife, or even two friends may do this; the husband sits in the lap of the wife. Friends' "goodbye" consists in raising the hand of the other to the mouth and gently blowing on it, reciprocally. At Matavai a full-dress greeting after long absence requires scratching the head and temples with a shark's tooth, violently and with much bleeding. This brief list could easily be enlarged by other anthropologists.

Kissing is Germanic, Graeco-Roman, and Semitic (but apparently not Celtic, originally). Greek and Roman parents kissed their children, lovers and married persons kissed one another, and friends of the same or different sexes; medieval knights kissed, as modern pugilists shake hands, before the fray. Kissing relics and the hand of a superior is at least as early as the Middle Ages in Europe; kissing the feet is an old habit among various Semites; and the Alpine peasant kisses his own hand before receiving a present, and pages in the French court kissed any article given them to carry.[2] Two men or two women exchange the "holy kiss" in greeting before meetings, in the earlier Appalachian-highland version of the snake-handling cult of the Southeast; the heterosexual kiss is a secular one, not used in public. Another admired gambit is to move the rattlesnake or copperhead back and forward across the face, and closer and closer, until the communicant's lips brush the flickering-tongued mouth of the snake; one Durham minister once offered to kiss the police officers who had raided a snake-handling meeting, to show "no hard feelings," but this offer was not accepted. Kissing, as is well known, is in the Orient an act of private lovemaking, and arouses only disgust when performed publicly: thus, in Japan, it is necessary to censor out the major portion of love scenes in American-made movies. Tapuya men in South America kiss as a sign of peace, but men do not kiss women (nor women, women) because the latter wear labrets or lip plugs. Nose-rubbing is both Eskimo and Polynesian. Djuka Negroes of Surinam show pleasure at a particularly interesting or amusing dance step by embracing the dancer and touching cheek to cheek, now on one side, now on the other—the identical attenuation of the "social kiss" (on one cheek only, however) between American women who do not wish to spoil each other's make-up. And one of the hazards of accepting a decoration in France is a bilateral buss in the name of the republic. Ona kissing in Tierra del Fuego is performed only between certain close relatives and young married couples or lovers; and not lip-to-lip, but by pressing the lips to the hand, cheek, or arm of the other, accompanied by a slight inward sucking.[3]

Sticking out the tongue is a kineme with indisputably diverse significance in varied cultures. In Sung Dynasty China, tongue protrusion was a gesture of mock terror, performed in ridicule; the tongue stretched far out was a gesture of surprise (at the time of the novel, *Dream of the Red Chamber*); in modern south China at least (Kunming), a quick, minimal tongue-protrusion and -retraction signifies embarrassment and self-castigation, as at some social *faux pas* or misunderstanding; it can vary in context from the humorous to the apologetic. Among the Ovimbundu of Africa, bending the head forward and sticking out the tongue means "you're a fool." In India, the long-protruding tongue in the statues of the goddess Kali signifies a monumental, welkinshattering rage, a demon-destroying anger as effective as a glance from the Saivite third eye in the forehead. In New Caledonia, in wooden statues of ancestors carved on houses, the protruded tongue means wisdom, vigor, and plenitude, since the tongue "carries to the outside the traditional virtues, the manly decision, and all the manifestations of life which the word bears in itself." Perhaps this is the meaning, in part, of similar New Zealand carvings, although here there may be other overtones of ancestral fertility, et cetera (the meaning of the connecting of the elongated nose and mouth to umbicilus and genitals in Melanesian carvings is unknown to me). In the Carolines, however, the gods are disgusted at the lolling tongues of suicides by hanging, and for this reason refuse entry to the souls of such among the deities. In at least one of the eighteen "Devil Dance" masks in Ceylon, specialized for the exorcistic cure in specific illnesses, the black mask has a protruding red tongue, probably synergistic (to judge from other cognates in the India area) with the extremely ex-ophthalmic eyes which are characteristic of all eighteen of these masks: to frighten out the demons regarded as causing the specific diseases. In Mayan statues of the gods, the protruded tongue signifies wisdom. In Tibet, the protruded tongue is a sign of polite deference, with or without the thrust-up thumb of the right hand, scratching the ears, or removing the hat.[4] Marquesans stick out the tongue as a sign of a simple negation. In America, of course, sticking out the tongue (sometimes accompanied by "making a face") is a juvenile quasi-obscene gesture of provocative mockery, defiance, or contempt; perhaps the psychiatrists can explain why this is chiefly a little girl's gesture, though sometimes used playfully by adult women, or by effeminate men. One might also conjecture a European "etymology" behind this gesture in American child-culture, based on this chronological sequence: apotropaic (a stone head with thrust-out tongue and "making a face" on a Roman fort in Hungary, although this etymon may also include a note of defiance as well), protective-defiant (gargoyles with thrust-out tongue on Gothic cathedrals), mock-affirmative (the subordinates of the demon Malcoda in Dante acknowledge a command by sticking out their tongues and making a rump-trumpet)—all with an obscure overtone of the obscenely phallic—whence the modern child-gesture of derision (and there comes to mind a similar "shame on you gesture," using the left-hand pointing gesture and using the similarly held right hand in an outward whittling movement, repeated). But such precarious kinemic "etymologies" must await more adequate ethnographic documentations, and these we largely lack. The Eskimo curl up the tongue into a trough or cylinder and protrude the tongue slightly, but this is not a kineme; it is rather a motor habit, used to direct a current of air when blowing a tinder into flame.

Gestures of contempt are a rich area for study also. A favorite Menomini Indian gesture of contempt is to raise the clenched fist palm downward up to the level of the mouth, then bringing it downward quickly and throwing forward the thumb and the first two fingers. Malayan Negritos express contempt or disgust by a sudden expiration of breath, like our "snort of contempt." Neapolitans click the right thumbnail off the right canine in a downward arc. The *mano cornudo* or "making horns" (first and little fingers of the right hand extended forward, thumb and other fingers folded) is primarily used to defy the "evil eye." The *mano fica* (clenched right fist with thumb protruding between the first and second fingers) is an obscene kineme symbolizing the male genitals; in some contexts its meaning is the same as the more massive slapping of the left biceps with the right hand, the left forearm upraised and ending in a fist[5]; a less massive, though no less impolite, equivalent is making a fist with all save the second ("social finger") and thrusting it upward. Mediterranean peoples are traditionally rich in such gestures; I believe, though with admittedly unsatisfactory evidence, that the "cocked snout" came from Renaissance Italy as a gesture of contempt about the same time as the fork arrived in England in the reign of Elizabeth.

Beckoning gestures have been little collected. In a restaurant, an American raises a well-bred right forefinger to summon a waiter. To express "come here!" a Latin American makes a downward arc with the right hand, almost identical with an American jocular gesture of "go away with you!" The Shans of Burma beckon by holding the palm down, moving the fingers as if playing an arpeggio chord. The Boro and Witoto beckon by moving the hand downward, not upward, as with us, in our face-level, wrist-flexing, cupped-hand "come here!" signal.

Gestures of politesse are equally sparse in the ethnographic sources. The Hindu palms-together, thumbs about the level of the chin, is a greeting, a "thank you," and a gesture of obeisance, depending on the context. A Shan, on being done a kindness, may bend over and sniff the sleeve of the benefactor's coat; the meaning is "how sweet you smell," not entirely unlike the Indian "shukriya" (sweetness) meaning "How sweet you are!" Curtseys and bows (almost infinitely graded in depth of bend in the Orient, to express a wide gamut of deference or mock-deference, depending on the social context) are both European and Asiatic. Indic and Oceanic peoples sit down to honor a social superior; Europeans stand up. In both Africa and Melanesia, hand-clapping is a gesture of respect to chiefs and kings. Covering and uncovering the head in deference to gods, kings, and social superiors, is complex, and sometimes contradictory in nature, in Europe and Asia. Taking off or putting on articles of clothing is also full of subtleties of politesse: in classic south India a woman uncovers the upper part of her body in deference, but in America a man puts on his coat to show respect to a lady. The psychology of clothes[6] and the motor habits in handling one's clothing can benefit from much more study: a Plains Indian warrior, for example, could express a wide variety of emotional states, simply through the manner in which he wore his outer robe or cloak. Quite as many gentlemen object to ladies hiking down their skirts or girdles, as ladies object to gentlemen hiking up their pants; and I once witnessed the interview with a young psychiatrist of a female hysteric in which a lively and wholly unconscious colloquy was carried on: she with various tugs at her bodice, skirt-hem, and other parts of her dress and underclothing, he with corresponding "business" with his tie, trousers, etc.[7] . . .

The Chinese have a complex gestural language of assignation, and most of the courtesans are very expert in their interpretation. A forefinger rubbed below the nose means that a man finds a woman attractive and would like to make a more intimate acquaintance; a forefinger tapping the tip of the ear means "No!" while the right hand slapping the back of the left hand means the same. Closed fists, but with the forefingers and second fingers of both extended and rubbed together as if sharpening knives, or putting the two hands together and shaking them like castanettes, have meanings easily imagined. The most infamous of these signs would only be used by the most vulgar of coolies: shoving the right forefinger in and out of the closed palm of the left hand. By means of signs the price and hours of meeting are also communicated; or else the fan is used to indicate the appropriate information. I have no doubt that similar signs are used on the Spanish Steps of Rome, but I do not know these; the "language of the fan" was known to all coquettes in eighteenth-century court circles in France. In Calcutta I was taught a gesture which effectively got rid of beggars that besiege Americans as insistently as flies, but unfortunately I never learned what it means.

In advertising, the hand symbol for a well known beer (to indicate "Purity, Body, Flavor" by touching forefinger and thumb, the last three fingers extended) is a gesture equally well known to kinesiologists as an ancient and obscene European gesture for coitus. Kinsey has also made a minor contribution to kinesiology in the following passage:

The toes of most individuals become curled or, contrariwise, spread when there is erotic arousal. Many persons divide their toes, turning their large toes up or down while the remaining toes curl in the opposite direction. Such activity is rarely recognized by the individual who is sexually aroused and actually doing these things, but the near universality of such action is attested by the graphic record of coitus in the erotic art of the world. For instance, in Japanese erotic art curled toes have, for at least eight centuries, been one of the stylized symbols of erotic responses.[8]

The erotization of body parts (foot, nape of neck, ear, etc.), on the other hand, appears to vary ethnographically quite widely.[9]

To my mind, the artist William Steig has an uncanny ability to portray psychiatric syndromes (especially in his classic, *The Lonely Ones*) largely through the postural tonuses of his figures.[10] From a study of daily column-wide wordless cartoons entitled "Tall Tales" that have appeared during the last two years, I am prepared to give, with exhaustive proofs, and in the appropriate context, a fairly complete psychiatric profile of the artist, Jaffe; I would venture the same, on the same grounds, for Gladys Parker of the series "Mopsy," and for Charles M. Schulz of "Peanuts." One of my students, expert in the Goodenough "Draw-a-Man" projective technique, applied this to the study of "Little Orphan Annie" with extraordinary results; and another has done a brilliant study on the psychological complexes of Pablo Picasso, through a study of his paintings.

The gesture language of the Japanese "tea ceremony" has been adequately described by ethnographers, but never sufficiently analyzed by kinesiologists.

A study of the approved stances and motor modalities in various sports might well be made from the point of view of kinesiology. Particularly absorbing to me has been the observation of the motor "business" and mannerisms of baseball, as observed in the Little League playing of my second son. Various athletes, I maintain, can be matched with their sport, by merely noting the way they sit in classrooms or walk across the campus; and like many other local fans I particularly admire the walking style of the Duke runner, David Sime, especially after he gave up football.

The Abbé Dubois made an exhaustive study of the motor acts of an orthodox Brahman, in connection with attendance to excretory acts.[11] Sex-dichotomized motor habits of this sort for men and women are well known to everyone in our society; but these are by no means the same for the appropriate sex in all societies.

Spitting in many parts of the world is a sign of utmost contempt; and yet among the Masai of East Africa it is a sign of affection and benediction, while the spitting of an American Indian medicine man is one of the kindly offices of the healer. The enormous variety and flexibility of male punctuational and editorial-comment spitting is especially rich, I believe, in Southern rural regions. Urination upon another person (as in a famous case at the Sands Point, Long Island, country club, involving the late Huey P. Long) is a grave insult among Occidentals,[12] but it is a part of the transfer of power from one medicine man to another in Africa, or to the patient in curing rituals and initiations.

Hissing in Japan (by sudden breath-intake) is a *politesse* to social superiors, implying the withdrawal of the subject's inferior breath in the presence of the superior person thus complimented. The Basuto applaud by hissing; but in England hissing is rude and public disapprobation of an actor or a political speaker.

The extraordinary complexity of motor and paralinguistic acts involved with drinking liquids in Africa is the subject of an article by A. E. Crawley.[13] The elaborate modesties of eating are also known to ethnologists with respect to India, Polynesia, and Africa.

The kinesic use of interpersonal physical distance will be familiar to this audience from the work of Edward T. Hall's indispensable text for all kinesiologists and paralinguists.[14]

APPLIED KINESIOLOGY

It is easy to ridicule[15] kinesiology as an abstruse, pedantic, and unimportant study by pure scientists. But I believe kinesiology is, on the contrary, one of the most important avenues for better understanding internationally. Consider, as one small example, how Chinese hate to be touched, slapped on the back, or even to shake hands; how easily an American could avoid offense by merely omitting these intended gestures of friendliness![16] Misunderstanding of nonverbal communication of an unconscious kind is one of the most vexing, and unnecessary, sources of international friction. (Consider, for example, the hands-over-the-head self-handshake of Khrushchev, which Americans interpreted as an arrogant gesture of triumph, as of a victorious prize-fighter, whereas Khrushchev seems to have intended it as a friendly gesture of international brotherhood.)

Gregory Bateson taught me in Ceylon the great value of attending Indian-made movies as an inexpensive kind of easily available fieldwork; and I have since, gratefully, assiduously attended foreign movies of all kinds. I should like to conclude, as a penultimate example, with some conjectures based on the Russian movie, "The Cranes Are Flying," which I believe explain somewhat the famous United Nations episode of Khrushchev's banging his shoe on a desk in the presence of that august body. I do not understand Russian, so that my comments are based entirely upon observation of the motor acts of the characters in two scenes of this movie. First scene: a soldier in a military hospital receives news that his sweetheart has married another man. Much uncontained total emotion, kinetically; raging, tearing at bandages with his teeth, so that there is potential danger to his war wounds; hospital manager is summoned in person to quell the one-man riot, and bring the social situation back to normal. No stiff-upper-lip Anglo-

Saxonism here! The assumption seems to be that the mere feeling of an emotion by a Russian is sufficient legitimation for the expression of it.[17] Anyone, even the highest authority in the context, it is assumed, can legitimately be called upon to help contain it, since the experiencer of the emotion cannot, need not, or is not expected to. (In this connection one recalls the finding of Gorer that the Russian infant is swaddled because, despite his small and unthreatening size, he is regarded as a center of dangerous and uncontained emotion; whereas Polish swaddling is done because the human being is an infinitely precious and fragile thing, in need of this protection.)

Second scene: a little ragamuffin boy, quite self-contained and stolid as a street-urchin alone in the snow, comes into a warm canteen full of Russian women; some minor contretemps in which the little boy's wish is crossed, then: not merely a simple temper tantrum in the child (panhuman phenomenon) *but* all the women begin running around, dropping everything else, as if it were the most natural and necessary thing in the world to help the exploding individual contain his emotion through attention and pacification. Hypothesis: if this is the expectancy of the Russian child in the enculturation experience and evidenced both in his behavior and in that of the soldier, is it possible that Khrushchev was unconsciously using a coercive modality, plausible and understood and unconsciously taken for granted in Russian culture, that wholly missed its mark, certainly for the Anglo-Saxon expectancies of Americans and British present? My reasoning is tenuous; it needs to be supported by masses of ethnographic fact before even being respectfully listened to. But the point I wish to make is that such kinesic and paralinguistic communication is of paramount importance in international relations. Would Pearl Harbor have occurred if we had been able to read the "Japanese smile" of the diplomats as they left their last fateful meeting with Secretary of the State Cordell Hull?

My last example has to do with a more modest and homely matter, the act of dunking doughnuts. During the last War there appeared in the North

African edition of *Stars and Stripes* a news picture, purporting to portray an American GI teaching an Arab the gentle art of dunking doughnuts. The American is obviously much self-amused, and the whole context of the picture is "See how good Americans make friends with anybody in the world!" by teaching the foreigner a homely aspect of the American's own culture. But, protests the cultural anthropologist, is this what is actually happening here? Is the GI really teaching, or even essentially teaching, the Arab *all there is to know* about doughnut-dunking? For doughnut-dunking also evokes Emily Post, a male vacation from females striving for vertical social mobility, Jiggs and Maggie, the revolt of the American he-man from "Mom" as the modern introject-source for manners in a neomatriarchate—and much else besides. The archly bent little finger (some obscure kineme? wonders the Arab) is an American lampoon of the effete tea-drinking Englishman and reminds us of 1776—and who, after all, won *that* war. It implies the masculine frontier, class muckerism, and effeminately tea-drinking Boston versus the coffee-drinking rest of the country. There may even be an echo of a robust Anglo-Saxon parody of Norman-French manners in Montmorencys and Percivals, and thus recall 1066 and all that. Underlying it all is the classless American society—in which everyone is restlessly struggling to change his social status, by persuading others that he is a "good guy" and a good average nonconformist-conformist. Doughnut-dunking is all this—and more!

Is the Arab, in fact, actually being "taught" all these intricate culture-historical implications of an alien tradition—about which, in all probability, our GI (who only finished high school) is neither conscious nor articulate? On the contrary, the Arab brings to the event his own cultural apperceptions and interpretations. To be sure, Arabs know all about coffee (and sugar too, for that matter) and knew it long before Europeans; in fact, the common European names for these two substances are all derived from the Arabic. The Arab is far more likely to be worried about another matter: is this oddly shaped breadstuff perhaps cooked (O abomination!) in pork-fat, thus is this eating not so much naughty-humorous as filthy blasphemous! But perhaps he may be reassured that the cooking fat does not derive from an unclean animal, and the Arab can be happy that it is cottonseed oil from good old South Ca'lina, or peanut oil, possibly laced with Tay-ex-us beef suet—none of which were prohibited by the Prophet. Where, then, can he search for an explanation of the GI's manifest amusement at himself in his doughnut-dunking? Ah! At last it is clear: the doughnut is an obscene symbol for the female (such as is common in Arab life), with coffee "black as night, hot as hell, and sweet as a woman," as the Arab prefers it. Now, perhaps, in universal male confraternity, the Arab can join with his GI friend in tasting the sweetness of women (O, of course, that powdered sugar is intended to symbolize the face powder of those obscenely bare-faced Christian women!). But these outlandish paynim kaffirs are certainly peculiar buzzards in their symbolisms! However, let us be reassured, for these are the Arab's ratiocinations, not ours. For all that we have been doing, the whole time, is sitting quietly here, with the best of good intentions, purely and simply dunking doughnuts!

NOTES

1. A number of examples are given in LaBarre, *Cultural basis*, pp. 50–51.

2. E. Crawley has a chapter on "The nature and history of the kiss," in his *Studies of savages and sex* (New York, n.d.), pp. 113–136.

3. Cooper, J. M., "The Ona," 143 *Bulletin, Bureau of American Ethnology* 1, pp. 107–125., especially p. 118.

4. The desirability of multiple sources on such a matter is indicated here: R. D. Mallery (ed.), *Masterworks of travel and exploration* (New York, 1948), p. 271 (Tibetans put out their tongue in polite deference to a police official in Lhasa investigating their provenience and purposes); p. 275 (Tibet-

ans scratched their ears and put out their tongues at Europeans when they break out their pictures, microscopes, et cetera, some with mouths open in awe); Hayes, op. cit., p. 223 ("In Tibet, customary greeting to a fellow traveler: thrust up thumb of right hand and thrust out tongue"); H. Bayley, *The lost language of symbolism*, 2 vols. (London, 1912), 2, 128 noted in Hayes, p. 226: "In Tibet a respectful salutation is made by removing hat and lolling out the tongue." See also: A. Sakai, *Japan in a nutshell*, 2 vols. (Yokohama, 1949), 1,131—"Formerly every *Sambaso* [a kind of prologue in a classical play, Kabuki as well an Bunraku] doll or mask had its tongue thrust out in accordance with the greatest obeisance performed in Tibet, from which, according to the late Rev. Ekai Kawaguchi, *Sambaso* was introduced."

5. The Boro and Witoto of Amazonia have a sign to express desire for coitus, but this is a mere jest or ribald suggestion: the right elbow is grasped with the left hand, the elbow being flexed so as to have the right hand extend upwards; it is, in fact, the letter Z of the deaf-and-dumb alphabet. Note that this is somewhat the opposite of the American obscenity, so far as right and left are concerned.

6. The British psychoanalyst, J. C. Flügle has shown an exquisite sensitivity to meanings in his monograph, *The psychology of clothes* (London, 1930). I have not seen E. B. Hurloch, *The psychology of dress*, 1929, or F. A. Parsons, *Psychology of dress* (1921).

7. In this same psychiatric clinic, at another time, I also observed a self-justifying male patient giving a song-and-dance about himself, while slightly to his rear beside him, his psychiatrist (of German origin) gave a complete editorial comment on his patient's story, entirely through facial gestures and motions of his head—fully as skillful a performance as John O'Hara's in the original short story version of "Pal Joey" in which a self-justifying heel condemns himself out of his own mouth.

8. Kinsey, A., et. al., *Sexual behavior in the human female* (Philadelphia-London), p. 620.

9. LaBarre, W., "The erotiz~ various cultures," address Club (1936).

10. LaBarre, W., "The apperceptio sponses to *The lonely ones* of Willia~. *ican Imago* 6 (1949), 3–43.

11. Dubois, Abbé J. A., *Hindu manners,* ~ *and ceremonies,* 3rd ed. (Oxford, 1906).

12. See, in this connection, the paper by Karl Abraham, comprising chapter XIII of his *Selected papers* (London, 1927), pp. 280–298; and also the references on the urethral personality in W. LaBarre, *They shall take up serpents: Psychology of the southern snake handling cult* (Minneapolis, 1962), p. 197, note 120.

13. Crawley, A. E. "Drinks and drinking," *Hastings encyclopedia of religion and ethics* 5: pp. 72–82.

14. Hall, E. T., *The silent language* (New York, 1959).

15. *Horizon* magazine, in 1959–1961, in a reference I cannot locate.

16. Consider, indeed, that the atomic bomb need never have been dropped, if an interpreter had only properly translated the Japanese word *mokusatsu* (W. LaBarre, *The human animal*, pp. 171, 348 [p. 360 in 4th and later printings]).

17. Is there any remote connection here with the Siberian "olonism" that S. M. Shirokogoroff (*Psychomental complex of the Tungus*, London, 1935) writes of: when the underprivileged underdog expresses the most violent and psychotic emotions, and the whole society turns out to recapture the run-away "wild man" in the forest and then attempts to pacify him? If he succeeds in influencing the people, he may become a shaman; if not, he is a psychotic, in need of cure by an established shaman.

The Time Dimension in Intercultural Communication

TOM BRUNEAU

INTRODUCTION

At a recent communication conference held in Tokyo, I began a presentation about time concepts, timing behavior, and tempo in organizations with a "time joke." I began by saying that I had just arrived in Tokyo from the island of Guam situated in the Western-Central Pacific. I went on to say that "Guam time" and "Tokyo time" were suddenly contrasted for me and were so very different. "In Guam," I said with naive confidence, "you are never late for a party or fiesta—even if you show up and everyone else has gone home." Well, to my surprise, the audience did not respond in laughing approval. In fact, it was like "no response at all" and I decided to not tell the second part of my joke about "Tokyo time." I had planned to say that "Tokyo time" was monolithic in nature. I was planning to explain that "Tokyo time" may be deriving its power from one large rock and that it was probably that a giant quartz crystal might be buried somewhere near the very heart of Tokyo. In retrospect, I am glad I skipped the second half of my joke. Besides, my talk was being timed to fit a fifteen minute time frame and "being on time" was being stressed.

From *Communication* 3 (August 1979), 169–181. Reprinted by permission of the publisher and the author. Mr. Bruneau is a member of the Department of Communication and Coordinator of the Center for Communication Studies at the University of Guam.

TIME AND CULTURAL DIFFERENCES: SOME GENERAL CONSIDERATIONS

Oswald Spengler once said that ". . . it is the meaning that it intuitively attaches to Time that one Culture is differentiated from another . . ." (1926, p. 130). Accepting this claim by Spengler, however, does not mean that we should also accept his viewpoint that certain temporal orientations are associated with "higher cultures," (pp. 117–60, Chap.: "The Idea of Destiny and the Principle of Causality"). The idea that one culture's temporality is somehow better than another culture's temporality appears to be a major basis for intercultural perceptions of inferiority and superiority. Seldom do people recognize that their perception of peoples from other cultures relates to their elitism or rigidity about their own cultural time orientation. People do compare their time orientations with those of other cultural groups.

Western literature about culture and intercultural perceptions seems to be replete with unconscious assumptions: Western time experiencing is most advanced, most useful, and best for future development. These assumptions seem to be resistant to deep questioning by cultural groupings which have accepted Newtonian and objective forms of temporality as their definition of time. Obviously, when a cultural group assumes that "their time" is superior to the time, timing, and tempo of other cultural groups, a basis is established for preferential judgments about cultural aspects of space, spacing, and motion through space (perhaps *including inner space or subjective, personal time experiencing*). Even languages can then become related to notions of temporal superiority and inferiority. In this regard, the widely respected and accepted symbolic philosophy of Cassirer includes the blunt presumption that "advanced" languages are those which are more elaborate is terms of *zeitworts* (time-words) than other, less developed languages (e.g.: Cassirer, 1953, pp. 215–26). From an intercultural communication perspective which is more temporally open and educated, however, who is to say, for certain, that there is necessarily more wisdom in a bee than in a butterfly? Is a clock necessarily better or worse than the rhythm of the tides and celestial bodies? Billions of people may believe that clocks are necessary evils at best.

In a splicing statement suggesting that the East and West could be conveniently and arbitrarily divided into time zones, Reyna (1971, p. 228) said ". . . one cannot constrain the Oriental conceptions of time into the delimiting frames familiar to the West" (1971, p. 228). In terms of traditional notions of time in the Orient (related to Hinduism, Buddhism, and their branches and splinter groups), this statement seems to make much sense. However, a modern viewpoint does not warrant such a dichotomous position. Even though many small, timeless-like temples and pagodas dot many of the urban areas of the Orient, the roar of automobiles and trains, the smell of oil, the crush of politics, and the shattering of jet propulsion shakes the quiet air. In Peking the horns blare, in Shanghai people are beginning to nervously flick their wrists watchward toward their eyes in order to pace their day, throughout China a postponed industrial evolution is beginning to be reconstructed using every workable clock the British left behind. Differences in the time of cultural groups are complex. Examples of differences in time conception, time perspective (past, present, future), and time-experiencing (timekeeping, timing, pacing, and temporal behavior (see taxonomy) between cultural groups are many and varied.[1] It appears that, at every level about the analysis of time, timing, and tempo cultures do differ. For example, one of my students from the Trukese District of Micronesia wrote me a poem recently:

A snail
A mountain
Ten thousand years[2]

He said it does not matter which lines are spoken first or last or in what order.

If we compare this poet's temporal perspective with a British-America (or Western-European) preoccupation with "What came first, the chicken or the egg?" perhaps we will observe two very different orientations toward the nature and importance of causality. From an American or Western-European viewpoint about temporality, when we deal with causality retrospectively and analytically, we can construct a particular kind of past which is based on certain assumptions about memory and memory processing. Indeed, the manner in which certain people imagine historicity or the manner in which cultural groups utilize their memories appears to be grounded in culturally bound time orientations. Various ways of remembering, as well as ways of utilizing nostalgia, incidently, appear to be culturally specific. The various needs to look backward are many and complex. The need to look backward for a certain purpose may vary from cultural group to cultural group. Our example is a case in point. If one sits long enough on white, dry, fossilized coral—with the distant and rhythmic roar of the surf pounding on and under the outer reef—the time-count becomes atemporal. The lush and persistent greens and deep blues in Micronesia seem "always" and "always have been." Even for a visitor or newcomer in such a hypnotic, natural environment, the days can become confused and the hours can be easily forgotten. This seems especially so in some rural areas of Micronesia which are not yet frequented by the noises of modern technology. Acausality appears to be encouraged in such environments. In such a temporal atmosphere, accounting for a sequential accuracy about the past by using retrospective analysis seems to be a futile task. In such an atmosphere, it can become difficult for certain persons to care for minutes, hours, weeks, months, and even years.[3]

FUTURISM AND INTERCULTURAL COMMUNICATION

Just as concepts about a past perspective of time seem to vary from culture to culture, so does the image of the future. The future is both conceptual and processual—as is the present and the past.

The massive study required to say how cultures differ in their futuristic, temporal orientations has yet to be begun. Futurism is a movement which is multidisciplinary in scope and it is rapidly developing into intensive and sustained efforts of major importance in many academic disciplines. The study of the future should utilize a great deal of scholarly energy on both the near and distant future. This new movement may someday be viewed as a major turning point in the history of the development of human thought. New avenues into unexplored ways of thinking ahead should develop. However, new ways in which to "think ahead" should produce a greater distance between cultures which are rapidly expanding their visions of the future (progressivism) and those cultures in which the image of the future is just beginning to change from traditional visions.

Some cultures seem to have a rigid fixity in their images of the future. The degree of fixity of the image of the future seems to vary between cultural groups. The examples of this are many. For example, some cultural groups have an almost disdainful glimpse of the future. For some cultural groups, the future is feared and hidden from one's reflections. In some cultures, thinking about the future is considered to be: a wasteful activity, a manner of idleness, an unnecessary kind of dreaming, a kind of foolish romantic activity, or even a kind of activity engaged in by strange people or evil people, etc.

In such a temporal environment, a stable and rigid image of a future can develop. When this does occur, the rigid futuristic image appears to function for the purpose of negating other views of the future. For instance, a clear image of "one's own life hereafter" (held by many different cultural groups) may prevent alternative images of the future from developing. The fixity of a cultural group's image of the future may even prevent or hinder members of that culture group from thinking in ways related to planning and alternate avenues of hoping. We do know that individuals within cultural groups can vary widely in their images of their own futures and, still, individuals do tend to develop future images which are similar to members of their culture group. Individuals within cultures seem to vary their images of the future as they grow older, according to their fears of death and the unknown or unpredictable, and according to their particular

abilities to think in futuristic modes.[4] There appears to be no reason why we should not begin to assume that each cultural group holds a particular image of the future which can be both similar and different from the images of the future held by members of other cultural groups. In short, the time conceptions and perspectives of different cultures are significant differences between cultural groups and deserve more attention by those studying intercultural communication.

The ability to anticipate consequences and delay gratification seem to be culturally reinforced activities and involve a futuristic perspective. Delay of gratification and the anticipation of consequences are highly related to a group's wealth, economic conditions, and the pace of life. This appears to be the case across most cultural groups. However, cultural groups appear to have traditionally characteristic ways of anticipating consequences as well as delaying gratification. These characteristic ways may interact with changing social and economic conditions and changes in the pace of life in many ways.

In some cultural groups, clear directions for future actions are given by establishing and using various kinds of itinerary, by following the steps provided by custom and practice, or by various ways of creating atmospheres of fate or chance. Sometimes the clash of future perspectives between cultures can be sharply contrasted. An extended example should clarify some of the above ideas:

The Intercultural Traffic Jam

Let us imagine that a person from one cultural background (Person A) buys his or her first automobile, learns to drive it, and develops a pattern of anticipation for traffic conditions, traffic signs and traffic signals. The pattern of anticipation developed for traffic signs and signals by Person A grew out of particular kinds of conceptions of "thinking ahead" which are positively valued in Culture A. Let us also imagine that Person A belongs to a cultural group which values positive attitudes about the "rewards of thinking ahead."

Person B, in buying his or her first automobile, however, comes from a cultural group which is only somewhat familiar with the anticipation of consequences of one's own actions required in terms of a quickened, urban pace of life. Person B happens to come from and is influenced by a cultural group where one operates immediately and in terms of immediately given or perceived conditions. In Culture B, the need to think ahead quickly is not traditionally necessary except for particular cultural customs and activities. It is not that Culture B people cannot think futuristically, it is that most people from Culture B need to do so only infrequently. Their futurism is clearly related to custom and they have developed behavioral patterns to cope with problems or new conditions in a spontaneous fashion. In other words, Person B does not value thinking ahead, has not experienced much positive reinforcement from his cultural group for thinking ahead, and his or her responses to traffic conditions are present-oriented, here-and-now, and immediate.

Now, imagine a situation where you are a person driving in traffic behind person A. If you are from Culture A, you have perhaps begun to anticipate that Person A in the automobile ahead of you will usually give a signal (hand or electronic) indicating that he or she will make a left turn. This signal will often be far enough in advance of the actual turn to give others more than adequate notice of the turning event. In driving behind Person A, one begins to anticipate the anticipatory responses of Person A. This seems to also happen for other persons who are from Culture A. Soon, these anticipatory responses turn into a set of expectations for drivers like Person A. Our expectancy level, if we are from Culture A, begins to be consistent and we can become confident and trustful about the driving of Person A.

However, from the viewpoint of a driver from Culture A, who happens to be driving behind an automobile driven by Person B, the "uncertainties of an intercultural traffic situation" become apparent. From a perspective of a Person A

driving behind a Person B, Person B appears likely to slow down quickly, slam on his or her brakes, and to turn quickly. These appear to be Person B's turning behaviors. Person B seems to turn when a cue of the "place to turn" appears (arrives in consciousness without expectation) in his or her immediate present. From Person A's perspective, Person B is likely to actually turn his or her vehicle when he or she begins to signal his or her wish to turn. The wish to turn is not a signal requiring a delay of action–from B's perspective. For B, the event and the wish are merged. In other words, Person B will often signal and begin his or her turn upon seeing the place to turn. In such a situation, three functions or aspects of an event seem to share the same moment. In comparison, A seems to divide his or her traffic events into anticipatory units. In contrast to Person A, Person B seems to blend traffic events into unitary action.

For Person B, driving behind a vehicle driven by a member of Culture A can be just as confusing. From Person B's perspective, a Person A driver appears to be always ready to turn and at any given moment. Person A seems to signal and then, never seems to turn. From B's perspective, some people from Culture A never seem to make up their minds as to when and where they will turn. B may think that people from Culture A confuse a simple act by over-anticipating and making complex.

Imagining a further traffic jam or a complex traffic situation requiring participation and cooperation between people from Cultures A and B, one can now begin to visualize and hear the heat of intercultural conflict. The consternation of red countenances grim with frustration in not being able to predict the temporal behaviors of other drivers would create an interesting image. But, a traffic conflict between persons from Cultures A and B is fairly safe and uncomplicated compared to multicultural situations. A bicultural image is rather uncomplicated and tame compared to a high density traffic situation where people from ten to twenty different cultural groups attempt to survive a drive in the same countryside on the same Sunday afternoon.

Fred Polak (1961) is a major thinker concerning the development of the image of the future. Polak appears, at first glance, to be extreme about the importance of a futuristic orientation in the shaping of cultures. Polak appears to be claiming that *different future perspectives are highly influential in the actual creation of particular kinds of cultures* (1961). In other words, time perspective is culturally specific, culturally bound, and central to cultural identity and functioning. Polak's major thesis about culture and future perspective is clearly stated:

Awareness of ideal values is the first step in the conscious creation of images of the future and therefore in the conscious creation of culture. For a value is by definition that which guides toward a "valued" future. . . . It becomes clear now that magic, religion, philosophy, science, and ethics might well owe their origin and further creative development largely to the basic need to get fore-knowledge of the future. In other words, these fundamental fields of culture may have been developed at first mainly as ways and means of visualizing and influencing the future. . . . The images of the future . . . are historic landmarks and cultural mirrors . . . (1961, p. 37).

Polak's image of the future in cultural perspective appears to be a healthy one. His viewpoints seem to hold deep respect and positive regard for the complexity and challenge of the futurism/culture interface.

TIMING AND TIMEKEEPING AMONG CULTURES

A major aspect of the time dimension concerns the manner and degree to which objective forms of timekeeping are utilized and how they influence temporal pacing or patterning in particular cultures.[5] Of even greater interest to us is how objective time restraints and constraints may influence people from different cultures with different time orientations differently. In other words, time devices, timekeeping methods, and objective formulations of time are at the core of a modern pace of life. A modern pace of life interacts with a culturally traditional pace of life—at any given decade. The clock may be a machine of all machines. This tiny machine which is carried about on one's wrist may be the most basic and powerful machine in the world. The clock appears to control all other machines and electronic devices.

The idea of an objective time as a true and real form of time is a significant development in the history of human conduct. As Mumford stated, "The clock . . . is the key machine of the industrial age [1962, p. 14]. . . . The first characteristic of modern machine civilization is its temporal regularity. From the moment of walking, the rhythm of the day is punctuated by the clock. Irrespective of strain or fatigue, despite reluctance or apathy, the household rises close to its set hour" (p. 269).

The widespread use of clocks and timekeeping devices may be growing into irreversible directions during the last half of this century. Such growth in timekeeping expansion is not without dangers to the health of people. Wright (1968, p. 7) states the danger concisely in the introduction of his book about the tyranny of clockworks: "This is the history of an increasing, unchecked, and now intolerable *chronarchy*. That word is not to be found in *The Oxford English Dictionary*. Its coiner should be entitled to define it. Let chronarchy, then, be merely 'rule by time,' but 'regimentation of man by timekeeping.' " Elsewhere, I expressed the danger to cultural identity posed by the threat of the growth of objective timekeeping throughout the world: the spread of objective time throughout the world has been rapid and is growing. The signification of this movement might best be expressed in two hypotheses: (1) Objective tempo, when largely accepted, tends to destroy cultures which are based in subjective temporality; (2) The widespread adoption of standards of objective temporality tends to neutralize cultural diversity (Bruneau, 1978a).

Clocks imply a standard by which events may be compared and how similar events may be judged to differ. When time is only viewed as timekeeping, timing devices become valued and their functioning becomes associated with activities which are, in turn, valued. In some cultures, certain methods of objective timekeeping are more valued than other forms of objective timekeeping. While reliance on clock time has grown with the rapid growth of intercultural contact and exchange since the beginning of this century, other forms of timekeeping are still popular for millions of people spread throughout the planet. A clock is only one form of "regularized" time and clock time can often clash with other kinds of objective timekeeping which are related to cycles of celestial and natural events or the biological repetitions and periodicities of human beings and other animals. To use a pleasant image about clocks cast forth by Dora Marsden: "The entire universe is weighted toward rhythm . . . everywhere, as in a cosmic dance, natural bodies are doing their rounds . . . the universe is littered with clocks" (1955, p. 12).

Each natural clock which is replaced with an artificial, objective measure of timekeeping may lose its utility and purpose. One form of timekeeping can replace another. When one form of objective time replaces another form unnecessarily, can the situation be said to have been changed for the better? When highly valued forms of timekeeping associated with customary behaviors of particular cultural groups are replaced, perhaps the behaviors change or become lost to oblivion. When a cultural group changes its timekeeping, it may very well change its more stable characteristics, too.

The manner in which different cultural groups value different kinds of objective timekeeping may establish particular kinds of potential communicative interaction. Cultural groups appear to widely differ in their valuation of the same objective time systems. The differences in the degree to which an objective timekeeping is valued may very well influence the manner in which peoples from different cultures comply with objective time standards or adhere to the dictates of those who control, manipulate, and interpret objective time.

Cultural differences in the valuation of objective time, then, can establish a basis for understanding a number of intercultural communication problems. This is especially so when it is understood that timekeeping and objective time standards can control space and motion through space—and often do so. The imposition of objective time by one or more cultural groups upon another cultural group can be considered as a form of intercultural influence or persuasion.

Media are very time related. Objective timing is highly involved in the structuring of various kinds of media. What is usually not so apparent, however, is that values related to certain forms of timekeeping seem to be unconsciously projected through the media to people from other cultures. People can be influenced to wear wristwatches even if they are not necessary in everyday living. It should not be surprising to find clock time projected as a valued process in all spheres of life which are projected or broadcast by Western and Western-influenced media. Clock time appears to be a *channel of media channels.* Objective forms of time are forms of media controlling other media forms. This fact has not yet seemed to have been recognized for its importance. Western media appear to be hopelessly based in rigid, objective time constraints. With the growth and spread of Western media throughout many non-Western cultural groups, it seems reasonable to assume that these groups will continue to be exposed to massive doses of the value of clock time being projected to them by Westernized media.

PACE OF LIFE, CULTURAL TEMPO, AND INTERCULTURAL COMMUNICATION

There are many kinds of time which make up an individual's temporal system: biological time, physiological time, perceptual time, objective time, conceptual time, psychological time, social time, and cultural time.[6] The manner in which these interdependent levels of time experiencing interact subsume a "chronemics" of human behavior (Bruneau, 1977, p. 3). Chronemics is a relatively new idea of communication study which can be defined as the meaning of human time experiencing as it influences and is influenced by human communication.[7]

The pace of life of a cultural group concerns the manner in which levels of time experiencing are integrated by individual members and aggregates of individuals in such groups. Further, the pace of life of a cultural group concerns the standards and habits of *temporal behavior* which underscore interaction between members of a cultural group. (It should be noted here that kinds and levels of temporal behavior will be outlined in the "Taxonomy of Temporal Environment.")

Especially important in the pace of life of a cultural group is the manner in which subjective and objective forms of time experiencing interact. In other words, the manner in which highly variable forms of time experiencing in given cultures interact with somewhat constant or consistent forms of time experiencing in given cultures, helps to determine the characteristic tempo of a culture. Some cultural groups are paced by a merging of subjective kinds of time experiencing with cyclic, periodic forms of objective time. Nilsson (1920) has described the importance of such periodic forms of objective time in many "primitive" cultural groups. Periodic, cyclic forms of objective time concern the repetition of biological, natural, and celestial movements. When certain forms of periodic and cyclic objective time interact with personal, social, and cultural activities and events, a particular "cultural tempo" develops and *becomes* the temporal environment of some cultural groups. Certain cultural groups with this particular temporal environment still exist. Fifty years ago, many such cultural groups existed.

Some cultural groups adopt fairly constant forms of objective time (e.g., clocks, timers, bells, daily schedules, etc.). These cultural groups develop characteristic temporal environments by merging such objective forms of time with personal, social, and cultural activities and events. Cultural groups which stress the importance of objective standards of time, the accuracy of such time, and the pacing of life associated with clocks, can become "clock-bound" cultural groups. A clock-bound cultural group seems to stress objective time forms more than it stresses more personal and subjective forms of time experiencing. Often, clock time conformity may be basic to many other kinds of conformity (e.g., proxemic and kinesic habits and customs). The relationship between a chronemics, a proxemics, and a kinesics has yet to be outlined—though such related areas will have to be conjoined eventually. A cultural stress on objective timekeeping may prevent other forms of time experiencing from finding expression. For example, contemplation is a form of subjective time experiencing which appears to be sacrificed in highly clock-bound cultures. As McLuhan once stated, "Clocks are mechanical media that transform tasks and create new work and wealth by accelerating the pace of human association" (1964, p. 143). Such haste is often valued in clock-bound cultures. However, Meerloo, in his analysis of time experiencing, adds a negative note: "Haste is compensation for doubt" (1970, p. 207). Wyndham could very well have been speaking of present-day, clock-bound cultures when he expressed his reservations about "trances of action" long ago:

Everything in our life to-day conspires to thrust people into prescribed tracks, in what can be called a sort of trance of action. *Hurrying, without any significant reason, from spot to spot at the maximum speed obtainable, drugged in the mechanical activity, how is the typical individual of this epoch to do some detached thinking for himself? All his life is disposed with a view to banishing reflection. To be alone he finds terrifying* (1927, p. vii).

Cultures which stress clock time and fairly constant forms of objective tempo seem to also extend these forms of tempo into activities and events not traditionally punctuated by clock time. In clock-bound cultures, a tendency seems to develop where temporal conditioning becomes a pervasive style of living. Temporal conditioning develops from the increased use of clocks, time indicators, and time regulators in everyday life (Bruneau, 1974). Highly clock-bound cultures appear to extend the use of clocks into a form of mania which could be called a "chronophilia." In a chronophiliac atmosphere, people value clock time very much, they value accuracy highly, and cherish the order assumed to exist under such standards. In such an atmosphere, temporal conditioning can take place—depending on the degree of chronophilia. In such an atmosphere of temporality, clocks are increasingly extended into pacers which regulate the flow and speed of activities. More and more areas of life-space are regulated and punctuated by clocks and their extensions. Spontaneous activity, creativity, and a number of subjective forms of tempo can quickly lose their credibility and value.[8] Objective time conditioning, when too rigid and pervasive, can evolve into a kind of behavioral puppetry. Under such a puppetry temporal cloaks and robes are placed on as masks to cover traditional and subjective forms of time experiencing. In such an environment, the play unfolds on a fixed stage, the composition and setting of which are predetermined. Behavioral puppetry seems to result in a kind of boredom which finds the actors seeking escape in repetitive compulsions and faster and faster routines. Chronophilia can become, literally, a "chronic" pathology where life can become a constant, dull, grey line of ennui. On such a dull linearity, the players intensify and quicken their dance in a futile effort to expand and enliven the line. However, to use one of Whitehead's more terse statements, the result of more and more intensive activities is clear: "Intensity is the reward of narrowness" (1929, p. 172).

The characteristic tempo of a cultural group can be compared with the range of temporality of each member of that culture group. Each individual must adjust his or her unique, personal temporality to the unique tempo of his or her cultural group. When persons of different cultural tempos attempt to communicate, the temporal environment becomes a merger of both personal and cultural tempos. In the intercultural communication situation, rates of behavior and the expectancies about these rates may vary from person to person. The values held toward different forms of objective and subjective kinds of time can provide a wide range of misunderstandings and misinterpretations in such situations. The temporal behaviors (see taxonomy) of each person in an intercultural communication situation may differ radically and still function unconsciously or out of the awareness of the communicators during intercultural exchanges.

When it is understood that both proxemic and kinesic behaviors appear to be based in the temporal beliefs, attitudes, motives, values, and temporal behaviors of all participants in the intercultural situation, it becomes apparent that the temporal dimension is a most significant factor in intercultural communication. Creative conceptualizing about the manner in which time orientations and perspectives interact with cultural identity, cultural behaviors, and intercultural communication should provide for years of research activity.

The many lines of analysis required for a detailed consideration of the time/intercultural communication interface is beyond the scope of this paper. In lieu of a detailed discussion, a taxonomy is provided. This taxonomy, if used to access intercultural communication situations, should provide images of many probable examples and, hopefully, provide a sounding board for actual intercultural events and situations.

A TAXONOMY OF TEMPORAL ENVIRONMENT

The taxonomy outlined below was initially developed as a partial attempt to define a "chronemics" of human behavior (Bruneau, 1978a). The taxonomy can be used to analyze and study the temporal behaviors and temporal environments of many forms of human interaction. Hopefully, such a taxonomy can be of benefit by providing a structure in which to help control observations in the complex world of time, timing, and tempo. Such a tool may provide necessary control for making temporal estimates and judgments (see taxonomy for these terms) in complex intercultural communication situations. It should be understood that the levels of temporality outlined below are highly interrelated and a hierarchy of levels of temporal behaviors is not necessarily advocated:

Temporal Drives: involving biorhythmic activity; hormonal and metabolic periodicities; ergic impulses (Cattell 1957; 1965); involving the reduction of physiological need tension, need tension patterning, etc.

Temporal Cues: pertaining to the initial sensing and recognition of one's own temporal drives and those of others.

Temporal Signals: involving the imposition of perceptual durations and intervals which give rise to individual senses of time; perceptual continuities and discontinuities which give rise to habitual and variable recognition of successions and durations; any durational or processual phenomena giving rise to the formation of perceptual information related to the pacing, control, regulation, or facilitation of human behavior; concerning the recognition of temporal characteristics of nonverbal behavior; etc.

Temporal Symbols: pertaining to the symbolic representation of succession and duration, change and permanence, or of temporal perspective and orientation; concepts of subjective and objective tempos; relating to the representation of objective time, timing, and times; concerning linguistic representations and functionings related to levels of time experiencing and all behaviors (including mental) subsumed under the taxonomic items presented here, etc.

Temporal Beliefs: pertaining to assumptions held about the nature of time and space; concerning degree of rigidity in the perception and conceptualization of space-time behavior; concerning the validity of temporal cues and estimates; concerning the validity of temporal information arising from temporal drives, temporal signals, and temporal symbolism; pertaining to the validity and nature of temporal judgments (see below); etc.

Temporal Motives: relating to psychological intention to influence temporal behavior; concerning

the intention to alter personal and objective tempos; concerning the process of altering personal and objective tempos; relating to the influencing of drives, needs, and motivations; intention related to goals and goal behavior; et cetera.

Temporal Judgments: pertaining to the validity of temporal beliefs, temporal motives, and temporal values (below) as exercised by individuals or groups of individuals in sociocultural contexts; et cetera.

Temporal Values: concerning valuation and evaluation of tempo, times (events) and timing as they relate to personal, social, and cultural behaviors.

NOTES

1. While examples of temporal differences between cultural groups are many, surprisingly little work has been done in this area of study. For those interested in the time/culture interface, two bibliographic sources exist which provide the listing of approximately 2,000 bibliographic items associated with the study of time (Doob 1971; Zelkind and Sprug 1974). Also the proceedings of the International Society for the Study of Time (J. T. Fraser, et al. 1972; 1975; and 1978) can provide a rich source of information for the study of time across cultural groups.

2. I wish to thank one of my students, Jack Sigrah, for writing this poem.

3. The Americans, the British, the French, the Japanese, the Australians, the New Zealanders, the Russians, and others with particular interests in Micronesia do not seem to have such atemporal-acausal orientations. This is especially so with those persons from many countries who seek all forms of modern day "business."

4. I have previously described this mode of thinking as "protension" in an attempt to develop a model of mind-time relativity (Bruneau 1976).

5. For an excellent account of timekeeping, timekeepers, and objective time, see: Fraser and

Lawrence, 1975, pp. 365–485, a special session of the International Society for the Study of Time on timekeeping.

6. Each of these major levels of time experiencing has been outlined elsewhere along with a representative bibliography for each level (Bruneau 1977). It is not in the scope of this article to outline these areas of time experiencing.

7. For a more comprehensive definition of a "Chronemics," see: Bruneau, 1977; 1978a; 1978b. Also see: Poyatos, 1976, p. 61.

8. A model of subjective temporality in terms of different kinds of mental modes of tempo is offered in a theoretically speculative article by Bruneau (1976). In this article, a model of modes of mental relativity is developed which are said to be related to different kinds of sociocultural time perspectives as well as being characteristic of thinking stances.

REFERENCES

Bruneau, Thomas, "Chronemics and the Verbal-Nonverbal Interface," *The Relationship of Verbal and Nonverbal Communication*, ed., Mary Ritchie Key (The Hague: Mouton Press, 1978).

———, "Chronemics: The Study of Time in Human Interaction (with a Glossary of Chronemic Terminology)," *Communication*, CAPUH, 6 (1977), 1–30.

———, "Chronemics: Time and Organizational Communication," paper presented at the Communication Association of the Pacific Conference, Tokyo, Japan, June 1978b.

———, "Silence, Mind-Time Relativity, and Interpersonal Communication," Third Conference, International Society for the Study of Time, Alpbach, Austria, July 1–10, 1976.

———, "Time and Nonverbal Communication," *Journal of Popular Culture* 8 (1974), 658–666.

Cassirer, Ernst, *The Philosophy of Symbolic Forms*, Vol. 1., *Language* (New Haven, CT.: Yale University Press, 1953).

Cattell, Raymond B., *Personality and Motivation Structure and Measurement* (N.Y.: Harcourt, Brace and World, 1957).

———, *The Scientific Analysis of Personality* (Harmondsworth: Penguin Books, 1965).

Doob, Leonard, *Patterning of Time* (New Haven, CT.: Yale University Press, 1971).

Fraser, J. T., et al., *The Study of Time*, Vol. I (N.Y.: Springer-Verlag, 1972).

Fraser, J. T. and N. Lawrence, *The Study of Time II* (N.Y.: Springer-Verlag, 1975).

Fraser, et al., *The Study of Time III* (N.Y.: Springer-Verlag, 1978).

McLuhan, Marshall, *Understanding Media: The Extensions of Man* (N.Y.: New American Library, 1964).

Marsden, Dora, *The Philosphy of Time* (Oxford: The Holywell Press, 1955).

Meerloo, Joost A. M., *Along the Fourth Dimension* (N.Y.: John Day, 1970).

Mumford, Lewis, *Technics and Civilization* (N.Y.: Harcourt, Brace and World, 1962).

Nilsson, Martin P., *Primitive Time-Reckoning* (Lund, CWK Gleerup, 1920).

Polak, Fred L., *The Image of the Future* (N.Y.: Oceana Publications, 1961).

Poyatos, Fernando, "Language in the Context of Total Body Communication," *Linguistics* 168 (1976), 49–62.

Reyna, Ruth, "Metaphysics of Time in Indian Philosophy and Its Relevance to Particle Science," in J. Zeman, ed. *Time in Science and Philosophy* (Czechoslovak Academy of Sciences, 1971), 227–239.

Spengler, Oswald, *The Decline of the West* Vol. 1, *Form and Actuality* (N.Y.: Alfred A. Knopf, 1926).

Whitehead, Alfred North, *Process and Reality* (N.Y.: Humanities Press, 1929).

Wright, Lawrence, *Clockwork Man* (N.Y.: Horizon Press, 1968).

Wyndham, Lewis, *Time and Western Man* (Boston: Beacon Hill, 1927).

Zelkind, Irving and J. Sprug, *Time Research: 1172 Studies* (Metuchen, N.J.: Scarecrow Press, 1974).

Sex Differences in Nonverbal Communication

BARBARA WESTBROOK EAKINS
R. GENE EAKINS

. . . People talking without speaking
. . . People hearing without listening

—*Paul Simon*

In addition to the spoken language that we hear daily, a host of silent messages continually occur around us. These messages make up a nonverbal code, which is used and responded to by us all. This language is not formally taught. A substantial portion of the nonverbal communication that takes place is not consciously noted. But it is an extremely important aspect of communication, for we make many important decisions on the basis of nonverbal cues.

Ray Birdwhistell estimates that in most two-person conversations the words communicate only about 35 percent of the social meaning of the situation; the nonverbal elements convey more than 65 percent of the meaning. Another estimate is that the nonverbal message carries 4.3 times the weight of the verbal message. This is not so surprising when we consider the many ways in which we communicate information nonverbally: through eye contact, facial expressions, body posture and body tension, hand gestures and body movements, the way we position ourselves in relation to

From Barbara Eakins and R. Gene Eakins, *Sex Differences in Human Communication*. Copyright © 1978 Houghton Mifflin Company. Used with permission of the publisher. Barbara Eakins teaches at the Ohio State University, and R. Gene Eakins teaches at Wright State University. Footnotes have been deleted.

another person, touch, clothing, cosmetics, and possessions.

Some time ago Freud said, "He that has eyes to see and ears to hear may convince himself that no mortal can keep a secret. If his lips are silent, he chatters with his finger tips; betrayal oozes out of him at every pore." To be more skillful communicators, we need to be aware of nonverbal cues and to use what has been learned to improve communication.

Micro-units of nonverbal communication, such as dropping the eyelids, smiling, pointing, lowering the head slightly, or folding the arms are often considered trivia. But some researchers believe these so-called trivia constitute the very core or essence of our communication interactions. They consider them elements in the "micropolitical structure" that help maintain and support the larger political structure. The larger political structure needs these numerous minutiae of human actions and interactions to sustain and reinforce it. These nonverbal cues fall somewhere on a continuum of social control that ranges from socialization or cultivation of minds, at one extreme, to the use of force or physical violence, at the other. There are some significant sex differences in nonverbal communication patterns and, as we shall see, they have important implications in the lives of women and men. . . .

SEX DIFFERENCES IN NONVERBAL COMMUNICATION

Women seem to be more sensitive than men to social cues. Research has shown that female subjects are more responsive to nonverbal cues, compared with verbal ones, than males. Not only have women been found to be more responsive to nonverbal stimuli, but they apparently read it with greater accuracy than males. One study used the Profile of Nonverbal Sensitivity, a test that utilizes film clips of a series of scenes involving people using body movement and facial expression and showing face, torso, both, or neither. Subjects heard scrambled voice, content-filtered speech with intonation features preserved, or no sound. They were to select the best of the written interpretations of the nonverbal cues after each scene. Females from fifth grade to adulthood obtained better scores than males, with the exception of men who held jobs involving "nurturant, artistic, or expressive" work. When body cues were included, women did better than men. Sensitivity to nonverbal cues appeared to be independent of general intelligence or test-taking skills.

One could hypothesize that nonverbal awareness is an inborn trait and that females are more sensitive and responsive to nonverbal cues from birth. However, it seems more likely that females learn to become nonverbally sensitive at an early age because of their socialization. Their greater receptivity to nonverbal cues from others may be related to their lower status in society and the necessity of this skill to their survival. Blacks, for example, have been shown to be better than whites at interpreting nonverbal signals.

When a group of teachers took the Profile of Nonverbal Sensitivity, those more sensitive to nonverbal communication scored as less authoritarian and more democratic in teaching orientation. Females were relatively better than males at interpreting negative attitudes. Since females may be placed in subordinate positions or be dependent on others in social situations more often, they may be forced to become adept at reading signs of approbation or displeasure from those on whom they depend. Perhaps more than men, they need to know what expectations for them are. Developing the ability to pick up small nonverbal cues in others quickly may be a defense mechanism or survival technique women unconsciously use. It is much more important to someone in a subordinate position to know the mood, the feelings, or intentions of the dominant one than vice versa. The office worker will immediately note and relay to other office subordinates the information that "the boss is in one of his moods again." Just a look, the manner of walk, or the carriage of the arms and shoulders may provide the clue for that anxious observer. Rare, however, is the authority figure who notices employees' moods or is even aware that they have them.

We are not taught nonverbal communication in school. Our schools emphasize verbal communication. Because we seldom examine how we send and interpret nonverbal messages, the nonverbal channel is a very useful avenue for subtly manipulating people. The manipulation does not have to be consciously perceived.

We are prevented from getting knowledge or understanding of nonverbal communication because a delineation of looks, gait, posture, or facial expression is not legitimate in describing interaction. Such items are surely not accepted as valid data in an argument. ("What do you mean, I look as if I don't approve? I said 'all right,' didn't I?") And yet nonverbal cues have more than four times the impact of verbal messages. Not only are women more sensitive to such cues, but their position in society and their socialization to greater docility and compliance may predispose them to be more vulnerable to manipulation and thus make them ideal targets for this subtle form of social control. It behooves both women and men to learn as much as possible about how nonverbal cues can affect people and can serve to perpetuate status and power relationships in society. With this concern in mind, let us examine the categories of nonverbal behavior.

Eye Contact

Research in the use of eye contact has shown sharp differences according to sex. In studies involving female and male subjects, women have been found to look more at the other person than men do. In addition, women look at one another more and hold eye contact longer with each other than men do with other men. Women look at one another more while they are speaking, while they are being spoken to, and while they are exchanging simultaneous glances. Whatever the sex of the other, women have been shown to spend more time looking at their partner than men do. What might account for this asymmetry, or difference, in looking behavior of the sexes? The usual explanation given is that women are more willing to establish and maintain eye contact because they are more inclined toward social and interpersonal relations. The gaze may be an avenue of emotional expression for women.

Another reason has been suggested for sex differences in eye behavior. Some experiments have found that in orienting their bodies in space women are more affected then men by visual cues. In other words, in tests where subjects must make judgments about horizontal and vertical position, women tend to use reference points in the environment rather than internal body cues. This physical characteristic could be generalized to social situations.

Let us consider the paradigm of asymmetrical behavior as an indicator of status. Among unequals the subordinate is the one most likely to want social approval, and it has been shown that people have more eye contact with those from whom they want approval. The kinds of clues or information women may get by observing a male's reactions or behavior are important in helping them gauge the appropriateness of their own behavior. Women may value nonverbal information from males more than males value nonverbal information from females. Furthermore, it has been found that in conversation, the listener tends to look more at the speaker, whereas the speaker often looks away while talking. Since some studies show that men tend to talk more in female-male pairs, women would spend more time listening and, therefore, probably more time looking at the other.

Also it has been shown that the more positive an attitude toward the person being addressed, the more eye contact there is. Increased eye contact with the person being addressed also occurs if that person is of higher status. In some cases males use more positive head nods, but females use more eye contact, when they are seeking approval. In an investigation involving mixed-sex pairs, when women were told their partner's eye contact exceeded normal levels, they had a more favorable evaluation of him. But when men were told their partner looked more than usual, they had a less favorable evaluation of her. These studies suggest that women may be using eye contact to seek approval and that perhaps both women and men perceive women to have less status than men. Perhaps, as one student commented, "They almost *ask* for the subordinate position by their behavior."

In our personal experience, we became acquainted with a graduate student and the woman he had just married. There was a discrepancy in educational background between the man, who was just beginning work on his Ph.D., and the woman, who had a high school education. Not only her uneasiness but her heavy reliance on nonverbal cues to her husband's reaction were evident at social gatherings. During conversation, her eyes would continually stray to his face. When speaking with her, it was difficult to establish eye contact, for during her comments or her answers to questions, her eyes would dart to her husband's face, as if to measure the appropriateness of her remark by his approbation or lack of it.

Some writers have observed that women tend to avert their gaze, especially when stared at by men. Although mutual eye contact between persons can indicate affiliation or liking, prolonged eye contact or staring can signify something quite different. Back in our youth, we sometimes engaged in "double whammy," a game in which we tried to outstare our partner. The first one to break the eyelock by looking away, dropping the eyes, or closing the eyes was the loser. It has been suggested that this kind of competitiveness is involved when two persons' gazes meet, such that "a wordless struggle ensues, until one or the other succeeds in establishing dominance." Dominance is acquiesced to and submissiveness signaled by the person who finally looks away or down. We might ask ourselves, in our last encounter with the boss, someone in very high authority, or a person whom we felt greatly "outclassed" us in position or wealth, who was the first to break the mutual gaze and glance away? Indeed, this is a " 'game' . . . enacted at [subtle] levels thousands of times daily."

Jane van Lawick-Goodall has observed behavior of chimpanzees for a number of years and has noted striking similarities in the behavior of chimpanzees and people, particularly in nonverbal communication patterns. She points out how a greeting between two chimpanzees generally re-establishes the dominance status of the one relative to the other. She describes how one female chimp, "nervous Olly," greets another chimp, "Mike," to whom she may bow to the ground and crouch submissively with downbent head. "She is, in effect, acknowledging Mike's superior rank," says Goodall. This would seem to be the extreme of avoiding eye gaze with one of superior rank. Goodall also indicates that an angry chimpanzee may fixedly stare at an opponent.

Some years ago, when our oldest daughter was quite young, she asked us earnestly, "Why is it baboons don't like you to stare at them?" The family was amused at this, and it became a standing joke at our home for years. But we had been to the zoo and, young as she was, our daughter had apparently noticed that the baboons she saw reacted in a disturbed manner to staring.

Research with humans has shown that staring calls forth the same kinds of responses found in primates and that it serves as threat display. Observations of averted eye behavior in autistic children suggest that the averted glance or downcast eyes may be a gesture of submissiveness in humans. Researchers noted to their surprise that autistic children were rarely attacked by the other children, although they seemed to be "easy targets." They concluded that the autistic child's avoidance of eye contact served as a signal much like the appeasement postures used by certain gulls, for example. That is to say, turning away the gaze and avoiding eye contact seemed to restrain or check aggressive behavior or threat display.

The power of the direct stare and the strength of the message it conveys, as well as the acquiescence that turning the eyes away can signify, was illustrated to us by a humorous incident at a cocktail hour for new faculty. One young couple was eager to please and be accepted because it was the hus-

band's first position after finishing graduate school. The wife was a hearty, direct young woman who had been reared in Iowa. She had a bluff, good-natured sense of humor and an amusing way with idioms that refused to stay tucked under the sedateness she tried in vain to assume for this "important" occasion. She was in a tight little circle with some of the tenured and dignified "old guard," when one of them commented upon the great pleasure of discovering that his young colleague had such a lovely wife. The young woman was pleased and began animatedly telling her elderly admirer she felt "as grateful as the cow who remarked to the farmer, 'Thank you for a warm hand on a cold morning.'" As she spoke, her husband fixed upon her a direct and piercing stare. The young woman then stopped her talk and turned her head slightly as she lowered her eyes and became very intent upon sipping her punch.

There may seem to be a contradiction in reporting that women tend to look at others more than men do and yet claim that they generally follow a pattern of submission in one-sided behavior interactions. But several explanations may be offered. First, more of women's looking consists of mutual eye contact. It is possible that during mutual eye contact women are the first to turn the eyes away, the signal of submission. For example, one observation in which a male stared at 60 females and males showed that females averted their gaze more often. About 40 percent of the females would return the stare, then immediately break eye contact, and then reestablish it—as many as four times in an encounter. Only one male of the group made repetitive eye contact in this way.

Second, it may be useful to identify the nature of the gaze and [to] distinguish between subordinate attentiveness and dominant staring. Women may do more looking or scanning of the other person's face for expressive cues when the other person's gaze is directed elsewhere, just as subordinates in the animal world must stay alert to cues from the powerful. But when that person returns the gaze, a woman may drop hers. Intermittent and repetitive eye contact may be the female's response to two conflicting tendencies: the inclination to avert the eyes in submission and the need to watch for visual cues from the powerful.

Third, people tend to do more looking while they are listening to another speak than when they themselves are speaking; and we have learned that women are listeners more often than talkers. So women may be doing more of their looking while listening (in the submissive role) to the other person talk.

Fourth, looking that is done by subjects in experimental lab situations may function differently from looking that occurs in more natural settings. Some informal studies of eye contact by persons passing one another in public showed 71 percent of the males established eye contact with a female but only 43 percent of the females established eye contact with a male. Other observations have shown a pattern of females averting the eyes from both female and male starers. In contrast, males generally stared back at female starers, although they avoided eye contact with other males.

Apparently two types of eye behavior characterize both dominance and submissiveness, but in different ways.

1. Dominant staring and looking away. Staring can be used by a superior in some situations to communicate power and assert dominance. But in other instances staring may not be needed. With subordinates, one can feel comfortable and secure in one's power. A superior need not anxiously scan the inferior's face for approval or feedback, but can instead look away or gaze into space as if the underling were not there.

2. Submissive watching and averting of the gaze. Careful watching by an underling can be used to communicate submission and dutiful attentiveness, as well as to gather feedback or attitude cues from the dominant. But in some cases looking is not useful or appropriate. When receiving the fixed stare of a powerful other, for example, a subordinate may signal submission by averting the eyes.

Finally, it is said that while looking directly at a man, a woman will often have her head slightly tilted. This may imply the beginning of a "present-ing" gesture, or enough submission to render the stare ambivalent if not actually submissive.

It is interesting to note that in a "Dear Abby" survey on what women notice first about men and what men notice first about women, the eyes rank third for both sexes. Comments included such sentiments from women as, "The eyes tell everything," or "You can tell more about a man's character from his eyes than from anything else. His mouth can lie, but his eyes can't." Males' comments included explanations such as, "It tells me whether or not she's interested in me," or "The eyes show kindness, cruelty, warmth, trust, friendliness and compassion—or lack of it."

Facial Expression

Women have been found to be more prone to reveal their emotions in facial expressions than men. A psychologist who conducted an experiment on this subject found that men tended to keep their emotions "all bottled up." Subjects in the experiment (students) were shown slides calculated to arouse strong feelings or emotions. The pictures included scenes that were unpleasant, such as a victim with severe burns; pleasant, such as happy children; unusual, a double-exposed photograph; scenic; or sexual. While the subjects were viewing the slides, their own facial expressions were being picked up over closed-circuit television. The researchers found that it was easier to tell what kind of picture was being shown from viewing the women's facial expressions than from viewing the men's expressions. They concluded that men are "internalizers." Some of the evidence suggesting that men keep their emotions inside were the faster heart beat and greater activity of the sweat glands of males during the experiment.

It is significant to note that while preschool children were found to react differently to pictures, this difference did not seem to occur according to sex but on the basis of individual personality differences. The implication is that while they are growing up males are conditioned by society not to show or express their feelings and females are conditioned to reveal theirs more freely. While perhaps less advantageous in terms of power, it would seem to be healthier to express one's emotions.

Women have been found to be better able to remember names and faces, at least those of high school classmates. A study tested subjects from ages 17 to 47, with men and women put into nine categories, depending on the number of years since they had graduated from high school. In all categories the women's memories were superior to men's in matching names and faces. One would conclude that women are conditioned to associate names with physical characteristics more so than men.

From her study of chimpanzees, Goodall has observed that many of the submissive and aggressive gestures of the chimpanzee closely resemble our own. The chimpanzees have some facial expressions for situations that seem to provide insight when considering the human social environment. One facial expression is the "compressed-lips face" shown by aggressive chimpanzees during a charging display or when attacking others.

Another expression is the "play face" shown during periods of frolicking. The front upper teeth are exposed, and the upper lip is drawn back and up. A "full open grin," with upper and lower front teeth showing and jaws open, is displayed when a chimpanzee is frightened or excited, such as during attack or when a high-ranking male "displays" close to a subordinate. A "low open grin," with the upper lip slightly relaxed to cover the upper front teeth, is shown when the chimpanzee is less frightened or excited.

When the chimpanzee is less frightened or less excited than in the previous situations, "a full closed grin," with upper and lower teeth showing but with jaws closed, may be shown. It is also displayed by a low-ranking chimpanzee, when approaching a superior in silence. Goodall remarked, "If the human nervous or social smile has its equivalent expression in the chimpanzee it is, without doubt, the closed grin." Elsewhere it has been observed that apes use a "rudimentary smile" as an appeasement gesture or to indicate submission. It apparently signals to an aggressor that the subordinate creature intends no harm.

Some writers have pointed out that women smile more than men do, whether or not they are really happy or amused. The smile may be a concomitant of the social status of women and be used as a gesture of submission as a part of their culturally prescribed role. Supposedly the smile is an indicator of submission, particularly from women to men. Silveira indicates two instances in which women are more likely to smile: when a woman and a man greet one another, and when the two are conversing and are only moderately well acquainted. In these situations, rather than indicating friendliness or pleasure, the smile supposedly shows that no aggression or harm is intended. One study found that women tended to smile and laugh more than men during laboratory conversations. Women may have smiled more to cover up uneasiness or nervousness or to meet social expectations. The men who smiled generally did so only after they felt comfortable and to express solidarity or union.

In an investigation of approval seeking, one member in each pair of communicators was instructed to try to either gain or avoid the approval of the other. Those who tried to gain approval used significantly more nonverbal acts, including smiles. There was no difference between the sexes in use of smiles in approval seeking. However, when subjects were instructed to behave so as to avoid the approval of the other, the women avoiding approval tended to smile more often than the men avoiding approval. Perhaps the women were unwilling to withhold this gesture because they believe smiling is expected of them socially, whatever the situation. Or it may be that the forced or ready smile was so much a part of the female subjects' socialization that they used it unconsciously, even when inappropriate for their purposes.

Research has shown that children tend to respond differently to female and male smiles. Children five to eight years old responded to women's smiles, as compared to men's smiles, in a neutral manner. Furthermore, children five to twelve years old tended to react to "kidding" messages, which included a negative statement spoken with a smile, as negative; and the negative interpretation was stronger when the speaker was a woman. Young children's different responses to the smiles of women and men in these studies probably reflect sex differences in the smiling communication patterns of adults.

In another experiment videotapes were made of parents with their children. Half the families in the sample had disturbed children and half had normal children. Ratings were made of the parents' words and smiling during interaction with their children. Results showed that fathers made more positive statements when they smiled than when they did not smile. But mothers' statements were not more positive when they were smiling than when they were not smiling, and sometimes in fact were even slightly more negative when smiling. The pattern was not related to child disturbance.

Mothers in lower-class families smiled considerably less than their middle-class counterparts. Whereas 75 percent of the middle-class mothers smiled more than once, only 13 percent of the lower-class mothers smiled more than once. There was no significant difference between lower- and middle-class fathers in amount of smiling. From the results of this study, it appears that fathers are more sincere when they smile, and they are more likely to be saying something relatively friendlier or more approving when smiling than when they are not smiling. When mothers smile at their children, they may be saying something no more evaluatively positive than when they are not smiling. One may conclude that children are probably "reading" adults accurately when they interpret more friendliness in a male's smile than in a female's smile.

What does the middle-class mother's public smile mean? The researchers suggest that the mother is trying to meet middle-class expectations for a "good" mother, which discourage open expression of negative feelings. Her culturally prescribed role calls for "warm, compliant behavior in public situations." The smile may be used as a kind of softener, or mitigator, of critical statements. Another explanation is that the woman may use a smile as "socially ingratiating behavior," rather than as an indicator of friendliness or approval. One writer suggests that both women and men are

"deeply threatened" by a female who does not smile often enough and who is apparently not unhappy.

A class project by Henley featured a field study in which students smiled at about three hundred persons (half females, half males) in public and recorded whether each individual smiled back or not. Seventy-six percent of the time people returned smiles. But different patterns of smiling could be identified for each sex. Women returned smiles more often, about 89 percent of the time; and they returned smiles more frequently to males (93 percent of the time) than to other females (86 percent). Males returned smiles only 67 percent of the time to females and were even more inhibited in smiling back at other males, which they did only 58 percent of the time. Henley concluded that some short-changing occurs in the tradeoff of smiles between the sexes: "Women are exploited by men—they give 93 percent but receive in return only 67 percent."

Shulamith Firestone represents an extreme but thought-provoking view concerning the smile as a "badge of appeasement." She terms the smile "the child/woman equivalent of the shuffle," since it indicates the acquiescence to power, and she describes her youthful efforts to resocialize herself. "In my own case, I had to train myself out of that phony smile, which is like a nervous tic on every teenage girl. And this meant that I smiled rarely, for in truth, when it came down to real smiling, I had less to smile about." Firestone describes her "'dream' action": ". . . *a smile boycott*, at which declaration all women would instantly abandon their 'pleasing' smiles, henceforth smiling only when something pleased them."

Posture and Bearing

It has been observed that among nonequals in status, superordinates can indulge in a casualness and relative unconcern with body comportment that subordinates are not permitted. For example, one researcher observed that doctors in the hospital had the privilege of sitting in undignified positions at staff meetings and could saunter into the nurses' station and lounge on the station's dispensing counter. Other personnel such as attendants and nurses had to be more circumspect in their bearing. We need no handbook to tell us that in most interactions the person whom we observe sprawling out, leaning back, or propping feet up while the other maintains more "proper" bearing probably has the authority or power role.

A number of nonverbal sex differences in bearing and posture seem to parallel this asymmetry between nonequals. Birdwhistell describes some posture differences between the sexes involving leg, arm, and pelvis positioning. He believes these are among the most easily recognizable American gender identification signals. In fact, he indicates that leg angle and arm-body angle can be measured exactly. Women giving off gender signals are said to bring their legs together, sometimes even to the extent that their upper legs cross or they stand knee over knee. The American male, however, tends to keep legs apart by a 10- to 15-degree angle. Anyone who has ever participated in physical fitness exercises and assumed "attention" and "at ease" stances knows that the male stance is a more relaxed one.

As for arm-body carriage, females are said to keep their upper arms close to the trunk, while the male moves the arms 5 to 10 degrees away from the body in giving gender cues. Males may carry the pelvis rolled slightly back and females slightly forward. In movement, females supposedly present the entire body from neck to ankles as a moving whole. Males, in contrast, move the arms independently from the trunk and may subtly wag the hips with a slight right and left movement involving a twist at the rib cage. The male bearing seems the more relaxed of the two. Johnny Carson once said of Dr. Joyce Brothers, "She sits as if her knees were welded together."

That these are socialized positions may be inferred from the fact that often as women and men grow older or become ill, their gender positions may become underemphasized or indistinguishable. An elderly woman may, for example, sit relaxed with her legs apart. Because this is an inappropriate gender signal, such an action appears bizarre or may be the object of humor. Carol Burnett, portraying an old woman in one of her comedy routines, sometimes uses this position to get laughs.

Research indicates that in social situations, men assume a more relaxed posture than women, no matter what the sex of the other partner is. Males have been found to assume more asymmetric leg positions and more reclining postures than females. Generally females tend to position their bodies more directly facing the person with whom they are communicating than male communicators do.

In one study males and females were asked to imagine themselves communicating with different persons and to sit the way they would if addressing those persons. Torso lean proved to be a distinguishing difference in some cases. There is less sideways lean in communications with high-status persons. Torso lean was more relaxed, more backward, when communicators addressed persons they disliked. Torso lean of the males was farther back than that of the females. Women used less arm openness with high-status persons than with low-status persons. Males showed no difference. Leg openness of female communicators was less than that of male communicators.

It appears from these and a number of related studies that males are generally more relaxed than females, just as higher-status persons are more relaxed than those in subordinate roles. Research also shows that communicators in general are more relaxed with females than with males. They show less body tension, more relaxed posture, and more backward lean. By their somewhat tenser postures, women are said to convey submissive attitudes. Their general bodily demeanor and bearing is more restrained and restricted than men's. But society seems to expect this. Greater circumspection in body movement appears to be required of women, even in all-female groups.

It is considered unfeminine or unladylike for a woman to "use her body too forcefully, to sprawl, to stand with her legs widely spread, to sit with her feet up, . . . to cross the ankle of one leg over the knee of the other." And depending on the type of clothing she wears, "she may be expected to sit with her knees together, not to sit cross-legged, or not even to bend over." Although restrictions on women have relaxed recently, these prescriptions of propriety still seem to be in force. Women who break them are not fully accepted.

The public posture, stance, and gait prescribed for and expected of women can be extremely awkward. In an effort to demonstrate to our classes how inconvenient some of the expected behaviors for women are, the authors have borrowed a six-item list of exercises for men for our male students to perform in class. While the result has often led to merriment over the inability of some males to deftly and convincingly perform these actions, the exercises have served to make both the women and the men aware of the extent to which many of our learned behaviors are unexamined.

The following six sets of directions illustrate the inconvenience of the public postures permitted to women:

1. Sit down in a straight chair. Cross your legs at the ankles and keep your knees pressed together.

2. Bend down to pick up an object from the floor. Each time you bend, remember to bend your knees so that your rear end doesn't stick up, and place one hand on your shirt-front to hold it to your chest.

3. Run a short distance, keeping your knees together. You will find you have to take short, high steps.

4. Sit comfortably on the floor. . . . Arrange your legs so that no one can see [your underwear]. Sit like this for a long time without changing position.

5. Walk down a city street. . . . Look straight ahead. Every time a man walks past you, avert your eyes and make your face expressionless.

6. Walk around with your stomach pulled in tight, your shoulders thrown back, and your chest out. . . . Try to speak loudly and aggressively in this posture.

Gesture

"Every little gesture has a meaning all its own." So go the lyrics of an old song. And though students of kinesics, like Birdwhistell, hasten to warn us that no position, expression, or movement ever carries meaning in and of itself, research in nonverbal communication seems to indicate that patterns of gesture can tell us a good deal about ourselves and others. An important consideration is this: "The more men and women interact in the way they have been trained to from birth without considering the meaning of what they do, the more they become dulled to the significance of their actions." Outsiders who observe a culture different from their own can sometimes spot behavioral differences, and the significance of these differences, which those engaged in the behaviors are not conscious of. Some observational studies help us get outside ourselves and draw our attention to details we might otherwise not notice.

In viewing nonverbal gestures of preschool children, one investigator discovered that girls exhibited more pronounced bodily behavior when they were with other girls than when they were with boys. When they were paired with boys, they tended to be quieter. She concluded that society's expectations of sex differences in social behavior are evident even in the very young child and that different behavior is expected from boys than from girls.

Hand gestures are generally considered to function as illustrators, and they also serve to reveal our emotional states, intentionally or unintentionally. Hand and foot movements can sometimes signal messages at variance with our words. There seems to be some indication that in approval-seeking situations, women use more gesticulations than do males. Since some studies have shown that males talk more, interrupt more, and in general dominate conversations more than females, perhaps women resort to nonverbal expression more frequently. Some have concluded that women are molded into more patterns of behavior than are men, for there are more implicit and explicit rules as to how females should act and behave. Although initiative, innovation, boldness, and action are encouraged in males, such qualities are discouraged in women. "Forced to submerge their individual impulses and energies, women tend to express themselves more subtly and covertly." The nonverbal channel may be an outlet for women's covert and more subtle expression.

Peterson did a videotaped study of nonverbal communication that occurred during verbal communication between male-male, female-female, and female-male pairs. Subjects pairs were university students, and each pair held a two-minute conversation on the topic of their choice. She studied number of gestures, kinds of gestures, gestures used primarily be females, and gestures used primarily by males. She focused on hand, leg, and foot movements.

She found that overall, the number of gestures displayed by males exceeded the number exhibited by females, regardless of the sex of the conversation partner. Males displayed about the same number of gestures when conversing with either sex. However, females displayed significantly more gestures with males than with other females.

As for differences between the sexes in the kinds of gestures used, she observed the following:

Females

tend to leave both hands down on chair arms more than males do

arrange or play with their hair or ornamentation more

Males

use sweeping gestures more than females

use arms to lift or move the body position more

use closed fist more

stroke chin more

sit with ankle of one leg crossing the knee of the other more

tend to exhibit greater amount of leg and foot movement

tap their feet more

In addition, certain gestures seemed to be performed exclusively by females and others by males in this study. An asterisk indicates a more frequently performed gesture.

Female

hand or hands in lap

tapping hands

legs crossed at knees*

ankles crossed, knees slightly apart

Male

stretching hands and cracking knuckles

pointing*

both feet on floor with legs apart

legs stretched out, ankles crossed

knees spread apart when sitting*

General observations that Peterson made in regard to nonverbal gestures and the sexes include the following:

1. Both males and females seemed to be more relaxed with the same sex than with the opposite sex, except in two cases where subjects knew each other previously. Subjects exhibited more nervous gestures with the opposite sex.

2. Exclusively male and exclusively female gestures seemed to be reserved for conversations with the same-sex partner. Pointing generally occurred only between males, and hands in the lap between females.

3. Some traits appeared related to gender display. Females handled their hair and clothing ornamentation a great deal more in front of men than women. Men were significantly more open with their leg position and kept their feet on the floor with legs apart when conversing with other males. With females, however, the men nearly always crossed one ankle over the other knee.

4. Both males and females tended to display a greater number and greater diversity of gestures

with the opposite sex. There seemed to be more foot movement with the same sex.

Peterson believed her study indicated that nonverbal communication fills a dual role in conversation for the sexes. Gesture serves as an illustrator and supplement to the verbal channel, and it acts as a means of gender display. Since certain movements occurred exclusively in same-sex pairs, it is possible that separate nonverbal languages are occurring. There seemed to be a greater display of dominant gestures by males—closed fist, pointing, sweeping gestures. Open and dominant gestures may be signals of power and status.

Clothing, Grooming, and Physical Appearance

Physical attractiveness and the artifacts that contribute to appearance affect communication and communication responses. One study explored the use of physical attractiveness by females as a means of obtaining higher grades from male college professors. The researcher found no differences in the scores of females and males on a Machiavellian scale, which attempts to get at traits associated with those who use any means (cunning, duplicity, or whatever) to achieve a goal. He hypothesized that cultural and social norms may prevent females from using obvious exploitative or deceptive tactics, so they utilize more socially acceptable, but more covert, means and take advantage of their physical attractiveness.

After comparing faculty ratings of women's pictures with their grade-point averages and position in the family, he found a correlation between physical attractiveness, grade point average, and being firstborn and female. Women who used more exhibiting behavior were probably more memorable to professors and thus fared better on grades. They tended to sit in the front of the room more often or come to see the professor after class or during the instructor's office hours more frequently. Using a series of questions about body measurements, the researcher determined that, as he had hypothesized, the firstborn females did indeed seem more aware of and socially concerned about their looks.

In some respects, claimed the researcher, he found the results "not at all surprising," for "the suggestion that *men* live by their *brains* and *women* by their *bodies* was made as far back as Genesis." He found the implications of these results "rather frightening" since the results suggest that the male college professor is a "rather put-upon creature, *hoodwinked* by the *male* students (later born) and *enticed* by the *female* students (first born)." [Italics added.] Whether the reverse is true for female college professors ought to be the subject for future research. As consolation, however, the writer noticed that when a sample of 22 faculty members was given the Machiavellian scale, their average scores, compared with the scores of students in the study, showed them to be significantly more manipulative.

In another experiment, a girl was made up to look unattractive in one setting and attractive in another. The girl read aloud and explained some questions to listeners. Results showed the attitudes of the male students were modified more by the girl in the attractive condition than in the unattractive condition. However, this result was true for a male audience only.

Several years ago, the authors videotaped two women and two men speakers giving persuasive pro and con speeches about the merits of debate. Each gave his or her speech twice: once when made up to look unattractive with nose putty; subtle, unflattering make-up touches; and poorly styled hair and again when made up to look attractive. Clothing was kept constant. The speeches were such that, in the first set, the pro speech was constructed as a cogent and well-reasoned talk and the con speech was poorly reasoned and dogmatic. In the second set, the pro speech was poorly reasoned and dogmatic, and the con speech was cogent and well-reasoned. Listeners, who were college students, took a pretest concerning their attitudes on the subject and then took a post-test following the talks.

Results showed that physical attractiveness did

have a persuasive effect on both sexes in their acceptance of the views of the speakers. Both speakers of the well-reasoned talks had a greater persuasive effect when made up in their attractive state, as was anticipated. An interesting result was a difference in persuasiveness that occurred between the females and males in their unattractive states, whether they gave the poorly reasoned or well-reasoned talk. The males made up unattractively were only slightly less effective than in their attractive state. However, there was considerable difference in the influence of the females, depending on physical state. Unattractiveness in the female caused a decidedly more negative reception of her views. In fact, in one of the videotaped versions the unattractiveness of the female who delivered the cogent pro talk weighed so heavily that the attractive female who answered with the poorly reasoned and ill-constructed con speech had the greater impact on listeners. Both females and males seemed more accepting of arguments or views from an unattractive male than from an unattractive female. Males were most negative toward the unattractive female's stand. Another study showed that regardless of sex, attractive people are rated high on character in credibility scales.

In a "Dear Abby" reader survey mentioned earlier, readers were asked to indicate what they noticed first about the opposite sex. Results indicated that women noticed physique first. Added the columnist: "But nearly every female who wrote that it is the first thing she *notices* about a man also wrote that it was certainly not the most *important*." A close second was grooming, including attire. Most women who wrote that they noticed a man's physical attributes first emphasized that it is "what's on the inside" that counts. Women placed much more importance on behavior than the men did in their survey. Responses from men indicated that men noticed bosoms first. After bosoms, a woman's figure, or whole torso, ranked next in importance, with some male respondents terming themselves "leg men" or "fanny fanciers."

These studies, as well as the casual responses to the "Dear Abby" column, seem to reflect our cultural emphasis on a man's activity—what he does—and on a woman's being—how she appears. This was graphically illustrated last year at Arizona State University, where one of the authors teaches. Several men stationed themselves in front of the student union with signs numbered from 4 to 9. They proceeded to rate women on campus by holding numbered signs over the women's heads as they passed. After the university police were summoned to investigate complaints, one of the self-appointed raters explained lamely. "It seemed to me that everyone in the area enjoyed what we did, except for one woman who asked for a sign so she could rate one of us. Of course I refused."

Perhaps women in our society are expected to be more visible and to reveal more of their bodies than men are. Men are sometimes described as more modest than women. This, at least, was the view of Hollywood dress designer Edith Head during an interview. Head has dressed stars from Cary Grant to Robert Redford, and Carole Lombard to Elizabeth Taylor. "Men for the most part are annoyingly modest in the fitting room if a woman is present," she says. "Women, however, will peel off to their panties and bras with male fitters present without batting an eye." She cited Clark Gable as one who was extremely modest. He could bare his chest, but if he had to unzip his trousers and expose his shorts, "he would bluster and blush and make amusing remarks about what he had to go through for his art." Head mentioned a friend who was the head nurse in a urology clinic. "She faces up to male modesty all day long and it's a bore. Women, for the most part, do not have false modesty about their bodies." The references to modesty in all instances refer to mixed company.

The significance of clothing should be noted in passing. Different clothing types for the sexes is believed by some to have important social ramifications. Of course, pants suits for women have been and are worn extensively today, along with skirts, yet pants remain the symbol of the male and skirts the symbol of the female. Some writers question the notion that skirts should be worn by females. The roles of both sexes are changing. Women are moving out of old patterns, acquiring more education, exercising control of their childbearing, and getting political power. Yet, say some, they are still dressed in an archaic manner, with hips, thighs, and stomach skirted protectively or defensively hidden. Specialists in the history of dress indicate that the differentiation of pants and skirts goes back many years. Skirts may have been important once to protect the one who bore children because in early ages humans were more at the mercy of the elements, dangerous animals, human enemies, and high infant mortality. Presumably then, men were in awe of women's life-giving power and felt it necessary to "protect women's gateway to birth with skirts."

The division of pants from skirts may have been made originally because men needed freedom of leg movement when hunting and working the soil. Women needed skirts to hide their children under if danger threatened, to protect their own bodies, and to form convenient carrying places to convey children or food. Moira Johnston, a clothing historian, believes that skirts later became a male constriction for females because men feared the power a woman's childbearing ability gave her. So they consigned her sexuality to hiding. Later on the skirt became a form of modesty and an attempt to conceal seductive areas.

According to Johnston, the silhouette loosens when morals are lowered, as for example in the Roaring Twenties with the loose flapper dress. After the Second World War, when women went back to the home and to childbearing, fashions became more constrictive and restrictive. Women wore clothing cinched at the waist, with long, full skirts and high-heeled shoes. In looking at the history of feminism, one writer notes the significance of clothing. Before the 1920s women's clothing was confining and cumbersome. Casting aside the old corsets and long skirts may have had more significance for women's emancipation than women's suffrage had.

Henley notes that women's clothing today is fashioned to be revealing, but it still restricts women's body movement. Women are not supposed to reveal too much, and this required guarded movement in many cases. Another concomitant of clothing designed to reveal physical features is that, unlike more loose-fitting men's clothing, there are not convenient pockets in which to carry belongings—hence women's awkward purses. Some men's clothing styles today are styled for closer fit, and this may account for the carrying bags and purselike cases made and sold for males in some places. A clothing historian hypothesized that women have not freed themselves more from skirts and other restrictive women's clothing styles because they fear "terror of disorientation, and dissolution of identity."

In reflecting upon contemporary feminine clothing styles, the authors of this book would add this thought: The popular pants suit has had a liberating effect upon females. No longer must knees be tightly drawn together when sitting. Pants allow much more freedom of movement when walking, sitting on the floor, or lounging on the arm of a chair. The traditional need to cover and protect the female genital area by posture and apparel has been reduced considerably.

The so-called unisex look in clothing has freed women's bosoms from the protective slouch and the provocative thrust. It would be interesting to do research on how attitudes of the wearer are changed when clothing habits are modified. Perhaps it is true that we are what we wear!

Use of Space

The way we use space can convey nonverbal messages. It has been observed that dominant animals and dominant human beings keep a larger buffer zone of personal space surrounding them that discourages violation than do subordinate animals and humans. Dominant persons are not approached as closely as persons of lesser status. But research has shown that women are approached by both sexes more closely than men.

In one study, university students carried tape measures with them and when approached by anyone who began a conversation, each student measured the distance nose-to-nose between themselves and each speaker. Distances between pairs varied according to sex, age, and race. It was found that generally women were approached more closely than men by both women and men. Perhaps the envelope of inviolable space surrounding women is generally less than men's, and women are perceived as less dominant. Further, compared with men, women stand more closely to good friends but farther away from those they describe just as friends. It has been suggested that perhaps women are more cautious until they have established close relationships. In addition, it has been found that less distance is maintained between women and members of both sexes when they are sitting. There are indications that compared with men, women perceive their own territory as being smaller and as being more open to influence by others. Both sexes have been found more wary of the approach of males than of females.

Studies on crowding offer some insight on differences in personal space between the sexes. One researcher observed groups of people in crowded and uncrowded rooms during one-hour periods of time. Results showed that generally men had more negative reactions to crowding. They liked others less and considered them less friendly. In general, they found the situation more unpleasant, and they became more contentious and distrustful. In contrast, women found the experience pleasanter, liked others more, and considered them friendlier than men did.

It appears that women's territory is perceived as smaller by both males and females. Women may be more tolerant of, or accustomed to, having their personal space breeched by others. This may also be an indication that they are considered to be of lower status by those with whom they interact.

Certainly control of greater territory and space is a characteristic we associate with dominance and status. Superiors have the prerogative of taking more space. They have larger houses, estates, cars, offices, and desks, as well as more personal space in body spread. Inferiors own less space and take up less space personally with their bodies. Females generally command less space. For example, a study showed that women are less likely to have a special and unviolated room in the home. The male may have his den where "nothing is to be touched." Some will counter that the woman has her territory—her kitchen or sewing room. But this space is often as infinitely invadable for the woman working in it as her time while she is doing so. We are all familiar with Archie Bunker's special chair. While men may have their own chair in a house, women rarely do.

Seating arrangement is another space variable. Research shows that female/male status is evident in the way people seat themselves. At rectangular tables, generally the "head" position (the seat at either end of the table) is associated with higher status. Subjects in a study were shown paper-and-pencil diagrams of rectangular tables and asked how they would locate themselves with regard to a person of higher, lower, or equal status and of either sex. When subjects were asked to choose the seat they would take upon arriving first and then to name the seat the other would then take, approximately twice as many females as males would sit side by side, and this was more frequent in relation to a low-status than a high-status person. When asked to choose which seat the other would take upon arriving first, respondents tended to put others at an "end" chair. This tendency was greater for a high-status male authority figure. Subjects were also told to imagine that either Professor Henry Smith or Professor Susan Smith were there. Twice as many subjects would choose the head chair for themselves when the female professor was there as when the male professor was there.

Students in one of our classes did some observational studies of female and male students walking across the Arizona State University campus during peak class-change times in the heavily trafficked mall areas. They found people of both sexes tend to cut across females' paths more frequently.

When female-male pairs approach each other on the street, apparently women are expected to walk around men, according to the results of one study. Nineteen woman-man pairs were observed, and in 12 out of the 19, the woman moved out of the man's way. In only 3 cases did the man move, and in the remaining 4 instances both moved.

When women approached women or men approached men, however, about half of the time both moved out of each other's way. The rest of the time only one person moved.

Also in regard to space, it has been observed that women's general body comportment is restrained. Often their femininity is judged according to how little space they take up. Women condense or compress; men expand. Whereas males use space expansively, women, by the way they cross their legs, keep their elbows to their sides, and maintain a more erect posture, seem to be trying to take up as little space as possible. Novelist Marge Piercy, describing a character teaching movement to a theater group, put it well:

Men expanded into available space. They sprawled, or they sat with spread legs. They put their arms on the arms of chairs. They crossed their legs by putting a foot on the other knee. They dominated space expansively. Women condensed. Women crossed their legs by putting one leg over the other and alongside. Women kept their elbows to their sides, taking up as little space as possible. They behaved as if it were their duty not to rub against, not to touch, not to bump a man. If contact occurred, the woman shrank back. If a woman bumped a man, he might choose to interpret it as a come-on. Women sat protectively using elbows not to dominate space, not to mark territory, but to protect their soft tissues.

Touch

Touch has been the object of some investigation. Most research seems to show that females are touched by others more than males are. Mothers have been found to touch their female children more than their male children from the age of six months on. In one study of touch, the researcher gave a questionnaire to students concerning which parts of the body are touched most often and by whom. He found that females are considerably more accessible to touch by all persons than males are. Friends of the opposite sex and mothers did the most touching.

Further investigation showed that mothers touched their sons more than fathers did, and fathers touched their daughters more than their sons. Daughters touched their fathers more than sons did, and sons touched their mothers more than they touched their fathers. In other words, fathers and sons tended to refrain from touching each other, but other touching interaction in the family was about equal. As for body regions, mothers touched daughters in more places than they did sons. Fathers touched daughters in more places than they did sons. Fathers also were touched by their daughters in more places than they were by their sons. Males touched their opposite-sex best friends in more regions than females reported touching their opposite-sex friends. So in three of the four comparisons, touch by fathers, touch by mothers, and touch by opposite-sex friends, females were touched more. The mean total being-touched score for women was higher than for men. Also, whereas women's opposite-sex friends touched them the most, men's opposite-sex friends touched them the least.

The pattern of greater touching by males has been interpreted by some as a reflection of sexual interest and greater sexual motivation of men. Henley does not accept this, since she finds research does not support greater sexuality in males than females. Rather, she regards touching as a sign of status or power. Touching is an invasion of one's personal space and involves the deference or lack of deference accorded to the space surrounding the body. Touching between intimates can symbolize friendship and affection. But when the pattern of touching is not reciprocal, and both parties do not take equal touch privileges, it can indicate power and status. An observer of the touch system in a hospital noted that although the doctors might touch other ranks to convey support or comfort, other ranks tended to feel it would be presumptuous to return a doctor's touch, and particularly to initiate it.

One investigation of touching involved some 60 hours of observing incidents of touching in public. Intentional touch with the hand was recorded, as well as whether the touch was returned. Sex, age, and approximate socioeconomic status of the persons observed was also noted. Results showed that higher-status persons touched lower-status ones significantly more frequently. Comparing touching between the sexes, men touched women at a greater rate, when all else (age and apparent socioeconomic status) was equal. When other things were unequal, for example if women had a socioeconomic status advantage, the women would be the more likely one to initiate touch.

The pattern of sexual status showed up primarily in outdoor settings (shopping plaza, beach, college campus, and so forth) rather than in indoor interaction (bank, store, restaurant, doctor's office, and so on). It was suggested that because outdoor interaction is more public, it may necessitate stricter attention to signals of power. Indoor interaction is more informal and encourages more relaxed power relationships. When people are indoors, power can probably be more easily communicated by other cues than touching. Subtle cues, such as eye movements, gestures, and voice shifts, can convey reminders of status easily. But outdoors gross, larger physical acts, such as touching, seem to be required.

Goodall describes one use of touch among chimpanzees. A chimpanzee, after being threatened or attacked by a superior, may follow the aggressor around, screaming and crouching to the ground or holding out his or her hand. The chimpanzee is begging a reassuring touch from the superior. Sometimes the subordinate chimpanzee will not relax until he or she has been touched or patted and embraced. Greetings also reestablish the dominance status of one chimpanzee in relation to the other. For example, Olly would greet Mike by holding out her hand toward him. By this gesture she was acknowledging his superior rank. Mike would touch, pat, or hold her hand or touch her head in response to her submission. These gestures of dominance and submission observed in primates seem to occur among humans as well. As with apes, the gestures used are probably used by humans to maintain and reinforce the social hierarchy by reminding lower-status persons of their position in the order and by reassuring higher-status people

that those of lesser rank accept their place in the pecking order.

An informal test of the significance of touch that is not reciprocated and the authority it symbolizes would be to ask ourselves which person in each of the following pairs would be more likely to touch the other—to lay a hand on the back, put an arm around the shoulder, tap the chest, or grasp the wrist: master and servant; teacher and student; pastor and parishioner; doctor and patient; foreman and worker; executive and secretary; police and accused; lawyer and client. If status can explain touch differences in other groups, it seems reasonable to accept this as a factor in female/male touch differences as well.

A considerable amount of touching of women is so much a part of our culture that it goes virtually unnoticed. It occurs when men guide women through the door, down the stairs, into the car, across the street; when they playfully lift women; when they pat them on the head, or playfully spank them; and in many other instances. Males seem to have greater freedom to touch others. When used with objects, touching seems to connote possession. This may apply to attitudes about women as well. As Henley and Thorne express it: "... the wholesale touching of women carries the message that women are community property. They are tactually accessible just as they are visually and informationally accessible."

It is interesting to consider the difference in interpretation of touch by the sexes. This difference seems to support the idea that touch is used as a sign of status or power among the sexes. The difference in female/male perspective can be shown by an illustration which Henley relates. A woman was at a party one evening and saw a male friend of both her and her husband. At various times in the evening he would come up and sit with his arm around her. This she interpreted as a friendly gesture, and she reciprocated the action with friendly intent. However, later the man approached her in private and made sexual advances. When the woman expressed surprise at his suggestions, he replied, "Wasn't that what you were trying to tell me all evening?" The point is that

Table 1 Asymmetrical Nonverbal Cues

Cues	Superior [male]	Subordinate [female]
Eyes	Look or stare aggressively Look elsewhere while speaking	Lower eyes, avert eyes, look away, blink Watch speaker while listening
Face	No smile or frown Impassive, not showing emotions	Smile Expressive facial gestures, showing emotions
Posture	Relaxed, more body lean	Tense, more erect
Bearing	Loose legs, freed arms, non-circumspect positions	Tight, legs together, arms close to body
Gestures	Larger, more sweeping, forceful, such as pointing	Smaller, more inhibited
Touch	Touches other	Does not touch other or reciprocate touch, cuddles, or yields to touch
Use of space	Expands, uses more space	Condenses, contracts, takes as little space as possible
Distance	Maintains larger envelope of space Closer Approaches closer, crowds Cuts across other's path Walks into other's path	Maintains smaller envelope of space More distant Approaches more distant, retreats, yields Gives way Moves out of the way
Clothing	Loose, comfortable	Constraining, formfitting

Source: Some of the material in this table was suggested by Nancy Henley, "Examples of Some Nonverbal Behaviors with Usage Differing for Status Equals and Nonequals, and for Women and Men," *Siscom '75: Women's (and Men's) Communication*, ed. Barbara Eakins, Gene Eakins, and Barbara Lieb-Brilhart (Falls Church, Va.: Speech Communication Association, 1976), Table 1, p. 39; and Henley, "Gestures of Power and Privilege. Examples of Some Nonverbal Behaviors with Usage Differing for Status Equals and Nonequals, and For Women and Men," *Body Politics: Power, Sex, and Nonverbal Communication* (Englewood Cliffs, N.J.: Prentice-Hall, 1977), Table 5, p. 181.

women do not interpret a man's touch as necessarily a sexual invitation, but men often interpret a woman's touch in that way. Touch, of course, can be either. It can be a gesture of power or of intimacy. But touch as a gesture of power will appear to be inappropriate if it is used by one not having power.

Since women are often subordinate, touching by women will be perceived as a gesture of intimacy or sexual invitation rather than power. One would not anticipate that they would be exercising power. In addition, viewing a woman's gesture as a sexual invitation in not only complimentary to the man, but it can put the woman at a disadvantage. By

putting a narrower sexual interpretation on what she does and placing her in the position of a sex object, she is effectively placed outside the arena of primary social interaction.

STATUS AND NONVERBAL COMMUNICATION

We have looked at a number of nonverbal behavior differences exhibited by females and males. One theoretical thread running through much of the discussion is the concept of asymmetry, or non-reciprocality of behavior, that exists between non-equals in status. Female/male differences have been seen to roughly parallel those between superiors and subordinates in status, suggesting a status and power differential behind the socialization of the sexes. Table 1, which is based on theory and some research cited previously, categorizes behavior cues used by females and males.

To a certain extent we may say that behavior is cued. Perhaps women give gestures of submission because they have been shown gestures of dominance. In some situations some people may use gestures of dominance because they have been shown gestures of acquiescence or ingratiation by the others with whom they interact. One writer had some sobering pronouncements to make concerning many of the so-called womanly gestures. She indicated that submission in women is conveyed by such behaviors as smiling, averting the eyes, or lowering or turning the head. Self-improvement specialists would grow pale on hearing her definition of charm: "Charm is nothing more than a series of gestures (including vocalizations) indicating submission!" Staunch feminists would probably add a hearty "amen."

Changing or manipulating the signals and indicators of power or subordination may not go very far toward transforming the inequities of society. But perhaps by becoming aware of what we are signifying or are responding to nonverbally, we can better gain control over our lives and more readily ensure that our actions and responses are more conscious, more voluntary or, at least, less automatic. We may surprise ourselves by the extent to which we can affect the patterns and relationships in our lives.

To Hear One and Understand Ten: Nonverbal Behavior in Japan

SHEILA RAMSEY

A cool fall afternoon somewhere in the middle of Tokyo, two American friends are exploring a Shinto shrine dedicated to a famous World War II Japanese general. The grounds are empty. Over to one side is a raised wooden ramp covered by a red carpet; it appears to be a passageway leading from the shrine to the priests' living quarters. Wanting to take a photograph, one woman, new to Japan, is about to step onto the ramp:

A: Hey, you shouldn't step up there!

B: Why not?

A: Because you just shouldn't.

B: I don't see any signs.

A: There are signs all around you.

B: Where?

A: The red carpet is a sign, the raised floor ... anyway, you almost never step up to another level in Japan without taking your shoes off.

B: Sorry, but how I am I supposed to know?

This essay, prepared especially for this volume, is a revised and condensed version of a presentation given at the Second International Conference on Nonverbal Behavior, Toronto, 1984. Permission to reprint must be obtained from the author. The original version appears in *Nonverbal Behavior: Perspectives, Applications, and Intercultural Insights*, A. Wolfgang (ed.), C. J. Hogrefe, Inc., Toronto, 1984. The author wishes to thank the many students and colleagues in Japan whose insights and research make this discussion possible. Dr. Ramsey is a trainer/consultant for the Intercultural Relations Institute, Palo Alto, California.

This brief, and seemingly insignificant, exchange is focused on disagreement about what constitutes a sign. Person B is expecting that rules will be made explicit in writing; by saying "I don't see any signs" she is looking for an actual sign post with DO NOT STEP HERE printed in bold letters. Person A "reads" the rules just as clearly as if they were written, but her "sign post" is the interrelationships among architecture, objects, and a total sense of presence interpreted through the experience of several years of living in Japan. Certainly there is no intent on the part of Person B to be rude or insensitive; she is simply not functioning with culturally appropriate assumptions about where to find meaning to guide her behavior. In her own defense, Person B asks a very critical question: "But how am I supposed to know?"

Examining this exchange can give rise to a particular perspective about the role of nonverbal behavior in Japanese daily life and how non-Japanese might begin to adapt more effectively to living and working with the Japanese. Basically, this incident illustrates that it is very necessary to learn about common Japanese nonverbal behaviors such as gestures or the dictates of architectural form, and also that it is critical to examine *how* such knowledge is to be learned. The process by which the learning occurs greatly affects how any understanding is applied to interactions with the Japanese.

"NONVERBAL JAPAN?"

It is especially interesting to examine the role of nonverbal behavior in the life of the Japanese because of their self-awareness as a people who *consciously* value and rely upon this channel of communication. Despite the fact that there are close to one million foreign residents in Japan and that dialectical differences sometimes make communication between Okinawa and Sapporo difficult, the Japanese do think of themselves as a very homogeneous "we." It is common to hear, "we Japanese prefer" or "It is the Japanese way to do it like that." A Japanese scholar explains the effects of such a view:

Others have tried to qualify Japan's homogeneity.... In spite of all this, no one would deny that present-day Japan is more homogeneous than any other foreign country in the world.... The members share a great many aspects of their daily life and consciousness. Thus, explanations through the medium of language often become unnecessary, and the intuitive, nonverbal communication of the sort that develops among family members living under the same roof spreads throughout the society. (Kunihiro 1976, p. 53)

Certainly it is true that people who have long-term and close-knit relationships develop an increased ability to "read between the lines" and use gestures or glances to convey meaning (Ramsey 1976). It is significant however that an entire culture of 120 million people would continually choose to value the similarity of goals and expressive behaviors necessary if reliance on the nonverbal channel is to be effective.

Morsbach provides insightful detail about the development of this view as he explains the influence of geographic and political isolation (Morsbach 1973). In early Japan, farming villages were isolated from each other; strangers rarely joined a village and members rarely left. In the process of mutual cooperation as rice was planted or seaweed harvested, villagers were intensely involved with each other. Nakane suggests the effects of such involvement:

With his social environment so limited, the sign of an individual's relations within his own group becomes proportionately more intensified. Obligations and expectations among the members of the group are exacting; members of a group know each other exceedingly well—one's family life, love affairs, even the limits of one's capacity for cocktails are intimately known to the others. Among fellow members a single word would suffice for the whole sentence. The mutually sensitive response goes so far that each easily recognizes the other's slightest change in behavior or mood and is ready to act accordingly. (Nakane, 1970, p. 121)

Japan is rightly known as a group-oriented, hierarchy-conscious society. Though the majority of the Modern Japanese live in very Westernized cities, each belongs to office, school, neighborhood, or social activity groups to which Nakane's description applies. A reliance on nonverbal over verbal expression not only follows from intimacy but is also used precisely to manage intimacy. Knowing that one will be working with or living next to the same people for a long time, it is important to pay careful attention to getting along amicably. Indeed the Japanese value *wa*—harmony—above objective truth or principle as they live daily in a *ningen kankei* (human relations) reality. "In order to attain an end, whether social or nonsocial, the creation, maintenance, or manipulation of a relevant social relationship is a foremost and indispensable means" (Lebra 1976, p. 4). The Japanese know that direct expression of emotions or explicitly stating an opinion or a preference may bring more negative than positive effects if one's relationship to the other is the primary concern. The meanings of nonverbal behaviors can be interpreted more ambiguously than those of words; by relying on behavior one can more safely suggest, hint, or imply an opinion or desire and check on how the other responds before continuing; it is much easier to avoid embarrassing confrontations when interpretation is left up to the receiver. These are only a few reasons why messages sent via nonverbal behavior are preferred over verbal messages in long-term well-acquainted groups where harmony is the most desired state.

Examining Japanese esthetic and moral attitudes toward communication uncovers the importance of restraint and of its extreme, suppression. The importance of nonverbal behavior again becomes clear, in that behavior must be carefully monitored and verbal communication is constrained. In *The Sony Vision* Lyons comments, "Frankness. That was the most difficult trait for the Japanese.... The American often wears his self on his face; the Japanese contains it, protects it" (Lyons 1976, pp. 129–130).

Exploring the adjustment difficulties of young Japanese who are living for a brief time in the United States, a recent study suggested that discomfort with why Americans "could not control their emotions" was a large problem (Hartung 1983). A well-known experimental study by Friesen illustrates that the Japanese show more expression on their faces in private than in public settings (Friesen 1972). When the Japanese are asked to compare their own nonverbal behaviors with those of Americans, they often make comments about not using "as much" as Americans. Such a measurement usually means that the Japanese do not see themselves as being overtly and outwardly expressive in the size of gestures used or in the expressiveness of facial muscle movement. If adults take on such "American" behavior they are felt to be childish and *kiza* or showy and foreign. A more mature person will take on a more quiet, refined style (Tada 1975).

The ideal of restraint is quite evident in the self-presentation of Japanese women. Modern schools of etiquette teach women how to move so that the lines of a *kimono* are kept straight and so that only the proper amount of skin is seen. Observations in coffee shops, classrooms, on the train, or in parks confirm that Japanese women are culturally required to take up less space than men and to restrain their emotions, thus conforming to more traditional definitions of femininity (Frieze and Ramsey 1976; Ramsey 1981). Several studies, done on the campus of an international university in Japan, illustrate how subtle the idea of restraint and suppression may be and how conforming to this ideal may be difficult for some Japanese women. (Chen et al. 1980 in Ramsey 1984). On this campus there are Japanese who enter at the "regular" time, April, and those who enter later, in September, because they have been studying abroad. They are labeled "Aprils" and "Septembers"; it is easy to identify, with a high degree of accuracy, women who belong to each group. Over a period of two years, experimental and observational studies have helped to uncover the nonverbal cues of dress and demeanor that are the basis for this distinction (see Table 1).

The "September" women are, basically, less restrained in their movements and in the amount of

Table 1

	Aprils	*Septembers*
Clothing	Polo shirts in summer Blouses buttoned to the top with lace and bows at the neck Bobby socks or knee-socks with skirts; nylon stockings under socks Dressy jeans Rubber rain boots in the rain	Shorts and tank tops in summer Low neck lines No socks with skirts and no nylons with socks; bare legs in summer Baggy jeans with patches as well as dressy jeans Infrequent use of rubber rain boots
Gesture	Axis of gesture at wrist Cover mouth when laughing Does not call or wave across a long distance	Axis of gesture at elbow or shoulder Open mouth when laughing—head thrown back Greets across distance with full-arm wave and calls out name
Posture: Seated	Upright in classroom chair; arms and legs symmetrical On grass: *seiza* (sit on knees) or legs folded to side, knees together	Asymmetrical arms and legs in chair; slouch down in seat On grass: tailor fashion, knees apart
Posture: Walking	Arms held close to body Hips relatively stable	Free-swinging arms Side-to-side hip motion

skin they are willing to expose; they take up more space as they walk and sit. The gesture of covering the face or mouth area when laughing, or hiding the head when embarrassed, is usually dropped by "Septembers." Another detailed study of the "Kinesics of Femininity" explored this particular behavior and found that Japanese and American women have very different feelings about such behavior. By Japanese "April" women, the behaviors were judged "cute," "polite," "shy," "feminine," and "childish" and were given positive evaluations. American women used such labels as "silly," "immature," "childish," and "vain"—the evaluation was more negative. The behavior produced similar labels but the interpretations and consequences of the behaviors varied greatly between the two cultures. A major variable in both these studies of the nonverbal behaviors of Japanese women is the role that restraint and suppression plays in determining how a woman should behave. It seems that the American equivalent of "sexy" is "cute" for

Japanese women. These ideas have very different psychological as well as behavioral connotations. Decisions about how to incorporate the Japanese expectations into daily behavior have serious consequences for "Septembers" who have lived abroad, as they attempt to re-enter Japanese culture (Muro 1983).

The value of suppression and restraint has deep historical roots for the Japanese. It is related to the *enryo* norm that has pervaded Japanese interpersonal relations. *Enryo* means hesitancy or restraint; it is written with two Chinese characters meaning "think" and "distance." This suggests the withdrawal of self for the sake of the relationship (Handa 1983). Controlling the emotions was an ideal for those of the *samurai* class during the Tokugawa Period (1603–1867). "It was considered unmanly for a *samurai* to betray his emotions on his face . . . calmness of behavior, composure of mind, should not be disturbed by passion of any kind" (Nitobe 1969, pp. 104–105). During the 250 years in which

Japan considered herself closed to outside influences, prescribed rules regulating dress, ways of sitting or standing, and even breathing were solidified. In explaining much of their present-day nonverbal behavior, the Japanese call on these restrictions on behavior to maintain hierarchy and class structure. After the Meiji Restoration of 1867–8, when Japan reopened her ports, many *samurai* became bureaucrats; their esthetic tastes and regulations governing behavior greatly influenced those of the common people.

Minimizing behavioral expressiveness as an ideal can also be found in the world of Japanese aesthetics. *Noh*, a form of masked theater dating back some seven hundred years and originally supported by the aristocratic class, seeks to communicate by silence and suggestion. A *Noh* actor says that he has just turned eighty years old and moves one foot slightly forward; in that half step the audience is to imagine the quality of his eighty years. A glance at a *Noh* mask reveals a "blank" face—it reveals no overt emotion. Upon close observation, the eyes seem somewhat sorrowful and the corners of the mouth curve upward as if in a slight smile. The same mask can actually display subtle shades of emotion ranging from grief to happiness, depending upon the angle of tilt. To express joy, the mask is tilted upward; for sorrow the mask is tilted downward. Holding of one or both hands over the mask conveys deep sorrow. Control is ever present, and "the suppressed expressions enable us to imagine deeper" (Masuda 1971, p. 26). The expectation that a listener or audience will infer meaning based on nonverbal cues helps in part to explain the style of modern Japanese advertising. In particular, television commercials may not begin with overt reference to the product; sometimes the detailed features of a product are totally lacking. The product may not be shown until the end of the scene and even then it may not receive direct attention. George Fields speaks about four characteristics of Japanese commercials (Yamaki 1980, p. 56).

1. The expression is ambiguous.

2. An indirect style is preferred over a direct one.

3. Overt declarations are intentionally avoided.

4. Form and formalities are emphasized.

The audience is required to participate in creating the link between the product and images that have no "logical" connection but rather create a mood associated with the use or qualities of the product. Japanese commercials do less overt thinking for the audience than do American commercials. One particular television commercial for a top-of-the-line Toyota shows the car being driven down a country lane; it stops, and a woman in a *kimono* and a man in a suit emerge. As they walk around the car the camera shows a close-up shot of a green leaf that had fallen on the windshield. There are drops of moisture on the leaf and the window; birds are heard in the background. The man and the woman walk up next to a potter who is looking at a recently fired bowl. Silence. The potter throws the bowl to the ground; it breaks. The couple get back in the car and drive away. Frequently, Western audiences react to such an ad by wondering first what the product is and secondly what such a scene has to do with selling a car. The implication is: perfection as it is associated with the skill of a master craftsman. This scene has no sound, except for the birds. The message is communicated completely through careful construction of visual environment and mood to tease the imagination and invite viewer involvement. Commercials that clearly spell out cost-benefit advantages, or supply a factual analysis of why Brand A is three times more effective than Brand D, represent a "say ten thoughts with ten thoughts" attitude, which leaves little for the receiver to do but decide whether or not to buy the product.

Although the previous example of the Toyota ad is not representative of all Japanese advertising, it clearly illustrates a highly valued form of expression. This preference is echoed in the seventeen syllable poetic form *haiku*, in which events or environments are described just as they are.

On a withered bough
A crow alone is perching;
Autumn evening now.

—*Bashō*

Brushing the leaves
A white camellia blossom
Fell into the dark well.

Each *haiku* usually has the three elements of where, what, and when; standardized words may be used to suggest season. "Cherry blossom" represents spring, and "dragonfly," summer. These conventions help to guide the reader's intuitive responses. In *haiku*, "There is no time or place explicitly for reflection, for judgments, or for observers' feelings. There is only speaking, impassioned object, with its 'extraordinary powers to set up echoes in the readers' mind' " (Yasuda 1957, pp. 30–31).

Japanese brush painting, *sumie*, is remarkable for the relationship between line and "empty" space, full of meaning. To "hear one and understand ten," based upon the nonverbal components of the situation, is a theme found repeatedly in "Westernized" Japan. A poignant example comes from the current visitor pamphlet to the Hamada folk craft museum in the well-known pottery town of Mashiko. The last sentence reads: "In consideration of the visitor's personal response, detailed aesthetic descriptions are omitted. The exhibits are given brief labels only."

Whether attending a *Noh* play or viewing a modern TV commercial, audiences become very involved, as they must watch carefully to infer meaning from the tilt of a mask or the elegance of a handmade bowl. This ability to "hear one and understand ten" is also historically valued. Present-day Japanese value catching on quickly to another's intention or desire before the thought is completely expressed verbally. *Haragei* (*hara*, belly, and *gei*, sensitivity) is described as *the* Japanese way of communication. The *hara* is a metaphor for intuitive pre-logical understanding cultivated by an effective communicator. *Ishin-denshin* (intuitive sense) is another referent for this preference. The Japanese communication scholar Ishii has developed the *Enryo-Sasshi* Communication Model to describe this process. *Enryo* means reserve or restraint while *sasshi* means to surmise or guess. The model explains the behavior of a Japanese sender who filters his own behavior and a Japanese receiver who pays great attention to what is not said, to what is suggested, in order to "expand the message" by filling in (Ishii 1973).

Japanese scholars are also quick to point out that a distrust of words can be traced back to ancient texts of the seventh or eighth century. The concept of *kotodama* (word-spirit) suggested that words were felt to have spirits of their own so that speaking about something could cause it to happen. *Kotoage*, or speaking boldly, was discouraged. During the Feudal Period (thirteenth—mid-nineteenth century) this belief in *kotodama* became less powerful, yet speaking out against superiors was still discouraged. There are many proverbs from this time, still quoted today, that caution that (1) the mouth is useful (so it can play tricks), (2) a wise man is silent, (3) a lie is expedient, and (4) one should rely on nonverbal messages. Examples include: "to say nothing is a flower"; "what is within is revealed by the color of the face"; "sounds like paradise, looks like hell"; "those who know do not speak, those who speak do not know"; and "with your mouth, you can build Osaka castle." There are very few proverbs that view oral communication as productive and meaningful (Kato 1961). As Morsbach summarizes, "Basically, the most ubiquitous lesson about speech in Japanese proverbs is 'shut up' " (Morsbach 1973).

As suggested previously, the Japanese often explain their present-day communication style by calling on their historical and religious past and on the peculiarities of geography. The Western linguist Roy Andrew Miller is quite skeptical about the historical foundations of this reliance on nonverbal behavior. In his book *Japan's Modern Myth: The Language and Beyond*, he attacks the myth of *Nihongo* and the "Antimyth of Silence." According to Miller, in the myth of *Nihongo* the Japanese claim that their language is unique from all others, having a special character that . . . "makes it possible for Japanese society to use it for a variety of supralinguistic or nonverbal communication not enjoyed by any other society" (p. 11). The "Antimyth of Silence" (Chapter 5) states that Japan is a nation "not of language, but of silence. Our forte is nonverbal communication. And if you thought our language was difficult to learn and impossible to master, then how, the antimyth taunts, can you ever hope to become fluent in our silence?" (p. 85). Miller claims that the *kotodama* theories, and the antimyth that Japan is "a land of mysterious, silent nonverbal communication," were the result of willful manipulation of a 1937 government document, *Kokutai no Hongi*, by a powerful fascist nationalist clique. This document proclaimed the official state teachings on matters of policy and culture. Miller comments that

The old texts were cited as if to prove that the earliest period of Japanese life had put a premium upon not expressing personal views and that it had valued not verbalizing opinions. The texts were invoked to make a virtue out of silence endured in the face of conflict . . . particularly those of a political nature. It would be difficult to find a more blatant example of the harm that can be done by twisting innocent passages in early texts in order to make them into "proof texts" that would appear to support goals totally unrelated to their original sense (Miller 1983, p. 100).

Whether or not the historical origins of Japan's reliance on nonverbal behavior are pure, the fact that the Japanese claim them to be is necessary in understanding modern Japan.

INTERACTING WITH THE JAPANESE

What kind of information about nonverbal behavior in Japanese life do non-Japanese need to know to facilitate effective interaction? In addition to a general acceptance of how the Japanese view the role of nonverbal behavior in their culture, data provided by Western and Japanese scholars is one place to begin.

Bond and his colleagues have conducted controlled studies, with Japanese subjects, investigating the dynamics of spatial invasion, the effect of forward and backward body lean on perceptions of status, and the differing consequences of direct eye

contact. Their data suggested that Japanese female subjects responded to spatial intrusion with longer pauses, fewer glances, and backward lean. They classify this as a pattern of withdrawal and conclude that the "blunting of responses to crowding often reported in the Orient is probably situation-specific" (Bond and Iwata 1976, pp. 124–5). Testing the influence of Japanese hierarchy consciousness on forward and backward lean of the interviewer, their Japanese female subjects tended to express anxiety through increased speaking. Male Japanese subjects tended to express anxiety through silence. A forward-leaning interviewer was perceived, by both sexes, to be more polite and flexible (Bond and Shiraishi 1974). A third study examined the consequences of gazing at another's eyes or having one's eyes gazed at by another. When male Japanese subjects gazed at the interviewer, their hand movements increased, suggesting discomfort. When subjects were gazed at, they signalled greater involvement by reduced torso movements and shortened response latencies. This response was present whether or not they returned the gaze; these effects may be due primarily to the knowledge of being gazed at and not to some particular properties of eye contact (Bond and Komai 1976).

When thinking of nonverbal behavior among the Japanese, the use of gestures comes quickly to mind. As mentioned previously, the ideal is a differentiation between *shigusa*, quiet refined movement, and *miburi* or unrestrained expression. Tada comments that repression of emotion is actually an indication of assertion since a great amount of self-control may be needed to suppress overt bodily expression (Tada 1975). In all cultures there are gestures with distinct meaning, emblems, that are used in daily conversation. Ishii looked at differences in understanding of Japanese emblems among Japanese, Hawaiian Japanese, and Caucasian mainland Americans (1976). As might be expected, the Caucasian subjects were not familiar with such Japanese emblems as:

1. "come here"—palm down and fingers moving toward the body (This was frequently understood to mean "go away.")

2. "robber/theft"—crooked index finger

3. "husband/man"—thumb up

4. "wife/girlfriend"—little finger up

5. "promise"—hooking little fingers with another person

6. "shame/discomfort"—rubbing/scratching the back of head or neck

7. "jealousy/anger"—index finger held up to temple area

8. "me"—index finger pointing at nose

9. "no"—hand waving back and forth in front of the face.

For Japanese and non-Japanese alike, cultural differences in the meaning of gestures is a popular topic (Passin 1982; Mizutani 1982; Nishiyama 1974; Nakano 1973). Attempts are made to relate meanings to value perspectives. Kobayashi suggests that the "shrug off" gesture used by Americans is infrequent among the Japanese because the gesture is based on a clear distinction between people rather than on an emphasis upon harmony (Kobayashi 1976). Suzuki points out that the American idiom "keep your chin up" means "don't be discouraged," but for the Japanese, to "stick out the chin" means to be totally exhausted (Suzuki 1978, p. 69). Tada makes a related statement about chins and jaws: "Europeans unconsciously stick out their chins to take an aggressive posture. They could not survive in the world otherwise. Japanese, on the contrary, pull in their chins to assume a low posture" (Tada 1925). Comparison of verbal idioms about the body can be an interesting way to uncover differing assumptions about nonverbal behavior.

As would be expected, research has also focused upon the perception and effects of crowding. Using a questionnaire methodology, Iwata suggested that for Japanese and for Americans of Japanese ancestry, the perception of "others" as strangers, of higher status and of different ethnic background, contributed to increased feelings of being crowded (Iwata 1974b). In subsequent research, Japanese undergraduate females who were generally well adjusted, trusting, and who desired affiliation showed less of a tendency to experience crowding (Iwata 1979). Female subjects who showed a strong territoriality orientation, exemplified by choosing the same seat in a classroom, high privacy orientation (for example not liking to expose the self to others), and a high external locus of control were more likely to experience feelings of being crowded than subjects without such orientations (Iwata 1980).

Although thought provoking, such data are incomplete in themselves because they are based on a questionnaire methodology in which subjects are asked to project about feelings of a "person like you." When subjects were actually placed in high-density situations, the findings were much less clear, though generally Japanese of American ancestry seemed more sensitive to crowding than did Caucasians (Iwata 1974a).

Effects of crowding are very much related to the role of physical contact in daily life. Comparing U.S. and Japanese greeting rituals, Tohyama found touching to be more prevalent between Americans, with the amount or frequency depending upon gender and intimacy. For the Japanese, context and formality were more important determinants of display (Tohyama 1983). The world of Dean Barnlund is formative in understanding self-disclosure via nonverbal channels (1975). His results, consistent with other studies (Elzinga 1975), show Japanese women being touched more and doing more touching of others than Japanese males. Barnlund stated that, in general, Americans seem to engage in twice as much bodily contact as do Japanese. This should not, however, be used to label Japanese as a "non-contact" culture (Watson 1970). Observational data in five different areas of Tokyo illustrate that the Japanese are actually involved frequently in bodily contact. Touching among peers of the same sex is more common than touching across sex lines (Luk 1979). Frequency of touch increases greatly under the influence of alcohol though it is still primarily between same-sex peers. However, a study of the role of touching in courtship in Tokyo does bring this norm into question. Subjects were asked to judge the degree of intimacy of a heterosexual couple from photographs. College-age Japanese students felt the arm-around-the-waist position to be the most intimate, while subjects over forty judged the couple standing 15 cm apart, with no physical contact, to be most intimate. A Sunday afternoon walk in any more fashionable district in Tokyo will attest to the rapidly changing norms regarding touch.

In public settings, there is a great deal of passive touching evident. The Japanese are very adept at quickly protecting the more private parts of the body as they ride for kilometers on very crowded trains or become one in the midst of thousands during a summer festival.

When an individual is with members of his *uchi* (inner group), close-knit psychological relationships manifest themselves in a preference for physical closeness as well. This has been clearly illustrated in early studies of sleeping patterns. Dore's study of urban Japanese of the 1960s noted the preference for "crowded" sleeping in the same room (Dore 1958). Caudill and Plath suggested that such behavior was only partially a consequence of lack of space and was more directly related to "strength of family bonds" (Caudill and Plath 1974, p. 277). Today young children usually sleep in the same room as their parents, especially when they are infants. Other studies by Caudill and his associates suggest that there is close physical contact between Japanese mothers and their infants as they sleep, bathe, and play together (Caudill and Weinstein 1969; Caudill and Schooler 1973). In addition to the continued practice of bathing with children, and of same-sex friends and family members sharing a bath, the majority of the Japanese find themselves in quite close proximity around the *kotatsu* in winter time. This is a low quilt-covered table with an attached infrared lamp-heater. It is usually placed in the center of a room and people sit on the floor, around the table, with the lower parts of their bodies tucked under the quilt. The close proximity, the possibility of touching, the physical warmth, and the "barrier" the small tables provide combine to create a sought-after psychological intimacy with others in one's *uchi* (Handa 1983). Such observations, more situational in nature, suggest that perceptions of feeling crowded, or deciding whether or not the Japanese are a "touching people," cannot be determined simply by relying on a well-controlled research paradigm. It becomes very clear that without reference to context, information about nonverbal behavior is perhaps misleading and is certainly not very useful to a newcomer who wonders what behaviors to modify or amplify to interact effectively with the Japanese.

In a review of state-of-the-art methodology used in Western nonverbal research, Knapp concludes that those studies that most closely "match our beliefs about daily interaction ... attempt to assess a variety of contextual elements..." (Knapp 1984). He suggests that many studies acknowledge the importance of context in theory only, primarily because context is very difficult to explore in any systematic way to meet the Western need for reliability and validity before data can be accepted. Japanese scholars have, over time, written much about nonverbal behavior but it is usually presented in anecdotal and impressionistic ways, and tied intimately to context, so that the "Western mind cannot trust the 'data' and is certainly made uncomfortable because the 'data' are not generalizable" (Ramsey 1984).

Addressing this need for attention to context are two studies done by student research groups at International Christian University in Tokyo, where the author was on the communication faculty from 1977 to 1981. These studies take a controlled and holistic approach in trying to understand the mechanics of daily behavior among the Japanese.

The first study looks at the relationship between proxemics and privacy in the Japanese public bath. It examines the elements of locker use, patterns of dressing and undressing, the process of getting in and out of the tub, body orientation in the tub, and the use of faucets. This study is remarkable because it begins to unravel the way in which the Japanese create privacy in this very public experience.

Any bathhouse is distinguishable by its consistent external architectural elements: the wide entrance, the *noren* (curtain) showing the symbol for "hot springs," the rows of shoe boxes, the *kanji* (Chinese character) for "men" or "women" above the separate entrances into dressing rooms, and the tall smoke stack that can be seen from a distance. A bather first enters the locker room and will ideally choose a locker to block self from view of the money collector, if the collector is of the opposite sex. Exceptions are the elderly or children who may dress or undress in the middle of the room. There is no direct eye contact with the money collector while dressing or undressing. Whether or not the locker room is crowded, people try to use alternating lockers. If people must use adjoining lockers they give each other privacy by not having direct eye contact, by turning their back or sides to each other, or by moving to another part of the room to finish dressing. All this is accomplished without a word, though a slight nod of the head can communicate appreciation and apology for the inconvenience caused to each other. When walking nude in the locker room or the bathing room the small washing towel is used to signal appropriate modesty. Young women drape the towel over their arm about chest level; it is held in similar fashion just below the waist for men and older women. In the bathing room, faucets along the wall are preferred over those in the middle of the room. When the bath becomes crowded, the faucets in the middle are chosen over those between two strangers. Mothers with children are exceptions; a child seems to help break the tension. Friends may sit side by side as they converse and wash each other's back. The distance between faucets is 126 cm; this is within the range of Hall's social distance (120–210 cm) preferred by Caucasian North Americans. Further research might explore other interactions that are regulated to take place within this range, and how the Japanese interpret this distance. The placement of faucets controls behaviors in additional ways: the most desirable faucets are not only along the wall but near the tub, away from the door. These faucets are furthest from the cold air of the entrance, and soapy water from this position washes down the trough toward others. When one has finished washing, it is appropriate not to walk around the room but rather to go directly to the tub. If the tub is full, one merely extends the washing time until a space is available. In the tub,

the center is usually the last space occupied; men seem more often to sit face to face, avoiding eye contact, than women do.

The other study concentrates on the contribution of dress, body ornamentation, dancing style, and space to the group life of the *Takenoko-zoku*, "Young Bamboo Shoots" (Varnes, Takeda, Nakamura, Alielieu 1980). This is the name of groups of young Japanese, 12 to 18 years old, who gather on Sunday afternoons in the *Harajuku* section of Tokyo. Hundreds of spectators gather to watch as they dance to disco music in bright flashy clothes of Oriental design. Though the peak of this fad was in the summer of 1980, they continue to gather and dance and, although the costumes may change, the group dynamics remain consistent. Each group has between ten and 35 members; friends wear identical make-up, jewelry, and dye their hair in a similar fashion. A badge clearly shows group membership; leaders may have the group name written on their clothing. A large stereo tape player and bags containing street clothes are placed in the center of a circle, and same sex members dance side by side within the circle. The leader, usually male, takes a position in the center and explains the music and dances for the day, regulates breaks, and reinforces rules about good behavior. The relationship between members follows the *sempai–kohai* (senior–junior) dictates of respect and authority. Members can easily leave a group just by not joining in on Sunday. Dance movements often mimic the movements of popular singers; there is little or no touching during dancing. Groups are very aware of each other; if the music of one group "invades" that of another, the groups will take turns so as not to completely inconvenience each other. These young people say that they dance for excitement, to release everyday tension, and to be different. They are given as examples of young peoples' needs for individuality (Chipra 1982). On one level this is certainly true but, with the exception of the fluid group membership and the practice of meeting only on Sunday, a foundation of traditional values remains. "Emphasis upon dress codes, group identification, hierarchical relationship, and sensitivity paid to accommodating other groups suggests that 'being different' is also more of 'being the same' (Ramsey 1984).

These two studies are primarily observational; while the methodologies may not be the most rigorous, they do approach an understanding, along with the studies about Japanese women mentioned earlier, of "how a culture values itself and others, in what ways it is appropriate for its members to interact in certain situations, and how its world of communication is organized" (Cooley 1983, p. 244). Edward Hall also speaks very succinctly about the need for different approaches to the study of human behavior:

Modern classification methods provide man with a lot of information that is difficult to integrate into a usable, intelligible pattern. This is a classic example of low-context information . . . whichever way we Westerners turn, we find ourselves deeply preoccupied with specifics . . . to the exclusion of everything else. . . . We must not only learn to integrate the two or more systems of observation, but have the courage to underwrite contextual thinking and contextual research (Hall 1977, p. 123).

If a major goal is understanding how to interact most effectively with the Japanese, studies that "place context squarely in the middle" of the investigation are crucial (Cooley 1983, p. 249).

In addition to the nature of the data generated, there is another reason that an understanding of context is absolutely necessary. Hall characterizes Japan as a high-context culture (Hall 1977) in which meaning communicated through the environment and through behavior is emphasized. This concept is extremely helpful in adapting to daily life in Japan. Viewing life with a "high-context consciousness," a Japanese person feels most comfortable in a state of "embeddedness" or "withness" rather than as an individual entity. In describing post–World War II Japan, Kumon notes that

Suddenly dislodged from the traditional "contexts" by diction of law, a Japanese was forced to become a bare "contextual" who would look for some firm context to belong to instead of emerging as a self "individual" (Kumon 1980).

The Japanese self identity is an "in relation to" identity whether it be group, school, a single individual, a role, or a situation. Some determinations are less changeable: "I am Sumitomo's Nakamura"; "I am *chonan* (eldest son) or *yome* (new bride) of the Nakamura family." Other distinctions fluctuate at every encounter as one judges the other to be *uchi* (inside) or *soto* (outside); *sempai* (senior), *kohai* (junior), or *dohai* (equal); *o-kyakusama* (honorable guest) or host.

Attention to context is not only an important component of self identity, it is also an attitude that is reinforced daily from the moment the Japanese begin to learn to read. Japanese adopted *kanji* (Chinese characters) from China in the fifth century; until then they had no script of their own. They later added two syllabaries (*katakana* and *hiragana*) which, when used with *kanji*, gave much more flexibility to their language. *Katakana* is used primarily for writing foreign words (except those of Chinese origin), slang or italicized words, and sometimes the name of plants, animals, or diseases. *Hiragana* is used in combination with *kanji* to create the *kun*, or Japanese reading. The *kanji* without *hiragana* is known as the *on*, or Chinese reading. For example, the character 山 came to Japan with the Chinese pronunciation of "shan" and was modified to "san." At the same time the character means "mountain," which in Japanese is "yama." The *on* reading of this character is "san" and the *kun* reading is "yama." Each *kanji* can have several *on* and *kun* readings. For example, the character 生 (sei) can have the following variants:

一生 *isshoo* (one's whole life)

学生 *gakusei* (student)

生きる *ikiru* (to live)

生まれる *umareru* (to be born)

生 *nama* (fresh)

(Sasaki and Sunakawa 1976)

The meaning of any character very much depends on and is embedded in its relationship to other characters or *hiragana* with which it appears. There are 1,850 characters, called *toyo kanji*, that have been officially prescribed by the Japanese Ministry of Education as the characters most essential for daily communication. With a knowledge of these characters, one can read a Japanese newspaper. Reading, for the Japanese, is not a black-and-white process; the meaning of any character is dependent upon the context in which it appears. Context refers not only to surrounding characters but also to the environment in which the character occurs. For example, in newspapers the use of *toppan*, or background devices, for headlines can give the immediate sense of the type of story. A circular *toppan* suggests a scandal, backgrounds of figures of flowers are used for "household hints," and ducks or toys for children's stories. *Toppan* serve as a type of editorial statement and provide even another level of context to decipher (Brown 1984).

Hall comments that "in high-context cultures, syncing is very noticeable (Hall 1977, p. 79). Extending his observation, it appears that synchrony is an integral mechanism of any culture that relies upon contextual relations as much as Japan does. Synchrony, achieved by joining in with the rhythms of others, may be thought of as a "social oil" lubricating interactions among the Japanese. As Hall emphasizes, "humans are tied to each other by hierarchies of rhythms that are *culture specific* and expressed through language and body movement" (Hall 1977, p. 24).

Examples of synchronous behavior abound in modern Japan. The abundance of uniforms for office ladies, cooks, bank tellers, surfers, golfers, construction workers, housewives, salesmen, and dating couples reinforces the expectation that people, by their very appearance, announce their occupation or where they are going or with whom they are affiliated. Continuity of environmental forms also creates a sense of rhythm: department stores have distinctive logos; the *tai* fish is always used during celebrations; military music signals a

pachinko parlor around the corner; strains of "Auld Lang Syne" announce the closing of a park, a museum, or a department store; a lighted red lantern signals a neighborhood snack shop; a string of pink lanterns signal a *robatayaki* (grilled food) restaurant; railway ticket punchers make a continuous 'clicking' sound; and a certain "crazy" architecture creates a love hotel. When applied to the Japanese, synchrony must be broadened to include the small group and societal levels as well as the inter- and intrapersonal levels.

An added feature of Japanese interpersonal synchrony is labelled here as "interactional syncopation" or rule-governed, time-linked behavior. Examples include the pounding of *o-mochi* (rice cake) at New Year time, the pouring of *sake* or beer for one's partners during a drinking party, bowing, and even gift giving. During the New Year time a special glutinous rice is eaten. It must be made into a particular consistency by pounding. Two men alternately pound the rice with long wooden mallets, while a third person reaches into the container, between pounding turns, and kneads the *o-mochi*. This is done without a word and each is closely attuned to the rhythm of all. When drinking together there is an unwritten rule that one gets one's glass filled by continually attending to the needs of others. Respect is communicated by paying close attention to the other. *Aizuchi* is another example: *aizuchi* literally means the hammering of two crows, and is used to refer to the ritualized synchronous head nodding between two conversational pairs. The message communicated is, "I hear you, I follow you, I am with you."

The Japanese constantly behave so as to announce their relationships and belongingness; synchrony speaks directly about this quality of being "with" others. People are reminded of their identities by the nonverbal environment. It is not only quicker but also safer to "know" another by noticing a lapel pin, seating arrangement, clothing style, or name card, rather than waiting until the other verbalizes who they are. Dressing alike, joining in *radio taiso* exercise each morning before work, or the group toast before a party begins are all rituals of synchrony that mark group boundaries and enhance feelings of oneness.

Synchrony with others cannot exist unless the majority of people within the group or culture agree on the meaning of environmental forms or behavior. In Japan, one gets the feeling that "not only are more behaviors and forms expressly coded, but also that rules about how to manage such behaviors and forms are more explicit than in cultures that give less overt sanction to synchrony" (Ramsey 1984). Japan is a culture that emphasizes form. Much attention is paid to the belief that one's inner character is manifest through outward signs. To follow form is to participate in the maintenance of harmony. Form serves many functions; it is "a buffer against surprise, a sign of membership, a sign of predictability" (Ramsey and Birk 1983). Rejection of the dictates of form can communicate lack of respect and can cause embarrassment to one's Japanese colleagues. A decision to become "in sync" with the Japanese can also have far-reaching implications for effective interaction. It may be difficult for Westerners to understand and then to begin to value the freedom that boundaries and structure can provide.

Returning now to an issue introduced in the beginning of this discussion, what is important to understand about nonverbal behavior to interact more effectively with the Japanese? Certainly it is important to become familiar with specific behaviors—gestures, bowing rituals, seating arrangements, or perceptions about crowding, as illustrated in this discussion. A variety of such data are available. Some of it is collected and presented based on the belief that rationality is the only useful paradigm. With this world view, information about nonverbal behavior is gathered using a self-assertive, dialectic, more digital style in searching for just the *correct* answers about often isolated segments of behavior.

Although this information is important, the real challenge in understanding the role of nonverbal behavior comes in the demands made in regard to learning style. It is important to realize that a persistent verbal "why" may drive answers further away. Without attention to the role of context, it is impossible to grasp the dynamics by which privacy can be created or to understand the powerful effect that the desire for harmony or a sense of "withness" has in molding behavior. How can one become attuned to the myriad, often confusing variables that are part of a contextual analysis? The Japanese have an acute sense of presence and are very sensitive to monitoring their behavior in relationship to the group or situation. This ability is the culmination of a carefully guided socialization process. Listening, watching, and actually *participating* in events with the Japanese, while adopting a more holistic, situation-oriented, and non-dialectic learning style, may provide entry for non-Japanese into this approach to reality. Entering this reality is absolutely necessary if effective interaction is the goal of studying about nonverbal behavior among the Japanese.

REFERENCES

Barnlund, D. *Public and Private Self in Japan and the United States*. Tokyo: Simul Press, 1975.

Bond, M. H. and Iwata, Y. "Proxemics and observation anxiety in Japan: Nonverbal and cognitive responses," *Psychologia*, 1976, 19, 3, 119–126.

Bond, M. H. and Komai, H. "Targets of gazing and eye contact during interviews: Effect on Japanese nonverbal behavior," *Journal of Personality and Social Psychology*, 1976, 34, 6, 1276–1284.

Bond, M. H. and Shirashi, N. "The effect of body lean and status of an interviewer on the nonverbal behavior of Japanese interviewees." *International Journal of Psychology*, 1974, 9, 2, 117–128.

Brown, H. Personal communication based on student research in "Principles in Editing" class at International Christian University, 1984.

Caudill, W. and Plath, D. "Who Sleeps By Whom? Parent-Child Involvement in Urban Japanese Families," in Lebra, T. and Lebra, W. (eds.), *Japanese Culture and Behavior*. Honolulu: University of Hawaii Press, 1974, pp. 277–312.

Caudill, W. A. and Schooler, C. "Child Behavior and Child Rearing in Japan and the U.S.: An Intern Report." *Journal, Nervous and Mental Diseases*, 1973, 15f, 323–338.

Caudill, W. A. and Weinstein, H. "Maternal Care and Infant Behavior in Japan and America." *Psychiatry*, 1969, 32, 12–43.

Chance, P. "Ads Without Answers Make the Brain Itch," *Psychology Today*, November 1975, p. 78.

Chipra, S. "Rebellion in Japan catches young, old out of uniformity." *Chicago Tribune*, July 4, 1982, p. 12.

Cooley, R. "Codes and Contexts: An Argument for their Description," in Gudykunst, W. (ed.), *Intercultural Communication Theory: Current Perspectives*. Intercultural Communication Annual, vol. VII, Beverly Hills: Sage Publications, 1983.

Dore, R. *City Life in Japan*. Berkeley: University of California Press, 1958.

Elzinga, R. H. "Nonverbal Communications: Body accessibility among the Japanese." *Psychologia*, 1975, 18, 205–211.

Friesen, W. "Cultural differences in facial expressions in a social situation: An experimental test of the concept of display rules," University of California San Francisco, Ph.D. dissertation, 1972.

Frieze, I. and Ramsey, S. "Nonverbal Maintenance of Traditional Sex Roles," *Journal of Social Issues*, 1976, 32, 33, 133–141.

Hall, E. *Beyond Culture*. Garden City, New York: Anchor, Doubleday, 1977.

Handa, I. "Nonverbal Communication Patterns in Japanese Culture." Unpublished paper, 1983.

Hartung, E. A. "Cultural Adjustment Difficulties of Japanese Adolescents Sojourning in the USA." *Occasional Papers in Intercultural Learning #5*. New York: AFS Publications, November 1983.

Ishii, S. "Characteristics of Japanese Nonverbal Communicative Behavior." *Journal of the Communication Association of the Pacific*, Special Issue, 1973, 2, 3, 1973.

Ishii, S. "Japanese Nonverbal Communicative Signs: A Cross-Cultural Survey." Unpublished paper presented at annual meeting of Communication Association of the Pacific, 1976.

Iwata, O. "Empirical Examination of the Perception of Density and Crowding." *Japanese Psychological Research*, 1974b, 16, 3, 117–125.

Iwata, O. "Factors in the Perception of Crowding." *Japanese Psychological Research*, 1974a, 16, 2, 65–70.

Iwata, O. "Selected Personality Traits as Determinants of the Perception of Crowding." *Japanese Psychological Research*, 1979, 21, 13, 1–19.

Iwata, O. "Territoriality orientation, privacy orientation, and locus of control as determinants of the perception of crowding." *Japanese Psychological Research*, 1980, 22, 1, 13–21.

Kato, H. "Koto wazakara miru Nihonjin no communication—Kan (Japanese Communication Values Seen in Proverbs)." *Gengo Seikatsu*, Chikuma Shobo, 1961, 112.

Knapp, M. "The study of nonverbal behavior vis-à-vis human communication theory," in Wolfgang, A. (ed.), *Nonverbal Behavior: Perspectives, Applications and Intercultural Insights*. Toronto: C. J. Hogrefe, Inc., 1984.

Kobayashi, Y. "Miburi-Gengo no Nichi Ei Hikaku (Comparative Study of English and Japanese Gesture Language)." Tokyo: *Eigo Kyoiku*, 1976.

Kumon, S. "Middle Class State?" Presented in Japan Speaks Symposium, Osaka, Japan, 1980.

Kunihiro, M. "The Japanese Language and Intercultural Communication." *The Japan Interpreter*, 1976, 10, 3–4.

Lebra, T. S. *Japanese Patterns of Behavior*. Honolulu: East-West Center, 1976.

Luk, L. Y. A. "A Study of Tactile Behavior in Tokyo: Its Meaning and Social Implication." Unpublished Senior Thesis, Tokyo, Japan: I.C.U. Communication Department, 1979.

Lyons, N. *The Sony Vision*. New York: Crown Publishers, 1976.

Masuda, S. *Noh no Hyogen* (The Expressions of Noh). Tokyo: Chuo Koronsha, 1971.

Miller, R. A. *Japan's Modern Myth: The Language and Beyond*. Tokyo: Weatherhill, 1982.

Mizutani, O. *Japanese: The Spoken Language in Japanese Life*. Ashley, J. (trans.). Tokyo: The Japan Times, Ltd., 1982.

Morsbach, H. "Aspects of Nonverbal Communication in Japan." *Journal of Nervous and Mental Diseases*, 1973, 157, 1, 262–277.

Muro, Y. "How It Feels to Be 'Not Quite Japanese.'" *Japan Times*, March 27, 1983.

Nakane, C. *Japanese Society*. University of California Press: Berkeley and Los Angeles, 1970.

Nakano, M. "Nichi eigo no hikaku (Gesture: Comparative Study of Japanese and English)." Tokyo: *Eigo Koiku*, 1973, 21, 11, 10–12.

Nishiyama, S. *Gokai to Rikai, Understanding and Misunderstanding*. Tokyo: Simul Press, 1974.

Nitobe, I. *Bushido, The Soul of Japan*. Tokyo: Tuttle, 1969.

Passin, H. "Body Language Among Japanese: A Primer." *Japan Society Newsletter*, 1982.

Ramsey, S. "Double Vision: Nonverbal Behavior East and West," in Wolfgang, A. (ed.), *Nonverbal Behavior: Perspectives, Applications and Intercultural Insights*. Toronto: C. J. Hogrefe, Inc., 1984.

Ramsey, S. "The Kinesics of Femininity in Japanese Women." *Language Sciences*, 1981b, 3, 1, 104–123.

Ramsey, S. "Nonverbal Behavior of Japanese Women." Presentation to International Feminists Forum, Tokyo, Japan, 1981.

Ramsey, S. "Prison Codes." *The Journal of Communication*, 1976, 26, 3, 39–45.

Ramsey, S. and Birk, J. "Training North Americans for Interaction with Japanese: Considerations of Language and Communication Style." In Brislin, R. and Landis, D. (eds.), *The Handbook of Intercultural Training, vol. II: Area Studies in Intercultural Training*. New York: Pergamon Press, 1983.

Sasaki, M. and Sunakawa, G. *Exploring Japanese*, supplement to *Easy Japanese*. Tokyo, 1976.

Suzuki, T. *Japanese and the Japanese: Words in Culture*. Miura, A. (trans.). Tokyo: Kodaisha, 1978.

Tada, M. *Shigusa no Nihonbunka, Gestures in Japanese Culture*. Tokyo: Chikuma Shoho, 1975.

Tohyama, Y. "A Semiotic Analysis of Meeting and Parting Rituals in Japanese and English." Tokyo: Unpublished paper, Japan Women's University, 1983.

Varnes, R.; Takeda, E.; Nokamura, T.; and Alielieu, E. "Takenoko-zoku and Japanese Culture." Tokyo: Unpublished research, I.C.U. Communication Department, 1980.

Watson, O. M. *Proxemic Behavior: A Cross-Cultural Study*. The Hague: Mouton, 1970.

Yamaki, T. "Advertising Creativity in Japan and Other Countries." *Dentsu's Japan Marketing Advertising*, January 1980, 16, 56.

Yasuda, K. *The Japanese Haiku*. Tokyo: Tuttle Books, 1957.

CONCEPTS AND QUESTIONS FOR CHAPTER 6

1. From your personal experiences can you think of additional ways that people in various cultures greet, kiss, show contempt, or beckon?

2. Are cultural differences that are based on linguistic problems harder or easier to overcome than the problems related to nonverbal actions?

3. In what ways do nonverbal behaviors reflect the values, history, and social organization of a culture?

4. What are some of the dangers of overgeneralizing from nonverbal communication?

5. Have you ever experienced situations where the nonverbal behavior of someone did not meet your expectations? How did you react? Could this have been a cultural problem?

6. How can we develop a theory of nonverbal behavior if we go beyond the anecdotal narration of bizarre behaviors?

7. Can you think of any cultural examples that would tend to support the notion that a culture's history influences its use of nonverbal communication?

8. What are the relationships between verbal and nonverbal forms of communication?

9. How might cultural differences in time conceptualization lead to intercultural communication problems?

10. What examples can you think of that illustrate differences between the sexes in nonverbal behavior?

11. How would you prevent the occurrence of intercultural communication problems that are brought about by the unconscious and unintentional performance of nonverbal behavior and that deeply offend members of another culture?

12. Using the Japanese as an example, discuss how differences in nonverbal behavior might frustrate the progress of an intercultural encounter between a Japanese and a North American engaged in a business negotiation.

SUGGESTED READINGS

Basso, K. H. "To give up on words: Silence in Western Apache Culture." *Southwestern Journal of Anthropology* 26 (1970), 213–230. This article looks at silence as a form of communication among the Western Apache. Basso examines how silence is used when meeting strangers, courting, greeting friends, cursing, and curing someone.

Boucher, J. D. "Display rules and facial affective behavior: A theoretical discussion and suggestions for research" in *Topics in Culture Learning*, Vol. 2. Honolulu: East-West Center, 1974. Boucher develops a theory of facial affective behavior in interpersonal intercultural interaction. Display rules for facial affective behavior are defined as a set of norms that the individual internalizes during socialization. Examples of behavior are discussed, with emphasis on the identification of contextual characteristics of people and setting.

Bruneau, T. "The time dimension in intercultural communication" in D. Nimmo, ed. *Communication Yearbook* 3. New Brunswick, N.J.: Transaction Books, 1979, pp. 423–433. This article examines differences in the conception of time, in timing, and in particular tempos of cross-cultural groups. A number of major aspects of human temporality are outlined and related directly to intercultural situations. A taxonomic schema is offered, which can be used as a tool for observing, analyzing, and studying the time experiencing of intercultural communication.

Burgoon, J. K., and T. Saine. *The Unspoken Dialogue: An Introduction to Nonverbal Communication.* Boston: Houghton-Mifflin, 1978, Chapter 5. This excellent text accomplishes two purposes for the student of intercultural communication. First, the authors present an overview of the entire field of nonverbal communication. And second, they focus on the cultural dimensions of nonverbal communication.

Efron, D. *Gesture, Race and Culture.* The Hague: Mouton, 1972. Here, Efron presents the results of his classic study of spatio-temporal and linguistic aspects of the gestural patterns of Eastern Jews and southern Italians in New York City.

Ekman, P. "Communication through nonverbal behavior: A source of information about an interpersonal relationship" in S. S. Tompkins and C. E. Izard, eds. *Affect, Cognition, and Personality.* New York: Springer, 1965, pp. 391–442. This book discusses basic concepts in nonverbal communication behavior and also explains how nonverbal expressions provide additional information for the interpretation of verbal systems.

Hall, E. T. *The Hidden Dimension.* New York: Doubleday, 1966. People use space to communicate in very much the same way they use words or gestures. In this volume, Hall sets forth his theory of proxemics and describes and discusses cultural variance in proxemic behavior.

Harper, R. G., A. N. Wiens, and J. D. Matarazzo. *Nonverbal Communication: The State of the Art.* New York: John Wiley, 1978. The importance of culture to nonverbal communication is stressed throughout this volume. Cultural differences are noted in facial expressions, kinesics, eye and visual behavior, and proxemics.

Jakobson, R. "Nonverbal signs for 'yes' and 'no.'" *Language in Society* 1 (1972), 91–96. In this article Jakobson describes how the nonverbal expressions of yes and no vary among three European cultural groupings. The extent of this difference is so great that a head motion taken to signify approval in one culture can indicate disapproval in another. Such differences are crucial to intercultural communicators who seek successful interactive outcomes.

Johnson, F. L., and R. White Buttny. "Listener's responses to 'sounding Black' and 'sounding White': The effect of message content on judgements about language." *Communication Monographs* 49 (1982), 33–49. The effects of sounding "black" or "white" were examined in this very interesting study. More specifically, the study asked if white listeners focus their perceptions differently depending on whether a speaker "sounds white" or "sounds black" and depending on whether message content is abstract or experiential. Results suggest that both stereotypic and egocentric filters shape listener response.

LaBarre, W. "The cultural basis of emotions and gestures." *Journal of Personality* 16 (1946), 49–68. Specific emotional expressions and gestures have their bases in culture, both in the appropriateness of the expression and in the manner of expression. In this classic essay, LaBarre discusses variations in these forms of nonverbal behaviors that result from cultural differences; he cites numerous examples and describes how different cultures have different nonverbal expressions for the same meaning.

LaFrance, M., and C. Mayo. *Moving Bodies: Nonverbal Communication in Social Relationships*. Monterey, Calif.: Brooks/Cole, 1978. Chapter 13 of this book looks at the role of culture in nonverbal communication. The authors examine cross-cultural similarities and differences in the use of nonverbal cues. Topics such as emotional displays, status differences, and intimacy are treated in detail.

Luce, T. S. "Blacks, whites and yellows: They all look alike to me." *Psychology Today* (November 1974), 105–106, 107. In this article, Luce describes studies he has conducted that reveal that the stereotype of members of other ethnic and racial groups all looking alike is widespread among racial and ethnic groups.

Mayo, C., and N. M. Henley, eds. *Gender and Nonverbal Behavior*. New York: Springer-Verlag, 1981. This book explores the relationship between nonverbal cues and gender. The authors maintain that people negotiate their sex roles through the subtle expression of nonverbal cues. Composed of thirteen chapters, this book contains original research reports, state-of-the-art literature reviews, and conceptual essays on new research arenas. Topics discussed include touching, seating arrangements, visual behavior, body movements, facial expressions, and nonverbal signals.

Mehrabian, A. *Silent Messages*. Belmont, Calif.: Wadsworth, 1971. Much of this book is concerned with cultural differences in performing and perceiving nonverbal communication. In nearly all classes of nonverbal behavior, Mehrabian has examined the role of culture.

Morris, D., et al. *Gestures, Their Origins and Distribution*. Briarcliff Manor, N.Y.: Stein and Day, 1979. Morris and his associates describe the historical development and use of 20 nonverbal behaviors. Although the research was conducted in Western Europe, it still offers countless specific examples of how gestures and other nonverbal codes shift from culture to culture.

Ramsey, S. "Nonverbal behavior: An intercultural perspective" in M. K. Asante, E. Newmark, and C. A. Blake, eds. *Handbook of Intercultural Communication*. Beverly Hills, Calif.: Sage Publications, 1979, pp. 105–143. Ramsey offers an extensive review and evaluation of research on nonverbal communication and its relationship to culture. She analyzes gestures, bodily contact, spatial behavior, seating, architecture, and so on.

Rich, A. L. "Interracial implications of nonverbal communication" in A. L. Rich. *Interracial Communication*. New York: Harper & Row, 1974. In Chapter 7 of her book, Rich explores the importance of nonverbal communication to interracial interaction. Most dimensions of nonverbal communication are examined in this selection—environment, proxemics, clothing, physical appearance and characteristics, posture, gesture, eye contact, facial expressions, and paralanguage.

Sussman, N. M., and H. M. Rosenfeld. "Influence of culture, language, and sex on conversational distance." *Journal of Personality and Social Psychology* 42 (1982), 66–74. This study assessed interpersonal distance between seated conversants from each of three cultures: Japanese, Venezuelan, and American.

Watson, M. O., and T. D. Graves. "Quantitative research in proxemic behavior." *American Anthropologist* 68 (1966), 971–985. Watson and Graves report an experimental study between Americans and Arabs that tested the hypothesis that Arabs interact closer physically than do North Americans. This study is important because it not only supports proxemic theory, it also gives insight into cross-cultural research methodologies.

Wolfgang, A., ed. *Nonverbal Behavior: Applications and Cultural Implications*. New York: Academic Press, 1979. This text is a collection of essays on topics such as expressive behavior, emotion and nonverbal behavior, and culture and interracial problems. Contributions include experts such as Scheflen, Argyle, and Hall.

ADDITIONAL READINGS

Arndt, J., S. Gronms, and D. Hawes. "Allocation of time to leisure activities: Norwegian and American patterns." *Journal of Cross-Cultural Psychology* 11 (1980), 495–511.

Ashcraft, N., and A. E. Scheflen. *People Space: The Making and Breaking of Human Boundaries.* New York: Anchor Books, 1976.

Boucher, J. D., and G. E. Carlson. "Recognition of facial expression in three cultures." *Journal of Cross-Cultural Psychology* 11 (1980), 263–280.

Brislin, R. W. "Seating as a measure of behavior: You are where you sit" in *Topics in Culture Learning*, Vol. 2. Honolulu: East-West Center, 1974.

Ekman, P., R. Sorenson, and E. Friessen. "Pan-cultural elements in facial displays of emotion." *Science* 164 (1969), 86–88.

Forston, R. F., and C. U. Larson. "The dynamics of space: An experimental study in proxemic behavior among Latin Americans and North Americans." *Journal of Communication* 18 (1968), 109–116.

Grove, C. L. "Nonverbal behavior: Cross-cultural contact and the urban classroom teacher." *Equal Opportunity Review* (1976), 1–5.

Hall, E. T. *The Silent Language*. Garden City, N.J.: Doubleday, 1959.

Johnson, K. R. "Black kinesics: Some non-verbal communication patterns in the black culture." *Florida FL Reporter* 9 (Spring/Fall 1971), 17–20, 57.

Jones, S. E., and J. R. Aiello. "Proxemic behavior of black and white first-, third-, and fifth-grade children." *Journal of Personality and Social Psychology* 25 (1973), 21–27.

McCann, L. D., and M. L. Hecht. "Verbal and nonverbal assessment of foreign students' communication apprehension." *The Journal of the Communication Association of the Pacific* 12 (1983), 67–76.

Montagu, A. *Touching: The Human Significance of the Skin*. New York: Columbia University Press, 1971.

Pagan, G., and J. R. Aiello. "Development of personal space among Puerto Ricans." *Journal of Nonverbal Behavior* 7 (1982), 59–68.

Pucel, J., and G. Stocker. "A nonverbal approach to communication: A cross-cultural study of stress behaviors." *The Journal of the Communication Association of the Pacific* 12 (1983), 53–65.

Ramsey, S. J. "The kinesics of femininity in Japanese women." *Language Sciences* 3 (1981), 104–123.

Rudden, M. R., and K. D. Frandsen. "An intercultural test of the generality of interpretations of nonverbal cues." *International Journal of Intercultural Relations* 2 (1978), 410–425.

St. Martin, G. M. "Intercultural differential decoding of nonverbal affective communication." *International and Intercultural Communication Annual* 3 (1976), 44–57.

Scheflen, A. E., and N. Ashcraft. *Human Territories: How We Behave in Space-Time.* Englewood Cliffs, N.J.: Prentice-Hall, 1976.

Seward, J. *Japanese in Action.* New York: John Weatherhill, 1968.

Shuter, R. "The gap in the military: Hand-to-hand communication." *Journal of Communication* 29 (1979), 136–142.

Shuter, R. "Gaze behavior in interracial and intraracial interactions." *International and Intercultural Communication Annual* 2 (1979), 48–55.

Shuter, R. "A study of nonverbal communication among Jews and Protestants." *The Journal of Social Psychology* 109 (1979), 31–41.

Part Four

Intercultural Communication: Becoming More Effective

Things do change. The only question is that since things are deteriorating so quickly, will society and man's habits change quickly enough?

—*Isaac Asimov*

In a sense, this entire volume has been concerned with the practice of intercultural communication. We have looked at a variety of cultures and a host of communication variables that operate when people from different cultures attempt to interact. However, our analysis thus far has been somewhat theoretical. Previous selections have concentrated primarily on the issue of understanding intercultural communication. We have not, at least up to this point, treated the act of practicing intercultural communication.

We have already pointed out many of the problems that cultural differences can introduce into the communication process. And we have shown how an awareness of not only other cultures but also of one's own culture can help mediate some of the problems. But intercultural communication is not exclusively a single party activity. Like other forms of interpersonal communication, it requires for its highest and most successful practice the complementary participation of all parties to the communication event.

When elevated to its highest level of human activity, intercultural communication becomes what David Berlo in 1960 described as "Interaction: The Goal of Human Communication": the communicative act in which "two individuals make inferences about their own roles and the role of the other at the same time."* Berlo calls this reciprocal role taking: in order for people to achieve the highest level of communication there must be a mutual reciprocity in achieving an understanding of each other. In intercultural com-

---

*David K. Berlo, *The Process of Communication*. New York: Holt, Rinehart & Winston, 1960, p. 130.

munication, this means that you must not only know about your culture and the culture of the one with whom you are communicating, but that that person must also know about his or her own culture and about your culture as well. Unless there is mutual acknowledgment of each other's cultures and a willingness to accept those cultures as a reality governing communicative interactions, intercultural communication cannot rise to its highest possible level of human interaction.

In this final section we have slightly modified our orientation so that we can include a discussion based on the activity of communication. For although the readings in this portion of the book will increase your understanding, their main purpose is to improve your behavior *during* intercultural communication.

The motivation for this particular section grows out of an important precept found in the study of human communication. It suggests that human interaction is a behavioral act in which people engage for the purpose of changing their environment. Inherent in this notion is the idea that communication is something people *do*—it involves action. Regardless of how much you understand intercultural communication, when you are communicating with someone from another culture you are part of a behavioral situation. You, and your communication counterpart, are doing things to each other. This final part of the book deals with that "doing." In addition, it is intended to help your communication become as effective as possible.

As you might well imagine, personal contact and experience are the most desirable methods for improvement. Knowledge and practice seem to work in tandem. The problem, however, is that we cannot write or select readings that substitute for this personal experience. Therefore, our contribution by necessity must focus on the observations of those who have practiced intercultural communication with some degree of success.

7

Communicating Interculturally

The primary purpose of this book is to help you become more effective intercultural communicators. To this end, the articles in this chapter offer advice and counsel aimed at improving the way you communicate when you find yourself in intercultural encounters. To help you achieve this goal, most of the essays discuss problems as well as solutions. Being alert to potential problems is the first step toward understanding. Once problems have been identified it is easier to seek means of improvement.

The first essay looks at both problems and solutions. In "Stumbling Blocks in Intercultural Communication," LaRay M. Barna deals with some specific reasons why intercultural communication often fails to bring about mutual understanding. She has selected six important causes for communication breakdown across cultural boundaries: language problems, nonverbal misunderstanding, the presence of preconceptions and stereotypes, the tendency to evaluate, and the high anxiety that often exists in intercultural encounters.

Brent D. Ruben in "Human Communication and Cross-Cultural Effectiveness" is concerned with ways to increase communication effectiveness in intercultural settings. He examines seven factors that contribute to effective communication behavior: the capacity to communicate respect, the capacity to be nonjudgmental, the capacity to personalize one's knowledge and perceptions, the capacity to display empathy, the capacity to be flexible, the capacity for turn-taking, and the capacity to tolerate ambiguity.

No matter how well we may appreciate the necessity of understanding the culture of another in order to engage successfully in intercultural communication, we will all be affected to some degree by "the constant and pernicious influence of cultural bias in interpreting unfamiliar acts in an alien setting." It is extremely difficult for us to shrug off our internalized cultural biases as we evaluate the behavior of people from other cultures. In "Decentering, Convergence, and Cross-Cultural Understanding," Dean C. Barnlund and Naoki Nomura explore the notions of decentering and convergence as means of helping overcome this cultural bias. Decentering refers to the temporary suspension of the constructs used to interpret events; convergence is the process of acquiring alternative constructs. Barnlund and Nomura believe that if people can learn to decenter and to converge, they will possess qualities that can vastly improve intercultural communication.

In "Prejudice in Intercultural Communication" Richard W. Brislin examines this problem while looking at the functions and forms of prejudice. He warns of five different forms of prejudice: redneck racism, symbolic racism, tokenism, arms-length prejudice, and the familiar and unfamiliar. Each of these forms must be understood and controlled to achieve successful intercultural communication.

In recent years there has been a steady increase in the number of people who, as a profession, train others to be more effective intercultural communicators. These trainers work with people from a variety of cultures, yet their aim is the same in all training sessions—to make the participants better communicators. Most trainers follow a rather systematic program in their attempts to introduce their clients to the cultural variables that mediate most intercultural encounters. Paul Pedersen, who is a professional trainer, suggests that the most successful programs follow six stages that are designed to accommodate cultural and role differences. These stages seek to combine the requirements of good training design with a sensitivity to cultural and role relationships in the training environment. Knowing these stages, and the content of each, should help you experience what these training sessions are like.

The final article deals with acculturation, a somewhat unique and often overlooked aspect of intercultural communication. Young Yun Kim examines this topic in her article "Communication and Acculturation." With approximately a million refugees immigrating to the United States each year, she is concerned that many of the immigrants' communicative modes, internalized from early childhood, may prove dysfunctional in their new communication environment. She, therefore, presents a discussion of both the problems and the solutions of acculturation. Her thesis is that one learns to communicate by communicating, and that much of that communication takes place between the immigrants and the American people. By understanding the acculturation process, Americans can help with the often difficult transition facing these new arrivals.

Stumbling Blocks in Intercultural Communication

LARAY M. BARNA

Why is it that contact with persons from other cultures so often is frustrating and fraught with misunderstanding? Good intentions, a friendly approach, and even the possibility of mutual benefits don't seem to be sufficient—to many people's surprise. One answer to the question might be that many of us naively assume there are sufficient similarities among peoples of the world to enable us to successfully exchange information and/or feelings, solve problems of mutual concern, cement business relationships, or just make the kind of impression we wish to make.

The tendency for all people to reproduce, group into families and/or societies, develop a language, and adapt to their environment is particularly deceiving because it leads to the expectation that the forms of these behaviors and the attitudes and values surrounding them will also be similar. It's comforting to believe that "people are people" and "deep down we're all alike," but a determined search for proof of this leads to disappointment.

The major similarities are biological ones, including the need for food, shelter, and safety (with radical variations as to type and amount of each). Eibl-Eibesfeldt lists as cross-cultural similarities the "sucking response, the breast-seeking automatism, smiling, crying and a number of reflexes."[1] There is also Pavlov's "orienting reaction"—the instantaneous bodily changes that occur when threat is perceived.[2] Such changes include the flow of extra adrenaline and noradrenaline into the system, increased muscle tension, cessation of digestive processes, and other changes that prepare the human animal to "fight or flee." Although this is a universal and a key adaptive mechanism that allowed survival in a hostile environment for early humans, it hinders rather than helps today's intercultural communication process, which calls for calm, considered exchanges.

None of the above universals are much help for purposes of communication. More promising are the cross-cultural studies seeking to support Darwin's theory that facial expressions are universal.[3] Ekman found that "the particular visible pattern on the face, the combination of muscles contracted for anger, fear, surprise, sadness, disgust, happiness (and probably also for interest) is the same for all members of our species."[4] This seems helpful until it is realized that a person's cultural upbringing determines whether or not the emotion will be displayed or suppressed, as well as on which occasions and to what degree.[5] The situations that bring about the emotional feeling also differ from culture to culture; for example, the death of a loved one may be a cause for joy, sorrow, or some other emotion, depending upon the accepted cultural belief.

There seem to be no universals of "human nature" that can be used as a basis for automatic understanding. The aforementioned assumption of similarity might be a common characteristic, however. Each of us seems to be so unconsciously influenced by our own cultural upbringings that we at first assume that the needs, desires, and basic assumptions of others are the same as our own. As expressed by Vinh The Do, "If we realize that we are all culture bound and culturally modified, we will accept the fact that, being unlike, we do not really know what someone else 'is.' This is another way to view the 'people are people' idea. We now have to find a way to sort out the cultural modifiers in each separate encounter to find similarity."[6]

The aura of similarity is a serious stumbling block to successful intercultural communication. A look-alike facade is deceiving when representatives from contrasting cultures meet, each wearing West-

Reprinted by permission of LaRay M. Barna. Professor Barna teaches at Portland State University.

ern dress, speaking English, and using similar greeting rituals. It is like assuming that New York, Tokyo, and Tehran are all alike because each has the appearance of a modern city. Without being alert to possible differences and the need to learn new rules for functioning, persons going from one city to the other will be in immediate trouble, even when acting simple roles such as pedestrian or driver.

Unless a foreigner expects subtle differences it will take a long time of noninsulated living in a new culture (not in an enclave of his or her own kind) before he or she can be jarred into new perceptual and nonevaluative thinking. The confidence that goes with the myth of similarity is much more comfortable than the assumption of differences, the latter requiring tentative assumptions and behaviors and a willingness to accept the anxiety of "not knowing." Only with the assumption of differences, however, can reactions and interpretations be adjusted to fit "what's happening." Otherwise someone is likely to misread signs and judge the scene ethnocentrically.

The stumbling block of assumed similarity is a "troubble," as one English learner expressed it, not only for the foreigner but for the people in the host country (United States or any other) with whom the international visitor comes into contact. The native inhabitants are likely to be lulled into the expectation that, since the foreign person is dressed appropriately and speaks some of the language, he or she will also have similar nonverbal codes, thoughts, and feelings. Thus, nodding, smiling, and affirmative comments will probably be confidently interpreted by straightforward, friendly Americans as meaning that they have informed, helped, and pleased the newcomer. It is likely, however, that the foreigner actually understood very little of the verbal and nonverbal content and was merely indicating polite interest or trying not to embarrass himself or herself or the host with verbalized questions. The conversation may even have confirmed a stereotype that Americans are insensitive and ethnocentric.

Unless there is overt reporting of assumptions made by each party, which seldom happens, there is no chance for comparing impressions and correcting misinterpretations. The university classroom is a convenient laboratory to make such discoveries. For example, U.S. students often complain that international student members of a discussion or project group seem uncooperative or uninterested. One such person who had been judged "guilty" offered the following explanation:

I was surrounded by Americans with whom I couldn't follow their tempo of discussion half of the time. I have difficulty to listen and speak, but also with the way they handle the group. I felt uncomfortable because sometimes they believe their opinion strongly. I had been very serious about the whole subject but I was afraid I would say something wrong. I had the idea but not the words.[7]

The classroom is also a good place to test whether one common nonverbal behavior, the smile, is actually the universal people assume it to be. The following enlightening comments came from international students newly arrived in the United States and a U.S. student:[8]

Japanese student: *On my way to and from school I have received a smile by non-acquaintance American girls several times. I have finally learned they have no interest for me; it means only a kind of greeting to a foreigner. If someone smiles at a stranger in Japan, especially a girl, she can assume he is either a sexual maniac or an impolite person.*

Korean student: *An American visited me in my country for one week. His inference was that people in Korea are not very friendly because they didn't smile or want to talk with foreign people. Most Korean people take time to get to be friendly with people. We never talk or smile at strangers.*

Arabian student: *When I walked around the campus my first day many people smiled at me. I was very embarrassed and rushed to the men's room to see if I had made a mistake with my clothes. But I could find nothing for them to smile at. Now I am used to all the smiles.*

U.S. student: *I was waiting for my husband on a downtown corner when a man with a baby and two young children approached. Judging by small quirks of fashion he had not been in the U.S. long. I have a baby about the same age and in appreciation of his family and obvious involvement as a father I smiled at him. Immediately I realized I did the wrong thing as he stopped, looked me over from head to toe and said, "Are you waiting for me? You meet me later?" Apparently I had acted as a prostitute would in his country.*

Vietnamese student: *The reason why certain foreigners may think that Americas are superficial—and they are, some Americans even recognize this—is that they talk and smile too much. For people who come from placid cultures where nonverbal language is more used, and where a silence, a smile, a glance have their own meaning, it is true that Americans speak a lot. The superficiality of Americans can also be detected in their relations with others. Their friendships are, most of the time, so ephemeral compared to the friendships we have at home. Americans make friends very easily and leave their friends almost as quickly, while in my country it takes a long time to find out a possible friend and then she becomes your friend—with a very strong sense of the term.*

Another U.S. student gives her view:

In general it seems to me that foreign people are not necessarily snobs but are very unfriendly. Some class members have told me that you shouldn't smile at others while passing them by on the street. To me I can't stop smiling. It's just natural to be smiling and friendly. I can see now why so many foreign people stick together. They are impossible to get to know. It's like the Americans are big bad wolves. How do Americans break this barrier? I want friends from all over the world but how do you start to be friends without offending them or scaring them off—like sheep?[9]

The discussion thus far threatens the popular expectation that increased contact with representatives of diverse cultures through travel, student exchange programs, joint business ventures, and so on will result in better understanding and friendship. Tests of that assumption have indeed been disappointing.[10] Recent research, for example, found that Vietnamese immigrants who speak English well and have the best jobs are suffering the most from psychosomatic complaints and mental problems and are less optimistic about the future than their counterparts who remain in ethnic enclaves without attempts to adjust to their new homeland. One explanation given is that these persons, unlike the less acculturated immigrants, "spend considerable time in the mainstream of society, regularly facing the challenges and stresses of dealing with American attitudes."[11]

After 15 years of listening to conversations between international and U.S. students and professors and seeing the frustrations of both groups as they try to understand each other, this author, for one, is inclined to agree with Charles Frankel, who says, "Tensions exist within nations and between nations that never would have existed were these nations not in such intensive cultural communication with one another."[12] It doesn't have to be that way. Just as more opportunities now exist for cross-cultural contact, so does more information about what will be likely to make the venture more satisfactory. There are more orientation and training programs around the country, more courses in intercultural communication in educational institutions, and more published material.[13] However, until the majority can put aside the euphoria of the expectation of similarity among all people of the world and squarely face the likelihood of difference and misunderstanding, they will not be motivated to take advantage of these resources.

Until recently the method used to improve chances for successful intercultural communication was just to gather information about the customs of the other country and a smattering of the language. Behaviors and attitudes of its people might be researched, but almost always from a secondhand source. Experts realize that information gained in this fashion is general, seldom sufficient, and may or may not be applicable to the specific situation and area that the traveler visits. Also, knowing "what to expect" often blinds the observer to all but what confirms his or her image. Any contradictory evidence that does filter through the screens of preconception is likely to be treated as an exception and thus discounted.

A better approach is to begin by studying the history, political structure, art, literature, and language of the country if time permits. Even more important, develop an investigative, nonjudgmental attitude and a high tolerance for ambiguity—which means lowered defenses. Margaret Mead suggests sensitizing persons to the kinds of things that need to be taken into account instead of developing behavior and attitude stereotypes. She reasons that there are individual differences in each encounter and that changes occur regularly in culture patterns, which makes researched information obsolete.[14]

Edward Stewart also warns against providing lists of "do's and don'ts" for travelers for several reasons, the main one being that behavior is ambiguous. Another reason is that the same action can have different meanings in different situations and no one can be armed with prescriptions for every contingency. Instead Stewart encourages persons to understand the assumptions and values on which their own behavior rests. This can then be compared with what is found in the other culture, and a "third culture" can be adopted based on expanded cross-cultural understanding.[15]

One way to follow Margaret Mead's suggestion of improving sensitivity to what might go wrong is to examine variables in the intercultural communication process. One stumbling block has already been discussed, the hazard of *assuming similarity instead of difference*. A second block is so obvious it hardly needs mentioning—*language*. Vocabulary, syntax, idioms, slang, dialects, and so on all cause difficulty, but the person struggling with a different language is at least aware of being in this kind of trouble.

A worse language problem is the tenacity with which someone will cling to just one meaning of a word or phrase in the new language, regardless of connotation or context. The infinite variations possible, especially if inflection and tonal qualities are added, are so difficult to cope with that they are often waved aside. The reason this problem is worse than simply struggling to translate foreign words is because each person thinks he or she understands. The nationwide misinterpretation of Khrushchev's sentence "We'll bury you" is a classic example. Even "yes" and "no" cause trouble. When a Japanese hears, "Won't you have some tea?" he or she listens to the literal meaning of the sentence and answers, "No," meaning that he or she wants some. "Yes, I won't" would be a better reply because this tips off the host or hostess that there may be a misunderstanding. Also, in some cultures, it is polite to refuse the first or second offer of refreshment. Many foreign guests have gone hungry because their U.S. host or hostess never presented the third offer—another case of "no" meaning "yes."

Learning the language, which most visitors to foreign countries consider their only barrier to understanding, is actually only the beginning. As Frankel says, "To enter into a culture is to be able to hear, in Lionel Trilling's phrase, its special 'hum and buzz of implication.'"[16] This suggests the third stumbling block, *nonverbal misinterpretations*. People from different cultures inhabit different sensory realities. They see, hear, feel, and smell only that which has some meaning or importance for them. They abstract whatever fits into their personal world of recognition and then interpret it through the frame of reference of their own culture. An example follows.

An Oregon girl in an intercultural communication class asked a young man from Saudi Arabia how he would nonverbally signal that he liked her. His response was to smooth back his hair, which to her was just a common nervous gesture signifying nothing. She repeated her question three times. He smoothed his hair three times, and, realizing that she was not recognizing this movement as his reply to her question, automatically ducked his head and stuck out his tongue slightly in embarrassment. This behavior *was* noticed by the girl and she expressed astonishment that he would show liking for someone by sticking out his tongue.

The lack of comprehension of nonverbal signs and symbols that are easy to observe—such as gestures, postures, and other body movements—is a definite communication barrier. But it is possible to learn the meanings of these messages, usually in informal rather than formal ways. It is more difficult to note correctly the unspoken codes of the other culture that are further from awareness, such as the handling of time and spatial relationships and subtle signs of respect of formality.[17]

The fourth stumbling block is the presence of *preconceptions and stereotypes*. If the label "inscrutable" has preceded the Japanese guest, it is thus we explain the Japanese constant and inappropriate smile. The stereotype that Arabs are "inflammable" causes U.S. students to keep their distance or alert authorities when an animated and noisy group from the Middle East gathers. A professor who expects everyone from Indonesia, Mexico, and many other countries to "bargain" may unfairly interpret a hesitation or request from an international student as a move to manipulate preferential treatment.

Stereotypes help do what Ernest Becker says the anxiety-prone human race must do—reduce the threat of the unknown by making the world predictable.[18] Indeed, this is one of the basic functions of culture: to lay out a predictable world in which the individual is firmly oriented. Stereotypes are overgeneralized beliefs that provide conceptual bases from which to "make sense" out of what goes on around us. In a foreign land their use increases our feeling of security and is psychologically necessary to the degree that we cannot tolerate ambiguity or the sense of helplessness resulting from inability to understand and deal with people and situations beyond our comprehension.

Stereotypes are stumbling blocks for communicators because they interfere with objective viewing of stimuli—the sensitive search for cues to guide the imagination toward the other person's reality. Stereotypes are not easy to overcome in ourselves or to correct in others, even with the presentation of evidence. They persist because they are firmly established as myths or truisms by one's own national culture and because they sometimes rationalize prejudices. They are also sustained and fed by the tendency to perceive selectively only those pieces of new information that correspond to the image held. For example, the Asian or African visitor who is accustomed to privation and the values of self-denial and self-help cannot fail to experience American culture as materialistic and wasteful. The stereotype for the visitor becomes a reality.

The fifth stumbling block and another deterrent to understanding between persons of differing cultures or ethnic groups is the *tendency to evaluate*, to approve or disapprove, the statements and actions of the other person or group rather than to try to comprehend completely the thoughts and feelings expressed from the world view of the other. Each person's culture or way of life always seems right, proper, and natural. This bias prevents the open-minded attention needed to look at the attitudes and behavior patterns from the other's point of view. A mid-day siesta changes from a "lazy habit" to a "pretty good idea" when someone listens long enough to realize the mid-day temperature in that country is 115° F.

The author, fresh from a conference in Tokyo where Japanese professors had emphasized the preference of the people of Japan for simple natural settings of rocks, moss, and water and of muted greens and misty ethereal landscapes, visited the Katsura Imperial Gardens in Kyoto. At the appointed time of the tour a young Japanese guide approached the group of 20 waiting Americans and remarked how fortunate it was that the day was cloudy. This brought hesitant smiles to the group who were less than pleased at the prospect of a shower. The guide's next statement was that the timing of the midsummer visit was particularly appropriate in that the azalea and rhododendron blossoms were gone and the trees had not yet turned to their brilliant fall colors. The group laughed loudly, now convinced that the young man had a fine sense of humor. I winced at his bewildered expression, realizing that had I come before attending the conference I, also evaluating the weather as "not very good," would have shared the group's inference that he could not be serious.

The communication cutoff caused by immediate evaluation is heightened when feelings and emotions are deeply involved; yet this is just the time when listening with understanding is most needed. This can be exemplified by the long deadlock in resolving the issue of the U.S. hostages in Iran. It takes both awareness of the tendency to close our minds and courage to risk change in our own perceptions and values to dare to comprehend why someone thinks and acts differently from us. As stated by Sherif, Sherif, and Nebergall, "A person's commitment to his religion, politics, values of his family, and his stand on the virtue of his way of life are ingredients in his self-picture—intimately felt and cherished."[19]

It is very easy to dismiss strange or different behaviors as "wrong," listen through a thick screen of value judgments, and therefore fail miserably to achieve a fair understanding. The impatience of the American public over the choice of the shape of the conference table at the Paris Peace talks is another example. There are innumerable examples of intercultural value clashes that result in a breach in interpersonal relationships. Two follow:[20]

U.S. student: *A Persian friend got offended because when we got in an argument with a third party, I didn't take his side. He says back home you are supposed to take a friend's or family's side even when they are wrong. When you get home then you can attack the "wrongdoer" but you are never supposed to go against a relative or friend to a stranger. This I found strange because even if it is my mother and I think she is wrong, I say so.*

Korean student: *When I call on my American friend he said through window, "I am sorry. I have no time because of my study." Then he shut the window. I couldn't understand through my*

cultural background. House owner should have welcome visitor whether he likes or not and whether he is busy or not. Also the owner never speaks without opening his door.

The sixth stumbling block is *high anxiety*, separately mentioned for the purpose of emphasis. Unlike the other five (assumption of similarity, language, nonverbal misinterpretations, preconceptions and stereotypes, and the practice of immediate evaluation), the stumbling block of high anxiety is not distinct but underlies and compounds the others. Different language and nonverbal patterns are difficult to use or interpret under the best of conditions. The distraction of high anxiety (sometimes called "internal noise") makes mistakes even more likely. As stated by Jack Gibb:

Defense arousal prevents the listener from concentrating upon the message. Not only do defensive communicators send off multiple value, motive, and affect cues, but also defensive recipients distort what they receive. As a person becomes more and more defensive, he becomes less and less able to perceive accurately the motives, the values, and the emotions of the sender.[21]

The stumbling blocks other than language and nonverbal are defense mechanisms in themselves, as previously explained, and as such would obviously increase under stress.

The present of anxiety/tension is common in cross-cultural experiences due to the number of uncertainties present and the personal involvement and risk. Whether or not the reaction will be debilitating depends on the level of activation and whether the feeling is classified as being pleasant (thought of as excitement or anticipation) or unpleasant (anxiety). Moderate arousal and positive attitudes prepare one to meet challenges with energy, but high arousal, caused by a buildup of continued moderate stress, depletes the body's energy reserve quickly and defense must be used whether or not the person wills it. If the stay in a foreign country is prolonged and the newcomer cannot let down his or her high alert level, the "culture shock" phenomenon occurs. Illness may result, the body forcing needed rest and recuperation.

Anxious feelings usually permeate both parties in a dialogue. The host national is uncomfortable when talking with a foreigner because he or she cannot maintain the normal flow of verbal and non-verbal interaction. There are language and perception barriers; silences are too long or too short; proxemic and other norms may be violated. He or she is also threatened by the other's unknown knowledge, experience, and evaluation— the visitor's potential for scrutiny and rejection of the host national and his or her country. The inevitable question, "How do you like it here?" which the foreigner abhors, is a quest for reassurance, or at least a "feeler" that reduces the unknown and gives grounds for defense if that seems necessary.

The foreign members of dyads are even more threatened. They feel strange and vulnerable, helpless to cope with messages that swamp them, to which "normal" reactions seem inappropriate. Their self-esteem is often intolerably undermined unless they employ such defenses as withdrawal into their own reference group or into themselves, screening out or misperceiving stimuli, rationalization, overcompensation, "going native," or becoming aggressive or hostile. None of these defenses leads to effective communication.

Fatigue is a natural result of such a continued state of alertness, but, too often, instead of allowing needed rest, the body then tenses even more to keep up its guard in the potentially threatening environment. To relax is to be vulnerable. An international student says it well:

During those several months after my arrival in the U.S.A., every day I came back from school exhausted so that I had to take a rest for a while, stretching myself on the bed. For, all the time, I strained every nerve in order to understand what the people were saying and make myself understood in my broken English. When I don't understand what American people are talking about and why they are laughing, I sometimes

have to pretend to understand by smiling, even though I feel alienated, uneasy and tense.

In addition to this, the difference in culture or customs, the way of thinking between two countries, produces more tension because we don't know how we should react to totally foreign customs or attitudes, and sometimes we can't guess how the people from another country react to my saying or behavior. We always have a fear somewhere in the bottom of our hearts that there are much more chances of breakdown in intercultural communication than in communication with our own fellow countrymen.[22]

Knowing that the aforementioned stumbling blocks are present is certainly an aid in avoiding them, but these particular ones cannot be easily circumvented. For most people it takes insight, training, and sometimes an alteration of long-standing habits or cherished beliefs before progress can be made. But the increasing need for global understanding and cooperation makes the effort vital. To show that it is not impossible a few general suggestions follow.

We can study other languages and learn to expect differences in nonverbal forms and other cultural aspects. It is also possible to train ourselves to meet intercultural encounters with more attention to situational details, using an investigative approach rather than preconceptions and stereotypes. We can gradually expose ourselves to differences so that they become less threatening. By practicing conscious relaxation techniques we can also learn to lower our tension level when needed to avoid triggering defensive reactions. In a relaxed state it is also easier to allow the temporary suspension of our own world view, a necessary step to experience empathy. What the intercultural communicator must seek to achieve is summarized by Roger Harrison when he says:

. . . the communicator cannot stop at knowing that the people he is working with have different customs, goals, and thought patterns from his own. He must be able to feel his way into intimate contact with these alien values, attitudes,

and feelings. He must be able to work with them and within them, neither losing his own values in the confrontation nor protecting himself behind a wall of intellectual detachment.[23]

NOTES

1. Eibl-Eibesfeldt, Irenaus, "Experimental Criteria for Distinguishing Innate from Culturally Conditioned Behavior," in *Cross-Cultural Understanding: Epistemology in Anthropology*, ed. F. S. C. Northrop and Helen H. Livingston (New York: Harper & Row, 1964), p. 304.

2. Furst, Charles, "Automating Attention," *Psychology Today* (August 1979), p. 112.

3. See Darwin, Charles, *The Expression of Emotions in Man and Animals* (New York: Appleton, 1872); Eibl-Eibesfeldt, Irenaus, *Ethology: The Biology of Behavior* (New York: Holt, Rinehart & Winston, 1970); Ekman, Paul, and Wallace V. Friesan, "Constants Across Cultures in the Face and Emotion," *Journal of Personality and Social Psychology* 17 (1971), pp. 124–129.

4. Ekman, Paul, "Movements with Precise Meanings," *Journal of Communication* 26 (Summer 1976), pp. 19–20.

5. Ekman, Paul, and Wallace Friesen, "The Repertoire of Nonverbal Behavior—Categories, Origins, Usage and Coding," *Semiotica*, 1, 1.

6. Personal correspondence. Mr. Do is a counselor at the Indochinese Center in Portland, Oregon, and a counselor-interpreter at the Indochinese Psychiatry Clinic.

7. Taken from student papers in a course in intercultural communication taught by the author.

8. Ibid.

9. Ibid.

10. See for example: Wedge, Bryant, *Visitors to the United States and How They See Us* (N.J.: D. Van Nostrand Company, 1965); and Miller, Milton, et al.,

"The Cross Cultural Student: Lessons in Human Nature, *Bulletin of Menninger Clinic* (March 1971).

11. Horn, Jack D., "Vietnamese Immigrants: Doing Poorly by Doing Well," *Psychology Today* (June 1980), pp. 103–104.

12. Frankel, Charles, *The Neglected Aspect of Foreign Affairs* (Washington, D.C.: Brookings Institution, 1965), p. 1.

13. For information see newsletters and other material prepared by the Society for Intercultural Education, Training and Research (SIETAR), Georgetown Univ., Washington, D.C., 20057. Sources are also listed in the *International and Intercultural Communication Annual*, published by the Speech Communication Association, 5205 Leesburg Pike, Falls Church, Virginia 22041; the *International Journal of Intercultural Relations*, New York: Pergamon Press; and *The Bridge*, 1800 Pontiac, Denver, Colorado 80220.

14. Mead, Margaret, "The Cultural Perspective," in *Communication or Conflict*, ed. Mary Capes (Association Press, 1960).

15. Stewart, Edward C., *American Cultural Patterns: A Cross-Cultural Perspective* (Intercultural Network, Inc., 906 N. Spring Ave., LaGrange Park, Illinois 60525, 1972), p. 20.

16. Frankel, *The Neglected Aspect of Foreign Affairs*, p. 103.

17. For an overview see Ramsey, Sheila J., "Nonverbal Behavior: An Intercultural Perspective," in *Handbook of Intercultural Communication*, ed. Molefi K. Asante, Eileen Newmark, and Cecil A. Blake (Beverly Hills/London: Sage Publications, 1979), pp. 105–143.

18. Becker, Ernest, *The Birth and Death of Meaning* (New York: Free Press, 1962), pp. 84–89.

19. Sherif, Carolyn W., Musafer Sherif, and Roger Nebergall, *Attitude and Attitude Change* (Philadelphia: W. B. Saunders Co., 1965), p. vi.

20. Taken from student papers in a course in intercultural communication taught by the author.

21. Gibb, Jack R., "Defensive Communication," *Journal of Communication* 2 (September 1961), 141–148.

22. Taken from student papers in a course in intercultural communication taught by the author.

23. Harrison, Roger, "The Design of Cross Cultural Training: An Alternative to the University Model," in *Explorations in Human Relations Training and Research* (Bethesda, Md.: National Training Laboratories, 1966), NEA No. 2, p. 4.

Human Communication and Cross-Cultural Effectiveness

BRENT D. RUBEN

A great deal has been written about problems sojourners encounter as they strive to adapt to the demands and challenges of a new or different cultural environment.[1] A topic of no less importance to many persons whose professional or technical roles take them to new cultures is the question of how one functions effectively with individuals from other cultures in work and work-related contexts. Especially for the many Western advisors, technical personnel, and sponsoring governmental and private agencies involved in projects in Third World countries, such concerns are of increasing importance. This paper addresses this issue in a very basic manner from the perspective of human communication. To indicate the relevance of communication to problems of skills and knowledge transfer, a prototypical case study is presented. The case highlights some barriers to effective transfer-of-skills, and provides the foundation for a discussion of the professional sojourner as a teacher. Next, a summary of some recent research on the role of particular communication be-

From the *International and Intercultural Communication Annual*, Vol. IV, December 1977, pp. 98–105. Reproduced by permission of the Speech Communication Association and the author. Brent D. Ruben is Associate Professor and Assistant Chairman of the Department of Human Communication at Rutgers University. The author gratefully acknowledges the contributions of Daniel Kealey and Pri Notowidigdo of the Canadian International Development Briefing Centre, and the support and encouragement of Pierre Lortie, Director of the Centre.

havior in cross-cultural effectiveness is presented. Finally, some implications and possible applications of these findings are explored.

A CASE STUDY

Mr. S has accepted a position as an advisor in a Third-world country. He will be working directly with Mr. Akwagara, a national. Together they will have administrative responsibility for their project. Mr. S is eager to arrive at his post. His work experience in the U.S. seems exceptionally well suited to the task he must accomplish in his post in the developing country, and his high level of motivation and record of consistently superior achievement reassures him—and those who selected him—that he will encounter little he can't handle in his assignment.

After having been on the job for several weeks, Mr. S is experiencing considerable frustration. To S, it appears that Akwagara and most of the subordinates lack both training and motivation. On a number of occasions S has endeavored to point out to Akwagara, tactfully, that his practices are both inefficient and ineffective. Akwagara's responses seemed to S to indicate total indifference. On one occasion, S suggested that he and Akwagara get together one evening for a few drinks, thinking that in an informal setting he might be more successful in making Akwagara aware of some of these problems. The two went out together, but nearly every effort to bring up the work situation by S was followed by Akwagara changing the subject to unrelated chatter about family and friends.

The problem became increasingly severe in the weeks that followed. It seemed to S the only way he could get the job done he was sent to do, was to do most of it by himself. Gradually, he assumed more and more of the responsibilities that had been previously performed by Akwagara. Though he feels some concern about this situation from time to time, these feelings are more than compensated for by the knowledge that he is getting the job done that he was sent to do.

Consider the question, is S succeeding or failing? The answer, of course, depends largely upon how one defines the role of the sojourner. If one takes the point of view that the task of the sojourner consists solely of getting the job done, we would probably conclude that S is functioning effectively. Viewed from another perspective, one cannot help but conclude that the advisor has failed sadly. The job is being done at the cost of successful transfer-of-skills. Probable consequences of his approach include the alienation of Akwagara, a loss of credibility for Akwagara among his subordinates he must supervise after S departs, and reinforcement of the view that Western advisors are insensitive, egocentric, and not sincerely interested in the welfare of the host country or nationals.

For S, the sponsoring agency, and the country, the consequence is a failure to be able to share knowledge and skills meaningfully. The ultimate tragedy is that S, with the best of intentions and motives, may in fact spend two years of his life believing that he is functioning as the ideal advisor. All the while, he may actually contribute to forces which retard the process of growth, change, and development in his project and in the country as a whole. As this case, and a number of writings and research well indicate, the ability to satisfactorily understand and relate to others in a cross-cultural setting is probably the single most critical ingredient necessary to an advisor's success, and essential if one is to translate one's own skills and knowledge into the idiom of the culture.

THE SOJOURNER AS TEACHER

In conceptualizing the role of the sojourner or technical advisor in terms of the effective transfer-of-skills, it seems useful to think broadly of the role as one of teacher. A teacher, after all, is a person who possesses particular knowledges and skills he or she wishes to impart to others. There are two distinct components of teaching—at least of effective teaching. First, the teacher must have an appropriate mastery of skills and knowledge in his or her field. Secondly, the teacher must be able to package and deliver those understandings to other persons in such a way that they will be able to accept, utilize, and integrate them. For the sojourner, these same components are crucial.

With regard to most technical advisors selected for overseas postings, the first component is well satisfied. Whether selected for an assignment to assist with the installation of a computer or electronic communication systems, the development of educational, governmental, agricultural, economic, or industrial policy, or any of a number of other less technical positions, job-related competencies are seldom a problem. The second ingredient necessary for effectiveness of the sojourner is a set of skills and knowledge totally unrelated to the job. These skills and understandings have to do with communication, and research and reports from the field indicate that such capabilities are even more critical to the success of an advisor and a project than his or her job skills. For convenience, one can refer to this needed set of skills as *communication competence*.[2] If job or role competence is the ability to complete a task efficiently, communication competence is the ability to effectively relate to other persons in the process. Achieving an integration of the two is important in the short and long run, and from both idealistic and practical points of view.

The importance of communication to effective cross-cultural functioning is well illustrated by the case of Mr. S. As a member of a Western culture, it is likely that to Mr. S time and money are important criteria for success; he may well view wealth and power as essential to the solution of most problems, consider democratic or majority rule as the appropriate form of governance, revere technology, regard competition as good and winning an important goal. He likely values material possessions, the scientific method, efficiency, organization, specialization, and a clear separation between work and leisure. In his communication style, he is likely to be reasonably aggressive, direct, impatient, self-assured, and to regard business as the topic of major importance in most of his interactions, attaching a lesser value to discussion of family and personal matters.

Depending upon Akwagara's cultural background, he is likely to have a quite different communicational framework. For him speech and efficiency may be irrelevant or negative values. Material possessions, competition and winning may be regarded with far less concern, and he may view extended family relationships as the primary source of power and status. The democratic model, technology, progress, and Western development may be viewed with cynicism and suspicion. Conditions of living may be regarded primarily as inevitable consequences of manifest destiny, leaving little room for individual initiative or impact. Work and leisure may well be blended, and he may be little concerned with systematic, or efficient organization, or specialization. In discussions, Akwagara may well be relatively passive, indirect, patient, and will likely place a much higher priority on the topic of family and friends, than upon business. He may also be accustomed to standing or sitting close to persons he is talking to, and to numerous gestures involving frequent physical contact. In such an instance, the two individuals have a great many barriers to overcome if either is to understand with much accuracy the words and actions of the other.

RELEVANT RESEARCH

There has been considerable research effort directed toward identifying communication behaviors which contribute to effectiveness within one's own culture. Wiemann[3] identified three main schools of thought about face-to-face interaction. The first he characterized as the human relations or T-group approach, typified by the work of Argyris,[4] Bochner and Kelley,[5] and Holland and Baird.[6] The second orientation, the social skill approach, is reflected especially in the work of Argyle and Kendon,[7] and the third is essentially a self-presentation approach suggested in the work of Goffman,[8] Rodnick and Wood,[9] and Weinstein.[10]

Though attempts to consider how these approaches generalize to cross-cultural interpersonal situations have been few, a number of researchers (such as Arensberg and Niehoff;[11]

Barna;[12] Brislin and Pedersen;[13] Gudykunst, Hammer, and Wiseman;[14] Bochner;[15] Cleveland and Mangone;[16] and others[17]) have suggested certain personal characteristics and/or skills thought to be crucial to effectiveness in such contexts. A synthesis of findings suggested in intra- and inter-cultural writings yields some consensus. For those concerned particularly with communication, a number of such behaviors seem important. Seven of these are: (1) capacity to communicate respect; (2) capacity to be nonjudgmental; (3) capacity to personalize one's knowledge and perceptions; (4) capacity to display empathy; (5) capacity to be flexible; (6) capacity for turn-taking; and (7) tolerance for ambiguity.

Research was undertaken by Ruben and Kealey[18] to determine the relative importance of these communication behaviors to cross-cultural effectiveness. The findings from in-the-field research suggest that an avoidance of extreme *task, self-centered*, and *judgmental behavior*—in that order—contribute most to effective transfer-of-skills. *A tolerance for ambiguity, the ability to display respect*, and a *personal orientation to knowledge*, are next in importance in cross-cultural effectiveness, followed by *empathy* and *turn-taking*. In the following sections, these communication dimensions will be discussed and their relationship to effective transfer-of-skills briefly explored.

TASK AND RELATIONAL BEHAVIOR

Roles, how they are enacted, and the impact they have, have been a concern to intra- and inter-cultural researchers alike.[19] Individuals function in a variety of roles within interpersonal, group, and organizational settings. Behaviors that involve the initiation of ideas, requests for information, seeking of clarification, evaluation of ideas, etc., are directly related to the group's task or problem-solving activities. Behaviors that involve harmonizing, mediation, gatekeeping, attempts to regulate the evenness of contribution of group members, compromising, etc., are related to the relationship-building activities of a group.

Some situations seem to call for an intense concern for "getting the job done." Other situations call for building group cohesiveness, encouraging participation, and making certain no one feels excluded from involvement. Westerners seem to learn to focus mostly on the former, and are typically not much concerned about how involved people feel in the process, how much group or organizational solidarity develops, how people value the products of their effort, etc. But as indicated previously, the transfer-of-skills requires not only getting a job done, but also the competence to get it done in such a way that people feel a part of the completed project and have learned something from witnessing the process. Research suggests strongly that too much concern for getting the job done can lead to failure in terms of effectiveness at skills-transfer.[20]

Here, the Akwagara case provides an excellent illustration. Mr. S has apparently mastered the skills often demanded for success in Western occupational roles. His style, appropriate to his own cultural background, is one of fast-paced problem-solving. Yet, in a developmental context, the very skills that were perhaps critical to his selection as a cross-cultural professional, may become a liability in a culture where rapid-fire problem-solving is less valued. From such a cultural perspective, S may well be viewed as impatient, over-zealous, insensitive, and lacking concern for people. The consequences of such a response may well be to foster feelings of resentment toward S, and thereby render his technical skills totally useless, and preclude effectiveness at transfer-of-skills.

SELF-ORIENTED BEHAVIORS

Other role behaviors sometimes displayed by individuals in an interpersonal context are individualistic or self-centered behaviors that function in negative ways from a group's perspective. Behaviors such as being highly resistant to ideas of others, returning to issues and points of view previously acted upon and/or dismissed by the group, attempting to call attention to oneself, seeking to project a highly positive personal image by noting achievements and professional qualifications. and attempting to manipulate the group by asserting authority, are dysfunctional in intra-cultural as well as in inter-cultural contexts.

While the S case makes no reference to what might be thought of as self-centered communicative behavior, research conducted by Ruben and Kealey suggests that such behavior patterns toward persons in one's own culture are a good predictor of potential problems at successful interaction with persons from differing cultures.[21]

NON-JUDGMENTALNESS

People like to feel that what they say is not being judged by someone else without having been given an opportunity to fully explain themselves and be sincerely listened to. When persons find themselves being interrupted before having finished speaking, or notice that someone is nodding in disagreement even before they have finished presenting their thoughts, barriers to effective relating are set in place. The likelihood of teaching or transferring skills in such a setting is greatly lessened.[22] Ideally, one would strive to avoid passing judgments on what others have to say until one has enough information to be fairly certain that his or her evaluations will be based on a reasonably complete understanding of the other's point of view. When persons believe they have been fully and attentively listened to, they are generally much more receptive to hearing reactions—whether positive or negative. In addition to being of use in improving the fidelity of information transmission, nonevaluative postures seem likely to increase the receiver's regard for the source of nonevaluative messages, and thereby improve the quality of the relationship.

Again, with S and Akwagara, it isn't clear from the information presented whether S was non-judgmental or not. One may infer, however, that had S invested a bit more effort in listening to and trying to understand Akwagara's viewpoint, some of the problems might have been alleviated. Apart from the case, it is interesting to note that persons

who are non-judgmental with others in their own culture will often be more effective in cross-cultural skills transfer than persons who are highly judgmental.[23]

TOLERANCE FOR AMBIGUITY

The ability to react to new and ambiguous situations with little visible discomfort can be an important asset when adapting to a new environment. Although most people probably do react with some degree of personal discomfort to new environments, some seem more able to adjust quickly to those around them. Excessive discomfort resulting from being placed in a new or different environment—or from finding the familiar environment altered in some critical ways—can lead to confusion, frustration, or even hostility. This may well be dysfunctional to the development of effective interpersonal relations within and across cultural boundaries. Colleagues and would-be friends—as with Akwagara—may easily become the unwitting and misplaced targets of verbal hostility during periods of adjustment; and while the frustrations are often short-lived, the feelings about the sojourner that they may have initiated, might not be. Learning to manage the feeling of frustration associated with ambiguity can thus be critical to effective adaptation in a new environment.[24] It is likely that a bit greater tolerance for ambiguity and tolerance for the lack of control one feels in a new environment would have aided S substantially in his efforts to integrate himself successfully into his new situation.

DISPLAY OF RESPECT

The ability to express respect and positive regard for another person has been suggested as an important component in effective interpersonal relations within and between cultures.[25] The expression of respect can be expected to confer status upon the recipient, contribute to self-esteem, and foster positive regard for the source of the communicated respect. People like to feel that others respect them, their accomplishments, their beliefs, and what they have to say. If one is able, through gestures, eye gaze, smiles, and words of encouragement, to indicate to others that he or she is sincerely interested in them, they are much more likely to respond positively to the person and what he or she has to say. In the case study, listening to Akwagara carefully, attentively, and encouragingly as he discussed family and friends, and reciprocating in kind, would have been an important means for S to have communicated his respect, and to begin to establish a strong foundation for an effective relationship—one that would be productive and satisfying on a day-to-day basis, and one that would facilitate the transfer of S's skills and knowledge, as he has intended.

PERSONALIZING KNOWLEDGE AND PERCEPTIONS

Different people explain themselves and the world around them in different terms. Some people tend to view their knowledge and perceptions as valid only for them; others tend to assume that their beliefs, values, and perceptions are valid for everyone. Presumably, the more a person recognizes the extent to which knowledge is individual in nature, the more easily he or she will be able to adjust to other people in other cultures whose views of what is "true" or "right" are likely to be quite different.

People who recognize that their values, beliefs, attitudes, knowledge, and opinions are their own—and not necessarily shared by others—often find it easier to form productive relationships, than persons who believe they know *The Truth*, and strive to "sell" their own perceptions, knowledge, skills, and values to others. If a person often begins sentences with phrases like "I think" or "I feel" or "In my own experience . . ." chances are he or she is aware more of the personal nature of their knowledge and values than if they are using introductions like "Africans tend to be . . ." or "Americans are . . ." or "Canadians believe . . ." Among persons whose ideas of what is *True* and *Right* differ

dramatically from that to which you've become accustomed, it is useful to keep in mind that one's beliefs, knowledge, and attitudes are products of their own experiences. Remembering also that one's "truths" may bear little in common to those of others—gives one an important advantage as a teacher.

It is in this area where S was perhaps weakest. He unwittingly assumed his job description, his timetable, his mode of operating, his distinctions between work and family, his definitions of "idle chatter," and so on, were in fact *the* understandings—ones which Akwagara *must* certainly share. The results are rather clear in the case study, as in so many other instances of relational problems with persons working within as well as across cultural boundaries.

DISPLAYING EMPATHY

The capacity to "put oneself in another's shoes," or to behave as if one could, has been often suggested as important to the development and maintenance of positive human relationships within and between cultures.[26] Individuals differ in their ability to display empathy. Some people are able to project an interest in others clearly and seem able to obtain and reflect a reasonably complete and accurate sense of another's thoughts, feelings, and/or experiences. Others may lack interest, or fail to display interest, and may be unable to project even superficial understanding of another's situation.

Many people are attracted to individuals who seem to be able to understand things from "their point of view." Certainly, since each individual has a unique set of past experiences, it is not possible to totally put oneself "in someone else's shoes." Through care in listening and observing, and with a sincere and diligent effort to understand the other person's communicational framework, one can, however, achieve some degree of empathy, a critical ingredient for effective teaching. Had Mr. S devoted more effort to establishing this sort of understanding of Akwagara, and had he been successful in reflecting the resulting awareness in his words and actions, many of the difficulties he encountered could have been avoided.

TURN-TAKING

People vary in the manner in which they "manage" (or fail to manage) interactions of which they are a part.[27] Some are skillful at governing their contribution to an interactive situation so that the needs and desires of others play a critical role in defining how the exchange will proceed. Effective management of interaction is displayed through taking turns in discussion and initiating and terminating interaction based on a reasonably accurate assessment of the needs and desires of others. Other individuals are less proficient at these dimensions and proceed in interactions with little or no regard for time sharing, and initiation and termination preferences of others. It is almost too obvious to note that people enjoy having an opportunity to take turns in discussion. This suggests strongly the need to avoid monopolizing conversations, and conversely, to resist the temptation to refuse to share responsibility for even participation. This simple factor is important to how one is perceived in one's own culture, as well as in other cultures, where reciprocity in discussion can serve to indicate interest in, and concern for, the other person.

SUMMARY

It has been the intention of the foregoing to provide a basic framework for discussing the role of communication in cross-cultural effectiveness. In simplifying these processes for purposes of discussion, there is the risk of neglecting important questions. Perhaps the most crucial of these has to do with the difficulty of generalizing findings from studies of one or two cultures to other cultures. The studies summarized in the last section of this article, for example, were concerned with Canadian technical personnel who worked in various jobs in Kenya. On the basis of these and other studies noted, we can speculate that the findings are likely relevant for "Westerners" working with individuals from the so-called "developing" countries.

Presumably, highly aggressive problem-solving behaviors would carry the same risks of ineffectiveness in many of the countries in Latin America, as in Kenya or other African countries, but further research is needed to verify these relationships.

There is another problem related to generalizing the research findings such as those discussed here. While one can argue that the *importance* of communication behaviors such as empathy, respect, non-judgmentalness, etc., transcends cultural boundaries, the way these are *expressed and interpreted* may vary substantially from one culture (or one subculture) to another. Thus, while prolonged eye contact or head nodding may well be a sign of respect in one culture, it may be interpreted in quite another—perhaps even in an opposite—way in other cultures. A final caution has to do with the difference between *knowing* and *doing*. Even within one's own culture, knowing that one *ought to be* respectful or empathic or non-judgmental does not guarantee that one will be able to perform the behavior, even with good intentions.

For persons who will work in cross-cultural situations, these three issues have a number of implications. The central theme that emerges from studies discussed in this paper is the need to be alert and sensitive to the needs, orientations, values, aspirations, and particularly communication styles of other persons with whom one interacts. One needs to know how respect, empathy, non-judgmentalness, turn-taking, orientation to knowledge, and group and organizational roles are *regarded* and *expressed* in a given culture. Of equal or greater importance to effectiveness at transfer-of-skills is the willingness to be introspective, and committed to see, to examine, and to learn from one's failures and weaknesses as well as one's successes and strengths. Only in this way can one's behavior be brought into congruence with what one believes and intends.

For those persons involved in cross-cultural training and selection, aspects of the studies discussed in this paper have important implications. First, findings underscore the importance of interpersonal communication skills to cross-cultural effectiveness, suggesting a need to attend more closely to interpersonal communication skills in selection and training. Secondly, the research indicates the usefulness of a person's communication behavior in his or her own culture as a predictor of his or her communication behavior in another culture. This seems to suggest a need in effectiveness training and research for relatively more attention to the individual, and perhaps relatively less attention to inherent differences between cultures. Thirdly, the discussion focuses attention on the difference between knowing and doing, underscoring the importance of training which is directed relatively more toward behaviorial effectiveness and relatively less toward theoretical and verbal mastery.

Each of these issues would seem to merit additional attention by researchers, as well. Perhaps most importantly, more study is needed to identify additional communication behaviors which may be significant for cross-cultural effectiveness. Further, research is needed to identify those communication behaviors which best generalize to a large number of cross-cultural situations. Such studies will serve to further strengthen the theoretical and pragmatic link beteen human communication and cross-cultural effectiveness suggested in this article.

NOTES

1. See C. M. Arensberg and A. H. Niehoff, *Introducing Social Change: A Manual for Community Development* (Chicago: Aldine-Atherton, 1971); R. B. Brislin and P. Pedersen. *Cross-Cultural Orientation Programs* (New York: Gardner Press, 1976); J. Gullahorn and J. Gullahorn, "An Extension of the U-Curve Hypothesis," *Journal of Social Issues* 19, No. 3 (1963), 33–47; E. T. Hall, *The Silent Language* (New York: Doubleday, 1959); and K. Oberg, "Culture Shock: Adjustment to the New Cultural Environments," *Practical Anthropology* 7 (1960), 177–182.

2. Systematic efforts to conceptualize "effective," "successful," or "competent" communication behavior have been relatively few in number. The notion of communication competence—used interchangeably with communication effectiveness—is discussed in this paper as a dyadic concept. For a particular interaction to be termed effective, or a person to be termed competent, the performance must meet the needs and goals of both the message initiator and the recipient. The term communication competence, as used in this paper, is based on the work of John Wiemann, who credits E. A. Weinstein as the originator of the term. See Brent D. Ruben, "The Machine Gun and the Marshmallow: Some Thoughts on the Concept of Effective Communication." Paper presented at the annual meeting of the Western Speech-Communication Association, Honolulu, Hawaii, 1972; and John M. Wiemann, "An Exploration of Communication Competence in Initial Interactions: An Experimental Study," Unpublished doctoral dissertation, Purdue University (1975).

3. John M. Wiemann (1975) provides an excellent summary and discussion of these orientations.

4. C. Argyris, "Explorations in Interpersonal Competence—1," *Journal of Applied Behavioral Science* (1965), 58–63.

5. A. P. Bochner and C. W. Kelley, "Interpersonal Competence: Rationale, Philosophy, and Implementation of a Conceptual Framework," *Speech Teacher* 23 (1974), 279–301.

6. J. L. Holland and L. L. Baird, "An Interpersonal Competency Scale," *Educational and Psychological Measurement* 28 (1968), 503–510.

7. M. Argyle and A. Kendon, "The Experimental Analysis of Social Performance," *Advances in Experimental Social Psychology* 3 (1967), 55–98.

8. Erving Goffman, *The Presentation of Self in Everyday Life* (Garden City: Doubleday, 1959); *Behavior in Public Places* (New York: Free Press, 1963); *Interaction Ritual* (Garden City: Anchor, 1967).

9. R. Rodnick and B. Wood, "The Communication Strategies of Children," *Speech Teacher* 22 (1973), 114–124.

10. E. A. Weinstein, "Toward a Theory of Interpersonal Tactics," in C. W. Backman and P. F. Secord (eds.), *Problems in Social Psychology* (New York: McGraw-Hill, 1966); "The Development of Interpersonal Competence," in D. A. Goslin (ed.), *Handbook of Socialization and Research* (Chicago: Rand McNally, 1969).

11. Arensberg and Niehoff (1971).

12. L. Barna, "Stumbling Blocks in Interpersonal Intercultural Communication." In David Hoopes (ed.), *Readings in Intercultural Communication*, vol. 1 (1972).

13. R. W. Brislin and P. Pedersen, *Cross-Cultural Orientation Programs* (New York: Gardner Press, 1976).

14. W. B. Gudykunst, M. Hammer, and W. B. Wiseman, "Determinants of the Sojourner's Attitudinal Satisfaction." In *Communication Yearbook* 1, B. Ruben (ed.), (New Brunswick, N.J.: Transaction-International Communication Association, 1977).

15. S. Bochner, "The Meditating Man and Cultural Diversity," *Topics in Cultural Learning* 1 (1973), 23–37.

16. H. Cleveland and G. J. Mangone (eds.), *The Art of Overseasmanship* (Syracuse: Syracuse University Press, 1957); and H. Cleveland, G. J. Mangone, and J. C. Adams, *The Overseas Americans* (New York: McGraw-Hill, 1960).

17. A review of writings on cross-cultural effectiveness is provided by Brent D. Ruben, Lawrence R. Askling, and Daniel J. Kealey in "Cross-Cultural Effectiveness," in *Overview of Intercultural Education, Training and Research*, vol. 1: Theory, David S. Hoopes, Paul B. Pedersen, and George W. Renwick (eds.), (Washington, D.C.: Society for Intercultural Education, Training and Research, 1977), 92–105.

18. The results discussed herein are based on a two-year study conducted in Canada and Kenya by Brent D. Ruben and Daniel J. Kealey, presented in preliminary form at the Third Annual Conference of the Society for Intercultural Education, Training and Research (Chicago: 1977) in a report entitled "Behavioral Assessment and the Prediction of Cross-Cultural Shock, Adjustment, and Effectiveness."

19. K. Benne and P. Sheats, "Functional Roles of Group Members," *Journal of Social Research* 4 (1948).

20. See discussion in Ruben and Kealey (1977).

21. Ruben and Kealey.

22. See Arensberg and Niehoff (1971); Barna (1972); Brislin and Pedersen (1976); and Gudykunst et al. (1977).

23. Ruben, Askling, and Kealey (1977); discussion of the role of this dimension in cross-cultural interaction is provided in P. S. Adler, "Beyond Cultural Identity: Reflections Upon Cultural and Multicultural Man," in *Topics in Culture Learning*, vol. 2 (1974), 23–41, and P. S. Adler, "The Transitional Experience: An Alternative View of Culture Shock," *Journal of Humanistic Psychology*, vol. 15. No. 3 (1975).

24. Aitken, T., *The Multinational Man: The Role of the Manager Abroad* (New York: Wiley, 1973) and G. M. Guthrie and I. N. Zektick, "Predicting Performance in the Peace Corps," *Journal of Social Psychology* 71 (1967), 11–21.

25. See R. R. Carkhuff, *Helping and Human Relations* (New York: Holt, Rinehart & Winston, 1969) and Arensberg and Niehoff (1971).

26. See R. R. Carkhuff (1969); Cleveland et al. (1960); Gudykunst et al. (1977).

27. John M. Wiemann and Mark L. Knapp, "Turn-Taking in Conversations," *Journal of Communication* 25, no. 2 (1975).

Decentering, Convergence, and Cross-Cultural Understanding

DEAN C. BARNLUND
NAOKI NOMURA

There is one pervasive factor that endangers the outcome of every cross-cultural encounter from the most casual to the most sophisticated: how to overcome the constant and pernicious influence of cultural bias in interpreting unfamiliar acts in alien settings. So intangible are the cultural norms that govern our meanings, yet so profound are their effects, that they can undermine the simplest conversation, the most delicate negotiation, and the most carefully conceived research.

What the members of any society share is a commitment to a system of assumptions and values, to a series of interactional rules, and to a set of symbolic codes for articulating their experiences. These cultural conventions comprise the frames into which all events are placed for interpretation; they are indispensable to making the world an intelligible and manageable place. It is this shared assumptive world that promotes consistency of meanings and facilitates cooperative activities within a society. Although the consistency of meanings within any community may be exaggerated, considerable interpretive commonality is evident in the distinctive institutions and practices that differentiate one society from another.[1]

Rarely, however, do cultures create identical paradigms of meaning—adopt the same perceptual focus, categorical imperatives, rules of logic, or evaluative criteria—hence problems of meaning are nearly inevitable whenever two ages or two cultures meet. Difficulties in communication arise between people of contrasting cultures not merely because events are so differently construed, but because the rules governing their constructions are so little understood. The members of every society tend to be oblivious to how they surround every object and event with an interpretative frame of their own authorship. And such interpretive frames are acquired so early in life, and assimilated so completely, that they operate automatically and unconsciously. Yet it is these frames, more than events themselves, that affect how we look at the world, how we label its features, how we link one event to another, the motives that accompany our experience, and the acts that seem appropriate in fulfilling them.

The idea that our most primal processes are permeated with cultural bias—that our meanings are created rather than received, given to the world rather than taken from it—is an unsettling and complicating observation. Those who work in cross-cultural contexts, whether as participants or researchers, face a unique communicative challenge arising from the necessity of commuting between two or more assumptive worlds, shifting perceptual and cognitive processes to maintain a sufficient margin of empathy to sustain communication.

The problem of cultural bias is one that permeates all intercultural contacts at all levels. No one is completely free of a myopia born of culture and class. The aim here is to elucidate the nature of such cultural biases, to describe some ways of obtaining insight into them and, hopefully, to lessen their control of our behavior. Such insight might lead to a greater appreciation of the cultural dynamic that governs institutions and activities of a society that in some ways are alien and confusing.

This original essay was written especially for this volume. All rights reserved. Permission to reprint must be obtained from the publisher and the authors. Dean C. Barnlund teaches at San Francisco State University and Naoki Nomura teaches at Stanford University.

DECENTERING AND CONVERGENCE

In pursuit of this aim we shall explore two notions: the first is the concept of decentering. As used here the term refers to the process of becoming aware of and temporarily suspending the constructs normally used to interpret events so as to consider fresh ways of construing them.[2] Habitual assumptions are held in abeyance in order to explore alternative ways of interpreting them.[3] When successful, this sort of conceptual shift is often accompanied by increased appreciation that meanings derive not from objects or acts, but from the way they are construed by the interpreter. To decenter, then, is to see that all people polarize events in distinctive ways, that these are products of a particular personal and cultural context, and that other polarizations are not merely possible but equally reasonable.

The second notion, that of convergence through successive approximation, refers to the process through which one acquires an alternative construct. Each communicant in an intercultural encounter tries to establish some foothold in the experiential world of the other; both try to project themselves imaginatively into the "foreign" context of the other. Through a series of successive experiments in meaning, a sort of symbolic trial and error, ways of calibrating or connecting diverse meanings may be found, ways that can subsume their separateness in an emerging commonality. The American poet John Ciardi once described such a dialogue between an engineer and a poet, each of whom could not fathom what the other really did; as the engineer resorted to explaining mechanics through metaphors, and the poet through a structural analysis of verse, both came to appreciate their seemingly unrelated professions. All learning—and role-playing in particular—demonstrates that it is possible to expand our experience by entering the unfamiliar world of another person; the cross-cultural encounter, however, constitutes a far more serious challenge, since not only the meanings to be shared (the "content" of com-

munication), but also the means of their expression (the "process" of communication) are foreign.

We shall explore these themes of decentering and convergence through research on the communicative behavior of Japanese and Americans. The studies we shall use to illustrate these processes deal with matters of communicative style and the specific strategies employed in giving compliments and criticism in these two cultures. Our emphasis upon research is not because it is a more impressive or esoteric way of explaining decentering or convergence, but because it is the most tangible and concrete way. In research, decentering and convergence are constant challenges that are faced explicitly and are, therefore, accessible to scrutiny.

Our aim is a broad and humanistic one: to describe as simply as possible the process of creating, conducting, and evaluating inquiry into the communicative manner of Japanese and Americans, and to use this experience to expose the stages in the evolution of cross-cultural insight and empathy. We shall conclude by noting some parallels between the interpretive crises faced by the researcher and by the ordinary visitor or resident in an alien culture. In our view both face similar challenges, and both may find in decentering and convergence some guidance in overcoming cultural biases.

FIRST STAGE: THE FOCUS OF INQUIRY

Cultural parochialism, and the challenge to decenter, confront one at the most primitive and earliest stage of study, when the researcher first begins to think about another culture. Initial questions about other societies tend not only to be global, but also to reflect the unstated but implicit premises behind commitment to Christian or Buddhist religions, capitalist or communist economics, linear or intuitive logics, individual or collective identities. These latent assumptions, rarely recognized and even less often articulated are, after all, all we have; they provide guidance in transforming the flux of sensations into an intelligible sequence of events. It is not surprising that such premises should appear not to be premises at all, but the hard outlines of an "objective" reality. So it is seductive, in encounters with people of alien cultures, to interpret their acts by the same standards that apply so naturally within one's own society.

The cultures of the West, for example, rest on the notion of a singular and indivisible self; this is a core assumption of Judeo-Christian thought, it permeates Western institutions and practices, it is the presumptive base on which legal and moral imperatives rest. It is hardly surprising, then, that Western behavioral sciences presume the existence of a "self," the psychic counterpart of the physical body. Without such an assumption there would be no studies of self-concept, self-disclosure, self-actualization. (And one rarely encounters such research outside Western cultures except when performed by scientists trained in the West.)

While it is a provocative basis for studying human behavior in Western societies, where the concept of self legitimizes all institutions and processes, it is awkward and misleading when applied to societies that function without this construct. In some the self is seen as incorporating persons from the past; ancestors may be psychically present and influencing every meaning and motive. In other cultures the self is inconceivable apart from those who comprise the family, the clan, or peer group. To impose the notion of a separate self upon another culture may accommodate their acts within Western modes of thinking, but may grossly distort their significance in another culture. A Japanese, for example, may find it confusing or impossible to think of himself as a separate and independent self instead of as a subordinate of his supervisor, son to his father, father to his son, brother to his sister, or peer of his schoolmates. The idea of one self for one person is foreign to many Japanese; people are expected to be different persons in different situations, and those who possess a single self for varying social occasions are regarded as immature. Presupposing a singular identity—and the inability to decenter from that notion—distances one from the very acts one seeks to understand.

The concept of integrity displays a similar cultural parochialism: in the West it is regarded as truthfulness to self, a profound respect for the validity of private experience. It implies a courageous assertion of one's convictions in spite of, or even against, the convictions of others. But some societies, even some whose languages include the word, view it differently: integrity refers instead to respect for the experience of others and a willingness to subordinate personal meanings to communal meanings. A related idea, that of sincerity, also travels poorly across some borders, and sometimes not at all. To be "sincere" in America is to mean what one says, and to say what one means; the criteria are found within the individual. To be "sincere" in Japan is to be sensitive to what others are saying and feeling, and the criteria lie outside oneself. As Ruth Benedict noted, self-respect in one society derives from the matching of the inner and the outer person, in another society from the matching of the outer person to the expected person (Benedict 1946).

A parallel difficulty arises, of course, when foreign constructs are used to account for Western behavior. The concept of *amae*, which possesses almost the same explanatory power in Japan as the concept of the self in the United States, seems inappropriate in explaining features of American behavior. There is not only a lack of verbal equivalence but, one suspects, a lack of experiential relevance. There is similar awkwardness in exporting such constructs as *giri*, *on*, and *enryo* when applied in alien contexts. Even when researchers find a word-for-word parallel, members of foreign cultures may feel puzzled or doubtful that their acts have been explained as they know and experience them.

Our point is sensitively stated by the art critic Carter Ratcliff. Given the task of reviewing an exhibition of Indian artifacts, he comments on the impossibility of doing this fairly. Faced with the baskets and carvings of another world, he asks, "Isn't our most convincing knowledge of boundaries created by our own ways of making sense of things?" He notes that the tools of his trade, the terms used to discuss works of art, actually distance us rather than bring us closer to these objects. Words like "art," "artist," "sculpture," and "portrait" have no meaningful referents in Indian society. Nor, we might add, do the words "cubist," "impressionist," and "expressionist" that are so often applied to African sculpture. Ratcliff closes his essay on a chord we wish to strike as well: "We may have to find our way to the meaning of these works through a gradually abandoned esthetic of bewilderment" (Ratcliff 1974, p. 52).

Finding one's way into another culture proceeds best, in our view, through a process of decentering and convergence. How might this apply at the initial stage of cultural research? The first issue concerns who should undertake such research; the second concerns what is to be the focus of the research. There are several strategies to help counteract preliminary assumptive biases in the investigators. One is to create cross-cultural teams of researchers, each capable of arguing the assumptive biases and investigative tactics of their own culture. As each articulates his or her unique perspective, others may argue for alternative constructs that seem to fit their cultures better. As a topic takes form, it is subject to the pushes and pulls of investigators from both cultures, and all may be forced to expand their analytic frames to accommodate the others. Such a collaboration may not only counteract the biases that could confound a specific study, but may help to cultivate a broader general capacity to decenter among the researchers.

Another alternative, and one that may become more feasible in the future, is to provide researchers with opportunities to work and live within the cultures they wish to study. In this case the aim is for the researcher to become increasingly bicultural in outlook and understanding, familiar with the communicative styles and intepretive constructs that operate in several cultures. This expanded empathy provides some protection against, or antidote to, a single cultural view dominating the research. In the studies cited here the researchers included members of both cultures being studied, enhanced by the fact that each had experience in the contrasting culture. Such collaboration by no means guarantees the elimination of cultural bias in the choice of a topic, but it lessens the probability of one perspective dominating the effort.

How does one identify a suitable topic for cross-cultural research? An obvious choice is to select some pan-cultural issue so that decentering is unnecessary. Some experiences, like birth and death, achievement and failure, health and illness, seem to exist in every culture. But rarely do they provoke the same meanings, and rarely do they have the same behavioral consequences.[4] The only human features where cultural influences might be safely disregarded would be in comparative studies of the skeletal, neurological, and serological properties of people as physical objects alone. Even such physical properties in a symbolizing organism appear subject to some cultural influences. Since there are no universal meanings, no consistent reactions to any event in all cultures, the search for pan-cultural topics, where universality of meaning can be taken for granted, should be viewed with skepticism.

An alternative is to select some behavior that is critical to survival in every society but may be differently performed or executed. For example, food production, child-rearing, and decision making are found in some form in all societies. Such a research topic is decentered in the sense that the behavior is not indigenous to a single community and then sought by other communities, but is a requirement of communal living. In this case the aim is to probe such events, to identify similarities and differences, but by employing modes of inquiry that are appropriate to each society studied. Comparing functionally similar acts places a common perimeter around the field of inquiry and provides a common focus for such inquiry. But even acts so essential that they appear in many societies are often prompted by different motives, occur in different settings, are executed by different persons, and carry different psychological and social consequences. Even after identifying comparable behaviors, it is necessary to proceed with caution.

A third source of themes for cross-cultural research lies at the point where members of different societies have difficulty dealing with each other.

These conflicts, frustrating as they may be, testify to the existence of cultural differences and provide a concrete point of entry to the cultural unconscious. In confusing conversations, in moments of hostility or indifference, in invasions of territory or invasions of privacy, in the ease or difficulty of repairing broken friendships, one may identify researchable issues of cross-cultural interest.

It is in this way that the studies noted here arose. In the first, one researcher was surprised, even shocked, at the intensity of personal confrontations in the United States, and particularly by the frequency with which friendships survived such attacks; a colleague was no less impressed by the absence of such direct criticism in Japan. In the second the researcher was startled by the unaccustomed flow of verbal compliments she received, reminding her colleague of the frustrations of working in a culture where fewer and less explicit comments gave little indication of how one was being evaluated. These observations, and the long discussions they provoked, led to focusing upon the determinants and character of criticism and compliments in Japan and the United States (Nomura and Barnlund, 1982; Araki and Barnlund, in press).

SECOND STAGE: IDENTIFYING CULTURAL VARIABLES

After selecting a specific behavior to study, such as the handling of criticism or compliments, one seeks to identify the variables that influence them and to probe their operation within the two cultures. What features of social settings are Japanese and Americans sensitive to? What importance do they attach to them? How do such attributes affect the frequency, form, and consequences of acts of criticism or praise? Identifying the variables that shape particular acts within a culture is a complicated and potentially confounding step in the pursuit of cross-cultural understanding. Perhaps for that reason, the roles of decentering and convergence are even more evident at this stage of inquiry.

The study of criticsm and compliments began

with efforts to isolate the features of each society that governed the manner and consequences of such acts. We began by conducting semi-structured interviews with individual Japanese and Americans, in which they were asked to describe in detail two incidents in which they were the instigators or recipients of such acts. The interviews were conducted by interviewers of the same culture as the interviewee, and participants were given great latitude in recounting such incidents as spontaneously and subjectively as they wished. Their accounts provided hundreds of concrete incidents as they were experienced and interpreted by people in both cultures.

Out of the mass of details, four factors stood out as shaping the character of compliments and criticism: (1) the "nature of the provocation," that is, the offense or trait that provoked someone to criticize or compliment another; (2) the "nature of the relationship" with one's partner; (3) the "form and content" of the criticism or compliment; and (4) the "physical setting" in which the incident occurred.

The aim of the interviews was to identify the factors that should later be incorporated into an interpersonal criticism questionnaire or complimentary mode questionnaire to permit wider and more objective assessment of cultural communicative styles. The necessity of further clarification in the study of criticism became apparent almost at once. For example, so many provocative incidents were reported as to be unmanageable; yet many of these were similar or nearly identical. It seemed essential to find some way to cluster incidents of similar types and to distinguish those of different types. The topical taxonomy of Sydney Jourard, an American psychologist, seemed a promising first approximation: opinions, tastes, work, money, personality, and physical (Jourard 1964). Unfortunately, the incidents described in the interviews failed to fit this pattern readily: some fit equally well into several categories, others fit into none of them. This first approximation, based on an American typology, was clearly unsatisfactory.

A second approximation, based on a continuum of personal dissatisfaction suggested in the writings

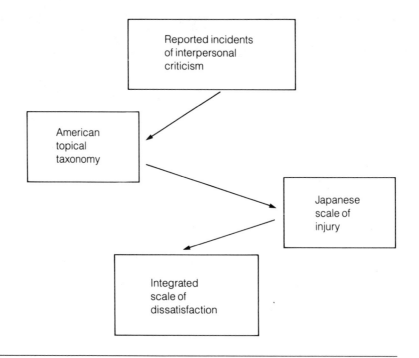

Figure 1 Process of Convergence through Successive Cultural Approximation

of a Japanese psychiatrist, Takeo Doi, was tried next (Doi 1973). All the reported incidents were arranged along a continuum from Direct Injury to Indirect Injury to No Injury. This idea proved acceptable to the Japanese but seemed an awkward ordering and presented difficulties for Americans. Thus the classification based on the degree of dissatisfaction seemed skewed toward the Japanese culture just as the topical ordering seemed skewed toward the American culture.

Finding a way of overcoming these biases seemed imperative if the Interpersonal Criticism Questionnaire was to work equally well in both countries, requiring a third approximation that derived from neither culture but that accommodated both. The new typology remained a scale of dissatisfaction, as consonant with the Japanese view, but differentiated between classes of dissatisfaction: (1) Injury (I have been wronged or harmed without justification); (2) Disappointment (You

have failed to live up to my expectations and have disappointed me); and (3) Disagreement (Your behavior undermines norms and beliefs that I value although it has no direct consequences for me). Thus the process of successive approximation started with the idea of an American psychologist, moved on to explore the perspective of a Japanese psychologist, and ended in a scale of dissatisfaction that emerged from neither culture but was an effort to accommodate both (see Figure 1).

A series of twelve situations, four of each type of provocation, based on the incidents actually reported by Japanese and Americans in the interviews, were then constructed to serve as the critical incidents designed to provoke critical responses in the questionnaires. All the people cited most often by Japanese or Americans in the interviews were designated alternative partners in these twelve situations: Mother, Father, Closest Male Friend, Closest Female Friend, Male Acquaintance, Female

Acquaintance, Male Stranger, and Female Stranger. Again it is important in any cross-cultural comparison that the range of partners reflect the normal span of associates in both cultures to avoid introducing another cultural bias in the results.

Perhaps the most critical feature of the Interpersonal Criticism Questionnaire concerned the formulation of alternative modes of expressing dissatisfaction. Respondents from both cultures should feel that the options open to them constitute natural and viable ways of offering criticism in their respective countries. Over seventy critical acts were noted in the interviews, but many were similar in form and content. Through successive reductions these were consolidated into twenty-four alternatives and were arranged along a continuum from active-aggressing to passive-withdrawing, a dimension that had proven useful in previous research on these two cultures (Barnlund 1975). This scale proved too cumbersome, and the twenty-four were compressed into a response scale of eleven distinct ways of expressive dissatisfaction from remaining silent to criticizing in an insulting way.

Although the eleven alternatives were common to both cultures, there was no way of knowing if Japanese and Americans would order them on an active-passive scale in identical ways. One culture might feel that expressing criticism "ambiguously" was more aggressive than to do so "humorously"; the other culture might reverse this, feeling that humor was more aggressive than ambiguity. To test this, a Q-sort was employed to enable a sample of Japanese and Americans to order the eleven modes of criticism along a scale from "most passive" to "most active." The results were almost identical, confirming the appropriateness of the original placement of the items.

However, there was an exception to this nearly parallel ordering of the modes of criticism, and it illustrates the necessity of decentering any instrument used in contrasting cultures. To criticize "logically" was seen by Americans as a less aggressive act than to criticize "constructively." To the Japanese, to criticize "logically" was seen as more aggressive than to do so "constructively." Thus the modes of criticism, while appropriate for each culture, were not completely compatible for comparison purposes. It is as if two foot-rulers were designed to be of the same overall length, but on one the eighth inch marker appeared between seven and nine, but on the other appeared between six and seven. Measurements "in feet" would be correct for both cultures, but measurement "in inches" would not be. And, since it was the comparison of cultural preferences for the eleven modes of criticism that was sought, this source of error had to be overcome.

Though it might appear to be a simple problem of translation, this is not the case: "logically" and "ronriteki na iikatade" are linguistically equivalent expressions. The problem is that the two terms trigger different intensities along an active-passive scale. Criticism expressed "logically" in Japan carries the possibility of provoking direct confrontation, and such confrontation has more serious consequences there than in the American society where confrontation is more frequent and less destructive in its long-term effects. This issue was finally resolved by removing "logically" altogether and substituting "in a direct manner," a mode of response that carried similar meanings and was similarly ordered along the response scale by both Japanese and Americans.

One final issue remained. Should the critical episodes used to study the exchange of criticism and compliments be based on recalled or projected behavior? Recalled incidents have the advantage of describing acts that have actually occurred, while projected incidents involve hypothetical acts. ("What did you *do*?" requires simple recollection; "What *would* you do?" asks for predicted acts.) On the surface it would seem that the former would introduce less distortion than the latter, but that is not necessarily so. Recalled incidents, while reflecting actual behavior, are subject to inaccurate recall, to the desire to report acts in socially approved ways. Most importantly, they make it difficult to standardize situations cross-culturally so that reactions to them can be compared. Projected incidents, on the other hand, can be identical for members of both cultures and can avoid reliance upon the reconstruction of past events by flawed memories; yet the disadvantage is that projected behavior may differ from actual behavior because of the tendency to select socially appropriate answers.

Situations that required respondents to project their behavior were employed in both studies described here. The chief reason was to utilize situations that would be identical for members of both cultures. The second and more compelling reason was that the length of recall was significantly different for respondents, particularly in the case of compliments. The interviews indicated that the average American would be recalling a compliment given or received within the last forty hours (1.6 days), while the average Japanese would be recalling one given or received more than 300 hours earlier (13 days). In the most extreme case American females would be reporting compliments within the same day, but Japanese males would be reporting compliments that occurred more than seventeen days earlier. Again, decentering requires that the cultural norms surrounding any act be taken into account in the manner of investigation.

THIRD STAGE: LINGUISTIC AND EXPERIENTIAL EQUIVALENCE

Nearly all efforts to describe another culture proceed through some sort of symbolic intervention: conversations, interviews, questionnaires, projective tests, simulations, laboratory experiments. Hence every effort at cross-cultural understanding must contend with the problem of equivalence in the symbol systems of investigator and investigated.[5]

As Kluckhohn has noted, "Anyone who has struggled with translation is made to realize that there is more to language than its dictionary" (Kluckhohn 1965, p. 135). Symbolic equivalence is rarely accomplished merely by substituting the words from one dictionary for those from another. A language is far more than a simple collection of words, a pool of terms for features of reality: it is

itself the shaper of reality; it promotes certain meanings and actions, and discourages and inhibits others. A linguistically naive person once asked how to say "son of a bitch" in Japanese. He was told that no direct translation was possible. Persisting, he asked for the Japanese words for "son," for "of," and for "bitch." He then combined them, insisting he had proved his point though Japanese who were present regarded the resulting expression as ludicrous. In less naive, but analogous, ways, we seek correspondence across language communities. Often we succeed; often we do not. Japanese terms like "on," "amae," "ma," and "mu" lose much of their cultural significance when ripped from their Japanese ontological context and cast into English as "obligation," "dependence," "space," and "nothingness."

The process of decentering any research instrument or procedure involves at least two complications: the first is to establish the symbolic equivalence of any stimulus used for comparative purposes across cultures; the second is to determine the experiential or behavioral equivalence. Again, this appears to involve a process of successive approximation, with the investigator moving back and forth between languages, adjusting one and then the other, seeking to bring them into closer and closer alignment.

In seeking the cross-cultural equivalence of research instruments, there are several possible courses of action. The first and most familiar is that of "forward" and "backward" translation (Brislin, Lonner, and Thorndike 1973, pp. 37–39; Triandis, Vassilou, Vassilou, and Shammagun 1972, p. 19). Once an original questionnaire or test has been designed, it is translated by competent bilinguals "forward" into the second language. This translated version is then given to another set of bilinguals to translate "backward" into the original language. The first and second versions of the original are then compared; any discrepancies in the two versions prompt alternative phrasings in the translated version. This alternation continues until the original and translated version are linguistically equivalent.[6] As Werner and Campbell note, "the semantic structure of the source language . . . is mapped onto the semantic structure of the target language" (1970, p. 402).

A second, more completely decentered, way of achieving equivalence begins not after a research tool has been designed in one language, but before this has been done. Investigators from both cultures independently and simultaneously construct items capable of measuring critical variables. These are then each translated into the alternate language. When discrepant in their meanings, efforts are made to rephrase items to make them increasingly appropriate for both cultures.

Whereas in the first method items are conceived in one language and the second language version is adjusted until it fits the first, in the latter the two cultural versions are generated independently, and both are adjusted until the research instrument has a common stimulus value for members of both cultures. Decentering appears more completely achieved in the latter case, but practical considerations have made it rarely attainable.

The second requirement is that any research tool or procedure be experientially or behaviorally equivalent. It is what Nida apparently refers to as "dynamic equivalence"—any item that on a questionnaire should carry a similar social meaning in both societies, and should tap actions that are functionally equivalent (Nida 1964, p. 166). Japanese and English contain suitable equivalents for "sword" and "gun," for "rice" or "potatoes," but the associations that surround these terms may sheer off in quite different ways. If in one culture coffee shops are a major place for socializing and in the other homes are, then no simple matching of vocabulary will prevent a cultural bias from creeping into the findings. There is no difficulty in phrasing a critical incident concerning air travel in Japan or the United States, but if air travel is common in one and train travel in the other, contrasting answers are a result of discrepant stimulus situations provided by the research instrument and not by life itself.

As should be the case in cross-cultural work, the first task was to assess the extent of agreement be-tween Japanese and Americans in their conceptions of "compliments" and "criticism." This was sought, first, by examining not only English and Japanese dictionaries, but also English-Japanese and Japanese-English dictionaries. While "criticism" appeared to present no major problems, "compliments" did. Compliments were defined in English as "expressions of praise, respect, affection, or admiration," but in Japanese the term subsumed two concepts with somewhat different colorations, "sanji" and "oseji." Pursuing these, it was found that "sanji" (sanbi no kotoba) was seen as "praise, compliment, kind remark, admiration," while "oseji" (aiso no yoi kotoba) was seen as "compliments, flattery, politeness, sugary words," a definition that veers toward flattery in English. Where Americans appear to sharply differentiate compliments and flattery, the Japanese incorporate overlapping meanings for both terms.

This was as far as lexical and linguistic clarification could carry us. Hence it was decided to probe the behavioral implications of compliments through interviews with Japanese and Americans. Each sample was asked to distinguish between "compliments" and "flattery" or between "sanji" and "oseji," respectively. Again, for Americans, compliments were clearly differentiated from flattery, as honest expressions of admiration given without manipulative intent; they clearly carried a positive valuation. Flattery was seen as a dishonest expression, calculated to impress others or to secure some future advantage; it consistently carried a negative evaluation. For the Japanese, the terms were less simple and less clear in their meanings: "sanji" also referred to honest praise or admiration, but with the implication that it be modestly and indirectly expressed; only when expressed in few words did it carry a clear positive evaluation. "Oseji" was rarely defined directly, but more often illustrated, suggesting its greater dependence upon the social context. It included the use of praise in complimenting, in smoothing human relationships, and in increasing a positive social atmosphere. "Oseji" need not be true; it also appeared to lack the strong negative values that Americans

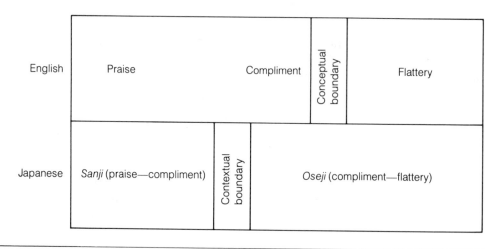

Figure 2 Compliments: Japanese and English Domains

attached to flattery. Figure 2 may clarify the semantic and experiential fields of these terms in Japanese and English.

It can be seen that Americans and Japanese have somewhat different interpretations of the words and of the function of the behaviors they suggest: Americans regard a larger proportion of statements of praise as compliments, a smaller proportion as flattery; the Japanese reverse this, interpreting a larger proportion of statements of praise as flattery. While Americans tend to distinguish more sharply between compliments and flattery, and to associate positive and negative evaluations with each, the Japanese tend to blur the boundary between them and tend not to strongly polarize their evaluations of them. Finally, while Americans tend to define the terms abstractly, the Japanese prefer to contextualize their meanings.

Every critical variable needs to be given the same careful scrutiny, or the labels of one culture will be misleading with regard to other cultures. Another problem in linguistic and experiential equivalence had to do with the communicative partners identified on the questionnaires. As might be expected, "Mother," "Father," "Closest Male Friend," "Closest Female Friend," and Male and

Female "Stranger" posed no problems. But Male and Female "Acquaintance" aroused some suspicion. Although the English term "acquaintance" and the Japanese term "chijin" are lexically equivalent, their behavioral implications may not be. Further interviews with Japanese and Americans clarified this issue: for Americans, "acquaintances" were persons with whom one had occasional social contact born of propinquity and opportunity to meet. These relationships were characterized by infrequent interaction, shallow disclosure, and superficial involvement. But increased frequency of meeting usually transformed "acquaintances" into "friends." For the Japanese as well, such relations were accidents of living or working in close proximity. And, somewhat similarly, it was the presence of "enryo" (restraint or holding back) that characterized these relations. Yet "acquaintances" rarely became "friends" simply because of increased contact. Although "acquaintance" and "chijin" were sufficiently similar to justify their use in the study of criticism, in the subsequent study of compliments the term was replaced by "casual friend," a term that seemed closer in meaning for both cultures.

Finally, are the research instruments culturally

reliable and cross-culturally reliable? Linguistic and experiential equivalence are of uncertain value unless repeated measures with the same instrument produce consistent results within and across the cultures compared. The steps taken to assess the reliability of the Interpersonal Criticism Questionnaire will illustrate this process.

The ICQ consisted of twelve critical incidents involving eight alternative partners. To reduce the length of the questionnaire, and the influence of fatigue in completing it, two matched forms were created: Form A comprised the twelve situations and four communicative partners; Form B utilized the same twelve situations with four alternative partners. Scores on alternate items on these two forms were used to test the reliability of the Japanese and English versions of the questionnaire. The reliabilities of both American and Japanese versions of the questionnaire exceeded .92; clearly, the instrument was a reliable one to use in both of the targeted cultures.

Cross-cultural consistency, however, is another matter. That is, are the scores of Japanese and Americans comparable? An instrument that may be highly reliable in each culture independently may measure erratically when used to compare contrasting cultures. The Japanese may consistently prefer some ways of manifesting criticism, and Americans may prefer other ways, but can these profiles be compared without prejudice to one or the other? To check for the cross-cultural consistency, bilinguals from both cultures (equally divided between those whose native language was Japanese and those whose native language was English) completed the questionnaire on two occasions. At the first testing, half the bilinguals completed Form A in Japanese and Form B in English, the other half Form A in English and Form B in Japanese; a month later the procedure was reversed with both groups, permitting comparison of the consistency of their scores (on both forms in both languages) with respondents familiar with both cultures. The resulting coefficients proved remarkably high for an instrument intended to be used cross-culturally. These figures indicated that decentering had been accomplished, and the results for members of both

cultures and both language communities could, with considerable confidence, be compared.

FOURTH STAGE: PURSUIT OF THE PATTERN

The object of inquiry, whether casual or systematic, is not the accumulation of data, interesting as they might be, but of insight into the cultural unconscious. It is not uncommon for displays of data and statistical acrobatics to distract attention from their role as means rather than ends. It is not uncommon, either, for less elaborate but equally penetrating observations to be dismissed because they lack statistical confirmation.

Yet there is something to be said for the careful and steady collection of cultural data, particularly when that process is linked to an effort to decipher their meaning. Data, however, do not explain themselves; they merely await and invite explanation. And at no other point in confronting another culture is the temptation to impose alien meanings harder to resist. To overcome ethnocentric temptations, the principles of decentering and convergence seem, again, to provide guidance. The effort to decenter will manifest itself in who interprets the data, what procedures are adopted to test such interpretations, and how inconsistent and discrepant findings are resolved.

Who should interpret the findings returns us to the original decisions concerning the qualifications for cross-cultural research. As before, it seems essential that the investigative team include insiders and outsiders. And, if feasible, it should include specialists whose cultural experience includes other comparable or contrasting societies. The presence of such cultural diversity should discourage ethnocentric myopia by expanding the range of explanatory hypotheses.

Assuming a bicultural investigator or, better still, a bicultural team of investigators, how might they proceed to interpret the findings? One way is simply to share their differing explanations of the data, allowing the push and pull of discussion to lead to more valid cultural inferences. The high incidence of compliments in one society and the low incidence in the other may lead one observer to link these to the encouragement of individuality in one culture and its inhibition in the other; another observer may see the data as symptomatic of the alienation that permeates an egocentric culture and the lack of alienation in the other. Such opposing perspectives may provoke efforts to find alternative hypotheses, to combine such explanatory inferences, or to initiate new research designed to test their relative validity.

One difficulty with this approach is that a greater aggressiveness or eloquence from one cultural perspective may color the conclusions disproportionately. This sort of argumentative advantage is lessened if investigators carry out their interpretations independently. Only after such independent appraisals had occurred would representatives of both cultures come together to confer and, through successive approximations, seek to accommodate divergent interpretations. In this case ethnic uniqueness is respected not only in the topic of investigation, and in the selection of variables and collection of data, but also in arriving at the meaning of behavior as it functions in its own cultural milieu.

A final suggestion that might enhance inquiry into human cultures is to invite participation from a variety of disciplines. There is little doubt that some of the integrity of any human act is lost when observed through the lens of a single academic specialty. As sociologists, communicologists, psychiatrists, and anthropologists, we are all "professionally centered" and suffer from a theocentric myopia that can be as disabling as an ethnocentric myopia. In its fullest sense, decentering is an effort to overcome all forms of paradigmatic isolation whether the isolation is born of culture or of discipline; all framings of human experience have their value, but all provide limited access to the human condition.

Once a decision is made as to who should be involved in interpreting cultural data, the nature of such interpretations becomes an issue. The unconscious framing of acts within the cultural context of the observer rather than of the participants is no-

where as difficult to resist as in explaining the behavior studied. There are, in our view, four configurations that hold promise in transforming a profusion of empirical data into cultural insight. These might be called the search for a cultural pattern, for the pattern within the pattern, for the comparison of patterns, and for discrepancies in the pattern.

The simple patterning of cultural observations is the most obvious first step. One searches for consistencies, trends, correlations, and for systematic shifts—in short, for whatever orderliness can be found. The data on Japanese communicative styles, for example, revealed a hierarchy of conversational topics, of communicative partners, of personal disclosure, and of defenses against threatening situations (Barnlund 1975). The study of Japanese compliments suggested that verbal praise was relatively rare and tended to focus on taste rather than on personality, and that nonverbal modes tended to dominate in close relationships (Araki and Barnlund, in press). The data on criticism suggested that negative evaluations were relatively rare among the Japanese, who, while less adapted to the form of provocation, were sensitively adapted to the status of their partners, meaning that direct criticism increased with intimacy and decreased with distance (Nomura and Barnlund 1982). In all three studies, culture rather than sex appeared to be more influential in regulating interaction.

Descriptions of this order are valuable because they reveal the regulative codes and norms of a society, many of which are unknown even to those who obey them. Yet their value is limited because, in revealing the conventions of meaning with regard to a specific rhetorical act in a specific setting, they fail to expose the cultural premises that make such norms necessary or desirable. They fail to reach beyond themselves to explain or predict other acts that derive from the same premises. We may grasp the dynamics of a specific act without grasping the dynamics of the culture that creates nourishes, or requires such acts.

For this reason a description of the interactional patterns of a culture invites a search for the pattern within the pattern, the underlying core assumptions or values that shape such acts. *Why* do Americans disclose and touch so much? *Why* do the Japanese limit contact and verbal disclosure? *Why* are compliments and criticism relatively rare in one society, and so prevalent in another? Perhaps in no other facet of cross-cultural work is it so vital to involve specialists of contrasting cultures in the pursuit of such questions; representatives of a single culture, like Plato's figures chained inside a cave, are rarely aware of their myopic view of the world. Members of other cultures provide a perspective that is unobtainable from inside a culture under study. To Americans, the level of contact and disclosure among the Japanese appears to reflect a repression of individual uniqueness; the Japanese, the constant contact and verbalization among Americans seems to reflect an effort to overcome an alienation that derives from excessive individuality. The relative absence of criticism among the Japanese strikes some Americans as a dishonesty born of excessive concern for social harmony; the constant flow of praise among Americans strikes the Japanese as equally dishonest and manipulative.

The data on compliments appeared puzzling to the Japanese researcher: Why do the Japanese compliment each other so rarely? This question cannot be answered by the data, nor is it obvious to members of a society that favors such norms. People in every society feel that their behavior is entirely natural and spontaneous. There is no more reason to justify such acts than to justify why one eats when hungry or sleeps when tired. And if questioned about the sources of such acts, insiders are often unable to provide a rationale, for the act and the explanation derive from the same system; figure and ground are indistinguishable.

A search for the pattern within the pattern regarding the wide cultural difference in the frequency of praise led to convergence on this explanatory principle: in a country like Japan, where social harmony is at a premium, compliments may be seen as discriminatory acts that separate the individual from the group, highlighting their virtues and implying a lower evaluation of others, thereby fostering a competitive rather than a harmonious atmo-

sphere; in a country like the United States, where individuality is prized, compliments may confirm the uniqueness of the person and promote competition among members of a group. Again, the pursuit of this underlying pattern proceeds through the positing of alternative hypotheses by representatives of both cultures. Great caution is essential, however, in seeking the pattern within the pattern, because higher order inferences about underlying motives always sheer away from concrete data and can easily be deflected by the ethnocentric inclination of the interpreters.

Another interpretive opportunity lies in examining the consequences of cultural acts when they appear in alien cultural contexts. Comparison of behavioral norms can permit prediction of their consequences when viewed through the interpretive lenses of a contrasting society. If verbal disclosure differs in Japan from the United States, one can predict that members of both countries may be uncomfortable in the presence of the other; one is distressed by the superficiality of the conversation, the other by an invasion of privacy. The frequent and exaggerated compliments of Americans may embarrass the Japanese, causing them to feel Americans are untrustworthy; the lack of criticism from Japanese colleagues may leave Americans feeling that Japanese are similarly untrustworthy. Again, cross-cultural collaboration provides a means of testing such predictions and of avoiding a prejudicial interpretation of the consequences of such acts.

Perhaps the most fascinating, and sometimes the most rewarding, findings in cross-cultural research are those that fall outside the pattern and fail to fit expectations. Such serendipitous data should not be dismissed or minimized; it is often just such aberrant findings that are clues to new or deeper cultural insights. To illustrate: the data on the handling of criticism by Japanese and Americans showed consistent cultural differences, the former preferring more passive and the latter more active ways of expressing dissatisfaction. Americans, as expected, frequently chose to criticize "in a direct way"; but the Japanese, surprisingly, also most often chose the Japanese equivalent of directness: "sotchoku na iikatade." This agreement was in some ways puzzling; there seemed to be a missing link somewhere. In pursuit of this missing link, a further survey of thirty-one Americans and twenty-six Japanese was instigated. A questionnaire was designed that asked respondents to write out exactly *how* they would express criticism "in a direct way" in three situations taken from the original Interpersonal Criticism Questionnaire: one involving injury, one involving disappointment, and one involving disagreement.

Analysis of the content of these cases of direct criticism not only provided the missing link, but also added another dimension to the research. Direct criticism by Americans was not only straightforward but incisive and trenchant in phrasing; Japanese direct criticism was somewhat straightforward, but more conciliatory and good-humored. In short, the same cultural patterns found *across* the repertoire of critical messages also held *within* a single form of criticism, with Americans preferring more assertive ways of expressing dissatisfaction and Japanese less assertive ways. The trends between categories and within categories appeared to reflect the same cultural predispositions.

To describe the acts of members of another society, and to see the sources and consequences of such acts in reference to the cultural milieu to which they belong, requires that investigators overcome biases inherent in their own acculturation; decentering and convergence offer practical guidance in the pursuit of the elusive and abstract goal of cross-cultural empathy.

STRANGER IN A STRANGE LAND

Are there any parallels between the requirements of formal research and the requirements of living or working in an alien culture? We believe there are, and that decentering and convergence are valid principles for the ordinary citizen to follow in adapting to life in a strange land. All of us are theorists of a sort, seeking to decipher the motives of others, collecting data to confirm or contradict our inferences about them, and using these to predict how they will act toward us. At any moment we may become painfully but provocatively aware of cultural differences and we may be challenged to accommodate such differences. The outsider who seeks to meet another culture on its own terms may find the pursuit of cultural empathy facilitated and accelerated by observing these principles.

When we cross the border into another country, we carry a great deal of undeclared (and largely unconscious) baggage with us, baggage that was useful in the culture we left behind but that may be useless or crippling in the one we are entering. Nonspecialists are no less prone than researchers to see foreign behavior through domestic lenses, to attach familiar meanings to unfamiliar acts. It is difficult to resist the temptation to interpret the acts of others by the same criteria we apply to our own.

Actually we know little yet about how to speed the process of adjustment for the ordinary person who is trying to gain access to the assumptive world of another society. We also know little about how to overcome the special blindness acquired in assimilating one's own culture. One obvious suggestion is to study and to become familiar with another society prior to entering it. Mead and Metraux, for example, have shown the extent to which it is possible to study "culture at a distance" (Mead and Metraux 1953). A classic demonstration of this is Benedict's profile of the Japanese, written without any first-hand experience in the culture (Benedict 1946). Through books, lectures, films, and artifacts, one can gain some idea of the political structure, religious beliefs, family life, and social practices of another country. Any of these may induce decentering by increasing the respect for the distinctive institutions and social attitudes of other peoples; it may also heighten awareness of the institutions and practices of one's own culture. New appreciation of the relativity of social structures and standards may cultivate the greater figure-ground elasticity that is essential to cross-cultural rapport.

The limitations of this approach are twofold.

The first is that such learning tends to be heavily intellectual. While decentering is to some extent a conceptual matter, it is not entirely so. To fully comprehend another way of life seems to require experiential involvement. Cultural relativity is not easily acquired; there are many well-informed provincials living in alien communities. A second limitation arises from the nature of learning; there is some evidence that prior information may retard learning from direct experience. Still, information about another society may expose its uniqueness and may thereby alert one to the complications of living inside it.

Another way to promote decentering is to form personal relationships with members of the contrasting culture who currently live in one's own community. This is often far more difficult than it sounds. Physical segregation of ethnic groups is found to some extent in almost all societies, but even where this is overcome there is often a social segregation that blinds us to the cultural diversity around us. The tendency to associate only with what the *New Yorker* once called PLUs (People Like Us)—people resembling us in income, age, interests, and values—is a powerful one. Getting acquainted with people of contrasting backgrounds forces us to confront different ways of seeing, hearing, thinking, caring, talking; interacting with them forces us to learn to accommodate such differences. The depth of cultural insight that can be obtained from such personal involvement is richly reflected in *Amazonian Cosmos*, a sensitive portrayal of the world view, symbolism, and practices of the Desana Indians through a deep personal relationship with only a single informant (Reichel-Dolmatoff 1971). Prior to living in another culture, then, a person may learn to decenter in a way that is not radically different from that of the researcher, by interacting and collaborating with someone from a different culture in an effort to grasp its dynamics. If impossible before departure, then the development of a personal relationship within the new culture may help in deciphering the confusions and failures that are bound to occur.

New opportunities for decentering arise when one begins to function in a foreign culture. Like the researcher, the visitor or resident must seek to understand the norms that shape a society's institutions and that shape interaction within them. Certain assumptions on the part of the observer appear to facilitate this sort of insight (assumptions that hold equally for the researcher). (1) No matter how alien it may appear to be, every culture works; most people in it find it a coherent and comprehensible way of life. (2) When the institutions or behaviors of another society seem incomprehensible or even reprehensible, there is a reasonable explanation for them. (3) Every interpretation of any event reflects and reports a relation between the observer and the observed; there is no way to comment on anything that does not incorporate the assumptive premises of the interpreter. (4) Through acculturation, all human beings have acquired distinctive ways of viewing life; hence, wider and deeper conflicts are probable in encounters between cultures. (5) Difficulties in living in alien cultures have as their source the distinctive unconscious premises of both outsider and insider; learning to recognize one's own cultural values is as constructive as learning the values of the new culture (indeed, neither insight proceeds very far without the other). (6) A demonological approach to cross-cultural encounters—the search for someone to blame for failures—is not merely unproductive, but counterproductive; the aim, instead, should be to collaborate in deciphering the cultural dynamics that provoke such contrasting motives and meanings.

All of this demands that the stranger in a strange land give high priority to observing the new culture. To observe without prejudice is, however, far more difficult than it appears. We have an immense capacity for deceiving ourselves when it serves our needs. Our simplest observations tend to be self-serving, operating to preserve and promote constructions of reality that have served in the past and in familiar settings. James Baldwin once described creative people as the "greatest of noticers," and one might urge that people entering a new culture actively cultivate their capacity for noticing. All the paraphernalia and procedures of science are efforts to overcome our tendency to see what we want to see or what we are accustomed to seeing.

Upon arrival, what, specifically, might the observer notice? This question is far too encompassing to answer here, but a few illustrations reveal the range of possibilities. First one would start where one is, in the streets, markets, buses, restaurants, wherever public life takes place most commonly. How people manage routines can be instructive, yet there are limitations in such observations: public encounters are often impersonal, dictated by functional needs, and conducted in routine ways. Still, this is the point of entry to a culture, and these are the daily affairs one must master first.

Encounters that may be more richly endowed with cultural significance are occasions such as birthdays, deaths, marriages, festivals, and rites of passage of various kinds. (More than one person has suggested that the most highly concentrated exposure to cultural values lies in a traditional marriage ceremony.) Perhaps the deepest exposure to cultural norms is likely to be found in close personal friendships or family relationships. One observational caution, however: outsiders tend to confuse the way insiders interact with them as being the way insiders interact with each other; many cultures observe slightly different rules for relating to foreigners, and this has sometimes led to misleading profiles of observed cultures.

Still, the problem is one of giving some sort of order to the multiplicity of acts one can observe, some familiar, some unfamiliar. (Unfortunately, the most familiar may carry unfamiliar meanings, and the unfamiliar, familiar meanings.) Again, like the researcher, the outsider might concentrate on carefully selected features of interaction. A few ways of focusing such observations may illustrate the possibilities: (1) Who talks to whom? People interact selectively, choosing associates with regard to age, sex, occupation, marital status, group membership, and so on. How is behavior adapted, if at all, to such differences in communicative partners? (2) What is talked about? Are some topics often discussed and others avoided? Do these change with

occasions and associates? Are verbal or nonverbal channels preferred for certain types of meanings? (3) How are differences managed? Are they confronted directly or indirectly? Are they resolved through orders, mediation, compromise, consensus? (4) How are positive or negative feelings expressed? How is criticism given to people of a different status or of the same status, between members of a family, between close and distant acquaintances? These are only a few facets of behavior that one might observe in trying to appreciate the norms that govern conduct in another society.

Yet the aim of the stranger, like that of the scientist, is to go beyond mere description. It is the significance of behavior, the explanatory base of such acts, that is the key to understanding another culture *on its own terms*. Sharing meaning is only possible when people can give an appropriate form to their experience and can predict the interpretations given to such forms by their associates. This is difficult enough within a society, but it requires added skill when attempted across societies. The outsider, whether scientist or not, must be capable of forward and backward "translations": the capacity to transform one's meanings into the vocabulary of another culture and to translate their forms into appropriate meanings. This deeper grasp of the cultural ethos marks the transition from outsider to insider; a transition from being one who only imitates the acts of members of another culture, to one who experiences the meanings of such acts and can participate spontaneously in the life of the culture. In some cases, adaptation may become assimilation, and one no longer moves back and forth between the two cultures but can function equally well in both.

This effort to grasp the cultural unconscious is the most difficult challenge to any outsider. And little is yet known about what nourishes this kind of cross-cultural competence. One aid to decentering lies in the daily encounters of the resident in the alien culture. There is continuous feedback, approval or rejection, mirrored in the faces, gestures, words, and silences of host nationals. Although it is easy to misinterpret such reactions, they provide some commentary on the visitor's efforts at successive approximation: one tries and fails, one tries again and fails less disastrously, one tries another alternative and partially succeeds. In a sense the serious outsider conducts continuous experiments in which his acts are the independent variable and the social consequences are the dependent variable. Gradually the dynamics of social interaction may become discernible. What seems critical to the success of this behavioral dialogue is that the outsider sees the process instructively rather than defensively; failures, when they are not devastating, appear far more informative than successes.

There are other sources that can assist the efforts to understand a foreign culture. Like the researcher who seeks collaborators from the culture to be studied, outsiders can also test their inferences by conferring with host nationals. Often a single close friend in the culture one has come to can mediate that experience; projected meanings and predicted consequences can be discussed and presumed motives can be confirmed or disconfirmed. This process not only benefits the outsider; the host national often obtains fresh appreciation of his own culture through the inquiries, enthusiasms, and frustrations of the outsider. Reichel-Dolmatoff writes that Antonio Guzman, his informant in the *Amazonian Cosmos*, reported that by "attempting to interpret it (his culture) to a stranger, he had acquired a comprehension of values and mechanisms he had not achieved before" (Reichel-Dolmatoff 1968, p. 252). Collaboration in decentering, then, need not become a one-way, exploitative affair, but may deepen the understanding of both people who seek the sources of their own cultural meanings. The contribution of one unique class of informant, the children, should be noted here: they make a special contribution, partly because in assimilating their own culture, they are often puzzled by the same questions outsiders pose, and partly because they are likely to be honest and direct in their answers.

In much the same manner as the researcher, though less systematically, the stranger searches for the pattern within the pattern, for trends, consistencies, and inconsistencies. Again, it is important to avoid premature explanation and to be on guard against ethnocentric interpretations, but the outsider is justified in assuming that there is orderliness in even the most discrepant acts. Every culture has some structure, underlying values, social norms, symbolic codes, and distinctive meanings. In searching for the threads that weave various facets of society into a coherent and integrated totality, we look for links between seemingly isolated phenomena, screen the familiar to be sure it does not mask an unfamiliar significance, examine the inconceivable to see if there is some equivalent parallel in our own culture, and try to separate the accidental from the intentional. We participate in the culture experimentally, and, when baffled, suspend interpretation to avoid premature denunciation, on the grounds that all acts serve some function and make some sense in context.

A simulation often used in intercultural training may help to display the steps and some of the hazards to be avoided in decentering. In the simulation called "Albatross," participants are exposed to an alien culture, but one of seeming simplicity and clarity.[7] Upon arrival they find themselves in a room with at one end a robed female and a male, the latter seated and the former kneeling beside him. Some of the participants sit on the floor, some on the few available chairs. A period of silence ensues. Then the robed male touches the back of the head of the kneeling female beside him and she bows, touching the floor with her forehead. Quietly and serenely they rise and move through the group, uttering "hms," "clicks," and "hisses" as they move females from the chairs to the floor and males to the vacant chairs. They return, repeat the bowing routine, and circulate once again. This time the robed male, with the female beside him, gestures for each male in turn to rise, places his hip against theirs, and engages them in a rhythmic movement up and down. Again they circle the group; this time the robed female takes the initiative, kneeling in turn beside each female, removing her shoes and caressing her feet and lower legs.

Upon returning to their places, the male again puts his hand behind his partner's head and she bows low again, touching the floor with her forehead. Then, in sequence, she offers a bowl of water (apparently for cleansing fingers) to her partner, and subsequently to all the males. She returns to her place, kneels and bows again, following the same pattern with a bowl of unfamiliar food and, after that, with a bowl containing a strange and bitter drink. In each case the routine is the same; bowing, serving her partner, next the males and finally the females.

When this has been concluded, the robed male and female, after bowing again, circle the group and the woman examines the feet of certain females. After selecting one, she is brought to the head of the room and both women kneel, one to the right and the other to the left of the seated male. Finally, the man places his hands behind the heads of both kneeling women and, depending on their reaction, both may bow to the floor. The central figures then quietly depart.

Many of our defenses against decentering may be seen in the discussion that follows. If the debriefing proceeds without direction, most of the participants promptly and adamantly characterize it as a sexist society (some males and females refuse to participate). Females are clearly "inferior": they must sit on the floor, must remove their shoes, and are served only after the males. The robed man and woman reflect and underscore these values: the male is seated while the female must kneel, the male is waited on while the female is not, the male "forces" the female to bow to the floor, demonstrating her enslavement.

All these reactions reveal the powerful tendency to see, to classify, to interpret, and to evaluate alien acts in ethnocentric terms. For it to serve as a cross-cultural learning experience and to demonstrate the process of decentering, the facilitator must control the debriefing. Participants are asked first to report only what they have *seen* and to do so in terms as culture-free as possible. (Males were seated on chairs and served first; females were seated on the floor and served second.) Even simple descriptions will introduce errors: meaningless acts, such as where the woman walked, may be seen as significant, but her serenity may be overlooked as

irrelevant; the clicking sounds may be read as signals of approval, and so on.

Only after summing up what has been observed are participants invited to comment on what the acts or cues might mean; with encouragement, a wide range of different and even contradictory inferences begin to seem plausible. Often there is some softening of dogmatic judgments at this point. Participants may next be asked how they *felt*, or how they perceived the Albatrossians to feel, during the unfolding of the exercise. At last they are encouraged to try to decipher the pattern within the pattern, to offer *explanations* of the cultural assumptions and values that might explain these acts. As this process goes on, there tends to be further softening of ethnocentric perspectives.

Finally the world view of Albatross is described: the earth rather than the heavens is the seat of the gods. Women are superior beings, hence sit directly on the earth, bare their feet, kneel and pray, for they alone have access to the gods. Males are inferior beings, must not touch the earth, relate to the gods only through the mediation of a female, are served first to protect females from any harmful or poisonous foods. In short, the simulation reveals how quickly, how silently, and how unconsciously strangers impose their own assumptive world onto events in a strange society, and, in decentering, how carefully the outsider needs to carry out the process of successive approximation; observing, inferring, comparing, predicting, and repeating this over and over until a wider understanding and deeper rapport emerge.

A FINAL COMMENT

Two processes seem to characterize successful efforts to grasp the alien world of another person or society. One is the concept of decentering, the other the process of convergence through successive approximation. The former signifies emancipation from having just one way of experiencing the world; the latter signifies the acquisition of new ways of experiencing it. They are not, in our view, independent of each other; each nourishes and is nourished by the other.

The approach of the serious investigator, if not the technology and procedures of scientific research, throws considerable light on the stages of cultural adaptation required in all encounters with people of a contrasting cultural heritage. Perhaps greater attention should be given to these processes, and to ways of promoting them, since they permeate both the most sophisticated and the most prosaic efforts to understand the dynamics of culture.

NOTES

1. The assumption of contextual consistency, that events and utterances elicit the same response throughout the members of society, is currently questioned by a growing number of scientists. They range from psychiatrists like Jay Haley to measurement specialists like Jane Mercer to ecologists like Roger Barker. All, in one way or another, question the assumption that one can presume that any event—whether a test of intelligence or a personal crisis—can be assumed to have the same meaning for everyone. The thrust of this criticism of contextual consistency is made succinctly by Jay Haley: "All attempts to classify individuals into types have assumed that they faced the same situations and that therefore differences must be within them" (Haley 1977, p. 41). If true, even within-cultural comparisons of people may be suspect; but that is the occasion for another paper, and outside the province of this one.

2. The importance of "detachment" as a condition for effective interaction within alien cultures was first mentioned by Clyde Kluckhohn, but the particulars through which such detachment might be gained were never developed in concrete form (Kluckhohn 1949, p. 39). Donald Campbell and Oswald Werner, as well as Richard Brislin in a later work, use the term "decentering" but limit its application to the achieving of linguistically equivalent instruments for cross-cultural research. Our effort is both to enlarge its scope and, at the same time, to clarify its particulars (Werner & Campbell 1970, pp. 398–420; Brislin, Lonner & Thorndike 1975, pp. 37–39).

3. In some ways this process resembles that experienced by members of an audience who shift identities with the characters in a play, the performers on a stage, or the musicians in an orchestra.

4. The diverse functions of superficially similar objects or acts are illustrated in the varied meanings that masks may evoke in various cultures (Boas 1955, p. 274).

5. Symbols are the most obvious and distinguishing feature of cultures. All meanings must be cast into some form—sound, color, gesture—to be displayed to others, and all such forms must carry conventional meanings to be interpreted similarly. Language is the most familiar of such symbolic codes, but far from the only one capable of giving form to meaning and meaning to form. Music, dance, painting, architecture, and artifacts are all capable of doing so and are often as culturally distinctive as languages themselves. All pose a similar problem of equivalance when studied cross-culturally.

6. This procedure can be described as asymmetrical since the primary language version of any instrument is treated as given, or correct, with the translator producing alternative phrasings in the second language until it matches the meaning of the first. The alternative, often described as symmetrical translation, regards neither language as primary and adapts both versions simultaneously until equivalence is attained (Werner & Campbell 1970, pp. 398–399).

7. The aim of this simulation is to decipher the dynamics of an unfamiliar culture without relying upon direct questions. (Theodore Gochenour. "The Albatross." In D. Batchelder & E. Warner [eds.], *Beyond Experience*. Brattleboro, Vermont: The Experiment Press, 1977.)

REFERENCES

Araki, Shoko, & Barnlund, Dean. *Intercultural Encounters: The Management of Compliments by Japanese and Americans*. In press.

Barnlund, Dean C. *Public and Private Self in Japan and the United States*. Tokyo: Simul Press, 1975.

Benedict, Ruth. *The Chrysanthemum and the Sword*. Boston: Houghton Mifflin, 1946.

Boas, Franz. *Race, Language and Culture*. New York: Macmillan, 1955.

Brislin, Richard, Lonner, Walter, & Thorndike, Robert. *Cross-cultural Research Methods*. New York: Wiley, 1973.

Doi, Takeo. *The Anatomy of Dependence*. Tokyo: Kodansha, 1973.

Haley, Jay. *Toward a Theory of Pathological Systems*. In P. Watzlawick and J. Weakland (eds.), *The Interactional View*. New York: Norton, 1977.

Jourard, Sidney. *The Transparent Self*. Princeton, New Jersey: Van Nostrand, 1964.

Kluckhohn, Clyde. *Mirror for Man: A Survey of Human Behavior and Social Attitudes*. Greenwich, Connecticut: Fawcett, 1965.

Mead, Margaret, and Metraux, Rhoda (eds.). *The Study of Culture at a Distance*. Chicago: University of Chicago Press, 1953.

Nida, Eugene A. *Toward a Science of Translation*. Leyden, Netherlands: E. J. Brill, 1964.

Nomura, Naoki, & Barnlund, Dean. "Patterns of Interpersonal Criticism in Japan and the United States." *International Journal of Intercultural Relation*, 1982.

Ratcliff, Carter. "American Indian Masterworks." *Art International*, February 1974, pp. 50–52.

Reichel-Dolmatoff, Gerardo. *Amazonian Cosmos*. Chicago: University of Chicago Press, 1968.

Triandis, Harry. *The Analysis of Subjective Culture*. New York: Wiley, 1972.

Werner, Oswald, & Campbell, Donald. "Translating, working through interpreters, and the problem of decentering." In R. Naroll and R. Cohen (eds.), *A Handbook of Method in Cultural Anthropology*. New York: American Museum of Natural History, 1970, pp. 398–420.

Prejudice in Intercultural Communication

RICHARD W. BRISLIN

THE FUNCTIONS OF PREJUDICE

When people react negatively to others on an emotional basis, with an absence of direct contact or factual material about the others, the people are said to behave according to prejudice. The concept of prejudice has been subjected to first-rate research investigations by psychologists and sociologists. One of the conclusions of this research is that "prejudice" is a far more complex concept than would be judged from the way the word is used in ordinary, everyday usage. This complexity has to be understood if the problems of prejudice are to be addressed effectively.

An understanding of prejudice can begin if its functions are analyzed. Katz[1] has written the clearest presentation of the functions of various attitudes which people hold, and these can be applied to the more specific case of prejudicial attitudes. In addition, the functions can be applied to the sorts of intercultural contact under scrutiny at this conference. In the past, the majority of research has dealt with interpersonal contact within countries, especially Black-White relations. The four functions that attitudes serve for people are:

1. *The utilitarian or adjustment function.* People

From *Intercultural Theory and Practice: Perspectives on Education, Training, and Research*, December 1979, pp. 28–36. Used with permission of the author. Footnotes have been renumbered. Richard W. Brislin is associated with the Culture Learning Institute, East-West Center, Honolulu, Hawaii.

hold certain prejudices because such attitudes lead to rewards, and lead to the avoidance of punishment, in their culture. For instance, people want to be well liked by others in their culture. If such esteem is dependent upon rejecting members of a certain group, then it is likely that the people will indeed reject members of the outgroup. Or, if jobs are scarce and if people from a certain group want those jobs, it is adjustive to believe that members of a certain group have no responsibility in work settings. Thus there will be less competition for the desired employment.

2. *The ego-defensive function.* People hold certain prejudices because they do not want to admit certain things about themselves. Holding the prejudice protects the people from a harsh reality. For instance, if a person is unsuccessful in the business world, (s)he may believe that members of a certain successful group are a scheming bunch of cheaters. This belief protects the individual from the self-admission that (s)he has inadequacies. Another example involves experiences that most people have during childhood, no matter what their culture. People believe, as part of their basic feelings of self-esteem, that they have grown up in a society where proper behavior is practiced. These people may look down upon members of other cultures (or social classes within a culture) who do not behave "correctly." This prejudicial attitude, then, serves the function of protecting people's self-esteem.

3. *The value-expressive function.* People hold certain prejudices becuse they want to express the aspects of life which they highly prize. Such aspects include basic values of people concerning religion, government, society, aesthetics, and so forth. Katz[2] emphasizes that this function is related to an individual's "notion of the sort of person he sees himself to be." For example, people who discriminate against members of a certain religious group may do so because they see themselves as standing up for the one true God (as defined by their own religion). As a more intense example, people have engaged in atrocities toward outgroup members so as to retain the supposed values of a pure racial stock (again, their own).

4. *The knowledge function.* People hold certain prejudices because such attitudes allow individuals to organize and structure their world in a way that makes sense to them. People have a need to know about various aspects of their culture so that they can interact effectively in it. But the various aspects are so numerous that various discrete stimuli must be categorized together for efficient organization. People then behave according to the category they have organized, not according to the discrete stimuli.[3] Often these categories are stereotypes that do not allow for variation within a category. For instance, if people believe that members of a certain cultural group are childlike and cannot be given any responsibility, they may employ that stereotype upon meeting a member of that group. Given a set of stereotypes, people do not have to think about each individual they meet. They can then spend time on the many other matters that compete for their attention during an average day. The prejudicial stereotypes thus provide knowledge about the world. The problem, of course, is that the stereotypes are sometimes wrong and always overdrawn.[4]

Certain prejudices can serve several functions, particularly so when an individual's entire life span is considered. Young children develop a prejudice to please their parents (adjustment), continue to hold it because of what they learn in school (knowledge), and behave according to the prejudice since they wish to express their view of themselves (value). Programs to change prejudice often fail because the most important function, or functions, are not recognized. Most change-oriented programs are concerned with presenting well-established facts about the targets of prejudice. But such a program will only change people's attitudes which serve the knowledge function. Much more work has to be done on finding ways to change prejudices that serve the other three functions. This is a research area that should yield very important payoffs to careful investigators.

THE FORMS OF PREJUDICE

In addition to an understanding of the functions of prejudice, it is also important to consider various forms that prejudice takes in its expression. The range of such expression is large.

1. *Red-neck racism.* Certain people believe that members of a given cultural group are inferior according to some imagined standard and that the group members are not worthy of decent treatment. The term "red-neck" comes from the Southern United States where world attention was focused on the White majority's treatment of Blacks during political demonstrations prior to the Civil Rights Act of 1964. The type of prejudice summarized by the term "red-neck," however, is found all over the world. This extreme form of prejudice has most often been assessed by asking people to agree or disagree with statements like this:[5] "The many faults, and the general inability to get along, of (*insert name of group*), who have recently flooded our community, prove that we ought to send them back where they came from as soon as conditions permit." "(*Insert name of group*) can never advance to the standard of living and civilization of our country due mainly to their innate dirtiness, laziness, and general backwardness."

All of us cringe at the thought of such tasteless, abhorrent sentiments. But we all know that such prejudices exist, and all of us can give many examples from the countries in which we have lived. Formal education has had a tremendous influence on lowering the incidences of red-neck racism. Research has shown that as the number of years of formal education increases, the incidence of racism decreases. However, I do feel that we need accurate figures on the current levels of such prejudice, and only large scale surveys can give us this information. It is possible that attendees at a conference such as this one underestimate the current levels of red-neck racism since they do not normally interact with people who hold such views.

2. *Symbolic racism.* Certain people have negative feelings about a given group because they feel that the group is interfering with aspects of their cul-

ture with which they have become familiar. The people do not dislike the group per se, and they do not hold sentiments that are indicative of red-neck racism. Symbolic racism[6] is expressed in terms of threats to people's basic values and to the status quo. When directly questioned, people will assert that members of a certain group are "moving too fast" and are making illegitimate demands in their quest for a place in society. Symbolic racism is expressed by responses to questions like these (the answer indicative of symbolic racism is noted in parentheses):

"Over the past few years, (*insert name of group*) have gotten more economically than they deserve." (agree)

"People in this country should support _____ in their struggle against discrimination and segregation." (disagree)

"_____ are getting too demanding in their push for equal rights." (agree)

Sentiments like these are probably more widespread than red-neck feelings among members of the affluent middle class in various countries. Again, however, exact figures are unavailable, and this lack hampers intelligent planning for programs to deal with this form of prejudice. It is important to understand the differences between red-neck and symbolic racism. People who hold symbolic sentiments do not view themselves as red-necks, and so programs aimed at changing extreme racist views (such programs are presently most common) are doomed to failure. McConahay and Hough[7] are accurate when they state that current change programs seem incomprehensible to holders of symbolic views "and they do not understand what all the fuss is about. This enables racism to be considered 'somebody else's' problem while holders of symbolic views concentrate upon their own private lives."

3. *Tokenism.* Certain people harbor negative feelings about a given group but do not want to admit this fact to themselves. Such people definitely do not view themselves as prejudiced and they do not

perceive themselves as discriminatory in their behavior. One way that they reinforce this view of themselves is to engage in unimportant, but positive, intergroup behaviors. By engaging in such unimportant behaviors people can persuade themselves that they are unprejudiced, and thus they can refuse to perform more important intergroup behaviors. For instance, Dutton[8] found that if people gave a small amount of money to an outgroup, they were less willing to later donate a large amount of their time to a "Brotherhood Week" campaign emphasizing intergroup relations and goodwill. Other people in the Dutton study donated time to the Brotherhood Week if they had previously not been asked to give the small sum of money. The small amount of money, then, was a token that allowed some people to persuade themselves that they are unprejudiced and so don't have to prove themselves again by engaging in the more important, time-consuming behavior.

4. *Arms-length prejudice.* Certain people engage in friendly, positive behavior toward outgroup members in certain situations but hold those same outgroup members at an "arm's length" in other situations. The difference across situations seems to be along a dimension of perceived intimacy of behaviors.[9] For semi-formal behaviors such as (1) casual friendships at a place of employment, (2) interactions between speaker and audience at a lecture, or (3) interactions at a catered dinner party, people who harbor an arms-length prejudice will act in a friendly, positive manner. But for more intimate behaviors such as (1) dating, (2) interactions during an informal dinner held at someone's home, or (3) relations between neighbors, people will act in a tense, sometimes hostile manner. Frankly, I have observed this sort of arm's-length prejudice at places where such behavior would ideally not be expected, as at the East-West Center. I have observed a Caucasian social psychologist (who has long lectured on prejudice), during a visit to my home, become non-communicative and ultimately rude when my Chinese-American neighbor unexpectedly dropped in for a visit. This form of prejudice is hard to detect since people who engage in it seem so tolerant of outgroup members much of the time.

5. *Real likes and dislikes.* Certain people harbor negative feelings about a given group because members of the group engage in behaviors that people dislike. This fifth category is derived from more common sense than scholarly literature, and it represents an expression of my feelings that not all prejudice should be looked upon as an indication of some sickness or flaw. People *do* have real likes and dislikes. No one person is so saintly as to be tolerant and forgiving toward all who engage in behaviors (s)he dislikes. For instance, littering really bothers me, and there are certain groups more likely to leave their trash on the ground after a picnic. Sometimes they are from cultures where servants or laborers are expected to do such cleanup. But my realization of the group's background does not lessen my dislike of litter. Seeing members of a certain group engage in such disliked behaviors, I am less likely to interact pleasantly with other members of the group in the future. My recommendation is to give more attention to this common, but heretofore neglected, type of everyday prejudice.

6. *The familiar and unfamiliar.* People who are socialized into one culture are likely to become familiar and thus comfortable with various aspects of that culture. These people, when interacting with members of another culture, are likely to experience behaviors or ideas that are unfamiliar and hence they are likely to feel uncomfortable. Consequently, the people are likely to prefer to interact with members of their own cultural group. What might seem like prejudice and discrimination to an onlooker, then, may be simply a reflection of people's preference for what is comfortable and nonstressful. In a study of interaction among members of nine ethnic groups on Guam,[10] I found that informants were able to verbalize this reason for people's choices of friends. An informant from the Marshall Islands wrote:

Culture makes these groups stick together. Somebody might not get along with one from another country. He likes to find some friends who have the same beliefs he has, and he could only find these characteristics with the people from his own country.

And a resident of Truk wrote about the type of strained conversation that can arise when members of different groups interact:

A Trukese who has never experienced the cold winter of the U.S. could not comprehend and intelligently appreciate a Statesider telling him the terrible winter they had in Albany anymore than a person from Albuquerque who has never seen an atoll could visualize the smallness of the islets that make up such an atoll. (Truk, of course, is an atoll.)

I believe that this sort of mild prejudice based on what is familiar and unfamiliar is the sort of phenomenon recently referred to by the United States Ambassador to the United Nations, Andrew Young.[11] In mid-1977, Young labeled a number of people as "racists,"[12] but in explaining his use of the term he clearly was referring to a lack of understanding and an insensitivity regarding other cultural groups. When questioned by the press, Young had to admit that the insensitivity and misunderstanding stem from unfamiliarity. As with the type of prejudice described under "real likes and dislikes," this everyday type of behavior deserves more attention from behavioral scientists and educators than it has heretofore received.

NOTES

1. D. Katz, "The functional approach to the study of attitudes," *Public Opinion Quarterly*, 1960, 24, pp. 164–204.

2. Katz, 1960, p. 173.

3. H. Triandis, "Culture training, cognitive complexity and interpersonal attitudes." In R. Brislin, S. Bochner, and W. Lonner (eds.). *Cross-Cultural Perspectives on Learning* (New York: Wiley/Halsted Division, 1976) pp. 39–77.

4. The fact that I use the term "prejudicial stereotypes" does not mean that stereotypes and prejudice are isomorphic. *Some* stereotypes stem from prejudicial attitudes, and only these are discussed in this paragraph. More generally, stereotypes refer to any categorization of individual elements that mask differences among those elements. Stereotypes are absolutely necessary for thinking and communicating since people cannot respond individually to the millions of isolated elements they perceive every day. They must group elements together into categories, and then respond to the categories. Stereotypes are a form of generalization that involve names of some group of people and statements about that group. Thus when we speak of "conservatives" or "academics" or "educators," we are using stereotypical categories that mask individual differences within those categories. Stereotypes will always be a factor in any sort of communication, a fact that must be realized in any analysis of communication between individuals from different backgrounds. I mention this because, recently, I have found difficulty in encouraging multicultural groups to discuss stereotypes since the link between prejudice and stereotypes has become so strong. Stereotypes have acquired a distasteful status. Refusal to deal with them, however, means a refusal to deal with one of the most basic aspects of thinking and communication.

5. These statements are adapted from the analysis of such questionnaire items by R. Ashmore, "The problem of intergroup prejudice," in B. Collins, *Social Psychology* (Reading, Mass.: Addison-Wesley, 1970) pp. 245–296.

6. J. McConahay and J. Hough, "Symbolic racism," *Journal of Social Issues*, 1976, 32(2), pp. 23–45.

7. McConahay and Hough, 1976, p. 44.

8. D. Dutton, "Tokenism, reverse discrimination, and egalitarianism in interracial behavior," *Journal of Social Issues*, 1976, 32(2), pp. 93–107.

9. H. Triandis and E. Davis, "Race and belief as determinants of behavioral intentions," *Journal of Personality and Social Psychology*, 1965, 2, pp. 715–725.

10. R. Brislin, "Interaction among members of nine ethnic groups and the belief-similarity hypothesis," *Journal of Social Psychology*, 1971, 85, pp. 171–179.

11. *Playboy*, July, 1977; also analyzed in *Newsweek*, June 20, 1977, p. 34.

12. An "unfortunate" use of the term, Ambassador Young eventually admitted.

The Transfer of Intercultural Training Skills

PAUL B. PEDERSEN

The trainer going to another culture is confronted with a *complexity* of environmental variables which will determine the success or failure of training. A balance of cultural variables mediates the success of training at several levels. First, there is the effect of difference in cultural background and perception that separates the trainer and participants from one another. These differences in socialization and value priorities will determine both the appropriate method and content of any training or consultation *before* any transfer of awareness or knowledge or skill can occur.

Second, there is the effect of role difference between the trainer on the one hand, with the participant, the sponsoring organization, or the funding agency on the other. These "role differences" function in ways similar to cultures, with some overlapping areas of interest and concern but considerable areas of contrary or even competing priorities (Miles 1976). The perspective of a service "provider" is significantly different from the service "consumer." The trainer will need to identify those areas of shared priority to establish a balance of roles and cultures.

A means-oriented "training culture," which lasts only as long as the training event, balances the contrary and competing interests of the participant's, sponsor's and trainer's differentiated agenda. If either the cultural differences or the role differences are disregarded in the development of a training program the resistance from special

From *International Journal of Psychology* 18 (1983), 333–345. Reprinted by permission of the *International Journal of Psychology* and the author. Dr. Pedersen teaches at Syracuse University.

interest groups is likely to confuse and complicate any measures of success.

Many intercultural training and development proposals fail either to meet the systematic requirements of good training design or the prerequisite balance of cultural and role relationships within the training environment. This article will attempt to identify both the cultural variables and the role relationship as they mediate the effectiveness of training within a systematic training design.

Lynton and Pareek (1976) describe training according to two dimensions that delineate the subject matter or knowledge being learned through training and another intersecting dimension of general understanding or insight on how people and things function. Since that publication many variations of training approaches have emerged (Goldstein 1980). During the 1970's general systems philosophy provided the most popular framework for discussing training issues. These systems emphasized instructional objectives, precisely controlled learning experiences and criteria for performance and evaluation of the training. There was an emphasis on measuring achievements, a within-systems framework to facilitate interaction between components of the system and finally a structure for interaction between the training program and its environment.

This article will follow a sequence of stages suggested by Hickerson and Middleton (1975) which has been translated into many other languages and cultures. The sequence moves through five stages, beginning with the job or task analysis, which identifies a discrepancy or "need." The second stage requires the setting of training objectives appropriate to the need. The third stage requires planning a training design appropriate to the objectives. The fourth stage requires implementing the training plan. The fifth stage requires evaluating the success or failure of the training.

With each stage in this sequence it will be useful to begin by developing a new awareness towards the desired change. After the necessary *awareness* has been achieved, the next step is to transfer *knowledge* through increasing information resources about the changes being considered.

Building on the new awareness and increased knowledge, it is then possible to transfer *skills* which will help to bring about the new changes through different behaviors, actions or interventions. The comprehensive training program will contain a balance of awareness, knowledge and skills.

1. THE NEEDS ASSESSMENT

The first stage of intercultural training begins with the "person" of the trainer. The trainer is in an awkward position to determine what kind of training would be appropriate in another culture. The trainer is an "outsider" both from the perspective of the host culture and from the point of view of the sponsoring organization. The trainer will need to balance the complex cultural and organizational components without losing his or her own legitimate identity. There is evidence that these boundary spanning activities by mediators, integrators or cultural brokers result in conflicting demands (Miles 1976), role ambiguity and role diffusion (Adler 1975). The trainer will need to learn a new cultural and organizational identity that will adapt to the unique training environment (Foa and Chemmers 1967). Before any communication on the training programs can begin, the trainer him- or herself will need to learn more about the host culture expectations that will define a uniquely new training role (Brislin and Pedersen 1976).

The greater the cultural and organizational differences, the more likely that barriers to communication will result in misunderstanding (Mishler 1965; LeVine and Campbell 1972). The problems are likely to become even more troublesome for the U.S. based trainer who is socialized into a culture where, as Stewart (1971) points out, the functional roles of parent/child, teacher/student, boss/employee and man/woman are much less formal and specified than in most other cultures.

The trainer who has gained acceptance in more than one culture will be able to function more effectively in issues that involve both cultures than persons without bicultural expertise (Useem and Useem 1967). In addition to knowing the home culture, the bicultural trainer will know the host culture's language, have a network of friends and colleagues within the host culture, be respected and accepted by significant members of the host culture community. Persons who have become bicultural or multicultural in this sense have tended to demonstrate better personal adjustment than monocultural individuals (Szapocznik and Kurtines 1980). Berry (1975) suggests that bicultural persons have the potential to function with greater cognitive flexibility and be more creatively adaptive in either of their two cultural settings. The trainer has to participate in more than one culture to function effectively in a bicultural or multicultural setting. As a compromise position, "mediators" or "cultural brokers" have sometimes been included in the training team as host culture counterpart interpreters or translators. Those go-between persons are in a position of considerable power to determine the success or failure of the training, and occasionally they may introduce their own private agenda independent of either the trainer or the host culture.

The appropriate trainer will need a balance of awareness, knowledge and skills to be successful. If the trainer has an appropriate *awareness* of the host culture, then the training will reflect appropriate attitudes, opinions and implicit assumptions from the host culture's point of view. Awareness relates to the trainer's grasp of the organizational and cultural complexity of this training assignment. If the trainer has appropriate *knowledge* of the host culture the training will appropriately adapt outside ideas in some cases and substitute indigenous alternative approaches where necessary. Knowledge relates to the trainer's access to information necessary for appropriate changes through training. If the trainer has appropriate *skills* in the host culture, the training will result in persons able to make appropriate interventions, behaviors or actions with positive results. Skills relate to helping trainees do something significant that they could not do before.

An appropriate needs assessment will also examine the balance of needs for awareness, knowledge and skill in the persons being trained. Most

of intercultural training begins by emphasizing a need for more "awareness" among the trainees. The needs assessment will emphasize attitudes, opinions, and perspectives that must be changed through training toward the host culture's point of view. In many cases, intercultural training does not go beyond increasing the trainee's new awareness in the hope that the trainee will then seek out the appropriate knowledge and develop the appropriate skills. Although appropriate awareness is extremely important to intercultural training, the needs assessment should also assess a need for new knowledge and information by the trainee that will document and support the new attitudes and opinions about what needs to be done. Finally, the needs assessment should identify the important skills which will allow the trainee to act appropriately and effectively in ways that were not possible before training. A comprehensive needs assessment must relate to the host culture perspective.

Cooper (1979) suggests several "common sense" suggestions for incorporating the host culture's perspective into an assessment of training needs. What is going to be the positive *and* negative impact of training on the trainee's family and community? If the training is successful in changing things, how might those changes require a readjustment of the balance in a trainee's home, work and community setting? What will be the impact of changes in a trainee's status resulting from the training? How will the new awareness, knowledge and skill be integrated into the community? How much local support will the trainee get for these new awareness, knowledge and skill changes?

The first stage of training requires an appropriate match of training/trainer resources and host culture needs. Unless this match is made appropriately the subsequent stages of training are not likely to succeed.

2. DEVELOPING TRAINING OBJECTIVES

The second stage of a discrepancy model is setting the training objectives. These objectives must be clearly stated and specific enough that their success or failure can be measured. For that reason performance objectives are usually "criterion-based" linking specific performance discrepancies with the success or failure of training. The objectives should be described in terms of what the trainee will be able to do at the end of successful training. Not only will clarity of objectives make it easier for a trainee to evaluate progress but also it will facilitate cooperation among the trainers who can now more clearly contribute to one another's objectives.

Behavioral objectives are action-oriented toward specific changes, they are people-oriented toward increased capability of meeting the training objectives, and they are responsibility-oriented in promising to accomplish specific tasks through training. Each behavioral objective is written in terms of specific outcomes, observable measurable actions, and with the "trainee" as the subject of an objective statement.

Intercultural training is complicated by having to balance the multiple cultural and organizational perspectives of success (Roberts 1970; Brein and David 1971; Stening 1979). Available research on establishing appropriate objectives is inconclusive because a variety of criteria are used to measure success, the methodologies do not allow for a comparison of data and because most research studies are limited to a single method or measure of analysis (Ruben and Kealey 1979). One frequent intercultural training objective has been to prevent "culture shock." However Ruben and Kealey (1979) suggest that in at least some cases the person who will be the most effective can expect to undergo intensive culture shock during transition. Regarding adjustment, they concluded that persons who express "respect" for persons within their own culture are also more genuinely tolerant, respectful toward and comfortable with persons from other cultures. Regarding effectiveness, persons who were excessively task-oriented toward problem solving and interpersonal interaction tended to be less effective than those who were less consistently task-oriented. Advisors who were non-judgmental, respectful, relativistic in their orientations to knowl-

edge and more tolerant of ambiguity were also more effective.

As examples of international awareness or affective objectives, Bloom (1956) suggests competencies which have been repeated in one form or another by much of the more recent literature. The affectively competent trainee is: (1) aware of other cultures, (2) willing to receive information about value systems different from his/her own and voluntarily selects articles and books about a different culture, (3) willing to respond to instructional materials about a different culture by asking questions and offering comments, (4) responding satisfactorily to information about another culture, (5) accepting the idea that it is good to know and understand other people of other cultures, (6) rejecting cultural isolationism and competing dogmatism, (7) weighing alternative international policies and practices against the standard of international understanding rather than narrow special interests.

As examples of international knowledge or cognitive objectives, Bloom (1956) likewise suggests competencies which have been borrowed by more recent research. The competent trainee knows or understands: (1) much of the history, language, customs and geography from cultures other than his or her own, (2) contributions of various cultures, (3) problem solving from an international perspective, (4) differences in social and economic circumstances across cultures, (5) similarities and differences between selected cultures, (6) culture specific and culturally general characteristics, (7) exceptions to generalizations about cultural data, (8) the importance of international interdependencies, and (9) the values of ideas from a multicultural perspective knowledge-base.

As examples of international skills or behavioral objectives, we would identify specific activities that would be appropriate for the organizational and cultural setting. Harris (1979) describes some sample skills as the ability to: (1) increase managerial effectiveness, (2) improve cross-cultural skills of employees to promote harmony, and (3) . . . increase an employee's job effectiveness in an intercultural setting. Harris (1979) also quotes a UNESCO study which includes the skills of negotiations, bargaining, conflict resolution, staff development and language skills. Kohls (1979) suggests, based on his research, that the most important skills to develop would be a "sense of humor," a "low goal/task orientation" and "the ability to fail," in that order.

The complexity of international and intercultural variables places special requirements on both the content and the process of setting training objectives. Having selected promising candidates for training, it is important to identify discrepancies that are both realistic and appropriate. The objectives will need to reflect a balance of variables that are sensitive to multiple cultural perspectives.

3. DESIGNING TRAINING

Phase three of the training plan relates to designing the training itself. The discrepancy model requires that trainees see why they should study the skill in a graduated sequence. The trainees proceed step by step, with each step more difficult than the previous one. Individual differentiation allows each trainee the opportunity to learn in his or her own style. The training of adults is quite different from the teaching of children. The term "androgogy" for the training of adults has been contrasted with "pedagogy" for the teaching of children (Knowles 1980). Pedagogy implies a superior–inferior relationship which puts the student or trainee in an inferior or dependent position. Adults need to be involved on a more equitable basis to increase their motivation and encourage them to take on more responsibility.

The graduated sequence builds on a trainee's resources and entry skills, teaching the component parts before combining them, teaching parts more familiar before teaching those less familiar to trainees, teaching [simpler] skills before more complex skills, demonstrating the skill before teaching it, teaching the theory and then applying the theory to practice or modeling the skill in a simulated interaction before trying it in a real situation. In each example the design duplicates the process of socialization in natural settings where members of our culture teach us as we "grow up." The design might typically move from awareness to knowledge to skill objectives.

In addition to the trainee, a design will have to satisfy the sponsoring organization. It will be possible to assess the importance of training from the organizational point of view by understanding how this training would contribute to the organization's mission, the importance of changes resulting from the training for corporate goals, the receptiveness by an organization for making changes based on successful training outcomes, and the commitment of organizational resources to the training. Ideally the training component will collaborate with other organizational components through clear divisions of responsibility, specified training populations, clearly stated limits or constraints and special financial provisions for the training project.

In an overview of education and training, Nath (1978) recommends a contingency approach to differentiating among types of training, depending on the organization's perspectives. Nath cites four stages of multinational organizational development. First there is the ethnocentric emphasis on the "national" perspective attempting to exploit the natural resources of a host country with little responsibility toward national development, where policy originates from the home office and foreign functionaries are given little or no freedom to interpret home office policy.

In a second stage, the foreign subsidiary acquires a semi-independent status, promotes local nationals to high management positions and makes contributions to national development in an "international" perspective. This stage frequently results in conflicts between home office and foreign subsidiaries on policy issues.

A third stage is the "multi-national" perspective where the subsidiary organization becomes almost autonomous in status and is allowed to develop its own policy with the home office coordinating and integrating information from the subsidiaries, with increased local control and representation among high level managers. Local interests are of primary importance.

The fourth stage reflects a "transnational" perspective with less distinction between home office and subsidiaries and a free flow of personnel from one location to another transcending national boundaries and issues. The European Common Market and the United Nations would be two examples of transnational development, although the ideals of this stage are reflected in many multinational organizations.

The differentiated requirements of training are contingent on the organization's stage of development. In the first stage the managers need to learn how to use authority in an absolute directive that enforces home office policy, while managers in second-stage organizations require skill at negotiation of policy issues and mediat[ing] conflict between the home office and the subsidiary, managing in the third stage organization requires managers to use a "consultation" style of leadership with coordination and integration skills, and managers in the fourth stage organization need participation in leadership. In each situation the organizational context as a comprehensive system needs to be considered to match the level of organizational development with the priority managerial and organizational skills.

There is frequently a well-defined multinational company policy that requires allegiance and loyalty from its employees which must be acknowledged by outside experts brought in for training. This ideology might frequently conflict with the values of *both* the host culture and the outside trainer, not to mention the perspective of their own company staff. Each organization develops its own culture (Harris and Moran 1979).

An appropriate training design will include a balance of perspectives from the trainee, the organization, the host culture and the trainer so that the needs of awareness, knowledge and skill will be met and so that the specified training objectives can be accomplished. A comprehensive design will include a balance of experiential approaches to increase awareness, lecture presentations to transfer knowledge, and simulated opportunities to practice skills. The degree of emphasis will depend on the training needs and objectives.

4. IMPLEMENTATION

In developing an effective training culture, intercultural training emphasizes the importance of harmonious interaction between the trainee and the trainer to develop a positive group climate. While the style of implementation will vary from one culture to another there are several important guidelines that have enhanced previous training programs.

Trainers bring their own expectations and values, needs and awareness which need to be skillfully incorporated into the curriculum. Each trainer has a different style which has developed over previous training experience. The primary task of the trainer is to define and develop shared and congruent expectations among trainers, supervisors and trainees interacting with one another. The establishing of a favorable training climate within the group is an extremely important prerequisite of effective implementation. There are many ways to develop this favorable climate. Amir (1969) cites considerable research which documents the necessity of favorable conditions such as *harmonious* contact that *enhances* status on *important* issues that are *mutually* rewarding for intergroup contact to have positive results.

There is a danger that the trainer might become so intent on meeting the specified objectives that the trainer might lose sight of the trainee as the center of concern. The trainee's perspective, expectations, and ultimate effectiveness back on the job must take top priority. Trainees will have specific expectations about the purposes, methods, trainer role and trainee role which must *constantly* be attended to. The trainee brings status and experience into the training session. Any training perceived as "experimenting" with, or patronizing the trainee in any way results in loss of status and a negative reaction to the training experience.

5. EVALUATION

The last stage of the intercultural model deals with follow-up and summative evaluation. The training cycle is completed by going back to the job description and looking at the original training objectives, discrepancies and outcomes to see if the training approach was successful or not. *Formative* evaluation is concerned with finding out how well and to what extent training objectives were reached and how well training activities are related to the training objectives. *Summative* evaluation, however, looks at whether the training objectives were the right ones to eliminate performance discrepancies and change job performance. Formative evaluation measures the relationship between training activities and the achievement of objectives throughout the course of the training at each point. Summative evaluation measures the relationship between those objectives and the performance discrepancies themselves, following the completion of training. Evaluation is therefore appropriate both as a part of the whole training program and at the conclusion of training. Because of cultural complexities, qualitative as well as quantitative evaluation measures will be necessary to monitor the impact of intercultural training.

The complexity of evaluating an intercultural training program is multiplied by the number of culturally complex intervening variables that define the objectives and values which determine the success of training. One important benefit of carefully setting training objectives is clarifying the expectations of trainees and trainers about the criteria of success for a training project.

An important aspect of evaluation is the follow-up support training can stimulate through post-training activities. The training has occurred in a unique, temporary, means-oriented culture of its own which incorporated aspects of the trainer's perspective, trainee's expectations, supervisor's requirements and the organizational environment's demands. The next task is to generalize what was learned in the "training culture" to the outside world. The training culture has provided peer support, constant guidance and resources for enhancing the skills as they were being learned so as to develop those support resources on the job.

The use of regular two-way communication as with newsletters, seminars, and trainer travel, the scheduling of follow-up training refresher courses, or continued technical assistance are some of the strategies for building bridges between the training culture and the job back home. Successful follow-up will result from the successful completion of the previous stages discussed. To some extent the cycle begins all over again duplicating many of the suggestions for job analysis in determining whether there are new discrepancies and/or whether the training objectives were adequately met. Consequently it should become increasingly obvious not only that evaluation is a constant consideration in each stage of the training process, but also that by changing the trainee through training, the whole back-home job context has been changed. One will need to consider changes in the whole cultural context as well as changes in the individual trainee, to assess the impact of the training experience.

6. CONCLUSION

The training of trainers for intercultural and international contact is complicated by the variety of sometimes conflicting expectations among those funding the experience, those benefiting from the training as well as the trainers and trainees themselves. By creating a temporary, means-oriented "training culture" a new set of systematic and specific guidelines can be generated that accommodates these otherwise conflicting interests. This training culture needs to be detached enough from reality to provide a safe environment to rehearse skills but also relevant enough to allow the generalization of those skills to the real world.

The intercultural trainer needs the *awareness* and *knowledge* to *skillfully* identify and balance the complicated interpersonal and organizational variables through the training experience. Several examples were presented demonstrating difficulties in successfully completing each of the stages. The training of trainers is therefore an especially important component of preparation for identifying discrepancies, developing appropriate objectives, implementing effective designs and generating accurate data to demonstrate the benefits of intercultural/international training through consultants, advisors and counterparts.

REFERENCES

Adler, P., 1975. The translational experience: an alternative view of culture shock. *Journal of Humanistic Psychology* 15 (3).

Amir, Y., 1969. Contact hypothesis in ethnic relations. *Psychological Bulletin* 71, 319–342.

Berry, J., 1975. "Ecology, cultural adaptation and psychological differentiation: traditional patterning and acculturative stress." In: R. Brislin, S. Bochner and W. Lonner (eds.), *Cross-cultural perspectives on learning*. New York: John Wiley (Halsted Division), pp. 207–231.

Bloom, B., 1956. *A taxonomy of educational objectives*. New York: McKay.

Brein, M. and K. H. David, 1971. Intercultural communication and the adjustment of the sojourner. *Psychological Bulletin* 76(3), 215–230.

Brislin, R. W. and P. Pederson, 1976. *Cross-cultural orientation programs*. New York: Gardner Press.

Cooper, C., 1979. The common sense of intercultural training. *The Micronesian Reporter* 27(3), 2–9.

Foa, U. and M. Chemmers, 1967. The significance of role behavior differentiation for cross-cultural interaction training. *International Journal of Psychology* 2, 45–57.

Goldstein, I., 1980. "Training in work organizations." In: *Annual Review of Psychology*, Washington, D.C.: Annual Reviews, pp. 229–272.

Harris, P. R., 1979. Cultural awareness training for human resources development. *Training and Development Journal* (March), 64–74.

Harris, P. R. and R. Moran, 1979. *Managing cultural differences*. Houston, TX: Gulf.

Hickerson, F. J. and J. Middleton, 1975. *Helping people learn: a module for trainers*. Honolulu: East-West Communication Institute.

Knowles, M., 1980. Malcolm Knowles on . . . Some thoughts about environment and learning—Educational ecology, if you like. *Training and Development Journal* (February), 34–36.

Kohls, L. R., 1979. *Survival kit for overseas living*. Chicago, IL: Intercultural Network, SYSTRAN.

LeVine, R. and D. Campbell, 1972. *Ethnocentrism: theories of conflict, ethnic attitudes and group behavior*. New York: Wiley.

Lynton, R. and U. Pareek, 1967. *Training for development*. Homewood, IL: The Dorsey Press.

Miles, R. H., 1976. Role requirements as sources of organizational stress. *Journal of Applied Psychology* 61(2), 172–179.

Mischler, A. L., 1965. "Personal contact in international exchanges." In: H. C. Kelman (ed.), *International behavior*. New York: Holt, Rinehart & Winston.

Nath, R., 1978. "Training international business and management personnel: a contingency approach." In: D. Hoopes, P. Pedersen and G. Renwick (eds.), *Overview of intercultural education, training and research*, Vol. II: *Education and training*. Washington, D.C.: Georgetown University, Society for Intercultural Education, Training and Research, pp. 135–147.

Roberts, K. H., 1970. On looking at an elephant: an evalution of cross-cultural research related to organizations. *Psychological Bulletin* 74(5), 327–350.

Ruben, B. D. and D. J. Kealey, 1979. Behavioral assessment of communication competency and the prediction of cross-cultural adaptation. *International Journal of Intercultural Relations* 3(1), 15–47.

Stening, E. W., 1979. Problems in cross-cultural contact. A literature review. *International Journal of Intercultural Relations* 3(3), 269–314.

Stewart, E., 1971. *American cultural patterns: a cross-cultural perspective*. Pittsburgh, PA: Regional Council for International Understanding.

Szapocznik, J. and W. Kurtines, 1980. "Acculturation ficulteerelism and adjustment among Cuban Americans." In: A. Padilla (ed.), *Acculturation: theory, models and some new findings*. Boulder, CO: Westwood Press.

Useem, J. and R. Useem, 1967. The interfaces of a binational third culture: a study of the American Community in India. *Journal of Social Issues* 23(1), 130–143.

Communication and Acculturation

YOUNG YUN KIM

ACCULTURATION

Human beings are sociocultural animals who acquire their social behaviors through learning. What we learn is defined largely by social and cultural forces. Of all aspects of human learning, communication is most central and fundamental. A great deal of our learning consists of communication responses to stimuli from the environment. We must code and decode messages in such a fashion that the messages will be recognized, accepted, and responded to by the individuals with whom we interact. Once acquired, communication activities function as an instrumental, interpretative, and expressive means of coming to terms with our physical and social environment. Communication is our primary means of utilizing the resources of the environment in the service of humanity. Through communication we adapt to and relate to our environment, and acquire membership and a sense of belonging in the various social groups upon which we depend.

Ultimately, it is not only the immigrant but also the host sociocultural system that undergoes changes as a result of the prolonged intercultural contact. The impact of immigrant cultures on the mainstream host culture, however, is relatively insignificant compared to the substantial influence of the host culture on the individual immigrant.

This original essay appeared in print for the first time in the third edition. All rights reserved. Permission to reprint must be obtained from the publisher and the author. Professor Young Yun Kim teaches at Governor's State University.

Clearly, a reason for the essentially unidirectional change in the immigrant is the difference between the number of individuals in the new environment sharing the immigrant's original culture and the size of the host society. Also, the dominant power of the host society in controlling its resources produces more impact on cultural continuity and change in immigrants. The immigrant's need for adaptation to the host sociocultural system, therefore, will be far greater than that of the host society to include elements of an immigrant culture.

Underlying an immigrant's acculturation process is the communication process. Acculturation occurs through the identification and the internalization of the significant symbols of the host society. Just as the natives acquire their cultural patterns through communication, so does an immigrant acquire the host cultural patterns through communication. An immigrant comes to organize himself or herself and to know and be known in relationship within the new culture through communication. The process of trial and error during acculturation can often be frustrating and painful. In many instances, an immigrant's native language is extremely different from that of the host society. Other communication problems fall broadly into a nonverbal category such as differences in the use and organization of space, interpersonal distance, facial expression, eye behavior, other body movement, and in the perceived importance of nonverbal behavior relative to verbal behavior.

Even when an immigrant has acquired a satisfactory blend of using the verbal and nonverbal communication patterns, he or she may still experience a more subtle and profound difficulty in recognizing and responding appropriately to the culturally sanctioned communication rules. The immigrant is rarely aware of the hidden dimensions of the host culture that influence what and how to perceive, how to interpret the observed messages, and how to express thoughts and feelings appropriately in different relational and circumstantial contexts. Cross-cultural differences in these basic aspects of communication are difficult to identify and infrequently discussed in public. They often seriously impede understanding between immigrants and members of the host society.

If we view acculturation as the process of developing communication competence in the host sociocultural system, it is important to emphasize the fact that such communication competence is acquired through communication experiences. *One learns to communicate by communicating.* Through prolonged and varied communication experiences, an immigrant gradually acquires the communication mechanisms necessary for coping with the environment. The acquired host communication competence of an immigrant has a direct bearing upon his or her overall acculturation. The immediate effect lies in the control that the immigrant is able to exercise over his or her own behavior and over the host environment. The immigrant's communication competence will function as a set of adjustive tools assisting the immigrant to satisfy basic needs such as the need for physical survival and the need for a sense of "belonging" and "esteem" (Maslow 1970, p. 47). Recent surveys of Korean and Indochinese immigrants in the United States clearly demonstrate the pivotal role that communication plays in the immigrants' psychological, social, and economic adjustment (Kim 1976, 1980).

The acculturation process, therefore, is an interactive and continuous process that evolves in and through the communication of an immigrant with the new sociocultural environment. The acquired communication competence, in turn, reflects the degree of that immigrant's acculturation. The degree to which an immigrant is acculturated is not only reflected in, but also facilitated by, the degree of consonance between his or her communication patterns and the sanctioned communication patterns of the host society. This does not mean that every detail of an immigrant's communication behavior can be observed in understanding his or her acculturation, nor that all aspects of the acculturation can be understood through his or her communication patterns. However, by focusing on a few key communication variables that are of crucial importance in the acculturation process, we can approximate, with a reasonable degree of accuracy, the reality of acculturation at a point in time, as well as predict the future development of acculturation.

COMMUNICATION VARIABLES IN ACCULTURATION

One of the most comprehensive and useful conceptual frameworks in analyzing an immigrant's acculturation from the communication perspective is provided by the systems perspective elaborated by Ruben (1975). In the systems perspective, the basic element of a human communication system is viewed as the person who is actively being, seeking, and desiring communication with the environment. As an open communication system, a person interacts with the environment through two interrelated processes—personal communication and social communication.

Personal Communication

Personal (or intrapersonal) communication refers to the mental processes by which one organizes oneself in and with one's sociocultural milieu, developing ways of seeing, hearing, understanding, and responding to the environment. "Personal communication can be thought of as sensing, making-sense-of, and acting toward the objects and people in one's milieu. It is the process by which the individual informationally fits himself into (adapts to and adopts) his environment" (Ruben 1975, pp. 168–169). In the context of acculturation, an immigrant's personal communication can be viewed as the organization of acculturation experiences into a number of identifiable cognitive and affective response patterns that are consistent with the host culture or that potentially facilitate other aspects of acculturation.

One of the most important variables of personal communication in acculturation is the complexity of an immigrant's *cognitive structure* in perceiving the host environment. During initial phases of acculturation, an immigrant's perception of the host culture is relatively simple; gross stereotypes are salient in the perception of the unfamiliar environment. As the immigrant learns more about the host culture, however, perception becomes more defined and complex, enabling the immigrant to detect variations in the host environment.

Closely related to the cognitive complexity is an immigrant's *knowledge* in patterns and rules of the host communication system. Sufficient empirical evidence supports the critical function of such knowledge (especially knowledge of the host language) in facilitating other aspects of acculturation. The acculturative function of the knowledge in the host communication system has been observed to be particularly important in increasing an immigrant's participation in interpersonal and mass communication networks of the host society (Breton 1964; Chance 1965; Richmond 1967; Kim 1977, 1980).

Another variable of personal communication in acculturation is an immigrant's *self-image* in relation to the immigrant's images of others. The relative position of the immigrant's self-image in relation to his or her images of the host society and the original culture, for example, provides valuable information about the immigrant's subjective reality of acculturation. Feelings of alienation, low self-esteem, and other similar psychological "problems" of immigrants tend to be associated with the greater perceptual distance between self and members of the host society (Kim 1980).

Also, an immigrant's *acculturation motivation* has been observed to be functional in facilitating the acculturation process. Acculturation motivation refers to an immigrant's willingness to learn about, participate in, and be oriented toward the host sociocultural system. Such positive orientation of an immigrant toward the new environment generally promotes participation in communication networks of the host society (Kim 1977, 1980).

Social Communication

Personal communication is linked to social communication when two or more individuals interact, knowingly or not. "Social communication is the process underlying intersubjectivization, a phenomenon which occurs as a consequence of public symbolization and symbol utilization and diffusion" (Ruben 1975, p. 171). Through social communication, individuals regulate feelings, thoughts, and actions of one another. Social communication can be classified further into interpersonal communication and mass communication. Interpersonal communication occurs through interpersonal relationships, which in turn represent the purpose, function, and product of an individual's interpersonal communication. Mass communication, however, is a more generalized process of social communication, in which individuals interact with their sociocultural environment without involvement in interpersonal relations with specific individuals. An individual's communication experiences through such media as radio, television, newspaper, magazine, movie, theater, and other similar public forms of communication, can be included in this category.

An immigrant's *interpersonal communication* can be observed through the degree of his or her participation in interpersonal relationships with members of the host society. More specifically, we can infer and predict an immigrant's acculturation from the nature of his or her interpersonal networks. An immigrant with a predominantly ethnic interpersonal network can be considered less acculturated and less competent in the host communication system than an immigrant whose associates are primarily members of the host society. In addition, the degree of intimacy in the relationships an immigrant has developed with members of the host society is an important indicator of his or her acquired host communication competence. We may further elaborate on an immigrant's interpersonal communication by observing his or her specific verbal and nonverbal communication patterns in interacting with members of the host society.

The acculturation function of *mass communication* is limited in relation to that of interpersonal communication (Kim 1979a). The immigrant's interpersonal communication experiences have intense and detailed influence over the immigrant's acculturation. Communication involving an interpersonal relationship provides the immigrant with simultaneous feedback, directly controlling and regulating the immigrant's communication behaviors. Though limited in its relative impact on an immigrant's acculturation, mass communication plays an important role in expanding the immigrant's experiences in the host society beyond the immediate environment. Through mass communication, an immigrant learns about the broader ranges of the various elements of the host sociocultural system. In transmitting messages that reflect the aspirations, myths, work and play, and specific issues and events of the host society, the media explicitly and implicitly convey societal values, norms of behavior, and traditional perspectives for interpreting the environment. Of the immigrant's various mass communication experiences, exposure to the content of information-oriented media such as newspapers, magazines, television news, and other informational programs has been observed to be particularly functional for acculturation when compared to other media that are primarily entertainment oriented (Kim 1977).

The acculturative function of mass communication should be particularly significant during the initial phase of an immigrant's acculturation process. During this phase, the immigrant has not yet developed a sufficient competence to develop satisfactory interpersonal relationships with members of the host society. The communication experiences in direct interpersonal contact with members of the host society can often be frustrating. The immigrant may feel awkward and out of place in relating to others: The direct negative feedback from the other person can be too overwhelming for the immigrant to experience pleasure in the interaction with members of the host society. The immigrant naturally tends to withdraw from such direct interaction and, instead, resorts to mass media as an alternative, pressure-free channel through which elements of the host environment can be absorbed (Ryu 1978).

Communication Environment

[Immigrants'] personal and social communication and their acculturative function cannot be fully understood in isolation from the communication environment of the host society. Whether the immigrant has resettled in a small rural town or a large metropolitan area, lives in a ghetto area or an affluent suburb, is employed as a factory worker or as an executive—all are environmental conditions that may significantly influence the sociocultural development the immigrant is likely to achieve.

An environmental condition particularly influential in an immigrant's communication and acculturation is the availability of his or her native ethnic community in the local area. The degree to which the ethnic community can influence the immigrant's behavior depends largely upon the degree of "institutional completeness" of the community and its power to maintain the distinctive home culture for its members (Taylor 1979). Available ethnic institutions can ameliorate the stresses of intercultural situations and provide context for acculturation under relatively permissive conditions. In the long run, however, an extensive involvement of an immigrant in the ethnic community without sufficient communication with members of the host society may retard the intensity and rate of the immigrant's acculturation (Broom and Kitsuse 1976).

It is ultimately the host society that permits the degree of freedom, or "plasticity" (Kim 1979b), for minority immigrants to deviate from the dominant cultural patterns of the host society and to develop ethnic institutions. Such permissiveness in the communication environment may vary even within the same country. In a relatively open and pluralistic society such as the contemporary United States, an immigrant may find a difference in the degree of receptivity and openness of the host environment between a large metropolitan area and a small town in a rural area.

ACCULTURATION POTENTIAL

Individuals respond to the new change in terms of their prior experience, accepting what promises to be rewarding and rejecting what seems unworkable or disadvantageous. Acculturation patterns are not uniform among all individuals but vary depending upon their *acculturation potential* as determined by their preimmigration characteristics. Some are more predisposed toward the host culture than others. Among the multitude of background characteristics, the following characteristics are considered important in contributing to greater acculturation potential.

The *similarity* of the original culture to the host culture is perhaps one of the most important factors of acculturation potential. An immigrant from Canada to the United States, for example, will have a greater acculturation potential than a Vietnamese immigrant from Southeast Asia. Even two immigrants from the same culture may have different subcultural backgrounds. An immigrant from a more cosmopolitan urban center is likely to have a greater acculturation potential than a farmer from a rural area. To the extent that we can understand the similarities and discrepancies between an immigrant's original cultural background and the host culture, we can better understand the immigrant's acculturation potential.

Among demographic characteristics, *age* at the time of immigration and *educational background* have been found to be significantly related to acculturation potential. Older immigrants generally experience greater difficulty in adjusting to the new culture and are slower in acquiring new cultural patterns (Kim 1976). Educational background of an immigrant prior to immigration facilitates acculturation (Kim 1976, 1980). Education, regardless of its cultural context, appears to expand a person's capacity for new learning and the challenges of life. In some cases, an immigrant's educational process in the home country includes training in the language of the host society, which gives the individual a basis for building communication competence after immigration.

On the psychological level, an immigrant's *personality factors*, such as gregariousness, tolerance for ambiguity, risk-taking, cognitive flexibility, open-mindedness, and other related characteristics, are likely to increase acculturation potential. These personality characteristics are likely to help restructure the immigrant's perception, feelings, and behaviors, facilitating acculturation in a new cultural environment.

Similarly, *familiarity* with the host culture prior to immigration through previous travel, interpersonal contacts, and through mass media may also increase the immigrant's acculturation potential.

FACILITATING ACCULTURATION THROUGH COMMUNICATION

So far, immigrant acculturation has been defined and explained from a communication viewpoint. Just as any native-born person undergoes the enculturation process through communication, so an immigrant is acculturated into the host culture through communication. Much of the acculturation process is to adapt to, and adopt, predominant patterns and rules of communication of the host culture. The acquired host communication competence, in turn, facilitates all other aspects of adjustment in the host society. Communication, therefore, is viewed as the major underlying process as well as an outcome of the acculturation process.

In order to understand an immigrant's acculturation, we must understand his or her communication patterns. Information about the immigrant's communication enables us to predict the degree and pattern of acculturation. As a conceptual framework to analyze the immigrant's communication patterns, the communication systems perspective has been presented. To summarize, the systems perspective recognizes the dynamic interaction processes of personal communication, social communication, and communication environment. Personal communication can be analyzed in terms of cognitive complexity, knowledge of the host communication patterns and rules, self-image, and acculturation motivation. Social communication is conceptualized in interpersonal communication and mass communication. Interpersonal communication is reflected in the nature and pattern of an immigrant's interpersonal networks and specific verbal and nonverbal communication behaviors. Patterns of use and participation in the host mass communication system, particularly the information-oriented contents of the mass media, are also useful indicators of acculturation. The sociocultural characteristics of the communication environment in which an immigrant carries out day-to-day activities influences the nature of the external communication stimuli that the immigrant is exposed to. Availability and strength of the ethnic community, as well as the plasticity of the host society, slow the acculturation process of an immigrant.

The acculturation potential of an immigrant prior to immigration may contribute to his or her subsequent acculturation in the host society. As discussed previously, acculturation potential is determined by such factors as: (1) similarity between the original culture and the host culture, (2) age at the time of immigration, (3) educational background, (4) some of the personality characteristics such as gregariousness and tolerance for ambiguity, and (5) familiarity with the host culture before immigration.

Once an immigrant enters the host society, the acculturation process is set in motion. The acculturation process will continue as long as the immigrant stays in direct contact with the host sociocultural system. All of the acculturative forces—personal and social communication, communication environment, and preimmigration acculturation potential—interactively influence the course of change in the immigrant's acculturation process. The acculturation process may not be a smooth linear process, but a forward-moving progression toward an ultimate assimilation, the hypothetical state of complete acculturation.

The extensive debate between "assimilationists" (who adhere to the "melting-pot" view) and "cultural pluralists" (proponents of conservation of ethnicity) loses its scientific relevance when we closely examine the inevitable adaptation of humans to their sociocultural environment. No immigrant, as long as livelihood or other needs are functionally dependent upon the host society, can escape acculturation completely. Acculturation, in this sense, is a "natural" phenomenon. A prolonged, direct contact by the immigrant with a new sociocultural environment leads to acculturative change. It is too simplistic to decree that one must be "either A or B," forced to accept or reject one of the two positions. In reality, ethnicity and accultura-

tion can be considered to be two sides of the same coin; they are interrelated and inseparable phenomena. What is important is that both the assimilationist and the pluralist perspectives acknowledge some changes in immigrants over time. When the changes are not complete, it is only natural that there remains a certain degree of ethnicity. Incomplete acculturation, depending on one's point of view, can be interpreted as evidence of (some) assimilation or (some) ethnicity.

Thus, the real issue between the two opposing views—assimilation vs. ethnicity—is not a scientific one, that is to say, whether or not there *is* such a phenomenon as acculturation. Rather, it is an ideological disagreement on the degree to which an individual immigrant *should* maintain (or lose) his or her original culture. Such ideological polarization along a continuum of acculturation among social scientists and social philosophers, however, does not interfere with the natural process of adaptive change or acculturation. Nor should the philosophical disagreement interfere with the ultimate right of an individual immigrant to determine how far to acculturate beyond the minimum, functional level. In reality, most immigrants tend to follow the folk wisdom, "When in Rome, do as the Romans do." They recognize and accept the fact that it is they who are joining an existing sociocultural system, and that the degree of success in building their new lives depends largely on their ability to acculturate into the host society.

Should an immigrant choose to increase his or her acculturative capacity and consciously try to facilitate the acculturation process, then the immigrant must realize the importance of communication as the fundamental mechanism by which such goals may be achieved. To facilitate communication competence in the host culture, the immigrant must develop cognitive, affective, and behavioral competence in dealing with the host environment. By developing a strong acculturation motivation, the immigrant becomes positively oriented to the host society and accepts the norms and rules of the host culture. Through learning the host communication patterns and rules and by being open-minded, the immigrant becomes tolerant of the differences and uncertainties of the intercultural situations. Also, the immigrant must attempt, whenever possible, to maximize participation in the host interpersonal and mass communication systems. Through active participation in the host communication systems, the immigrant will develop a more realistic understanding of, and a more positive outlook on, a new way of life.

The immigrant, however, cannot accomplish his or her acculturative goals alone. The process of acculturation is an interactive process of "push and pull" between an immigrant and the host environment. But members of the host society can facilitate an immigrant's acculturation by accepting the original cultural conditioning of the immigrant, by providing the immigrant with supportive communication situations, and by making themselves patiently available through the often strenuous intercultural encounters. The host society can more actively encourage immigrant acculturation through communication training programs. Such training programs should facilitate the immigrant's acquisition of the host communication competence.

Although prolonged involvement in an ethnic community may ultimately delay the acculturation process, the ethnic community can play a significant acculturative function for the new immigrants in their early stages of acculturation. Ethnic communities can provide support systems to assist new arrivals in coping with the stresses and initial uncertainties and can guide them toward effective acculturation. Studies are beginning to investigate the coping, ego strength, and adaptation mechanisms that are built by natural support systems—family, neighborhood, ethnic associations, and self-help groups (Giordano and Giordano 1977).

All in all, the acculturation process of an immigrant can be facilitated by cooperative effort among the immigrants themselves, the members of the host society, and the ethnic community. At the heart of interactive acculturation lies the communication process linking the individual immigrants to their sociocultural milieu. The importance of communication to acculturation cannot be overemphasized. Acquisition of communication competence by the immigrant is not only instrumental to all other aspects of his or her adjustment, but also vital for the host society if it is to effectively accommodate diverse elements and maintain the necessary societal unity and strength. As long as common channels of communication remain strong, consensus and patterns of concerted action will persist in the host society. As Mendelsohn (1964) describes it, communication makes it possible to merge the minority groups into one democratic social organization of commonly shared ideas and values.

REFERENCES

Adler, P. S. "Beyond Cultural Identity: Reflections on Cultural and Multicultural Man." In *Intercultural Communication: A Reader*, 2nd ed., ed. L. A. Samovar and R. E. Porter. Belmont, Calif.: Wadsworth, 1976, pp. 363–378.

Breton, R. "Institutional Completeness of Ethnic Communities and the Personal Relations of Immigrants," *American Journal of Sociology* 70 (1964), 193–205.

Broom, L., and J. Kitsuse. "The Validation of Acculturation: A Condition to Ethnic Assimilation." In *Ethnicity: A Conceptual Approach*, ed. D. E. Weinberg. Cleveland: Cleveland Ethnic Heritage Studies, Cleveland State University, 1976, pp. 135–146.

Chance, N. A. "Acculturation, Self-Identification, and Personality Adjustment." *American Anthropologist* 67 (1965), 373–393.

Giordano, J., and G. Giordano. *The Ethno-Cultural Factor in Mental Health: A Literature Review and Bibliography.* New York: Institute on Pluralism and Group Identity of the American Jewish Committee, 1977.

Herskovits, M. J. *Cultural Dynamics.* New York: Alfred A. Knopf, 1966.

Kim, Y. Y. "Communication Patterns of Foreign Immigrants in the Process of Acculturation: A Survey Among the Korean Population in Chicago." Ph.D. Dissertation, Northwestern University, 1976.

———. "Communication Patterns of Foreign Immigrants in the Process of Acculturation."

Human Communication Research 4, 1 (1977), 66–77.

————. *Indochinese Refugees in the State of Illinois. Volume IV. Psychological, Social and Cultural Adjustment of Indochinese Refugees.* Chicago: Travelers Aid Society of Metropolitan Chicago, 1980.

————. "Mass Media and Acculturation: Toward Development of an Interactive Theory." Paper presented at the annual conference of the Eastern Communication Association, Philadelphia, Pennsylvania, May 1979a.

————. "Toward an Interactive Theory of Communication-Acculturation." In *Communication Yearbook* 3, ed. D. Nimmo. New Brunswick, N.J.: Transaction Books, 1979b, pp. 435–453.

LeVine, R. A. *Culture, Behavior, and Personality.* Chicago: Aldine, 1973.

Maslow, A. H. *Motivation and Personality*, 2nd ed. New York: Harper & Row, 1970.

Mendelsohn, H. "Sociological Perspectives on the Study of Mass Communication." In *People, Society and Mass Communication*, ed. L. A. Dexter and D. M. White. New York: Free Press of Glencoe, 1964, pp. 29–36.

Peterson, T., J. Jensen, and W. Rivers. *The Mass Media and Modern Society.* New York: Holt, Rinehart & Winston, 1965.

Richmond, A. H. *Post-War Immigrants in Canada.* Toronto: University of Toronto Press, 1967.

Ruben, B. D. "Intrapersonal, Interpersonal, and Mass Communication Process in Individual and Multi-Person Systems." In *General Systems Theory and Human Communication*, ed. B. D. Ruben and J. Y. Kim. Rochelle Park, N.J.: Hayden, 1975.

Ryu, J. S. "Mass Media's Role in the Assimilation Process: A Study of Korean Immigrants in the Los Angeles Area." Paper presented to the annual meeting of the International Communication Association, Chicago, May 1978.

Schutz, A. "The Stranger: An Essay in Social Psychology." In *Identity and Anxiety: Survival of the Person in Mass Society*, ed. M. R. Stein, A. J. Vidich, and D. M. White. New York: Free Press, 1960, pp. 98–109.

Taylor, B. K. "Culture: Whence, Whither and Why?" In *The Future of Cultural Minorities*, ed. A. E. Alcock, B. K. Taylor and J. M. Welton. New York: St. Martin's, 1979.

CONCEPTS AND QUESTIONS FOR CHAPTER 7

1. If you were going to travel abroad, what preparations would you make to ensure the best possible opportunity for effective intercultural communication?

2. What specific suggestions can you make that could improve your ability to interact with other ethnic or racial groups in your community? How would you go about gaining the necessary knowledge and experience?

3. What are the six stumbling blocks in intercultural communication discussed by LaRay Barna? How can you learn to avoid them?

4. Can you think of instances when you have been guilty of assuming similarity instead of difference?

5. How would a "non-judgmental attitude and a high tolerance for ambiguity" help intercultural communication? Is there such a thing as a "non-judgmental attitude"?

6. Can you think of any mannerisms, behaviors, or styles that the U.S. businessperson reflects that are apt to stifle intercultural communication?

7. What kind of training program could be developed that would foster favorable attitudes toward other cultural groups? How would you persuade others to enroll in such a program? What should be done about those who refuse to enroll (and who just may need it the most)?

8. How might you go about developing the traits of decentering and convergence?

9. Why is it important to try to locate similarities between cultures as well as differences?

10. What current television programs and commercials encourage false media stereotyping?

11. Can you think of examples for each of the forms of prejudice discussed by Brislin?

12. What specific behaviors can you engage in that will help the immigrant in the acculturation process?

SUGGESTED READINGS

Abe, H., and R. Wieman. "A cross-cultural confirmation of the dimensions of intercultural effectiveness." *International Journal of Intercultural Relations* 7 (1983), 53–67. This study attempts to examine the topic of "intercultural effectiveness." It compares American sojourners with Japanese sojourners according to 24 personal abilities suggested by a review of literature. Once similarities and differences are found between the Americans and the Japanese, perceptions of intercultural effectiveness are discussed.

Amir, Y. "Contact hypothesis in ethnic relations." *Psychological Bulletin* 71 (1969), 319–342. In what has become a classic piece, Amir explores the assumption that ethnic contact will reduce ethnic prejudice and intergroup tension, and improve relations among various ethnic groups. His findings suggest that specific conditions are required if contact is to result in tension reduction. Practical applications are also considered.

Kohls, R. L. *Survival Kit for Overseas Living*. LaGrange Park, Ill.: Intercultural Network, 1979. This is a practical "how-to" book that deals with the topics of working and living abroad. Kohls offers a number of suggestions that examine the import of values, stereotyping, cultural shock, and so on.

Stening, B. W. "Problems in cross-cultural contact: A literature review." *International Journal of Intercultural Relations* 3 (1979), 269–313. This excellent article reviews the literature "bearing on the matter of misunderstanding between persons engaged in cross-cultural relationships." The author looks at such factors as stereotyping, ethnocentrism, and prejudice.

Trifonovitch, G. J. "On cross-cultural orientation techniques" in *Topics in Culture Learning*, vol. 1. Honolulu: East-West Center, 1973. This article deals specifically with cross-cultural orientation techniques used by the author in the last eight years with American personnel who were preparing to assume duties and responsibilities in Micronesia. Although the cultural orientation is limited in scope, the techniques and methods can be generalized to training programs for a variety of cultures.

Webb, M. W. "Cross-cultural awareness: A framework for interaction." *Personnel and Guidance Journal* 16 (1983), 498–500. In order to facilitate cross-cultural understanding, this essay offers a framework for interaction. It focuses on personal experience, attribution theory, and Gullohorn's "W-curve" concept. It is suggested that these concepts can be useful in intercultural communication.

ADDITIONAL READINGS

Atkeson, P. "Building communication in intercultural marriage." *Psychiatry* 33 (1970), 396–408.

Bennett, J. "Transition shock: Putting culture shock in perspective." *Intercultural Communication Annual* 4 (1977), 45–52.

Brown, I. C. *Understanding Other Cultures*. Englewood Cliffs, N.J.: Prentice-Hall, 1963.

Casse, P. *Training for the Cross-Cultural Mind*. Washington, D.C.: Sietar, 1979.

Clark, M. L., and W. Pearson, Jr. "Racial stereotypes revisited." *International Journal of Intercultural Relations* 6 (1982), 381–393.

Close, D. et al. *Interviewing Immigrants*. Melbourne: Clearing House on Migration Issues, 1978.

Dyel, J. A., and R. Y. Dyel. "Acculturation stress and coping." *International Journal of Intercultural Relations* 5 (1981), 301–328.

Fontaine, G., and E. Dorch. "Problems and benefits of close intercultural relationships." *Interna-*

tional Journal of Intercultural Relations* 4 (1980), 329–337.

Hwang, J., S. J. Chase, and C. W. Kelley. "An intercultural examination of communication competence." *Communication: The Journal of the Communication Association of the Pacific* 9 (1980), 70–79.

Kim, J. K. "Explaining acculturation in a communication framework: An empirical test." *Communication Monographs* 47 (1980), 155–179.

Kitao, K. "Difficulty of intercultural communication between Americans and Japanese." *Communication: The Journal of the Communication Association of the Pacific* 9 (1980), 80–89.

Loveridge, D. "Communication between people." *Hong Kong Psychological Society Bulletin* 9 (1982), 19–26.

Nann, R. C., ed. *Uprooting and Surviving: Adaptation and Resettlement of Migrant Families and Children*. Boston: D. Reidel Publishing Company, 1984.

Neff, C., ed. *New Directions for Experiential Learning: Cross-Cultural Learning*, No. II. San Francisco: Jossey-Bass, 1981.

Sell, D. K. "Research on attitude change in U.S. students who participate in foreign study experiences: Past findings and suggestions for future research." *International Journal of Intercultural Relations* 7 (1983), 131–147.

Tseng, W., et al., eds. *Adjustment in Intercultural Marriage*. Honolulu: University of Hawaii Press, 1977.

8

Ethical Considerations and Prospects for the Future

The goal of this book is to help you understand intercultural communication and to assist you in appreciating the issues and problems inherent in interactions involving people from foreign and alien cultures. To this end we have examined a series of diverse essays that presented a variety of variables operable during intercultural encounters. But what we have looked at up to now is what is already known about intercultural communication. We now shift our emphasis and focus on two issues that are much harder to pin down. These are the ethical considerations that must be inherent in intercultural interactions and the future prospects of this developing field of study. In short, this chapter examines some of the following questions: What do we need to accomplish, what may we expect to accomplish, what philosophical issues must we deal with, and what kinds of personalities must we develop if we are to improve the art and science of intercultural communication during the remainder of this century?

To set the tone for this final chapter, we begin with Gerald R. Miller and Milton J. Shatzer's "Communication Scholarship and the Pursuit of a World Humanism" that calls for the development of a set of goals and ideas by communication scholars that will lead to the furthering of a "world humanism." The phrase "world humanism" is seen as a concerted common effort by all the world's societies to improve the quality of life for all humankind. Miller and Shatzer help us recognize that although we are not unified in the sense of language, culture, or ideology, humanity does share many elements of a common vision of the kind of world it would like to create for its children and grandchildren. This humanistic ideal and its achievement are fraught with conflict, but effective communication is a primary means by which it may be achieved. "The pursuit of a world humanism is probably best carried forward in the context of an informed international citizenry who understands the communicative strategies and the expected impacts of the messages bombarding it." To this end, Miller and Shatzer set forth a few of the ways they believe improved communication abilities can lead to the ideal of "world humanism."

In the second selection, "The Cross-Cultural Arena: An Ethical Void," Dean C. Barnlund raises a number of questions concerning the ethical dimensions of intercultural communication. Barnlund sees countless ethical considerations inherent in two of the premises of this book. First, all human contact involves choices, and second, that contact produces a response. In the intercultural context these choices and responses take on added significance. For, as Barnlund points out, "Morality tends to be culture-specific." This being the case, each individual approaches a person from another culture with a set of values and norms that are part of his or her cultural heritage. These standards are acted out in the intercultural transaction and, as noted, will influence the communication partner. So the question asked is: How should the individual behave? To be more specific, Barnlund queries: "to bribe or not to bribe; to respect class distinctions or to resist them; to employ deception or to insist upon honesty; to express differences or to remain silent?" These and countless other issues are put into perspective in this thought-provoking essay.

Our next essay by Young Yun Kim is based on one of the basic themes of this book—that today's interconnected and fast-changing world demands that we all change our assumptions about culture and our individual place within that culture. Recognizing these changes, Kim advances a philosophical orientation that she calls "Intercultural Personhood." For Kim intercultural personhood combines the key attributes of Eastern and Western cultural traditions. Using these attributes she presents a model of intercultural personhood. This model takes into account basic modes of consciousness, cognitive patterns, personal and social values, and communication behavior. The notion of intercultural personhood also leads us into the concept of the multicultural person as set forth in the next and final article of the text.

We have ended the three previous editions of this book with an article we originally selected because it not only expressed our philosophy toward intercultural communication but also gave a bright perspective for the future. We have again selected Peter S. Adler's "Beyond Cultural Identity: Reflections on Cultural and Multicultural Man" as the final article because it continues to express our viewpoint and because it introduces the notion of the *multicultural person*. We still find this notion highly attractive because the multicultural person is one whose identifications and loyalties have transcended the boundaries of nationalism and ethnocentrism and whose commitments are based on a vision of the world as a global community. A multicultural person is a person of the world—an international person who feels at home anywhere in any culture—who may be the prototype of the individual most suited to successful intercultural communication, and, if the need should ever arise, interstellar or intergalactic communication.

It might be well to view this exploration of ethics and the future as only a sampling of the many issues that confront those involved in intercultural communication. The field is still so new and the challenges so varied that it is impossible to predict future directions with any degree of assurance. Our intent in this chapter, therefore, is simply to introduce you to a few of the issues and concepts.

One final note. Much of what is offered in this chapter may appear naive and unrealistic. Neither we nor the authors of the articles apologize for suggesting that in intercultural contracts each person should aim for the ideal. What we present here are some challenges to develop new ways of perceiving oneself and others. In so doing we all can help make this complex and shrinking planet a more habitable and peaceful place for its 4.5 billion residents.

Communication Scholarship and the Pursuit of a World Humanism

GERALD R. MILLER
MILTON J. SHATZER

When Marshall McLuhan first penned the phrase "the Global Village," the tenor of his words was more pessimistic than optimistic.[1] McLuhan wrote that the new electronic interdependence resulting from increased communication and telecommunication would create a world in the image of a "tribal" village. Unless individuals were aware of this dynamic, the world would be thrown into a phase of panic terrors, which McLuhan posited was the normal state of any oral society (for in it everything affects everything all the time). One needs only to scan the news headlines to wonder if, in fact, McLuhan's prophecies are not being fulfilled. Are we heading toward a world filled with terror and fear, or are we moving toward a world where the worth and dignity of humankind are based on the capacity for self-realization through reason? It is our fervent desire that, as newly-found members of the Global Village, we will guide humankind along the latter path. Though we are not as one in language, culture, or ideology, we believe humanity shares many elements of a common vision of the kind of world it would like to create for its children and grandchildren. Moreover, we suspect that most

This original essay appears here in print for the first time. All rights reserved. Permission to reprint must be obtained from the publisher and the authors. Gerald Miller and Milton Shatzer can be reached at Michigan State University.

people would agree that effective communication constitutes one primary means of achieving it. What better opportunity, then, to speculate about the role of communication study and of the scholarship that pursues a world humanism?

Since the phrase "world humanism" will conjure up many different meanings in the minds of readers, we must first share with you the way we use it. "World humanism" refers to a common effort by all the world's societies to improve the quality of life for all humankind. Since the phrase "quality of life" is also extremely ambiguous, we must go further in our explication; our intended meaning for "quality of life" embraces two dimensions of human existence, which can be identified through quotations.

An often-repeated Biblical quotation, "Man does not live by bread alone," implies that one avenue that can be pursued to improve the quality of life for all humankind is to provide opportunities to engage in liberating, self-expanding, esthetic, and cultural experiences—to experience great art and architecture, music, dancers, poetry and novels, or, for that matter, the physical artistry of great athletes.

It is instructive to note two characteristics of this side of the phrase "quality of life." First, these esthetic and cultural experiences are, in essence, communicative, consisting of reactions to verbal and nonverbal messages. Second, there is a universality to these experiences that transcends national boundaries: regardless of cultural or political heritage, we can all marvel at, and be inspired by, a Michelangelo or Hokusai painting, a song by Um-Khartoum or a symphony by Beethoven, a passage from Octavio Paz, Li Po, or Gibran Khalil Gibran, the intricate movements of Mikhail Baryshnikov or Margot Fonteyn, a building by Frank Lloyd Wright or I. M. Pei, and the athletic feats of Pelé or Earvin "Magic" Johnson. Thus, in a very real sense, communication does not *play a role* in the pursuit of this dimension of quality of life; rather, communication of a certain genre is *synonymous with* quality of life. Because of the universality of these communicative experiences, the roots of a world humanism are firmly planted; the task of this and future generations is to nourish and extend them to all our planet's inhabitants.

There is, however, a second vital dimension to the phrase "quality of life," which is captured by the words of an anonymous author who extended the Biblical quotation: "Humanity does not live by bread alone, but it most certainly can't live without it." This quotation implies that a second avenue through which to improve the quality of life for all humankind consists of providing for basic physiological, economic, and social needs—a nutritious, palatable diet, an architecturally adequate, psychologically satisfying residence, a physically nurturant program of preventive and curative health care, and a cognitively expanding, self-actualizing education.

Despite our best intentions, we travel this second avenue haltingly and perilously. Ideological lane changes are frequent; economic street repairs are commonplace. We disagree on the meaning of street signs: should we bear left, bear right, or continue straight ahead? Indeed, if our goal of a world humanism is to be achieved, it may be necessary to reach the avenue's end by alternate routes: just as a prior point in history gave rise to the expression, "All roads lead to Rome," so we must realize that the route to physiological, economic, and social welfare for all humanity is charted by different societal road maps. In attempting to assimilate this cultural diversity, while at the same time continuing our common quest for humanity's collective security and enhancement, communication study and scholarship play numerous crucial roles.

First, certain elements in the theoretical and empirical writings of communication scholars from numerous societies have the potential of providing us with some common frames of reference for talking about the complex process of communication. One need not accept the extreme position of the Whorfian Hypothesis to grant that how we talk about a phenomenon has an influence on how we think about it. For instance, if we verbally describe communication as the act of selecting and transmitting those symbols that convey the "correct" meaning of words to other individuals, we are predisposed to think in certain ways about both the task we are engaged in, and the responsibility for and consequences of, successful and unsuccessful communication. By contrast, if we verbally conceive of communication as the act of stimulating and/or establishing shared meanings—a conception that accepts the arbitrariness of symbols and suggests that people often have numerous meanings for a given symbol—we are predisposed to think quite differently about the task *and* about the responsibility for, and consequences of, success and failure.

Our major premise is that common frames of reference for talking about communication promote a richer, consensually shared understanding of the process, and this understanding enhances our ability to communicate more effectively. Perhaps even more important, in terms of our quest for a world humanism, it enables us to deal with the inevitable instances of less-than-successful communication more civilly and rationally. We are not suggesting that understanding the process of communication is either a necessary or a sufficient condition to ensure effective communication. Rather, the thrust of our argument is best captured in an anecdote related by one of the first author's most respected professors, Donald C. Bryant. Following a "communication breakdown" that occurred between Professor Bryant and a female acquaintance, the woman queried accusatively, "How is it that an expert on communication like yourself can do such a poor job of communicating?" "Madam," replied Professor Bryant, "I've never laid an egg, either, but I'm a better judge of an omelette than any chicken."

The wisdom in Bryant's rejoinder is that it is unrealistic to assume a necessary relationship between conceptual understanding of communication and success as a practical communicator. Nevertheless, a thoughtful, analytical frame of reference for talking about communication (a heuristic metacommunication, if you will) is not only valuable in its own right, it increases the likelihood of successful communication and heightens the communicator's creative potential for dealing with instances of unsuccessful communication. In pursuing the goal of world humanism as we have defined it, humanity needs all the creative potential it can muster.

Let us now mention a second role of communication study and scholarship in the pursuit of a world humanism. Despite the admitted limitations of current knowledge as it is generated by communication scholars and scholars from related disciplines, research can still tell us a good deal about the way communication actually functions, the variables that influence the act of communicating, and the consequences of these communicative acts themselves. We know of few, if any, scholars who would not agree that communication is at least, in the language of the philosopher, "softly deterministic"; that is, students of communication generally believe that communicative processes and outcomes are at least partially governed by some set of empirical generalizations—whether we choose to call these generalizations "laws," "rules," or by some other label. In order to traverse the path to world humanism, we believe that effective communication—"effective" in the sense that it yields predicted, desired outcomes—is a necessity. Moreover, this necessity can only be realized as students of communication continue to expand the boundaries of our knowledge about the empirical regularities that foster effective communication transactions.

These empirical regularities can not be discovered by using one, and only one, research methodology. Different questions demand congruent research methodologies. For certain questions, a more ethnomethodological, anthropological type of research is needed. For example, to discover the "rules" or regularities that govern human communication in various cultures and societies, researchers may need to become internal observers of the social interactions of people to be able to identify normative procedures. From this type of research, testable generalizations can be inductively generated about the nature and "quality" of effective communication. For other questions, a more experimenter-controlled, laboratory-type research is required. This type of research allows the researcher to focus on specific variables and their effect on efficient communication, for example, Machiavellianism, alienation, dogmatism, and ethnocentrism. Laboratory experiments can be used to test and quantify the generalizations that are made inductively in more naturalistic settings.

In addition, communication researchers should look at societal influences and pressures on the individual that, in turn, direct and constrain the communicative interactions of people. For example, the idea of "achievement motivation" may be more a function of the social system and of pressure placed upon individuals (for example, in a dictatorial governmental regime) than a function of the psychological predisposition of the person (almost all normal people desire better outcomes for themselves).

We are well aware that some voices decry all empirical research in communication and related fields as a tool used mainly in the hands of Western imperialists and transnational corporations. These critics argue vehemently that empirical research is one of the main obstacles to the type of world humanism we have been advocating. To these dissidents the focus on the more traditional social psychological style of research, which investigates individual communication variables, has blinded researchers to the harsh realities of societal, political, and geo-political constraints upon the individual. In the area of communication and international development, for example, much of the blame for underdevelopment has been placed on the individual for being "unmotivated" or "backward," rather than blaming social factors that limit the potential for development. Their point is well taken. But to suggest the complete rejection of empirical research in favor of more philosophical theorizing is throwing out the baby with the bath water. Our philosophical theories of humanity and human societies must be put to the test of empirical comparison, or else communication researchers will produce arguments about as profound as those of the Middle Ages: disputes that center on the number of angels able to dance on the head of a pin.

We know that we are treading on highly controversial ground. There are those who would cogently argue that such knowledge, if placed in the hands of the wrong forces, could inhibit, rather than further, the pursuit of a world humanism as we have defined it. We grant this possibility, but counter it with two rejoinders, one admittedly evaluative and the other primarily factual.

From the evaluative perspective, the argument that it is dangerous to acquire further knowledge about how communication works seems to rest on the assumption that ignorance is preferable—indeed, in this case, morally superior—to understanding. We resist this value judgment for several reasons. A fair amount of knowledge about the workings of communication is already available, and we face the danger that this knowledge may be misapplied even in the absence of further information. Moreover, if indeed communication is at least softly deterministic, ignorance of the set of empirical generalizations that partially govern it will not lessen the behavioral impact of these generalizations at all—to argue that is like suggesting that if we did not understand the biological process of nutrition, people would no longer be required to eat. Instead, what will happen is that those with greater intuitive capabilities or a richer fund of human or material resources will fathom these generalizations and become their sole guardians. The means of effective communication then will indeed be elitist and potentially Machiavellian.

The preceding assertion gives rises to a factual rejoinder: As Miller and Burgoon note in their book, *New Techniques of Persuasion*, knowledge may also be liberating, not just coercive.[2] Knowledge that may be used to persuade can also be used to resist persuasion. Indeed, one formidable barrier to a stable set of empirical generalizations about communicative effects can be found in the self-reflexive dilemma: if a person knows how he or she is predicted to behave, that person is likely to behave differently. Stated another way, knowledge about the variables influencing communicative effects is often itself a relevant variable that can alter the predicted outcomes. As outlined in this essay, the pursuit of a world humanism is probably best carried forward in the context of an informed international citizenry that understands the communicative strategies and the expected impacts of the messages bombarding it.

We end this essay with two disclaimers intended to underscore our awareness of the limits and problems inherent in the view we have sketched above. First, unlike some of the more zealous of the early general semanticists, we realize that not all of the problems blocking the path to a world humanism are problems of communication. People sometimes understand each other perfectly yet persist in disagreeing on the best path to follow. Second, whether we label it "marvelously complex" or . . . "an unnatural act," most people realize that conceptual, empirical, and practical mastery of the communication process poses a monumental challenge to communication scholars and communication practitioners of all societies. Moreover, as people extend symbolic commerce beyond national boundaries, this challenge is intensified. In spite of these complexities and limitations, we conclude with the optimistic claim that communication study and scholarship does play an important role in pursuing a world humanism, and we commend all students and practitioners for their contributions to unlocking its mysteries. Hopefully, their efforts will lead to an improvement in the quality of life for all inhabitants of our "Global Village," both in terms of our esthetic and ethical sensibilities and our physical well-being.

NOTES

1. Marshall McLuhan, *The Gutenberg Galaxy: The Making of Typographic Man* (New York: New American Library, 1969), pp. 43–44.

2. Gerald R. Miller and Michael Burgoon, *New Techniques of Persuasion* (New York: Harper & Row, 1973), pp. 102–106.

The Cross-Cultural Arena: An Ethical Void

DEAN C. BARNLUND

Explorers of tropical areas of the world once employed what were called "dew driers" who preceded them into the jungle and facilitated their exploration by drying the dew that accumulated on the heavy foliage the previous night. They also cut away the less substantial underbrush so that the tougher and more tenacious obstacles that blocked the way might be visible. It is this role of dew drier that I have chosen to assume today; even should I succeed, however, we shall only stand in clearer appreciation of the tenuous path before us. . . . I hope my colleagues will then cut [their way] through.

This conference is far from premature. It is evident from the words of our philosophers, our politicians, our scientists and technicians, that life in the twentieth century has acquired a new dimension; that we are, in effect, rushing into a new world order with no more than the slightest idea of where we are headed or how to manage the transition. There is only a growing suspicion that the cultural enclaves of the past—our clans, tribes, villages, cities and states, self-sustaining and independent of the rest of humanity—are no longer adequate. Whether our preoccupation is with the management of physical resources—of water, oil, food, space, or weather—or with the management

From *Ethical Perspectives and Critical Issues in Intercultural Communication*, edited by Nobleza C. Asuncion-Lande. Reprinted by permission of the Speech Communication Association and the author. Professor Barnlund teaches at San Francisco State University.

of symbolic resources—information, media, ideas, morality—these can no longer be entrusted to the unilateral decisions of any single source.

Yet the record of the past reveals a tedious and tragic picture of accommodation to conflicting ideologies. Every age has sought novel solutions to this problem. It is discouraging to note, however, that new methods of arbitrating cultural differences have rarely replaced earlier ones; they have only multiplied the alternatives available. The physical destruction of other cultures through war is still with us; domination through occupation and police control is still with us; exploitation of land and resources is still with us; alteration of cultural identity through religious or political conversion is still with us. And our new technology would appear to make the control of cultures even more feasible now through the manipulation of information and ideas. The promise of such agencies as the League of Nations and the United Nations is still unfulfilled. It is not an attractive or encouraging picture.

Nor is the picture any brighter with respect to the management of relations between persons of different cultural identities. Over a billion people were on the move on this planet last year; nearly a quarter of a billion traveled to foreign countries; millions took up residence temporarily or permanently in an alien culture. Yet to date there has been no serious exploration of the ethics of interpersonal encounters of the cultural kind. There have been few international conferences devoted to the subject, and even less research undertaken to propose guidelines.

Consider even the simplest dimensions of this problem: there are almost no limitations—other than financial—on the right to travel; no compensating sensitivity or set of responsibilities accompanies this right. Discharging a thousand cruise ship passengers on islands populated by a few dozen Cuna Indians is seen as no more than a problem in logistics. There are a number of places in the world, often some of the most appealing, where the numbers of visitors in a single week exceeds the total permanent population; no one has yet articulated a critical threshold for cultural extinction

or proposed protective legislation. Are the only endangered species to be nonhuman? Or is the loss of a life style, an art form, a language, or a religious experience at least as precious and perhaps as critical to our survival?

Nor has anyone yet, except as a private individual, examined the moral aspects of such commonplace activities as eating, drinking, dressing, working, playing, worshipping, or rearing children, when these are carried out in the context of an alien culture. Yet sensitive residents of foreign cultures are constantly reminded that even their most mundane activities—unconsciously performed in their home cultures—may not only embarrass members of other cultures but may powerfully undermine the system of values that shape the ethos of that culture.

Technical innovations and scientific discoveries have been found to produce severe dislocations when transplanted into other cultures; less visible, but no less profound, may be the shock waves flowing from introducing alien patterns of friendship, of male-female relations, of attitudes toward work, of unfamiliar modes of decision making. The dissemination of short-grain wheat may have less disastrous moral consequences than the dissemination of attitudes toward child-rearing; barbed wire fences may be more easily assimilated than the refusal to conform to status and sex differences.

Communication between any two persons involves a certain risk, for exposure to new meanings can vitalize or undermine existing values and behavior patterns. When such encounters take place within a culture there is some protection in the fact that communicants employ symbols with some consistency, but more importantly that they share a system of rules governing such encounters. When these encounters involve persons of different cultures this protection is largely lacking; communicants interact not only in an unfamiliar medium, but each brings to the situation a divergent set of contextual rules. The magnitude of risk, and the possibility of harmful interaction, is therefore multiplied. In cross-cultural communications psychic and social injury may result from the highest motives; demoralizing consequences often accompany the most laudable intentions.

It might be helpful to examine some of the parallels between the intercultural and the therapeutic encounter. In professional therapy two or more people converse about significant events in ways designed to promote introspective examination of their assumptions and values leading to some reorganization of the personality. It should be noted that this type of interaction, prevalent in some form in most cultures of the world, is regarded as so serious a form of communication that it is restricted to a body of highly trained professionals and surrounded by a set of legal and moral restraints. Training in intercultural communication, and intercultural encounters themselves, commonly provoke the same sort of introspective examination of underlying assumptions and values and frequently trigger some reorganization of the personality. As of yet the cross-cultural encounter is protected by no standards of ethical adequacy. (I am aware of important differences between therapeutic and intercultural encounters, and by no means would argue for a parallel set of restrictions, but people participating in intercultural encounters often go through intensive, and insightful or destructive, experiences that are not unlike those occurring in professional therapy.)

All of this is more or less familiar, depending on the length and depth of our immersion in other cultures. But is there anything distinctive, anything unprecedented, about the ethical issues that arise in cross-cultural work? Are they any different than those that confront a person, anywhere or anytime, who is trying to act with respect and compassion for others? Human acts always involve choices and some estimate of their consequences. Are these decisions any more complicated when they arise in cross-cultural contexts?

They are, indeed. At least in my present view. The moral issues that attend intercultural encounters are not simply more complicated, they are of an entirely new dimension. Despite the pervasiveness of cross-cultural contact, these complications remain overlooked and unexplored in any systematic way.[1] The ethical vacuum that confronts us reflects not merely a failure of specialists within this evolving field, nor the negligence of outside agencies to give support to such ethical study, but is due in large part to difficulties that are inherent in the cross-cultural context.

The number of these complications may be very great, but there are five that can be identified in some detail at this time. The first, perhaps the foremost, complication is that no commonly shared metaethic exists to which members of diverse cultures can repair when facing dilemmas of action arising out of conflicting frames of references.

Cultures are, in effect, systems. Perhaps the most complex of all structures created by human beings. They are comprised of many elements and variables, most of which have a sensitive and deep dependence upon each other. Damage to or removal of any critical feature—physical or symbolic—can impair or strengthen the viability of that system. But our intercultural sophistication is scarcely of an order yet that permits us to forecast even the short-range repercussions of such disturbances to a culture.

As with every system, cultures create and maintain boundaries. Sometimes they are territorial, but more often psychological. The most critical of these may be the communicative boundaries within which human interaction is decipherable and meaningful; outside of which it becomes indecipherable and meaningless. The *sine qua non* of any human organization is the creation and maintenance of these patterns of meaning. What we call "morals" or "values" are simply the particular set of meanings involving evaluation, invested with more than ordinary emotional significance, that members of a particular culture share. They are, in a sense, the most meaningful of our meanings. They provide the motive for thought and action; they surround and make intelligible every communicative act.

Meanings and morals, however, tend to stop at the borders of every society; ethical principles represent, in a sense, a territorial imperative. Within a community of persons one acts with consideration, for moral consequences tend to inhere in a context of shared meanings. Acts have a more or less consistent interpretation, and tend to be viewed from the same ethical premises. Outside these boundaries the consequences are difficult to predict, and evaluations rest upon a multiplicity of often conflicting ethical premises.

It is not surprising that one of the great intellectual enterprises in every culture has been the articulation of a set of ethical precepts. Some of these frames of reference have been economic—feudalism, communism, capitalism, socialism; others have been philosophical—idealism, hedonism, rationalism, pragmatism; still others have been religious—Hinduism, Animism, Christianity, Buddhism. Each of them, through their appeal to human needs, their impassioned advocacy, or their forceful imposition, have diffused across diverse cultures. Generally they have had the negative effect of homogenizing cultures coming under their sphere of influence, and the positive effect of providing a common moral climate for evaluating human actions. But even the most extensive and influential of these ethical structures has failed to supply an ethic for more than a tenth of the world's population, and in these instances did so only through the application of one kind of force or another.

Morality tends to be culture-specific, as arbitrary and as bound to culture as all our symbols and meanings are. When people communicate across cultures they tend to approach moral dilemmas in one of two ways: one is to evaluate the behavior of the other by adopting the perspective of their own moral assumptions, that is by assuming an external frame of reference and moralizing about their behavior; the second is to evaluate the behavior of the other by adopting the perspective of their moral assumptions, that is by assuming an internal frame of reference and empathizing with them. Either fosters a truncated morality that is incomplete and ethnocentric, for it subordinates the ethical premises of one culture or the other. And it thereby fails to fully illuminate or to fairly adjudicate conflicts in which people of different moral orientations must accommodate their differences and create ways of collaborating on common tasks. (Those who have worked abroad are familiar with such dilemmas: to

bribe or not to bribe; to respect class distinctions or resist them; to employ deception or to insist upon honesty; to express differences or to remain silent.)

The formulation of what is ethically responsible in intercultural encounters is as formidable as it is indispensable in the years ahead. The ethical systems we know are each tied to and reflect the premises of a particular body of people, and few of them enjoy the loyalty of more than a minority of the world's population. Until a metaethic—one that prescribes standards for relations between cultures—can be articulated in ways that gain wide allegiance, or until a common ethic emerges from the thousands of daily confrontations, confusions, and antagonisms that now characterize such encounters, we shall continue to conduct intercultural affairs in a moral vacuum.

Which brings me to the second condition that complicates the formulation of such an ethic. Moral vacuums are transient affairs; they tend to be filled at once by moralists of one persuasion or another. But the cultures which might make important contributions to such an ethical dialogue are far from equal in power or influence, and the validity of their claims tends to be proportionate to the importance of their geography, resources, level of technology, and capacity of military destruction. Specialists in communication are well aware of the difficulty of collaborating—or even of achieving understanding—when communicants are grossly unequal not only in power, knowledge, and experience, but when they also control the channels of communication. An intercultural dialogue requires that those with something to say be given access to the platform and be taken seriously by those who might listen. Freedom to participate in such a global discourse is relatively meaningless today for such access is limited to nations with the financial resources, the technological facilities, and the sophistication to employ the media effectively. There is not merely an unfavorable balance of trade in material goods, but a more serious unfavorable balance of trade in ideas. Such a mutual exchange of ideas cannot develop, according to Hidetoshi Kato, until the channels of influence open to cultures of only thirty material objects compare more favorably with those open to cultures of five hundred thousand objects.[2] The unaided human voice is without much impact in a world dominated by those who control television, radio, and the press.

Related to the disproportionate influence that cultures have upon intercultural relations is the extent to which cultures are accessible to such influence. If ethical dialogue can be monopolized, it can also be blocked. Not all cultures of the world agree upon the desirability of exposing their values to the scrutiny of, or commerce with, alien moralities.

Societies differ, in short, in the degree to which they constitute open or closed systems. In some the cultural ethic is nearly unknowable by outsiders, for control of the social system and its rules regarding interpersonal relations are in the hands of a minority of the population. In others the underlying ethic derives from a philosophy or religion that is monolithic in character and cannot tolerate the relativistic assumption on which collaboration depends. In still others, morality has derived from actions that have acquired a deeply sacred character that places such principles beyond the range of rational deliberation. And in others ethical standards are so woven into the economic and familial fabric of society that exposure to alternatives may threaten the entire system.

It should not be surprising therefore that there are cultures which do not permit the entry of any outsiders; others which permit entry only of aliens capable of providing critical skills and information. Some cultures open their borders, but control the movements of aliens; others regulate the frequency and occasions of interaction with their own people. In some it is dangerous for the outsider to speak openly; in others it is dangerous for citizens to listen [to] or be seen with foreigners. In very few societies today is it possible to be legally accepted as a citizen with full political and economic rights, or to be psychologically accepted with full social privileges and opportunities.

It is impossible of course to explore the moral aspects of intercultural encounters when they are not permitted to occur; but it is not automatically possible even when they are. We must be wary of assuming the world is populated with cultures all of whom are eager for moral dialogue. Even in encounters between two people both of whom were nurtured in societies that are open and tolerant, the exploration of differing moral standards is still imbued with deep feelings that often trigger defensive reactions. How much more difficult or impossible such discussion becomes when one or both parties present closed systems of thought. Yet every culture is, to some extent and on some issues, resistant to alternative views; strong identification with and commitment to cultural values are deeply rooted in even the most tolerant of people. Any viable intercultural ethic will have to take into account such political and personal realities.

Seemingly outside the scope of this paper, but unfortunately not irrelevant to the issues it explores, is the interdependence of intercultural and international relationships. It is appealing to pretend that they can be separated—intercultural communication focusing upon the informal encounters between citizens of differing cultural identities, and international communication focusing upon formal encounters in which official representatives of national interests make political and economic policy—but they cannot. No such neat line of demarcation divides the two areas ethically. Many of the conditions that promote and stifle communication—the movement of people, the occasions for interaction, the topics to be discussed, the alliances and marriages that result—are seen to have political implications and are assumed to be the rightful province of government.

There is even a complication within this complication. Is the same ethical stance appropriate toward cultures ruled by a minority through force and cultures in which the will of the people is capable of affecting public policy? In popular governments, official actions tend more or less to reflect majority sentiment; in unpopular governments the majority may be silenced through military or police control. At what point is outside influence or intervention ethically justified, and at what point is such interference unethical and destructive of cultural values? Are there differences ethically between a popular and unpopular dictatorship, a temporary or permanent dictatorship? Few countries contain a single and homogeneous culture within their borders: Are the same ethical principles to apply when subcultures support or threaten national unity?

The intercultural dialogue we seek concerning ethical standards is compounded, finally, by our diverse concepts of the nature and potential of communication in mediating these values. The rhetorical premises of the West—our belief in the value of rational discourse, our faith in the emergence of truth from competing arguments, our confidence in the values of collaboration—do not enjoy universal respect. Setting aside for the moment those cultures who refuse to contribute to such a dialogue, there remain many others who claim an intuitive truth that is higher than reason, who reject collaboration (especially among equals), who are unimpressed with arguments and mistrustful of words. If the content of such an ethical dialogue—that is the diverse opinions we have of what constitutes moral human behavior—were the only diversity, our task might be easier. But it is not. Even the processes through which these issues might be explored reflect a multiplicity of approaches, and these, too, carry ethical implications.

While this is not the occasion to articulate a set of ethical specifics, in the face of such urgency and complexity can some modest recommendations be made? Perhaps. One of them is to expand the number of such conferences and the variety of cultures participating in them. People who have experienced ethical dilemmas arising from their residence, their study, or their research in foreign cultures need to share these conflicts in a setting that supports such exploration.

Much more needs to be done to stimulate research on the communicative styles of various cultures so we may become familiar with their dynamics and their cross-cultural consequences. We need to identify the underlying commonalities among cultures whose outward forms and practices differ, and to discover differences that lie beneath the surfaces of cultures whose institutions and behavior are superficially alike. To formulate any truly humane ethic in the absence of such knowledge seems predestined to fail.

Finally we need to confront a task that is as delicate as it is formidable. And that is to create—or to synthesize from existing cultures—a superordinate set of guidelines for regulating communication between cultures. And one that can attract popular support from the widest number of cultures possible. The metaethic should incorporate the minimal consensus required to discourage the grossest forms of destructive interaction while promoting the widest variations of behavior within cultures. Such a beginning might curtail the most injurious forms of intercultural contact that originate in a moral void while leaving space and time for more constructive alternatives to evolve.

NOTES

1. An exception to this may be found in the "Symposium of Humane Responsibility in Intercultural Communication" held at International Christian University, January, 1976, Tokyo, Japan. The papers presented at this Symposium are published in John C. Condon and Mitsuko Saito (Eds.), *Communicating Across Cultures for What?* Tokyo: Simul Press, 1976.

2. Kato, Hidetoshi, "Are Materials Immaterial?" in John C. Condon and Mitsuko Saito (Eds.), *Communication Across Cultures for What?* Tokyo: Simul Press, 1976, p. 109.

Intercultural Personhood: An Integration of Eastern and Western Perspectives

YOUNG YUN KIM

Today we live in a world of global community. Rigid adherence to the culture of our youth is neither feasible nor desirable. The tightly knit communication web has brought cultures of the world together closer than ever before. Strong cultural identity is more a nostalgic conception than a realistic assessment of our attributes. Indeed, we live in an exciting time in which we are challenged to examine ourselves critically. As Toffler (1980) states in *The Third Wave*, "Humanity faces a quantum leap forward. It faces the deepest social upheavel and creative restructuring of all time. Without clearly recognizing it, we are engaged in building a remarkable new civilization from the ground up" (p. 10).

Reflecting the interactive realities of our time, a number of attempts have been made to explore ideologies that are larger than national and cultural interests and that embrace all humanity. As early as 1946, Northrop, in *The Meeting of the East and the West*, proposed an "international cultural ideal" to provide intellectual and emotional foundations for what he envisioned as "partial world sovereignty." Among contemporary critics of culture, Thompson (1973) explored the concept of "planetary culture" in which Eastern mysticism was integrated with Western science and rationalism. Similarly, Elgin (1981), proposed "voluntary simplicity" as an emerging global "common sense" and a practical lifestyle to reconcile the willful, rational approach to life of the West and the holistic, spiritual orientation of the East.

In this frame of ideas, the present writer has presented the concept "intercultural person" as an image of future human development (Kim 1982; Gudykunst & Kim 1984). The intercultural person represents a type of person whose cognitive, affective, and behavioral characteristics are not limited but are open to growth beyond the psychological parameters of his or her own culture. Other similar terms such as "international" (Lutzker 1960), "universal" (Walsh 1973), and "multicultural" (Adler 1982) person have also been used to project an essentially similar image of personhood with varying degrees of descriptive and explanatory utility.

To envision how we may renew ourselves and grow beyond our own cultural conditioning in this intercultural world, we need to comprehend and to seek meaning and order in the complexity of the fundamental human condition. Our task is to look at both Eastern and Western cultures in their "original form" rather than in their contemporary cultural patterns. The linking back to the origin not only enables us to see the respective foundation of the two cultures clearly, but also creates the possibility of recognizing and bringing into play new lines of development. In this essay, we will examine the basic cultural *a priori* or world view of East and West, concepts deeply rooted in the religious and philosophical traditions of the two cultural groups. Once we rediscover the cultural roots of Eastern and Western worlds, we will then be able to develop a broad perspective on the ground-level human conditions without being restricted by our own cultural "blind spots." Such a pan-human understanding will enable us to construct an image of intercultural personhood—a way of life that is called for by the increasingly intercultural realities of our world.

This original essay appears here in print for the first time. All rights reserved. Permission to reprint must be obtained from the publisher and the author. Young Yun Kim is University Professor of Communication at Governors State University, Park Forest South, Illinois.

EASTERN AND WESTERN WORLD VIEWS

Traditional cultures throughout Asian countries including India, Tibet, Japan, China, Korea, and Southeast Asia have been profoundly influenced by such religious and philosophical systems as Buddhism, Hinduism, Taoism, and Zen. On the other hand, the Western European nations have historically followed the Greek and the Judaeo-Christian traditions. Of course, any attempt to present the cultural *a priori* of these two broadly categorized civilizations inevitably sacrifices specific details and the uniqueness of variations within each group. No two individuals or groups are identical in their beliefs and behaviors, and whatever we characterize about one culture or cultural group must be thought of as variable rather than as rigidly structured. Nevertheless, there are several key factors in the two perspectives that distinguish each group clearly from the other. To examine these factors is to indicate the equally evident interconnectedness that ties different nations together to constitute the Eastern or Western cultural group.

The characterization of Eastern and Western world views in this section and throughout this article is based on the observations of many authors. Of the existing comparative cultural analyses, Northrop's *The Meeting of the East and the West* (1946/1966), Gulick's *The East and the West* (1963), Nakamura's *Ways of Thought of Eastern Peoples* (1964), Oliver's *Communication and Culture in Ancient India and China* (1971), Capra's *The Tao of Physics* (1975), and Elgin's *Voluntary Simplicity* (1981) have provided a particular influence.

Universe and Nature

One of the most fundamental ways culture conditions our existence is through explicit and implicit teachings about our relationship to the nature of the universe and to the non-human natural world. Traditional Eastern and Western perspectives diverge significantly in this basic premise. As Needham (1951) observed in his article, "Human laws and the laws of nature in China and the West," people in the West have been dominated by the view that the universe was initially created, and has since been externally controlled, by a divine power.

In this sense, the Western view of the universe is characteristically dualistic, materialistic, and lifeless. The Judaeo-Christian tradition sets God apart from this reality; having created it and set it into motion, God could then be viewed as apart from His creation. The fundamental material of the universe is thought to be elementary particles of matter that interact with one another in a predictable fashion. Furthermore, since the foundation of the universe is seen as consisting of matter, it is viewed as essentially non-living. It is seen as an inanimate machine in which humankind occupies a unique and elevated position among the sparse life-forms that exist. Assuming a relatively barren universe, it seems only rational that humans exploit the lifeless material universe (and the lesser life-forms of nature) on behalf of those who live most intensely—humankind itself.

On the other hand, the Eastern view is profoundly holistic, dynamic, and spiritual. From the Eastern perspective, the entirety of the universe is a vast, multidimensional, living organism consisting of many interrelated parts and forces. The universe is conscious and engaged in a continuous dance of creation: the cosmic pattern is viewed as self-contained and self-organizing. It unfolds itself because of its own inner necessity and not because it is "ordered" to by any external volitional power.

What exists in the universe is a manifestation of a divine life force. Beneath the surface appearance of things, an ultimate reality is continuously creating, sustaining, and infusing our worldly experience. The all-sustaining life force that instant by instant creates our manifest universe is not apart from ourselves or our worldly existence. Rather, it is continuously creating and intimately infusing every aspect of the cosmos—from its most minute details to its most grand scale features.

Thus, the Eastern view reveres the common source out of which all things arise, and at the same time recognizes that everything in this dynamic world is fluid, ever-changing, and impermanent. In

Hinduism, all static forms are *maya*, that is, they exist only as illusory concepts. This idea of the impermanence of all forms is the starting point of Buddhism. The Buddha taught that "all compounded things are impermanent," and that all suffering in the world arises from our trying to cling to fixed forms—objects, people, or ideas—instead of accepting the world as it moves. This notion of the impermanence of all forms and the appreciation of the aliveness of the universe in the Eastern world view is strongly contrasted with the Western emphasis on the visible forms of physical reality and their improvement through social and material/technological progress.

Knowledge

Since the East and the West have different cosmic patterns, we can expect a different approach to knowledge. In the East, because the universe is a harmonious organism, there is a lack of any dualism in the cosmic pattern as well as in epistemological patterns. The Eastern view places an emphasis on perceiving and knowing things and events holistically and synthetically, rather than analytically. Furthermore, the ultimate purpose of knowledge is to transcend the apparent contrasts and to "see" the interrelatedness and underlying unity of all things.

When the Eastern mystics tell us they experience all things and events as manifestations of a basic oneness, this does not mean they consider all things equal. They recognize the individuality of things but at the same time are aware that all differences and contrasts are relative within an all-embracing unity. The awareness that all opposites are polar, and thus a unity, is seen as one of the highest aims of knowledge. Suzuki (1968) writes, "The fundamental idea of Buddhism is to pass beyond the world of opposites, a world built up by intellectual distinctions and emotional defilements, and to realize the spiritual world of non-distinction, which involves achieving an absolute point of view" (p. 18).

Since all opposites are interdependent, their conflict can never result in the total victory of one side, but will always be a manifestation of the interplay between the two sides. In the East, therefore, a virtuous person is not one who undertakes the impossible task of striving for the "good" and eliminating the "bad," but rather one who is able to maintain a dynamic balance between the two. Transcending the opposites, one becomes aware of the relativity and polar relationship of all opposites. One realizes that good and bad, pleasure and pain, life and death, winning and losing, light and dark, are not absolute experiences belonging to different categories, but are merely two sides of the same reality—extreme aspects of a single whole. This point has been emphasized most extensively by the Chinese sages in their symbolism of the archetypal poles, yin and yang. And the opposites cease to be opposites in the very essence of Tao. To know the Tao—the illustrious way of the universe—is the ultimate purpose of human learning.

This holistic approach to knowledge in the East emphasizes understanding concepts and the aesthetic components of things by intuition. A concept by intuition is one of complete meaning and is something immediately experienced, apprehended, and contemplated. Northrop (1946/1966) described it more accurately as the "differentiated aesthetic continuum." Within the total differentiated aesthetic continuum, there is no distinction between subjective and objective. The aesthetic continuum is a single all-embracing continuity. The aesthetic part of the self is also an essential part of the aesthetic object, whether it is a person or a flower. With respect to the immediately apprehended aesthetic nature, the person is identical with the aesthetic object; only with respect to his differentiation is the self other than the aesthetic object.

In this orientation, Taoism pursues the all-embracing, immediately experienced, emotionally moving aesthetic continuum with respect to its manifestations in the differentiated, sensed aesthetic qualities of nature. Confucianism pursues the all-embracing aesthetic continuum with respect to its manifestations in human nature and its moral implications for human society. The Taoist claim is that only by seeing the aesthetic continuity in its all-embracing-ness as ultimate and irreducible will we properly understand the meaning of the universe and nature. The Confucian claim, similarly, is that only if one takes the same standpoint, that of recognizing the all-embracing aesthetic whole to be an ultimate and irreducible part of human nature, will we have a compassionate feeling for human beings other than ourselves.

The ultimate, irreducible, and undifferentiated aesthetic continuum is the Eastern philosopher's conception of the constituted world. The differentiations within it, such as particular scenes, events, or persons, are not the irreducible atomic identities, but merely arise out of the ultimate undifferentiated reality of the aesthetic continuum. Sooner or later, they fade back into it again and thus are transitory and impermanent. When Eastern sages insist that one must become self-less, they mean that the self consists of two components: one, a differentiated, unique element, distinguishing one person from any other person; and the other, the all-embracing, aesthetically immediate, emotionally moving, compassionate, undifferentiated component. The former is temporary and transitory, and the cherishing of it, the desire for its immortality, is the source of suffering and selfishness. The part of the self that is not transitory but rather immortal is the aesthetic component, and it is identical not merely in all persons, but in all aesthetic objects throughout the universe.

While the East has concentrated its mental processes on the all-embracing, holistic, intuitive, aesthetic continuum, the Western pursuit of knowledge has been based on the doctrine of a dualistic world view. Since in the West the world and its various components came into existence through the individual creative acts of a God, the fundamental question is, how can I reach out to the external inanimate world or to people? In this question, there is a basic dichotomy between the knower and the things to be known.

Along with this epistemological dualism, the West has emphasized rationality in the pursuit of knowledge. Since the Greek philosopher Plato "discovered" reason, virtually all subsequent Western thought—the themes, the questions, and the terms—exists in essence in the writing of Plato (Wei 1980). Even Aristotle, the great hero of all anti-Platonists, was not an exception. Although Aristotle did not have, as Plato did, a realm of eternal essences that were "really real" and that guaranteed the primacy of reason, he was by no means inclined to deny this realm.

Thus, while the East has tended to emphasize the direct experience of oneness via intuitive concepts and contemplation, the West has viewed the faculty of the intellect as the primary instrument of worldly mastery. While thinking in the East tends to conclude in more or less vague, imprecise statements with existential flexibility, Western thinking emphasizes clear and distinct ideas by means of categorization and the linear, analytic logic of syllogism. While the Eastern view expresses its drive for growth in spiritual attainment of oneness with the universe, the Western view expresses its drive for growth in material progress and social change.

Time

Closely parallel to the differing perception of the nature of knowledge, the perception and experience of time differs significantly between Eastern and Western traditions.

Along with the immediate, undifferentiated experiencing of here and now, Eastern time orientation can be portrayed as a placid, silent pool within which ripples come and go. Historically the East has tended to view material existence as cyclical and has often characterized worldly existence with the metaphor of a wheel. The "wheel of existence" is continually turning but is not seen as going in any predetermined direction. Although individuals in the world may experience a rise or fall in their personal fortunes, the lot of the whole is felt to be fundamentally unchanging. As Northrop (1946/1966) illustrated, "the aesthetic continuum is the great mother of creation, giving birth to the ineffable beauty of the golden yellows on the mountain landscape as the sun drops low in the late afternoon, only a moment later to receive that differentiation back into itself and to put another in its place without any effort" (p. 343).

Because worldly time is not experienced as going anywhere and because in spiritual time there is nowhere to go but to eternity within the now, the future is expected to be virtually the same as the past. Recurrence in both cosmic and psychological realms is very much a part of Eastern thought. Thus, the individual's aim is not to escape from the circular movement into linear and profane time, but to become a part of the eternal through the aesthetic experience of here and now and the conscious evolution of spirituality in knowing the all-embracing, undifferentiated wholeness.

Whereas the East traditionally has perceived time as a dynamic wheel with circular movements and the "now" as a reflection of the eternal, the West has represented time either as an arrow or as a moving river that comes out of a distant place and past (not here and now) and goes into an equally distant place and future (also not here and now). In this linear view of time, history is goal-directed and gradually progressing in a certain direction, such as toward universal salvation and the second coming of Christ or, in a secular form, toward an ideal state such as boundless freedom or a classless society.

Closely corresponding to the above comparison of Eastern and Western time orientations is the recent work of anthropologist Edward Hall in his *Beyond Culture* (1976) and *The Dance of Life: The Other Dimension of Time* (1983). Hall considers Asian cultures "polychronic" and Western cultures "monochronic." The polychronic system is less inclined to adhere rigidly to time as a tangible, discrete, and linear entity; it emphasizes completion of transactions here and now, often carrying out more than one activity simultaneously. On the other hand, the monochronic system emphasizes schedules, segmentation, promptness, and standardization of human activities. The traditional Eastern orientation to time depends on the synchronization of human behavior with the rhythms of nature. The Western orientation to time depends on the synchronization of human behavior with the rhythms of clocks or machines.

Communication

The historical ideologies examined so far have made the empirical content of the East and the West what they are. Eastern and Western perspectives on the universe, nature, knowledge, and time are reflected in many specific activities of individuals as they relate themselves to fellow human beings—how individuals view "self" and the group and how they use verbal and nonverbal symbols in communication.

First, the view of self and identity cultivated in the Eastern view of reality is embedded within an immutable social order. People tend to acquire their sense of identity from an affiliation with, and participation in, a virtually unchanging social order. The sense of "self" that emerges from this social context is not the strongly differentiated "existential ego" of the West, but a more weakly distinct and unchanging "social ego" as pointed out in many contemporary anthropological studies. Thus, individual members of the family tend to be more willing to submit their own self-interest to that of the family. Individuals and families are often expected to submit their views to those of the community or the state.

Also, the Eastern view accepts hierarchy in social order. In a hierarchical structure, individuals are seen as differing in status although all are equally necessary for the total system and its process. A natural result of this orientation is the emphasis on authority—the authority of the parents over the children, of the grandparents over their descendants, and of the official head of the community, the clan, and the state over all its members. Authoritarianism is a distinct feature of Eastern life, not only in government, business, and family, but also in education and beliefs. The more ancient a tradition, the greater its authority.

Furthermore, the Eastern view asserts that who we are is not limited to our physical existence. Consciousness is seen as the bridge between the finite and differentiated (our sense of uniqueness) and the infinite and undifferentiated (the experience of wholeness and eternity). With sufficient training, each person can discover that who we are is correlated with nature and the divine. All are one and the same in the sense that the divine, undifferentiated, aesthetic continuum of the universe is manifested in us and in nature. Through this aesthetic connection, we and nature are no other than the Tao, Ultimate Reality, the divine life force, nirvana, God.

On the other hand, the Western view—in which God, nature, and humans are distinctly differentiated—fosters the development of autonomous individuals with strong ego identification. The dualistic world view is manifested in an individual's view of his or her relationship to other persons and nature. Interpersonal relationships, therefore, are essentially egalitarian—cooperative arrangements between two equal "partners" in which the personal needs and interests of each party are more or less equally respected, negotiated, or "compromised." While the East emphasizes submission (or conformity) of the individual to the group, the West encourages individuality and individual needs to override the group. If the group no longer serves the individual's needs, it—not the individual—must be changed. Thus, the meaning of an interpersonal relationship is decided primarily by what functions each party performs to satisfy the needs of the other. A relationship is considered healthy to the extent that it serves the expected function for all parties involved. As anthropologist Frances Hsu (1981) notes, individualism is a central theme of the Western personality, which distinguishes the Western world from the non-Western.

This functional, pragmatic interpersonal orientation of the West is contrasted with the Eastern tradition—where group membership is a "given" that goes unchallenged—in which individuals must conform to the group in the case of conflicting interest. Members of the group are encouraged to maintain harmony and to minimize competition. Individuality is discouraged while moderation, modesty, and "bending" of one's ego are praised. In some cases, individual and group achievement (in a material sense) must be forsaken to maintain group harmony.

In this social milieu, the primary source of interpersonal understanding is the unwritten and often unspoken norms, values, and ritualized mannerisms relevant to a particular interpersonal context. Rather than relying heavily on verbalized, logical expressions, the Eastern communicator "grasps" the aesthetic "essence" of the communication dynamics by observing the various nonverbal and circumstantial cues. Intuition rather than logical reasoning plays a central role in the Eastern interpersonal understanding of how one talks, how one addresses the other and why, under what circumstances, on what topics, in what varied styles, with what intent, and with what effect. Verbal articulation is less important than nonverbal, contextual sensitivity and appropriateness. Eastern cultures favor verbal hesitance and ambiguity to avoid disturbing or offending others (Doi 1976; Cathcart & Cathcart 1976). Silence is often preferred to eloquent verbalization even in expressing strong compliments or affection. Sometimes individuals are suspicious of the genuineness of excessive verbal praise or compliments since, to the Eastern view, true feelings are intuitively apparent and therefore do not need to be, nor can be, articulated. In this sense, the burden of communicating effectively is shared equally between all parties involved.

While interpersonal meaning in the Eastern perspective resides primarily in the subtle, implicit, nonverbal, contextual realm and is understood aesthetically and intuitively, the Western communicative mode is primarily a direct, explicit, verbal realm, relying heavily on logical and rational perception, thinking, and articulation. Communicators are seen as distinct individuals, expressing their individuality through verbal articulation and assertiveness. Feelings inside are not to be intuitively "grasped" and understood, but to be clearly verbalized and discussed. In this sense, the burden of communicating effectively lies primarily in the speaker.

The above characterization of communication patterns in the Eastern and the Western traditions parallels the notion of "high-context" and "low-context" communication proposed by Hall (1976). Hall's conceptualization is based on empirical studies of many cultures, and it focuses on the degree to which information is either embedded in physical context or internalized in the person communicating. In this scheme, a low-context communication—more prevalent in the West than in the East—is when most of the interpersonal information is carried in the explicit, verbalized codes.

A SYNTHESIS

So far, a number of basic dimensions of cultural *a priori* in the Eastern and the Western traditions have been examined. To recapitulate, the many differences between the two civilizations stem fundamentally from their respective premises on the reality of the universe, nature, time, and communication. Based on an organic, holistic, and cyclic perspective, the East has developed an epistemology that emphasizes direct, immediate, and aesthetic components in human nature's experience of the world. The ultimate aim of human learning is to transcend the immediate, differentiated self and to develop an integrative perception of the undifferentiated universe; that is, to be spiritually one with the universe and to find the eternal within the present moment. In this view, the present moment is a reflection of the eternal, and the eternal resides in the present moment.

On the other hand, the West, founded on the cosmology of dualism, determinism, and materialism, encourages an outlook that is rational, analytic, and indirect. History is viewed as a linear progression from the past into the future. The acquisition of knowledge is not so much for spiritual enhancement as for utilization to improve the human condition.

These different world views, in turn, have been reflected in the individual conception of the self, of others, and of the group. While the East has stressed the primacy of the group over the individual, the West has stressed the primacy of the individual over the group. Interpersonally, the Eastern concept of self is less differentiated and more deeply merged in "group ego," while the West encourages distinct and autonomous individuality. Explicit, clear, and logical verbalization has been the most salient feature in the Western communication tradition, compared to the implicit, intuitive, nonverbal messages in the East.

Thus, the mechanistic Western world view has helped to systematically describe and explain the physical phenomena we encounter daily. It has proved extremely successful in technological and scientific development. The West has also learned, however, that the mechanistic world view and the corresponding communication patterns are often inadequate for the subtle, complex phenomena of human relationship—causing alienation from self and from others. The West has also learned that its dualistic distinction between humanity and nature has brought about alienation from nature. The analytical mind of the West has led to modern science and technology, but it has also resulted in knowledge that is departmentalized, specialized, fragmented, and detached from the fuller totality of reality.

The East has not experienced the alienation the West has been experiencing in recent centuries. But, at the same time, the East has not developed as much science and technology since its view of the world does not promote material and social development. It does not encourage worldly activism or promote the empowerment of individuals to fundamentally change the social and material circumstances of life. Furthermore, instead of building greater ego strength and the capacity for more self-determining behavior, the Eastern view tends to work toward ego extinction (transcendence). It also tends to encourage ego dependency and passivity since people feel locked into an unchanging social order.

It should be stressed at this point that the Western emphasis on logical, theoretical, dualistic, and analytic thinking does not suggest that it has been devoid of an intuitive, direct, purely empirical, aesthetic element. Similarly, emphasizing the Western contributions (of worldly dynamism and sociomaterial development) does not suggest that the East has been devoid of learning in these areas. The differences are not in diametric opposition: rather they are differences in emphasis. As a result, the range of sophistication of Western contributions to the sociomaterial process far exceeds the historical learning of the East. Conversely, the aesthetic and holistic view and self-mastery of the East offers a greater depth and range of human experience vis-à-vis other humans, the natural world, and the universe, than the West.

Thus, East and West are not competing views of reality, but are, instead, intensely complementary. It needs to be emphasized that the values, behaviors, and institutions of the West should not be substituted for their Eastern counterparts, and vice versa. The West should no more adopt the world views of the East than the East should adopt the world views of the West. Our task is not to trade one view for another—thereby repeating the excesses of the other—but to integrate. Our task is to find our human unity and simultaneously to express diversity. The purpose of evolution is not to create a homogeneous mass, but to continuously unfold a diverse yet organic whole.

COMPLEMENTARITY

To explore the possibilities of integrating the two cultural traditions in a limited space, we need to take a one-sided perspective by focusing on significant limitations in either of the two and then projecting the complementary aspects from the other. In the following discussion, then, we will look critically at possible limitations of the Western cultural orientation, and attempt to integrate the complementary Eastern cultural insights.

A growing realization of limitations in the Western world view is expressed by many writers. Using the term "extension transference," Hall (1976) points out the danger of the common intellectual maneuver in which the extensional systems—including language, logic, technology, institutions, and scheduling—are confused with or take the place of the process extended. For instance, the tendency in the West is to assume that the remedy for problems with technology should not be the attempt to minimize our reliance on technology, but the development of even more technology. Burke (1974) calls this tendency of extension transference "technologism":

There lie the developments whereby "technologism" confronts its inner contradictions, a whole new realm in which the

heights of human rationality, as expressed in industrialism, readily become "solutions" that are but the source of new and aggravated problems (p. 148).

Criticisms have also been directed at the rigid scientific dogmatism that insists on the discovery of "truth" based on mechanistic, linear causality and "objectivity." In this regard, Thayer (1983) comments:

What the scientific mentality attempts to emulate, mainly, is the presumed method of laboratory science. But laboratory science predicts nothing that it does not control or that is not otherwise fully determined. . . . One cannot successfully study relatively open systems with methods that are appropriate only for closed systems. Is it possible that this is the kind of mentality that precludes its own success? (p. 88)

Similarly, Hall (1976) points out that the Western emphasis on logic as synonymous with "truth" denies that part of the human self that integrates. Hall sees logical thinking as only a small fraction of our mental capabilities, and he suggests that there are many different and legitimate ways of thinking that have tended to be less emphasized in Western cultures (p. 9).

The criticisms raised by these and other critics of Western epistemology do not deny the value of rational, inferential knowledge. Instead, they relate to the error in traditional Western philosophy and science, of regarding concepts that do not fit into its mode as not equally valid. It refers to the arrogance or over-confidence of believing that scientific knowledge is the only way to discover "truth," when, in reality, the very process of doing science requires immediate, aesthetic experience of the phenomenon under investigation. Without the immediately apprehended component, the theoretical hypotheses proposed could not be tested empirically with respect to their truth or falsity and, therefore, would lack relevance to the corresponding reality. As Einstein once stated:

Science is the attempt to make the chaotic diversity of our sense-experience correspond to a logically uniform system of thought. In this system single experiences must be correlated with the theoretic structure in such a way that the resulting coordination is complete and convincing (Northrop, 1946/1966, p. 443).

In this description of science, Einstein is careful to indicate that the relation between the theoretically postulated component and the immediately experienced aesthetic component is one of correspondence.

In fact, the wide spectrum of our everyday life activities demands both scientific and aesthetic modes of apprehension: from critical analysis to perception of wholes; from doubt and skepticism to unconditional appreciation; from abstraction to concreteness; from the general and regular to the individual and unique; from the literalism of technical terms to the power and richness of poetic language, silence, and art; from casual acquaintances to intimate personal engagement. If we limit ourselves to the traditional Western scientific mode of apprehension, and if we do not value and practice the Eastern aesthetic mode, we are limiting the essential human to only a part of the full span of life activities.

One potential benefit of incorporating the Eastern aesthetic orientation into Western life is a heightened sense of freedom. As discussed earlier, the aesthetic component of human nature is in part indeterminate, and it is this aesthetic component in us that is the basis of our freedom. We would also transcend the clock-bound worldly time to the Eternal Now, the timeless moment embedded in the center of each moment. By withdrawing into the indeterminate aesthetic component of our nature, away from the determinate, transitory circumstances, we may in part overcome the pressures of everyday events and creatively integrate them as a basis for the renewal of our life spirit. The traditional Eastern practice of meditation is designed primarily for the purpose of moving one's consciousness from the determinate to the indeterminate, freer state.

Second, the Eastern view would bring the West to a heightened awareness of the aliveness of the universe. The universe is engaged in a continuous dance of creation at each instant. Everything is intensely alive—brimming with a silent, clear energy that creates, sustains, and infuses all that exists. With the expanded perspective on time, we would increase our sensitivity to rhythms of nature such as the seasons and the cycles of birth and decay.

Third, the holistic, aesthetic component, in human nature and in the nature of all things, is a factor that pacifies us. Because of its all-embracing oneness and unity, the indeterminate aesthetic continuum also tends to make us compassionate and flexible human beings with intuitive sensitivity—not only for other humans but for all of nature's creatures. In this regard, Maslow (1971) refers to Taoistic receptivity or "let-be" as an important attribute of "self-actualizing" persons:

We may speak of this respectful attention to the matter-in-paradigm as a kind of courtesy or deference (without intrusion of the controlling will) which is akin to 'taking it seriously.' This amounts to treating it as an end, something per se, with its own right to be, rather than as a means to some end other than itself; i.e., as a tool for some extrinsic purpose (p. 68).

Such aesthetic perception is an instrument of intimate human meeting, a way to bridge the gap between individuals and groups. In dealing with each other aesthetically, we do not subject ourselves to a rigid scheme but do our best in each new situation, listening to the silences as well as to the words of the other, and experiencing the other person or group as a whole living entity without being biased by our own egocentric and ethnocentric demands. A similar attitude can be developed toward the physical world around us, to strengthen our determination to achieve maximum ecological and environmental integrity.

TOWARD INTERCULTURAL PERSONHOOD

The movement from a cultural to an intercultural perspective in our individual and collective consciousness presents one of the most significant and exciting challenges of our time. As Toffler (1980) convincingly documented and articulated in *The Third Wave*, there are numerous indications today that point clearly to the need for us to actively pursue a new personhood and a culture that integrates Eastern and Western world views. Toffler notes:

This new culture–oriented to change and growing diversity–attempts to integrate the new view of nature, of evolution and progress, the new, richer conceptions of time and space, and the fusion of reductionism and wholism, with a new causality (p. 309).

Similarly, Gebser's "integral consciousness" (Mickunas 1973) projects an emerging mode of experiencing mode of experiencing reality in which "rational," "mythological," and other modes of consciousness are integrated.

If we are to actively participate in this evolutionary process, the dualism inherent in our thinking process, which puts materialism against spiritualism, West against East, must be transcended. The traditional Western emphasis on the intellect and on material progress need not be viewed as "wrong" or "bad." Rather, the Western orientation is a necessary part of an evolutionary stage, out of which yet another birth of higher consciousness—an integration of East and West—might subsequently evolve. We need to acknowledge that both rational and intuitive modes of experiencing life should be cultivated fully. When we realize that both types of concepts are real, ultimate, and meaningful, we also realize that Eastern and Western cultures have given expression to something in part true. The two seemingly incompatible perspectives can be related and reconciled without contradictions in a new, higher-level, intercultural perspective—one that more closely approximates the expression of the whole truth of life.

As Jantsch (1980) observes, "Life, and especially human life, now appears as a process of self-realization" (p. 307). With an openness toward change, a willingness to revise our own cultural premises, and the enthusiasm to work it through, we are on the way to cultivating our fullest human potentialities and to contributing our share in this enormous process of civilizational change. Together, the East and the West are showing each other the way.

REFERENCES

Adler, P. "Beyond cultural identity: Reflections on cultural and multicultural man." In L. Samovar and R. Porter (eds.), *Intercultural Communication: A Reader*, 3rd ed. Belmont, Calif.: Wadsworth, 1982, pp. 389–408.

Burke, K. "Communication and the human condition." *Communication* 1, 1974, pp. 135–152.

Capra, F. *The Tao of Physics*. Boulder, Colo.: Shambhala, 1975.

Cathcart, D., and Cathcart, R. "Japanese social experience and concept of groups." In L. Samovar and R. Porter (eds.), *Intercultural Communication: A Reader*, 2nd ed. Belmont, Calif.: Wadsworth, 1976, pp. 58–66.

Doi, T., "The Japanese patterns of communication and the concept of amae." In L. Samovar and R. Porter (eds.), *Intercultural Communication: A Reader*, 2nd ed. Belmont, Calif.: Wadsworth, 1976, pp. 188–193.

Elgin, D. *Voluntary Simplicity*. New York: Bantam Books, 1981.

Gudykunst, W., and Kim, Y. *Communicating with Strangers: An Approach to Intercultural Communication*. Reading, Mass.: 1984.

Gulick, S. *The East and the West*. Rutland, Vt.: Charles E. Tuttle, 1963.

Hall, E. *Beyond Culture*. Garden City, New York: Anchor Books, 1976.

Hall, E. *The Dance of Life: The Other Dimension of Time*. Garden City, New York: Anchor Press, 1983.

Hsu, F. *The Challenges of the American Dream*. Belmont, Calif.: Wadsworth, 1981.

Jantsch, E. *The Self-Organizing Universe*. New York: Pergamon, 1980.

Kim, Y. "Becoming intercultural and human development." Paper presented at the annual conference of the International Communication Association, Boston, Mass., May 1982.

Lutzker, D. "Internationalism as a predictor of cooperative behavior." *Journal of Conflict Resolution* 4, 1960, pp. 426–430.

Maslow, A. *The Farther Reaches of Human Nature.* New York: Viking, 1971.

Mickunas, A. "Civilizations as structures of consciousness." *Main Currents* 29, no. 5, 1973, pp. 179–185.

Nakamura, H. *Ways of Thought of Eastern Peoples.* Honolulu: University of Hawaii Press, 1964.

Needham, J. "Human laws and laws of nature in China and the West." *Journal of the History of Ideas* XII, 1951.

Northrop, F. *The Meeting of the East and the West.* New York: Collier Books, 1966 (1946).

Oliver, R. *Communication and Culture in Ancient India and China.* New York: Syracuse University Press, 1971.

Suzuki, D. *The Essence of Buddhism* Kyoto, Japan: Hozokan, 1968.

Thayer, L. "On 'doing' research and 'explaining' things." *Journal of Communication* 33, no. 3, 1983, pp. 80–91.

Thompson, W. *Passages About Earth: An Exploration of the New Planetary Culture.* New York: Harper & Row, 1973.

Toffler, A. *The Third Wave.* New York: Bantam Books, 1980.

Walsh, J. *Intercultural Education in the Community of Man.* Honolulu: University of Hawaii Press, 1973.

Wei, A. "Cultural variations in perception." Paper presented at the Sixth Annual Third World Conference, Chicago, Ill., March 1980.

Beyond Cultural Identity: Reflections on Cultural and Multicultural Man

PETER S. ADLER

INTRODUCTION

The idea of a multicultural man[1] is an attractive and persuasive notion. It suggests a human being whose identifications and loyalties transcend the boundaries of nationalism and whose commitments are pinned to a vision of the world as a global community. To be a citizen of the world, an international person, has long been a dream of man. History is rich with examples of societies and individuals who took it upon themselves to shape everyone else to the mold of their planetary dream. Less common are examples of men and women who have striven to sustain a self process that is international in attitude and behavior. For good reason. Nation, culture, and society exert tremendous influence on each of our lives, structuring our values, engineering our view of the world, and patterning our responses to experience. No human being can hold himself apart from some form of cultural influence. No one is culture free. Yet, the conditions of contemporary history are such that we may now be on the threshold of a new kind of person, a person who is socially and psychologically a product of the interweaving of cultures in the twentieth century.

We are reminded daily of this phenomenon. In

From *Topics in Culture Learning*, Vol. 2 (August 1974), pp. 23–40. Reprinted with permission of the author and the East-West Center. Dr. Adler is with the Office of Participant Affairs, The East-West Center, Honolulu, Hawaii.

410   Chapter 8 Ethical Considerations and Prospects for the Future

the corner of a traditional Japanese home sits a television set tuned to a baseball game in which the visitors, an American team, are losing. A Canadian family, meanwhile, decorates their home with sculptures and paintings imported from Pakistan, India, and Ceylon. Teenagers in Singapore and Hong Kong pay unheard of prices for American blue-jeans while high school students in England and France take courses on the making of traditional Indonesian batik. A team of Malaysian physicians inoculates a remote village against typhus while their Western counterparts study Auryvedic medicine and acupuncture. Around the planet the streams of the world's cultures merge together to form new currents of human interaction. Though superficial and only a manifestation of the shrinking of the globe, each such vignette is a symbol of the mingling and melding of human cultures. Communication and cultural exchange are the pre-eminent conditions of the twentieth century.

For the first time in the history of the world, a patchwork of technology and organization has made possible simultaneous interpersonal and intercultural communication. Innovations and refinements of innovations, including mass mail systems, publishing syndicates, film industries, television networks, and newswire services have brought people everywhere into potential contact. Barely a city or village exists that is more than a day or two from anyplace else; almost no town or community is without a radio. Buslines, railroads, highways, and airports have created linkages within and between local, regional, national, and international levels of human organization. The impact is enormous. Human connections through communications have made possible the interaction of goods, products, and services as well as the more significant exchange of thoughts and ideas. Accompanying the growth of human communication has been the erosion of barriers that have, throughout history, geographically, linguistically, and culturally separated man from man. As Harold Lasswell (1972) has recently suggested, "The technological revolution as it affects mass media has reached a limit that is subject only to innovations that would substantially modify our basic perspectives of one

another and of man's place in the cosmos." It is possible that the emergence of multicultural man is just such an innovation.

A NEW KIND OF MAN

A new type of person whose orientation and view of the world profoundly transcends his indigenous culture is developing from the complex of social, political, economic, and educational interactions of our time. The various conceptions of an "international," "transcultural," or "interculture" person have all been used with varying degrees of explanative or descriptive utility. Essentially, they all define a type of person whose horizons extend significantly beyond his or her own culture. An "internationalist," for example, has been defined as a person who trusts other nations, is willing to cooperate with other countries, perceives international agencies as potential deterrents of war, and who considers international tensions reducible by mediation (Lutzker, 1960). Others have researched the internationality of groups by measuring their attitudes towards international issues, i.e., the role of the U.N., economic versus military aid, international alliances, etc. (Campbell et al., 1954). And at least several attempts have been made to measure the world-mindedness of individuals by exploring the degree to which persons have an international frame of reference rather than specific knowledge or interest in global affairs (Sampson and Smith, 1957; Garrison, 1961; Paul, 1966).

Whatever the terminology, the definitions and metaphors allude to a person whose essential identity is inclusive of life patterns different from his own and who has psychologically and socially come to grips with a multiplicity of realities. We can call this new type of person multicultural because he embodies a core process of self verification that is grounded in both the universality of the human condition and the diversity of man's cultural forms. We are speaking, then, of a social-psychological style of self process that differs from others. Multicultural man is the person who is intellectually and emotionally committed to the fundamental unity of all human beings while at the same time he recognizes, legitimizes, accepts, and appreciates the fundamental differences that lie between people of different cultures. This new kind of man cannot be defined by the languages he speaks, the countries he has visited, or the number of international contacts he has made. Nor is he defined by his profession, his place of residence, or his cognitive sophistication. Instead, multicultural man is recognized by the configuration of his outlooks and world view, by the way he incorporates the universe as a dynamically moving process, by the way he reflects the interconnectedness of life in his thoughts and his actions, and by the way he remains open to the imminence of experience.

Multicultural man is, at once, both old and new. He is very much the timeless "universal" person described again and again by philosophers through the ages. He approaches, in the attributions we make about him, the classical ideal of a person whose lifestyle is one of knowledge and wisdom, integrity and direction, principle and fulfillment, balance and proportion. "To be a universal man," writes John Walsh (1973), "means not how much a man knows but what intellectual depth and breadth he has and how he relates it to other central and universally important problems." What is universal about the multicultural person is his abiding commitment to essential similarities between people everywhere, while paradoxically maintaining an equally strong commitment to their differences. The universal person, suggests, Walsh, "does not at all eliminate culture differences." Rather, he "seeks to preserve whatever is most valid, significant, and valuable in each culture as a way of enriching and helping to form the whole." In his embodiment of the universal and the particular, multicultural man is a descendent of the great philosophers in both the East and the West.

What is new about this type of person and unique to our time is a fundamental change in the structure and process of his identity. His identity, far from being frozen in a social character, is more fluid and mobile, more susceptible to change and open to variation. The identity of multicultural man is based, not on a "belongingness" which implies either owning or being owned by culture, but on a style of self consciousness that is capable of negotiating ever new formations of reality. In this sense multicultural man is a radical departure from the kinds of identities found in both traditional and mass societies. He is neither totally *a part of* nor totally *apart from* his culture; he lives, instead, on the boundary. To live on the edge of one's thinking, one's culture, or one's ego, suggests Paul Tillich (1966), is to live with tension and movement. "It is in truth not standing still, but rather a crossing and return, a repetition of return and crossing, back-and-forth—the aim of which is to create a third area beyond the bounded territories, an area where one can stand for a time without being enclosed in something tightly bounded." Multicultural man, then, is an outgrowth of the complexities of the twentieth century. Yet unique as he may be, the style of identity embodied by multicultural man arises from the myriad of forms that are present in this day and age. An understanding of this new kind of person, then, must be predicated on a clear understanding of cultural identity.

THE CONCEPT OF CULTURAL IDENTITY: A PSYCHOCULTURAL FRAMEWORK

The concept of cultural identity can be used in two different ways. First, it can be employed as a reference to the collective self-awareness that a given group embodies and reflects. This is the most prevalent use of the term. "Generally," writes Stephen Bochner (1973), "the cultural identity of a society is defined by its majority group, and this group is usually quite distinguishable from the minority sub-groups with whom they share the physical environment and the territory that they inhabit." With the emphasis upon the group, the concept is akin to the idea of a national or social character which describes a set of traits that members of a given community share with one another above and beyond their individual differences. Such traits most always include a constellation of values and attitudes towards life, death, birth, family, children, god, and nature. Used in its collective sense, the concept of cultural identity includes typologies of cultural behavior, such behaviors being the appropriate and inappropriate ways of solving life's essential dilemmas and problems. Used in its collective sense, the concept of cultural identity incorporates the shared premises, values, definitions, and beliefs and the day-to-day, largely unconscious, patterning of activities.

A second, more specific use of the concept revolves around the identity of the individual in relation to his or her culture. Cultural identity, in the sense that it is a functioning aspect of individual personality, is a fundamental symbol of a person's existence. It is in reference to the individual that the concept is used in this paper. In psychoanalytic literature, most notably in the writing of Erik Erikson (1959), identity is an elemental form of psychic organization which develops in successive psychosexual phases throughout life. Erikson, who has focused the greater portion of his analytic studies on identity conflicts, has long recognized the anchoring of the ego in a larger cultural context. Identity, he suggests, takes a variety of forms in the individual. "At one time," he writes, "it will appear to refer to a conscious sense of *individual identity*; at another to an unconscious striving for a *continuity of personal character*; at a third, as a criterion for the silent doings of *ego synthesis*; and, finally, as a maintenance of an inner *solidarity* with a group's ideals and identity." The analytic perspective, as voiced by Erikson, is only one of a variety of definitions. Most always, however, the concept of identity is meant to imply a coherent sense of self that depends on a stability of values and a sense of wholeness and integration.

How, then, can we conceptualize the interplay of culture and personality? Culture and personality are inextricably woven together in the gestalt of each person's identity. Culture, the mass of life patterns that human beings in a given society learn from their elders and pass on to the younger generation, is imprinted in the individual as a pattern of perceptions that is accepted and expected by others in a society (Singer, 1971). Cultural identity is the symbol of one's essential experience of oneself as it incorporates the world view, value system,

attitudes, and beliefs of a group with whom such elements are shared. In its most manifest form, cultural identity takes the shape of names which both locate and differentiate the person. When an individual calls himself an American, a Christian, a Democrat, a male, and John Jones, he is symbolizing parts of the complex of images he has of himself and that are likewise recognizable by others. The deeper structure of cultural identity is a fabric of such images and perceptions embedded in the psychological posture of the individual. At the center of this matrix of images is a psychocultural fusion of biological, social, and philosophical motivations; this fusion, a synthesis of culture and personality, is the operant person.

The center, or core, of cultural identity is an image of the self and the culture intertwined in the individual's total conception of reality. This image, a patchwork of internalized roles, rules, and norms, functions as the coordinating mechanism in personal and interpersonal situations. The "mazeway," as Anthony Wallace calls it, is made up of human, non-human, material and abstract elements of the culture. It is the "stuff" of both personality and culture. The mazeway, suggests Wallace (1956), is the patterned image of society and culture, personality and nature all of which is ingrained in the person's symbolization of himself. A system of culture, he writes, "depends relatively more on the ability of constituent units autonomously to perceive the system of which they are a part, to receive and transmit information, and to act in accordance with the necessities of the system. ..." The image, or mazeway, of cultural identity is the gyroscope of the functioning individual. It mediates, arbitrates, and negotiates the life of the individual. It is within the context of this central, navigating image that the fusion of biological, social, and philosophical realities, then, form units of integration that are important to a comparative analysis of cultural identity. The way in which these units are knit together and contoured by the culture at large determines the parameters of the individual. This boundary of cultural identity plays a large part in determining the individual's ability to relate to other cultural systems.

All human beings share a similar biology, universally limited by the rhythms of life. All individuals in all races and cultures must move through life's phases on a similar schedule: birth, infancy, adolescence, middle age, old age, and death. Similarly, humans everywhere embody the same physiological functions of ingestion, irritability, metabolic equilibrium, sexuality, growth, and decay. Yet the ultimate interpretation of human biology is a cultural phenomenon; that is, the meanings of human biological patterns are culturally derived. Though all healthy human beings are born, reproduce, and die, it is culture which dictates the meanings of sexuality, the ceremonials of birth, the transitions of life, and the rituals of death. The capacity for language, for example, is universally accepted as a biological given. Any child, given unimpaired apparatus for hearing, vocalizing, and thinking, can learn to speak and understand any human language. Yet the language that is learned by a child depends solely upon the place and the manner of rearing. Kluckhohn and Leighton (1970), in outlining the grammatical and phonetic systems of the Navajo Indians, have argued that patterns of language affect the expression of ideas and very possibly more fundamental processes of thinking. As Benjamin Whorf has suggested (1957), language may not be merely an inventory of linguistic items but rather "itself the shaper of ideas, the program and guide for the individual's mental activity."[2]

The interaction of culture and biology provides one cornerstone for an understanding of cultural identity. How each individual's biological situation is given meaning becomes, then, a psychobiological unit of integration and analysis. Man's essential physiological needs, hunger, sex, activity, and avoidance of pain, are one part of the reality pattern of cultural identity; similarly with those drives that reach out to the social order. At this, the psychosocial level of integration, generic needs are channeled and organized by culture. Man's needs for affection, acceptance, recognition, affiliation, status, belonging, and interaction with other human beings are enlivened and given recognizable form by culture. We can, for example, see clearly the intersection of culture and the psychosocial

level of integration in comparative status responses. In America economic status is demonstrated by the conspicuous consumption of products; among the Kwakiutl Indians, status is gained by giving all possessions away in the "potlatch"; and contempt or disrespect for the status of old people in many Asian societies represents a serious breach of conduct demanding face-saving measures.

It is the unwritten task of every culture to organize, integrate, and maintain the psychosocial patterns of the individual, especially in the formative years of childhood. Each culture instruments such patterns in ways that are unique, coherent, and logical to the premises and predispositions that underlie the culture. This imprinting of the forms of interconnection that are needed by the individual for psychosocial survival, acceptance, and enrichment is a significant part of the socialization and enculturation process. Yet of equal importance in the imprinting is the structuring of higher forms of individual consciousness. Culture gives meaning and form to those drives and motivations that extend towards an understanding of the cosmological ordering of the universe. All cultures, in one manner or another, invoke the great philosophical questions of life: the origin and destiny of existence, the nature of knowledge, the meaning of reality, the significance of the human experience. As Murdock (1955) has suggested in "Universals of Culture," some form of cosmology, ethics, mythology, supernatural propitiation, religious rituals, and soul concept appears in every culture known to history or ethnography. How an individual raises and searches for ultimate answers is a function of the psychophilosophical patterning of cultural identity. Ultimately it is the task of every individual to relate to his god, to deal with the supernatural, and to incorporate for himself the mystery of life itself. The ways in which individuals do this, the relationships and connections that are formed, are a function of the psychophilosophical component of cultural identity.

A conceptualization of cultural identity, then, must include three interrelated levels of integration and analysis. While the cultural identity of an individual is comprised of symbols and images that signify aspects of these levels, the psychobiological, psychosocial, and psychophilosophical realities of an individual are knit together by the culture which operates through sanctions and rewards, totems and taboos, prohibitions and myths. The unity and integration of society, nature, and the cosmos is reflected in the total image of the self and in the day-to-day awareness and consciousness of the individual. This synthesis is modulated by the larger dynamics of the culture itself. In the concept of cultural identity, then, we see a synthesis of the operant culture reflected by the deepest images held by the individual. These images, in turn, are based on universally human motivations.

Implicit in any analysis of cultural identity is a configuration of motivational needs. As the late Abraham Maslow (1962) suggested, human drives form a hierarchy in which the most prepotent motivations will monopolize consciousness and will tend, of themselves, to organize the various capacities and capabilities of the organism. In the sequence of development, the needs of infancy and childhood revolve primarily around physiological and biological necessities, i.e., nourishment by food, water, and warmth. Correspondingly, the psychosocial needs of the individual are most profound in adolescence and young adulthood when the individual is engaged in establishing himself through marriage, occupation, and social and economic status. Finally, psychophilosophical drives are most manifest in middle and old age when the individual can occupy himself with creativity, philosophic actualization, and with transcendental relationships. As Cofer and Appley (1964) rightly point out, Maslow's hierarchy of needs is not an explicit, empirical, verifiable theory of human motivation. It is useful, however, in postulating a universally recognized but differently named process of individual motivation that carries the individual through the stages of life. Each level of integration and analysis in cultural identity, then, can be viewed as both a part of the gridwork of the self image as well as a developmental roadmap imprinted by the culture.

The gyroscope of cultural identity functions to orchestrate the allegiances, loyalties, and commitments of the individual by giving them direction and meaning. Every human being, however, differentiates himself to some degree from his culture. Just as no one is totally free of cultural influence, no one is totally a reflection of his culture. The cultural identity of an individual, therefore, must be viewed as an integrated synthesis of identifications that are idiosyncratic within the parameters of culturally influenced biological, social, and philosophical motivations. Whether, in fact, such unity ever achieves sufficient integration to provide for consistency between individuals within a given culture is an empirical matter that deals with normalcy and modal personality. The concept of cultural identity, then, can at best be a schema for comparative research between (rather than with) cultures. This schema of cultural identity is illustrated in Figure 1. Though admittedly a fundamental rule of social science must be human variation and the unpredictability of models and theories, a schema of cultural identity and the interplay of psychological and cultural dynamics may lay a groundwork for future research and conceptualization. Particularly useful may be the "eiconic" approach proposed by Kenneth Boulding (1956). His typology of images which include the spatial, temporal, relational, personal, value, affectional, conscious-unconscious, certainty-uncertainty, reality-unreality, and public-private dimensions, may add important perspectives to the comparative study of cultural identity.

THE MULTICULTURAL IDENTITY

The rise of multicultural man is a significant phenomenon because it represents a new psychocultural style of self process. He arises amidst the metamorphosis of both traditional and mass societies, in a transitional time in which man is redefining himself politically, socially and economically. Multicultural man is a radically different sort of human being. Three characteristics distinguish his style of personality from the traditional structure of cultural identity. First, the multicultural person is psychoculturally adaptive; that is, he is

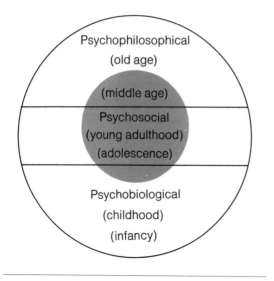

Figure 1

situational in his relationships to others and his connections to culture. He maintains no clear boundaries between himself and the varieties of personal and cultural contexts he may find himself in. The multicultural identity is premised, not on the hierarchical structuring of a single mental image but rather on the intentional and accidental shifts that life's experiences involve. His values and attitudes, world view and beliefs, are always in reformation, dependent more on the necessities of experience than on the predispositions of a given culture. For multicultural man, attitudes, values, beliefs, and a world view are relevant only to a given context (as is usually learned as a result of the culture shock process) and cannot be translated from context to context. Multicultural man does not judge one situation by the terms of another and is therefore ever evolving new systems of evaluations that are relative to the context and situation.

Second, the multicultural person is ever undergoing personal transitions. He is always in a state of "becoming" or "un-becoming" something different than before while yet mindful of the grounding he has in his own cultural reality. Stated differently, multicultural man is propelled from identity to identity through a process of both cultural learning and cultural un-learning. Multicultural man, like

Robert J. Lifton's concept of "protean man" (1961), is always recreating his identity. He moves through one experience of self to another, incorporating here, discarding there, responding dynamically and situationally. This style of self process, suggests Lifton, "is characterized by an interminable series of experiments and explorations, some shallow, some profound, each of which can readily be abandoned in favor of still new, psychological quests." The multicultural man is always in flux, the configuration of his loyalties and identifications changing, his overall image of himself perpetually being reformulated through experience and contact with the world. Stated differently, his life is an ongoing process of psychic death and rebirth.

Third, multicultural man maintains indefinite boundaries of the self. The parameters of his identity are neither fixed nor predictable, being responsive, instead, to both temporary form and openness to change. Multicultural man is capable of major shifts in his frame of reference and embodies the ability to disavow a permanent character and change in his social-psychological style. The multicultural person, in the words of Peter Berger (1973) is a "homeless mind," a condition which, though allowing great flexibility, also allows for nothing permanent and unchanging to develop. This homelessness is at the heart of his motivational needs. He is, suggests Lifton, "starved for ideas and feelings that give coherence to his world . . .," that give structure and form to his search for the universal and absolute, that give definition to his perpetual quest. The multicultural man, like great philosophers in any age, can never accept totally the demands of any one culture nor is he free from the conditioning of his culture. His psychocultural style, then, must always be relational and in movement. He is able, however, to look at his own original culture from an outsider's perspective. This tension gives rise to a dynamic, passionate, and critical posture in the face of totalistic ideologies, systems, and movements.

Like culture-bound man, multicultural man bears within him a simultaneous image of societies, nature, personality, and culture. Yet in contrast to the structure of cultural identity, multicultural man is perpetually re-defining his mazeway. No culture is capable of imprinting or ingraining the identity of multicultural man indelibly; yet, likewise, multicultural man must rely heavily on cultures to maintain his own relativity. Like human beings in any period of time, multicultural man is driven by psychobiological, psychosocial, and psychophilosophical motivations that impel him through life. Yet the configuration of these drives is perpetually in flux and situational. The maturational hierarchy, implicit in the central image of cultural identity, is less structured and cohesive in the multicultural identity. For that reason, his needs and his drives, his motivations and expectations are constantly being aligned and realigned to fit the context he is in.

The flexibility of multicultural man allows great variation in adaptability and adjustment. Adjustment and adaptation, however, must always be dependent on some constant, on something stable and unchanging in the fabric of life. We can attribute to multicultural man three fundamental postulates that are incorporated and reflected in his thinking and behavior. Such postulates are fundamental to success in cross-cultural adaptation.

1. Every culture or system has its own internal coherence, integrity, and logic. Every culture is an intertwined system of values and attitudes, beliefs and norms that give meaning and significance to both individual and collective identity.

2. No one culture is inherently better or worse than another. All cultural systems are equally valid as variations on the human experience.

3. All persons are, to some extent, culturally bound. Every culture provides the individual with some sense of identity, some regulation of behavior, and some sense of personal place in the scheme of things.

The multicultural person embodies these propositions in the living expressions of his life. They are fundamentally a part of his interior image of himself and the world and as much a part of his behavior.

What is uniquely new about this emerging hu-

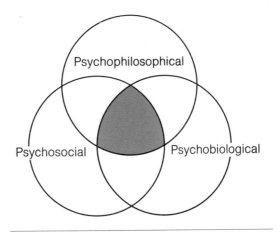

Figure 2

man being is a psychocultural style of self process that transcends the structured image a given culture may impress upon the individual in his or her youth. The navigating image at the core of the multicultural image is premised on an assumption of many cultural realities. The multicultural person, therefore, is not simply the person who is sensitive to many different cultures. Rather, he is a person who is always in the process of becoming *a part of* and *apart from* a given cultural context. He is very much a formative being, resilient, changing, and evolutionary. He has no permanent cultural character but neither is he free from the influences of culture. In the shifts and movements of his identity process, multicultural man is continually recreating the symbol of himself. The concept of a multicultural identity is illustrated and differentiated from the schema of cultural identity in Figure 2.

The indefinite boundaries and the constantly realigning relationships that are generated by the psychobiological, psychosocial and psychophilosophical motivations make possible sophisticated and complex responses on the part of the individual to cultural and subcultural systems. Moreover, this psychocultural flexibility necessitates sequential changes in identity. Intentionally or accidentally, multicultural persons undergo shifts in their total psychocultural posture; their religion, personality, behavior, occupation, nationality, outlook, political persuasion, and values may, in part or completely, reformulate in the face of new experiences. "It is becoming increasingly possible," writes Michael Novak (1970), "for men to live through several profound conversions, calling forth in themselves significantly different personalities. . . ." The relationship of multicultural man to cultural systems is fragile and tenuous. "A man's cultural and social milieu," continues Novak, "conditions his personality, values, and actions; yet the same man is able, within limits, to choose the milieus whose conditioning will affect him."

Who, then, is multicultural man? Four different variations of the multicultural identity process can be seen in the following case studies. While two of these individuals have been interviewed extensively by the author,[3] the other two are figures of contemporary importance. Each of these persons, in their own unique way, represents the essential characteristics of multicultural man in a vivid and dramatic manner.

1. *C.K.* is a talented musician, an excellent student, a deeply spiritual disciple of an Indian mystic, and at once, both a teacher and a friend to a number of other students. Though outgoing, humorous, and articulate he is likewise a private, almost quiet person who appears to exert a high degree of control over his life. Coming from a large family in which his father, an engineer, spent a good deal of time abroad, C.K. had an early opportunity to both live and study in a foreign culture. Following high school C.K. spent his college years in the Middle East where he purposely stayed away from other Americans in order to facilitate both contacts with the local people and language learning. His first years in the Middle East were significant: "It was at this point that I began to *see* where I grew up and not just *know* that I had been raised in America." In high school, C.K. had been intensely interested in mathematics and physics; his college career, however, brought about a shift. Increasingly, he found himself interested in music, an interest that would later carry him East both academically and spiritually. It was during his college years that C.K. also became aware of American policy abroad; though never entirely a political activist, C.K. was outspoken and critical of American foreign policy

and critical of the Viet Nam war. After completing his B.A., C.K. enrolled in graduate studies in ethnomusicology, concentrating his work on the Indian flute. With his wife he then spent a year and a half in India studying under an Indian teacher. His Indian experiences were important. Living and studying in a traditional setting, C.K. became progressively more involved with the philosophic traditions of the country and eventually met a well-known Indian mystic. His encounters with the meditations of this teacher influenced him profoundly. After months of study, meditation, and living with this religious leader and his other disciples, C.K. himself became a disciple. The dissolution of his marriage which he calls "an amicable and agreeable parting" came at roughly the same time. After returning to America to continue his graduate studies in music, C.K., still very much a disciple of his teacher, has continued to both practice and teach meditation. C.K. is very warm and articulate in discussion. He describes life as a series of peaks and valleys, what he calls the "mountain climbing" model of existence. "Life is a series of mountains in which you must go down one mountain in order to go up yet another. Each ascent and descent is difficult but one must be able to experience both the top and the bottom if one is to grow." C.K. is an exceptional person. His friends to whom he teaches meditation come from a variety of disciplines and countries, including some from India and Japan. In his day-to-day experiences, C.K. seems to react situationally. In his own words, he makes every attempt to "be in the here and now," to relate to people individually, and to live as simple and uncomplicated an existence as possible. Though he rejects much talk about mysticism, C.K. lives an ascetic and "feeling" style of life in which he aspires to bring himself in contact with the largest rhythms of nature and of the universe.

2. *Y.N.* is Japanese, an expatriate now residing in Hawaii, and a quiet intelligent individual. Though he initially is shy with strangers, Y.N. likes very much to play host for his friends. In conversation he will demonstrate techniques of ju-jitsu, in which he holds a high ranking belt, and talk about the incidents that have occurred to him in his travels

throughout Asia and America. Brought up in a middle-class, relatively traditional home, Y.N. finished high school and taught ikebana, the art of flower arrangement. Qualified as a teacher in this and several other aesthetic and martial arts, Y.N. came to America. In high school and his first years in college, Y.N. had become a member of a splinter faction of the Zengakuren, the militant student movement in Japan, and had participated actively in numerous demonstrations and student revolts. He describes this time in his life "both a high and low for myself." Though his commitment to the radical movement was deep, he felt strongly the urge to live contemplatively and reflectively as his various masteries had taught him to do. In the tension that surrounded the late 1960's in Japan, and amidst conflicts with his father who was opposed to his radical leanings, he "escaped" to America where he has every intention of remaining until he "finds another place to live." Having disavowed himself from both the aesthetic arts and radical political causes, Y.N. is today employed in a hotel as a means of supporting himself through school. Since coming to the United States, Y.N. has undergone, in his words, a "transformation." He is completely different and realizes that he is no longer able to return to Japan to become reconciled with his family and culture. Nor is he totally at home in the U.S. Instead, he sees the U.S. as a temporary place for himself and considers the world to be his home. At one point, several years after being in the U.S., Y.N. returned to Japan, but his anxieties rapidly cascaded into a nervous breakdown. Returning to the U.S., he underwent intensive psychotherapy and again resumed his studies, and with an undergraduate degree in history, may move to Australia. Though unsure of his future, he hopes to utilize his studies of history in teaching and writing and seems confident that his inner struggles have prepared him for further changes which he sees as inevitable.

3. *Carlos Castaneda* (1969, 1971, 1972), familiar through his writings about don Juan, the Yaqui Indian sorcerer, is an anthropologist by training, a Brazilian by birth, and an elusive, intensely private individual. He is known solely through his books and the articles about him that have appeared in popular literature. Castaneda spent most of his life in Argentina and came to the United States to do graduate work in anthropology. Interested in the cultural uses of psychotropic drugs, he began field work with don Juan Mateus, a Yaqui Indian reputed to be a medicine man of great power. After a year of studying with don Juan, Castaneda entered an apprenticeship under the sorcerer and spent the next twelve years working, living, and studying under the old man. His first books documented his experiences with mescalin, peyote, and jimson weed and his progressively deeper involvement with the cultural context in which such drugs are used. In attempting to understand their use, Castaneda had to struggle with a "non-ordinary reality." His writings, taken in series, document his struggles to understand another way of life, his resistances, his failures, and his occasional successes. A trained Western scientist, Castaneda's apprenticeship led him deeper and deeper into the world of the "brujo," a reality which is as much comprised of phantoms and spirits as it is rattlesnakes and cactus. Progressively more jolted by the extraordinary things he encountered in the world of don Juan, Castaneda documented his experiences, which read like the dream-logs of Jungian psychologists. Throughout his twelve years of apprenticeship, don Juan has progressively brought Castaneda deeper into the "becoming of a man of power and knowledge." At least one of the ongoing lessons of don Juan has been responsibility, to personally be accountable for every movement and thought, every behavior and action. To pick the leaves of a plant, to disturb pebbles in the desert, or to shiver in the cold are all ultimate acts of the man who has control of himself. Nothing is chance; yet nothing can be explained logically or rationally. Castaneda, who is somewhat publicity shy, is known only through his writings, and these are quite controversial. Studying, writing, and existing on the far fringe of academic respectability, Castaneda seems comfortable in his relationships to several different cultures.

4. *Norman O. Brown,* born in Mexico of American parents, educated in both England and America, at one time a researcher for the Office of Strategic Services (forerunner of the CIA) is presently a professor of comparative literature and a prominent left-wing thinker. Brown is a fiercely intentional, highly provocative writer whose major contributions have been in fields where he had limited academic training. At one time an obscure teacher of literature, Brown became immersed in a penetrating study of Freud in the late 1950's. Out of his encounters with the psychoanalytic school of psychology, Brown wrote his first book, *Life Against Death* (1959), which sought nothing less than a total overhaul of psychological, social, economic, and political thinking. Using his thoughts on the Freudian concept of repression as a departure point, Brown has attempted to formulate a social theory that is determined to remove all barriers to human liberation. Having jumped freely into the domain of psychologists, sociologists, and political scientists, Brown has come to see hope in madness and in the Dionysian model. His apocalyptic vision encompasses, in his own words, "a shaking of the foundations" which bind man to repetitious, self-destructive behavior. Brown is a visionary in the school of Nietzsche and, like Nietzsche, finds liberation in the ultimate destruction of all boundaries. Brown and his writings cannot be encapsulated in a discipline. He overlaps, expands, and bursts areas of study and purposely seeks to shock his intellectual peers with thinking that is often bizarre, usually outrageous, and always rigorous. He draws from the sources of metaphor: myths, dreams, religion, symbols, and the undercurrents of the unconscious; in drawing together sources from philosophy, theology, psychology, and history he weaves together a theoretical perspective that is both analytic and polemic. Brown is a spokesman for liberation, his enemy the "politics of sin, cynicism, and despair," his goal the ultimate unification of man and nature. Far from being a gadfly, Brown is accepted as a deep and penetrating thinker whose writings have thrust him in the role of both counter-culture hero and enemy of the academic establishment. More than anything else, however, Brown has jumped across disciplines,

theories, and traditions in an effort to free the human mind from its blinders. His ultimate vision comes to rest in poetry and in the sublime, if unchallengeable, processes of dialectical confrontation with the barriers of his time.

Each of these individuals, C.K. Y.N., Castaneda, and Brown, share significant elements of the multicultural identity. Each, in their own way, can be understood only contextually, that is, only in relation to the particular time, place, and system we choose to focus on. Each of these individuals has undergone shifts in identity, in some cases quite radical breaks with their previous "selves." C.K. and Castaneda, for example, have followed a course that involves a search for heightened personal consciousness. Y.N. and Brown, on the other hand, have pursued a series of identity changes that have carried them into and through a radical political posture. But in all four of these individuals it is possible to see that there have been fracture points in which the constellation of values, attitudes, world view, and outlook that we call identity has changed. Each of these individuals, different as they are, have embraced, only to let go, one frame of reference in favor of yet another.

Neither C.K., Y.N., Castaneda or Brown are "usual" persons. All of them have perched themselves precariously close to the boundaries of the system. In the case of Y.N., this has involved self-exile from his native country; for Brown, this has meant a departure from the perimeters of his training and expertise; for C.K., the experience of self has meant embracing a religious order that is antipodal to the Western tradition; and for Castaneda, it has involved an agonizing indoctrination into an order of experience that carries him far from the careful, methodical schooling of anthropology. Each of these persons is in some sense or another an outsider, intentionally or accidentally dislocated from one frame of reference to another, from one environment of experience to a different one. Though they differ drastically in their personalities, orientations, political values, and personal objectives, they share a similar process of identity change. And though they share a similar process of identity style, they differ greatly in their handling of the stresses and strains, the tensions and problems that ensue from such a fluidity of self. Y.N. has obviously been severely disturbed by the demands placed on him through conflicts in loyalty. Brown has glorified the infantile ego and taken refuge in an intellectual process that necessitates the smashing of all boundaries without regard for the functions such boundaries may perform. Castaneda has removed himself totally from the public view while C.K. has submitted himself to what one might call a dogmatic totalism.

STRESSES AND TENSIONS

The unprecedented dynamism of multicultural man makes it possible to live many different lives, in sequence or simultaneously. But such psychocultural pliability gives rise to tensions and stresses unique to the conditions which allow such dynamism in the first place. Multicultural man, by virtue of the fact that his boundaries are indefinite, his experience more intense, and his lifetime telescoped into modules of congruency, is subject to stresses and strains that are equally unique. At least five of these stresses bear mentioning.

First, multicultural man is vulnerable. In maintaining no clear boundary and form multicultural man is susceptible to confusing the profound and the insignificant, the important and the unimportant, the visionary and the reactionary. "Boundaries can be viewed," suggests Lifton (1967), "as neither permanent nor by definition false, but rather as essential. . . . We require images of limit and restraint, if only to help us grasp what we are transcending. We need distinctions between our biology and our history, all the more so as we seek to bring. these together in a sense of ourselves. . . ." Without some form of boundary, experience itself has no shape or contour, no meaning and importance; where the individual maintains no critical edge to his existence everything can become confusion. Experience, in order to be a particular experience, must take place amidst some essential polarity in

which there is tension between two opposing forces. Where there is no sense of evil, there can be no sense of the good; where nothing is profane, nothing can be sacred. Boundaries, however indefinite, give shape and meaning to the experience of experience; they allow us to differentiate, define, and determine who we are in relation to someone or something else.

Second, multicultural man can easily become multiphrenic, that is, to use Erikson's terminology, a "diffused identity." Where the configuration of loyalties and identifications is constantly in flux and where boundaries are never secure, multicultural man lays himself open to any and all kind of stimuli. In the face of messages which are confusing, contradictory, or overwhelming, the individual is thrown back on himself and his own subjectivity with which he must integrate and sort out what he allows himself to take in. Where the multicultural man is incapable of doing this he is pulled and pushed by the winds of communication, a victim of what everyone else claims he is or should be. It is the task of every social and cultural group to organize messages, images, and symbols into terms that the individual can translate into his own existence. But where the messages and stimuli of all groups are given equal importance and validity, the individual can easily be overwhelmed by the demands of everyone else.

Third, multicultural man can easily suffer from a loss of the sense of his own authenticity. That is, multicultural man, by virtue of the fact that he is psychoculturally adaptive, can potentially be reduced to a variety of roles that bear little or no relationship to one another. Multicultural man can lose the sense of congruence and integrity that is implicit in the definition of identity itself. Roles, suggest psychologists, are constellations of behaviors that are expected of an individual because of his place in particular social or cultural arrangements. Behind roles are the deeper threads of continuity, the processes of affect, perception, cognition, and value, that make a whole of the parts. Multicultural man can easily disintegrate into a fragmented splinter who is unable to experience life along any dimension other than institutional-ized, routinized expectations placed on him by family, friends, and society.

Fourth, and related to this, is the risk of being a gadfly and a dilettante. Multicultural man can very easily move from identity experience to identity experience without committing himself or his values to real-life situations. The energy and enthusiasm he brings to bear on new situations can easily disintegrate into superficial fads and fancies in which the multicultural person simply avoids any deeper responsibilities and involvements. Flexibility can easily disguise a manner of self process in which real human problems are avoided or in which they are given only superficial importance. Especially in the Western societies, where youth is vulnerable to the fabricated fads of contemporary culture, the multicultural identity process can give way to a dilettantism in which the individual flows, unimpaired, uncommitted, and unaffected, through social, political, and economic manipulations of elites.

Fifth, and finally, the multicultural person may take ultimate psychological and philosophical refuge in an attitude of existential absurdity, mocking the patterns and lifestyles of others who are different from himself, reacting, at best in a detached and aloof way, and at worst as a nihilist who sees negation as a salvation for himself and others. Where the breakdown of boundaries creates a gulf that separates the individual from meaningful relationships with others, the individual may hide behind a screen of barbed cynicisms that harbors apathy and insecurity. In such a condition nothing within and nothing outside of the individual is of serious consequence; the individual, in such a position, must ultimately scorn that which he cannot understand and incorporate into his own existence.

These stresses and strains should not be confused with the tensions and anxieties that are encountered in the process of cross-cultural adjustment. Culture shock is a more superficial constellation of problems that results from the misreading of commonly perceived and understood signs of social interaction. Nor is the delineation of these tensions meant to suggest that the multicultural person must necessarily harbor these various difficulties. The multicultural style of identity is premised on a fluid, dynamic movement of the self, an ability to move in and out of contexts, and an ability to maintain some inner coherence through varieties of situations. As a psychocultural style, multicultural man may just as easily be a great artist or neurotic; he is equally as susceptible, if not more so, to the fundamental forces of our time. Any list of multicultural individuals must automatically include individuals who have achieved a high degree of accomplishment, i.e., writers, musicians, diplomats, etc., as well as those whose lives have, for one reason or another, been fractured by the circumstances they failed to negotiate. The artist and the neurotic lie close together in each of us suggests Rollo May (1969). "The neurotic," he writes, "and the artist—since both live out the unconscious of the race—reveal to us what is going to emerge endemically in the society later on . . . the neurotic is the 'artiste Manque,' the artist who cannot transmute his conflicts into art."

The identity process of multicultural man represents a new kind of person unfettered by the constricting limitations of culture as a "totalistic" entity. Yet, like men in any age, multicultural man must negotiate the difficulties of cross-cultural contacts. The literature of cross-cultural psychology is rich with examples of the kinds of problems encountered when people are intensely exposed to other cultures. Integration and assimilation, for example, represent two different responses to a dominant culture, integration suggesting the retention of subcultural differences and assimilation implying absorption into a larger cultural system. The relationship between assimilation, integration, and identification, write Sommerlad and Berry (1973), "suggests that if an individual identifies with his own group, he will hold favourable attitudes towards integration; on the other hand, if he identifies with the host society, he should favour assimilation." Related to this are the various negative attitudes, psychosomatic stresses, and deviant behaviors that are expressed by individuals in psychologically marginal situations. "Contrary to predictions stemming from the theory of Marginal Man," writes J. W. Berry (1970), "it tends to be those persons more traditionally oriented who suffer the most psychological marginality, rather than those who wish to move on and cannot." Multicultural man is, in many ways, a stranger. The degree to which he can continually modify his frame of reference and become aware of the structures and functions of a group while at the same time maintaining a clear understanding of his own personal, ethnic, and cultural identifications may very well be the degree to which the multicultural person can truly function successfully between cultures. . . .

Although it is difficult to pinpoint the conditions under which cultural identities will evolve into multicultural identities, such changes in psychocultural style are most likely to occur where the foundations of collective cultural identity have been shaken. "Communities that have been exposed too long to exceptional stresses from ecological or economic hardships," writes J. W. Cawte (1973), "or from natural or man-made disasters, are apt to have a high proportion of their members subject to mental disorders." Cawte's studies of the Aboriginal societies of Australia and Turnbull's studies of the Ik in Africa (1972) document how major threats to collective cultural identity produce social and psychological breakdown in individuals. Yet, potentially, multicultural attitudes and values may develop where cultural interchange takes place between cultures that are not totally disparate, or where the rate of change is evolutionary rather than immediate. The reorganization of a culture, suggests J. L. M. Dawson (1969), "results in the formation of in-between attitudes" which Dawson considers "to be more appropriate for the satisfactory adjustment of individuals in transitional situations." The multicultural style, then, may be born and initially expressed in any society or culture that is faced with new exposures to other ways of life.

Conceptualization of a multicultural identity style in terms of personality types, behavior patterns, traits, and cultural background is at best impressionistic and anecdotal. Yet, the investigations of cross-cultural psychologists and anthropologists give increasing credence to the idea of a multicultural man who is shaped and contoured by the stresses and strains which result from cultural interweaving at both the macro- and microcultural levels. Seemingly, a multicultural style is able to evolve when the individual is capable of negotiating the conflicts and tensions inherent in cross-cultural contacts. The multicultural person, then, may very well represent an affimation of individual identity at a higher level of social, psychological, and cultural integration.

Just as the cultures of the world, if they are to merit survival amidst the onslaught of Western technologies, must be responsive to both tradition and change, so too must the individual identity be psychoculturally adaptive to the encounters of an imploding world. There is every reason to think that such human beings are emerging. Multicultural man, embodying, as he does, sequential identities, is open to the continuous cycle of birth and death as it takes place within the framework of his own psyche. The lifestyle of multicultural man is a continual process of dissolution and reformation of identity; yet implicit in such a process is a sequence of growth. Psychological movements into new dimensions of perception and experience tend very often to produce forms of personality disintegration. But disintegration, suggests Kazimierez Dabrowski (1964), "is the basis for developmental thrusts upward, the creation of new evolutionary dynamics, and the movement of personality to a higher level. . . ." The seeds of each new identity of multicultural man lie within the disintegration of previous identities. "When the human being," writes Erikson (1964), "because of accidental or developmental shifts, loses an essential wholeness, he restructures himself and the world by taking recourse to what we may call 'totalism.'" Such totalism, above and beyond being a mechanism of coping and adjustment, is a part of the growth of a new kind of wholeness at a higher level of integration.

CONCLUSIONS AND SUMMARY

This paper does not suggest that multicultural man is now the predominate character style of our time. Nor is it meant to suggest that multicultural persons, by virtue of their uninhibited way of relating to other cultures, are in any way "better" than those who are mono- or bi-cultural. Rather, this paper argues that multicultural persons are not simply individuals who are sensitive to other cultures or knowledgeable about international affairs, but instead can be defined by a psychocultural pattern of identity that differs radically from the relatively stable forms of self process found in the cultural identity pattern. This paper argues that both cultural and multicultural identity processes can be conceptualized by the constellation and configuration of biological, social, and philosophical motivations and by the relative degrees of rigidity maintained in personal boundaries and that such conceptualization lays the basis for comparative research.

Two final points might be noted about the multicultural man. First, the multicultural person embodies attributes and characteristics that prepare him to serve as a facilitator and catalyst for contacts between cultures. The variations and flexibility of his identity allows the multicultural person to relate to a variety of contexts and environments without being totally encapsulated or totally alienated from the particular situation. As Stephen Bochner (1973) suggests, a major problem of cultural preservation in Asia and the Pacific "is the lack of sufficient people who can act as links between diverse cultural systems." These "mediating" individuals incorporate the essential characteristics of multicultural man. "Genuine multicultural individuals are very rare," he writes, "which is unfortunate because it is these people who are uniquely equipped to mediate the cultures of the world." The multicultural person, then, embodies a pattern of self process that potentially allows him to help others negotiate the cultural realities of a different system. With a self process that is adaptational, multicultural man is in a unique position to understand, facilitate, and research the psychocultural dynamics of other systems.

Second, multicultural man is himself a significant psychological and cultural phenomenon, enough so as to merit further conceptualization and research. It is neither easy nor necessarily useful to reconcile the approaches of psychology and anthropology; nor is there any guarantee that inter-disciplinary approaches bring us closer to an intelligent understanding of the human being as he exists in relation to his culture. Yet, the multicultural man may prove to be a significant enough problem in culture learning (and culture unlearning) to force an integrated approach to studies of the individual and the group. "Psychologists," write Richard Brislin et al. (1973), "have the goal of incorporating the behavior of many cultures into one theory (etic approach), but they must also understand the behavior within each culture (emic approach)." Empirical research based on strategies that can accurately observe, measure, and test behavior, and that incorporate the "emic versus etic" distinction will be a natural next step. Such studies may very well be a springboard into the more fundamental dynamics of cross-cultural relationships.

We live in a transitional period of history, a time that of necessity demands transitional forms of psychocultural self process. That a true international community of nations is coming into existence is still a debatable issue; but that individuals with a self consciousness that is larger than the mental territory of their culture are emerging is no longer arguable. The psychocultural pattern of identity that is called for to allow such self consciousness, adaptability, and variation opens such individuals to both benefits and pathologies. The interlinking of cultures and persons in the twentieth century is not always a pleasant process; modernization and economic development have taken heavy psychological tolls in both developed and third-world countries. The changes brought on in our time have invoked revitalistic needs for the preservation of collective, cultural identities. Yet, along with the disorientation and alienation which have characterized much of this century comes new possibility in the way human beings conceive of their individual identities and the identity of man as a species. No one has better stated this possibility than Harold Taylor (1969), himself an excellent example of multicultural man:

There is a new kind of man in the world, and there are more of that kind than is commonly

*recognized. He is a national citizen with
international intuitions, conscious of the age
that is past and aware of the one now in being,
aware of the radical difference between the two,
willing to accept the lack of precedents, willing to
work on the problems of the future as a labor of
love, unrewarded by governments, academies,
prizes, and position. He forms part of an invisible
world community of poets, writers, dancers,
scientists, teachers, lawyers, scholars, philosophers,
students, citizens who see the world whole and
feel at one with all its parts.*

NOTES

1. Despite the fact that men and women share an equal investment in psychological developments of our time, it is virtually impossible to express certain concepts in language that is sexually neutral. The idea of a multicultural "man" and other references to the masculine gender are to be considered inclusive of men and women alike.

2. A technical reference to the controversial literature examining the "Sapir-Whorf Hypothesis" can be found in "Psycholinguistics" by G. Miller and D. McNeill in Volume 3 of the *Handbook of Social Psychology*, edited by G. Lindzey and E. Aronson (Reading: Addison-Wesley Publishing Company, 1968).

3. The examples of both C. K. and Y. N. are condensed from a number of longer case studies done by the author as part of his research on identity changes that result from cross-cultural experiences. The full case studies are included in his Ph.D. thesis entitled *The Boundary Experience*.

REFERENCES

Berger, P. and Berger, B. *The Homeless Mind*. New York, Random House, 1973.

Berry, J. W. "Marginality, Stress and Ethnic Identification," *Journal of Cross Cultural Psychology*, 1970, 1, 239–252.

Bochner, S. "The Mediating Man and Cultural Di-

versity," *Topics in Culture Learning*, 1973, vol. 1, 23–37.

Boulding, K. *The Image*. Ann Arbor: The University of Michigan Press, 1956.

Brislin, R., Lonner, W., and Thorndike, R. *Cross-Cultural Research Methods*. New York: John Wiley & Sons, 1973.

Brown, N. *Life Against Death*. Middleton, Conn.: Wesleyan University Press, 1959.

Campbell, A., Gurin, G., and Miller, W. E. *The Voter Decides*. Evanston: Row, Peterson and Co., 1954.

Castaneda, C. *Journey to Ixtlan*. New York: Simon and Schuster, 1972.

Castaneda, C. *A Separate Reality*. New York: Pocket Books, 1971.

Castaneda, C. *The Teachings of Don Juan*. New York: Ballantine Books, 1969.

Cawte, J. E. "A Sick Society," In G. E. Kearney, P. R. de Lacey, and G. R. Davidson (Eds.), *The Psychology of Aboriginal Australians*. Sydney: John Wiley & Sons Australasia Pty Ltd., 1973, 365–379.

Cofer, C. and Appley, M. *Motivation: Theory and Research*. New York: John Wiley & Sons, Inc., 1964.

Dabrowski, K. *Positive Disintegration*. Boston: Little, Brown, & Co., 1964.

Dawson, J. L. M. "Attitude Change and Conflict," *Australian Journal of Psychology*, 1969, 21, 101–116.

Erikson, E. *Insight and Responsibility*. New York: W. W. Norton and Company, 1964.

Erikson, E. "The Problem of Ego Identity," *Psychological Issues*, 1959, vol. 1, No. 1, 101–164.

Garrison, K. "Worldminded Attitudes of College Students in a Southern University," *Journal of Social Psychology*, 1961, 54, 147–153.

Kluckhohn, C. and Leighton, D. "The Language of the Navajo Indians." In P. Bock (Ed.), *Culture Shock*. New York: Alfred A. Knopf, 1970, 29–49.

Lasswell, H. *The Future of World Communication: Quality and Style of Life*. Honolulu: East-West Center Communication Institute, 1972.

Lifton, R. *Boundaries*. New York: Vintage Books, 1967.

Lifton, R. *History and Human Survival.* New York: Vintage Books, 1961.

Lutzker, D. "Internationalism as a Predictor of Cooperative Behavior," *Journal of Conflict Resolution,* 1960, 4 (4), 426–430.

Maslow, A. *Toward a Psychology of Being.* Princeton: D. Van Nostrand Company, Inc., 1962.

May, R. *Love and Will.* New York: Dell Publishing Co., Inc., 1969.

Murdock, G. "Universals of Culture." In J. Jennings and E. A. Hoebel (Eds.), *Readings in Anthropology.* New York: McGraw-Hill Book Company, 1955, 13–14.

Novak, M. *The Experience of Nothingness.* New York: Harper & Row, 1970.

Paul, S. "Worldminded Attitudes of Panjab University Students," *Journal of Social Psychology.* 1966, 69, 33–37.

Sampson, D. and Smith, H. "A Scale to Measure World-Minded Attitudes," *Journal of Social Psychology,* 1957, 45, 99–106.

Singer, M. "Culture: A Perceptual Approach," In D. Hoopes (Ed.), *Readings in Intercultural Communication*, Pittsburgh: RCIE, 1971, 6–20.

Sommerlad, E. and Berry, J. W. "The Role of Ethnic Identification." In G. E. Kearney, P. R. de Lacey, and G. R. Davidson (Eds.), *The Psychology of Aboriginal Australians.* Sydney: John Wiley & Sons Australasia Pty Ltd., 1973, 236–243.

Taylor, H. "Toward a World University," *Saturday Review*, 1969, 24, 52.

Tillich, P. *The Future of Religions.* New York: Harper & Row, 1966.

Turnbull, C. *The Mountain People.* New York: Simon and Schuster, 1972.

Wallace, A. Revitalization Movements: Some Theoretical Considerations for Their Comparative Study," *American Anthropologist*, 1956, 58, 264–281.

Walsh, J. *Intercultural Education in the Community of Man.* Honolulu: The University of Hawaii Press, 1973.

Whorf, B. In J. B. Carroll (Ed.), *Language, Thought, and Reality.* Cambridge, Massachusetts: Technology Press of MIT, 1957.

CONCEPTS AND QUESTIONS FOR CHAPTER 8

1. What do you see as most necessary to the improvement of intercultural communication during the next decade?

2. How can intercultural communication be improved domestically? Internationally? Is one form more important than the other? Why?

3. Given all the complexities associated with intercultural communication, do you think there is really any hope for the future?

4. Do you agree with Miller and Shatzer when they say communication study and scholarship can foster world humanism?

5. What does Barnlund mean when he writes of "an ethical void" in intercultural communication?

6. What are the important ethical questions that communicators must ask themselves as they engage in intercultural communication?

7. What does Kim mean when she refers to a holistic approach to knowledge in the East and how does this approach differ from Western tradition?

8. Explain how Kim views Eastern and Western views of reality as complementary rather than competitive.

9. What fundamental differences are there between Kim's notion of intercultural personhood and Adler's multicultural man?

10. What does Adler mean by "multicultural man"? Is such a state ever possible?

11. Can you think of examples of people who might fit the description of the multicultural person?

12. What are some of the difficulties in becoming a multicultural person?

SUGGESTED READINGS

Asante, M. K. "Intercultural communication: An inquiry into research directions" in D. Nimmo, ed. *Communication Yearbook* 4. New Brunswick, N.J.: Transaction, 1980, pp. 401–410. In this paper Asante explores two prevalent schools of thought in intercultural communication scholarship, the cultural dialogist and the cultural critic. He notes that most intercultural communication theories have a Eurocentric bias, which he explicates along with alternatives to this perspective.

Asuncion-Lande, N.C. *Ethical Perspectives and Critical Issues in Intercultural Communication.* Falls Church, Va.: Speech Communication Association, 1979. This book contains a collection of essays developed at a conference entitled "Ethics, Responsibility, and Standards in Intercultural Communication, Education, Training, and Research." The organizers of the conference and the editor believe that "a new set of ethical questions has attained a new degree of urgency," in the interactions among peoples of different cultures.

Brislin, R. W., S. Bochner, and W. Lonner, eds. *Cross-Cultural Perspectives on Learning.* New York: Halsted Press, 1975. This book contains a collection of essays from a conference on culture and learning sponsored by the Culture Learning Institute of the East-West Center at the University of Hawaii. It includes essays that deal with the problems of learning another culture, studies of perception and cognition, and a variety of different perspectives for approaching intercultural communication.

Conangelo, N., C. H. Foxley, and D. Dustin, eds. *Multi-Cultural Nonsexist Education: A Human Relations Approach.* Dubuque, Iowa: Kendall/Hunt, 1979. Here are principles of human relations applied to teaching. The text contains articles from individual authors on such topics as human emotions and feeling, discovering empathy, mediating cultures, multicultural aspects of human relations, designing multicultural programs, the legal vicissitudes of bilingual communication, and racism. A comprehensive bibliography is included.

Condon, J. "Values and ethics in communication across cultures: Some notes on the North American case." *Communication* 6 (1981), 255–265. The author argues that for an examination of ethics in intercultural communication, one begins not with broad statements of ethical principles, but with a narrower analysis of cultural values and the range of behavior that is permissible in cultures. Within this range it should be possible to identify preferred behaviors and to deduce from them the underlying ethical principles. To illustrate this point, Condon looks at a number of value items in the U.S. and contrasts them with several other cultures.

Feagin, J. R. *Racial and Ethnic Relations.* Englewood Cliffs, N.J.: Prentice-Hall, 1978. This text contains outlines of the history, education, religion, arts, economy, and so on, of Irish-, Italian-, Jewish-, Mexican-, and Japanese-Americans. Typical conflicts are discussed with suggested remedies.

Jervis, R. *Perception and Misperception in International Politics.* Princeton, N.J.: Princeton University Press, 1976. Although this book is concerned primarily with international relations, it nevertheless deals with many issues that are central to any study of cross-cultural relations. Jervis discusses how decision makers perceive information for cultures that are foreign to their own. He also points out some common misperceptions and various ways these problems can be avoided in international politics.

Rogers, E. M., and F. F. Shoemaker. *Communication of Innovations: A Cross-Cultural Approach*, 2d ed. New York: Free Press, 1971. This book is concerned with the question of how innovations (ideas, products, and practices perceived as new by an individual) diffuse to the members of a social system. The new ideas range from tractors in Turkey to family planning techniques among Hindu housewives.

Samovar, L. A., R. E. Porter, and N. Jain. *Understanding Intercultural Communication.* Belmont, Calif.: Wadsworth, 1980, Chapter 8. In the last chapter of this book, entitled "Futurism: What Is Next, and Next, and Next . . . ," the authors focus on a number of needs and challenges facing intercultural communication, and offer their philosophy about how to treat the ethical implications of intercultural communication.

Sowell, T. *Essays and Data on American Ethnic Groups.* The Urban Institute, 1978. This text is a helpful resource of demographic information on Black-, Chinese-, Japanese-, Filipino-, Italian-, Jewish-, Mexican-, Puerto-Rican-, and West Indian-Americans. It gives demographics on income, fertility rates, occupational distribution, numbers of children, education, and so on.

Triandis, H. C., and W. W. Lambert, eds. *Handbook of Cross-Cultural Psychology*, vol. 1. Boston: Allyn & Bacon, 1980. The last chapter of this book deals with the politics and ethics of cross-cultural research, providing guidelines about study design and corroboration, researchers' responsibilities, and professional responsibilities.

Wedge, B. "Communication analysis and comprehensive diplomacy" in A. S. Hoffman, ed. *International Communication and the New Diplomacy.* Bloomington: Indiana University Press, 1968, pp. 22–47. This article stresses the theme that "misunderstandings of the most concrete and literal kind have played a large role in conflicts between nations." It is Wedge's contention that these conflicts are usually based on differing value systems and orientations. To illustrate this point, actual cases in international diplomacy are examined.

ADDITIONAL READINGS

Allport, G. *The Nature of Prejudice.* New York: Doubleday, 1958.

Benjamin, R. L. "Accountability as a basis for communication ethics." *The Journal of the Communication Association of the Pacific* 8 (1979), 30–36.

Brislin, R. W. "Cross-cultural research in psychology." *Annual Review of Psychology* 34 (1983), 363–400.

Brueing, W. "Racism: A philosophical analysis of a concept." *Journal of Black Studies* 5 (1974), 3–17.

Cherry, C. *World Communication: Threat or Promise.* New York: John Wiley, 1971.

Condon, J. C., and S. Mitsuko, eds. *Communication Across Cultures for What? A Symposium on Human Responsibility in Intercultural Communication.* Tokyo: Simual Press, 1976.

Critchfield, T. M., and C. Paik. "Where is the line? Ethics in intercultural translation." *Communication: The Journal of the Communication Association of the Pacific* 9 (1980), 112–116.

Edelstein, A. C. *Comparative Communication Research.* Beverly Hills, Calif.: Sage Publications, 1982.

Fisher, G. *American Communication in a Global Society.* Norwood, N.J.: Ables, 1979.

Ganley, O. H., and G. D. Ganley. *To Inform or to Control: The New Communications Network.* New York: McGraw-Hill, 1982.

Glenn, E., R. Johnson, R. Kimmel, and B. Wedge. "A cognitive interaction model to analyze culture conflict in international relations." *Journal of Conflict Resolution* 14 (1970), 35–48.

Hanney, R. G. *An Attainable Global Perspective.* New York: Center for Global Perspectives, 1976.

Harwood, K. "Ethical limits of multinational communication." *Communication: The Journal of the Communication Association of the Pacific* 10 (1981), 83–86.

Johnnesen, R. *Ethics in Human Communication.* Manhasset Hills, N.Y.: Avery Publishing Group, 1978.

Lovall, O. S., ed. *Cultural Pluralism Versus Assimilation.* Northfield, Minn.: Norwegian American Association, 1977.

Maruyama, M., and A. Harpkins. *Cultures of the Future.* Paris: Mouton, 1978.

Miller, J. *Many Voices: Bilingualism, Culture, and Education.* Boston: Routledge & Kegan Paul, 1983.

Nordenstreng, K., and H. Schiller. *National Sovereignty and International Communication.* Norwood, N.J.: Ablex, 1979.

Pratte, R. *Pluralism in Education: Conflict, Clarity, and Commitment.* Springfield, Ill.: Charles C. Thomas, 1979.

Rhinesmith, S. H. *Bring Home the World.* New York: AMACOM; American Management Association, 1975.

Rogers, E. M., ed. *Communication and Development: Critical Perspectives.* Beverly Hills, Calif.: Sage, 1976.

Schramm, W., and D. Lerner, eds. *Communication and Change: The Last Ten Years—and the Next.* Honolulu: University of Hawaii Press, 1976.

Smith, A. *The Geopolitics of Information: How Western Culture Dominates the World.* New York: Oxford University Press, 1980.

Triandis, H. C. "Reflections on trends in cross-cultural research." *Journal of Cross-Cultural Psychology* 11 (1980), 35–58.

Walsh, J. E. *Humanistic Culture Learning.* Honolulu: University of Hawaii Press, 1979.

Wendt, J. R. "Uncle Sam on the bad news bears: Human rights as intercultural communication" in M. Burgoon, ed. *Communication Yearbook* 5. New Brunswick, N.J.: Transaction Books, 1982, pp. 571–589.

Epilogue

We introduced the topic of intercultural communication by pointing out both its boundaries and its territory. By looking at what intercultural communication is and is not, we were able to establish some guidelines for our investigation. In general terms, we suggested that intercultural communication occurred whenever a message sender is a member of one culture and a message receiver is of another culture. Once this broad definition was presented we were able to survey some specific refinements. We noted that culture was the sum total of the learned behaviors of a particular group and that these behaviors (attitudes, values, language, and so forth) were transmitted from generation to generation. Differences among international, interracial, and cross-cultural communication also were examined.

Following our general introduction to intercultural communication, we focused on one of the conceptual threads woven through this book. This concept suggests that to understand intercultural communication one must realize the impact and influence of past experience. Anyone who has observed human interaction will have little trouble accepting the notion that where people come from—their cultural histories—is crucial to communication. Your prior experiences, structured by your culture, help to determine what you value, what you see, and how you behave. In short, what your culture has taught you, in both conscious and unconscious ways, will be manifest during intercultural communication. For example, Navajo Indians believe that the universe is full of dangers and that illness is a price to be paid for disorder and disharmony. These particular views are bound to be reflected in Navajo intercultural interactions. In another example, people from some cultures deem men more important than women. These people's behavior toward each sex will be influenced by this orientation. Even one's background colors what is perceived. Judgment of beauty is an example. In the United States, the slim, statuesque female represents the cultural stereotype of beauty. Yet in many Eastern European countries, a heavier, stockier body reflects the ideal. These examples—and there are countless others—point out that your culture gives the framework for your experiences and values. They, in turn, define your view of the world and dictate how you interact within that world.

Because people share cultural experiences in a symbolic manner, we explored the two most common symbol systems—verbal and nonverbal. Representing ideas and feelings by symbols is a complex and complicated procedure at best. When the dimension of culture is added to the encoding and decoding process, however, the act of sharing internal states becomes even more intricate. To help you understand this act, we sought to demonstrate the relationship between three closely related axioms: (1) language helps shape thoughts and perceptions (Whorf's linguistic relativity hypothesis), (2) diverse cultures have *different* words with *similar* meanings (foreign languages), and (3) cultures can have the same word with vastly *different* meanings (subcultural use of vernacular and argot). We noted that the problems of coding systems plague actions as well as words. Even a simple hand motion can convey a host of unrelated meanings and interpretations. The hand gesture used by a hitchhiker in the United States is apt to produce a punch in the nose in Ghana. In short, the symbols used to share cultural experiences may often be subject to confusion and ambiguity.

In the next section of the book we examined ideas and techniques that contribute to successful intercultural communication. We proceeded on the assumption that intercultural communication is, by its very definition and nature, an action and an overt activity. Intercultural communication is, in short, something people do to and with each other. Because of advances in technology, such as improved air travel and communication satellites, all people seem to be engaging in more and more of this activity. In addition to increased communication among foreign cultures, the late 1960s and 1970s revealed that there were a number of subcommunities within the boundaries of the United States. Subcultures such as the blacks, the urban poor, women, gays, the elderly, youth, Chicanos, and Asians wanted and demanded

contact and dialogue with the main culture. Consequently, all Americans are engaging in intercultural communication at an accelerating rate. If this interaction is to be significant, and if intercultural communication is to foster increased understanding and cooperation, then potential problems must be avoided.

Finally, we extended our analysis toward the future. This is due, in part, to the fact that most intercultural interactions and meetings lie in the future. The success of your communication experiences may well depend on your philosophy and attitude toward intercultural communication. The way you behave around others is often a reflection of your philosophy toward life and toward yourself. Yet each person is capable of change from day to day and from situation to situation. Individual alterations represent a gift that accompanies personal liberty. As Plutarch noted over two thousand years ago, "All things are daily changing." If intercultural exchanges are to be considered worthy of time and energy, each person must begin to realize that such change is possible.

But change, as everyone knows, is not simple. Many attitudes and behaviors are deeply ingrained. And many of them are subject to ethnocentric influences. By this we mean that as each person learns a cultural pattern of behavior that person is, in both obvious and subtle ways, acquiring a corresponding subjective and normative value judgment associated with that behavior. Many people are guilty of assuming that their cultural group, whatever it may be, is superior to all other groups. Everyone therefore judges other cultures by his or her own standards. How often do people say, "Our way is the right way"? Or they may foolishly assume that their ideas and solutions to problems are the only correct ones. This attitude is often manifest in such ideas as are expressed by the statement, "If you are not part of the solution, you are part of the problem." This shortsighted notion fails to recognize that most social problems are complex and must be solved by many ideas and many approaches. The danger of such a philosophy should be self-evident. It is indeed difficult to achieve mutual understanding if one's culture is placed in a central position of priority or worth. How foolish to assume that because one culture prays on Saturday while another worships on Sunday, one is superior to the other. Or take, for example, the cultural values of competition and winning. Because they are important values to North Americans, many assume that all cultures ought to strive to win and to be first. There are numerous cultures, however, where competition and winning are unimportant. On the contrary, cooperation and sharing are valued highly. To be guilty of ethnocentrism is to doom intercultural communication to failure.

The new mode of communicative behavior should not only be void of ethnocentrism, but it also ought to reflect an attitude of mutual respect and trust. We emphasize that intercultural communication will not be successful if, by actions or words, the communicators appear to be condescending. Every individual and every culture wants to believe it is as worthy as any other. Actions that manifest the opposite will diminish the worth and tend to stifle meaningful interaction.

The changes required are not easy. They require that we all possess a willingness to communicate, have empathy toward foreign and alien cultures, be tolerant of views that differ from our own, and develop a universalistic, relativistic approach to the universe. If we have the resolve to adopt these behaviors and attitudes and the desire to overcome ethnocentrism and feelings of superiority, we can begin to know the feelings of exhilaration that come when we have made contact with someone far removed from our own sphere of experiences. Intercultural communication offers the arena for this interpersonal contact. Our ability to change, to make adjustments in our communication habits, give us the potential tools to make that contact successful.

Index of Names

Index of Subjects